Project Management for Business, Engineering, and Technology

Project Management for Business, Engineering, and Technology

Principles and Practice
3RD EDITION

John M. Nicholas
Loyola University Chicago

Herman Steyn
University of Pretoria

AMSTERDAM • BOSTON • HEIDELBERG • LONDON • NEW YORK • OXFORD
PARIS • SAN DIEGO • SAN FRANCISCO • SINGAPORE • SYDNEY • TOKYO

Butterworth-Heinemann is an imprint of Elsevier

Butterworth-Heinemann is an imprint of Elsevier
The Boulevard, Langford Lane, Kidlington, Oxford, OX5 1GB
30 Corporate Drive, Suite 400, Burlington, MA 01803, USA

First edition 2008
Reprinted 2008

Notice
No responsibility is assumed by the publisher for any injury and/or damage to persons
or property as a matter of products liability, negligence or otherwise, or from any use
or operation of any methods, products, instructions or ideas contained in the material
herein. Because of rapid advances in the medical sciences, in particular, independent
verification of diagnoses and drug dosages should be made

British Library Cataloguing in Publication Data
A catalogue record for this book is available from the British Library

Library of Congress Cataloging-in-Publication Data
A catalog record for this book is available from the Library of Congress

ISBN: 978-0-7506-8399-9

For information on all Butterworth-Heinemann publications
visit our website at www.elsevierdirect.com

Printed and bound in *Hungary*

08 09 10   10 9 8 7 6 5 4 3 2

Working together to grow
libraries in developing countries

www.elsevier.com | www.bookaid.org | www.sabre.org

ELSEVIER   BOOK AID
             International   Sabre Foundation

Front cover photograph of the Nelson Mandela Bridge by Jorge Jung. Background puzzle
Image courtesy of iStock/starfotograf.

To Sharry, Julia, Joshua, and Abigail
John M. Nicholas

To Karen and Janine
Herman Steyn

BRIEF CONTENTS

CONTENTS

PART V: PROJECT MANAGEMENT IN THE CORPORATE CONTEXT   575

PREFACE

When people see something impressive—a bridge arching high over a canyon, a space probe touching down on a distant planet, a graceful curlicue ramp on a freeway, a motion picture (so real you think you're there!), or a nifty computer the size of your hand—they wonder "how did they do that?" By *they*, of course, they are referring to the creators, designers, and builders, the people who thought up and actually made those things. Seldom do they wonder about the *managers*, the people who organized and lead the efforts that brought those wondrous things from a concept or idea into reality and without whose talent, skills, and hard work most neat ideas would never amount to anything. This book is about the managers—project managers, the mostly unsung heroes of business and technology who stand outside the public eye but are behind practically every collective effort to create, develop, or produce something.

Although the project manager is but one of numerous people involved in the shaping of each of society's products, systems, and artifacts, he (or she) is usually the one in the middle, the one who gets all of the others involved and then organizes and directs their efforts so everything will come out right. Sometimes, though rarely, the manager and the creator happen to be the same: Burt Rutan, Woody Allen, and Gutzon Borglum are examples; their life work—in aerospace, motion pictures, and monumental sculptures, respectively—represent not only creative or technological genius, but leadership and managerial talent as well.

The last few decades have seen businesses transform from domestic, nationalistic enterprises, and markets into multinational enterprises and a single global market. As a result, no matter what your perspective there is more of everything to contend with—more ideas, competitors, resources, constraints, and, certainly, more people doing and wanting things. The rate of technological change is accelerating and products and processes are evolving at a more rapid pace; as a result, the life cycles of most things society uses and relies upon are getting shorter. This "more of everything" plus the accelerated rate of technological change has had a direct impact on the conduct of projects—including projects to develop products, systems, or processes that compete in local, domestic, and international markets; projects to create and implement new ways of meeting demand for energy, recreation, housing, communication, transportation, and food; and projects to answer basic questions in science and resolve problems such as hunger, disease, pollution, and climate change. All of this project activity has spurred a growing interest in project management—in ways to plan, organize, and control projects to better meet the needs of customers, markets, and society within the bounds of limited time and resources.

Associated with this interest is the growing need to educate and train project managers. In the past and still today, project managers were chosen for some demonstrated exceptional capability, although not necessarily managerial. If you were a good engineer, systems analyst, researcher, architect, or accountant, eventually you would become a project manager. Somewhere along the way, presumably, you would pick up the "other" necessary skills. The flaw in this reasoning is that project management encompasses a broad range of skills—managerial, leadership, interpersonal—that are much different and independent of skills associated with technological competency. And there is no reason to presume that the project environment alone will provide the opportunity for someone to "pick up" these other necessary skills.

As a text and handbook, this book is about the "right" way to manage projects. It is intended for advanced undergraduate and graduate university students, and for practicing managers in business, engineering, and technology. As the title says, it is a book about principles *and* practice, meaning that the topics in it are practical and meant to be applied. It covers the big picture of project management—origins, applications, and philosophy, as well as the nitty-gritty, how-to steps. It describes the usual project management topics of schedules, budgets, and controls, but also the human side of project management, including leadership and conflict.

Why a book on business, engineering, *and* technology? In our experience, technical specialists such as engineers, programmers, architects, chemists, and so on, often have little or no management training. This book, which includes many engineering and technology project examples, provides somewhat broad exposure to relevant business concepts and management specifics to help these specialists get started as project managers.

What about those people involved in product-development, marketing, process-improvement, and related projects commonly thought of as "business projects"? Just as students of engineering and technology seldom receive formal management training, rarely are business students exposed to common practices in technology projects. This book reveals not only how "business" projects are conducted, but also concepts and necessary steps in the conception and execution of engineering, construction, and other kinds of "technology" projects.

Of course, engineering and technology projects are *also* business projects: they are conducted in a business context and involve business issues such as customer satisfaction, resource utilization, deadlines, costs, profits, and so on. Virtually all projects—engineering, technology, and business—are originated and conducted in similar ways, conceptualized in this book using a methodology called the Systems Development Cycle (SDC). The SDC serves as a general framework for discussing the principles and practices of project management, and illustrating commonalities and differences among a wide variety of projects.

This book is an outgrowth of the authors' combined several decades of experience teaching project management at Loyola University Chicago and University of Pretoria to business and engineering students, preceded by several years working in business and technology projects, including design and flight test work in the aircraft industry, large-scale process facility construction projects, and software applications development and process improvement projects. From our practical experience we developed an appreciation not only for the business-management side of project management, but also for the human and organizational side as well. We have seen the benefits of good communication, trust, and teamwork, as well as the costs of poor leadership, emotional stress, and group conflict. In our experience, the most successful projects are those where leadership, trust, communication, and teamwork flourish, regardless of the formal planning and control systems in place; this book largely reflects these personal experiences. Of course, comprehensive coverage of the project management field required that we look much beyond our own experience and draw upon the published works of many other authors and the suggestions of colleagues and reviewers.

In this third edition we have revised and added substantial new material to incorporate new topics of interest, current examples, and the growing body of literature in project management. Every chapter has been revised and updated. The most significant changes are as follows: Introduction includes a table showing locations in the book addressing PMBOK knowledge areas. Chapter 1 has new examples and case studies of projects and project managers. Chapter 2 includes new material and a new appendix on systems engineering. Chapters 3 and 4 have new coverage of front-end topics such as preparation of RFPs, proposals, charters, and definition of user needs, requirements, and specifications. Chapter 5 includes a new section on procurement management. Chapter 6 has been substantially revised to cover precedence diagramming. In Chapter 7, coverage of constrained-resource scheduling, the critical-chain method, and multiple-project scheduling based on the Theory of Constraints has been expanded. Chapter 9 is completely new and addresses methodologies and practices for project quality assurance. Chapter 11 is expanded and combines the topics of project execution and control. Chapter 12 is completely revised and covers project communications, review meetings, and system implementation and project close-out. Part V—Chapters 16 to 18—is completely new: Chapter 16 addresses 4 topics of growing recent interest: project management methodology, maturity, and knowledge management, and the project management office; Chapter 17 deals with methods for project selection and managing projects in a portfolio; and Chapter 18 covers the management of projects that are "international", "global", or "overseas." Numerous new examples and 11 new end-of-chapter case studies have been added throughout the book.

Our goal in writing this book is to provide students and practicing managers the most practical, current, and interesting text possible. We appreciate hearing your comments and suggestions. Please send them to us at jnichol@luc.edu and herman. steyn@up.ac.za.

ACKNOWLEDGMENTS

Writing a book is a project and, like most projects, reflects the contributions of many people. Here we want to acknowledge and give special thanks to those who contributed the most. First, thanks to our research assistants. Research assistants in general do a lot of work—academic as well as gofer work, and without their toiling efforts most professors would accomplish far less. We have been fortunate to have had the assistance of several such bright and capable people, particularly Elisa Denney, Hollyce James, Miguel Velasco, Gaurav Monga, Cary Morgan, and Louis Schwartzman.

Special thanks to current and former colleagues at Loyola University Chicago and the University of Pretoria. In Chicago, thanks to Dr Gezinus Hidding for his enthusiasm, interest, and contributions to the field of project management; and to Drs Enrique Venta, Harold Dyck, Samuel Ramenofsky, and Donald Meyer, and to Carmen Santiago, Elaine Strnad, Paul Flugel, John Edison, Sharon Tylus, Lewis Lancaster, and Debbie Gillespie for their support for this and earlier editions. In Pretoria, thanks to Drs Calie Pistorius, Roelf Sandenbergh, Antonie de Klerk and Tinus Pretorius for encouraging education and research in project management at the Graduate School of Technology Management. I (Herman) also want to express appreciation to Giel Bekker, Philip Viljoen, Dr Pieter Pretorius, Dr Krige Visser, and Dr Michael Carruthers for their direct and indirect contributions to this book and for all that I have learned from them. I (John) want to acknowledge the influence of three of my professors, Charles Thompson and Gustave Rath at Northwestern University, and Dick Evans at the University of Illinois, whose philosophies and teachings helped shaped this book.

Our wives Sharry and Karen also get special thanks. Sharry provided numerous suggestions to the first edition and helped reduce the amount of "techno-jargon" in the book; she managed the home front, was a steadfast source of support, and freed up time so that I (John) could pursue and complete this project. Karen provided wifely support and encouragement; as in the case of so many other projects I (Herman) have been involved in, had not it been for her support, my contribution to this project would not have materialized.

Thanks also to the folks at Butterworth-Heinemann, and especially to Maggie Smith for her support of this publication.

There are other colleagues, students, and friends, some mentioned in endnotes elsewhere throughout the book that provided support, encouragement, and reference materials; to them we say thank you. Despite the assistance of so many people and our own best efforts, there are still likely to be omissions or errors. We had final say and accept responsibility for them.

John M. Nicholas

Herman Steyn

ABOUT THE AUTHORS

JOHN NICHOLAS is professor of operations management and former associate dean of the Graduate School of Business at Loyola University Chicago. He is an active teacher, writer, and researcher in project management and manufacturing management, and conducts executive seminars and has been a consultant on project management and process improvement. John is the author of numerous academic and technical publications, and five books including *Competitive Manufacturing Management* (1998) and *The Portal to Lean Production* (2006). He has held the positions of engineer and team leader on aircraft development projects at Lockheed-Martin Corporation, business analyst on operations projects at Bank America, and research associate on energy-environmental research projects at Argonne National Laboratory. He has a BS in aeronautical and astronautical engineering and an MBA in operations research from the University of Illinois, Urbana-Champaign, and a PhD in industrial engineering and applied behavioral science from Northwestern University.

HERMAN STEYN is professor of project management in the Graduate School of Technology Management, University of Pretoria, South Africa. He has been involved in project management in industry since 1975, has managed a variety of large and small engineering projects (system, product, and process development) in the minerals, defense and nuclear industries, and has also managed project portfolios. In 1996, he was appointed to his current position at the University of Pretoria where he initiated a masters' program in project management and a comprehensive continuing-education program in project management. Besides teaching graduate courses, consulting, and conducting research in project management, over the last decade Herman has conducted more than 80 seminars and workshops on project management. He has a bachelor's degree and graduate diploma in metallurgical engineering, an MBA, and a PhD in engineering management.

Introduction

> **Project** *(praj' ekt, ikt) n. a proposal of something to be done; plan; scheme 2. an organized undertaking; specif., a) a special unit of work, research, etc., as in school, a laboratory, etc., b) an extensive public undertaking, as in conservation, construction, etc.*
>
> —*Webster's New World Dictionary*

I.1   IN THE BEGINNING

Sometime during the third millennium B.C., workers on the Great Pyramid of Cheops set the last stone in place. Certainly they must have felt jubilant, for this event represented a milestone of sorts in one of humanity's grandest undertakings. Although much of the ancient Egyptians' technology is still a mystery, the enormity and quality of the finished product remain a marvel. Despite the lack of sophisticated machinery, they were able to raise and fit some 2,300,000 stone blocks, weighing 2 to 70 tons apiece, into a structure the height of a modern 40-story building. Each facing stone was set against the next with an accuracy of 0.04 inch, and the base, which covers 13 acres, deviates less than 1 inch from level (Figure I-1).[1]

Equally as staggering was the number of workers involved. To quarry the stones and transport them down the Nile, about 100,000 laborers were levied. In addition, 40,000 skilled masons and attendants were employed in preparing and laying the blocks and erecting or dismantling the ramps. Public works were essential to keep the working population employed and fed, and it is estimated that no less than 150,000 women and children also had to be housed and fed.[2]

Figure I-1
The Great Pyramid of Cheops, an early (circa 2500 B.C.) large-scale project.
(Photo courtesy of Arab Information Center.)

But just as mind-boggling was the managerial ability of the Egyptians—the planning, organizing, and controlling that were exercised throughout the 20-year duration of the pyramid construction. Francis Barber, a nineteenth century American naval attaché and pyramid scholar, concluded that:

> it must have taken the organizational capacity of a genius to plan all the work, to lay it out, to provide for emergencies and accidents, to see that the men in the quarries, on the boats and sleds, and in the mason's and smithies shops were all continuously and usefully employed, that the means of transportation was ample, . . . that the water supply was ample, . . . and that the sick reliefs were on hand.[3]

Building the Great Pyramid is what we today would call a large-scale project, and stands representative of numerous projects from early recorded history that required massive human works and managerial competency. The Bible provides accounts of many projects that required orchestration of thousands of people and the transport and utilization of enormous quantities of materials. Worthy of note are the managerial and leadership accomplishments of Moses. The scriptural account of the exodus of the Hebrews from the bondage of the Egyptians gives some perspective on the preparation, organization, and execution of this tremendous undertaking. Supposedly Moses did a magnificent job of personnel selection, training, organization, and delegation of authority.[4] The famed ruler Solomon, among other accomplishments, was the "manager" of numerous great construction projects. He transformed the battered ruins of many ancient cities and crude shantytowns into powerful fortifications. With his wealth and the help of Phoenician artisans, Solomon built the Temple in Jerusalem. Seven years went into the construction of the Temple, after which Solomon took 13 years more to build a palace for himself. He employed a workforce of 30,000 Israelites to fell trees and import timber from the forests of Lebanon.[5] That was almost 3,000 years ago. About 600 years later, Nehemiah completely rebuilt the wall around Jerusalem—in just 52 days.

With later civilizations, most notably the Greeks and Romans, the number of activities requiring extensive planning and organizing escalated. These societies undertook extensive municipal and government works programs such as street paving, water supply, and sewers. To facilitate their military campaigns and commercial interests, the Romans constructed networks of highways and roads throughout Europe, Asia Minor, Palestine, and northern Africa so that all roads would "lead to Rome." The civilizations of Renaissance Europe and the Middle and Far East undertook river engineering, construction of canals, dams, locks, and port and harbor facilities. With the spread of modern religions, construction of churches, temples, monasteries, mosques, and massive urban cathedrals was added to the list of projects. Remains of aqueducts, bridges, temples, palaces, fortifications, and other large structures throughout the Mediterranean, Asia Minor, and China testify to the ancients' occupation with large-scale projects.

With the advent of industrialization and electricity, the projects of humankind took on increasing complexity. Projects for the construction of railroads, electrical and hydroelectrical power facilities and infrastructures, subways, and factories became commonplace. In recent times, development of large systems for communications, defense, transportation, research, and information technology have spurred different, more complex kinds of project activity.

As long as humankind does things, there will be projects. Many projects of the future will be similar to those in the past. Others will be different either in terms of increased scale of effort or more advanced technology. Representative of the latter are three recent projects—the English Channel tunnel (Chunnel), the international space station, and SpaceShipOne. The Chunnel required tremendous resources and took a decade to complete. The international space station (Figure I-2) has required development of new technologies and the efforts of the US, Russian, European, Canadian, and Japanese space agencies. SpaceShipOne is the venture of a small California company aimed at developing a vehicle and launch system for future space tourism.

Figure I-2
The international space station, a modern large-scale project.
(Photo courtesy of NASA/Johnson Space Center.)

I.2 WHAT IS A PROJECT?

From these examples it is clear that humankind has been involved in project activities for a long time. But why are these considered "projects" while other human activities, such as planting and harvesting a crop, stocking a warehouse, issuing payroll checks, or manufacturing a product, are not?

What *is* a project? This is a question we will cover in much detail later. As an introduction though, below are listed some characteristics that warrant classifying an activity as a project:[6]

1. A project involves a single, definable *purpose* and *well-defined end-items, deliverables*, or *results*, usually specified in terms of cost, schedule, and performance requirements.
2. Every project is *unique* in that it requires doing something different than was done previously. Even in a "routine" project such as home construction, variables such as terrain, access, zoning laws, labor market, public services, and local utilities make it unique. A project is a one-time activity, never to be exactly repeated again.
3. Projects are *temporary* activities. Each is an ad hoc organization of personnel, material, and facilities assembled to accomplish a goal within a scheduled time frame; once the goal is achieved, the ad hoc organization is disbanded.
4. Projects *cut across organizational and functional lines* because they need skills and talents from multiple functions, professions, and organizations.
5. Given that each project is unique, it also involves *unfamiliarity* and *risk*. It may encompass new technology or processes and, for the organization undertaking it, possess significant elements of uncertainty and risk.
6. The organization usually has something *at stake* when doing a project. The work calls for special scrutiny or effort because failure would jeopardize the organization or its goals.
7. A project is the *process* of working to achieve a goal; during the process, projects pass through several distinct phases called the *project life cycle*. The tasks, people, organizations, and other resources involved in the project change as the project moves from one phase to the next.

The examples described earlier are for familiar kinds of projects such as construction (pyramids), development (transportation and information technology), or a combination of both (space station). In general, the list of activities that qualify as projects is long and includes many that are commonplace. Weddings, remodeling a home, and moving to another house are certainly projects for the families involved. Company audits, major litigations, corporate relocations, and mergers are also projects, as are new product development and system implementations. Military campaigns also meet the criteria of projects; they are temporary, unique efforts directed toward a specific goal. The Normandy Invasion in World War II on June 6, 1944 is a good example:

> The technical ingenuity and organizational skill that made the landings possible was staggering. The invasion armada included nearly 5,000 ships of all descriptions protected by another 900 warships. The plan called for landing 150,000 troops and 1,500 tanks on the Normandy coast *in the first 48 hours*. There were large-scale air operations with bombers, gliders, paratroopers, and fighter support. There was PLUTO, the Pipe Line Under the Ocean, to bring the flood of petroleum the armies would need. And there was Mulberry Harbor. Since the French ports were not large enough to handle

the traffic anticipated to follow the invasion (12,000 tons of stores and 2,500 vehicles *per day*), the idea evolved to tow two monstrous break-waters and floating quays (Mulberries) across the English Channel, each making a complete port the size of Dover.[7]

Most artistic endeavors are projects, too. Composing a song or symphony, writing a novel, or making a sculpture are one-person projects. The unusual (and somewhat controversial) works of the artist Christo—draping portions of the Grand Canyon, several islands in Biscayne Bay, and 1,000,000 square feet of Australian coastline with colored plastic—are projects also, but on a larger scale. So is the making of motion pictures, whether they are home movies or the releases of major production studios. Some large artistic projects have also involved the skills of engineers and builders: Mount Rushmore, the Statue of Liberty, and the Eiffel Tower are examples.

Many efforts at saving human life and recovering from man-made or natural disasters become projects. Examples are the massive cleanup following the Soviet nuclear accident at Chernobyl, and rescue and recovery operations following disastrous earthquakes in Mexico City, Turkey, Armenia, and Kobe, Japan, and the Indian Ocean tsunami of December 2004.

Figure I-3 shows generalized project endeavors and examples of well-known projects. Notice the diversity in the kinds of efforts. The figure shows approximately where projects fall with respect to the degree of complexity and uncertainty involved. Complexity is roughly measured by magnitude of the effort, number of

Figure I-3
A typology of projects.

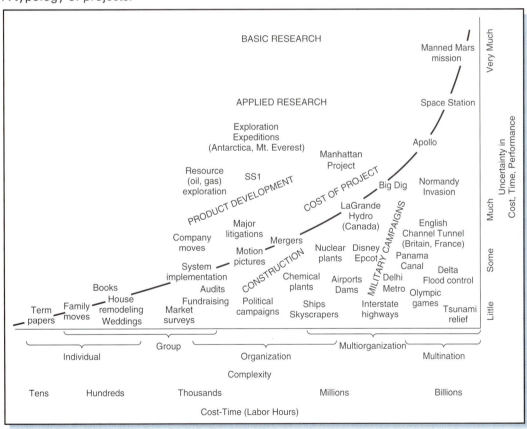

groups and organizations that need to be coordinated, and diversity in skills or expertise needed to accomplish the work. Time and resource commitments tend to increase with complexity.

Uncertainty is measured roughly by the difficulty in predicting the final outcome in terms of the dimensions of *time*, *cost*, and *technical performance*. In most projects there is some uncertainty in one or two dimensions, at least in the initial stages of planning (e.g., weddings and world fairs). The most complex projects have uncertainty in all three dimensions (e.g., the space station).

Generally, the more often something is done, the less uncertainty there is to doing it. This is simply because people learn by doing and so improve their efforts—the "learning curve" concept. Projects that are very similar to previous ones and about which there is abundant knowledge have lower uncertainty. These are found in the lower portion of Figure I-3 (e.g., weddings, highways, dams, system implementation). As manned missions to Mars become frequent, they too will move down the uncertainty scale.

The cost curve indicates that the expense of projects increases roughly in proportion to both complexity and uncertainty. Cost, represented in terms of time or economic value, is at the level of tens or hundreds of labor hours for projects with low complexity and uncertainty, but increases to millions and billions of hours for projects with the greatest complexity and uncertainty.

When the uncertainty of a project drops to nearly zero, and when the project effort is repeated a large number of times, the work is usually no longer considered a project. For example, building a skyscraper is definitely a project, but mass construction of prefabricated homes more closely resembles a scheduled, repetitive process than a project. Admiral Byrd's exploratory flight to the South Pole was a project, but modern daily supply flights to Antarctic bases are not. When in the future tourists begin taking chartered excursions to Mars, trips there will not be considered projects either. They will just be ordinary scheduled operations.

In all cases, projects are conducted by organizations that after the project is completed go on to do something else (construction companies) or are disbanded (Admiral Byrd's crew, the Mars exploration team). In contrast, repetitive, high-certainty activities (prefabricated housing, supply flights, and tourist trips to Antarctica or Mars) are performed by permanent organizations that do the same thing over and over, with little change in operations other than rescheduling. That projects differ greatly from repetitive efforts is the reason they must be managed differently.

I.3   PROJECT MANAGEMENT: THE NEED

Although humankind has been involved in projects since the beginning of recorded history, obviously the nature of projects and the environment have changed. Many modern projects involve great technical complexity and require much diversity of skills. Managers are faced with the problem of putting together and directing large temporary organizations while being subjected to constrained resources, limited time schedules, and environmental uncertainty. To cope with complex kinds of activities and great uncertainty, new forms of project organization and new practices of management have evolved.

Two examples of activities that required project organization and management are the Manhattan Project to develop the first atomic bomb and the Pathfinder Mission to land and operate a rover vehicle on the surface of Mars. Projects such as these are not only unparalleled in terms of technical difficulty and organizational complexity, but also in terms of the requirements circumscribing them. In ancient times, project requirements were more flexible. If the Pharaohs needed more workers, more slaves or more of the general population were conscripted. If funding ran out during construction of a Renaissance cathedral, the work was stopped until more money could be raised (indeed, this is one reason some cathedrals took decades or centuries to complete). If a king ran out of money while building a palace, he simply raised taxes. In other cases where additional money could not be raised, more workers could not be found, or the project could not be delayed, the scale of effort or the quality of workmanship was simply reduced to accommodate the constraints. There are many early projects of which nothing remains simply because the work was shoddy and could not withstand the rigors of time.

In projects like Manhattan and Pathfinder, the requirements were not so flexible. First, both projects were subject to severe time constraints. Manhattan, undertaken during World War II, required developing the atomic bomb in the shortest time possible to end the war. For Pathfinder, the mission team was challenged with developing and landing a vehicle on Mars in less than 3 years time and on a $150 million budget. This was less than half the time and one-twentieth the cost of the last probe NASA had landed on Mars. Both projects involved advanced research and development and explored new areas of science and engineering. In neither case could technical performance requirements be compromised to compensate for limitations in time, funding, or other resources; to do so would increase the risk to undertakings that were already very risky. However, constraints and uncertainty in project work are not restricted to large-scale government science programs. They are common, everyday experiences in business and technology where organizations continually strive to develop and implement new products, processes, and systems, and to adapt to changing requirements in a changing world.

Consider, for instance, Dalian Company's development of "Product J," an example of a product development project that companies everywhere must do to remain competitive, indeed, to survive. In the past, the Dalian Company had relied upon trial and error to come up with new products: in essence, whatever worked was used again; whatever failed was discarded. In recent years the company had begun to lose market. Although it had had many innovative concepts on the drawing board, all had failed because it had been too slow to move them into the marketplace. Dalian was now considering development of Product J, a promising, but radically new idea. To move the idea from concept to product would require the involvement of engineers and technicians from several Dalian divisions and suppliers. Before approving the budget, Dalian management wanted assurances that Product J could be introduced early enough to put it well ahead of the competition. It was apparent that a new approach would be needed to develop Product J. The project would need a systematic development process guided by project management.

Another example is Shah Alam Hospital's installation of a new employee benefits plan. The new plan would better suit employee needs, add flexibility and value to the benefits package, and reduce costs. The project would be big—it would involve developing new policies, upgrading the training of staff workers, familiarizing 10,000 employees with the plan, and installing a new computer network and database, and require active participation from personnel in human resources, financial service, and information systems, as well as experts from two consulting firms. This project is typical of "change" projects everywhere—projects initiated in response to changing needs and with the goal of transforming the organization's way of doing things. For the hospital, the project would be different from anything it had done before.

As a final example, consider that virtually every company in the world now has or will have a website. Website addresses appear everywhere on printed and broadcasted advertising as companies scramble to inform customers they have become part of the e-business phenomenon. Behind each are multiple projects to develop or enhance the website and to integrate electronic business technology into the company's mainstream marketing and supply-chain operations. Such projects are also examples of organizations' need to change, in this case, to keep pace with advances in information technology and business processes.

Activities such as these defy traditional management approaches for planning, organization, and control. They are representative of activities that require modern methods of project management and organization to fulfill difficult technological or market-related performance goals in spite of severe limitations on time and resources.

As a distinct area of management practice, project management is still a new idea, and its methods are still unknown to many experienced managers. Only 50 years ago, its usage was restricted largely to the defense, aerospace, and construction industries. Today, however, project management is being applied in a wide variety of industries and organizations. Originally applied only in large-scale, complex technological projects such as the Apollo Program to put men on the moon, today project management techniques are being applied to any project-type activity, regardless of size or technology. Methods of modern project management would have been as useful to early Egyptian and Renaissance builders as they are to present-day contractors, engineers, systems specialists, and managers.

I.4 RESPONSE TO A CHANGING ENVIRONMENT

Project management has grown in response to the need for a managerial approach that deals with the problems and opportunities in modern society. The salient characteristics that distinguish modern society from earlier periods of history are risk and uncertainty arising from rapidly changing technology, rising costs, increasing competition, frequent resource shortages, and numerous interest groups with opposing views.[8]

Project management is a departure from the management of simpler ongoing, repetitive operations where the market and technology tend to be predictable, anticipated outcomes are more certain, and fewer parties or organizations are involved. In situations like these, which are somewhat stable and predictable, "mechanistic" organizational forms and management procedures—forms that rely on centralized decision making and adherence to hierarchical authority—work well. When, however, situations require adaptability and rapid response to change—change spurred, for example, by changing technologies or markets, then "organic" forms of organization and management work much better. These forms, which include project management, provide the diversified technical and managerial competency and decentralized communication and decision making necessary to meet the challenges of complex, unfamiliar, high-stakes activities.

I.5 SYSTEMS APPROACH TO MANAGEMENT

A system is a collection of interrelated elements that in combination do something. The systems approach is a way of looking at and understanding a phenomenon that involves identifying all the contributing components and the way they interact to cause the phenomenon. In the systems approach to management, a goal or solution to a problem is regarded as the end-result or outcome of a system. The approach starts by defining the goal, identifying all of the contributors and constraints to achieving the goal, and then managing those contributors so as best to achieve the goal. Emphasis in the systems approach is on the desired end-result and taking into account everything possible that aids or hinders achieving that result—including things that can be controlled or manipulated as well as those that cannot. Always the focus is on achieving or optimizing the performance and goal of the overall *system*, not of the components.

Project management is a systems approach to management. A project is a goal-oriented system of interrelated components—tasks and stakeholders—functioning in a larger environment; the purpose of project management is to unify or integrate the components—the interests, resources, work efforts of many stakeholders, as well as schedules, budgets, and plans—to accomplish the project goal.

I.6 PROJECT GOAL AND PROJECT MANAGEMENT BENEFITS

For virtually every project the goal is to hit a three-dimensional target: complete the work for a customer or end-user in accordance with *budget*, *schedule*, and *performance requirements*. The budget is the specified or allowable cost for the project. The schedule is the time period over which the work is to be done, dates for specific tasks, and the target completion for the project. Performance requirements are the required features of the project end-item, deliverables, or final result, including necessary attributes of the final product or service, technological specifications, quality and quantity measures, and whatever else is important to the customer or end-user. As shown in Figure I-4, the goal can be conceptualized as a target point in three-dimensional space. The goal represents a

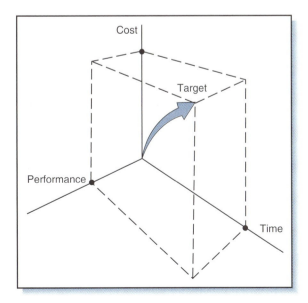

Figure I-4
Three-dimensional project goal. (Adapted from Milton Rosenau, *Successful Project Management* (Belmont, CA: Lifetime Learning Publications, 1981): 16.)

commitment to deliver a certain something, by a certain date, for a certain cost. The purpose of project management is to hit the target.[9]

Unfortunately, technological complexity, changing markets, and an uncontrollable environment make it easy to miss the target. Time, cost, and technical performance are interrelated, and exclusive emphasis on any one will likely undermine the others. In trying to meet schedules and performance requirements, costs increase; conversely, in trying to contain costs, work performance erodes and schedules slip. In earlier times, one or two aspects of the goal were simply allowed to slide so that the "most fixed" could be met. Most projects, as the Pathfinder, Dalian Company, and Shah Alam Hospital examples show, do not have this luxury. Time, cost, and performance must receive equal emphasis.

Project management offers a way to maintain focus on all three dimensions and control the tradeoffs among them. As a systems approach it integrates resources and enables simultaneous emphasis on the "whole" project goal—time, cost, and technical performance.

If project management succeeds in hitting the three-dimensional target, the benefit is more or less obvious: The project has met the requirements of its stakeholders—the customers, contractors, and others who have an interest in the project. Assuming the requirements at which the project aimed were correctly defined, the customers, users, contractors, and, ideally, society as a whole will all be satisfied. A well-managed project will meet the profit, market share, and service objectives of the customer, as well as the profit, reputation, or service objectives of the contractor. Good project management increases the likelihood that a project will succeed, and when a project succeeds, everyone with a stake in it benefits.

I.7 PROJECT MANAGEMENT: THE PERSON, THE TEAM, THE METHODOLOGY

Three key features distinguish project management from traditional forms of management: the person, the team, and the methodology.

The Person

The most important feature about project management is the role of the project manager. Within this, overall responsibility to *plan*, *direct*, and *integrate* the efforts of all stakeholders to achieve project goals lies with a single person, the project manager. In fast-changing environments it is increasingly difficult for organizations like Dalian and Shah Alam to relate facts about technology, production methods, costs, and markets; the number of issues and decisions to be processed is simply too large for traditional hierarchical organizations to effectively handle. In the role of project manager, one person is held accountable for the project and is totally dedicated to achieving its goals. The project manager coordinates the efforts across all of the involved functional areas and organizations, and oversees the planning and control of costs, schedules, and work tasks.[10]

The Team

Project management is bringing together individuals and groups to form a single, cohesive team working toward a common goal. Perhaps more than any other human endeavor, project work is teamwork. It is accomplished by a group of people, often from different functional areas and organizations, who contribute wherever and whenever they are needed. Depending on project requirements, the size and composition of the team may fluctuate, and the team may disband after the project is completed.

The Methodology

The project manager and the project team utilize a "project management methodology." This methodology is composed of organization structure, information processing, and practices and procedures that permit integration of all project elements—tasks, resources, information, stakeholders, etc. It provides for *integrated planning and control*, which according to Archibald refers to

> the pulling together of all important elements of information related to (1) the products or results of the project, (2) the time, and (3) the cost, in funds, manpower, or other key resources. Further, this information must be pulled together for all (or as many as practical) phases of the project. Finally, integrated planning and control requires continual revision of future plans, comparison of actual results with plans, and projection of total time and cost at *completion* through interrelated evaluation of all elements of information.[11]

As projects move from one phase to the next, resource requirements (labor, facilities, capital, etc.) and organizational responsibilities shift. The project management methodology provides the means for (1) identification of tasks, (2) identification of resource requirements and costs, (3) establishing priorities, (4) planning and updating schedules, (5) monitoring and controlling end-item quality and performance, and (6) measuring project performance.[12]

1.8   About This Book

Philosophy and Objectives

As a philosophy and an approach, project management is broader and more sophisticated than traditional management of repetitive activities. The history of the theory and practice of project management reveals its roots in many disciplines, including management science, systems theory, accounting, operations management, organizational design, law, and applied behavioral science. What has evolved, and will continue to evolve, are a philosophy, approach, and set of practices, the *sum total* of which comprise project management. Some managers fail to understand this, believing that application of techniques alone, such as "Gantt charts," "PERT," or "matrix management" (all explained later), makes for successful project management. Project management is much more than these.

C.P. Snow wrote an essay entitled "Two Cultures" about the cultural gap that separates scientists from the rest of society. He wrote of the conflict of ideas, the problems of communication, and the lack of understanding between scientists and other intellectuals.[13] Managers and management scholars also tend to see the world from either of two perspectives: some see the world in "hard," quantitative terms; others in "soft" or behavioral terms. The "quantitativists" tend to view projects in terms of costs, dates, and economic variables; their approach is to structure problems mathematically and to follow some prescribed set of procedures to arrive at a solution. The "behaviorists" view problems in terms of peoples' behavior, skills, and attitudes, and systems of organization; their approach is to try to motivate attitudinal and behavioral change, and to alter the processes and structure of teams, groups, and organizations.

The intent of this book is to give a comprehensive, balanced view that emphasizes both the behavioral and quantitative sides of project management. The philosophy of his book is that for managers to "do" project management, they must gain familiarity with four topical areas: system methodology; systems development process; management methods, procedures, and systems; and organization and human behavior. All four are essential to project management; correspondingly, the objectives of this book are to cover in depth:

1. The principles and philosophy that guide project management practice.
2. The logical sequence of stages in the life of a project.
3. The methods, procedures, and systems for defining, planning, scheduling, controlling, and organizing project activities.
4. The organizational, managerial, and human behavioral issues relevant to project management.

In recent years the scope of project management has grown to encompass more than the management of individual projects, recognizing that project success involves more than the skills and talent of a good project manager; hence, a fifth objective of this book is to describe responsibilities of the *organization* for effective project management and successful projects. Within the five stated objectives, both the quantitative and behavioral sides of project management are addressed.

This book is intended for "general" project managers. It is comprehensive in the sense that it provides an understanding of project management concepts and techniques widely recognized and applicable to virtually any industry or project situation. It is not the intent of this book to dwell on particular methodologies and techniques used only in specific industries or organizations. This would be difficult because many industries—construction, information systems, product development, social work, and so on—have modified "traditional" project management practices or adopted other approaches to satisfy their unique project needs. Many of these methodologies and techniques are described in texts devoted to construction, product management, software development, research management, and so on.

Just as many of the project management practices described in this book were developed in certain industries to be later recognized and adopted for more general usage, there are probably many valuable practices currently in practice about which most of us are ignorant of. These remain to be "exposed" and to appear in textbooks like this in the future.

The Study Project

The best way to learn about project management is to actually participate in it or, failing that, to witness it. At the end of every chapter in this book are two kinds of questions: the first kind are the usual chapter review questions, the second are called "Questions About the Study Project." The latter are intended to be applied to a particular project of the reader's choosing. This will be called the "study project." The purpose of these questions and the Study Project is to help the reader relate concepts from each chapter to real-life situations.

The study project questions should be used in two ways:

1. For readers who are currently working in projects as managers or project team members, the questions can be related to their current work. The questions serve to increase the reader's awareness of key issues surrounding a particular project and to guide managers in the conduct of project management.

2. For readers who are currently full- or part-time students, the questions can be applied to "real-life" projects they are permitted to observe and research. Many business firms and government agencies are happy to allow student groups to interview managers of projects and collect information about their projects. Though secondhand, this is nonetheless an excellent way to learn about project management practice (and mismanagement).

Organization of This Book

Beyond this introductory section, the book is divided into five main parts. The first part is devoted to the basic concepts of project management. It describes project management principles, systems methodologies, and the systems approach—the philosophy that underlies project management. Also covered are the origins and concepts of project management, situations where it is needed, and examples of applications. The second part describes the logical process in the creation and life of a system. Called the Systems Development Cycle, it is the sequence of phases through which all human-made systems move from birth to death. The cycle is described in terms of its relation to projects and project management. The third part is devoted to methods and procedures for planning, scheduling, cost estimating, budgeting, resource allocation, controlling, and terminating a project. The topics of resource planning, computer and web-based project management, and project evaluation are also covered. The fourth part is devoted to project organizations, teams, and the people in projects. It covers forms of project organization, roles and responsibilities of project managers and team members, styles of leadership, and methods for managing teamwork, conflict, and emotional stress. The last part covers topics that lie beyond the project manager but are crucial for project success and, more broadly, the success of the organizations and communities that sponsor and undertake projects. It also covers a topic that spans most other topics in this book but requires special attention, managing projects in different countries.

The five stated objectives of this book are roughly divided among chapters in the book's five parts:

1. Basic concepts and systems philosophy: Chapters 1 and 2.
2. Systems development and project life cycle: Chapters 3 and 4.
3. Methods, procedures, and systems for planning and control: Chapters 5 through 12.
4. Organization, management, and human behavior: Chapters 13 through 15.
5. Project management maturity, the PMO, project selection and portfolio management, and international project management: Chapters 16 through 18.

The Appendices provide examples of three topics mentioned throughout the book: request for proposal (Appendix A), project proposal (Appendix B), and project master plan (Appendix C).

I.9 PMBOK

Several project management professional organizations have sprouted around the world. In general, these organizations have served to improve the practice of project management by establishing standards, guidelines, and certifications, and have advanced project management from being a simple title or role to a recognized, respected profession. Among the more well known among these organizations are IPMA (International Project Management Association), the UK's APM Group

(Association for Project Management), and the PMI (Project Management Institute). In 1985, PMI—the largest of these organizations—gathered up all the known, accepted best practices in the profession and later published them in a document called *A Guide to the Project Management Body of Knowledge* (PMBOK), which has since been updated and expanded.[14] The APM and IPMA have since also created versions of the PMBOK. Although none of the PMBOKs covers everything about project management (which they couldn't even if they tried), they have become the recognized standards about what minimally a project manager should know in practice and for attaining professional certification. The PMI calls its project management certification PMP—Project Management Professional.

The PMI's *Guide* to PMBOK divides project management knowledge into nine areas:

- Project integration management
- Project scope management
- Project time management
- Project cost management
- Project quality management
- Project human resource management
- Project communications management
- Project risk management
- Project procurement management

For readers interested in the PMI's PMBOK or seeking PMP certification, Table I-1 shows the correspondence between PMBOK knowledge areas as published in the PMI's *Guide* and the chapters in this book that address them.

I.10   STUDY PROJECT ASSIGNMENT

Select a project to investigate. You should select a "real" project; i.e., a project that has a real purpose and is not contrived just so you can investigate it. It can be a current project or one already completed; whichever, it must be a project for which you can readily get information.

If you are not currently involved in a project as a team member, you must find one for which you have permission to study (collect data and interview people) as an "outsider." The project should include a project team (a minimum of five people) with a project leader and be at least 2 or 3 months in duration. It should also have a specific goal in terms of a target completion date, a budget limit, and a specified end-item result or product. In general, larger projects afford better opportunity to observe the concepts of project management than smaller ones.

If you are studying a project as an outsider it is also a good idea to do it in a team with four to six people and an appointed team leader (i.e., perform the study using a team). This, in essence, becomes your *project team*—a team organized for the purpose of studying a project. You can then readily apply many of the planning, organizing, team building, and other procedures discussed throughout the book as practice and to see how they work. This "hands-on" experience with your own team combined with what you learn from the project you are studying will give you a fairly accurate picture about problems encountered and management techniques used in real-life project management.

Table I-1 Book chapters versus the PMI's PMBOK knowledge areas.

Book chapters	Introduction	Project Life Cycle and Organization	Project Management Process	Project Integration Management	Project Scope Management	Project Time Management	Project Cost Management	Project Quality Management	Project Human Resource Management	Project Communication Management	Project Risk Management	Project Procurement Management
Introduction	P	*	*									
Chapter 1: What Is Project Management?	P		*									
Chapter 2: Systems Approach and Systems Engineering			*	*	*							
Chapter 3: System Development Cycle and Project Conception		P	*	*							*	P
Chapter 4: Project and System Definition		*			P							
Chapter 5: Planning Fundamentals		*	*	*	P					*		P
Chapter 6: Project Time Planning and Networks	*		*			P						
Chapter 7: Advanced Project Network Analyses and Scheduling			*			P					*	
Chapter 8: Cost Estimating and Budgeting			*				P					*
Chapter 9: Project Quality Management			*	*				P				
Chapter 10: Managing Risks in Projects			*								P	
Chapter 11: Project Execution and Control			*	*	*	*	*			P		*
Chapter 12: Project Evaluation, Communication, Implementation and Closeout	*		*							P		*
Chapter 13: Project Organization Structure and Integration	*	P										
Chapter 14: Project Roles, Responsibilities, and Authority		*	*						*			
Chapter 15: Managing Participation, Teamwork, and Conflict		*	*						P			
Chapter 16: The Management of Project Management	*	*		*								
Chapter 17: Project Selection and Portfolio Management	*									*	*	*
Chapter 18: International Project Management	*			*	*	*	*		*	*	*	*

Key:
P = PMBOK Knowledge Area is a major focus of this chapter
* = PMBOK Knowledge Area is addressed in this chapter

(PMBOK Guide — PMBOK Knowledge Areas)

REVIEW QUESTIONS

1. Look at websites, newspapers, magazines, or television for examples of items that pertain to projects. Surprisingly, a great number of newsworthy topics relate to the status of current or future projects, or to the outcome of past projects. Prepare a list of these topics.

2. Prepare a list of activities that are not projects. What distinguishes them from project activities? Which activities are difficult to classify one way or the other?

3. Because this is an introductory chapter, not very much has been said about why projects must be managed differently, and what constitutes project management—the subject of this book. Now is a good time to speculate about these: Why do you think that projects need to be managed differently than non-projects? What do you think are some additional or special considerations necessary for managing projects?

ENDNOTES

1. Peter Tompkins, *Secrets of the Great Pyramids* (New York: Harper & Row, 1976): 233–234; Rene Poirier, *The Fifteen Wonders of the World* (New York: Random House, 1961): 54–67.
2. Ibid., 227–228.
3. Francis Barber, *The Mechanical Triumphs of the Ancient Egyptians* (London: Tribner, 1900) as described by Tompkins, ibid., 233.
4. Claude S. George, *The History of Management Thought* (Upper Saddle River, NJ: Prentice Hall, 1968): 11.
5. Chaim Potok, *Wanderings* (New York: Fawcett Crest, 1978): 154–162.
6. See Russell D. Archibald, *Managing High-Technology Projects* (New York: Wiley, 1976): 19; Jack R. Meredith and Samuel Mantel, *Project Management: A Managerial Approach,* 3rd ed. (New York: Wiley, 1995): 8–9; Daniel D. Roman, *Managing Projects: A Systems Approach* (New York: Elsevier, 1986): 2–10; John M. Stewart, "Making Project Management Work,"*Business Horizons* 8, no. 3 (Fall 1965): 54–68.
7. See John Terraine, *The Mighty Continent* (London: BBC, 1974): 241–242.
8. D.I. Cleland and W.R. King, *Systems Analysis and Project Management*, 3rd ed. (New York: McGraw-Hill, 1983): 5–6.
9. See Meredith and Mantel, *Project Management*, 3; Milton D. Rosenau, *Successful Project Management* (Belmont, CA: Lifetime Learning, 1981): 15–19.
10. Harold Kerzner, *Project Management: A Systems Approach to Planning, Organizing, and Controlling* (New York: Van Nostrand Reinhold, 1979): 6.
11. Archibald, *Managing High-Technology Projects*, 6–7.
12. Kerzner, *Project Management*, 7.
13. C.P. Snow, *The Two Cultures and a Second Look* (Cambridge, England: Cambridge University Press, 1969).
14. *A Guide to the Project Management Body of Knowledge (PMBOK Guide)*, 3rd ed., Project Management Institute, November 2004.

Part

I

Philosophy and Concepts

CHAPTER 1

What Is Project Management?

CHAPTER 2

Systems Approach and Systems Engineering

*T*he two chapters in this part describe the philosophy and concepts that differentiate project management from traditional, nonproject management. Project management is an application of what has been called the systems approach to management. This section introduces features associated with project management and describes the principles, terminology, and methodology of the systems approach. It forms the foundation of the book and sets the stage for more detailed coverage in later parts.

Both of these chapters address what PMBOK refers to as project management "process." Although Chapter 2 covers topics not explicitly included in PMBOK, topics in the chapter fall broadly under the PMBOK areas of project integration management and project scope management.

Chapter 1

What Is Project Management?

> *Making a film is a lot like carrying out a space mission. Both are big-ticket items produced by teams, which come into existence with budgetary and schedule constraints. The technical skills necessary to land a spacecraft on a planet are close to the ones required to create the illusion of that landing.[1]*

—M.G. LORD,
Astro Turf

*T*he projects mentioned in the Introduction—the Great Pyramid of Cheops, the international space station, the Chunnel, and the development of Product J—all have something in common with each other and with every other undertaking of human organizations: they all require, in a word, *management*. Certainly the resources, work tasks, and goals of these projects vary greatly; yet without management, none of them could happen. This chapter contrasts project management and non-project management and looks at the variety of ways and places where project management is used. It also serves as an introduction to the concepts and topics of later chapters.

1.1 FUNCTIONS AND VIEWPOINTS OF MANAGEMENT[2]

The role of management is to plan, organize, and integrate resources and tasks to achieve project goals. Although the specific responsibilities of managers vary greatly, all managers—whether they are corporate presidents, agency directors, line managers, school administrators, movie producers, or project managers—have this same role.

Management Functions

The activities of a manager can be classified into the five functions identified in Figure 1-1. First, the manager decides what has to be done and how it will be done. This is the *planning* function, which involves setting a purpose or goal and establishing the means for achieving it consistent with available organizational goals, resources, and constraints in the environment.

Second and related to planning is arranging for the work to be done, which is the *organizing* function. The manager must (1) hire, train, and gather people into a system of authority, responsibility, and accountability relationships; (2) acquire and allocate facilities, materials, capital, and other resources; and (3) create an organization structure that includes policies, procedures, reporting patterns, and communication channels.

Third, the manager directs and motivates people to attain the goal. This is the *leadership* function. The manager focuses on workers, groups, and their relationships to influence work performance and behavior.

Fourth, the manager evaluates work performance with respect to the goal or some standard and takes necessary action to correct for deviation from the goal; this is the *control* function. For effective control, the manager relies upon information about performance with respect to costs, schedules, and goal criteria.

All four functions are performed to accomplish the goal, which implies a fifth function: assessing the four functions to determine how well they, the functions, are doing and where *change* is needed, either in the functions themselves or the goal.

On a day-by-day basis, rarely do managers perform the functions in Figure 1-1 in strict sequence. Although planning should precede the others, there is always a need to organize activities, direct people, and evaluate work, regardless of sequence. Managers constantly face change, which means that plans, activities, performance standards, and leadership styles must also change. Managers oversee a variety of work tasks simultaneously, and for each one they must be able to exercise any of these functions at a given time.

Different managers' jobs carry different responsibilities depending on the functional area and managerial level of the job. Some managers devote most of their time to planning and organizing, others to controlling, and others to directing and motivating. No process or set of prescriptive functions seems to apply equally well in all management cases. Managers must be adaptable to the situation. This is the *contingency viewpoint* of management.

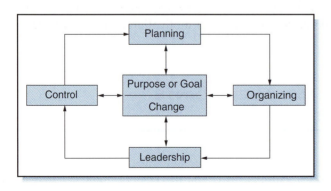

Figure 1-1
The functions of management.

Viewpoints of Management

The contingency viewpoint is but the latest in an evolving series of management propositions and methodologies. The earliest, called the *classical* viewpoint, originated at the start of the twentieth century. This held that there was one *best way* to manage with a corresponding set of universal bureaucratic and scientific management principles that could be applied to all situations. The classical viewpoint established formal principles for planning, organizing, leading, and controlling. In theory, the principles outline all the kinds of things managers should do. The drawback is that they presume much more order and rationality than actually exists in organizations and, therefore, provide poor guidance about what managers should do in different situations.

The 1930s brought the *behavioral* viewpoint in which the emphasis shifted from work principles to the human and social aspects of organizations. One of the early proponents of this viewpoint, Elton Mayo, introduced the concept of "social man"—the worker who is motivated by social needs and relationships with others and is responsive to work group norms and pressures.[3] The contribution of this viewpoint is that it highlighted the importance of leadership style, group dynamics, and social environment, concepts not even acknowledged by the classical theorists. But the behaviorists, like their classical counterparts, tended to look at management rather narrowly. Human and organization behavior are more complex than they presumed, and many behaviorist theories concerning satisfaction, morale, and productivity are too simplistic to be of practical use. In the end, managers still have to rely on their own best judgment.

During World War II the third viewpoint, called the *systems approach*, was introduced. Whereas the first two viewpoints sought to simplify management through concepts that would fit all situations, the systems viewpoint acknowledges complexity and causal relationships. Simply stated, before the manager can prescribe action, she must first understand the system and its relationship with the environment. Rather than give a new set of rote prescriptions about how to manage, the approach suggested ways to understand the elements and dynamics of a situation, and models to help clarify problems and identify courses of action. But even this approach could not always be relied upon to tell the manager what to do because it could not adequately represent "non-quantifiables" such as human motivations, emotions, and values. Even the systems viewpoint must be supplemented by the judgment of the manager.

All three viewpoints represent different perspectives, all make valuable contributions to management theory and practice, and all have limitations. The current *contingency* viewpoint recognizes that none of them alone can guide a manager in all aspects of the job in every situation. The current viewpoint, which includes ideas like situational leadership[4] and the contingency approach to management,[5] stresses that all three views can be applied independently or in some combination, *depending upon the situation*. Simply, the contingency viewpoint suggests that for management practice to be effective, it must be consistent with the requirements of the environment, the tasks to be performed, and the motivation and skills of the people who perform them.

1.2 PROJECT VIEWPOINT VERSUS TRADITIONAL MANAGEMENT

The purpose of project management is to manage a system of tasks, resources, people, and organizations to accomplish the project goal; this is what makes it a systems approach to management. Nonetheless, project management also relies upon elements of the classical and behavioral viewpoints. It is, in fact, a good example of the contingency approach because it is a management philosophy and methodology oriented toward accomplishment of just one type of undertaking—projects.

Characteristics of Projects

A project was defined in the Introduction as:[6]

1. Involving a single, definable purpose and well-defined end-items or deliverables.
2. Unique.
3. Somewhat or largely unfamiliar.
4. Utilizing skills and talents from multiple professions and organizations.
5. A temporary activity.
6. Something at stake.
7. The *process* of working to achieve a goal.

Perhaps the most significant distinguishing characteristics are the second, third, and fourth: every project is unique and unfamiliar in some sense, and requires multi-functional or multi-organizational involvement. These create uncertainty and risk, and decrease the chances of achieving the desired result. In non-project, repetitive activities like mass production or delivery of services, which involve procedures that are seldom changed and are performed by the same people, day-in, day-out, the results are more certain and the risks low.

Projects need a different kind of management.

Characteristics of Project Management

Looking at the characteristics of a project, the question from a management perspective is: How do you manage such a thing? The answer: use project management.

The key features of project management are:[7]

1. A single person, the project manager, heads the project organization and functions independently of the normal chain of command. The project organization reflects the cross-functional, goal-oriented, temporary nature of the project.
2. The project manager is *the* person who brings together all efforts to meet project objectives.
3. Because each project requires a variety of skills and resources, the actual project work might be performed by people from different functional areas or by outside contractors.
4. The project manager is responsible for integrating people from the different functional areas or contractors who work on the project.
5. The project manager negotiates directly with functional managers who might be responsible for the individual work tasks and personnel within the project.
6. While the project manager focuses on delivering a particular product or service at a certain time and cost, functional managers must maintain an ongoing pool of resources in support of organizational goals. As a result, conflict may arise between project and functional managers over the time and talent to be allotted to a project.
7. A project might have two chains of command, one functional and one project, and people in a project report to both a project manager and a functional manager.

8. Decision making, accountability, outcomes, and rewards are shared between the project team and supporting functional units.
9. Although the project organization is temporary, the functional or subcontracting units from which it is formed are permanent. When a project ends, the project organization is disbanded and people return to their functional or subcontracting units.
10. Project management sets into motion work in numerous supporting functions such as HR, accounting, procurement, and IT.

Because projects involve the coordinated efforts of different units from within and outside the organization, the traditional *vertical* chain of command for authority and communication is not very effective. To get a project done, managers and workers in different units and at different levels need to associate directly with each other. In traditional organizations, communication and authority run vertically. In project organizations, formal lines of communication and authority are frequently bypassed and a *horizontal hierarchy* is created that augments the vertical hierarchy. This horizontal hierarchy enables members of the project organization from different functional areas and outside organizations to communicate and work directly with each other as needed.

Managers in traditional organizations tend to be specialized and responsible for a single functional unit or department, which works well for optimizing the efficiency of the department. A project, however, needs the support of many departments and, hence, someone from outside these departments to take responsibility for meeting the project's goals. That person is the project manager. This emphasis on project goals versus the performance of each functional unit is a major distinguishing feature between project managers and functional managers.

Project managers often depend upon people who are not "under" them but who are "assigned" to them from different areas of the organization as needed. Thus, the task of project managers is more complicated and diverse than for departmental managers. A project manager must know how to use diplomacy, resolve conflicts, be an effective leader, and able to function without the convenience of always having the same team reporting to him.

Example 1: Project Management in Construction

Construction projects are often in the news—sometimes because of problems owing to cost overruns or schedule slippages. Although many factors are cited (labor union problems, materials shortages, weather, inflation), the real cause is frequently poor management and lack of control. Often, the manager of a construction project is either the architect or the contractor. This works on small, less complex jobs, but on big construction jobs it is a bad arrangement because architects and contractors each represent the interests of separate "functional areas." When things go wrong and arguments arise, both tend to be self-serving; there is no one who is impartial and can reconcile differences in the best interests of the building and its owner.

A better arrangement is when the developer or the owner appoints an independent construction project manager. The project manager is the owner's agent during the entire design and construction process. The role is similar to that of the ancient master builders whose responsibility covered virtually all aspects of design and construction. Notice in Figure 1-2 the central position of the project manager in the project organization, a position that enables her to monitor and coordinate all design and building tasks in accordance with the owner's or developer's goals. The project manager's role is to ensure that the architect's designs are within the developer's cost allowances and building requirements, and that the contractor's work is executed according to contract specifications and at a

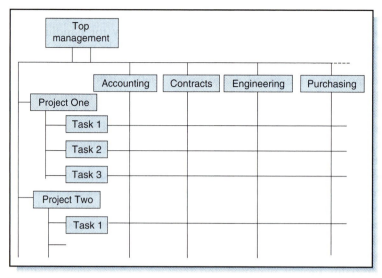

Figure 1-3
Vertical and horizontal elements of a matrix project organization.

- *Matrix managers*: Their purpose is to achieve *unity of direction*. Although they serve the same purpose as the first two, they also have authority to plan, motivate, direct, and control project work. Matrix managers direct people located administratively in functional departments, and the resulting crisscross pattern of vertical-functional and horizontal-project reporting relationships create what is called a *matrix organization*, illustrated in Figure 1-3. The manager of a construction project whose company both designs and constructs the building is such a manager. She relies upon managers in the architectural and construction departments to assign personnel to her project; these personnel report to her about the project and for as long as they are needed on the project. The same personnel may also work on other projects and report to other project managers.

- *Pure project managers*: These managers direct *pure project* organizations of people who report directly to them. Their purpose is to achieve *unity of command*. They are primarily integrators and generalists rather than technical specialists. They must balance technical factors of the project with schedules, costs, resources, and human factors. In the course of a project, they actively deal with top management, functional managers, vendors, customers, and subcontractors. The manager of a large construction project who is hired by the developer and delegated the authority to make major decisions (such as selecting and contracting with the architect and the contractor) has this role.

The last two types are most in keeping with the project management concept, although the other two are also widely found. All are discussed further in later chapters.

1.4   WHERE IS PROJECT MANAGEMENT APPROPRIATE?[9]

Project management originated in construction and aerospace because the environments and kinds of activities in those industries demand flexible forms of management. But what about other industries and other environments? Certainly there must be many applications of project management beyond the familiar ones cited. Fact is, project management is now used almost everywhere, and there are relatively few industries or situations where project management is not being applied at least some of the time. This section identifies conditions and situations where a project-type organization is more applicable (or essential) than a traditional, functional organization.

Project management can be applied to any ad hoc undertaking. As shown in the Introduction, Figure I-3, an "ad hoc undertaking" includes activities that range from writing a term paper or remodeling a kitchen, to fund-raising and constructing a theme park such as Walt Disney's Epcot. For most of these, project management is desirable or necessary. Generally, the more unfamiliar or unique the undertaking, the greater the need for project management to ensure nothing gets overlooked; the more numerous, interdisciplinary, and interdependent the activities in the undertaking, the greater the need for project management to ensure everything is coordinated, integrated, and completed.

Customers such as major corporations or the US government frequently request or mandate project management because they believe it offers better cost, schedule, and quality control, and they prefer having a single point of contact—the project manager—with whom to deal. In most cases, however, the contractor has the option of deciding when to use project management.

Criteria

Cleland and King list five general criteria for determining when to use project management techniques and organization:[10]

1. Unfamiliarity

By definition, a project is something different from the ordinary and routine. A project always requires that different things be done, that the same things be done differently, or both. For example, continuous minor changes in products such as small improvements in automobile parts can usually be accomplished without project management. But modernizing a plant, which calls for nonroutine efforts such as revising the facilities, replacing equipment, retraining employees, and altering policies and work procedures would certainly require project management.

2. Magnitude of the Effort

When a job requires substantially more resources (people, capital, equipment, etc.) than are normally employed by a department or organization, project management techniques may be necessary. Examples include relocating a facility, merging two corporations, or developing or substantially redesigning a product and placing it on the market. Even when the job lies primarily within the realm of one functional area, the task of coordinating the work with other functional areas might be large and mandate project management. For example, a corporate software installation project might *seem* to fall entirely within the functional area of IT, yet in reality it will require a continuous meshing of the procedures and resources of all the departments affected by the installation and may involve hundreds of people.

3. Changing Environment

Organizations in industries such as computers, electronics, pharmaceuticals, and communications face a rapidly changing environment—an environment characterized by high innovation, frequent product changes, and shifting markets and consumer behavior. Other industries such as chemicals, biotechnology, and aerospace also exist in an environment that, though less volatile, is highly competitive and dynamic. Project management and organization provides the necessary flexibility to deal with emerging threats and opportunities of the business environment.

4. Interrelatedness

Functional areas tend to be self-serving and work independently. When a multifunctional effort is required, project management builds lateral relationships between the areas to expedite work and reconcile any conflicts. The project manager coordinates the efforts of internal areas with each other and with those of outside subcontractors and vendors.

5. Reputation of the Organization

If failure to satisfactorily complete the project will result in financial ruin, loss of market share, damaged reputation, or loss of future contracts, there is a strong case for project management. Project management does not guarantee success but it does provide for better planning and control to improve the odds. It can do much to reduce the inherent risks in large, complex undertakings.

Example 2: Renovating the Statue of Liberty[11]

Ninety-five years after the Statue of Liberty was presented to the American people, its surface and interior structure had become so badly corroded that it was judged structurally unsound. To oversee restoration of the statue and other buildings on nearby Ellis Island, the US Department of Interior established a foundation.

Very little of the work qualified as "standard." Renovation of the statue involved highly specialized skills, such as erection of scaffolding, construction of a new torch, building of windows for the crown, and replacement of the interior framework—expertise that tends to be found in smaller firms. As a result, the work was accomplished by a legion of over 50 small businesses; many workers were immigrants or descendants of immigrants whom the statue had welcomed to America.

There were myriad notable features about the job. The scaffolding surrounding the statue never touched it at any point. Constructed of hundreds of thousands of pieces of aluminum, it qualified for the *Guinness Book of World Records* as the largest free-standing scaffolding ever built. To renovate the statue's interior, 1,699 five-foot bars were painstakingly fashioned from 35,000 pounds of stainless steel, then individually installed. Around the crown 25 windows were replaced. Each was handcrafted and had to be treated as a project unto itself. To fashion an entirely new torch, French artisans practiced an ancient copper shaping technique. The project was truly a marriage of art and engineering.

The 30-month, $31 million renovation effort involved thousands of tasks performed by hundreds of people. Most of the tasks were nonroutine and interrelated, and all had to be completed within a tight budget and schedule—certainly a situation that called for project management. (Chapter 15 discusses the company responsible for managing the renovation.)

Where Project Management Is Not Appropriate

The obverse of all of this is that the more familiar the undertaking, the more stable the environment, the less unique and more standardized the end-item, and the lower the stake in the result, the less the need for project management. Production of standardized industrial and agricultural products, for example, is generally more efficiently managed by tried and true operations planning and control procedures than by project management. This is because for standardized, repetitive operations, there is greater certainty in the process and outcome, and standardized, routine production procedures, schedules, and budgets are well suited.

1.5 MANAGEMENT BY PROJECT: A COMMON APPROACH

Though not appropriate for managing every situation or even every kind of project, project management does apply to a great many situations not only in large-scale, infrequent undertakings, but in all kinds of smaller, more frequent activities as well. Whenever an undertaking involves doing several activities that are unique or unfamiliar, and require cooperation from several parties, project management might apply.

For example, consultants in any industry perform work on a project-by-project basis; whenever these projects call for coordinated participation of several groups, project management applies. The more people or groups involved, the more disparate their tasks and the greater need for coordination, the greater the applicability.

Similarly, groups that work on the development or implementation of anything new (product, system, or service) also work on a project-by-project basis. The larger, riskier, more complex, costly, innovative, or different the thing being developed or implemented, the more applicable is project management.

Further, any group that performs unique work on a *client-by-client basis* (so-called made-to-order, or made-to-engineer) is also performing project work. If the end-item requires coordinated efforts from different parties, project management usually applies.

Think about these situations for a moment and you start to realize the many cases where projects happen and project management applies.

Managing any kind of work as a discrete project activity is referred to as "managing by project," or MBP.[12] With MBP, an undertaking or set of activities is planned and managed as if it was a project. In particular, MBP implies that the undertaking will have well-defined objectives and scope, firm requirements for the objectives and end-results, a completion date, a budget for the cost of required resources, and a plan to review progress and final results. A team is formed for the sole purpose of performing the work, and a project manager or team leader assigned to guide and coordinate the work. Work progress is carefully tracked and compared to the project plan to assess performance in terms of end-results, schedules, and costs.

At some time, all organizations use project approaches. Even in stable repetitive industries, small informal projects involving a few individuals are always in progress: new machines are installed, old ones are repaired; the office is remodeled; the cafeteria is relocated. It is when larger or more special undertakings arise, such as the development of a totally new product, the move of a company, or installation of major equipment that a more formalized project group must be formed.

Example 3: Relocation of Goman Publishing Company

Many companies regardless of size (headquarters for a multi-billion dollar corporation or a storefront family restaurant) at some point face the decision to relocate. Relocation requires planning and coordination of numerous tasks involving many individuals, departments, and outside contractors. It is an important event that if done properly can be an exciting and profitable experience, but if done poorly can lead to financial loss or ruin. It also is representative of innumerable situations wherein a company must do something it does not ordinarily do.

Consider Goman Publishing, a company experiencing rapid growth and soon to exceed the capacity of its current facility. The initial task in relocating the company was to decide between two options: buying land and constructing a new building, or leasing or buying an existing structure. After deciding to build, the next task was to select a site. The main selection criteria were purchase expense, distance from current location, prestige and size of the new location, and access to major highways. Next was the relocation planning, which had two major phases: design and construction of the new facility, and the physical move, each involving numerous considerations. For example, Goman wanted to retain its current employees, and so as to maximize the new facility's appeal it chose to build an indoor employee parking area and a large, well-appointed cafeteria. Among the many move-related considerations were furniture procurement, special handling of computer equipment, hiring movers, distributing information to employees and clients about the move, and maintaining corporate security. Further, the relocation would have to be scheduled to minimize downtime and interruption of operations.

To oversee the project and ensure that construction and the physical move went according to plan, Goman appointed a project manager and support staff. The project manager worked with architects and building contractors during the design and construction phases, and later with moving contractors and representatives from functional departments who kept him abreast of problems and progress. Despite the scope and unfamiliarity of the project, Goman was able to complete the construction and physical move according to schedule and within budget.

1.6 DIFFERENT FORMS OF PROJECT MANAGEMENT

Project management has been termed different names, including systems management, task force management, team management, ad hoc management, matrix management, and program management. Regardless, all these forms of management share two features: (1) a *project team* or project organization created uniquely for the purpose of achieving a specific goal, and (2) a single person—the *project manager*—assigned responsibility for seeing that the goal is accomplished. Beyond these, features differ somewhat depending on the application.

The following sections highlight these differences. In the first section, the term "basic" project management refers to what is the most commonly understood concept of project management. The other sections cover variants of or management forms similar to project management.

Basic Project Management

The most common project approach places the project manager and functional managers on the same organizational level so that both report to the same person. The project manager is given formal authority to plan, direct, organize, and control the project from start to finish. The project manager may work directly with any level and functional area of the organization to accomplish project goals. She reports to the general manager or owner and keeps him apprised of project status. Although sometimes the project manager has authority to hire personnel and procure facilities, more often she negotiates with functional managers to "borrow" these.

Basic project management is implemented in two widely used forms—pure project and matrix. In pure project management a complete, self-contained organization is created. Resources belong to the project and do not have to be borrowed. In matrix management, the project organization is created from resources allotted (borrowed) from the functional units. The project must share these resources with other concurrent projects and with the functional areas from which they are borrowed. These two project management forms will be described further in Chapter 13.

Although often found in construction and technology industries, basic project management could readily be applied to small, non-technical activities as well, including in the arts and social sciences. Adams, Barndt, and Martin cite examples where basic project management could (but has yet to) be applied:[13]

- Health, Education, and Welfare (HEW) performs social work largely on the basis of grants allocated through state and local agencies. Associated with each grant are time, cost, and performance requirements of the funding agencies. In essence, each grant results in a project or projects—to which the concepts of project management apply.

- When an advertising firm conducts a promotional campaign it utilizes the support of marketing research, accounting, graphics, sales, and other units. Several projects are usually underway at any given time, each in a different stage of its life cycle. These campaigns are similar to the projects and programs in other industries that commonly practice project management.

- A good deal of work performed in education development can be considered project work. Like HEW, much of this work is funded by grants with target goals and cost and time constraints. Also, the work requires coordination among many educators and researchers—a task for which project management is ideally suited.

Program Management

The term "program management" is often used interchangeably with project management due to the similarities of programs and projects: both (1) are defined in terms of goals or objectives about what must be accomplished; (2) emphasize the time period over which goals or objectives are to be pursued; and (3) require plans, budgets, and schedules for accomplishing the goals. In short, projects and programs both work toward goals specified in terms of a desired product or service output, a date of accomplishment, and a budget.

But for definitional purposes in this book, programs and projects are different. A program extends over a longer time horizon and consists of several parallel or sequential work efforts or projects that are coordinated to meet a program goal. The projects within a program share common goals and resources, and often they are interdependent. As examples, an urban development program may include several projects such as housing rehab, job and skill training, and small business consulting assistance; a planetary exploration program may include several projects for unmanned probes to Mars and its moons, Phobos, and Diemos, followed by a manned mission to Mars. Actually, some of these projects might grow to become so large that they themselves would have to be set up as full-fledged programs, as was the case with the Apollo Lunar Program. The Manhattan Project was really a "program."

Another distinction is that projects are oriented to producing and delivering a product or service, after which the project organization is dissolved. The project organization develops and delivers the end-item, but afterward the end-item's operation is somebody else's responsibility. Similarly, the contractor who develops the end-item is usually not responsible for maintaining it afterwards. In a program, however, once the end-item product or service has been delivered, it is up to program management to ensure that it is integrated with other systems and operational for as long as needed. For example, several contractors might produce and deliver a work in government projects is performed by contractors, the project manager's role is largely administrative. Though he is responsible for checking on the contractors' progress, the project manager has little control over technical matters. Project managers may oversee and coordinate multiple, related projects within a larger system; in other words, they are program managers.

Military Project Management

Similar to government projects, most military projects involve testing and evaluating hardware developed by contractors. Evaluation is often based on the "weapons systems" approach whereby each project is part of a larger systems program and hardware is evaluated for its contribution to the mission of the overall system. The major criteria for evaluating projects are technical and political; costs are of lesser importance and profit is not a consideration. Project managers are military officers. Because their tour of duty is limited, officers typically do not oversee a project for its full life cycle. Thus the military must train, transfer, or promote people with the administrative and technical competence to carry on the job.

Civilians are often employed to provide technical support and managerial continuity. This arrangement is a source of strife because civilians are not subject to the same rotation of assignments and are often paid more, despite their formal "subordinate" status to military project managers.

Many organizations exist in multiple project environments (such as government/military and commercial) and utilize a variety of management forms—project, program, matrix, task force, and committee.

1.8 PROJECT MANAGEMENT IN INDUSTRIAL SETTINGS

The following cases show typical applications of project management in three industrial settings: product development, manufacturing, and construction. They are intended to portray the diversity in scope and size of typical project management situations in industry.

SpaceShipOne and the X-Prize Competition[16]

In April 2003, SpaceShipOne (SS1) and its mothership White Knight were rolled out to the public. Simultaneously it was announced that SS1 was entering the $10 million X-Prize competition against 23 other teams from seven countries to be the first manned vehicle to successfully make two trips into space in less than 2 weeks (Figure 1-5). Space is internationally recognized as beginning at 100 kilometers, or about 62 miles up (commercial jets fly at about 8 kilometers). The brainchild of celebrated aerospace engineer and visionary Burt Rutan and the culmination of almost 8 years of design and development work, it was but the first step in Rutan's broader dream to build vehicles to carry paying passengers into space. Rutan's major challenge was not just winning of the prize, but designing and building a *complete space launch system*—spacecraft, aerial launch vehicle, rocket motor, and all support subsystems—without having many hundreds of engineers to do it and many millions of dollars in government support. Rutan would try to do it with his own company of 130 people, a small handful of subcontractors, and the backing of a single investor, billionaire Paul Allen, cofounder of Microsoft.

Figure 1-5
SpaceShipOne beneath its mothership, White Knight. (Photo courtesy of John Nicholas.)

Besides Rutan and Allen, the principal stakeholders in the program included the Ansari Foundation, Sir Richard Branson, and the Federal Aviation Administration (FAA). Allen, an aviation enthusiast, committed $25 million to the project in return for ownership of Rutan's spaceship technology. The Ansari Foundation is the sponsor of the X-Prize competition. Its long-term goal is to spur innovations that will make space travel safe, affordable, and accessible to everyone, and its X-Prize requirements were for "a non-government-funded program to put three people safely into space twice within 2 weeks with a reusable spacecraft." Sir Richard Branson, founder of the Virgin Group, is Rutan's and Allen's customer; his plan is to buy from them spaceships and associated technology for his fledgling space airline, Virgin Galactic. Branson has estimated Virgin will be able to turn a profit if it can carry 3,000 customers into suborbit over a 5-year period at about $190,000 a ticket—to include medical checks, 3 days of preflight training, custom-molded seats, and five minutes of floating weightless while in space. (By comparison, a trip aboard the Russian Soyuz will cost you about $20 million.) Paying passengers are another stakeholder group. Although none would be aboard SS1, the vehicle was designed with them in mind. For instance, SS1's cabin is designed to provide a "shirtsleeve" environment, which means passengers do not have to wear spacesuits. The FAA is also a stakeholder; it imposes a long list of requirements necessary for the spaceship to be "certified" and commercially viable.

As in most technical projects, SS1 is managed by a project engineer and a project manager. The project engineer is responsible for identifying functional requirements, overseeing design work, system integration, and testing. All this and what is left for the project manager to do will become clearer in later chapters.

Product Management: The Development of Product J[17]

The future of Dalian Company depends on its ability to continuously develop and market new products. Dalian specializes in food and drink additives, but it is representative of all kinds of firms in industries such as pharmaceuticals, food products, biotechnology, home and commercial appliances, computer and entertainment electronics, and communications that continuously need to generate new ideas to survive in a changing, competitive environment.

Dalian Company was concerned about maintaining market share for "Product N," a mainstay that accounted for the majority of its profits. It was known that other companies were developing substitutes for Product N that might be less expensive. To beat the competition, Dalian had to develop its own improved substitute, "Product J."

Facilitating the product development process is a department called, appropriately, the New Product Development Department. The department is a "project office" firms—fictitiously called CPAone and CPAtwo—project management is used to plan and control auditing and management consultation projects. A third example shows project management applied to a nonprofit fund-raising campaign.

Improving Auditing Efficiency at CPAone

The auditing division at CPAone generates financial statements to meet generally accepted accounting principles. In large audits, the size of the task and the range of problems require the involvement of many people. In the audit of a national corporation, for example, numerous auditors with diverse specialties are required to investigate all aspects of operations in various geographic areas. Given the number of people and the variety of skills, expertise, and personalities involved, a project manager is needed to oversee and conduct the audit efficiently. Every audit begins by assigning the client to a partner, usually someone who is familiar with the client's business. The partner becomes the audit's "project director," responsible for the project's initiation, staffing, scheduling, and budgeting.

The project director begins by studying the client's income statement, balance sheet, and other financial statements. If the client has a bad financial reputation, the project director can make the decision for CPAone to refuse the audit. If the client is accepted, the director prepares a proposal that explains the general approach for conducting the audit and designates the completion date and the cost estimate.

In determining the general approach for conducting the audit, the project director considers the company's size and number of departments. Auditors are then assigned on a department-by-department basis. The audit team is a pure project team, created anew for every audit, composed of people who have the skills best suited to the needs of the audit. Generally, each audit team has one or two staff accountants and one or two senior accountants. Before the proposal is even accepted, the director specifies who will be performing each task within a given time frame. The project cost estimate is based on estimated labor hours multiplied by employees' hourly wages.

During the audit the director ensures that all work adheres to the Book of Auditing Standards and is completed on schedule. Each week the client and project director meet to review progress. When problems arise that cannot be solved immediately, the director may call in people for CPAone's tax or consulting divisions. Service is sometimes provided after the audit is completed: should the IRS request an examination, the project director sees to it that the client is represented.

Management Consulting at CPAtwo

CPAtwo uses project management in its management consulting division (MCD). MCD projects are classified into seven areas: systems planning, business planning, profit improvement, contract management, data security, executive management, and human resources.

In the systems planning area, projects focus on determining the best system (e.g., payroll processing) to satisfy a firm's needs or objectives. Systems analysis methodology (described in Chapter 2) is applied to define system characteristics, evaluate benefits, and assign priorities for implementation. A typical project begins by first reviewing the client's present system, followed by a proposal summarizing the findings and suggesting options for a new system. If the proposal is accepted, MCD management determines who will be assigned to the project, when the project should be completed, and the cost. A partner or senior manager is assigned as project leader based on his familiarity with the client or the system. From then on, the project leader has complete responsibility, including to select people from MCD to work on the project team. The project leader creates the plans and schedules, and determines costs based upon employee hourly rates and hours needed to complete the job.

When the division has sufficient internal expertise, a pure project organization of MCD personnel is formed; when it does not, a matrix form of project organization is used, with other divisions supplying people with the needed skills. The project leader directs the team in project matters, and keeps MCD management informed of progress—much the same as do project directors at CPAone and Dalian.

Nonprofit Fund-raising Campaign Project: Archdiocese of Boston[20]

American Services Company, a fund-raising consulting firm for nonprofit organizations, contracted with the Archdiocese of Boston to manage a 3-year campaign to raise $30 million for education, social and health care services, building renovations, and a clergy retirement fund. American Services appointed a project manager to prepare the campaign strategy and to organize and direct the campaign staff. The project manager had to deal with issues concerning three groups: donors, the Archdiocese Board of Directors, and campaign volunteers. Potential target donors had to be identified and provided with evidence to show how their financial commitment would benefit the community and the Archdiocese; the board and church leadership had to be involved in and kept apprised of campaign planning and progress; and volunteers had to be identified, organized, and motivated.

One of the project manager's first tasks was to conduct a feasibility study to determine whether there was sufficient leadership capability, volunteer willingness, and "donor depth" within the Archdiocese community to achieve the $30 million goal. Following the study, which indicated that the goal was achievable, pastors were invited to a kick-off luncheon at which time the Cardinal of the Archdiocese introduced the campaign. During the meeting, influential church personnel were signed up and the process of identifying potential donors and volunteers started.

The project manager provided guidance for establishing a campaign leadership team and project office, enlisting volunteers, forming campaign committees, and recruiting and training volunteers. In addition to organizational matters, he convened several "reality sessions" with chairpersons to remind them of the importance of the campaign and renew their commitment to the campaign goal, and organized frequent meetings with the volunteers to instill a sense of pride and involvement in the campaign.

1.10   PROJECT AND PROGRAM MANAGEMENT IN GOVERNMENT AND THE PUBLIC SECTOR

The following two illustrations about disaster recovery and NASA organization illustrate how project management and program management are performed in large public sector and joint government/commercial undertakings.

Disaster Recovery

The aid assistance, cleanup, rebuilding, and return-to-normalcy efforts following a disaster involve the labors of numerous organizations. A large disaster such the integrate, and test-flight hardware, it relies upon its own considerable in-house management and technical competence to monitor and work with contractors. Because NASA projects call for a diversity of technical and managerial competency, project managers practice the philosophy of "participative responsibility"—an integration of technical and managerial competency across industry, academia, and NASA laboratories. Regardless of location, NASA brings in experts from its own field installations, from universities, and from other government laboratories to assist contractors in tackling difficult problems. This participative team approach avoids the usual delays caused by working across boundaries that separate government, commercial, and military organizations. The concept utilizes teamwork, central control, and decentralized execution, but respects the semi-autonomous status of NASA's field installations.

NASA defines a *program* as a series of undertakings, which over several years is designed to accomplish broad scientific or technical goals. Responsibility for programs is assigned by NASA headquarters. A *project* is an undertaking within a program with a scheduled beginning and end, and normally involves design, construction, and/or operation and support of specific hardware items.

NASA uses a dual system of responsibility. Perhaps the single greatest contributor to a project's success is the person upon whom final responsibility rests, the *project manager*. She is the official responsible for executing the project within the guidelines and controls of NASA, and for day-to-day supervision, execution, and completion of projects, whether conducted by NASA, its contractors, or university scientists. Although most of the workers on a project are outside of the administrative authority of the project manager, nonetheless they take directions *on project matters* from the project manager.

The project manager has a counterpart in Washington, the *program manager*, who is the senior NASA staff official responsible for developing and administering headquarter's guidelines and controls with respect to a given project. He must fight the battles for resource allocation within headquarters, work with all organizations participating in the project, relate the project to NASA's broader goals, and testify to or justify authorizations from Congress or the President. The success of a project depends on both the project and program manager and the quality of their relationship.

1.11 SUMMARY

This chapter addressed the question, "What is project management?" by describing the characteristics that distinguish projects, project environments, and project managers from non-project forms of activities and managers. All managers "manage" tasks and resources: they translate organizational goals into specific objectives, prepare plans for the tasks and resources needed to achieve objectives, organize the resources, and direct, evaluate, and control work tasks and resources to ensure objectives are met.

Project management is a systems/contingency approach to organization and management; it applies elements of classical and behavioral management and uses organizational forms and management roles best suited to the unique environment of projects.

The most important aspect of project management is the project manager. This person functions to unify project-related planning, communications, control, and direction to achieve project goals. The project manager is an integrator-generalist who ties together the efforts of functional areas, suppliers, and subcontractors, and keeps top management and the customer apprised of project progress. Project management includes the organizations, systems, and procedures that enable the project manager to perform this function.

Project management can be applied to any temporary, goal-oriented activity, but it becomes more essential as the magnitude, unfamiliarity, and stake of the undertaking increase. Organizations in rapidly changing business and technology environments especially need project management.

Project management takes on a variety of forms: larger efforts typically utilize pure project, matrix, and program management forms; smaller efforts are handled by ad hoc committees and task forces. New venture and product management forms used in consumer-oriented firms are similar to project management. Project management is applied in much the same way in commercial, nonprofit, government, and military projects, with variations to account for differences in the environments.

Project management is a "systems approach" to management. The next chapter describes what that means and discusses the systems philosophy and methodologies that underlie a large part of project management theory and practice.

REVIEW QUESTIONS

1. Describe five functions of management. Are any of these not performed by managers? How do you think each of these functions comes into play in the course of a project?

2. Describe the classical and behavioral viewpoints of management and how they differ from the systems approach. The classical and behavioral viewpoints originated decades ago. Are they still of use today? (For a better idea of how the viewpoints differ, refer to current popular management references or texts.)

3. Explain what distinguishes the contingency approach to management from the other three viewpoints.

4. List the main characteristics of "projects." How do these features distinguish projects from other, non-project activities?

5. What are the characteristics of "project management?" Contrast these to functional and other types of non-project management.

6. What makes project management more suitable to project environments than traditional management and organization?

7. Where did project management methods and organization originate? What happened during the twentieth century that made project management necessary?

8. What are the four types of project management roles? Describe the responsibilities and authority of managers in each role. Are all four roles ever used in the same organization?

9. What are the five criteria that Cleland and King suggest for determining when to use project management? From these, describe briefly how a manager should know when project management is appropriate for the task.

10. When is project management clearly not appropriate? List some "project-type" activities where you think project management should *not* be used. Describe organizations or kinds of work where both project and non-project types of management are appropriate.

11. Briefly compare and contrast the following forms of project management: pure project, matrix, program, new venture and product. Give at least one illustration of an organization where each is used.

12. What are some of the problems of being a project leader in commercial, government, and military projects? Where do organizations in these environments get project leaders?

13. In the industry, service sector, and government examples in this chapter, what common characteristics of the environment, the project goals, and the project tasks make project management appropriate (or necessary)? Also, what seem to be the common characteristics of the roles and responsibilities of the project managers in these examples? What are the differences?

14. Now that you know a little about projects and project management, list some government and private organizations where you think project management might be useful. You might want to check to see if, in fact, they *are* using project management.

QUESTIONS ABOUT THE STUDY PROJECT

1. In the project you are studying, what characteristics of the company, project goals, tasks, or necessary expertise make the use of project management appropriate or inappropriate? Consider the project size, complexity, risk, and other criteria in answering this question.

2. How does the project you are studying fit the definition of a project?

3. What kind of project management is used—program, product, matrix, pure, or other? Explain. Is it called "project management" or something else?

4. What kind of role does the project manager have—an expeditor, coordinator, pure project, or matrix manager? Explain. What is his or her title?

Case 1-1   *Disaster Recovery at Marshall Field's*[24]

Early one morning, basements in Chicago's downtown central business district began to flood. A hole the size of an automobile had developed between the Chicago River and an adjacent abandoned tunnel. The tunnel, built in the early 1900s for transporting coal, runs throughout the downtown area. When the tunnel flooded, so did the basements connected to it, some 272 in all, including that of major retailer Marshall Field's.

The problem was first noted at 5:30 A.M. by a member of the Marshall Field's trouble desk who saw water pouring into the basement. The manager of maintenance was notified and immediately took charge. His first actions were to contact the Chicago Fire and Water Departments, and Marshall Field's parent company, Dayton Hudson in Minneapolis. Electricity—and with it all elevator, computer, communication, and security services for the 15-story building—would soon be lost. The building was evacuated and elevators

were moved above basement levels. A command post was set up and a team formed from various departments such as facilities, security, human resources, public relations, and financial, legal, insurance, and support services. Later that day, members of Dayton Hudson's risk management group arrived from Minneapolis to take over coordinating the team's efforts. The team's goal was to ensure the safety of employees and customers, minimize flood damage, and resume normal operations as soon as possible. The team hoped to open the store to customers 1 week after the flood began.

An attempt was made to pump the water out; however, as long as the tunnel hole remained unrepaired, the Chicago River continued to pour back into the basements. Thus, the basements remained flooded until the tunnel was sealed and the Army Corps of Engineers gave approval to start pumping. Everything in the second-level basement was a loss, including equipment for security, heating,

28   **Part I   Philosophy and Concepts**

ventilation, air-conditioning, fire sprinkling, and mechanical services. Most merchandise in the first-level basement stockrooms was also lost.

Electricians worked around the clock to install emergency generators and restore lighting and elevator service. Additional security officers were hired. An emergency pumping system and new piping to the water sprinkling tank were installed so the sprinkler system could be reactivated. Measures were taken to monitor ventilation and air quality, and dehumidifiers and fans were installed to improve air quality. Within the week, inspectors from the City of Chicago and OSHA gave approval to reopen the store.

During this time, engineers had repaired the hole in the tunnel. After water was drained from Marshall Field's basements, damaged merchandise was removed and sold to a salvager. The second basement had to be gutted to assure removal of contaminants. Salvageable machinery had to be disassembled and sanitized.

The extent of the damage was assessed and insurance claims filed. A construction company was hired to manage restoration of the damaged areas. Throughout the ordeal, the public relations department dealt with the media, being candid yet showing confidence in the recovery effort. Customers had to be assured that the store was safe and employees kept apprised of the recovery effort. The team overseeing the recovery initially met twice a week to evaluate progress and make decisions, then slowly disbanded as the store recovered.

This case illustrates crisis management, an important element of which is having a team that moves fast to minimize losses and quickly recover damages. At the beginning of a disaster there is little time to plan, though companies and public agencies often have crisis guidelines for responding to emergency situations. Afterwards they then develop more specific, detailed plans to guide longer-term recovery efforts.

QUESTIONS

1. In what ways was the Marshall Field's flood disaster recovery effort a project? Why are large-scale disaster response and recovery efforts projects?
2. In what ways do the characteristics of crisis management as described in this case correspond to those of project management?
3. Who was (were) the project manager(s) and what was his or her (their) responsibility? Who was assigned to the project team and why were they on the team?
4. Comment on the appropriateness of using project management for managing disaster recovery efforts such as this.
5. What form of project management (basic, program, and so on) does this case most closely resemble?

Case 1-2   *Flexible Benefits System Implementation at Shah Alam Medical Center*[25]

To reduce the cost and improve the value and service of its employee benefits coverage, the management committee of Shah Alam Medical Center decided to procure and implement a new benefits system. The new system would have to meet four goals: improved responsiveness to employee needs, added benefits flexibility, better cost management, and greater coordination of human resource objectives with business strategies. A multifunctional team of 13 members was formed with representatives from the departments that would rely most on the new system—Human Resources (HR), Financial Systems (FS), and Information Services (IS). Representation from these departments was important to assure all of their needs would be met. The team also included six technical experts from the consulting firm of Hun and Bar Software (HBS).

Early in the project a workshop was held with team members from Shah Alam and HBS to clarify and finalize project objectives and develop a project plan, milestones, and schedule. Project completion was set at 10 months. In that time HBS had to develop and supply all hardware and software for the new system; the system had to be brought on-line, tested, and approved; HR workers had to be trained how to operate the system and load existing employee data; all Shah Alam employees had to be educated about and enrolled in the new benefits process; and the enrollment data had to be entered in the system.

The director of FS was chosen to oversee the project. She had the technical background and had previously worked in the IS group in implementing Shah Alam's patient care information system. Everyone on the team approved of her appointment as project leader, and many team members had worked with her previously. To assist her she selected two team leaders, one each from HR and IS. The HR leader's task was to ensure that the new system met HR requirements and the needs of Shah Alam employees; the IS leader's task was to ensure that the new software interfaced with other Shah Alam systems.

Members of the Shah Alam team worked on the project on a part-time basis, spending roughly 50 percent of the time on the project and the rest on their normal daily duties. The project manager and team leaders also worked on the project part time, although when conflicts arose the project took priority. Shah Alam's top-management committee had made it clear that meeting project requirements and time deadlines was imperative. The project director was given authority over functional managers and project team members for all project-related decisions.

QUESTIONS

1. What form of project management (basic, program, etc.) does this case most closely resemble?

2. The project manager is also the director of FS, only one of the departments that will be affected by the new benefits system. Does this seem like a good idea? What are the pros and cons of her selection?

3. Comment on the team members' part-time assignment to the project and the expectation that they give the project top priority.

4. Much of the success of this project depends on the performance of team members who are not employed by Shah Alam, namely the HBS consultants. They must develop the entire hardware/software benefits system. Why was an outside firm likely chosen for such an important part of the project? What difficulties might this pose to the project manager in meeting project goals?

ENDNOTES

1. M.G. Lord, *Astro Turf* (New York: Walker & Co., 2005): 166.
2. Adapted from Andrew Szilagyi, *Management and Performance*, 2nd ed. (Glenview, IL: Scott, Foresman, 1984): 7–10, 16–20, 29–32.
3. One of the earliest discussions of this viewpoint appeared in F.J. Roethlisberger and W.J. Dickson, *Management and the Worker* (Boston: Harvard University Press, 1939).
4. See, for example, Paul Hersey and Ken Blanchard, *Management of Organizational Behavior: Utilizing Human Resources*, 4th ed. (Upper Saddle River, NJ: Prentice Hall, 1982). This volume presents the "situational leadership" theory and applications.
5. See Don Hellriegel and John Slocum, "Organizational Design: A Contingency Approach," *Business Horizons* 16, no. 2 (1973): 59–68.
6. Russell D. Archibald, *Managing High-Technology Projects* (New York: Wiley, 1976): 19; Jack R. Meredith and Samuel Mantel, *Project Management: A Managerial Approach*, 3rd ed. (New York: Wiley, 1995): 7–9; Daniel D. Roman, *Managing Projects: A Systems Approach* (New York: Elsevier, 1986): 2–10; John M. Stewart, "Making Projects Management Work," *Business Horizons* 8, no. 3 (Fall 1965): 54–68.
7. David Cleland and William King, *Systems Analysis and Project Management*, 3rd ed. (New York: McGraw-Hill, 1983): 191–192.
8. Keith Davis, "The Role of Project Management in Scientific

Manufacturing,"*IEEE Transactions of Engineering Management* 9, no. 3 (1962): 109–113.

9. Portions of this section are adapted from Richard Johnson, Fremont Kast, and James Rosenzweig. *The Theory and Management of Systems*, 3rd ed. (New York: McGraw-Hill, 1973): 395–397.

10. Cleland and King, Systems Analysis and Project Management, 259.

11. Based upon W. Hofer, "Lady Liberty's Business Army,"*Nation's Business* (July 1983): 18–28.

12. Dick Sharad, "Management by Projects, and Ideological Breakthrough,"*Project Management Journal* (March 1986): 61–63.

13. John Adams, Stephen Barndt, and Martin Martin, *Managing by Project Management* (Dayton, OH: Universal Technology, 1979): 12–13.

14. Szilagyi, Management and Performance, 489–490.

15. This section is adapted from Daniel Roman, *Managing Projects: A Systems Approach* (New York: Elsevier, 1986): 426–429, with the permission of the publisher.

16. This and examples in later chapters of SpaceShipOne illustrate concepts. While much factual information about the project and the systems is available from published sources, information about the design and development of the systems is confidential. SpaceShipOne, the X-Prize, and the stakeholders described are all true-life; however, for lack of information portions of this and subsequent examples are hypothetical.

17. Based upon information compiled by Jenny Harrison from interviews with managers in Dalian Company (fictitious name).

18. Based upon information compiled by Cary Morgan from interviews with managers of the LogiCircuit Corporation (fictitious name).

19. Based upon information compiled by Darlene Capodice from interviews with managers in two accounting firms.

20. Information about this project contributed by Daniel Molson, Mike Billish, May Cumba, Jesper Larson, Anne Lanagan, Madeleine Pember, and Diane Petrozzo.

21. "Disaster Response. Lesson 7: Emergency Operations Support," University of Wisconsin, Disaster Management Center, http://dmc.engr. wisc.edu/courses/response/BB08-07. htmlhttp://www.dmc.engr.wisc. edu/courses/response/BB08-07.html.

22. "India: Emergency Tsunami Reconstruction Project," The World Bank Group May 3, 2005, Press Release No. 453/SAR/2005, *ReliefWeb*, http://www.reliefweb.int/rw/RWB.NSF/ db900SID/VBOL-6C3CF8?OpenDocument& rc=3&cc=indhttp://www.reliefweb.int/rw/ RWB.NSF/db900SID/VBOL-6C3CF8?OpenD ocument&rc=3&cc=ind.

23. Portions of this section are adapted from Richard Chapman, *Project Management in NASA: The System and the Men* (Washington, DC: NASA SP-324, NTIS No. N75-15692, 1973).

24. Information about this case contributed by Jennifer Koziol, Sussan Arias, Linda Clausen, Gilbert Rogers, and Nidia Sakac.

25. Information about this case contributed by Debbie Tomczak, Bill Baginski, Terry Bradley, Brad Carlson, and Tom Delaney. Organizational names are fictitious but the case is factual.

Chapter 2

Systems Approach and Systems Engineering

There is so much talk about the system.
And so little understanding.

—ROBERT M. PIRSIG
Zen and the Art of Motorcycle Maintenance

One thing leads to another.

—THE FIXX

A project is a system of people, equipment, materials, and facilities organized and managed to achieve a goal. Much of the established theory and practice about what it takes to organize and coordinate a project comes from a perspective called the "systems approach"; at the same time, work done in projects is often for the purpose of *creating* systems. In projects, especially those in product and software development, engineering, or research in technology industries, methodologies such as "systems analysis,""systems engineering," and "systems management" are commonplace. This chapter introduces concepts that form the basis for project management and the systems methodologies commonly used in technical projects.

2.1   SYSTEMS THINKING

Systems thinking is a way of viewing the world. The key distinguishing feature of systems thinking is focus on the "whole organism" rather than just the parts. It is the *opposite* of analytical thinking, which breaks things into progressively smaller parts to better understand the parts. Although systems thinkers look at the parts too and try to understand the processes among them, they always go back to see how the parts fit into the whole.[1]

Systems thinking means being able to perceive the "system" in a situation—to take a seemingly confused, chaotic situation and perceive some degree of order or harmony in it. As such, it is a useful way for dealing with complex phenomena, especially human-created systems and endeavors such as large projects.

Although project managers must be familiar with and able to coordinate the individual parts of the project, the responsibility for each of the parts is largely delegated to managers and technicians who specialize in them. Project managers are concerned with the "big picture"—the whole project with its stakeholders and environment; as such, they must be systems thinkers.

2.2   DEFINITION OF SYSTEM

To some people "the system" means a computer, to others it means a bureaucracy. The term is so commonly used that it could refer to almost everything. By definition, however, a system is "an organized or complex whole; *an assemblage of parts interacting in a coordinated way.*" The parts could be players on a football team, keys on a keyboard, or components in a DVD. The parts need not be physical entities; they can be abstract or conceptual entities, such as words in a language or steps in a procedure. The term is associated with such disparate things as river systems, planetary systems, transportation and communication systems, nervous and circulatory systems, production and inventory systems, ecosystems, urban systems, social systems, economic systems, ad infinitum. Thus, a system *can* be just about anything—but not quite: besides being an "assemblage of parts" a system has three other features:[2]

1. parts of the system *affect the system* and *are affected* by it,
2. the assemblage of parts *does* something,
3. the assemblage is of particular interest.

The first feature means that in systems the whole is more than the sum of the parts. The human body, e.g., can be analyzed in terms of separate components—the liver, brain, heart, nerve fibers, and so on; yet if any of these are removed from the body, both they and the body will change. Parts of the body cannot live outside the body; nor can the body live without the parts. The name given to viewing things in terms of their "wholeness," or the whole being more than the sum of the parts is *holism*. Holism is the opposite of *reductionism*, the philosophy that things can be understood simply by breaking them into pieces and understanding the pieces. Certainly many things cannot be understood just by understanding the pieces. Knowing that hydrogen and oxygen are gases does not lead you to know that combined they form a liquid. The idea of the parts affecting the whole and vice versa is central to systems thinking. Related ideas appear elsewhere. Psychologists use the term *Gestalt* to describe theories and practices that emphasize the whole person and the surrounding situation. Another term, *synergy*, describes situations where several components work together to produce a combined effect. Take any organism—a cell, animal, or organization—and it is easy to see that its behavior is more than just the sum of the behaviors of its pieces.

The second feature of systems is that they are dynamic—they exhibit some kind of *behavior*—they *do* something. The kind of behavior they exhibit depends upon the particular kind of system at hand, but usually can be observed in the outputs of the system or the way the system converts inputs to outputs (although sometimes that process may be quite obscure).

Third, systems are conceived by the people looking at them, which means they exist in the eye (or mind) of the beholder.[3] This is not to say that they do not exist unless someone is there to see them, but rather that the conception of a system can be altered to suit one's purpose. For example, in diagnosing the illness in a patient, a doctor may see the whole human body as "the system." The doctor may send the patient to a specialist, who sees only the digestive tract as "the system." If the diagnosis is food poisoning and the patient files suit, her attorney's view of "the system" might include the restaurant where the person last ate.

2.3 SYSTEMS CONCEPTS AND PRINCIPLES

The following concepts, principles, and terms apply to all systems.

Natural versus Human-Made Systems

Systems can be classified as *natural systems* or *human-made systems*. Natural systems came into being by natural processes (e.g., animal organisms and planetary systems). Human-made systems are designed and operated by people (e.g., communication systems and human organizations). Projects exist for the purpose of creating human-made systems.

Natural systems can be altered by or become intertwined with human-made systems. An example is the alteration of a river system and formation of a lake by building a dam; another is the alteration of the atmospheric composition, climate, and ecosystem through CO_2 and pollutants introduced by human-made machines.

Human-made systems are embedded in and utilize inputs from natural systems, and both systems interact in important and significant ways. In recent years, the appearance of large-scale human-made systems has had significant, mostly undesirable, impact on the natural world. Examples abound, such as global warming, acid rain, and toxic contamination of water systems. Such consequences, called "side effects," arise largely because system designers and users fail to consider (or choose to ignore) the impacts of their systems on the natural environment.

Goals and Objectives

Human-made systems are designed to *do* something; they have goals and objectives that are conceived by people. For the intentions of this book, a *goal* is defined as a broad, all-encompassing statement of the purpose of a system, and an *objective* as a more detailed, usually quantifiable statement of purpose pertaining to some aspect of the system. The system goal is met by achieving a group of system objectives. Hence, in designing a human-made system, the place to start is with a definition of the goal of the system, and then with a hierarchy of objectives that relate to aspects of the system.

For instance, a project can be conceptualized as a system that exists for the purpose of creating a human-made system. The goal of the project may be defined as, e.g., "build a space station." Starting with that goal, the project can then be defined in terms of a hierarchy of many objectives such as "select overall configuration for the station,""select prime contractors,""train crew,""launch components into orbit,""assemble components,""spend at most $15 billion,""complete in 10 years," and so on. The objectives are further broken down into subobjectives, which are broken down into *requirements*. Requirements are the criteria to which the work tasks and subsystems must conform for the system to meet its goals and objectives.

Elements and Subsystems

Systems can be broken down into smaller and smaller parts. These parts in combination form "the assemblage of parts" that constitutes the system. The smallest part of a system is an *element*. Systems also can be broken down into parts which themselves are systems, called *subsystems*. A subsystem is a system that functions as a component of a larger system. When it is not necessary to understand or reveal its inner workings, a subsystem can simply be thought of as an element. Figure 2-1, a common organization chart, illustrates: the production department may be viewed as an "element" in the company; if we choose to delve into it, however, production becomes

Figure 2-1
A company portrayed in terms of systems, subsystems, and elements.

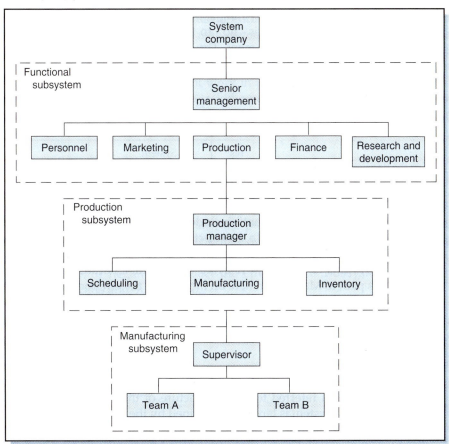

factors such as weather and natural phenomena (the environment). Inputs that originate from the system itself are called feedback. For example, all systems produce information; usage of that information for guiding system behavior is called feedback input.

Process is the means by which the system physically converts or transforms inputs into outputs. An important aspect of system design is to create a process that effectively produces the desired outputs and meets system objectives, yet minimizes consumption of inputs and production of wasteful outputs.

In a hierarchical structure where systems are divided into subsystems, the subsystems each have their own inputs, process, and outputs, which are interconnected in some way. In Figure 2-1, e.g., the marketing subsystem uses customer surveys and sales reports as input to generate demand forecasts (output), and these forecasts serve as one input for the production subsystem.

Constraints and Conflicts

All systems have *constraints* or limitations that inhibit their ability to reach goals and objectives. Time and money are two universal constraints in projects; without them, almost any project objective imaginable would be attainable. Trouble is, most times project objectives must be achieved within a limited time period and budget.

In human-made systems, and especially in projects, the objectives of the subsystems are sometimes in *conflict*, which reduces the chances that they or the objectives of the overall system will ever be realized. Conflict in objectives is especially prevalent between different levels and functions in project systems. Removing the conflict between the objectives of subsystems to enable meeting the objectives of the overall system is called integration.

Integration

For any system to perform effectively and achieve its goal, all of its elements, the "assemblage of parts," must work in unison. Designing, implementing, and operating a system that achieves its prespecified objectives and requirements through the coordinated (so-called "seamless") functioning of its elements and subsystems is called *system integration*. Project management seeks to integrate tasks and resources to achieve project goals. In technological projects, project management also addresses the integration of the physical components and modules that compose the project end-item. The subject of systems integration is covered in Chapter 13.

Open Systems and Closed Systems

Systems can also be classified as *closed* or *open*. A closed system is one that is viewed as self-contained, and "closed-systems thinking" means to focus on the internal operation, structure, and processes of a system without regard to the environment. For many kinds of machines, closed-system thinking applies: to understand how the machine functions, you need only study the machine and its components, and not anything else. This does not mean that the environment does not affect the system, but only that the person looking at the system has chosen to ignore the environment. In fact, for analyzing or improving the design of many kinds of machines, closed-system thinking works fairly well.

But what about organizational and social systems that interact with and must adapt to the environment? These are open systems. To understand their behavior and functioning, you cannot ignore the environment. Any system that must be adaptable to its environment must be treated (analyzed, described, or designed) as an open system.

Of course, machines rely upon resources from and inject byproducts (e.g., pollutants) into the environment, so in many cases they too should be treated as open systems.

2.4 HUMAN ORGANIZATIONS[4]

Most people belong to organizations—employers, clubs, congregations, sports teams, and so on. Organizations can be looked at as systems—interacting parts, human and nonhuman, generally working toward common (though sometimes vague or uncertain) goals. All organizations have a goal or mission, stated or otherwise; it is the reason they exist.

Organizations as Open Systems

Organizations are *open* systems: They interact with the environment, utilize as inputs people, materials, information, and capital, and produce as outputs goods, services, information, and waste byproducts. Certain features characterize organizational systems; we will consider those relevant to project organizations:

1. For just about any "realistic" [5] goal that a person can conceive, a project organization can be developed to work toward it. Unlike biological systems, organizations do not necessarily die; they can be altered and reformed to sustain life and pursue different objectives. Once a project has achieved its objectives, the project organization (its elements, technology, and structure) can be changed to pursue other objectives.

2. Since organizations are open systems, their *boundaries* are permeable and tend to fluctuate with different objectives and types of activities. The boundaries of large project organizations are sometimes difficult to define, especially when one considers all of the contractors, subcontractors, suppliers, customer representatives, and local and government regulatory groups that might be involved. Some of these elements are more involved than others, but all are part of the project system.

   Project managers are "boundary agents": they work at points of contact between subsystems where there is transfer of information and resources. Their role is to integrate the elements of the project (energy, people, materials, money, etc.), and to integrate the project with the larger environment.

3. Organizations, like all complex systems, are *hierarchical*—they are composed of lower-order subsystems and are part of a higher-order suprasystem. Within an organization, people combine to form organized groups, and groups combine to form departments or project teams. These make up a company that is part of an industry, which is within an economy, and so on. Hierarchy exists for both structure (units and relationships) and processes (lower-level tasks and activities combine to make up higher-level tasks and activities). Project planning and scheduling utilizes the concept of hierarchy.

4. To maintain stability in changing environments, organizations depend upon *feedback* of information from their internal elements and the environment. Negative feedback is information signaling that the system is deviating from its objectives and should adjust its course of action. In a project, managers continually gather and interpret feedback information to keep the project on course; this is the role of project review and control.

5. Organizations have been called *socio-technical systems*, which means they consist of a social subsystem of people with a culture and a mission, as well as

a technology subsystem of equipment, facilities, tools, and techniques. The two subsystems are interdependent. Although it is the technology subsystem that influences the types of inputs and outputs of the organization, it is the social subsystem that determines the effective utilization of the technology. This is why it is just as important to manage the behavioral and social aspects of a project as it is the technology. To the detriment of project goals, some managers behave as if the social subsystem does not exist.

Organizations and Environment

Organizations interact with stakeholders in the environment, including customers, suppliers, unions, stockholders, and governments, and they rely upon the environment for inputs of energy, information, and material. In turn, they export to the environment outputs of goods, services, and waste (represented in Figure 2-4). Point is, in establishing goals and methods of operation, organizations have to account for and deal with the environment. Sometimes, however, managers function as if the organization were isolated from the environment—as if the organization were a closed system. They do not learn about the environment, or fail to utilize what they already know.

As an open system, any organization must choose goals and conduct its operations so as to respect opportunities presented and limitations imposed by the environment. Cleland and King call this the "environmental problem," meaning that a manager must:[6]

1. appreciate the need to assess forces in the environment;
2. understand the forces that significantly affect the organization;
3. integrate these forces into the organization's goals, objectives, and operations.

Every project is influenced by outside forces. The project manager must understand the forces influencing the project but, having done that, be able to guide the project to its goal. A project that is predominantly influenced by divergent forces in the environment will be difficult to control and likely to fail.

Example 1: Life and Death of an Aircraft Development Project

The systems concepts described thus far can be related by way of a study by Law and Callon of a large British aerospace project.[7] The study traces the evolution of the project in terms of two systems: the global system and the project system. The *global system* represents parties and organizations outside the

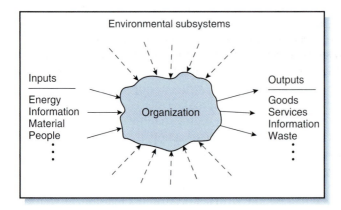

Figure 2-4
Organization as an input–output system.

project organization that have a stake in the project; it is the project environment. The *project system* represents the creation and conduct of the project itself and the organizations contracted to do the project.

The Global System

The project was initiated when the Royal Air Force (RAF) posted a request for a new supersonic aircraft with short take-off capability. Besides the RAF, the other principle stakeholders in the global system were:

1. The Ministry of Defense (MOD), which had mandated that the aircraft could *not* be a bomber. The RAF, wanting *some kind* of aircraft, complied by specifying that the aircraft would be a "tactical strike and reconnaissance *fighter*"—called TSR.
2. The Treasury, which wanted the aircraft to be inexpensive and have market appeal for sale outside the UK, such as to the Royal Australian Air Force (RAAF).
3. The Royal Navy, which actually wanted to procure *a different* aircraft but that the RAF hoped would ultimately buy the TSR instead.
4. The Ministry of Supply (MOS), which wanted an aircraft that would consolidate the efforts of several airframe and engine manufacturers into one large consortium.

As typical of most projects, each stakeholder in the global system conceptualized the project differently: to the RAF and MOD it would yield an aircraft for a specific mission; to the Treasury it would fit the defense budget and generate revenue; to the Navy it was a competitive threat to the aircraft they really wanted; and to the MOS it was an instrument of industrial policy. The parties had different reasons for contributing resources and support: economic (in return for funds, an aircraft would be built); political (in return for a demonstrated need, objections of the Navy would be overruled); technical (in return for engineering and technical effort, the aircraft would meet RAF performance requirements); and industrial (in exchange for contracts, the aircraft industry would be consolidated).

The Project System

The Treasury would not approve project funding until aspects of the project were better defined, including the aircraft's basic design and its manufacturer, cost, and delivery date. The RAF and MOD begin to create a project system comprised of contractors, tasks, schedules, and so on. They sent requests to the aircraft industry for design ideas, and selected two manufacturers; Vickers Corp. and English Electric (EE). They favored Vickers for its integration capability (combining aircraft, engine, armaments, and support equipment into a single "weapons package"), but they also liked EE's design and experience with supersonic aircraft. Hence, they decided to contract with both companies and adopt a design that would utilize features from both. The idea was presented to the rest of the global system, which approved and released funding.

The project system grew as Vickers and EE organized and expanded their design teams, production teams, management teams, subcontractors, and so on. Under the encouragement from MOS, Vickers, EE, and several other contractors merged to form a single new organization called the British Aircraft Corporation (BAC).

Designers initially faced two problems: some wanted to locate the engines in the fuselage to minimize aerodynamic problems, but others worried about fire risks and wanted them on the wings. Also, they were unable to design a wing that would meet the requirement for both supersonic speed and short take-off capability. Compromises were made, requirements relaxed, and eventually the designs were completed and sent to the factory.

Relationships Between the Global System and the Project System

As the project system expanded, so did the problems between it and the global system. MOS wanted centralized control over all aspects of the project and all transactions between the project system and the global system. Although BAC was the prime contractor and in principle responsible for managing the project, MOS would not vest it with the necessary management authority. Rather, MOS formed a series of committees to represent government agencies in the global system and gave them primary responsibility for managing the project. This led to serious problems:

1. The committees were allowed to make or veto important project related decisions. For example, important contracts were awarded by MOS, not BAC, and often the RAF changed its mind or requirements without consulting with BAC.
2. The committees lacked information, knowledge, or both. Technical committees made decisions without regard to costs, and cost committees made decisions without regard to technical realities. Decisions did not reflect "systems thinking"; they did not account for impacts on other parts of the project or the project as a whole.

Eventually distrust grew between BAC and MOS, and neither was able to effectively integrate the resources, information, and decisions flowing between parties in the global system and the project system. For example, the project ran into problems with development of the TSR engine. MOS had specified the engine requirements in general terms and expected the development to be routine, but the new engine needed much greater thrust than anticipated. One of the test engines exploded and it would take years to understand the cause.

Subcontractors were difficult to control. Many ignored BAC and appealed directly to MOS for favorable treatment; some colluded directly with the RAF; and many doubted that the plane would ever fly, overcharged the project, or gave it low priority.

Global System Reshaped

Everyone connected with the project knew it was in trouble. The RAF and MOD recognized that the engine would likely remain unproven for some time, and the Treasury, which had hoped for an inexpensive aircraft, saw its costs double. In addition, the RAAF announced that instead of the TSR it was ordering the US-built F-111. Still, RAF and MOD remained strong supporters, and as long as the funding continued so would the project. But opponents were aware of the project's troubles, and they decided to take them to a broader arena, the Labour Party. A general election was coming, and the Labour Party promised that if elected it would review the project.

The emergence of these two new elements in the global system—the F-111 and the Labour Party—clinched the fate of the project. The Labour Party won the election and immediately began assessing the TSR project, which included comparing it with the F-111—considered by now an alternative to the TSR. As cost overruns and schedule delays continued, MOS slowly withdrew support. The RAF also withdrew support when it discovered that the F-111, which was already in production, met all of its requirements. TSR was canceled.

Conclusions

The lesson suggested is that the nature and fate of large technological projects depend upon the global system, the project system, and the interface between them as handled by project management. Law and Callon, the study authors, concluded that the TSR project failed because BAC project management was not able to control the project or the information and resources flowing between it and the global system. Parties in the global system were able to interfere with the structure and management of the project, and subcontractors in the project system were able to circumvent project management and deal directly with parties in the global system, each to maximize its own interests, although usually to the detriment of the project.[8]

2.5 SYSTEMS APPROACH

Systems thinking is a way to visualize and analyze physical and conceptual systems, but more than that it is an *approach* for *doing* things—a framework for conceptualizing problems and solving problems.

Systems Approach Framework

The framework utilizes systems concepts such as goals and objectives, elements, subsystems, relationships, integration, and environment. The systems approach formally acknowledges that the behavior of any one system element may affect other elements and no single element can perform effectively without help from the others. This recognition of *interdependency* and *cause–effect* among elements is what most distinguishes the systems approach.[9]

For example, as an element of the "world system" the internal combustion engine can be viewed in terms of the multiple effects it has triggered in other elements and subsystems:

- Development of rich economies based largely on the production and distribution of petroleum.
- Industrialization of previously nomadic societies and redistribution of political power among world nations.
- Development of new modes of transportation that have altered patterns of world travel, commerce, markets, and population distribution.
- Alteration of the chemical composition of the atmosphere, causing ecological consequences such as altered weather patterns, global warming, and smog.

Managers who practice the systems approach recognize the multitude of "elements" in the systems they manage or the problems they wish to solve; the inputs, outputs, and relationships among the elements; and reciprocal influences between human-made systems and the environment. As a result, they are better able to grasp the full magnitude of a problem and anticipate consequences of their actions. This reduces the chances that important elements in a situation or consequences of actions will be overlooked.

The systems approach keeps attention on the big picture and the ultimate goal; it allows focus on the parts, but only in regard to the contribution of the parts to the whole. For instance, a university system can be viewed as separate elements of students, faculty, administrators, and alumni, and actions can be taken regarding any of them while ignoring impacts on the others or the environment. But actions that focus exclusively on parts of the system are likely not optimal for the total system because they disregard negative repercussions on other parts of the system. For example, although curtailing the hiring of faculty reduces costs, it can also lead to classroom overcrowding, less faculty research time, fewer research grants, disgruntled students, lower prestige to the university, and ultimately, lower enrollments and less revenue. Similarly, enacting laws is one way to reduce air pollution, but laws

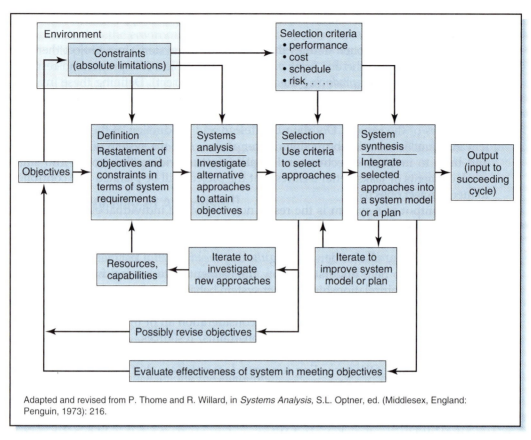

Adapted and revised from P. Thome and R. Willard, in *Systems Analysis*, S.L. Optner, ed. (Middlesex, England: Penguin, 1973): 216.

Figure 2-5
The systems approach.

simple checklist. An example of a *physical model* is a model airplane. It is a scaled-down abstraction of the real system. It includes some aspects of the system (configuration and shape of exterior components) and excludes others (interior components and crew). Another kind of model is a *conceptual model*; it depicts the elements, structure, and flows in a system. The conceptual model in Figure 2-6, e.g., helps biologists to understand relationships among the elements contributing to population size and make limited predictions.[14]

Figure 2-6
A generalized population sector model.

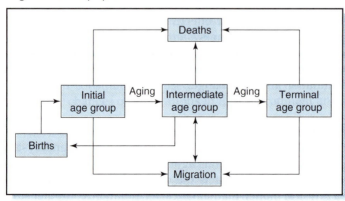

Models are used to conduct experimentation and tests. Many human-made systems are too expensive or risky to do "real life" experiments on. The model permits assessment of various alternatives and their consequences before committing to a decision. Engineers use model airplanes in wind tunnel tests, for instance, to try out design alternatives and measure the effect of different design parameters on airplane performance. A good model allows designers and analysts to ask "what if" questions and explore the effects of altering the various inputs. This exploration is called *sensitivity analysis*. A good model takes into account the requirements, relevant elements, resources, and constraints, and allows the consequences of different alternatives to be compared in terms of costs and benefits. Models for quality assurance are discussed in Chapter 9.

Systems Life Cycle

Systems change over time. The change tends to be systematic and evolutionary, with similar kinds of systems following similar cycles of evolution. One basic cycle, that of all organisms, is the pattern of conception, birth, growth, maturity, senescence, and death. Historically, even past civilizations and societies have followed this pattern. Another cycle, that of all nonliving, electro-mechanical systems, is that of design, fabrication, installation, burn-in, normal operation, and deterioration or obsolescence. Similarly, all products follow a similar pattern—the "product life cycle." They are conceived, designed and developed, produced, launched into the market, capture market share, then decline and are discontinued. Some products such as home computers have life cycles of only months; others (Kool-Aid and Levi's jeans) have decades-long cycles.[15]

The *development* of a system also follows a series of phases. A key feature of the systems approach is recognition of the logical order of thought and action that go into developing systems, whether commercial home products, public works, or military weapons systems. The more general development of a system according to a prescribed series of logical, structured steps is called the *systems development cycle*. This cycle is similar to those of organisms and products, and includes the phases of conception, definition, design and development, fabrication and testing, installation or launch, production, operation and maintenance, and, finally, enhancement, replacement, or cancellation. The prescribed process for large-scale development projects is called *systems engineering*. Most human-made systems start out as projects, and the early and mid phases of the development life cycle constitute the phases of the *project life cycle*.[16] The systems development and project life cycles are discussed in the next chapter.

2.6 SYSTEMS ENGINEERING

Systems engineering has been defined as "the science of designing complex systems in their totality to insure that the component subsystems making up the system are designed, fitted together, checked and operated in the most efficient way."[17] It refers to the conception, design, and development of complex systems where the *components themselves* must be designed, developed, and integrated together to fulfill the system objectives. Systems engineering is a way to *bring a whole system into being* and to *account for its whole life cycle*—including operation and phase-out—during its early conception and design.

Modularization: Iterative Analysis–Synthesis–Evaluation Cycle[21]

The process of creating a system concept that will meet requirements is a series of steps to define the subsystems and elements that will comprise the system. The process involves an iterative cycle of (1) *top-down analysis* of details (i.e., decomposing the system into smaller parts), (2) *bottom-up synthesis* (building up and integrating the parts into successively larger parts), and (3) *evaluation* (checking to see that results meet requirements); this is illustrated by Forsberg and Mooz's "V-model" in Figure 2-8.[22]

Systems are designed and assembled out of subsystems that themselves are systems designed and assembled out of subsystems, and so on. The practice, called *modularization*, is what makes the design, assembly, and operation of complex systems feasible and practical. Herbert Simon gives the example of a watchmaker who assembles a watch out of 100 parts. The process requires concentration and is time-consuming and expensive. If the watch should need repair, finding and fixing the problem might be difficult. If instead the watch were made of 10 modules, each with 10 parts, assembly will be simple. If the watch develops a problem, the repair will be simple: just identify the module with the malfunction and replace it.[23]

The downstroke of the V represents the subdividing of functions of the system into subfunctions and requirements. At each lower level the process of working with customers to define requirements repeats, except the "customer" becomes the function at the next higher level and the question becomes, what must the lower-level functions do to meet the requirements of the higher-level function? In this way, requirements are set for functions at all levels.

Systems are designed by designing subsystems or modules that each performs a necessary function of the system. Functions are attributes of the system; they are the means by which a system meets its objectives and requirements. In everyday systems it is easy to identify the modules and the functions they perform. A desktop computer is almost completely modularized: it has a processor and controllers, drives, and peripheral devices that each performs a specialized function such as data processing, data storage, and input/output processing.

The way system functions are grouped into modules is called the *system architecture.* The architecture of an airplane is an example: An airplane must perform several

Figure 2-8
Forsberg and Mooz's V-model.

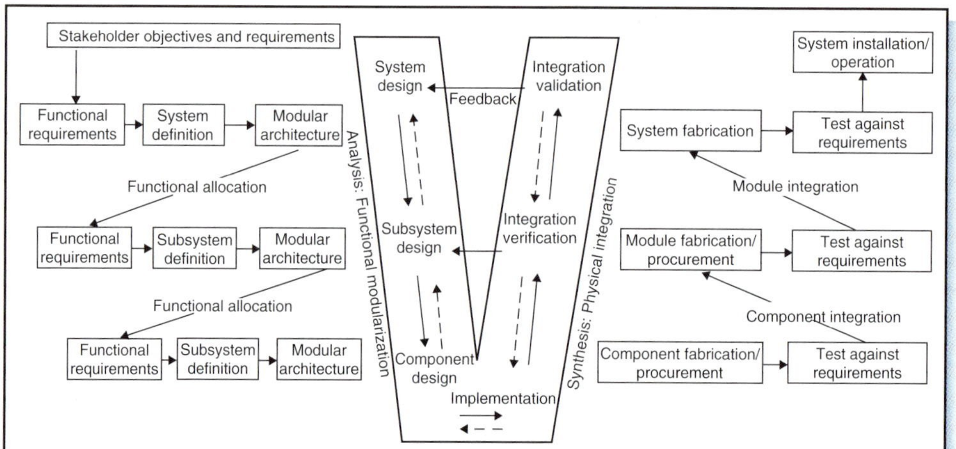

Adapted from K. Forsberg and H. Mooz in *Software Requirements Engineering*, 2nd ed., R. Taylor, M. Dorfman, and A. Davis eds. (Los Alamitos, CA: IEEE Computer Society Press, 1997): 44–77.

major functions including propulsion, lift, and payload stowage; the visibly familiar modules of engines, wings, and fuselage serve these functions. But each function is itself a composite of several subfunctions, hence each module is comprised of several submodules. A wing, e.g., is subdivided into ailerons, flaps, spoilers, etc., each that performs a specific aerodynamic function.

The upstroke of the V represents assessing "design alternatives" to satisfy requirements, implementing design decisions, converting designs into physical parts, integrating the parts, and verifying that the integrated parts meet the requirements. Design alternatives are the potential solutions to problems; they are the courses of action for meeting requirements; ultimately they show up in the final system as pieces of hardware and software. The chosen alternatives result in procuring or designing and building component parts. Components are checked individually and then assembled into modules; modules are tested, then combined with others and tested again.

If tests reveal that parts or modules are not meeting requirements, the process returns to the downstroke of the V to determine why, and the analysis–synthesis–evaluation cycle repeats. The process is anything but smooth flowing, as illustrated by the many feedback arrows in Figure 2-8. Within each down- and upstroke, the process moves back and forth; at times during the upstroke it loops back and over to the downstroke.

One rule of the systems approach is "Don't rush to solutions! Look for alternatives." Ideally, a wide range of alternative solutions is considered—innovative and creative as well as familiar and available. Interdisciplinary teams are good at this; they combine knowledge from experts in disparate areas and can generate alternatives that transcend any one person's or field's area of expertise.

The design and development of a complex technical system can be a vexing problem, but the systems approach offers an approach. Readers interested in systems engineering should see the Appendix to this chapter.

2.7 RELEVANCY OF THE SYSTEMS APPROACH TO PROJECT MANAGEMENT

Systems Management[24]

Project management is a form of "systems management," which is the management and operation of organizations *as* systems. Four major features characterize systems management. First, it is total-system oriented and emphasizes achievement of the *overall system* mission and objectives. Second, it emphasizes decisions that optimize the *overall system* rather than the subsystems. Third, it recognizes interaction and synergy among systems and subsystem—that outputs from one system or subsystem provide inputs to other systems and subsystems. Fourth, it is responsibility oriented; the manager of each subsystem is given specific assignments so that inputs, outputs, and contributions to *total system* objectives can be measured. Systems management works to ensure that organizations, responsibilities, knowledge, and data are integrated toward achieving overall objectives. The systems manager recognizes interactions and interdependencies between subsystems and with the environment, and accounts for them in making plans and taking action. This contrasts with the more typical management view, which is to focus on individual functions and tasks, and to try to enhance the performance of units or departments, even though it might be at the expense of the total organization.

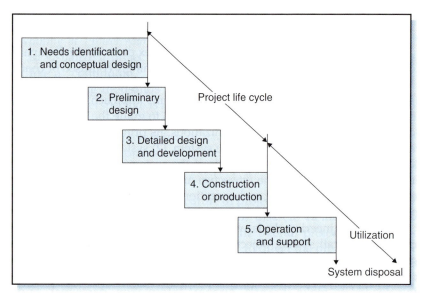

Figure 2-9
Phases of the systems engineering process.

(Stages 1 through 4, which coincide with the project life cycle), the other with the *utilization* of the system (Stage 5).

STAGE 1: NEEDS IDENTIFICATION AND CONCEPTUAL DESIGN[32]

The main tasks of this stage are to define stakeholder needs and requirements, perform feasibility analysis, and perform high-level requirements analysis, system-level synthesis, and a system design review. The process moves top-down to identify the needs and objectives of stakeholders, and the requirements and functions of the system; then it moves bottom-up to assess the functions and synthesize them into groups. The result is a "functional baseline" design or list of all high-level requirements and high-level functions of the system.

Stakeholders and Needs Identification

Systems engineering deals with poorly defined problems. The customer may feel that something is wrong or something new is required but be unclear about the source of problem or need, or how the system should look or what it should do. Sometimes it is not even clear *who* has the problem or need. The first step in systems engineering is *identification*—identifying the stakeholders and translating fuzzy ideas into clear definitions of the needs, problems, and objectives. Systems engineering addresses the needs of not only the client or customer (the party paying to develop the system and its future owner and operator), but also of others who are affected by or able to impact (contribute to, support, or block) the system. Even identifying the "customer" is not trivial; the customer might be an organization, but within the organization only certain parties have the authority to make decisions relating to the system, or will use, operate, or be impacted by it. These parties must be singled out and their needs identified.

Developing a clear conception of the need or problem begins by asking basic questions:[33]

1. How did the problem or need arise?
2. Who believes it to be a problem or feels the need?
3. Is this the root problem or need, or is it a manifestation of some other, deeper problem?
4. Why is a solution important? How much money (or time, etc.) will it save? What is the value of the system?
5. How important is the need? Would resources be better applied to another need?

The systems engineer (system developer or contractor) works with the customer to answer these questions and prepares a preliminary description of the system, including performance requirements, cost, and schedule. The customer reviews the description and perhaps redefines the need, in which case the contractor must redefine the system description. The process continues back and forth until the need definition and system description are set.

Requirements Definition

Requirements specify what the system must do and become the targets that system designers seek to hit. High-level requirements should incorporate everything important about the system—its objectives, life cycle, operational modes, constraints, and interfaces with other systems.

Objectives: Objectives elaborate on the need and define the overarching aim of the system. It is usually necessary to define several objectives to fully specify the system. Each objective is then elaborated in terms of a set of requirements.

Life cycle: There are many issues regarding the system's life cycle and how the system will be built or produced, tested, distributed, marketed, financed, operated, maintained, and ultimately disposed of. This leads to consideration of ancillary issues such as "side items"—spare parts and training of users—and environmental impacts. The requirements must address all of these.

Operational modes: Many systems operate in multiple environments and in different ways, termed "operational modes" or "scenarios of operation." An airplane, e.g., is used for passengers and cargo transport and for crew training; and it must be maintained, repaired, and tested. Each of these constitutes a different operational mode and set of requirements.

Constraints: Every system is constrained by policies, procedures, and standards; available materials, knowledge, and technology; and limited time, funding, and resources. These must all be defined as requirements.

Interfaces: Every system interfaces with other systems in the environment. An interface occurs whenever a system receives input from or provides output to other systems. Requirements specify the interfaces and the mandated or prespecified inputs or outputs at each.

The requirements should address the needs of all the stakeholders—producers, suppliers, operators, and others who will ultimately use, benefit from, manage, maintain, and otherwise impact or be impacted by the system. They reflect the different interests and perspectives of the different stakeholders: corporate customers who are interested in the system's market, capacity, and operating and capital costs; operators who are interested in its performance, durability, reliability, parts availability, etc.; and users who care about its comfort, safety, and usability.

The initial requirements, stated in the language of the stakeholders, are compiled in a list called the *stakeholder requirements document* (SRD). Anyone reading the SRD should be able to readily understand the mission and application of the intended system. The project should not be started until the principle stakeholders have reviewed and endorsed the SRD.

Example A1: SRD for the Spaceship[34]

As an example, let's revisit the X-Prize competition and SpaceShipOne described in Chapter 1. The criteria of the competition were to send a reusable vehicle capable of carrying three people into space twice within 2 weeks. Besides winning the competition, a goal of developer Burt Rutan and customer Sir Richard Branson was to develop technology that would enable low-cost space tourism. Among the constraints were a relatively small budget and a small development company with limited resources. Hence, the SRD would likely include the following:

1. develop a spaceship that can minimally attain 100 kilometers altitude;
2. develop a spaceship that carries three people;
3. develop a spaceship that provides comfortable flight;
4. develop a spaceship that is relatively inexpensive to design, build, and launch;
5. develop a spaceship that can be turned around in 2 weeks or less;
6. develop a spaceship that is inherently safe to operate.

Feasibility

Given the defined needs, objectives, constraints, and requirements, the question arises, What are the available alternatives to satisfy them, and are the alternatives feasible? Thus, the next step is to identify alternative high-level (system-level) solutions for the needs and requirements. The alternative solutions are evaluated in terms of costs, risks, effectiveness, and benefits using studies and models, and the most feasible solutions recommended to customers and supporters.

System Requirements Analysis

With approval of the project and system-level alternatives, the next step is to specify what *the system must do* to be able to meet the requirements on the SRD; this is the purpose of system requirements. For example, the stakeholder requirement that the spaceship "provide comfortable flight" implies a system requirement that the spaceship's cabin temperature, humidity, and pressure all remain at "comfy" levels throughout the flight. This implies that the spaceship will be equipped to perform the necessary functions to make this happen. Whereas the SRD specifies the system in terms of stakeholder wants or needs, the system requirements tell the designer the functions the system must perform and the physical characteristics it must possess to meet the SRD. The process of defining requirements is called *requirements analysis*; the result of this analysis is a document called *the system specification,* described later. Requirements analysis addresses three kinds of requirements: functional, performance, and verification.

Functional Requirements

Functional requirements specify the functions that the new system must perform to meet all the requirements in the SRD, including those to support, operate, and maintain the system. A popular tool for analyzing and defining functional requirements is the functional flow block diagram, FFBD, illustrated in Figure 2-10. Each block represents a function that the system must perform to satisfy objectives or requirements. As illustrated, each function is defined in greater detail by decomposing it into subfunctions; e.g., as shown function 3 is logically comprised of five subfunctions,

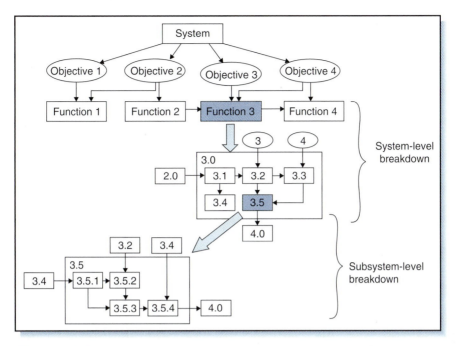

Figure 2-10
FFBD for decomposing system-level functions into lower-level functions.

3.1 through 3.5. In the conceptual design stage the decomposition of functions into smaller, better-defined subfunctions proceeds only to the next level (e.g., subdivides function 3 into 3.1–3.5). Later, in the preliminary design stage, the decomposition will resume and continue to whatever level necessary to arrive at the best possible requirements definition. In the figure, this is shown by decomposing function 3.5 into functions 3.5.1–3.5.4.

Notice the numbering scheme used in Figure 2-10: each and every function has a unique identifier that enables it to be traced to the original system-level function; e.g., function 3.5.4 contributes to function 3.5, which contributes to function 3. This "traceability" of functions is essential because throughout the system life cycle numerous changes will be made to components and functions. For each of these changes it is necessary to know the impact on higher- and lower-level functions. This helps prevent mistakes that could lead to later problems. In the Apollo 13 spacecraft, the cryogenic tanks were originally designed to operate at 28 volts. Later on, the Apollo's design required that certain controls be changed to 65 volts. This involved changes to numerous components including the cryogenic tanks, but somehow the required changes were not traced back to the tanks, and the changes there never made. During the mission this oversight caused a thermostat to malfunction and a tank to explode, which ruined the mission and nearly cost the lives of the three astronauts.

Example A2: Functional Requirements Breakdown for the Spaceship

Figure 2-11 shows a portion of the FFBD for the spaceship, and decomposition of the system-level functions that address stakeholder requirements 3 and 5. The other system-level functions would be decomposed as well.

Performance and Verification Requirements

Associated with each functional requirement are several performance requirements and verification requirements. Whereas a functional requirement states *what* the

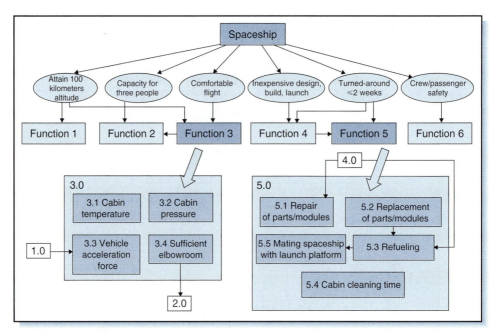

Figure 2-11
System-level breakdown of functions for spaceship.

system must do, a performance requirement states *how well* it must do it. Performance requirements are usually specified in physical parameters such as speed, acceleration, weight, accuracy, power, force, or time. They are the targets on which designers set their sights. For example, the stakeholder requirement "provide comfortable flight" has many functional requirements, including some for temperature and pressure. The associated performance requirements for these are:

3.1 Cabin temperature: 75–85 degree Fahrenheit
3.2 Cabin pressure: 4.2–3.2 pounds per square inch

Accompanying each performance requirement is a set of verification requirements; these are the procedures, measures, and tests to verify that the performance requirement has been met. In the example, verification requirements specify the kinds of tests necessary to prove that cabin temperature and pressure will remain at the required levels during spaceflight.

Throughout the conception stage reviews are conducted to verify and approve the system-level requirements. Requirements are categorized as mandatory, important, desirable, or optional. This gives designers flexibility: later on, when faced with constraints, they will know which requirements must be met and which can be modified or ignored.

Synthesis

Up until now the systems engineering process has been focused on top-down analysis, resulting in a big list of functional, performance, and verification requirements. The next step, synthesis, looks at relationships among the system-level requirements and alternative ways of satisfying the requirements. One question is, can these requirements be satisfied using existing, "off the shelf" (OTS) designs and products, or must new and different designs or technologies be employed? An OTS item is one that can be readily purchased or built; if it meets the requirements, an OTS item is often preferable to one that must be newly designed because it is readily available and usually less costly. Sometimes there is no OTS and to create a new design that meets the requirements would be very costly, risky, or time-consuming; in such cases the requirements must be revised.

The result of synthesis is called the "system specification," which is a comprehensive list of all the functions the new system must satisfy, as well as a firm or tentative solution (to be developed or bought) for each function. The system specification serves as a guide for designers in the stages of preliminary and detailed system design. Often these designers are subcontractors or suppliers; the subsystem specification defines the requirements they must meet.

Example A3: System Specification for Spaceship Motor

A decision must be made about the kind of rocket motor the spaceship will have. Among the functional requirements for the motor are:

1.1 Must provide thrust of x
4.1 Cost of fuel and fuel handling must be economical
5.3 Refueling procedure must be simple
6.1 Fuel, fuel system, and fuel ignition must be inherently safe

A check of existing OTS rocket motors used to launch satellites shows that none fit the requirements; all are too costly to fuel and operate and somewhat dangerous. Hence, a new rocket motor must be developed—one that will be simple to fuel, inexpensive to operate, inherently safe, and provide the necessary thrust. Experiments reveal one promising solution: a motor that uses ordinary rubber as the fuel and nitrous oxide (laughing gas) as the oxidant; both materials are stable, safe, inexpensive, and easy to handle. The decision is made to adopt the technology and design and build a completely new motor. Thus, one system specification for the spaceship (of many hundreds) is that the rocket motor burns nitrous oxide and rubber.

The system specification is reviewed and checked against the functional requirements at a formal meeting. When approved, it becomes the *"functional baseline"* or template for all subsequent design work.

STAGE 2: PRELIMINARY DESIGN[35]

In the preliminary design stage the system-level functional requirements are translated into design requirements for the subsystems. Tradeoff studies are performed of the high-level elements comprising the system, and the system-level requirements are *allocated* among the subsystems.

Functions of Subsystems

The FFBD process illustrated in Figure 2-11 now repeats to decompose the system-level functions into subsystem-level functions and, as before, to define functional, performance, and testing requirements for each functional block. The degree of detail of the FFBDs is whatever is necessary to completely define each subsystem and permit decisions about whether each function can be met with an OTS design or product or must be designed and built from scratch.

In this stage of the design process, there is a subtle shift in focus away from *what* the system will do to *how* it will do it. The shift is from the *functional* design to the *physical* design.

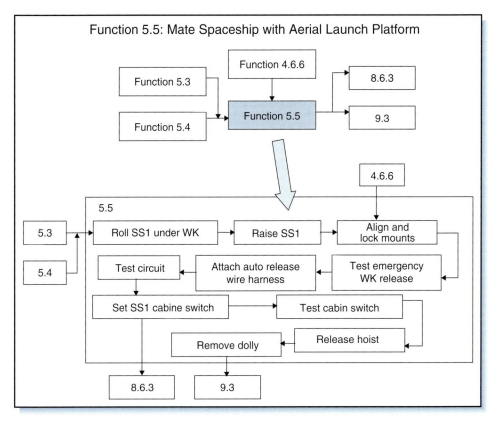

Figure 2-12
FFBD for mating spaceship and launch platform.

Example A4: Decomposing Functions into Subfunctions

Figure 2-12 shows the fictional FFBD for function 5.5, mating the spaceship with the launch platform. This requirement is derived from the system-level requirement of "turn-around in 2 weeks or less." Suppose the performance requirement for mating (attaching) the spaceship to the underbelly of the mothership is set at 10 hours. Having decomposed the function into all of the subfunctions in the procedure, planners are able to set time requirements for the subfunctions so that the mating procedure will not exceed the allotted 10 hours.

Grouping of Functions: Architecture and Configuration Items

The next step is to group the identified functions and requirements according to the *physical architecture* of the system. In general, the term "architecture" refers to the major components in a system and how they are configured or arranged to satisfy the functions of the system. As an example, the architecture most people have in mind for a bicycle is:

Major components: two wheels, frame, seat, pedals and chain, handle bar.
Configuration: wheel attached at each end of frame; front wheel pivots on frame; seat mounted on frame; pedals attached to frame, linked by chain to rear wheel; etc.

Sometimes the architecture "looks right," sometime not. Often, in order to satisfy unique requirements, designers are forced to stray from the commonplace architecture, the result being an architecture that "looks funny."

The spaceship will have airplane features of a fuselage and wings, although it will also have spacecraft features, namely, a rocket motor and ability to maneuver in space. Unlike an airplane where the cabin and fuselage walls are the same, the cabin in a spaceship is a separate "pressure vessel" fitted inside the fuselage. The spaceship architecture will include the following subsystems:

- *Fuselage*: Structure in which other subsystems are contained (hydraulics, avionics, motor, fuel, cabin, landing gear, etc.) or attached (wing, flight control surfaces, etc.).
- *Cabin*: Location for pilot and passengers; includes seats, storage space, instruments and flight controls, and environmental control system.
- *Rocket motor*: Main propulsion system, fuel system, attachments to fuselage and fuel system, and motor controls.
- *Avionics*: Aviation electronics; computers and subsystems for communication, navigation, automatic flight controls, in-flight and auxiliary power systems.
- *Wing/aerodynamic surfaces*: Main wing, tail, ailerons, flaps, spoilers, rudders, stabilizers, and hydraulic/electronic actuators.
- *Controls for spaceflight*: Thrusters or reaction jets.
- *Landing gear*: Gear doors, braces, skids or tires, brakes.

Each major subsystem will perform a major function or set of system-level functions from the functional baseline. From this point onward, each of these subsystems will be called a *configuration item* or CI. In general, a CI is a subsystem or component whose history is documented and monitored throughout the system's complete life cycle—its design, production, and usage. The purpose of this documenting and tracking, referred to as *configuration management*, is to ensure that any changes in the design, production, or usage of the CI do not alter or degrade its ability to meet the functional requirements. Configuration management utilizes "traceability" to prevent snafus, such as the voltage change that caused the Apollo 13 incident. Configuration management pertains not only to major subsystems, but also to any items identified as critical to the system, high risk, "special," or costly. Configuration management is discussed further in Chapters 9 and 11.

Requirement Allocation

As of this point, the design consists of: (1) a list of the functional requirements and (2) a high-level design of the system—the major subsystem or CIs (the system architecture). The next step is to "allocate" the functional requirements to the CIs, which means to *assign* responsibility for each functional requirement to one or more of the CIs. The purpose here is to ensure that every functional requirement will be addressed (and hopefully satisfied) by at least one of the subsystems or CIs. The resulting allocations are shown in an "allocation matrix" or "traceability matrix." As shown in Figure 2-13, the columns are the subsystems responsible for meeting the requirements; the rows are the requirements the subsystems must fulfill.

With this allocation the transition from functions to physical items accelerates. Since each of the CIs represents something that will ultimately be a physical item—a piece of hardware, software, or both, the assignment of functional requirements to CIs represents a transition in thinking from *what* must be done (e.g., travel 100 kilometers above the Earth) to *how* the system will do it (in a spacecraft that has a fuselage, cabin, wings, and engine, configured in a certain way).

Notice in Figure 2-13 that some of the functional requirements are the shared responsibility of more than one CI. For example, the weight of the system (requirement 1.5) is shared by all the CIs. That is to say, the spacecraft weight is the sum of the weights of all the CIs, and if the weight of any one is changed, so is the weight

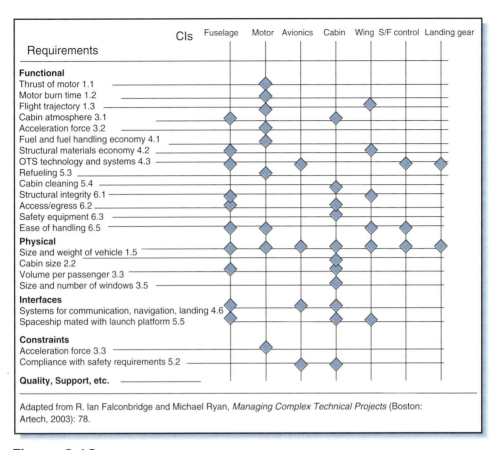

Adapted from R. Ian Falconbridge and Michael Ryan, *Managing Complex Technical Projects* (Boston: Artech, 2003): 78.

Figure 2-13
Allocation or traceability matrix.

of the spacecraft. If the maximum loaded weight of the spacecraft is set at 3,600 kilograms, each CI must be designed so that all of the CIs combined will not exceed that requirement.

Example A6: Allocation of Weight among CIs

Question: How do you design and develop all of the CIs such that in the end the total weight (shared requirement) does not exceed 3,600 kilograms? *Answer*: estimate the percentage of the total spaceship weight that each CI should account for, and set that as the "target" design weight for the CI. For example, allocate, say, 30% of the total system weight to the fuselage and contents, 20% to the motor, 20% to the wings, 10% to avionics, and 10% for everything else. Hence, the fuselage target weight would be 0.30 × 3,600 kilograms = 1,080 kilograms, the motor target weight is 0.20 × 3,600 kilograms = 720 kilograms, and so on. Since achieving these targets is critical, each is designated as a *Technical Performance Measure*, or TPM, which means that for the remainder of the project the estimated and actual weights of the CIs will be closely monitored versus the targets. If at some point in the project it becomes clear that a target cannot be achieved (and this will surely happen), then the allocations are readjusted. If, say, the weight of the motor cannot be held to its target but must be increased by, say, 30 kilograms, then the allotted weights for other subsystems must correspondingly be reduced, or else the target weight for the spaceship increased by 30 to 3,630 kilograms. Throughout the development process it will be necessary to adjust the CI targets and allocations. The TPM process, described in Chapter 11, guides such adjustments.

Interfaces

None of the subsystems functions independently. All rely on the outputs of other functions and, in turn, provide inputs to still others; in a word, they *interface*. Part of preliminary design is to identify all interfaces in the system and establish requirements for the interfaces. A main source of information about interfaces is FFBDs. For example, the FFBD in Figure 2-12 shows that function 5.5 *receives* input from functions 5.3, 5.4, and 4.6.6 and *provides* input to functions 8.6.3 and 9.3. Each arrow represents an interface and the "flow" of something between functions. The "thing" flowing can be:

- *Physical*: mechanical connections, physical joints and supports, pipes
- *Electronic*: analog or digital signals
- *Electrical*: electricity
- *Hydraulic/pneumatic*: liquid or gas
- *Software*: data
- *Environment*: temperature, pressure, humidity, radiation, magnetism
- *Procedural*: completion of a procedural step so another next step can begin

Identifying the interfaces is necessary for setting requirements on the inputs and outputs of every subsystem and element. For example, since the fuselage of the spacecraft contains the motor and also supports the wings, neither wings nor motor can be designed without also considering the design of the fuselage, and vice versa. The requirements for each interface (e.g., allowable maximum or minimum flow or physical strength) are set by a design team that includes representatives from the subsystems at both sides of the interface.

Synthesis and Evaluation

Designing each of the CIs and its subsystems and elements involves choosing among design alternatives and, again, deciding whether to buy or modify an OTS design or product, or to develop a new design from scratch. An OTS design or product that meets all or most of the requirements for a CI and is not too costly will be purchased; otherwise the CI must be designed and built from scratch.

The selection of alternatives in the preliminary design stage must consider the synthesis of components—the impacts of each design decision on other components and the overall system. Following is an example.

Example A7: Tradeoffs in Determining Spaceship Weight

The weight requirement for a spacecraft is a big deal because the greater the weight, the more thrust required of the rocket motor to propel the vehicle into space and the greater the load-carrying capacity of the mothership to carry it aloft. At some point early in the conceptual design the maximum weight will be set, although as the design progresses every effort will be made to find ways to reduce it. Consider a few of the tradeoff decisions that designers face.

How big should the cabin be? In general, the cabin should be roomy enough to hold three people, instruments and controls, and stowage; a bigger cabin would be more comfortable for the occupants, but it would also weigh more. Suppose a cabin of volume m is chosen, which will result in an estimated weight of w for the spaceship. Suppose also that to propel a vehicle of weight w into space will require a rocket motor with thrust of y (Figure 2-14(a and b)). Note that if the cabin size is increased, then the thrust of the rocket motor must also be increased—unless weight can be reduced somewhere else in the spaceship.

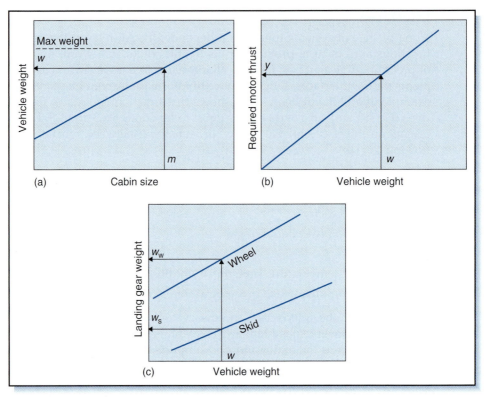

Figure 2-14
Impact of cabin size on vehicle weight, rocket thrust, and landing gear.

Now consider the impact of vehicle weight on another decision: landing gear. The more the vehicle weighs, the stronger the required landing gear; but, all else equal, the stronger the gear, the heavier the gear. If the weight of a typical wheeled landing gear strong enough to support the vehicle is deemed too high, then an alternative must be considered, such as a skid (Figure 2-14(c)). The skid has no wheels and weighs less than the wheeled gear. If the skid meets other functional requirements, it would be chosen over a wheeled landing gear.

Such tradeoff decisions will be necessary for all the CIs and other components. As the decisions are made, a design evolves that meets the requirements. The form and configuration of the CIs starts to evolve, and the physical appearance of the system begins to take shape. By the end of the preliminary design stage the system architecture will have been established and all system-level requirements allocated among the major subsystems (CIs). Combined, the architecture and allocation form the "allocated baseline" design (example, Figure 2-15).

STAGE 3: DETAILED DESIGN AND SYSTEM DEVELOPMENT

The stage of detailed design involves further description of subsystems, assemblies, components, and parts of the main system and support items. Everything up to

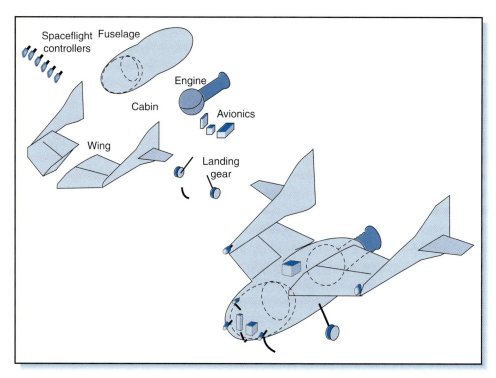

Figure 2-15
Pictorial representation of major subsystems (CIs) and allocated baseline design.
(The "funny looking" architecture derives from the spaceship having to meet
many requirements. On reentry, the wings rotate upward, making the spacecraft
one big airbrake that floats to earth like a shuttlecock, thus avoiding high speed
and high temperature. Nearer to the ground the wings tilt back and the ship
glides to a landing.)

this point has been analytical in nature. With detailed design, the move is from
"concepts on paper"—the SRD and system specifications—to a design that is ready
for fabrication or production. Decisions are made about whether subsystems and
components will function manually or automatically; whether components will be
electronic, mechanical, or hydraulic; whether input/output will be manual, keyboard,
disks; etc. Available, OTS components selected on the basis of surveys or comparison tests in a laboratory, and components being newly developed are tested exper-
imentally using "breadboards," i.e., test models that enable designs to be verified
by trial and error. Breadboards are used to develop individual pieces of equipment
that will subsequently be mated and integrated into the overall system. A "prototype" system—a nearly complete system assembled for purposes of developmental testing—may then be used to evaluate the overall system in terms of satisfying
requirements. Much of the development work, even with the use of breadboards
and prototypes, is done on computers. Prototypes and other models are described in
Chapters 4 and 9.

System development and design testing and evaluation includes:[36]

- Checking the operation of subsystems when combined in a complete system.
- Evaluating the validity of design assumptions.

- Paying close attention to the interfaces:
  (a) "cross talk" among subsystems
  (b) feedback among subsystems
  (c) adjustments and calibrations
  (d) serviceability and maintenance.

The system is checked under a variety of conditions and operational modes. Notable problems previously overlooked in the design process often come to light during these tests. Modifications often are necessary to correct for oversights, eliminate deficiencies, and simply improve the system.

Example A8: Testing SpaceShipOne

Numerous ground and flight tests of SpaceShipOne resulted in many changes; among them:

- In one test flight SS1 began to pitch wildly, and only with great difficulty was the pilot able to regain control. Engineers diagnosed the cause as being a too small tail, which they quickly redesigned. (Problem was the small company did not have a wind tunnel in which to test it. Undeterred, they mounted the tail assembly on a Ford pickup truck and checked it by racing up and down the runway.)
- A three-man crew was sealed in the cockpit for 3 hours, and to test cabin pressure sensitive ultrasound equipment scanned the cabin for the "hissing" sound of leaks.
- The nose skid showed excessive wear after tests and was replaced with a stronger material.

When there is not enough time or money to build a prototype, the first few manufactured models are subjected to developmental testing and design evaluation. Gradually, after modifications are made and the design is approved, full-scale production begins. Design and development testing is phased out; quality control is phased in to ensure the end-item system as produced conforms to design specifications.

The design of the capability (facilities and related resources) to produce the system (the "process design") also begins during this phase so that as soon as the system is fully developed it can be produced (Stage 4). It includes the design of new (or redesign of old) facilities and manufacturing processes, selection of specific materials and pieces of equipment, and preparations for production control, quality testing, manufacturing tooling, product transportation, personnel hiring and training, and data collection and processing.

STAGE 4: SYSTEM CONSTRUCTION AND/OR PRODUCTION

During Stage 4 the system is either (1) mass produced, (2) produced in limited quantities with different features, or (3) built as a single item. This stage begins as soon as the design is approved and "frozen." The stage involves acquiring materials, managing inventory, and controlling production/construction operations to uphold performance, quality, reliability, safety, and other requirements.

Stage 5: System Operation and Support

Stage 5 completes the system development life cycle. Here the customer operates the system until it ultimately wears out or becomes obsolete. The developer might provide support in the following ways: assistance in deploying, installing, and checking out the system; assisting day-to-day operation with field service and maintenance support; modification and enhancement of the system to ensure continued user satisfaction; and support in closing, phasing out, and disposing of the system at the end of its life cycle. The last way, close-out and disposal of the system, is often a major consideration in the design and operation of the system, especially so for systems that have potential to degrade the surrounding environment. One example is nuclear reactors, the design of which must take into account the way each reactor will be shut down and the facility closed out. Another is mines for metals and coal, which scar the land, leave hazardous deposits, and pollute ground water and watersheds. Their closeout must be accompanied by measures to restore the land, clean up wastes, and remove toxins from soil and water. Such measures can be expensive and time-consuming, and extend the system life cycle by many years or even decades.

Example A9: Life Cycle of SpaceShipOne

Preliminary development of SS1 and its support systems—White Knight, navigation system, flight simulator, etc.—began in 1999, and full development began in April 2001, albeit in total secrecy. Exactly 2 years later Dick Rutan announced intentions to capture the X-Prize and flight testing began (Figure 2-16).

In May 2004, Mike Melville piloted the craft on a test above 100 kilometers, making him the world's first civilian astronaut. On October 29 he again flew SS1 into space, and less than 2 weeks later so did pilot Brian Binney, winning the $10 million X-Prize for the SS1 team (Figure 2-17). Today SS1 hangs in display at the Smithsonian Air & Space Museum in Washington DC. Sir Richard Branson has announced plans to spend up to $100 million for development of a bigger spaceship, SS2, and a bigger mothership, WK2. He will operate his fleet of spaceships from a site located near the town of Truth or Consequences, New Mexico.

Figure 2-16
SS1 beneath mothership White Knight. (Photo courtesy of John Nicholas.)

Figure 2-17
Designer Burt Rutan (center) and pilots Mike Melville (left) and
Brian Binney. (Photo courtesy of John Nicholas.)

REVIEW QUESTIONS

1. What distinguishes systems thinking from analytical thinking? Is systems thinking something new or is it just another perspective? Explain.
2. Define system. What notable features enable you to see something as a system?
   Describe briefly the legal or education system in terms of these features.
3. How can several people looking at the same thing see the "system" in it
   differently?
4. Describe the following concepts and explain how they fit into systems thinking:
   objectives, elements, subsystems, attributes, environment, boundary, structure,
   inputs, outputs, process, and constraints.
5. Describe the difference between open and closed systems, and between human-
   made and natural systems. Are all natural systems open systems?
6. Is a space vehicle an open system? Is an organization an open system? Explain.
7. Why are organizations called socio-technical systems? Are they ever just social
   systems?
8. Describe the features and properties that distinguish human organizations from
   other systems.
9. What is the manager's environmental problem?
10. Describe the systems approach. Where does the systems approach apply?
    Explain in a sentence what a manager does in the systems approach that she
    might not do otherwise.
11. What is the "environmental fallacy?"
12. What things does the problem solver keep in mind when applying the systems
    approach?

13. Describe how the following elements of the systems approach apply to projects and project management: objectives, environment, resources, subsystems, and management.

14. Describe the systems approach in Figure 2-5.

15. Give some examples of physical models; of graphical models; of mathematical models.

16. What is the systems life cycle? What is the systems development cycle?

17. Discuss the dimension of systems engineering in Figure 2-7.

18. What is modularization? What are its benefits in system design and operation?

19. In systems engineering the first stage is identification. Identification of what?

20. Who are the stakeholders in systems engineering?

21. What are requirements? What aspects of the system or stakeholder needs should the requirements incorporate?

22. Distinguish stakeholder requirements and system requirements.

23. Describe the stages of systems engineering in Figure 2–9. Think of some projects and describe the stages of systems engineering in these projects.

24. Distinguish the following: functional requirements, performance requirements, and verification requirements. Give an example of a functional requirement and its associated performance and verification requirements.

25. What is meant by the term "traceability?"

26. Think of a simple system like a mousetrap, tape dispenser, or can opener. Draw a simple high-level functional flow block diagram for it. If possible, decompose each of the functions into subfunctions.

27. What is the emphasis in systems management? How does it differ from just management?

28. What is the relevancy of the systems approach to project management?

QUESTIONS ABOUT THE STUDY PROJECT

1. Conceptualize the project organization (the project team and the parent organization of the team) you are studying as a system. What are the elements, attributes, environment, and so on? What are its internal subsystems—functional breakdown and management-hierarchy subsystems? What is the relevant environment? Who are the decision makers?

2. Describe the role of the project manager with respect to these subsystems, both internal and external. What is the nature of his or her responsibilities in these subsystems? How aware is the project manager of the project "environment" and what does he or she do that reflects this awareness?

3. Now, conceptualize the output or end-item of the project as a system. Again, focus on the elements, relationships, attributes, subsystems, environment, and so on. All projects, whether directed at making a physical product (e.g., computer, space station, skyscraper, research report) or a service (e.g., giving consultation and advice), are devoted to producing systems. This exercise will help you better understand what the project is doing. It is also good preparation for topics in the next chapter.

4. If the study project involves engineering or integration of many components, was the systems engineering process used? Is there a section, department, or task in the project called systems engineering? If so, elaborate. Are there functions or phases of the project that seem to resemble the systems engineering process?

As described in this chapter, besides the main end-item or operating system (i.e., the output objective of the project), systems engineering also addresses the support system—that system which supports installation, operation, maintenance, evaluation, and enhancement of the operating system. Describe the support system in the study project and its development.

5. Were the stakeholder requirements clearly defined at the start of the project? Were system requirements clearly defined? What are the requirements? In your opinion, were stakeholders identified and involved early in the project. Were their needs identified and addressed? Did the project deliver a system that met their needs?

6. What aspects of the project or parent organization appear to use systems management? What aspects do not use systems management? Describe the appropriateness or inappropriateness of systems management in the project you are studying.

Case 2-1 Glades County Sanitary District

Glades County is a region on the Gulf Coast with a population of 600,000. About 90 percent of the population is located in and near the city of Sitkus. The main attractions of the area are its clean, sandy beaches and nearby fishing. Resorts, restaurants, hotels, retailers, and the Sitkus/Glades County economy in general rely on these attractions for tourist dollars.

In the last decade, Glades County has experienced a near doubling of population and industry. One result has been the noticeable increase in the level of water pollution along the coast due primarily to the increased raw sewage dumped by Glades County into the Gulf. Ordinarily, the Glades County sewer system directs effluent waste through filtration plants before pumping it into the Gulf. Although the Glades County Sanitary District (GCSD) usually is able to handle the county's sewage, during heavy rains the runoff from paved surfaces exceeds sewer capacity and must be diverted past filtration plants and directly into the Gulf. Following heavy rains, the beaches are cluttered with dead fish and debris. The Gulf fishing trade also is affected since pollution drives away desirable fish. Recently, the water pollution level has become high enough to damage both the tourist and fishing trade. Besides coastal pollution, there is also concern that as the population continues to increase, the county's primary fresh water source, Glades River, will also become polluted.

The GCSD has been mandated to prepare a comprehensive water waste management program that will reverse the trend in pollution along the

Gulf Coast as well as handle the expected increase in effluent wastes over the next 20 years. Although not yet specified, it is known that the program will include new sewers, filtration plants, and stricter anti-pollution laws. As a first step, GCSD must establish the overall direction and mission of the program.

Wherever possible, answer the following questions (given the limited information, it is okay to advance some logical guesses; if you are not able to answer a question for lack of information, indicate how and where, as a systems engineer, you would get it):

1. What is the system? What are its key elements and subsystems? What are the boundaries and how are they determined? What is the environment?

2. Who are the decision makers?

3. What is the problem? Carefully formulate it.

4. Define the overall objective of the water waste management program. Because the program is wide ranging in scope, you should break this down into several subobjectives.

5. Define the criteria or measures of performance to be used to determine whether the objectives of the program are being met. Specify several criteria for each subobjective. As much as possible, the criteria should be quantitative, although some qualitative measures should also be included. How will you know if the criteria that you define are the appropriate ones to use?

6. What are the resources and constraints?

7. Elaborate on the kinds of alternatives and range of solutions to solving the problem.

8. Discuss some techniques that could be used to help evaluate which alternatives are best.

ENDNOTES

1. Peter Schoderbek, Asterios Kefalas, and Charles Schoderbek, *Management Systems: Conceptual Considerations* (Dallas: Business Publications, 1975): 7–8.

2. John Naughton and Geoff Peters, *Systems Performance: Human Factors and Systems Failures* (Milton Keynes, Great Britain: The Open University, 1976): 8–12.

3. Ibid., 11. Innumerable systems can be perceived from any one entity. Kenneth Boulding, *The World as a Total System* (Beverly Hills: Sage, 1985), describes the world as physical, biological, social, economic, political, communication, and evaluative systems.

4. See Fremont Kast and James Rosenzweig, "The Modern View: A Systems Approach," in *Systems Behavior*, 2d ed., John Beishon and Geoff Peters, eds. (London: Harper & Row, 1976): 19–25.

5. "Realistic" is relative: given more time and resources, formally unrealistic objectives may become feasible and realistic. It is possible to uniquely structure an organization that is "best suited" for working toward any particular goal, whether or not that goal is ever achieved.

6. David Cleland and William King, *Management: A Systems Approach* (New York: McGraw-Hill, 1972): 89.

7. This section is adapted from J. Law and M. Callon, "The Life and Death of an Aircraft: A Network Analysis of Technical Change," in *Shaping Society/Building Technology*, W. Bijker and J. Law, eds. (Cambridge, MA: MIT Press, 1992).

8. Ibid.

9. C. West Churchman, *The Systems Approach and Its Enemies* (New York: Basic Books, 1979).

10. Ibid., 4–5.

11. Much of the discussion in this section is based on C. West Churchman, *The Systems Approach* (New York: Dell, 1968): 30–39.

12. P.G. Thome and R.G. Willard, "The Systems Approach: A Unified Concept of Planning," in *Systems Analysis*, S.L. Optner, ed. (Middlesex, England: Penguin Books, 1973): 212.

13. Ibid., 212–215.

14. H. R. Hamilton et al., *Systems Simulation for Regional Analysis* (Cambridge: The MIT Press, 1972).

15. The life cycle of technological products and their impact on competition is eloquently described by Richard Foster in *Innovation: The Attacker's Advantage* (New York: Summit Books, 1986).

16. As common parlance, the term project life cycle is recognition that all projects tend to follow a similar sequence of activities, start to finish. Since every project, however, has a start and finish, when referring to a particular project the more precise term is "project life span."

17. G.W. Jenkins, "The Systems Approach," in *Systems Behavior*, 2nd ed., John Beishan and Geoff Peters, eds. (London: Harper & Row for the Open University Press, 1976): 82

18. Sunny Auyang, *Engineering—An Endless Frontier* (Cambridge, MA: Harvard University, 2004): 175–189.

19. Frederick Brooks, *The Mythical Man Month* (Reading, MA: Addison Wesley, 1995): 199.

20. Auyang, Engineering—An Endless Frontier, 183.

21. Ibid., 192–197.

22. K. Forsberg and H. Mooz, in *Software Requirements Engineering*, 2nd ed., R. Taylor, M. Dorfman, and A. Davis eds. (Los Alamitos, CA: IEEE Computer Society Press, 1997): 44–77; V-model adapted from reprint in Auyang, ibid., 197.

23. Herbert Simon quoted in Auyang, ibid., 194.

24. Cleland and King, *Management: A Systems Approach*, 171–173; and R. Johnson, F. Kast, and J. Rosenzweig, *The Theory and Management of Systems*, 3d ed. (New York: McGraw-Hill, 1973): 135–36.

25. Robert Gilbreath, *Winning at Project Management* (New York: John Wiley & Sons, 1986).

26. Ibid., 95–96.

27. Ibid., 98–102.

28. Ivars Avots, "Why does project management fail?,"*Harvard Business Review* XII, no. 1 (1969): 77–82.

29. Eric Chaisson, *The Hubble Wars* (New York: HarperCollins Publishers, 1994): 347, 348.

30. "Systems management" sometimes pertains to systems that are designed to operate within a defined organizational boundary, whereas project management extends beyond the boundary of the organization responsible for mission accomplishment. Project management thus relies more upon persuasion than formal authority to coordinate and organize activities. See Johnson, Kast, and Rosenzweig, *The Theory and Management of Systems*, 395.

31. This section is derived from five sources: R. Ian Falconbridge and Michael Ryan, *Managing Complex Technical Projects: A Systems Engineering Approach* (Boston: Artech House, 2003): 9–93; Benjamin Blanchard and Walter Fabrycky, *Systems Engineering and Analysis* (Upper Saddle River, NJ: Prentice Hall, 1981): 18–52; Robert Boguslaw, *The New Utopians: A Study of System Design and Social Change* (Upper Saddle River, NJ: Prentice Hall, 1965): 99–112; Harold Chestnut, *Systems Engineering Methods*: 1–41; G. W. Jenkins, *The Systems Approach*, 78–101.

32. R. Ian Falconbridge and Michael Ryan, ibid., 29–65.

33. G.W. Jenkins, *The Systems Approach*, 88.

34. The SpaceShipOne (SS1) examples in this book illustrate concepts. While there is much factual information about the project available from published sources, information about the actual design and development of the spaceship is confidential. SS1, the X-Prize, and the stakeholders described are all true life, however for lack of information portions of this and subsequent examples are hypothetical. Information for this and other examples of SS1 are drawn from news articles and the SS1 website at Scaled Composites, www.scaled.com/projects/tierone/index.htmhttp://www.scaled.com/projects/tier-one/index.htm.

35. Adapted from R. Ian Falconbridge and Michael Ryan, *Managing Complex Technical Projects*, 67–96.

36. Harold Chestnut, *Systems Engineering Methods* (New York: John Wiley & Sons, 1967): 33.

Part II

Systems Development Cycle

CHAPTER 3

Systems Development Cycle and Project Conception

CHAPTER 4

Project and System Definition

Most systems move inexorably through a process or series of developmental stages. In planned human systems, development occurs through an intentional, logical sequence of prescribed activities called the systems development cycle. Project management takes place within the context of this cycle and is the function responsible for planning development activities and organizing and guiding their execution. The two chapters in this part introduce the systems development cycle and describe the first two phases, conception, and definition. They cover the PMBOK topics of *procurement management* and *scope management*.

Chapter 3

Systems Development Cycle and Project Conception

There is . . . a time to be born, and a time to die; a time to plant, and a time to reap; a time to kill, and a time to heal; a time to break down, and a time to build up . . .

—ECCLESIASTES 3:1

A key feature of the systems approach is the concept of "life cycle"—the basic pattern of change that occurs throughout the life of a system. Two ways the systems approach accounts for this are to (1) recognize the *natural process* that occurs in all dynamic systems—that of birth, growth, maturity, and death and (2) incorporate such recognition into the planning and management of systems. The practice of project management does both.

For any human-made system, the process of developing, implementing, and operating it happens through a logical sequence of phases called the *systems development cycle*. As a system itself, each project also follows a progression of phases from beginning to end called the *project life cycle*. This chapter and the next describe both of these cycles and their phases: This chapter gives an overview of the system development cycle and focuses on the first phase, conception; the next covers the second phase, definition. Subsequent chapters describe the other phases.

Systems are dynamic—they change over time. The change tends to follow a distinct pattern that is repeated again and again. Mentioned in Chapter 2 was the obvious life cycle of organisms—birth, growth, maturity, senescence, and death, and its similarity to cycles in human-made products and systems. Recognizing this life cycle pattern enables managers to better plan for systems, create them, and guide their actions.

Project Life Cycle

Projects are undertaken for the purpose of developing systems—either to create new ones or improve existing ones. The natural life cycle of systems gives rise to a similar life cycle in projects called the *project life cycle*. Each project has a starting point and progresses toward a predetermined conclusion during which the state of the project organization changes. Starting with project conceptualization, projects are characterized by a buildup in "activity" that peaks eventually and then declines until project termination—the typical pattern shown in the lower curve in Figure 3-1 (the upper "S-curve," shows cumulative activity). This activity can be measured in various ways, such as the amount of money spent on the project, the number of people working on it, or the amount of materials being used.

Besides changes in the level of activity, the nature and emphasis of the activity also vary. For example, consider the mix of project personnel: customers and planners dominate during early stages of the project; designers, builders, and implementers are in charge during middle stages; users and operators take over in later stages.

Despite changes in level and mix of activity, three measures of project activity that apply throughout a project's full span are *time*, *cost*, and *performance*. Time refers to the temporal progress of activities and extent to which schedules and deadlines are being met. Cost refers to the rate of resource expenditure as compared to budgeted resources. Performance refers to outputs of the project as compared to objectives, specifications, and requirements (e.g., speed and range of an aircraft, consumer appeal of a new product, poll results for a candidate running for office). Ability to meet performance requirements is one measure of the *quality* of the project output.

Figure 3-1
Level of activity during the project life cycle.

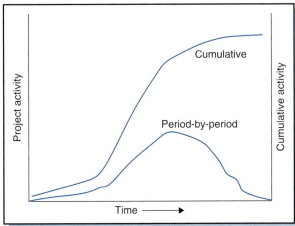

The project organization attempts to achieve time, cost, and performance requirements as it advances through phases of the project life cycle.

Managing the Project Life Cycle

Managing the project life cycle requires special treatment. Unlike in non-project, repetitive operations where everything tends to be somewhat familiar and stable, most things in projects—resources, schedules, tasks, etc.—are somewhat unfamiliar or in a constant state of change. Little that is done in a project can be considered repetitive or even routine. Work schedules, budgets, and tasks must be tailored to fit each phase and stage of the project life cycle.

All life cycles contain an element of uncertainty. Unforeseen obstacles, some virtually inevitable, can cause missed deadlines, cost overruns, and poor project performance. Management must anticipate problems and plan for them, and then replan activities and shift resources as unforeseen problems occur.

Often organizations undertake several projects at once, and at a given time the projects are at different stages of their life cycles: some are just being started while others are underway or are being closed out. Management must be able to continuously balance resources among the projects so each gets what it needs, yet the sum does not exceed the resources available.

3.2 SYSTEMS DEVELOPMENT CYCLE

The life cycle of a human-made system can be segmented into a logical series of phases and stages, each representing a group of tasks or activities that typically happen in that phase, regardless of the particular system. Figure 3-2 shows one way of dividing the life cycle into four phases, called the *systems development cycle*:

1. Conception phase (Phase A)
2. Definition phase (Phase B)
3. Execution phase (Phase C)
4. Operation phase (Phase D)

Figure 3-2
Four-phase model and stages of the systems development cycle.
The project life cycle is Phases A, B, and C.

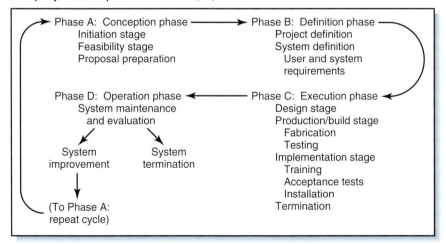

Virtually all of the projects described in Chapter 1 can be fit into this four-phase cycle.

The Phases

The four-phase model encompasses the total developmental life cycle of all human-made systems. The phases overlap and interact, yet are clearly differentiable. They reflect the natural order of thought and action in the development of all human-made systems, whether consumer products, space vehicles, information systems, or company relocations.

For some systems the development cycle overlaps identically with the project life cycle. A project typically spans Phases A through C—the conception, definition, and execution phases of the cycle. Hence, the first three phases of the systems development cycle overlap with the project life cycle. When Phase C ends upon implementation of the system, so does the project. At that point the system transits from being the end-result of a project to an operational entity.

Virtually all projects progress through Phases A, B, and C, though not necessarily through the stages as shown in Figure 3-2. The actual stages in the life cycle depend on the system or end-item being developed. For some projects, some of the stages might receive little emphasis or be entirely skipped; most projects, however, *do* pass through the stages shown in Figure 3-2, even if informally. For instance, although many projects do not involve formal proposal preparation, every project starts with a proposal from *someone*. Similarly, while not all projects require design, manufacturing, or construction, every project does require conceptualization and bringing together the pieces of something (even if only information) to produce a final result. In a consulting project, for example, the situation must be conceptualized, analyzed, and laid out (design), the consultant's suggestions compiled and edited into a final report (production), and the report presented to the client (implementation).

Sometimes between the phases of the life cycle are points at which decisions are made concerning the preceding phase and whether continuation to the next phase should be approved or the project abandoned. Referred to as "gating," the project is assessed at the end of each phase and a go/no-go decision made.

In some large-scale endeavors where the development cycle spans years—such as urban renewal, product development, and space exploration, the cycle is treated as a *program* and the phases within it as separate *projects*—sometimes each conducted by a different contracting organization. For example, Phase A would be treated as a project and conducted by one organization, Phase B as another project conducted by another organization, and so on, each phase with its own project manager. The bond holding them together and keeping them all moving forward are common program goals of the program manager.

Stakeholders

Within the systems development cycle are many stakeholders (actors and interested parties):

1. System *customers* or clients, including
   (a) Customer management
   (b) Users and operators

2. The *contractor* (also called the systems development organization (SDO), developer, promoter, or consultant), which includes
    (a) Contractor top management (corporate and functional managers)
    (b) Project management (project manager and staff)
    (c) The doers—professional, trade, assembly, and other workers

Customers are the persons or groups for whom the project is being done and who will acquire and/or operate the system when it is completed. Customer management pays for and makes decisions about the project, whereas users and operators will utilize, maintain, or in other ways be the immediate recipients of the project end-item. It is important to identify the users since, ultimately, it is for them that the system is created. Here on we will use the terms somewhat interchangeably, keeping in mind this simple distinction:

- The customer *pays* for the system
- The users *use* it

The contractor or developer is the group that performs the project, the group that studies, designs, develops, and installs the system. The contractor is usually external to the user organization, although, of course, it might well reside within the same organization as the user, as is the case of internal consulting/support groups. Since the contractor is usually an *organization*, we sometimes refer to it as the SDO. Because in most cases the customer *pays* the contractor to perform the project, you can think of the customer as the *buyer* and the contractor as the *seller*. Use of these terms makes more sense when you think of a project in the context of being a contract between two parties wherein one agrees to provide services to another in return for payment. The project manager usually works for the contractor, although the customer might have a project manager also.

Besides these, the life cycle involves other key parties—individuals, groups, and organizations with vested interests and/or influence on the conduct of the project. Anyone who is affected by the project or potentially can alter its outcome is broadly termed a *stakeholder*. Customers and contractors are considered internal stakeholders; other parties outside the project (in the environment) are considered external stakeholders.

Phase A: Conception

Every project is part of an attempt to solve a problem. The first step in solving a problem is recognition and acceptance that it exists. After that, the person or group facing the problem—the customer and users—seek out someone who can help. The steps taken after that—soliciting people to do the work, evaluating their proposals, and reaching an agreement are all part of the *procurement management* process.

If the customer organization has an internal group capable of solving the problem, it turns the problem over to them. If not, it looks for an outsider to handle the problem, possibly by sending out to contractors a formal request for help called a *request for proposal* or *RFP*. Each contractor examines the customer's problem, objectives, and requirements as stated in the RFP and determines the technical and economic feasibility of undertaking the project. If the contractor decides to respond to the request, it presents the customer a proposed solution (system concept) in a formal *proposal* or *letter of interest*. The customer then examines the proposal—or in the case where several contractors responded, all the proposals—and makes a choice. The result is a formal agreement between the chosen contractor and the customer. But most ideas or potential systems never get past Phase A; they are judged as

```
+-----------------------------------------------------------------------+
|                          Statement of work                            |
|  (a) Description of problem, need, or general type of solutions to be  |
|      investigated.                                                     |
|  (b) Scope of work to be performed by contractor, work to be included, |
|      work excluded, and work restrictions; criteria of acceptance for  |
|      results or end-items.                                             |
|  (c) Requirements for the solution, results, or end-item, including    |
|      specifications and standards; description of how work will be     |
|      measured; expected relationship between user and contractor;      |
|      expected completion date; constraints on cost of work to be       |
|      performed.                                                        |
|                         Proposal requirements                         |
|  Conditions placed on the proposal such as proposal contents and       |
|  format, data requirements, sample forms to include, and submission    |
|  location and deadline.                                                |
|                         Contractual provisions                        |
|  Type of contract to be awarded, sample contract, and nondisclosure    |
|  provisions.                                                           |
|                      Technical information or data                    |
|  Any additional data, or name of a contact person for requesting       |
|  additional data, necessary to develop a solution and prepare the      |
|  proposal or price quote.                                              |
+-----------------------------------------------------------------------+
```

Figure 3-4
Contents of a RFP.

it wins significantly affect its company overhead since expenses for those proposals not awarded must be charged to overhead. Only in rare cases such as major defense contracts are the winning contractors reimbursed for proposal expenses.

The likelihood of winning and undertaking a project depends on a number of factors:

- Have competitors gotten a head start?

- Does the contractor have sufficient money, facilities, and resources to invest in the project?

- Will performance on the project be good for (or damaging to) the contractor's reputation?

- Other factors similar to the criteria employed by the customer in the initial investigation.

Sometimes a contractor will submit a proposal knowing full well that it cannot possibly win the project, doing so to maintain its relationship with the customer, remain on the customer's bidders list, or keep the field competitive. Sometimes a customer sends out an RFP with *no intention* of ever signing with a contractor, doing so simply to gather ideas. Obviously this is a situation of which respondent contractors must be wary.

Contractors can also submit proposals to potential customers without an RFP. Whenever a developer believes it has a system or solution that satisfies a need or solves a problem, the project manager works with his marketing department to identify prospective customers, and to these he sends an *unsolicited proposal* describing the merits of the new system. Unsolicited proposals are also sent to current customers for potential follow-up work on current projects.

The Feasibility Study[6]

As mentioned, the feasibility study can happen at multiple times and with different parties in a project: minimally the customer performs a study to determine if the project is worth supporting; if the project work is to be done externally, the contractor also performs one to determine if the job is worth pursuing. In this section we consider the latter, although the steps described apply equally to the customer or anybody doing a feasibility study.

The statement of the problem as defined in the initiation stage is frequently incomplete, vague, or even incorrect. If an RFP has been received it will likely contain such a statement. Thus, one of the contractor's first steps in responding to an RFP is to develop a definition of the problem that is more concise, accurate, and complete than the one on the RFP.

The prime source of information about the problem is interviews and documented information provided by the customer and user. It is thus important that the contractor identifies who the *real user* really is. Surprisingly, this is not always obvious. The "real" user is often confused with persons of rank and position who only represent the user. If the customer is an organization, the contractor must determine the individual parties whose needs are to be met. The contractor will be working closely with the user throughout the feasibility study, so it is important that users are found who are familiar with both the problem and the workings of the organization. Sometimes, however, the RFP specifies that in order to keep the competition "fair" competing contractors must maintain an "arms-length" relationship with the customer. Even then, however, the contractor is usually permitted to make inquiries to or seek additional information from a customer contact person.

Needs Definition

One way to ensure that the idea, problem, or solution stated by the customer is concise and accurate is to start with a list of user needs. Problems originate from needs (Definition: a problem is an unsatisfied need), and so do solutions (Definition: a solution is a way to satisfy a need), so it is important that the solution adopted for the project addresses the right needs. Hence, the process of conducting a feasibility study and preparing a proposal should begin with defining user needs. J. Davidson Frame,[7] one of the best authors on defining needs in the project context, suggests the following steps:

1. *Ask the user to state the needs as clearly as possible.* The user is often not clear about the needs.

2. *Ask the user a complete set of questions to further elicit the needs.* These are questions a competent contractor would know to ask. They include:

> Are these real needs, or are there other, more fundamental ones?
> Are the needs important enough to pursue?
> Are we capable of fulfilling these needs, or is someone else better suited?
> If the needs are fulfilled, will they give rise to other needs?
> Will satisfying these needs also satisfy others, or instead, would satisfying other needs indirectly fulfill these, also?
> What effect do the unmet needs have on the organization and the user?
> What other parties are affected by these needs and how will they react to our efforts?

3. *Conduct research to better understand the needs.* "Research" means probing to gain the best understanding possible. It involves gathering whatever information necessary to understand the needs, define the problem, and propose a solution. Sources include interviews, organizational reports, memos, observations, models, and analysis of technical data or empirical test results.

the need for "a reusable three-person vehicle that can be launched into space twice within a 2-week period" can be defined by the following simple set of objectives:

"Develop a spaceship that

1. can minimally attain 100 kilometers altitude (space)
2. is reusable
3. carries three people
4. can be turned around in 2 weeks."

Each objective is then elaborated in terms of a set of requirements. The requirements must account for whatever the users and other stakeholders think will be significant throughout the expected life cycle of the system, cradle to grave. Thus, the requirements should incorporate issues regarding the system's design, development, building, testing, distribution, marketing, financing, support, training, enhancement, upkeep, environmental impacts, and disposal.

Requirements for Operational Modes

Included in this life cycle thinking are the different ways and kinds of environments in which the system will be operated; these are referred to as *operational modes* or *scenarios of operation*. For example, the modes for a reusable spacecraft include:

- Flight mode

    Launch and boost into space

    In-space

    Return from space

    Landing

- Turn-around between flights mode
- Crew training mode
- Ground transport mode
- Maintenance and testing mode

The system will be expected to perform different functions and satisfy different conditions in each of the modes, and these functions and conditions must be specified in the requirements.

Requirements for Constraints and Interfaces

Every system is subject to constraints such as mandated policies, procedures, and standards, and limited materials, knowledge, technology, time, funding, and resources. In addition, it faces constraints imposed from the environment, including technological requirements, regulations, laws, and even social norms and customs. For instance, among the numerous constraints and interfacing systems to which the spaceship must conform are FAA regulations, technical standards of the aerospace industry, and local noise and pollution limits. Also, the spaceship must be able to interface with existing systems for air traffic control and radio communication.

Ideally, the requirements address the needs of not only customers and supporters, but also builders, suppliers, operators, and anyone else who will ultimately use, benefit from, manage, maintain, or in other ways be impacted or influenced by the system. Defined using the language of the customer and stakeholders, the enumerated requirements are combined into a list called the *user's requirements*. The project should not be started until the customer and contractor have agreed on these requirements.

The Current System

Conceptually, a need arises because of inadequacies within the *current system*; a gap exists between the present system's output and the desired output. Thus, another aspect in the feasibility stage is to *fully understand* and *document* the present system. The documentation should identify key system elements (inputs, outputs, functions, flows, subsystems, components, relationships, and attributes), resources, and constraints and use schematics and charts. The schematic in Figure 3-5, for example, was developed during a hospital project to find ways of improving efficiency and reducing procurement and operating costs of surgical facilities and supplies. It shows components and flows in the present system, and was useful for identifying areas of cost and procedural inefficiency.

Through the process of needs definition and documenting the current system, the contractor and customer develop a good understanding of the problem and are better able to determine the user requirements, and to delimit the project scope to only those areas essential to solving the problem.

Alternative Solutions

Given the defined needs, objectives, constraints, and requirements, the question arises, What alternative solutions are available to satisfy them, and are they feasible? Therefore the next step is to identify alternative high-level (system-level) solutions to the problem. The solutions are developed using studies and models taking into account what the system must do (user requirements), how it can be done (technical

Figure 3-5
System schematic: flow of supplies to the operating room.

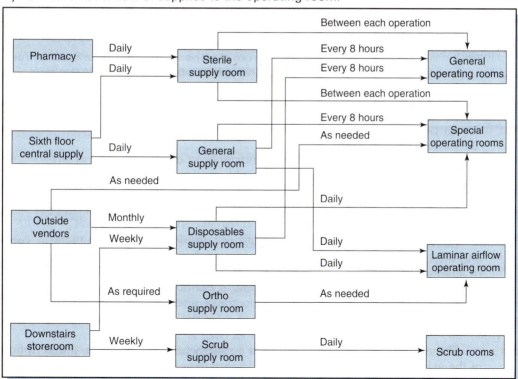

Executive summary

Perhaps the most important part of the proposal, this section must convince the customer that the remainder of the proposal is worth reading. It should be more personal than the proposal, briefly state the qualifications, experience, and interests of the contractor and draw attention to the unique or outstanding features of the proposal, the price and the contractor's ability to do the project. In case the customer has questions, the contractor "contact" person is identified here. From reading this section the customer decides whether or not to examine the rest of the proposal.

Technical section (SOW)

(a) Indicates the scope of the work—the planned approach. It must be specific enough to avoid misunderstandings and demonstrate the method and appropriateness of the approach, yet not so specific as to "give away" the solution. It should also discuss any problems or limitations inherent to the approach.

(b) Describes realistic benefits in sufficient detail to demonstrate that user needs will be fulfilled, but not so specific or enthusiastic as to promise benefits that might be difficult to deliver.

(c) Contains a schedule of when end-items will be delivered. It should be based upon a work breakdown structure and include the major project phases and key tasks, milestones, and reviews. In developmental projects, portions of this section might have to be negotiated.

Cost and payment section

Breaks down projected hours for direct, indirect, and special activities and associated labor charges, materials expenses, and price of project. The preferred or required contractual arrangement and method of payment are also included.

Legal section

Contains anticipated, possible, or likely problems, and provisions for contingencies; e.g., appropriate procedures for handling changes to the scope of the project and for terminating the project.

Management/qualifications section

Describes the background of the contractor, related experience and achievements, and financial responsibility. Also includes organization of management, and resumes of project manager and key project personnel.

Figure 3-6
Contents of a proposal.

Selecting the Winning Proposal[12]

Having received proposals from multiple contractors, the customer must now review and evaluate them. Choosing the best, reaching an agreement with the contractor, and committing funds are all part of the "project selection" process. Most companies follow a prescribed procedure for evaluating and comparing proposals. The procedure is somewhat more intricate when it involves assessing each proposed project for its contribution to a *portfolio* of projects; this includes looking at the project's contribution to company strategic goals, the resources it will require, and its comparative benefits (expected financial return or cost–benefit ratio). The topics of project selection and portfolio management are covered in depth in Chapter 17. Here we give a brief overview of proposal evaluation and project selection.

In general, priority and selection of projects is based upon consideration of:

- Project price
- Solution's ability to satisfy stated needs
- Return on investment

- Project plan and management
- Reputation of contractor
- Likelihood of success or failure (risks)
- Fit to contractor resources and technological capability

Because many users take it on faith that a competent contractor with a good plan will do a good job, choice of the best proposal is sometimes based more on the project plan, project management, and qualifications and reputation of the contractor than on the proposed solution or technical approach. Thus, it is important that the schedule section of the proposal includes a rudimentary plan with key activities to be performed, and start and end dates and deliverables for each. Methods for preparing the plan are discussed in Chapters 5 through 10.

Among the many approaches for selecting the best proposal, one is a prescreening method that rejects proposals that fail to meet minimal requirements, such as a too-high price tag, a too-low rate of return, or a contractor with insufficient experience. Proposals that survive prescreening are subjected to closer scrutiny; a common method employs a checklist to rate proposals according to several evaluation criteria.

Each proposal is reviewed and given a score s_j for each criterion j. The overall score for the proposal is the sum of the scores for all criteria,

$$S = \sum S_{j'}, \text{ where } j = 1, 2, \dots, n$$

The proposal that receives the highest overall score wins. This method is called *simple rating*.

One limitation of the method is that all evaluation criteria are treated as equally important. When some criteria are clearly more important than others, a method called *weighted rating* is used instead wherein the relative importance of each criterion j is indicated with an assigned weight w_j. After a given criterion has been scored, the score is multiplied by the weight of the criterion, $s_j \cdot w_j$. The overall score for the proposal is the sum of the $s_j \cdot w_j$ for all criteria,

$$S = \sum S_j w_j, \text{ where } j = 1, 2, \dots, n$$

$$\sum w_j = 1 \text{ and } 0 \le w_j \le 1.0$$

The procedures for the two methods are illustrated in Example 4.

Example 4: Evaluating the Proposals at MPD Company

In response to the RFP sent to several contractors (Appendix A, end of book), MPD received proposals from three companies: Iron Butterfly Contractors, Inc.; Lowball Company; and Modicum Associates. The proposals were reviewed and rated by a group of executives, facility managers, and operations experts at MPD's Chicago and New York offices. The proposals were each rated on five criteria using a 4-point scale as follows:

Criteria	1	2	3	4
Technical solution approach	Poor	Adequate	Good	Excellent
Price of contract	≥1.8	1.6–1.8	1.4–1.6	≤1.4
Project organization and management	Poor	Adequate	Good	Excellent
Likelihood of meeting cost/schedule targets	Poor	Adequate	Good	Excellent
Reputation of contractor	Poor	Adequate	Good	Excellent

Simple Rating

The results of the group assessment for the three proposals were as follows:

	Scores		
Criteria	Iron Butterfly	Lowball	Modicum
Technical solution approach	3	1	4
Price of contract	4	4	1
Project organization/management	4	2	3
Likelihood of meeting cost/schedule targets	3	2	4
Reputation of contractor	3	3	4
Sum	17	12	16

Based on the sum of simple ratings, Iron Butterfly was rated the best.

Weighted Rating

Lowball's proposal was clearly the worst, but Iron Butterfly and Modicum were considered too close to make an objective decision. The rating group then decided to look at the criteria more closely and to assign weights based on the relative importance of each of them:

Criteria	Weight
Technical solution approach	0.25
Price of contract	0.25
Project organization and management	0.20
Likelihood of meeting cost/schedule targets	0.15
Reputation of contractor	0.15
	1.00

Taking the weights into account, the proposals scored as follows:

		Iron Butterfly		Modicum	
Criterion	Weight (w)	S	$(s)(w)$	s	$(s)(w)$
Technical solution approach	0.25	3	0.75	4	1.0
Price of contract	0.25	4	1.0	1	0.25
Project organization/management	0.20	4	0.8	3	0.6
Risks of solution	0.15	3	0.45	4	0.6
Reputation of contractor	0.15	3	0.45	4	0.6
	Sum		3.45		3.05

Using the sum of the weighted ratings, Iron Butterfly Contractors stands out as having the superior proposal.

Assessment of proposals can also include evaluation of project risk, especially when the proposed solutions and associated levels of risk differ significantly between proposals. Methods for identifying and assessing risks are discussed in Chapter 10.

Selection of the best proposal and awarding a contract often depend more on the contractor than on the proposed solution. Among factors the customer considers are:[13]

- Is the contractor big enough to do the project?
- Is it adequately financed to do the project?
- Does it have a good track record with this kind of project?

- Does it have a good reputation in the industry?
- Has it been involved in litigations and arbitrations?
- Will the company's management be accessible?
- Is it ISO 9000 certified?
- Will the relationship with the company likely be amicable or touchy?

Proposal finalists are notified and competing contractors might be requested to provide more data, meet for interviews, or give presentations or live demonstrations of their proposed solution or system. The preferred contractor is recommended to top management and, if approved, awarded the contract. If several contractors receive equal marks, or if some terms in the proposal are unspecified or questionable, then the parties must negotiate to settle upon the final terms. If none of the proposals is acceptable or the feasibility studies reveal that the project would be too costly, risky, or time-consuming or provide insufficient benefit, the process ends.

Project Initiation: Variations on a Theme

Projects are always initiated in response to a need, but they do not always involve an RFP or even a proposal. The RFP/proposal process as described largely applies to projects where the work is *contracted out*; i.e., where the customer and the contractor are not in the same organization. For internal projects—projects where the organization has the internal capability to perform the work on its own—the initiation happens with a *business case study*. Common examples of this are projects in product development and IT—two areas where companies often exhibit significant internal prowess. In the former, the "need" is manifest as the desire or mandate to fill a perceived market niche or a growing market, or respond to a competitive threat. The business case study, similar to a feasibility study, analyzes the market, competition, product alternatives, risk, cost, and returns, and argues in favor of launching a new product development effort. If the business case is approved and funded, the project is turned over to the new product development department to begin work. The business case study serves as feasibility study and project proposal combined. In similar fashion, business case studies are used to initiate IT solutions.

The department that would do the project if it were approved (product development or IT) oversees preparation of the case study and argues in favor of the proffered end-item or solution. Final approval or denial of the project involves rating the business case against other competing cases using criteria such as resources required, benefits in terms of strategic goals, or the immediacy or priority of needs—the process described in Chapter 17. If the project is approved a project charter is created.

The RFP/proposal process as described earlier represents projects with relatively few stakeholders, viz., a single, clearly identified customer and its potential contractors. In large technical projects that touch many stakeholders the process is more complex and protracted. The TSR project in Chapter 2 is an example that illustrates the relative difficultly of defining all the stakeholders and meeting their multiple, sometimes conflicting needs. Other examples include projects for infrastructure and transportation systems (Boston Big Dig, Delhi Metro, telecommunication systems, Chunnel), complex technical products where subsystems and even the components must be developed from scratch (commercial aircraft, SpaceShipOne, and medical devices) and large-scale property developments (resorts and planned communities).

In such cases, the RFP/proposal process includes a "front-end" component of initially identifying all the important stakeholders, capturing their needs, and incorporating the needs into stakeholder requirements that subsequently appear in RFPs. The organization gathering the stakeholder requirements is not necessarily

Negotiating the Contract[17]

The purpose of negotiation is to clarify technical or other terms in the contract and to reach agreement on time, schedule, and performance obligations. Negotiation is not necessary for standardized projects for which the terms are simple and costs are fairly well known, but for complex systems that require development work or are somewhat risky it is. Different contractual agreements offer advantages to the customer and contractor, depending on the nature of the project. These agreements are discussed in the Appendix to this chapter; they are, briefly:

- *Fixed Price Contract*: The price paid by the customer for the project is fixed regardless of the costs incurred by the contractor. The customer knows what the project will cost.

- *Cost-Plus Contract*: The price paid by the customer is based on the costs incurred in the project plus the contractor's fee. The contractor is assured his costs will be covered.

- *Incentive Contract*: The amount paid by the customer depends on the contractor's performance in comparison to the target price, schedule, or technical specification: the contractor either receives a *bonus* for exceeding the target or it must pay the customer a *penalty* for falling short of the target. This arrangement affords the contractor opportunity to make a higher profit and reduces the customer's risk of the contractor not meeting requirements.

The specific type of contract agreement negotiated with subcontracts depends on the type of agreement between the customer and the prime contractor. If the prime contract is fixed price (FP), then subcontracts should also be FP, otherwise the prime contractor risks being charged more by subcontractors than the customer will pay him. For prime contracts that are cost-plus or incentive, the contractor has more latitude in using a variety of agreements for subcontracts.

Although contract negotiation is the last activity before an agreement is reached, the process actually begins much earlier, often during proposal preparation, because the terms in the proposal must be consistent with the kind of contract acceptable to both customer and contractor. During negotiation, terms in the proposal related to specifications, schedules, and price are converted into legal, contractual agreements. Final negotiation is the last opportunity to correct misperceptions that might have slipped through the RFP/proposal process. (Customers are always negotiating—usually informally—for a better deal, even after the contract is signed and the project is underway. The contractor must always be careful about saying and writing anything that might be construed as a promise or agreement to deliver more than specified in the contract.)

Performance, schedule, and cost are interrelated, and a "package" agreement must be reached wherein all three parameters are acceptable to both parties. In highly competitive situations, the customer will try to play one contractor against the other, raising performance specifications while shortening the schedule and decreasing the price. Raising performance requirements, however, may increase costs to a level unacceptable to the contractor. In that case, the project manager must take on the role of salesperson and push the merits of his proposal. Throughout negotiation, his goal is to obtain an agreement to the best advantage of his company. In countering any customer objections to the proposal, the project manager's best defense is a well thought-out project plan that clearly shows what can or must be done to achieve the desired parameters. A detailed project plan is often used to define which parts of the plan are relatively "fixed"—the work and the schedule, and which are somewhat flexible and negotiable.

To be in the most knowledgeable and competitive position, the project manager must learn as much as possible about the customer and the competition. She should determine, for example, if the customer is under pressure to make a particular decision, needs the system soon, faces an impending fiscal deadline, or has historically shown preference for one particular approach or contractor over others. The project manager should also try to learn about the competition—their likely approach to the problem, costs, and competitive advantages and disadvantages. She learns this from historical information, published material, or employees who once worked for competitors. (Relying on the last source is ethically questionable and, of course, works against the contractor whenever competitors hire its employees.)

To be able to negotiate tradeoffs, the project manager must be intimately familiar with the technical details of the system design, its fabrication, and related costs. Sometimes the contract will include incentive or penalty clauses as inducements to complete the project before a certain date or below a certain cost. To competently negotiate such clauses, the project manager must be familiar with the project schedule and time–cost tradeoffs.

The signed contract becomes the binding agreement for the project. Any changes thereafter should follow formal change mechanisms, including change notices, reviews, customer approvals, and, sometimes, contract renegotiation—topics discussed in Chapter 11.

Contract Statement of Work and Work Requisitions

The contract contains a SOW that is similar to the SOW in the original RFP or the winning proposal, or is a restatement of either to reflect negotiated agreements. This so-called *contract statement of work* (CSOW) legally defines the expected performance of the project in terms of scope of work, requirements, end-results, schedules, costs, and so on. The CSOW must clearly specify the conditions under which the deliverables or end-results will be accepted by the customer or user. Failure to state these conditions can lead to later disputes and delay in completing the project.

On contracts with suppliers and subcontractors for procured items, the contracts also include a CSOW, responsibilities and liabilities of all parties, specifications and quantities, delivery schedules, costs and conditions, payment schedules, indemnities and method for handling changes or variations, and responsibilities for damages.

Once the user and the contractor both agree on the CSOW, the project is considered "approved" and ready to go. Before the work can actually begin, however, the work must be divided among the different departments and organizations. Requirements that have been specified in the CSOW must be summarized and translated into terminology and expressions understandable to personnel in the SDO and its subcontractors, i.e., personalized SOWs. These translations, aimed at parties who will perform the work, must have identical interpretations to the requirements and scope statement specified in the CSOW.

The document containing the personalized SOW for each work group is called a *work requisition* or *work order*. This document serves two purposes: (1) to notify each party in the project, in the language it understands, about the work expected and (2) to authorize the work to begin. This topic is discussed further in Chapter 11.

Signing the contract marks the completion of Phase A and approval to proceed to Phase B. The project is then prioritized with other previously approved projects according to availability of capital funds, resources needed, and criticality of the project. The steps in Phase A are summarized in Figure 3-8.

The process of initiating projects, preparing proposals, and negotiating and finalizing contracts sometimes involves substantially more than is possible to cover in a chapter. The following story illustrates.

Figure 3-10
Apollo spacecraft. (Photo: John Nicholas.)

saw the final bill. With less than 6 weeks to go he picked John Paup to be Apollo program manager, someone he thought perfect for the role, a "witty, engaging person who could tell a great story" and understood the technology. For the next month Paup listened to lectures and presentations 18 hours a day, slept on a cot, and ate from vending machines. Every morning he gathered his team for a stand-up meeting; anyone not there by 7:45 was locked out. No coffee, no seats, he wanted to hear the problems and how each would be fixed within 24 hours.

The proposal was encyclopedic in size, and NASA wanted dozens of copies submitted no later than 5 P.M., 2 days before the presentation. The whole bundle, weighing 100 pounds, was hand delivered just under the wire. Next day Paup and his team, looking like zombies from lack of sleep, boarded the company plane for the presentation in Virginia. NASA gave each company 60 minutes to present its proposal to an evaluation team of 75 top engineers, some of them legends. Unintimidated, Paup, witty and charming as ever, hit all the presentation high points and finished 10 minutes early.

Days later Storms received a telegram: NASA wanted to know how, given NA's second-stage contract, it could possibly handle Apollo too? The response at 20 pages was too long to telegraph back so Storms and Paup jumped on a plane to hand deliver it. This violated an unwritten rule that a contractor does not meet with the customer evaluating the proposal. But Storms had little regard for such rules, especially with so much at stake.

Meantime NA headquarters had determined what the proposal cost—5 times the allotted $1 million—and it was fuming. But to say the overrun was worth it would be an understatement. North American had won the competition, though it would take another year to formalize the contract: in return for a target $884 million in costs and a fee of $50 million, NA was to deliver several mock-ups, test versions, and flight-ready Apollo spacecraft (Figure 3-10). The contract was cost-plus of course since the unknowns of sending humans to the moon were overwhelming. By the time the program ended 10 years later with the return of the seventh crew from the moon, NA as prime contractor had earned the sum of $4.4 billion—about $20 billion in 2005 dollars.

3.8 SUMMARY

A common theme among human-made systems is a development process or life cycle divided into four phases: conception, definition, execution, and operation. The first three of these phases constitute the project life cycle

The first phase of the systems development cycle, conception, includes formulating the problem, defining needs and user requirements, evaluating alternative solutions, and preparing a proposal to conduct the project. At the start of this phase most activities are in the hands of the customer; by the end of the phase, the activities have been taken over by the contractor or system developer. The relationship between the customer and the contractor is cemented through the process of solicitation (RFPs), proposal preparation and evaluation, and contract negotiation.

Phase A is the "foundation" part of the systems development cycle; it establishes the needs, objectives, requirements, constraints, agreements, and patterns of communication upon which the remaining phases are built. It is a crucial phase and the place where often the seeds of project success or failure are planted.

APPENDIX: KINDS OF CONTRACTS

A contract is an agreement between two parties wherein one party (the contractor) promises to perform a service, and the other party (the client) promises to do something in return—typically make payment for the service. Both the service requirements and the payment must be clear and unequivocally spelled out in the contract.

Different kinds of contracts provide different advantages to the client and the contractor. Depending on the risk of the project and the degree of difficulty in estimating costs, the client and contractor try to negotiate the type of contract that best serves their own interests. In some cases, for example, the client can protect herself by imposing penalty clauses or incorporating incentives into the contract.

The two fundamental kinds of contacts are *fixed price* and *cost-plus* contracts. In the FP contract, the price is agreed upon and remains fixed as long as there are no changes to the scope or provisions of the agreement. In the cost-plus contract, the contractor is reimbursed for all or some of the expenses incurred during the performance of the contract, and as a result, the final price is unknown until the project is completed. Within these two types, several variations exist including some with built-in incentives for the contractor to meet cost, time, or performance targets.[19]

Variables

The variables specified in a contract may include the following:

C_{ex} and C_{ac}	Target (expected) cost and actual cost. "Cost" represents monies expended by the contractor in performing the work. C_{ex} and C_{ac} are the negotiated target cost and the actual cost of the project under normal circumstances.
Fee	Amount paid to the contractor in addition to reimbursable costs.
Price	The price the client pays for the project. Price includes reimbursable costs (or a percentage thereof) incurred by the contractor, plus the contractor's profit or fee.
CSR	The cost sharing ratio. When costs are to be shared by the client and the customer, this is the percentage of the cost that each agrees to share (the sum is 100%).

21. Describe how a contractor can be both the receiver and sender of an RFP. How can a contractor both prepare and submit proposals, and receive and select a winning proposal?

22. When a contractor contracts out work to a subcontractor, to whom is the subcontractor obligated—the end-user customer or the contractor?

23. What does the project manager need to know to be able to effectively negotiate a contract? Consider aspects of the customer, the competition, and technical content of the proposal.

24. Discuss the difference between the SOW, CSOW, and work requisition or work order.

25. Describe the different kinds of contracts (refer to chapter Appendix). What are the relative advantages and disadvantages of each to the user and the contractor?

QUESTIONS ABOUT THE STUDY PROJECT

As appropriate, answer questions 1 through 13 regarding your project. Also answer the following questions: How are contracts negotiated and who is involved in the negotiation? What kinds of contracts are used in the project?

Case 3-1   *West Coast University Medical Center*

(This is a true story.) West Coast University Medical Center (pseudonym) is a large university teaching and research hospital with a national reputation for excellence in health care practice, education, and research. Always seeking to sustain that reputation, the senior executive board at the Medical Center (WCMC) decided to install a comprehensive medical diagnostic system. The system would be linked to WCMC's computer servers and be available to physicians via the computer network. Doctors and staff would be able to access the system from WCMC as well as from their homes or private-practice offices. By simply clicking icons to access a medical specialty area, then keying answers to queries about a patient's medical symptoms and history, a physician could receive a list of diagnostics with associated statistics.

The senior board sent a questionnaire to managers in every department about needs in their areas and how they felt the system might improve doctors' performance. Most managers

felt the system would save the doctors time and improve their performances. The hospital IS group was assigned to investigate the cost and feasibility of implementing the system. They interviewed medical-center managers and software vendors who specialized in diagnostic systems. The study showed high enthusiasm among the respondents and a long list of potential benefits. Based on the study report, the senior board approved the system.

The IS manager contacted three well-known consulting firms that specialized in medical diagnostic systems and invited each to give a presentation. Based on the presentations, he chose one firm to assist the IS group in identifying, selecting, and integrating several software packages into a single, complete diagnostic system.

One year and several million dollars later the project was completed. However, within less than a year it was clear that the system had failed. Although it did everything the consultants and software vendors had promised, few doctors accessed the system, and those who did complained that many of the system "benefits" were irrelevant, and that certain features they desired were lacking.

QUESTIONS

1. Why was the system a failure?
2. What was the likely cause of its lack of use?
3. What steps or procedures were absent or poorly handled in the project conception phase?

Case 3-2 X-philes Data Management Corporation: RFP Matters

X-philes Data Management Corporation (XDM) is preparing to contract out work to outside consultants for two large projects: Scully and Mulder. Although the projects are comparable in terms of size, technical requirements, and estimated completion time, they are independent and will have their own project managers and teams.

Two managers at XDM, one each assigned to Scully and Mulder, prepare RFPs for the projects and send them to several contractors. The RFP for Scully includes a SOW that specifies system performance and quality requirements, a maximum price, a completion deadline, and contract conditions. As an incentive, the contractor will receive a bonus for exceeding minimal quality measures and completing the project early, and will be penalized for poor quality and late completion. The project will be tracked using precise quality measures, and the contractor will have to submit detailed monthly status reports. In contrast, the RFP for Mulder includes a SOW, a maximum budget, and the desired completion date.

Based on proposals received in response to the RFPs, the managers responsible for Scully and Mulder each select a contractor. Unknown to either manager is that they select the same contractor, Yrisket Systems. Yrisket is selected for the Mulder Project because its specified price was somewhat below the budget limit specified in the RFP, and its reputation in the business is good. Yrisket was chosen for the Scully Project for similar reasons—good price and reputation. In responding to the Scully RFP, Yrisket managers had to work hard to get the price down to the maximum specified, but they felt that by doing quality work they could make a tidy profit on the incentive offered.

A few months after the projects are underway some of Yrisket's employees quit. Thus, to meet their commitments to both projects Yrisket workers have to work long hours and weekends. It is apparent, however, that these extra efforts might not be enough, especially because Yrisket has a contract with another customer and will have to start a third project in the near future.

QUESTIONS

1. What do you think will happen?
2. How do you think the crisis facing Yrisket will affect the Mulder Project? The Scully Project?

Case 3-3 Proposal Evaluation for Apollo Spacecraft[24]

Five proposals were submitted to NASA to design and build the Apollo spacecraft. An evaluation board of more than 100 specialists reviewed the proposals and ranked them as follows (maximum = 10):

Chapter 4

Project and System Definition

> When one door is shut, another opens.
>
> —CERVANTES, DON QUIXOTE

The result of Phase A is a formalized systems concept. It includes: (1) a clear problem formulation and list of user requirements, (2) a rudimentary but well-conceptualized systems solution, (3) an elemental plan in the proposal for the project, and (4) an agreement between the customer and the contractor about all of these. The project is now ready to move on to the "middle" and "later" phases of systems development and to bring the systems concept to fruition.

4.1   PHASE B: DEFINITION

Phase B, Definition, can be called the "analysis of the solution" phase because it is here that the *solution* is first scrutinized in great detail. Most of the effort in Phase A was devoted to investigating the *problem*—what is it, is it significant, should it be resolved, and can it be resolved in an acceptable fashion. Despite the effort and expense devoted to initial investigation and feasibility studies, most of this work remained focused on the problem. Any work on the solution was preliminary and rudimentary.

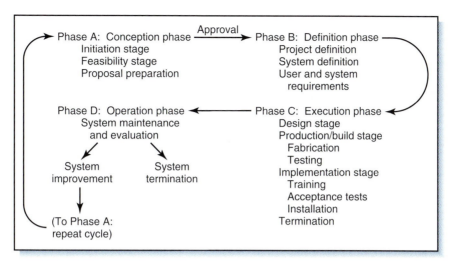

Figure 4-1
Four-phase model of systems development cycle.

As Figure 4-1 shows, given approval of the project in Phase A, the thrust of the effort is now turned toward definition, design, production, and implementation of the solution. In Phase B the system solution is analyzed and defined in sufficient detail such that designers and builders can produce a system with the greatest likelihood of solving the user's problem. The definition phase has two objectives: determination of detailed system requirements and specifications, and preparation of a detailed project plan.

Project Definition versus System Definition

There are two ways of looking at a project: one is to see the end-item or *result* of the project, the other to see the *effort* directed at achieving that result. Both are necessary: if you focus too much on the end-item and too little on the effort, chances are the project will run into problems for lack of preparation, coordination, and control over resources, costs, and schedules. But if you focus primarily on the effort and less so on the end-item, chances are you will still run into problems, this time for not meeting user requirements. System definition aims at achieving a good understanding of what the end-item must do to be able to meet user requirements; project definition aims at specifying what must happen in the project to produce the end-item. The two are inextricably linked and happen in iterative fashion. It is not surprising that much of the literature on project planning is preoccupied with project definition, although what is surprising is how little attention is given to system definition. This is puzzling because the simple fact is, a good plan cannot be prepared without first having a good definition of the project end-item.

System definition begins with defining user needs and requirements; project definition begins with addressing those requirements in a proposed solution—the project proposal. Hence, some of the definition work necessary for a project is initiated in Phase A. Phase B continues with the definition work and concludes with a set of system specifications and a project plan—a full suite of everything necessary to execute the project in Phase C.

Project Kickoff

The project formally begins with a kickoff meeting, which is the first formal meeting of the project team members and key stakeholders. The purpose of the meeting is to announce that the project is about to commence, communicate what the project is about, develop common expectations, and generate enthusiasm and commitment to project goals and deliverables. The project manager plans and runs the meeting. Attendees include the project team (or, if too large, only managers, team leads, and project staff), supporters, and others who should know that the project is about to begin. For a multi-location project, multiple kickoffs at each location or a video or phone conference might be necessary. The kickoff runs 1.5 to 2 hours and is mostly a formal presentation with a question-and-answer period at the end.

Invited attendees should be formally notified in advance and provided with information about the meeting agenda, a list of invited participants and their project roles, and a rudimentary project plan. The meeting should address the following topics: the project manager; the project statement of work (SOW), goals, and deliverables; the proposed project plan—budget, schedule, main work packages; constraints and risks; the customer and other key stakeholders, and their needs and requirements; the project organization structure and key team members; and immediate next steps and who is to do what. Much of this information will have been worked out for the project proposal; if it hasn't, the project manager should identify the key people who will be working on the project and request their assistance in preparing it prior to the meeting.

Every project—and every major effort associated with it—should start with a kickoff meeting. For a large project, the effort to prepare the proposal will itself be a project and should be preceded by a kickoff meeting; similarly, each large work package can be initiated with a kickoff.

Important to emphasize is that the purpose of the kickoff is to inform and provide information, not to reach consensus of opinions, develop working relationships, or establish guidelines so team members can work together effectively. The latter is the purpose of team building, for which a subsequent meeting should be held shortly after the kickoff. Teambuilding is discussed in Chapter 15.

Project Name

Every project has a name, although sometimes the name just happens without anyone having given it much thought. But a project's formal name is important because it is the first thing that people hear about the project, often without any accompanying explanation.[1] The name will appear again and again in virtually all communication and persist for as long as the project—and perhaps longer. A carelessly chosen name can cause misunderstanding or a blank stare about what the project is supposed to do; it can cause people to confuse the project with other projects; and it can influence the way they react to the project. Unless the intention is to obfuscate the project's purpose ("Manhattan Engineering District"—the atomic bomb project; "Have Blue"—the F-117 stealth fighter project), the name should clearly suggest what the project is about.

It is okay to give the project a subtitle if it helps clarify the picture in people's minds. Burt Rutan titled his project "Tier One" to imply that suborbital human spaceflight—the purpose of the project—is the first tier to space tourism; he could as well have named it "Tier One: Commercial Suborbital Spaceflight." (He intends in the future to undertake "Tier Two: Commercial Orbital Spaceflight.")

Clever or cute names or acronyms should be avoided; they tend to be ambiguous and, sometimes, annoying to all but the namers. All projects are apt to acquire nicknames, which tend to indicate how people *feel* about the project ("Project from Hell") but not much else. The formal name should be more robust than the nickname; if, however, the nickname gains widespread usage, then sometimes the sensible thing is to formally adopt it. (Boston's Central Artery/Tunnel became the "Big Dig"—not to be confused with Canada's "Big Dig", the Wascana Lake Urban Revitalization Project in Saskatchewan. The 1960s geological research project to drill completely through the earth's crust to the Mohorovicic discontinuity was aptly named Project Mohole; as political and technical problems mounted, it became known as "Project Nohole.") An obvious way to name a project is for a place or person, or the end-item it creates (Bandra-Worli Sea Link Bridge; Petronas Towers), and for long-named end-items to adopt an acronym (BWSL). But it is a good idea to check first the name's acronym before adopting the name; a serious project should not make people laugh whenever they see the acronym (*Automated Network for Uniform Security*).

4.2   PROJECT DEFINITION

Project definition addresses the question: What must the project do to deliver the system concept and satisfy the user and system requirements? Actually, the question is comprised of several sub-questions such as What work must be done, Who will do it, How will they do it, How much time will they have, How much money will they have, What resources will they need?, etc. These questions are largely answered in one place: the project plan.

Project definition and system definition happen concurrently and cyclically. The work to be done in the project plan must meet the system specifications, but the system specifications must conform to the constraints, methods of work, technological capabilities, and risks as specified in the project plan.

Detailed Project Planning

Prior to Phase B a portion of the project definition will already have been done: at minimum, some amount of project definition was necessary in Phase A to prepare project plans and system requirements for inclusion in the proposal. But at best that definition effort will have resulted in a detailed outline of what is to come. During Phase B that outline must be filled in, expanded, and elaborated in detail. The renewed definition effort will involve identifying the work tasks and necessary resources, creating schedules, budgets, and cost control systems, and identifying the project team and its leaders, supervisors, subcontractors, and support staff.

The project team begins to evolve from the skeletal group that worked on the proposal, sometimes following a cascade pattern: the project manager selects team leaders who, in turn, select team members to fill positions under them. The project manager negotiates with functional managers to get specific individuals or the requisite expertise assigned to the project. Sometimes she seeks the customer's approval in adding members to the project team; this is advisable whenever the customer must work closely with the team or when the customer might have an objection. Good user–project team rapport is crucial to maintaining a healthy user–contractor relationship.

Project Master Plan

As key members of the project team are assembled they begin preparing the detailed project plan or project "master plan." The plan includes:

- A scope statement or SOW that includes high-level user requirements and system requirements.
- Work breakdown structure and work packages or tasks.

- Project organization and responsibility assignments.
- Assignments of key personnel to work packages and other areas of the project.
- Project schedules showing events, milestones, or points of critical action.
- Budget and allocation to work packages.
- Quality plan for monitoring and accepting project deliverables.
- Risk plan and contingency or mitigation measures.
- Procurement plan.
- Work review plan.
- Testing plan.
- Change control plan.
- Documentation policy/plan.
- Implementation plan to guide conversion to or adoption of deliverables.

Ultimately all of the elements of the plan must be integrated, meaning that each is tied to, compatible with, and supportive of the others. Details of these elements are discussed in Part III, starting with the next chapter. A sample project plan is in Appendix C.

In large projects most of the planning is delegated to subordinate members of the project team. The project manager coordinates and oversees their efforts to ensure that all subplans are thorough and tie together. The final plan is reviewed for approval by contractor top management and the customer. Contractor top management makes sure that the plan fits into existing and upcoming organizational projects and capabilities, and the customer checks the plan for conformity with user requirements and conditions as stated in the contract.

Anxious to get the project underway, many contractors avoid reviewing the project plan with the customer. This is shortsighted because the plan might contain elements to which the customer objects. Often the project is not conducted and implemented in isolation but within the customer's ongoing system. Everything in the plan must fit: The project schedule must fit the customer's schedule; project cash flow requirements must meet the customer's payment schedule; the contractor's personnel and procedures must complement those of the customer; and materials and work methods must be acceptable to the customer. To avoid later problems, the customer and user should be allowed to carefully review the plan before starting work.

Once the project plan and systems specifications have been approved by management and the customer, the project team turns its attention to the detailed design and building of the system, which happen in Phase C, covered in Chapters 11 and 12. As we will explain later, however, project planning never stops; it continues throughout the project life cycle.

Phased Project Planning

Phase B represents a major thrust to develop the project plan, but seldom does it produce a comprehensive, detailed plan for the entire project. The fact is, despite all the effort devoted to the plan in Phase B, the plan is developed in stages, not all at once. This is because there are too many unknowns at the start of a project and it is impossible to specify exactly for the whole project what will happen and what should be done. Only as the project progresses do the unknowns decrease, allowing details in the plan to be filled in. The situation is analogous to planning the route to some ultimate destination, but without the benefit of knowing the obstacles ahead. Since you can only see the landscape you first encounter, you can only plan the early part of the route in detail; beyond that, however, the route is vague. This is represented by Phase I in Figure 4-2a. As you move through Phase I, you start to see more of the

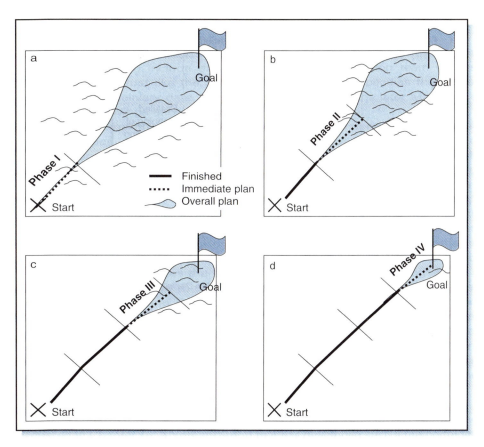

Figure 4-2
Phased project planning.

obstacles ahead, which enables you to plan for next part of the route, Phase II (b). The process continues, filling in details of the route, phase by phase, until you reach the destination (c and d).

In a project, the initial plan is somewhat rough and perhaps vague (analogous to the shaded blob in Figure 4-2), although it is adequate for managers to have estimated project resources, time, and cost, and to show all these to the customer. But as the project progresses, another, more-detailed plan is created, but for *the most immediate phase* of the project only (dotted line, Figure 4-2). Whereas the rough plan is based upon information from similar projects, estimates, and forecasts, the detailed plan is based upon facts about upcoming work, facts identified as the approaching work gets closer—similar to seeing obstacles in the terrain ahead.

At the onset of a project the customer wants to know the project cost and finish date, but these can be estimated only by preparing a rough plan. For highly unique projects, the rough plan should be seen as just that—a rough indication of project deliverables, cost, and delivery date, but not a commitment. The rough plan specifies the project phases and the deliverables of each. For the most immediate phase the "terrain" is clearly visible, hence it is possible to chart a clear path through it. Unlike the rough plan, the impending work includes a commitment to a date and cost based on a detailed plan of the necessary work, who will do it, and how long it will take. In the project life cycle, the rough plan is first prepared during the feasibility study or business case study. As the project moves through the successive phases and stages, detailed plans are prepared with more-specific deliverables and schedules.

The *last phase, stabilization,* consists of extensive internal and external (beta) testing of the product—the combined, integrated sets of features developed in the previous phase. No new features are added at this time, unless the features of emerging competitive products make such additions essential. "Zero-bug release" occurs when no more bugs remain. Either all bugs are fixed, or features with remaining bugs are removed from the product (to be fixed later and included in subsequent product versions). This phase concludes with the release of a "golden master" disk from which manufacturing will make copies. The project concludes with the project team's preparation of a postmortem report that outlines what worked well and what did not.

Relocation of a Company Division[8]

Over recent years the information systems division of a large corporation had grown such that relocation to a larger work area had become a necessity. The main activities of the relocation closely paralleled the phases of the systems development cycle: Phase I, project *concept* (recognize the necessity to relocate); Phase II, project *definition* (find a new location, define facility and equipment needs, and obtain designs and construction drawings); Phase III, *acquisition* (new facility construction and equipment purchase); and Phase IV, *implementation* (relocate the division and monitor it during a settling-in period).

Phase I happened by mandate: The division either would be relocated or it would be "suffocated" out of business. Phase II started with a needs analysis to determine the requirements for the new site, which included space for 100 employees and a new computer room. Preliminary budget figures were prepared for the required square footage of 300,000 square feet for leased and purchased space. It was decided that space should be leased, and three sites were considered. The company hired a real estate broker and legal consultant to help select the site and conduct contract negotiations. A preliminary space design was prepared for each site, showing location of workstations and work flow. A detailed budget was prepared with leasing arrangements, improvement and construction expenses, furniture, fixtures, and telecommunication costs, moving expenses, and plant and office costs. Based upon budget and design considerations, a site was selected.

Later in Phase II, detailed design and construction drawings were obtained for company offices and the computer room. A detailed needs analysis was performed and the space design was analyzed in greater detail. For the computer room, requirements for power, air-conditioning, and corporate and local data inputs to the system were defined. Bids were secured from local distributors and installation groups, and a furniture manufacturer was selected. After the final interior design was selected, bids were taken on general construction drawings for space design, HVAC engineering, electricity, architecture, lighting, telephone, and computer equipment, and contracts signed.

In Phase III the preliminary construction work was completed. The phase also involved equipment needs analysis and purchase, vendor selection, and employee training. Numerous vendors performed the electrical, sheet metal, dry wall, painting, HVAC, plumbing, plastering, and carpentry work. A team of corporate and general contractor personnel oversaw and supervised the construction.

Meantime, bids from several moving companies were reviewed, a company was selected, and a moving schedule was prepared. At the same time, bids were received and contracts signed for procurement and installation of computer workstations, photocopy machines, vending machines, and security systems.

Under the supervision of the project management team, Phase IV (relocation to the new site and equipment installation) were performed according to schedule. Before and during the move an orientation program was conducted for division employees. After the move a final check-out was conducted to ensure that all steps had been completed and that all equipment was working properly. During the last phase, management established amicable working relationships with the local municipality and services environment—city hall, the community college, the fire department, and utilities companies.

Overhaul of Human Services Administration

Small projects in the service sector follow a series of phases that is roughly *analogous* to the systems development process. These phases nominally include *initiation and problem definition, analysis of solutions, implementation,* and *operation.* The following example is an illustration.[9]

Human Services Administration (HSA) is a city welfare agency that provides limited financial assistance in the form of money, medical care, and drug rehabilitation treatment to eligible recipients. In administering these services, HSA became plagued by a number of bureaucratic problems, the worst being:

- Inefficient control measures that allowed for mismanagement and errors in payments.
- High increases in the annual cost of the system.
- Inadequate control in applicant approvals leading to fraudulent client abuse.
- Employee productivity below 40 percent.
- Excessive tardiness and absenteeism among employees.

The city's mayor allotted $10 million annually for the implementation and maintenance of a new administrative system to resolve the problems. A group of outside professionals would be hired as a project team to overhaul the system. After the team had resolved the problems it would become a permanent part of HSA.

The project was to be conducted in four phases. During the first phase, *initiation,* HSA would define overhaul objectives and hire the professionals who would form the project team. In the second phase, *analysis,* the project team would identify problems and related objectives, and recommend solutions. In the third phase, *implementation,* the solutions would be executed, giving priority to the most severe problems. In the fourth phase, *operation,* the project team would be interweaved into the existing organization and become an ongoing staff function.

During the initiation phase, the following project objectives were stated:

1. Create a project management team with clear-cut responsibilities and authority. Conforming to this objective, outside professionals were hired and a project management team was created.
2. Eliminate opposition by some members of the existing organization to the planned overhaul.
3. Produce solutions to smaller problems so confidence could be gained and talent identified for working on larger problems.
4. Gain taxpayer confidence through media attention to the overhaul project.

In the second phase the project management team identified specific problem areas and divided them into five categories: new applications, photo identification, addicts, eligibility, and fraud. It then reorganized HSA to create a task force for each category. Each task force was to define problems, document the system, and suggest long-range recommendations and alternatives to the current system. Problems needing immediate attention were singled out and worked on first.

Part III

Systems and Procedures for Planning and Control

*S*uccessful project management goes far beyond defining requirements and objectives; it also involves creating a project organization, identifying the necessary work tasks and project resources, and providing leadership and direction to ensure the tasks get done. Overall project goals and system requirements need to be articulated into shorter-term objectives with carefully plotted plans, schedules, and budgets to accomplish them. Controls are then needed to make sure plans and schedules are carried out as intended.

Over the years an impressive collection of methods has been developed to help project managers collect and use information for defining and directing work. The next 8 chapters describe these methods, including techniques and procedures for defining, scheduling, and budgeting project activities, assessing risks, organizing and keeping records, and monitoring and controlling work to achieve project quality, time, and cost goals.

Procedures are best conducted within the framework of a system to ensure that all elements are accounted for, properly organized, and executed. The so-called project management system and the various structures, activities, and frameworks that comprise it—work breakdown structures, cost accounting systems, management information systems, and many others—are all described in this section.

Chapters in this part address all of the PMBOK knowledge areas: Integration management, Chapters 5 and 11; human resource management, Chapter 5; scope management, Chapter 5; time management, Chapters 6 and 7; cost management, Chapter 8; quality management, Chapter 9; risk management, Chapter 10; communication management, Chapters 11 and 12; and procurement management, Chapters 5, 11, and 12.

Chapter 5

Planning Fundamentals

> Big fleas hath smaller fleas upon their backs to bite 'em
> And these fleas have smaller fleas
> And so ad infinitum.

—Jonathan Swift

*O*ne distinguishing feature of projects is that each is tailored toward some unique end-item or end-result. That uniqueness implies that every project must be defined anew and a scheme created telling everyone involved *what to do.* Deciding and specifying what they have to do is the function of *project definition*, the output of which is a project plan. Making sure they do it right is the function of *project control.*

Three things occur in the planning and control process: (1) during the conception and definition phases, a *plan is prepared* specifying the project requirements, work tasks, responsibilities, schedules, and budgets; (2) during the execution phase the work in the *plan is performed* and project *progress is tracked* and assessed; if necessary (3) *corrective action is taken* or the requirements or plan are revised. This chapter gives an overview of the planning process, project scope definition, and the concept of the integrated project plan.

5.1 PLANNING STEPS

Top management authorizes planning to begin shortly after a business need, contract request, or request for proposal (RFP) has been received. This authorization releases funds so that an initial plan, schedule, and budget can be prepared for inclusion in the project proposal. Approval of the project or signing the contract justifies full-scale funding and work authorization for the entire project, and, starting with the definition of detailed system requirements, the preparation of a detailed project master plan. For internal projects, the *project charter* will be released to announce and briefly describe the project to stakeholders.

A project manager, if not already assigned or involved, is now identified to oversee the planning process, which proceeds from here on and elaborates on the initial plan as prepared for the proposal, business case study, or charter.

Because every project is somewhat different, there is never an a priori, established way that specifies how each and every project should be done. New projects pose new questions, and the purpose of planning is to answer them. For starters, the project team needs to answer questions regarding *what*, *how*, by *whom*, in *what order*, *for how much*, and by *when*. The formalized planning process answers these questions in the following steps:

1. **What, for how much, and by when?**
   Define the project *objectives, project scope, and system requirements*. These specify the project deliverables, end-items, and other sought results, as well as the time, cost, and performance targets. The scope and requirements include criteria the customer will use to determine the acceptability of deliverables or end-items at project completion.

2. **How?**
   Define the specific *work activities*, tasks, or jobs to be done to achieve the objectives and requirements. The activities must include everything necessary to create and deliver the promised end-item or deliverables, including activities for planning, control, and administration of the project.

3. **Who?**
   Create the *project organization* that will perform and manage the work. This involves identifying the departments, subcontractors, and managers that will comprise the project, and specifying their responsibilities.

4. **When, in what order?**
   Prepare a *schedule* showing the timing of work activities, including deadlines and milestone dates.

5. **How much and when?**
   Prepare a *budget* and *resource plan* that allocates funding and other resources to support work activities as necessary according to the project schedule.

6. **How well?**
   Prepare a plan to review and control work performance after the project has begun to keep the project on track, i.e., to ensure that it conforms to schedule, budget, and user and system requirements.

7. **Repeat: How Much, When, and How Well?**
   As needed, revise and fill in aspects of the plan to reflect recent information, current project progress, and updated estimates of the time and cost to complete the project.

With familiar projects, many of these questions can be answered based on past experience and historical records; with first-of-a-kind projects, getting the answers is more difficult and proceeds from scratch. But rarely are projects *completely* familiar or first-of-a-kind; in most projects some portions of the plan can be based upon experience from previous projects while in others they must be created anew.

Planning for the project begins early in the project life cycle—even before the project is authorized. In most cases it begins with preparation of the proposal, during which a rudimentary project team is organized and major decisions about the necessary resources are made. The team prepares a project summary plan for inclusion in the proposal using the same, albeit more abbreviated, procedures that will be used later to develop a more-elaborate and more-detailed master plan. The difference between the summary plan in the proposal and the project master plan is that the former is intended for the customer, the latter for the project team.[1] During proposal preparation the planning effort is directed at estimating the work and resources needed for the project, and the project duration and cost. The summary plan in the proposal contains just enough information to provide the customer an overview of the project and its price.

In contrast, the purpose of preparing the project master plan is to work out the details of the project and create a roadmap that will *guide* the project team throughout the execution of the project. As mentioned in Chapter 4, the plan usually contains details only for the immediate, upcoming phase of the project, about which the most is known. The plan for later phases of the project is filled in as necessary information becomes available and details can be determined.

Contents of Master Plans

The contents of master plans vary depending on the size, complexity, and nature of the project. Figure 5-1 shows a template of the contents of a typical master plan as outlined in Chapter 4.[2] Depending on the client or type of project contract, some plans require additional, special items not outlined here;[3] in small or low-cost projects, it is possible to bypass some of the sections, taking care not to overlook the crucial ones. It is usually good practice to systematically review every item in the template even if only to verify that some of them are "N/A" (not applicable). An example of a project master plan is given for the LOGON Project in Appendix C.

You might notice a similarity between the sections of the plan and the contents of the proposal described in Figure 3-6. Though the format is different, there is indeed a similarity. In some cases the proposal, after revision and update to reflect agreements and contract specifications, becomes the project master plan. Other times, when the project master plan must be expanded and defined in great detail, the proposal serves only as the outline. Because the primary audience of the project master plan is the project team and not the user, the technical section of the master plan is usually much larger and more detailed than in the proposal.

As illustrated in the following example, functional areas of the organization and subcontractors to be involved in the project assist in the planning effort. The development of the project master plan is an evolutionary, multidisciplinary process.

Example 1: Developing a Project Plan at Master Control Company

The Master Control Company (MCC), a medium-sized engineering firm, was approached by Bier Publishing Company to develop a control unit for tracking the production process of two multistage, high-efficiency printing presses. Bier's engineering department initiated the project by sending MCC a list of requirements for power, wiring, performance, and possible future enhancements for the unit. MCC appointed a project manager to oversee design and development of the unit and to prepare a proposal.

MCC's engineering group conceived an initial, theoretical design that covered all requirements. Throughout the design process they consulted with engineers at

I. Scope, charter, or statement or work
Overview description of the project oriented toward management, customer, and stakeholders, includes a brief description of the project, objectives, overall requirements, constraints, risks, problem areas, and solutions, master schedule showing major events and milestones.

II. Management and organization section

Project organization, management, and personnel requirements:
A. *Project management and organization*: key personnel and authority relationships.
B. *Manpower*: workforce requirements estimates—skills, expertise, and strategies for locating and recruiting qualified people.
C. *Training and development*: executive development and personnel training necessary to support the project.

III. Technical section
Major project activities, timing, and cost:

A. High-level *user requirements* and *system requirements*.
B. *Work breakdown structure*: Work packages and detailed description of each, including resources, costs, schedules, and risks.
C. *Responsibility assignments*: List of key personnel and their responsibilities for work packages and other areas of the project.
D. *Project schedules*: Generalized project and task schedules showing major events, milestones, and points of critical action or decision.
E. *Budget,* cost accounts, and sources of financial support: Estimates and timing of all capital and development expenses.
F. *Quality plan*: Measures for monitoring quality and accepting results for individual work tasks, components, and end-item assemblies.
G. Areas of uncertainty, and *risk plan*: Risk strategies, contingency and mitigation plans for areas posing greatest risk.
H. *Work review plan*: Procedures for periodic review of work, what is to be reviewed, by whom, when, and according to what standards.
I. *Testing plan* (may be included in work review plan): Listing of items to be tested, test procedures, timing, and persons responsible.
J. *Change control plan*: Procedures for review and handling of requests for changes or de facto changes to any aspect of the project.
K. *Documentation policy/plan*: List of documents to be produced, format, timing, and how they will be organized and maintained.
L. *Procurement policy/plan*: The policy, budget, schedule, plan, and controls for all goods, work, and services to be procured externally.
M. *Implementation plan*: Procedures to guide customer conversion to or adoption of project deliverables.

Figure 5-1
Template for project master plan.

Bier and altered the design several times. Included with the final design were blueprints, a manual of operations specifications, and a bill of materials for parts.

With this design, MCC's manager of marketing performed a detailed analysis of the price of parts and cost of labor. MCC's production manager also examined the design, and with the project manager prepared a work breakdown structure (WBS) and tentative project plan outlining the major work tasks.

The project manager convened a meeting with representatives from engineering, marketing, and production to review the design, project plan, and costs. The production department supplied information about the kind of labor expertise needed, parts availability, and an estimate of the time required to produce the unit. Marketing provided information about the costs of labor, parts and supplies, and the overall project. Having this information the project manager was able to complete the project plan, develop a bid price, and combine the two into a proposal. Notice that, in terms of the systems development process, the stages of initiation, feasibility, definition, and most of the design were completed before the proposal was even sent.

Following negotiation and contract signing, the project manager and production manager developed a detailed master plan. This plan contained much the same information as the proposal, but was updated and expanded to include schedules for materials and parts procurement, a plan for the labor distribution across work tasks, a management and task responsibility matrix, and a detailed master schedule.

As this example shows, the project plan is developed gradually, expanded and modified as information is accumulated; in due course, it should also be reviewed and agreed to by all key project participants.

Learning from Past Projects

Oftentimes organizations view themselves and their projects as being *too* unique (they think, "we are different") and ignore the lessons of history—the dilemmas, mistakes, and solutions of the past.[4] While developing a project plan it makes sense for the project manager to refer to earlier, similar projects (plans, procedures, successes, and failures). To be able to do this, ideally the project manager is provided with planning assistance in the form of lessons learned, best practices, suggested methodologies and templates, and even consulting advice derived from experience in past projects. Sometimes the project manager has to seek these out, and sometimes she is provided them by the organization; indeed, this latter is a function of the project management office (PMO), described in Chapter 16. Lessons learned and suggested best practices often come from the so-called *post-project summary* or *project post-mortem* report, which is a formal retrospective report about a project created at close-out and describing what went well, what went wrong, and the lessons learned (described in Chapter 12). These provide guidance in planning projects and help managers avoid reinventing the wheel and repeating past mistakes.

5.3 SCOPE AND STATEMENT OF WORK

Project planning starts with determining the objectives, deliverables, and major tasks of the project; in combination these define the overall size of the project and the range or extent of work it encompasses, a concept called *project scope*. Determining the project scope begins during project conception, first in project initiation and then in the initial description of the project (the RFP/proposal process, if the project is contracted), and it continues again during project definition. In each case, user needs and requirements are compared to constraints of time, cost, resources, and technology to determine what, exactly, the project should and can encompass. The process of setting the project scope is called scope definition.

Scope Definition

Scope definition is the process of specifying the breath of the project and its full span of outputs, end-items, or deliverables; these sought-after requirements and end-results are termed "inclusions," referring to what is to be *included* in the project. Sometimes, to ensure clarity about expected outcomes, the scope definition also specifies items, conditions, or results *not* to be included within the project, i.e., "exclusions" (a project to construct a building, for example, might exclude interior decorating and landscaping). Distinguishing between inclusions (contractor responsibilities) and exclusions (possible customer responsibilities) is important to prevent misunderstanding and false expectations. Scope definition focuses primarily on project outputs and deliverables, not on time and cost—although certainly time and cost delimit or dictate the deliverables; as such, time and cost are often listed as "constraints" in the scope definition.

The result of scope definition is a *scope statement*, which besides the main deliverables of the project and some background about the problem being addressed or the opportunity being exploited might also contain project objectives, functions to be fulfilled by the deliverables, user requirements or high-level specifications, assumptions and constraints (to provide the rationale as to why the project has these deliverables and not others), and high-level project tasks or major areas of work. Necessary information for scope definition includes user needs and requirements, a business case or other expression of needs, and constraints and assumptions; ideally the principal subsystems and components of the end-item will also have been identified.[5] Everything considered as part of the project or contract, including support, side-items, as well as related areas of work or deliverables not considered part of the project (exclusions) are mentioned. Sometimes the scope statement also lists results or consequences to be *avoided,* such as negative publicity, interference with other systems, pollution, or damage to vegetation, soil, or wildlife. Vague terms that preclude measurement or direct observation should be avoided in the scope statement.

The scope statement is initially determined during project initiation and is expanded and specified in detail during project definition. When the project is unique, this preliminary scope statement may be somewhat vague; it should however be revised and clarified while the detailed plan for the first phase is being developed. In programs and large projects, separate scope statements are developed for the program, individual projects that form the program, and major activities within projects.

Rather than repeat requirements and specifications, the scope statement normally refers to or incorporates the documents that contain them. Once the scope statement has been approved as a baseline, it becomes a controlled document and, as such, can only be modified through a formal change process (Chapters 9 and 11).

Example 2: Scope Statement for the LOGON Project

The RFP for Midwest Parcel Distribution Company's (MPD's) LOGON project (see Appendix A at back of book) specifies "The Contractor's responsibility shall be for furnishing expertise, labor, materials, tools, supervision, and services for the complete design, development, installation, checkout, and related services for full operational capability of the LOGON system." It also specifies technical performance requirements for the system, as well as exclusions, e.g., "Removal of existing storage, placement, and retrieval equipment will be performed under separate contract . . ."

During proposal preparation Iron Butterfly Contractors decided that the system that would best meet MPD's needs is one that will employ robotic transporter units for placing and retrieving shipping containers from racks as instructed by a computerized neural-network system. Analysis of MPD's requirements and budget constraint and a preliminary system design effort lead Iron Butterfly to create the following scope statement for the LOGON proposal.

1. Background: (Short description of MPD's Chicago distribution facility, and of the purpose and objectives of the LOGON system).
2. Description of the work to be done: design, fabrication, installation, test, and checkout of a transport, storage, and database system for the automatic placement, storage, and retrieval of standardized shipping containers.
3. Deliverables and main areas of work:
   (a) *Overall system*: Create basic design. Reference requirements A and B.
   (b) *Racks and storage-bucket system (termed "Hardware A")*: Develop detailed design. Storage-bucket system is Model IBS05 modified to meet requirements C.1 through E.14.

(c) *Robotic transporter units and track system (termed "Hardware B")*: Develop detailed design. RTU is Model IBR04 modified to meet requirements F.1 through G.13.

(d) *Neural-network, database, and robotic-controller system*: Develop software specifications. Reference requirements H.1 through H.9 and K.3.

(e) *Hardware A and Hardware B*: Procure software, subassemblies, and components. Reference requirements K.1 through L.9.

(f) *Hardware A and Hardware B*: Fabricate at Iron Butterfly site. Reference requirement M.

(g) *Overall system*: Install and check-out at MPD site. Reference requirement Y.

Items (a) through (g) represent deliverables for different stages of the project; associated with each are specific requirements (the "reference requirements"), which are check-off or acceptance criteria listed in a separate document and appended to the scope statement. For example, the detailed designs noted in items 2 and 3 must be sufficiently comprehensive to enable subcontractors to produce components and subassemblies for Hardware A and Hardware B; the reference requirements C.1 through E.14 and F.1 through G.13 specify the level of detail necessary for that to happen. The scope statement will also contain exclusions as noted in the RFP or identified later.

The scope statement provides a reference document for everyone in the project to review and reach agreement about the expected objectives, outcomes, and deliverables for the project. It will also become the basis for making decisions about resources needed for the project, and, later, determining whether or not required or requested changes to work tasks and deliverables fall within the agreed upon project scope. A common tendency in projects is *scope creep*, which means to keep adding to the project scope (increasing the number and/or size of deliverables). Scope creep, if not controlled, can lead to runaway project budgets and schedules.

The project scope statement appears in any document intended to provide an overview or broad description of the project, including the project charter and the statement of work (SOW).

Statement of Work

The SOW is a description of the project, including its objectives, scope (major deliverables and work tasks), impact, justification, and management. Sometimes the SOW contains much more—specifications and requirements on the deliverables, management procedures for planning and handling risks and changes, budgets, schedules for deliverables, staffing, and responsibilities for key administrative and work tasks; in such cases the SOW is effectively a mini- or high-level version of the project master plan.

The SOW is usually associated with contracted projects and contract work, and it appears in documents associated with the contracting process. The RFP, proposal, contract, and project master plan all contain a SOW, each an updated, more refined version of the one in the previous document. The project charter, described in Chapter 3, might also contain a SOW.

5.4 WORK DEFINITION

Once project objectives and deliverables in the scope statement have been set, the next step is to translate them into specific, well-defined elements of work; these are the tasks, jobs, and activities the project team must do. Particularly for large, unique projects it is easy to overlook or duplicate activities. To insure that none are missed and that every activity is well understood and clearly defined, a systematic procedure called the "WBS" is used.

Work Breakdown Structure

Complex projects consist of numerous smaller subprojects, interrelated tasks, and work elements. As the rhyme at the beginning of the chapter alludes, the goal, main end-result or deliverable of a project can be thought of as a system that consists of subsystems, which themselves consists of components, and so on. The procedure for subdividing the overall project into smaller elements is called the *work breakdown structure* or *WBS*, and its purpose is to define the total project into "pieces of work" called *work packages*. Dividing the project into work packages makes it easier to prepare project schedules and cost estimates, and to assign management and task responsibilities.

The first step in creating a WBS is to divide the total project into major categories. These major categories then are divided into subcategories that, in turn, are subdivided, and so on. This level-by-level breakdown continues so that the scope and complexity of work elements is reduced with each level of breakdown. The objective of the procedure is to reduce the project into work elements that are so clearly defined that they, individually, can be accurately budgeted, scheduled, and controlled.

A typical WBS might consist of the following four levels (the number of levels varies, as does the name of the element description at each level; different project methodologies use different terms):

LEVEL	ELEMENT DESCRIPTION
1	Project
2	Subproject
3	Activity
4	Work Package

Level 1 represents the total project. At Level 2 the project is broken down into several (usually between 4 and 10) major elements or subprojects. These subprojects should conform to the deliverables or work areas specified in the scope statement. All of the subprojects when taken together must make up the *total project effort*. Each subproject, in turn, is broken down into activities, the sum of which must comprise everything in the subproject. When the process is completed, the tasks at the *lowest* levels, whatever the levels might be, are termed *work packages;* these work packages become the basis for further planning steps. In the table above, that the term "work package" that appeared at Level 4 is for illustration only. The actual number of levels in the WBS varies, as does the name of the element description at each level. In fact, the levels and names are often prescribed by the project methodology in use. Figure 5-2 shows a typical WBS. Note the different levels and usage of different names for each.

The WBS process happens somewhat naturally, starting with the list of requirements and specifications. These requirements and specifications suggest the main end-item, deliverable, or system of the project and its major subsystems and components; they also specify which of the requirements will be met externally (by suppliers/ subcontractors) and which internally. These major subsystems or components appear as boxes on the WBS. Those boxes are then logically subdivided into smaller components of the system and into the work tasks necessary to create or acquire them. For technical and engineering projects, the WBS should include all the configuration items (CIs) and major components of the system, as well as the work tasks to design, develop, build, and test them.[5]

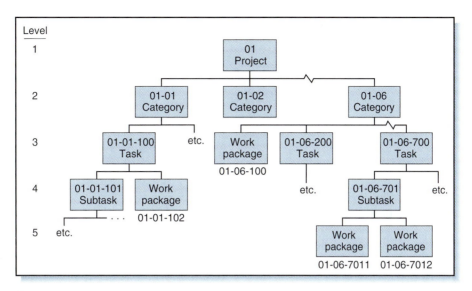

Figure 5-2
Elements of a WBS.

The WBS becomes the basis for assigning project responsibility and contracting. For contracted work, responsibility for each subproject or activity is assigned to a subcontractor, and a contract agreement exists between the subcontractor and the project manager. For internal projects, each subproject or activity is assigned to an in-house department, and a formal agreement exists between the department manager and the project manager.

To facilitate communication and prevent unnecessary complexity in budgets and schedules, the number of levels in the structure should be limited. A five-level structure is appropriate for large projects, although for most small projects three or fewer levels are adequate.

Figure 5-3 illustrates the WBS for the construction of a house. The top part of the figure shows the project objective (Level 1) and the major categories of items (Level 2) necessary to accomplish it. Implicit in the objective are the user requirements. Notice that, for the most part, the items in the breakdown are physical pieces or components of the house. In other words, the top levels of the WBS identify the physical deliverables, hardware, or products to be produced. By subdividing a project like this, according to physical deliverables, it is easy to attach performance, cost, and time requirements to each deliverable and to assign responsibility for meeting those requirements. This is necessary so that other parts of the master plan, including the project budget and schedule, can be prepared.

The middle part of Figure 5-3 shows an alternative way of breaking down the project: into functions (e.g., carpentry), not deliverables. In development projects, project *phases* can be used instead of functions, i.e., the first level breakdown would consist of the phases of conceptual design, detailed design, development and fabrication, and testing. The problem with a functional- or phase-based WBS is that associated with each function or phase (e.g., carpentry) are numerous deliverables (e.g., frame, cabinets, walls, floors, trim, doors, stairs, windows, etc.) that all will require work that must be budgeted and scheduled. Thus, if you start with a functional breakdown, eventually you will have to breakout from each function the *deliverables* or *products* to which it contributes. Easier is to simply start at the top of the WBS with deliverables or products and then only later in the WBS (at lower levels) identify the functions that will contribute to them.

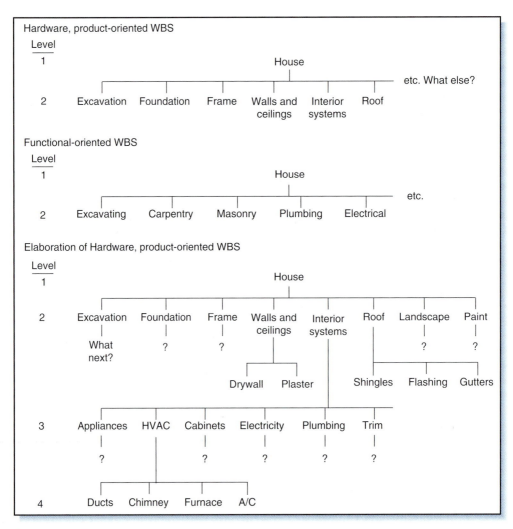

Figure 5-3
Example of WBS for building a house.

There are some places in the WBS where a *task-oriented* breakdown might be necessary or desirable. Whenever tasks such as "design," "engineering," and "management" apply to more than one element or deliverable (e.g., for *integrating* multiple deliverables), those tasks should be identified in the WBS as separate work packages. Hence the WBS will likely contain boxes for, e.g., project management, project engineering, etc., which are then subdivided into smaller elements, tasks, and deliverables. Whether the WBS starts with a deliverable-, functional-, phase-based, or other breakdown is a matter of personal choice or, sometimes, recommended or stipulated by the organization's project methodology or WBS templates.

Continuing with the example, the bottom part of Figure 5-3 shows Level 2 elements subdivided into Level 3 elements, and a Level 3 element (HVAC) subdivided into Level 4 elements. Concurrent with the breakdown process is *definition of the work elements*. As each element of the WBS is identified and further broken down, project work is further elaborated and more clearly specified. By the time the WBS is completed, all of the work in the project will have been defined.

During the WBS process the questions "What else is needed?" and "What's next?" are constantly being asked. The WBS is reviewed again and again to make sure everything is there. Supplementary or missed elements are identified and added to the WBS at appropriate levels. For example, the WBS in Figure 5-3 nowhere includes blueprints, budgets, and work schedules, even though construction cannot happen without them. These are deliverables associated with planning the project and designing the house, which of course must be largely completed before construction can begin. These deliverables can be included in the WBS by expanding Level 2 and inserting categories for "design" and "administration and management," and then inserting "blueprints" at Level 3 under design and "budget and work schedules" at Level 3 under "administration and management." Level 2 might be further expanded to include other considerations such as site location, permits and licenses, environmental impact and mitigation plans, building maintenance plans, and so on. As described later, the WBS should reflect any procured deliverables (contracted, outsourced) as well as those produced internally.

Figure 5-4, the WBS for the Spaceship project, exemplifies the WBS for large engineering development projects where the main deliverable and many of its subsystems and components must be developed, built, integrated, and tested from scratch.

Project participants should check the WBS to ensure that nothing is missed. In standardize projects like building a house the likelihood of overlooking something is remote. However, in larger or less standardized projects, the chance of missing something is easier and the WBS more valuable. In big projects the initial WBS is usually rather course and indicates only the major phases and components of work

Figure 5-4
WBS for spaceship project.

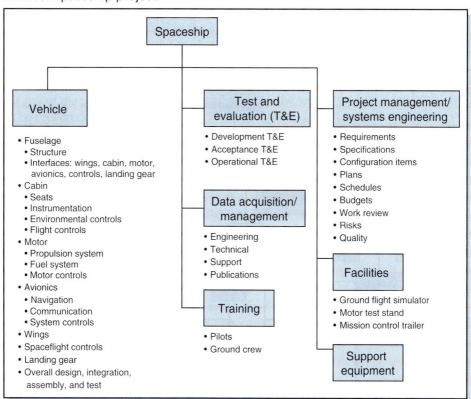

the project. Each work package is the focal point of management planning and control and, as such, requires paperwork, time, and cost to plan, execute, and monitor. Thus, a large number of tasks requires greater time and cost to manage than fewer tasks.

Companies that routinely perform similar kinds of projects will employ roughly the same Level 2 or Level 3 breakdown for every project and create a WBS "template" standardized for each kind of project. The template is created from experience acquired with projects that share commonalities in areas of work. Templates, which simplify the WBS process and serve as project checklists, are created and maintained by the PMO. Nonetheless, it is good to remember that every project is unique, and that that uniqueness will become apparent at some level, maybe at Level 3, 4, or 5. Hence, the WBS for each project should never be a mere template or complete copy of the WBS for a previous project. No matter how similar projects might seem, scrutiny should go into identifying the places where they differ. Nowhere is the saying "the devil is in the details" more appropriate than in projects, and the WBS is *the* tool for identifying the details wherein the devil might be hiding. As a measure to reduce oversights, it is a good practice to have two or more teams each create a WBS independently, and then combine them into one.

Ideally, work packages represent jobs of about the same magnitude of effort and of relatively small cost and short duration compared to the total project. To reduce the proliferation of work packages in large projects, sometimes several related work packages are aggregated on the basis of cost and time. For example, DOD/NASA guidelines specify that work packages should be of 3 months' duration and not exceed $100,000 in cost. These are guidelines, however, not strict limits. The actual dollar size and duration of work packages depend on many factors, including the stage of the project (design work packages are usually long duration; fabrication work packages are large cost) and the size of the project (smaller projects have smaller work packages).

Each work package represents either a contract with a subcontractor or supplier, or an internal agreement with an inside functional unit. Although several functional or subcontracting units might share responsibility for a work package, ideally each work package is the responsibility of a single subcontractor or functional unit. This simplifies work planning and control, and insures accountability.

Example 4: Work Package Definition for LOGON Project

The LOGON project was divided into 19 work packages, denoted in the boxes lettered H through Z in Figure 5-5. Below is an example of the contents of a typical work package, Work Package X: test of Robotic transporter unit (Hardware B).

1. *SOW*: Perform check-out, operational test, and corrections as necessary for sign-off approval of four Batman robotic transporter units, Model IBR04.
2. *Resource requirements*:
   - Labor (full-time commitment for 3 weeks): Test manager, two test engineers, three test technicians.
   - Procured materials: track for mock-up; all other materials on hand.
   - Facility: Iron Butterfly test room number 2 for 3 weeks.
3. *Time*: 3 weeks scheduled; (time critical) start December 2; finish December 23.
4. *Costs (Cost account RX0522)*:

Labor: Manager, 75 hours + 25% OH	=	$9,750
Engineers, 1,125 hours + 25% OH	=	135,000
Technicians, 1,125 hours + 25% OH	=	112,500
Material:		70,000
Subtotal:		327,250
10% G&A:		32,725
Total:		$359,975

5. *Responsibility*:
   - Oversee tests, B.J., manager of robotic assembly.
   - Approve test results B.O.B., manager of Fabrication Department.
   - Notify of test status and results: J.M., project engineer, F.W.N., site operations.
6. *Deliverables*: Four (4) tested and approved Batman robotic transporters, Model IBR04. Refer to specifications (number 9).
7. *Inputs*:
   - Predecessor: Assembly of Batman robotic transporter unit (work package V).
   - Preconditions: Test room number 2 setup for robotic transporter.
8. *Quality assurance*: Refer to entry, process, and exit conditions for work package X in the LOGON quality plan.
9. *Risk*: RTU will not meet test requirements because of assembly/integration problems/errors. Likelihood: low. Contingency reserve: one additional week has been included in the schedule as allowance, if needed.
10. *Specifications*: Test specs, refer to test document 2307 and LOGON contract specification sheets 28, 36, and 41; robotic specs, refer to contract requirements G.9 to G.14.
11. *Work orders*: None, pending.
12. *Subcontracts and purchase orders*: No subcontracts; purchase order 8967–987 for track testing material.

Table 5-1 gives information about estimated time, cost, and weekly labor requirements for all the work packages in the LOGON project. This information would be developed for each work package on an individual basis.

Table 5-1 Activities, time, cost, and labor requirements (result of work breakdown analysis).

Activity	Time (Weeks)	Weekly Direct Cost ($K)	Total Cost ($K)	Weekly Labor Requirement (Workers)
H	10	10	100	5
I	8	8	64	4
J	6	16	96	8
K	4	4	16	2
L	2	18	36	6
M	4	21	84	3
N	4	20	80	2
O	5	10	50	5
P	5	12	60	6
Q	5	16	80	2
R	5	0	0	0
S	3	0	0	0
T	3	0	0	0
U	1	14	14	9
V	5	16	80	14
W	2	12	24	6
X	3	12	36	6
Y	8	13	104	14
Z	6	11	66	5

Total Direct Cost—$990K

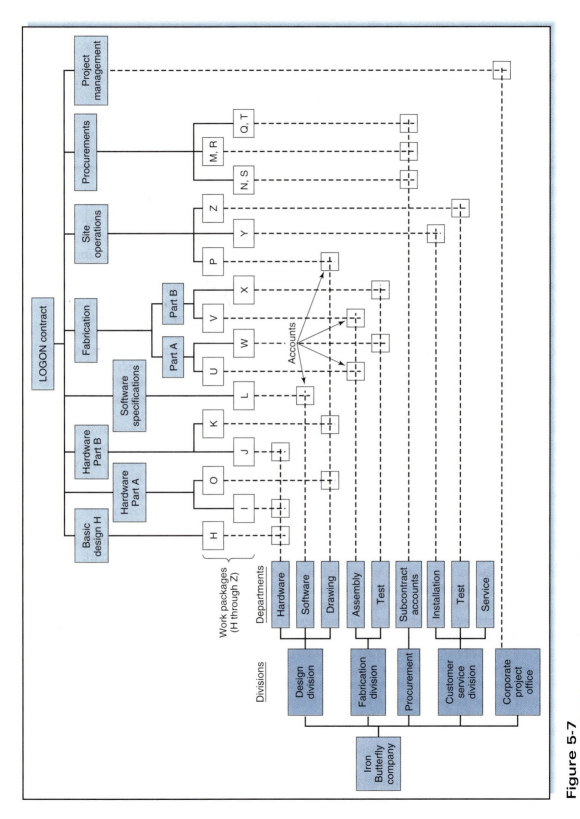

Figure 5-7
Integration of WBS and project organization.

Iron Butterfly, Corp.

Elegant design. Built to last.

Responsibility Code

P Primary responsibility
S Secondary responsibility
N Must be notified
A Must give approval

	Persons Responsible																												
		Project Manager																											
			Project Engineer																		Fabrication Manager								
			Design				Drawing					Software				Site Operations						Assembly A				Assembly B			
Project Task or Activity	F.W.	J.M.	S.E.H.	R.L.Q.	P.J.	D.V.R.	R.I.P.	O.E.M.	P.V.P.R.	D.M.N.	R.L.	L.S.F.	L.L.L.	J.R.S.	D.V.Q.	F.W.N.	J.M.M.N.	L.O.T.	A.U.A.	D.A.R.	B.O.B.	E.N.	G.G.F.	R.T.T.	B.V.L.	B.J.	T.T.Y.	H.R.D.	B.V.-Purchasing
Project coordination	P	S																			S								
Project development	A	P																											
Project design		A	P				A					N				A					N								N
H Basic design	N	A	A	P	S	S	N					N				N													
I Hardware design A			A		P	S																							
J Hardware design B			A	P		S						N																	
K Drawings B							A	S	P												N								
L Software specs		N	A									A	P	S	S														
M Parts purchase B		N																			A								P
N Parts purchase A		N																			A								P
O Drawings A							A			S	P										N								
P Installation drawings							A	P		S						N													
Q Software purchase		N																			A								P
U Assembly A		N																			N	A	P	S	S				
V Assembly B		N																			N					A	P	S	
W Test A		N														N					A	P							
X Test B		N														N					A					P			
Y Final installation		N														A	P	S	S										
Z Final test		N														A		P		S									

Figure 5-8
Sample responsibility matrix for LOGON project (with initials of persons responsible).

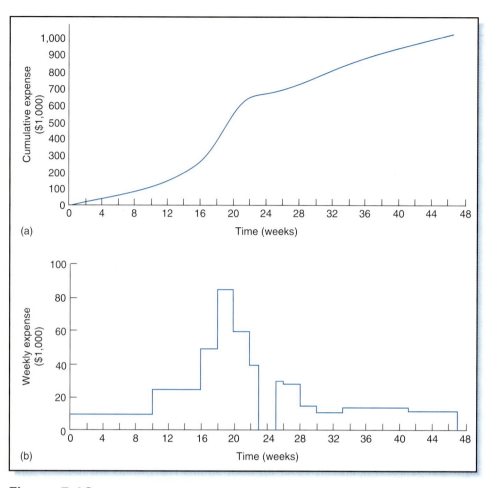

Figure 5-13
Planned (a) cumulative and (b) weekly expenses for the LOGON project (Table 5-11).

by the three levels in Figure 5-14. In terms of the project levels in Figure 5-5, the top-level chart would show the principle subprojects, the intermediate-level chart would show major activities within each subproject, and the bottom level would show work packages or smaller tasks within each activity. Milestones and target dates can be displayed at any level.

Each level chart expands on the details of the chart of the level above it. Charts of intermediate or bottom level are necessary to permit project and functional managers to plan labor and resource allocations.

The bottom-level charts are the most-detailed, showing the daily (and even hourly) schedules of the tasks within work packages. These schedules are used by work package leaders and technical specialists and correspond to the task schedules mentioned earlier. Figure 5-15 is a multilevel schedule, showing both the higher-level activities of the project (denoted by "summary" bars) as well as detailed tasks within each activity (denoted by "task" bars).

Disadvantages of Gantt Charts

One disadvantage of the Gantt chart is that it does not necessarily show the relationships among work elements, i.e., it does not necessarily reveal the effect of one work

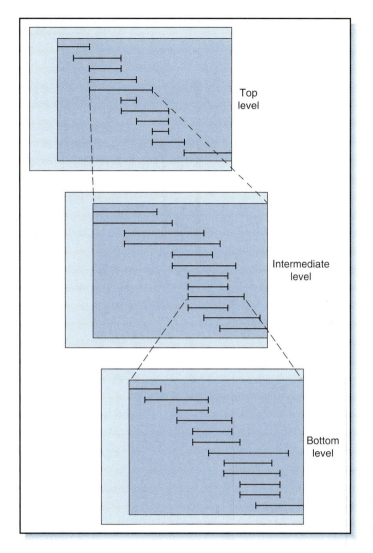

Figure 5-14
A hierarchy of bar charts.

element falling behind schedule on other work elements. In most projects, certain work elements must be completed by a specific date for the project to be completed on target, while others can fall behind without delaying the project. Gantt charts alone provide no way of distinguishing which elements cannot be delayed from those that can.

Gantt charts are often maintained manually, which is easy and an advantage in small projects, but a burden and disadvantage in large projects. For large projects especially, Gantt chart creation and update should be done with software. Assuming input data is accurate and up-to-date, computer-generated Gantt charts can be updated frequently to display progress.

5.8   LINE OF BALANCE

While a project is by definition a unique, one-time endeavor, some projects contain repetitive work elements. Examples from the construction industry include erecting

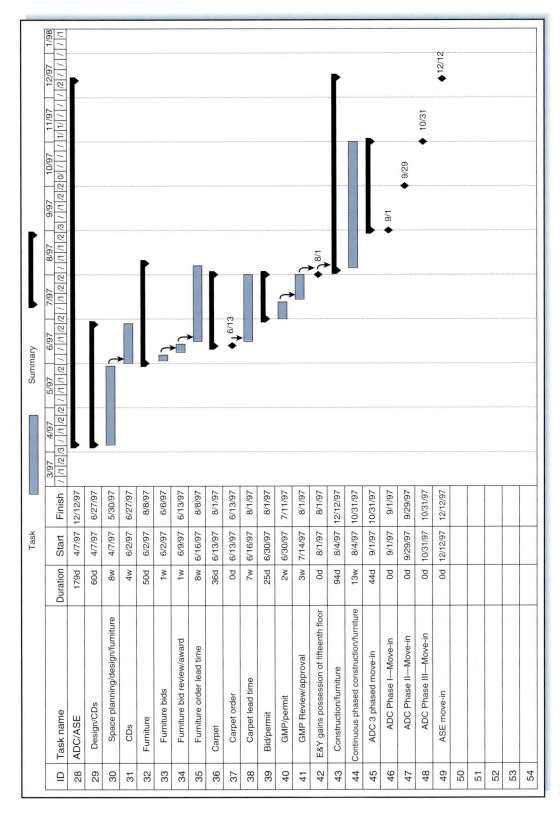

ID	Task name	Duration	Start	Finish
28	ADC/ASE	179d	4/7/97	12/12/97
29	Design/CDs	60d	4/7/97	6/27/97
30	Space planning/design/furniture	8w	4/7/97	5/30/97
31	CDs	4w	6/2/97	6/27/97
32	Furniture	50d	6/2/97	8/8/97
33	Furniture bids	1w	6/2/97	6/6/97
34	Furniture bid review/award	1w	6/9/97	6/13/97
35	Furniture order lead time	8w	6/16/97	8/8/97
36	Carpet	36d	6/13/97	8/1/97
37	Carpet order	0d	6/13/97	6/13/97
38	Carpet lead time	7w	6/16/97	8/1/97
39	Bid/permit	25d	6/30/97	8/1/97
40	GMP/permit	2w	6/30/97	7/11/97
41	GMP Review/approval	3w	7/14/97	8/1/97
42	E&Y gains possession of fifteenth floor	0d	8/1/97	8/1/97
43	Construction/furniture	94d	8/4/97	12/12/97
44	Continuous phased construction/furniture	13w	8/4/97	10/31/97
45	ADC 3 phased move-in	44d	9/1/97	10/31/97
46	ADC Phase I—Move-in	0d	9/1/97	9/1/97
47	ADC Phase II—Move-in	0d	9/29/97	9/29/97
48	ADC Phase III—Move-in	0d	10/31/97	10/31/97
49	ASE move-in	0d	12/12/97	12/12/97
50				
51				
52				
53				
54				

Figure 5-15
Multilevel schedule.

184

a number of pylons for a new transmission line, construction of a number of housing units that are largely identical, and erecting a building with a number of identical floors. Other examples include the opening of a number of identical retail stores, or production of a batch of computers, locomotives, or airplanes. A method for planning and controlling these repetitive elements is the *line of balance*—LOB.

Example 5: Cranes for Construction

A supplier of construction cranes must deliver 12 cranes according to the schedule in Table 5-3, where "deliver" includes training an operator for each crane, and testing and commissioning the crane with the trained operator. From the WBS for manufacturing one crane, the Gantt chart in Figure 5-16 is prepared.

Of course, meeting the crane delivery schedules also requires that Activities A–F also meet schedules. For example, from Table 5-3 it is clear that by week 2 a total of three cranes must be delivered; the question is, how many power units (Activity B) should be delivered by then? From the Gantt chart it can be seen that a power unit must be delivered 2 weeks before delivery of each crane. Looking at the right-hand column of Table 5-3 and moving down 2 weeks from February 14, it can be seen that all 12 power units need to be delivered. In the same way it can be seen that by February 14 all 12 sets of "other components" (Activity C) and all 12 sets of structural components (Activity A) should already have been completed since they must be ready 3 weeks prior to crane delivery. Since operators need to be trained (Activity F) 1 week before delivery, the number of operators that need to be trained by February 14 is determined by looking at the right-hand column of Table 5-3 and moving one week down from February 14, which shows 7. Likewise, by February 14 seven cranes (Activity E) must have been assembled.

Table 5-3   Delivery schedule for cranes.

Week	Date	Delivery Quantity	Cumulative Delivery Quantity
1	February 7	1	1
2	February 14	2	3
3	February 21	4	7
4	February 28	5	12

Figure 5-16
Gantt chart of tasks for delivery of one crane.

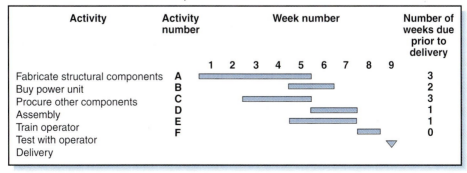

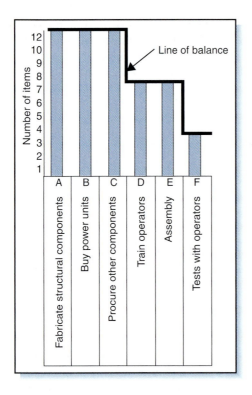

Figure 5-17
Number of deliverables required by
February 14 per type of activity.

Figure 5-17 summarizes the results and the number of units required by February 14 for Activities A–F. The cost center, function, or vendor responsible for each activity can use this figure to estimate the resources it will need to meet the schedule for units and to plan for production and delivery of each component.

An alternative approach is to depict the number of units for a specific operation (or type of activity) completed per time period. For example, dates and quantities for the assembled cranes and structural components are illustrated in Figure 5-18. Actual units produced can be plotted on the same graph as planned units.

Figure 5-18
Alternative presentation of a Line of Balance schedule.

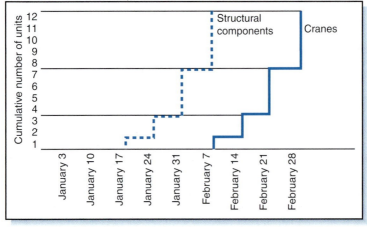

This provides handy checkpoints for the completion of intermediary stages of production batches and is useful as a "management by exception" tool.

5.9 PROCUREMENT MANAGEMENT[9]

Most projects involve some procurement of goods and materials and subcontracting of project work. Indeed, in some projects everything is "procured" and virtually nothing is produced "internally." Whether the work should be performed internally or procured from outsiders is the result of a make-or-buy analysis of the end-items, subsystems, and components or other project deliverables, and of work packages and tasks identified in the WBS.

Certainly, the management of procured materials and outsourced work is every bit as important to project success as work done internally: procured items that run over budget, are delayed, or fail to meet requirements cause cost and schedule overruns for the entire project.

Procurement management refers to planning and control of the following:[10]

1. Equipment, materials, or components designed and provided by vendors specifically for the project. The procured items might involve portions of work packages or entire work packages (e.g., design work, environmental impact study, soil analysis), or even major portions of the project wholly outsourced in a "turnkey" arrangement (suppliers and subcontractors fully design, build, and install equipment or components for the project end-item).
2. Off-the-shelf (OTS) equipment and components supplied by vendors. These represent products that are readily available and not specifically produced for the project.
3. Bulk materials (cement, metal tubing or framing, wire, stone, piping, etc.).
4. Consumables (nails, bolts, rivets, fuel) or loose tools used for construction or fabrication.
5. Equipment for construction, fabrication, etc., not already owned by the contractor; includes cranes, supports, scaffolding, and equipment for machine shops, welding, and testing.
6. Administrative equipment not already owned by the contractor; includes computers, project office facilities, and office equipment.

Procured items are usually classified as goods, work, or services (GWS). Goods represent raw materials or produced items, work means contracted labor, and services means consulting. To simplify we lump them together here and refer to them as procured GWS. Planning, budgeting, scheduling, and follow-up control of these items all fall under the heading of procurement management.

Although we use the term "procurement" to represent activities related to purchased, bought, or subcontracted items, other terms are also used, although with the following distinctions: "acquisition" refers to the purchase of an *entire complex system*, including its design and development, ramp-up and production; "procurement" to the purchase of a component or subsystem (*less than entire system*), including its design and/or production; and "buying" to the purchase of a *standardized item or part*. Hence it would be appropriate to say the "acquisition of a nuclear power plant," the "procurement of an automatic shut-down safety device," and "buying a batch of standard 1 inch nails."

Soliciting and Evaluating Bids

Once the decision is made to procure goods or services, potential vendors are solicited to offer bids. A customer who has a long-term relationship with a supplier or contractor will usually approach the contractor and negotiate a contract. Alternatively, the customer can advertise for bids in newspapers and other media, or solicit bids from a short list (bidder's list) of preferred or qualified suppliers. For a large or somewhat undefined system that requires design work or other intellectual input, the normal means of solicitation is an RFP; for a well-defined or simple item, it is an RFQ (request for quotation—a simple price quote). Acceptance of a bid will result in a formal contract with content and conditions as described in Chapter 3. When the procured item is hardware, the contract specifies at what point the supplier is no longer responsible for damage or loss and the buyer becomes responsible.

The basic types of contracts are described in Chapter 3, although certain industries require specific contract formats.[11] Procurement management is a specialized function that requires legal and contract administration skills, and in some organizations is handled by a specialized procurement division. [12]

Procurement Planning and Scheduling

The first step in procurement planning is to estimate the procured GWS needs for the project—the items, labor, or services mentioned above. Associated with every work package are procured GWS requirements, some that will be shared with other work packages. Items to be procured are identified during the WBS process, either from detailed planning of the work and resources needed for particular work packages, or from knowing that whole work packages must be outsourced. In the former case, managers responsible for each work package identify the materials or work within the package that must be procured (e.g., the work package "build wing" will require fiberglass, aluminum, and other materials from suppliers); in the latter case, managers will recognize that certain (sometimes significant) portions of the project (*entire* work packages) will have to be outsourced (e.g., the work package "develop rocket motor" will require development, fabrication, and testing—*all* to be provided by a contractor).

Associated with each procured item will be a schedule specifying when the item will be needed, and when procurement activities must begin. Everything to be procured in the project must be scheduled in advance to allow enough time to conduct the RFP/proposal process (described in Chapter 3) and select suppliers, and for suppliers to deliver (or design, build, and then deliver) the items at the time needed. The Gantt chart schedule in Figure 5-19 shows the considerations in scheduling procured GWS items. The schedule is prepared by working backwards, starting with event 10, the date when the item *must* be available for the project. This schedule is then integrated with the project schedule to assure that everything in the procurement process happens far enough in advance so that all procured items will be available when needed.

Of course, preparing such a schedule requires knowing the lead times for each of the procurement activities—the time needed, e.g., for suppliers and subcontractors to prepare proposals, for the project manager to evaluate proposals and issue contracts and work orders, and for suppliers/subcontractors to fulfill the work orders (which could involve their designing, building, and testing of equipment or components). Not uncommon (especially in international projects) is for these times to be grossly underestimated and, subsequently, the project delayed.

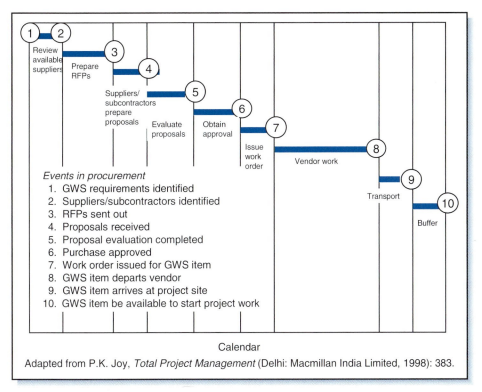

Events in procurement
1. GWS requirements identified
2. Suppliers/subcontractors identified
3. RFPs sent out
4. Proposals received
5. Proposal evaluation completed
6. Purchase approved
7. Work order issued for GWS item
8. GWS item departs vendor
9. GWS item arrives at project site
10. GWS item be available to start project work

Calendar

Adapted from P.K. Joy, *Total Project Management* (Delhi: Macmillan India Limited, 1998): 383.

Figure 5-19
Procurement activities schedule.

Note that the schedule in Figure 5-19 starts at the point where GWS requirements have been identified. To get to that point, however, the system end-item or deliverable must first have been somewhat well defined, meaning that the system requirements and system specifications must have been defined—another reason for careful definition of the system early in the project life cycle.

Procured GWS items require the same treatment in project planning as internal aspects of the project; hence matters such as the responsibility, budget, quality, and risk for procured items must also be addressed in the plan. These topics are discussed in later chapters.

Logistics Plan

Logistics includes everything related to the transport and storage of materials for the project. In projects that are materials intensive, the loading, unloading, transportation, inspection, clearances and approvals, and storage of materials can be major issues. For example, consider a large construction project and the importance of timing the arrival of materials (steel, pipes, concrete slabs, etc.) to coincide with when those materials will be needed for the building. Obviously the materials cannot arrive late because that will delay the project. But equally serious is when the materials arrive early. Where do you *put* them? In congested urban areas there simply is no space, and even when there is, materials delivered early are subject to damage, deterioration, and theft. Whenever GWS items cannot be scheduled to arrive *just in time* (exactly when needed), provision must made to store and protect them until they are needed.

5.10 SUMMARY

The purpose of project planning is to determine the way in which project goals will be achieved—what must be done, by whom, when, and for how much. Project planners strive to minimize uncertainty, avoid cost and scheduling overruns, and uphold project performance requirements.

The project scope statement and WBS are ways that managers and planners answer the question "What must be done?" The scope statement outlines the main areas of work to be done and the deliverables or end-items. The scope statement appears commonly in two places, the SOW or the project charter. The SOW is a summary description of the project used for contracted work; it appears in the RFP, proposal, contract, and project master plan. The charter is a document used for internal projects to describe, announce, and formally authorize the project to begin.

The WBS process subdivides the project into work packages or other work elements, each small enough to be well understood, planned, and controlled. Virtually all elements and functions of project management—scheduling, budgeting, resource allocation, tracking, and evaluation—are subsequently carried out with reference to the WBS and work packages.

The responsibility matrix integrates the project organization with the WBS; it prescribes which units and individuals, both internal and among subcontractors, have project responsibility and the kind of responsibility for each. It is valuable for achieving consensus, ensuring accountability, and reducing conflict among project participants.

Project schedules show the timing of work and are the basis for resource allocation and performance tracking. Depending on the amount of detail required, different types of schedules are used: project-level schedules show only high-level tasks and work packages; task-level schedules show the jobs needed to complete an individual work package or smaller work elements. The most common form of schedule is the Gantt chart. As a visual planning device it is effective for showing when work should be done and whether work elements are behind or ahead of schedule.

Project plans must account for all materials, work tasks, and services necessary for the project, including those procured (provided by suppliers and contractors) and that require lead time for services, transportation, and storage. Procured items and the procurement process must be included in all elements of the project plan—the WBS, schedule, responsibility matrix, budget, and so on.

The concepts and techniques in this chapter are foundation tools for planning and scheduling. The next few chapters look at techniques that augment these ideas and compensate for their limitations. Later we will consider the role of WBS, work packages, and project schedules in cost estimating, budgeting, and project control.

REVIEW QUESTIONS

1. What questions must be answered every time a new project is planned? What are the steps in the planning process that answer these questions?
2. What is the purpose of a project master plan? At what stage of the project should this plan be prepared?
3. Can a project be undertaken without a master plan? What are the possible consequences?
4. Which items, if any, could be eliminated from the master plan for projects with small budgets? Which could be eliminated for projects of short duration (a few weeks or months) that have relatively few tasks?

5. The subsection on "areas of risk and uncertainty" is frequently left out of the project master plan. What do you think are the potential pitfalls of doing this?

6. What is the purpose of the project scope statement? What information is used to create the scope statement? How is the scope reflected on the WBS?

7. What is the SOW? In what documents does the SOW appear?

8. What is included in the project charter? What is the purpose of the charter?

9. Think of a somewhat complicated task that you are familiar with and develop a WBS for it. (Examples: a wedding, a high school reunion, a questionnaire survey, a motion picture or stage play, etc.) Now do the same for a complicated job that you are not very familiar with. At what point would you need the assistance of "functional managers" or specialists to help you break down subtasks?

10. In a WBS, how do you know when you have reached the level where no further breakdown is necessary?

11. Could the WBS in Figure 5-5 have started with different elements at Level 2 and still ended up with the same work packages? In general, can different approaches to a WBS end with similar results?

12. In what ways is the WBS important to project managers?

13. What is the role of functional managers in developing a WBS?

14. What is the impact of altering the WBS after the project has started?

15. What should a "well-defined" work package include?

16. What is the relationship between the WBS and organization structure? In this relationship, what is the meaning of an "account?"

17. Figure 5-8 shows some possible types of responsibilities that could be indicated on a responsibility matrix. What other kinds of responsibilities or duties could be indicated?

18. Using the WBS you developed in question 9, construct a responsibility matrix. In doing this, you must consider the project organization structure, the managerial/technical positions to be assigned, and their duties.

19. What function does the responsibility matrix have in project control?

20. Do you think a responsibility matrix can be threatening to managers and professionals? Why?

21. Distinguish between an event and an activity. What problems can arise if these terms are confused by people on a project?

22. Distinguish between an interface event and a milestone event. What are some examples of each? When is an interface event also a milestone event?

23. How are project level and task level schedules prepared? What is the relationship between them? Who prepares them?

24. Construct a Gantt chart similar to the LOGON project in Figure 5-10 using the following data:

Task	Start Time (Weeks)	Duration (Weeks)
A	0	5
B	6	3
C	7	4
D	7	9
E	8	2
F	9	8
G	12	7

When will the last task be completed?

25. How must the Gantt chart you drew in problem 24 be changed if you were told that C and D could not begin until B was completed, and that G could not begin until C was completed? What happens to the project completion time?

26. Is the Gantt chart an adequate tool for planning and controlling small projects?

27. For problem 24, suppose the weekly direct expenses are as follows:

Task	Direct Expense ($1,000/Week)
A	10
B	15
C	25
D	35
E	10
F	20
G	10

Construct charts, as in Figure 5-13, showing weekly and cumulative direct expenses. Use the start dates given in problem 24.

28. Repeat problem 27 using the assumptions given in problem 25. What is the effect on weekly and cumulative expenses?

29. In a hierarchy of charts, how does changing a chart at one level affect charts at other levels?

30. How would you decide when more than one level of charts is necessary for planning?

31. If a hierarchy of charts is used in project planning, explain if there should be a corresponding hierarchy of plans as well.

32. What kinds of items or aspects of the project fall under "procurement management?" Why is management of procured items no less important to project success than internal items? What are the issues in scheduling procured items?

33. Consider the statement: The management of procured items sometimes poses greater difficulties than that of internal items. Do you agree or disagree, and why?

QUESTIONS ABOUT THE STUDY PROJECT

1. Describe the project master plan for your project (the plan developed at the *start* of the project). What is in the contents? Show a typical master plan.

2. Who prepared the plan?

3. At what point in the project was the plan prepared?

4. What is the relationship between the master plan and the project proposal? Was the plan derived from the proposal?

5. Is there a project scope statement? Who prepared it? Do the major areas of work and deliverables of the project correspond to the scope statement?

6. Is there an SOW or project charter? Describe its purpose and contents.

7. How, when, and by whom was the WBS prepared? Describe the process used in preparing the WBS.

8. How was project management included in the WBS?

9. Was the concept of work package used? If so, describe what was included in a work package. How was the work package defined?

10. How were ongoing activities such as management, supervision, inspection, and maintenance handled? Was there a work package for each?

11. How were responsibilities in the WBS assigned to the project organization (i.e., how was it determined which functional areas would be involved in the project and which tasks they would have)?

12. How were individual people assigned to the project? Describe the process.

13. Was a responsibility matrix used? Show an example.

14. How were activities in the WBS transferred to a schedule? How were times estimated? Who prepared the schedules?

15. Show examples of project-level and task-level schedules. Who prepared each one? How were they checked and integrated?

16. How were procured items managed? How were they first identified and then integrated into the project plan? Did procured items pose any difficulties to the project?

Case 5-1   Barrage Construction Company: Sean's WBS

Sean Shawn was recently appointed project planner at the Barrage Construction Company, which specializes in custom-made garages. He had worked for 2 years in the company's human resources department while completing his MBA and was now in the newly created project office. Barrage is considering branching out to building standard two-car and three-car garages as well as custom-designed garages. Sean was asked to determine the feasibility of moving into the standard-garage market. Skimming a book on project management, he discovered the WBS concept, which he thought would be helpful for developing cost estimates for the standardized garages. Even though he had never worked on a garage construction project, he felt he knew the process well enough just from having talked to people in the company. He sat down and drew the WBS in Figure 5-20. To estimate the costs for each work category in the WBS, he reviewed cost records from three recent two-car garage projects that he thought were similar to standard garages and computed the average. He then apportioned these costs among the categories in the WBS. For a three-car garage, he increased the cost estimates for the two-car garage by 50 percent. When he tallied the costs for all the categories he arrived at a total of $143,000 for a two-car garage and $214,500 for a three-car garage. Compared to competitors, he discovered, these costs were more than 10 percent higher than their *prices*. However, he believed because his estimates had been based on custom garages, his cost figures were probably at least 20 percent higher than for standard garages. He thus lowered all his estimates by that percentage and concluded that Barrage would be able to price its garages competitively and still make a 10 percent profit.

QUESTION

1. What is your opinion of Sean's approach to creating a WBS and estimating project costs? Please elaborate.

Garage			
Site	Construction	Electrical	Finish up
Excavation	Walls	Lights	Paint
Foundation	Roof	Door opener	Clean up
Floor	Windows		
	Doors		

Figure 5-20
Sean's garage project WBS.

Case 5-2   Startrek Enterprises, Inc.: Project Plan

Deva Patel is the project manager at Startrek Enterprises, Inc. for planning and coordinating the move of company offices into a new wing currently under construction. Deva wants the move to commence as soon as the construction supervisor indicates the building is ready for occupancy, which is estimated to be on June 1, still 2 months away. The entire move is to be completed within 1 week. The move will affect four departments and 600 people. Because timing is critical, Deva starts her planning by preparing a Gantt chart. At the project level she draws a bar 1 week (7 days) long, then subdivides it into three major categories: (1) pack office supplies, equipment, and furniture (3 days allotted); (2) move everything (2 days allotted); and (3) unpack and arrange it at new location (2 days). She then prepares an estimate of the total amount of boxes, equipment, and furniture that will have to be moved in 2 days and gives it to the moving contractor, who then gives her a price quote. For assistance in packing and unpacking boxes and equipment, Deva intends to hire workers from a temp agency. She estimates the number of workers needed to complete the move in 1 week and gives it to the agency for a price quote.

Deva gives her manager her complete plan and asks him to review it. The plan consists of the Gantt chart and a budget, which is based on the amount to be charged by the moving company and the temp agency.

QUESTIONS

1. What do you think about Deva's approach to scheduling the move and estimating the costs?
2. If you were Deva's manager, would you consider her plan comprehensive?
3. How would *you* prepare a plan for the move and what would your plan include?

ENDNOTES

1. Some organizations use the term "project charter" to refer to a "master plan." Our preference is the more common usage, i.e., the charter being a somewhat brief document to announce and authorize the decision to undertake the project, the master plan a much more comprehensive document to guide the project team though project execution.

2. Contents of master plans are listed in D.I. Cleland and W.R. King, *Systems Analysis and Project Management*, 3d ed. (New York: McGraw-Hill, 1983): 461–469; J. Allen

and B.P. Lientz, *Systems in Action* (Santa Monica: Goodyear, 1978): 95; H. Kerzner, *Project Management*, 5th ed. (New York: Van Nostrand Reinhold, 1995): 570–573.

3. See, for example, Cleland and King, Systems Analysis and Project Management, 461–469.

4. Seymour Sarason in *The Creation of Settings and The Future Societies* (San Francisco: Jossey-Bass, 1972) argues the importance of knowing the beginnings, origins, and history of any new "setting" before initiating work; especially important is to learn about and prepare for struggles, obstacles, and conflicts that might later be encountered.

5. In technical projects, the components are the "CIs" identified during preliminary design studies in systems engineering, as described in Chapter 2.

6. Cleland and King, *Systems Analysis and Project Management*, 258.

7. R. Archibald, *Managing High-Technology Programs and Projects* (New York: John Wiley & Sons, 1976): 65, 156.

8. Quality function deployment (QFD) methodology discussed in Chapter 4 can be used to identify the precedence relationship between jobs.

9. Portions of this section adopted from P.K. Joy, *Total Project Management* (Delhi: Macmillan India Limited, 1998): 378–400.

10. Ibid., 378–380.

11. Examples are: NEC or New Engineering Contract, published by The Institution of Civil Engineers, *The Engineering and Construction Contract* (London: Thomas Telford, 1995); and FIDIC, published by the International Federation of Consulting Engineers, Lausanne, Switzerland. See http://www1.fidic.orghttp://www1.fidic.org

12. Roy Whittaker, *Project Management in the Process Industries* (New York: John Wiley & Sons, 1995).

Chapter 6

Project Time Planning and Networks

I know why there are so many people who love chopping wood.
In this activity one immediately sees the results.

—ALBERT EINSTEIN

You can't always get what you want.

—ROLLING STONES

Project scheduling involves much more than just displaying tasks on a Gantt chart. It is an integral part of project planning, and often involves a trial-and-error process of adjusting work tasks to meet the constraint of limited resources while trying to meet project deadlines. While Gantt charts are good for displaying project schedules, as a tool for project planning they are limited because they do not explicitly show the relationships among activities or the effects of delaying activities or shifting resources on the overall project. Network methods as described in this chapter do not have this limitation; they clearly show interdependencies and what happens to the project when resources are altered or individual activities delayed. With these methods alternative schedules can be analyzed and the project planned to satisfy resource constraints and deadlines. This chapter and the next discuss the most widely used network-based approaches to project scheduling and planning.

6.1 NETWORKS DIAGRAMS

A network diagram shows a group of activities or tasks and their logical relationships—i.e., the "precedence relationship" or "dependency" among the tasks. Figure 6-1 is a network diagram for "getting up in the morning and getting dressed" (for a male!). The boxes represent activities or tasks, and the arrows connecting them show the order in which they should occur, e.g., put on shirt *before* tie, put on pants *and* socks *before* shoes, etc. (The diagram in Figure 6-1 is of course intended for illustration only; any real life attempt to plan work in such detail would be "micro management" and a real time-waster!) In a project, the activities shown in the network would be the work packages or other tasks as defined in the work breakdown structure (WBS) according to the guidelines in Chapter 5.

Network diagrams describe a project in terms of sequences of activities and events. An *activity* represents a work task or work element—normally a work package or job of smaller size. Depending on the desired detail, however, the activities in the network can represent work at any level of the WBS, including projects in a program, subprojects belonging to a project, or the work packages belonging to a project, project phase, subproject, or specific facility.

Networks also show *events*. As described in Chapter 5, an event represents an *instant* in time, an "announcement" that something has happened or will happen. Typically it signifies the start of an activity or the end of an activity. An activity with a very short duration can sometimes be regarded as an event. A significant event such as the completion of a project phase is a *milestone*.

Two common methods for constructing network diagrams are *activity-on-node (AON)*—also called *precedence diagramming method (PDM)*, and *activity-on-arrow (AOA)*. Both were developed independently during the late 1950s—AON for the Critical Path Method and AOA for the PERT method. Most of our discussion will center on the more-commonly used AON method. The AOA method is addressed in the Appendix to this chapter.

AON Diagrams

Figure 6-2 shows how an activity is represented using the AON method. The *node* (the block in the figure) is the activity; inside the node is information about the activity, such as its duration, start time, and finish time.

Figure 6-1
Logic diagram for getting up and getting dressed.

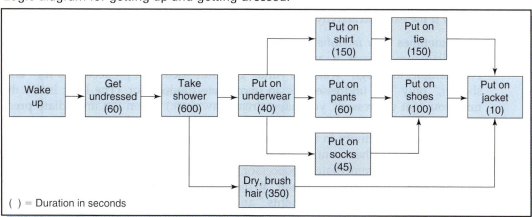

( ) = Duration in seconds

Computer software eases the task of creating networks for small projects, but for large projects it is a necessity. The resulting network should be reviewed for accuracy and omissions, and for mistakes in data entry. As a rule of thumb, the network should be created only after a suitable scope statement and WBS have been developed (i.e., the list of work tasks should be created before—not while—the network is created).

6.2 THE CRITICAL PATH

The strength of project networks is their utility as a tool for project planning and control. They are good for estimating project duration, scheduling of activities within the project, and making commitments regarding the due date of a project, in other words for determining *how long* the project will take (the *expected project duration*), *when* each activity should be scheduled, and the *likelihood* of completing a project on time.

In general, the expected project duration, T_e, is determined by finding the *longest path* through the network. A "path" is any route comprised of one or more activities connected in sequence. The longest path from the project start node to the end node is called the *critical path*; its length is the expected project duration. Should any activity that forms part of the critical path (critical activity) take longer than planned (because of delays, interruptions, lack of resources, whatever), the entire project will take longer than planned. Thus, the critical path indicates to the project manager which activities are most critical to completing the project on time.

These concepts are illustrated in the following example. The firm of Kelly, Applebaum, Nuzzo, and Earl, Assoc. (KANE) is working on the Robotics Self-Budgeting (ROSEBUD) project. Table 6-4 lists the project activities, and Figure 6-5 shows the network. (Parts (a) and (b) of Figure 6-5 are very similar; for now look only at (a).) The first phase in the project is systems design (represented by Activity J), followed by the simultaneous phases of (1) robotics hardware purchase, assembly, and installation (Activities M–V–Y), and (2) software specification and purchase (L–Q). The last phase of the project is system test and user test of both the hardware and software (W–X).

How long will this project take? The first Activity, J, takes 6 weeks. As shown in Figure 6-5, after J has been completed both the "hardware activities" and "software

Table 6-4 Activities for the ROSEBUD project.

ACTIVITY	DESCRIPTION	IMMEDIATE PREDECESSORS	DURATION (WEEKS)
J	System design	—	6
M	Hardware purchase and delivery	J	4
V	Hardware assembly and test	M	6
Y	Hardware installation	V	8
L	Software specification	J	2
Q	Software purchase and delivery	L	8
W	System test	Y, Q	1
X	User test	W	1

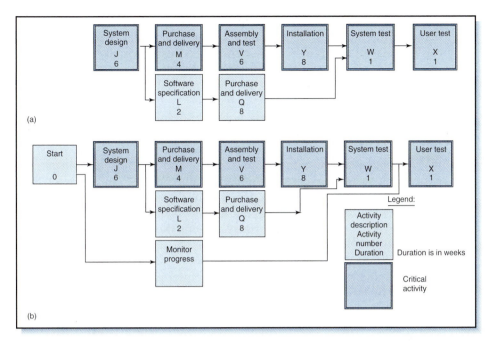

Figure 6-5
Network for ROSEBUD project: (a) Network for ROSEBUD project and
(b) Network for ROSEBUD project with hammock.

activities" can begin. It will take $4 + 6 + 8 = 18$ weeks to do the hardware activities (Path M–V–Y), and $2 + 8 = 10$ weeks to do the software activities (Path L–Q). Because Activity J takes 6 weeks, the *hardware* will be ready for Activity W (system test) in $6 + 18 = 24$ weeks, and the *software* will be ready for Activity W in $6 + 10 = 16$ weeks. Because Activity W requires that *both* the hardware and the software be finished, the earliest Activity W can begin is after 24 weeks. Activity W will be completed 1 week later, and Activity X (user test) will be completed 1 week after that. Thus, the duration (denoted as T_e) of the ROSEBUD project is $T_e = 24 + 1 + 1 = 26$ weeks.

Notice from Figure 6-5(a) that there are two paths from the start node (J) to the end node X. The shorter path J–L–Q–W–X is 18 weeks long; the longer path, J–M–V–Y–W–X, is 26 weeks long. In general, *the longest path gives the project duration*. The longest path is called the *critical path*, and the activities that comprise it are called *critical activities*. The critical path should be highlighted as in the example, where the critical activities are the ones with "framed" boxes.

Should it be necessary to reduce the project completion time, any reduction effort (e.g., shortening the duration of an activity) must be directed at the critical path. Shortening any critical activity by, say, 1 week would have the effect of shortening the project duration by 1 week. In contrast, shortening activities *not* on the critical path would have no effect on project duration. For example, if either L or Q were reduced by 1 week, then the software activities would be completed in week 15 instead of week 16, but since Activity W must still wait on completion of hardware activities—which won't happen until after week 24—there would be no change in project duration.

The critical path is important for another reason: *any* delay among the activities in the critical path will result in a delay in the completion of the project. Should any critical activity be delayed by, say, 1 week, the project completion will be delayed by

1 week. Note, however, that noncritical activities *can* be delayed somewhat without delaying the project. In fact, in the example noncritical Activities L and Q together can be delayed by up to 8 weeks. This is because normally they will be completed in 16 weeks, which is 8 weeks earlier than the hardware activities (24 weeks). Thus, although the software activities can be completed in as early as 16 weeks, it is okay if they are completed in as late as 24 weeks.

The critical path is important, but that doesn't mean it should receive exclusive focus. As activities not on the critical path are delayed, the length of noncritical paths gets longer. When the length of a noncritical path grows to exceed the critical path, the former noncritical path becomes critical and the (former) critical path becomes noncritical. In other words, the critical path changes.[1] In a project these changes can take place without warning, leaving the project manager to focus on the wrong activities. One solution is to provide warning signals when noncritical activities are at risk of becoming critical; the *critical chain* method discussed in Chapter 7 provides a way to do this.

Figure 6-5 also illustrates an activity that "spans" multiple other activities, called a *hammock*. In Figure 6-5(b) the activity "Monitor progress" is a hammock; it specifies that all activities in the project except "user test" must be monitored, implying that the project manager is responsible for the progress on every activity in the project except "user test." The duration of a hammock is determined by the duration of the longest path of activities over which it spans, which in Figure 6-5(b) is $6 + 4 + 6 + 8 + 1 = 25$ weeks. Note, however, that although a hammock spans a portion of the longest path, it is not considered a critical activity.

A final example of the critical path is in Figure 6-6. This network has four paths leading from start node H to the end node Z:

(a) H–J–P–Y–Z
(b) H–J–K–V–X–Y–Z
(c) H–J–M–R–V–X–Y–Z
(d) H–J–L–Q–T–Z

Figure 6-6
Example network showing the critical path (developed with Project Scheduler 8.5 software).

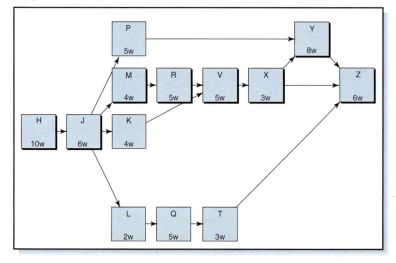

The lengths of the four paths are, respectively: 35, 42, 47, and 32; the critical path is the longest path, Path c, as indicated by the "shadowed" boxes, and $T_e = 47$.

Multiple Critical Paths

Can a project have more than one critical path? There is no reason why not. Suppose the duration of Activity L in Figure 6-6 were 17 weeks instead of 2 weeks. In that case, the durations of path M–R–V–X–Y and path L–Q–T would both be 25 weeks, and the project would have *two* critical paths, both with duration 47 weeks; a delay along *either* path would extend the project. Suppose, however, you wanted to *reduce* the project duration to less than 47 weeks; given that you have two critical paths, you would then have to shorten *both* of them. This means you would reduce the time on Activities H, J, or Z, or, if you want to, reduce M, R, V, X, or Y by a certain amount and *also* reduce L, Q, or T by the same amount. A problem with multiple critical paths is that they dilute management focus because there are more things of critical importance to keep track of.

Early Times: Early Start Time and Early Finish Time

Scheduling each activity in a project involves at minimum specifying when the activity must be started and finished. The usual assumption is that an activity is started at the *beginning* of a period and finished at the *end* of a period. For example, if an activity has a duration of 5 working days and starts on Monday morning, it would be finished on Friday afternoon. If Monday is Day 1 and Friday is Day 5, the activity would start at the beginning of Day 1 and finish at the end of Day 5:

$$\text{Finish time} = \text{Day 1 (Monday)} + 5 \text{ days (Duration)} - 1$$
$$= \text{Day 5 (Friday)} = 1 + 5 - 1 = 5$$

The formula is:

$$\text{Finish time} = \text{Start time} + \text{Duration} - 1$$

This is represented on the network by two "early times" for the activity: (1) the *early start time* (ES), and (2) the *early finish time* (EF), which represent the earliest possible times that the activity can be started and completed.

But the ES of an activity depends on the activity's immediate predecessors, in particular the finish times of its immediate predecessors. These times are found by summing the durations of the predecessor activities along the paths leading to the activity in question; when more than one path leads to that activity, the ES will be the time along the *longest path*. This is shown with another example in Figure 6-7. Suppose the ES for the first activity, H, is week 1 (i.e., the project starts at the *beginning* of week 1). Since the duration is 10 weeks, the early finish, EF, of H must then be at the *end* of week 10. This was determined from the formula:

$$EF = ES + \text{Duration} - 1$$

ES is shown in the upper left of each node; EF on the upper right.

Given that the EF for H is at the end of week 10, the ES for Activity J will be at the beginning of week 11, and the EF will be at the end of week 16. Similarly, ES for activities K, M, and L will be the beginning of week 17. The ES for Activity V will happen after all of its immediate predecessors have been completed: the length of the path going through Activity K is $10 + 6 + 4 = 20$, which is the EF for Activity K; the

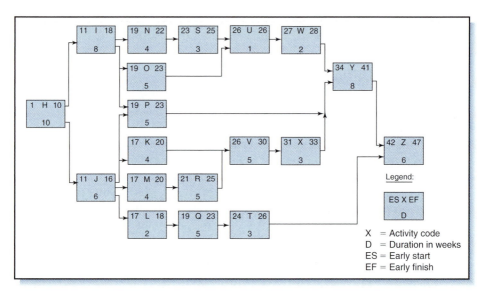

Figure 6-7
Example network showing ESs and EFs.

length of the path going through Activities M and R is $10 + 6 + 4 + 5 = 25$, which is the EF for Activity R. The ES of Activity V will depend on the longer of the two paths leading to it, which is through Activity R. Since EF for Activity R is week 25, ES for Activity V is week 26.

The same happens at Activity Y: ES = week 34, which is computed by using the longest path leading it—the path through Activity X. For Activity Y to start, all three of Y's immediate predecessor Activities, W, P and X, must have been completed. Activity P will be completed after 23, W after 28, and X after 33 weeks. Hence, the earliest that Activity Y can be started is in week 34. For Activity Z, the last in the project, the ES is at the start of week 42 and EF at the end of week 47. Notice that 47 weeks is also the project duration, T_e.

In summary, ESs and EFs are computed by taking a "forward pass" through the network. When an activity has only one immediate predecessor, its ES is simply the period following the EF of the predecessor. When an activity has several immediate predecessors, its ES is based on the *latest* EF of all its immediate predecessors.

Late Times: Late Start Time and Late Finish Time

As discussed earlier, an activity that is not on the critical path can be delayed without delaying the project; the question is, by how much can it be delayed? To answer that we must determine the "late times," that is, the latest allowable times that the activity can be started and finished without delaying the project completion. Just as in the case of ES and EF, every activity also has a *late start* time, LS, and a *late finish* time, LF. Referring to Figure 6-8, we will show that the method for calculating LF and LS is the reverse of calculating ES and EF.

To determine the late times, begin by assigning a *target completion date*, T_s, to the last node in the network. In general, for projects that have to be completed *as soon as possible*, the figure used for T_s is always the same as the T_e calculated in a forward pass, which is the EF of the last activity. For projects with a due date set by the customer, T_s is the due date.

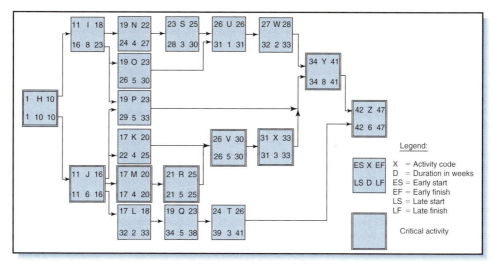

Figure 6-8
Example network showing LFs and LSs.

To determine the late times, start at Activity Z in Figure 6-8 and make a "backward pass" through the network using the formula:

$$LS = LF - Duration + 1$$

If T_s is 47 weeks, then LS for Activity Z must be $47 - 6 + 1 = 42$. Activity Z must start at the beginning of week 42 in order not to delay the project. Still moving backwards, for Activity Y, the LF must be 41 weeks, and EF for Y must be $41 - 8 + 1 = 34$. Continue moving backward through each path, computing LF and LS for each activity.

Whenever we encounter an activity that has *multiple* paths leading back to it (i.e., it has multiple immediate successors), it is the *longest backward path* that determines the activity's LF. In other words, it is the backward path (immediate successor) with the *smallest* LS that determines the activity's LF. For example, there are four paths leading back to Activity J:

- for Activity P the LF is 33 weeks (because LS for Activity Y is week 34); thus LS for P is $33 - 5 + 1 = 29$ weeks (beginning of week 29);
- for Activity K the LF is 25 weeks (since LS for Activity V is week 26), thus LS = $25 - 4 + 1 = 22$ weeks;
- similarly, for Activity M, LS = $20 - 4 + 1 = 17$ weeks;
- for Activity L, LS = $33 - 2 + 1 = 32$ weeks.

Notice, it is the longest path back that gives the smallest LS, which is 17 weeks. Thus, the LF for Activity J is 16 weeks (i.e., Activity J must finish by end week 16 so as not to delay Activity M, whose LS = 17 weeks). LF = 16 weeks is the latest J can be finished to allow enough time to complete the longest sequence of remaining Activities M–R–V–X–Y–Z by the target date of 47 weeks.

In summary, calculations for LFs and LSs start at the last node of the project network and work backward. When an activity has more than one path leading back to it, the smallest value of LS among all its immediate successors becomes the basis for determining the activity's LF. Having completed both forward and backward passes through the network, we now have the earliest possible and latest allowable scheduled times for every activity in the network. Note that hammock activities are excluded from the forward and backward pass calculations. Only after both the forward pass and backward pass calculations have been completed are the durations of hammock activities calculated.

Total Slack

Referring to Figure 6-8, notice the activities where the ES and LS are not the same. The difference between LS and ES (or LF and EF) is referred to as the *total slack* time (or the "float" or simply "slack") of an activity. Slack is the amount of allowable deviation between when an activity *must* take place at the latest and when it *can* take place at the earliest:

$$\text{Total slack} = \text{LS} - \text{ES}$$
$$= \text{LF} - \text{EF}$$

In Figure 6-8, the total slack for Activity H is $0 - 0 = 0$ weeks; for Activity I, total slack is $15 - 10 = 5$ weeks; for Activity J it is $10 - 10 = 0$, and so on. Slack is the amount of time an activity can be delayed without delaying the project. Notice that activities on the critical path in Figure 6-8 have zero slack; hence, critical activities cannot be delayed by any amount, else the project will be delayed. (Sometimes critical activities do have slack, but this is discussed later.) The activities that do have slack (which, as it turns out, are the *noncritical activities*) can be delayed by their total slack time without delaying the project completion.

When activities lie in sequence on a subpath, a delay in earlier activities will result in a delay to later ones, which is the equivalent of reducing slack for the remaining activities. In Figure 6-8, for example, Activities L, Q, and T all lie on the same subpath and all have the same slack time of 15 weeks. But if Activity L, the first one in the sequence, is delayed by 5 weeks, then Activities Q and T will also be delayed by 5 weeks and, thus, will have only 10 weeks of slack remaining, not 15. If, in addition, Activity Q is delayed by 10 weeks, then Activity T will have no remaining slack and must be started immediately upon completion of Q. Having used up all their slack, Activities L, Q, and T would then all become critical activities.

Total slack time is the maximum allowable delay that can occur for noncritical activities. Once this slack is used up, noncritical activities become critical and further delays of these activities will delay the project completion. The practical implication of slack is that the project management team has some flexibility regarding exactly when noncritical activities can be scheduled: any schedule is feasible as long as activities occur somewhere within the available slack time—somewhere between their computed late and early times. Knowing the amount of flexibility is important for managing resource workload. By starting some activities as early as possible and moving others back to later dates, the workload can be smoothed. This concept is discussed later.

In general, if sufficient resources are available then noncritical activities should be scheduled as early as possible (their ESs); this preserves slack time and minimizes the risk that delays in noncritical activities will cause a project delay. (Another method, the *critical chain*, specifies that activities should be scheduled as late as possible but provides "buffers" to protect them. This is discussed in the next chapter.)

Notice that decisions concerning exactly when to schedule activities require knowing both the late and early times for the activities. The implication is that a network diagram and network analysis should have been done *before* creating a Gantt chart. Most project management software develops the network and Gantt chart simultaneously, and automatically schedules activities using the early start times. As discussed later, however, not all activities in a project should or can be scheduled according to the early times.

Free Slack

While *total slack* refers to the amount of time an activity can be delayed without delaying the project, the term *free slack* refers to the amount of time an activity can be delayed without delaying *the early start of any successor activity*. Free slack of an activity is determined by the following formula:

$$\text{Free slack for activity} = \text{ES (earliest successor)} - \text{EF (activity)} - 1$$

For example, in Figure 6-8 Activity I has a total slack time of 5 weeks but free slack time of 0 weeks because *any* delay in it will delay the start of other activities, namely N, O, and P. Activity O, on the other hand, has free slack of 2 weeks because its EF of 23 weeks can be delayed to 25 weeks without delaying the ES of its successor, Activity U, which is 26 weeks.

Knowing the free slack, managers can quickly identify activities where slippages have consequence for other activities. When an activity has zero free slack, *any* slippage will cause at least one other activity to also slip. If, for example, Activity L slips, then so will Q and T, and teams working in Q and T (specified in the responsibility matrix) must be notified of the delay.

As with total slack, the amount of free slack available to an activity assumes the activity starts at its ES time. Thus, the free slack for Activity O is 2 weeks as long as Activity I, its immediate predecessor, is completed at EF = 18 weeks. If Activity I is delayed by any amount, then Activity O's free slack will be reduced by the same amount.

Table 6-5 summarizes these concepts, showing ES, LS, EF, and LF, and total and free slack times for the LOGON project in Figure 6-8. Notice that everywhere on the critical path the total slack and free slack times are zero.

The Effect of Project Due Date

We assumed in discussing total slack time that the target completion date, T_s, was the same as the earliest expected completion date, T_e. The target completion date can actually be varied to make it either later or earlier than T_e to reflect wishes of the client.

Setting the target date to *later* than T_e has the effect of *increasing* total slack for every activity in the project by the amount $T_s - T_e$. Although possibly no longer zero, the slack time on the critical path will still be the *smallest* slack anywhere in the network. For example, if the target completion date T_s for the project in Figure 6-8 were increased to 50 weeks, then the total slack in Table 6-5 would be $50 - 47 = 3$ weeks for all critical activities, and 3 *additional* weeks for all noncritical activities.

If T_s is set *earlier* than T_e, then the total slack times throughout the network will be reduced by the amount $T_s - T_e$, and activities along the critical path will have *negative* slack times. Negative slack on the critical path occurs whenever the customer sets a due date earlier than T_e. The size of this negative slack is the amount of time by which the project duration must be reduced to meet the target date. All of this has no influence on free slack times, which depend on early start and finish times, both of which are affected by the same amount when changing T_s.

In general, projects have to be completed either as soon as possible or by a predetermined due date. For projects that have to be completed as soon as possible, the project manager does a forward pass calculation through the network, then commits

Table 6-5 LOGON project time analysis (from Figure 6-8).

Activity (1)	Duration (Weeks) (2)	Start Node ES(Start of Week) (3)	Start Node LS (Start of Week) (4)	Finish Node EF (End of Week) (5)	Finish Node LF (End of Week) (6)	Slack Total* (7)	Slack Free** (8)	Note
H	10	1	1	10	10	0	0	CP
I	8	11	16	18	23	5	0	
J	6	11	11	16	16	0	0	CP
K	4	17	22	20	25	5	5	
L	2	17	32	18	33	15	0	
M	4	17	17	20	20	0	0	CP
N	4	19	24	22	27	5	0	
O	5	19	26	23	30	7	2	
P	5	19	29	23	33	10	10	
Q	5	19	34	23	38	15	0	
R	5	21	21	25	25	0	0	CP
S	3	23	28	25	30	5	0	
T	3	24	39	26	41	15	15	
U	1	26	31	26	31	5	0	
V	5	26	26	30	30	0	0	CP
W	2	27	32	28	33	5	5	
X	3	31	31	33	33	0	0	CP
Y	8	34	34	41	41	0	0	CP
Z	6	42	42	47	47	0	0	CP

Total Slack, (7) = (4) − (3) = (6) − (5)

Free Slack, (8) = [(3) of earliest successor] − (5) − 1

Total slack is the spare time on an activity that if used will affect the slack on succeeding jobs (i.e., will delay successors and reduce their slack), and if used up and delayed further will affect the project as a whole.
**Free slack* is the spare time on an activity that if used up will not affect the early start time of any succeeding activities (i.e., will not affect the total slack nor delay any successor).

to the resultant T_e. For projects that must meet a predetermined due date, the project manager substitutes T_s at the last event, then works backward through the network, noting the feasibility of speeding up activities in the project and the steps necessary to do so.

6.3 GANTT CHARTS AND CALENDAR SCHEDULES

Converting the information from a table such as Tables 6-1 – 6-4 to a network with start and finish times is a simple step-by-step procedure that requires no management decisions and is readily be performed by computer software. But to be usable, however, the times in the network must be converted into calendar dates (day, month, year), either on a Gantt chart or actual calendar. For a few reasons, converting

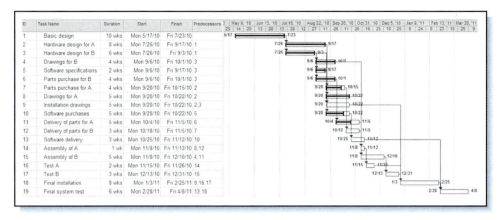

Figure 6-9
LOGON project schedule adjusted for holidays and weekends.

network times to a Gantt chart or calendar schedule is *not* a simple procedure and *does* require management decisions.

For starters, the calendar schedule must account for *non-working time* such as weekends, holidays, and vacations. Figure 6-9 shows the LOGON project schedule as produced by Microsoft Project software and incorporating time off for weekends and holidays.

In addition, the calendar schedule must account for issues that involve analysis and decisions; examples include:

- *Resource constraints*: a work package must be delayed because the resources it needs are unavailable or must be shared with other, parallel activities.

- *Change risk*: a design activity is postponed to reduce the potential effects from changes in other design activities, project scope, or developing technologies.

- *Cash flow*: the procurement of an expensive item is delayed in order to defer cash outlay, improve cash flow, enable investments to generate income, or, if procured from another country, await exchange rate improvement.

- *Logistics*: the acquisition of bulky items for construction is delayed until space becomes available at the construction site.

Although computer software can readily generate the project network, Gantt chart, and calendar schedule, it cannot, of its own, know about or account for issues like those above; as a consequence the resulting project schedule will likely be infeasible, unworkable, or overly risky. The point is, the project schedule should result from sound management judgment about issues surrounding the project and not be merely a computer-generated variation of the project network.

6.4 MANAGEMENT SCHEDULE RESERVE

The contractual or committed target completion time T_s is usually *not* simply the estimated completion time T_e plus allowance for non-working time; instead, it is some time *after* that and includes a *management schedule reserve* or *time buffer*. This chapter has treated activity durations as if they are fixed. Of course, each project is a unique endeavor, and until it has actually been completed its duration is no more than a mere estimate. All durations (of projects and the activities that compose them) are subject to uncertainty. The greater the uncertainty of the project, the larger the potential uncertainty in the project completion date. To account for that uncertainty, a management schedule reserve and budget reserve are created; together they comprise a "safety buffer" or "project buffer" that the project manager can use to compensate for project delays or cost overruns. The size and placement of these reserves or buffers are discussed in Chapter 7.

6.5 PRECEDENCE DIAGRAMMING METHOD[2]

The network scheduling procedures discussed so far assumed a strict sequential relationship wherein the start of an activity is predicated upon the completion of its immediate predecessors. Such is the case illustrated in the diagram in Figure 6-10 where Activity B starts upon completion of Activity A. This strict start-only-when-the-predecessors-are-finished relationship is called *finish-to-start, FS*. The limitation of the FS network representation is that it precludes those kinds of tasks that can be started when their predecessors are only *partially* (but not fully) completed. For example, when a company relocates to a new facility the activity "employee move-in" should be able to start after *some* of the activity "move office furniture" has been done. Although it might be necessary to have completed "move furniture" before completing "employee move-in," the point is that "employee move-in" can begin *before* its immediate predecessor "move furniture" has been completed. The *PDM* allows for this and similar such situations. Besides the usual FS relationship, PDM permits the relationships of start-to-start (SS), finish-to-finish (FF), and start-to-finish (SF). It also allows for time lags between when multiple activities must be started or finished. These special relationships are described next.

Start-to-Start

In an SS relationship between two Activities A and B, the start of B can occur n days at the earliest after the start of its immediate predecessor, A. This is diagrammed in Figure 6-11. The n days delay is called the *lag*. In the case of an acceleration instead of a delay, it is called a *lead* (lead is the mathematical negative of lag).

Using the example from Figure 6-10, suppose that "employee move-in" can begin 5 days after the start of "furniture move-in;" the network diagram and associated Gantt chart for the two activities would appear as in Figure 6-12.

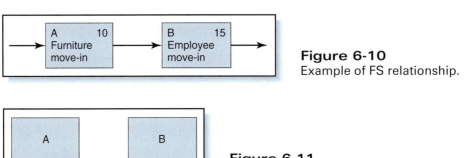

Figure 6-10
Example of FS relationship.

Figure 6-11
PDM representation of SS relationship with n day lag.

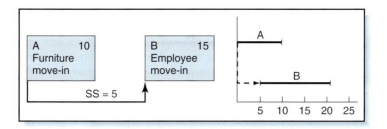

Figure 6-12
Example of SS relationship.

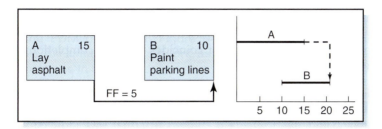

Figure 6-13
Example of FF relationship.

Finish-to-Finish

In an FF relationship between two Activities A and B, B will finish *n* days, at the latest, after A finishes. An illustration is in Figure 6-13 where "paint parking lines" (B) must be finished within 5 days after "lay asphalt" (A) has been finished. Where two or more activities have to finish at the same time, an FF relationship with zero lag is often used.

Start-to-Finish

In an SF relationship, the finish of Activity B must occur *n* days at the latest after the start of Activity A. For example, "phase-out old system" (B) cannot be finished until 25 days after "test new system" (A) begins. This is shown in Figure 6-14.

Finish-to-Start

In an FS relationship, the start of Activity B can occur *n* days at the earliest after the finish of Activity A. For example, "tear-down scaffolding" (B) can start no sooner

Figure 6-14
Example of SF relationship.

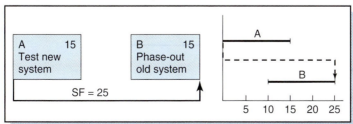

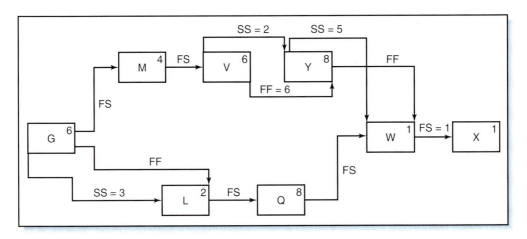

Figure 6-20
PDM network for the ROSEBUD project.

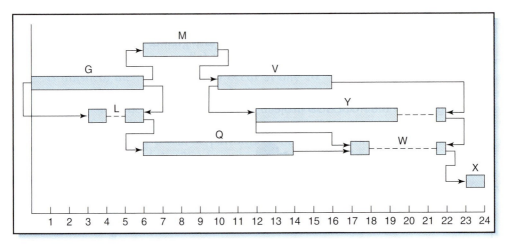

Figure 6-21
Time-based network for the ROSEBUD project revised for PDM.

the critical path and slack times is not so simple either. Complex precedence relationships also cause counterintuitive results. For example, in a simple network the way to reduce the project completion time is to reduce the time of activities along the critical path; however, doing the same thing in a PDM network does not necessarily produce the desired result. In the previous example, the critical path is path G–M–V–Y–W–X. Suppose we decide to reduce the time on Activity Y. Because the precedence requirement is that Y cannot be finished sooner than 6 days before V is finished, the completion date of Y cannot be changed. Thus, any shortening of the duration of Y serves to *move back* the start date of Y. Because of the precedence requirement, moving back the start date of Y results in moving back the start date of W and, as a result, the start date of X. In other words, shortening critical Activity Y actually causes an *increase in the project duration*.

In general, interpreting a PDM network requires more care than ordinary AON networks. However, these and other difficulties are relatively inconsequential when the PDM network is generated with project management software.

Every activity requires resources such as working capital, people, equipment, material, and even space. Until now, our coverage of scheduling has assumed implicitly that any resources needed to do the work would always be available when needed. But of course, resources are not always available. We now consider project scheduling with resource constraints, and the effect of constraints on workload fluctuation and project duration.

Resource Availability and Project Duration

In many cases it is the availability of skilled workers, machinery, equipment, and working capital that dictates whether activities can be scheduled at their early time or must be delayed. This is especially true when multiple activities that require the same resources are scheduled for the same time. When resources are not sufficient to satisfy the needs of all of them, some activities must be delayed. Figure 6-22 illustrates: (a) the network, and (b) the project schedule without considering resources. Suppose Activities B and C both require the same resource, but the resource can be applied to only one of them at a time. In that case, the schedule must be revised, and the two *resource-constrained* schedules in Figure 6-22(c) are alternatives.

In general, projects tend to be either *resource constrained* or *time constrained*. A project is resource constrained when its resources are limited in some way, and its completion date is determined by the availability of those resources. A project is time constrained when it *must* be completed by a required due date, though it is assumed to have sufficient resources to meet that date. A project that is both resource and time constrained might not have sufficient resources to be completed by the required date.

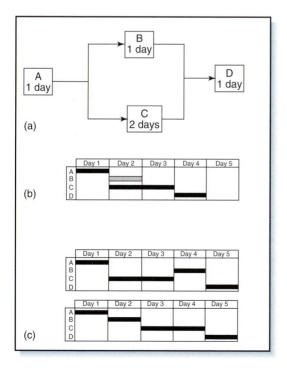

Figure 6-22
The effect of a constrained resource on schedule.

Resource Allocation, Workload, and Loading

The terms resource allocation, workload, and resource loading convey related but different concepts. *Resource allocation* refers to assigning one or more resources to an activity or project. *Workload* refers to the amount of work imposed on a resource. *Resource loading* refers to the amount of a particular resource necessary to conduct all the activities in a project to which it is allocated. For an *individual resource* (such as a person), the workload can be specified either as a percentage of the resource's full workload potential, or more commonly in units such as labor hours. For a *facility* or *labor category* (such as a department or pool of workers with a specific skill), the workload is specified in terms of number of workers. Since people in a labor category (such as "computer programmer") rarely have exactly the same skills, ordinarily it is better to allocate a specific person (a specific programmer) rather than a labor category to an activity. (The usual assumption when allocating from a labor category is that everyone in the category is equally capable, though often after the work begins it soon becomes evident that some workers are more capable than others.) The workload that an individual can handle in a year is computed as the number of working days (excluding public holidays and all types of leave) times the number of productive (working) hours per day. Many companies have guidelines stating the number of hours an individual should work on projects per week, month, or per year. In a matrix organization the functional managers are responsible for ensuring that each worker's time is well utilized and that her workload does not exceed the recommended maximum hours.

Workload is always from the perspective of the particular resource; in contrast, loading is from the perspective of the *project*. It is the number of hours, people, or other units of a particular resource needed at a given time in a project (or in multiple concurrent projects). Resource loading is important because virtually all resources are finite and many are scarce. Thus, the resource loading (the total amount of the resource needed for a project or projects at a given time) cannot exceed the amount available. When resources are scarce, their allocation is constrained, and sometimes activities in a project must be rescheduled to accommodate the scarcity. The example in Figure 6-22 is such a case: Activities B and C require the same resource, but there is not enough of the resource to do both. Resources that are available in sufficient quantity do not pose an issue (air is an example—unless the project is being conducted under water or in outer space where air is limited) and can be ignored for scheduling purposes.

In the following sections we consider two cases where the project schedule must be altered to accommodate resources. The first is called *resource leveling* in a *time-constrained project*. In this case, there is always enough of the resource to complete the project on time; however, the amount of the resource needed fluctuates dramatically throughout the project, making it difficult to manage the resource or pool of resources. The objective of resource leveling is to balance or level the amount of the resource needed throughout the project. The second case is the situation mentioned before, not having enough of a resource to do multiple activities at once (a resource-constrained project) and adjusting the schedule to accommodate the constraint.

Leveling of a Time-Constrained Project

Because the loading for a particular resource depends on the amount of the resource needed by individual activities and the timing of those activities in the project, the loading for a particular resource tends to vary throughout a project as different activities are started and completed. A common resource-loading pattern in a project is a steady buildup in the amount of the resource needed, a peak, and then a gradual decline. Thus, relatively little of the resource is needed early and late in the project, but much is needed in the middle. This is problematic for functional managers who are responsible for a stable, uniform pool of workers and equipment and results in periods where the pool is underworked or overworked. Certainly better would be a relatively uniform workload on the resource pool. This is the purpose of resource leveling: to alter the schedule of individual project activities such that the resultant amount of a required resource is somewhat constant throughout the project.

Figure 6-23 shows the loading of a resource for the LOGON project—the resource being a particular skill or trade (programmer, steel worker, etc.). The diagram is created with the Gantt chart in Figure 6-23 and weekly labor requirements in Table 6-6 by adding requirements for all activities scheduled each week, on a

Figure 6-23
Schedule and corresponding worker loading for the LOGON project.

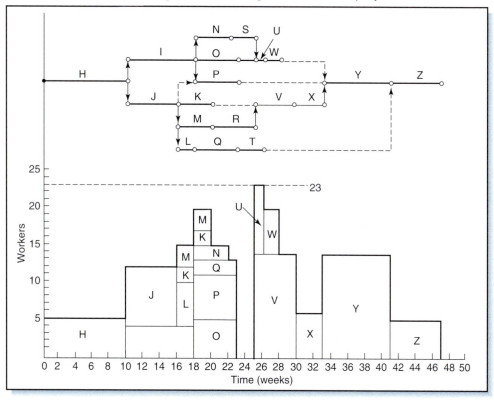

Table 6-6 LOGON project weekly labor requirements.

Activity	H	I	J	K	L	M	N	O	P	Q	R	S	T	U	V	W	X	Y	Z
Duration (weeks)	10	8	6	4	2	4	4	5	5	5	5	3	3	1	5	2	3	8	6
Weekly Labor Requirements (workers)	5	4	8	2	6	3	2	5	6	2	0	0	0	9	14	6	6	14	5
Weekly Equipment Requirements (hours)	8	2	6	1	2	2	0	0	6	0	4	4	0	8	8	8	8	8	8

week-by-week basis. For example, for the first 10 weeks only Activity H is scheduled, so the loading for those weeks stays at five workers (the weekly requirement for H). Over the next 6 weeks, Activities I and J are scheduled, so the loading becomes $4 + 8 = 12$, and so on.

Looking at Figure 6-23, you can see that the loading for the LOGON project might pose a problem because it fluctuates so much, varying from a maximum of 23 workers in week 26 to a minimum of zero workers in weeks 24 and 25 (since Activities R, S, and T do not require any workers). The problem facing the manager allocating these workers to LOGON is what to do with excess workers during slow periods and where to get additional workers during busy periods. One way to handle this problem is to balance the worker loading so it is more "level" throughout the project.

The problem is addressed by "juggling" activities around, which is done by taking advantage of slack times and moving noncritical activities to later than their early times so as to reduce workload peaks and to fill in workload valleys. For example, the somewhat smoothed workload in Figure 6-24 is achieved by delaying Activities P and Q each by 2 weeks, and U and W each by 5 weeks. (A perfectly level loading is not usually possible.)

Although resource leveling is often necessary to ease difficult-to-manage workload situations, it potentially increases the risk of project delays due to moving activities back and reducing slack time. In Figure 6-24 delaying Activities U and W makes them critical, and thereafter a delay in either will delay the project.

Figure 6-24
Smoothed worker loading for the LOGON project.

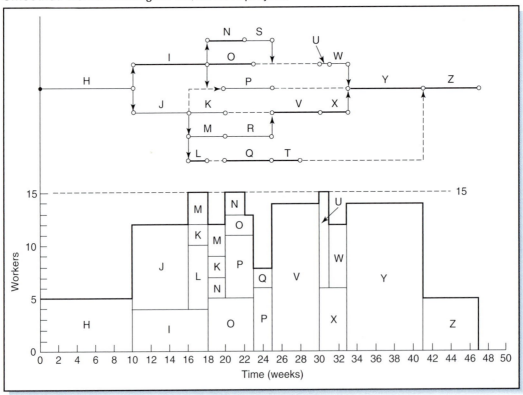

Splitting Activities, Multitasking, and Hand-Over Points

In the previous example an even-more uniform loading could have been achieved if each activity were split and the pieces scheduled at different times. Whether this is feasible depends on whether each job, once started, can be interrupted and then restarted later. As discussed earlier, definition of project activities and work packages takes place during the WBS process, and the resultant activities become the basis for establishing schedules, budgets, responsibility, and so on. Once an "activity" has been defined in the WBS, it should not be arbitrarily later "split" because doing so might also require splitting budgets, responsibilities, etc., for the activities.

But even though activity splitting can lead to a more uniform loading, the downside is that it can lead to wasted time and longer activity durations. Figure 6-25 illustrates what happens when an activity is split. Uninterrupted, the activity starts slowly but then builds momentum as it moves ahead. Split, each piece starts slowly and never gathers much momentum. The sum of the durations of the pieces in (b) exceeds the duration in (a). The effect, known as *multitasking*, leads to slower-paced work on average and extends the activity duration. The moral is, once an activity has been started, it is usually better to finish it uninterrupted.

Multitasking wherein the work is stopped and then resumed should not be confused with work that continues uninterrupted but has multiple *hand-over points*. The hand-over concept is illustrated in Figure 6-26 where the design and build activities each proceed interrupted, though multiple hand-over points (called "laddering") enable the build activity to start and continue well before the entire design activity

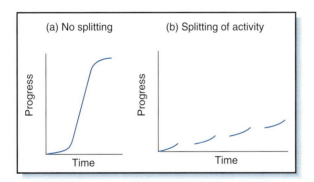

Figure 6-25
The effect of splitting of an activity on duration.

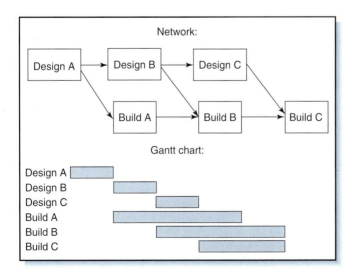

Figure 6-26
Multiple hand-over points of an uninterrupted activity.

(encompassing Design A + Design B + Design C) is completed. Although the activities appear to be split (Design A, Design B, Build A, Build B, etc.), in fact they are not. The method greatly reduces the project duration and facilitates interaction between designers and builders, the concurrent engineering approach described in Chapters 4 and 13.

Leveling Multiple Resources

Leveling is easy for a single resource but can be difficult for several resources simultaneously. Because work packages usually require resources from more than one functional unit or subcontractor, a schedule that provides a level loading for one organizational unit may cause overloading or difficult-to-manage fluctuations for others. For example, based on the weekly equipment requirements for LOGON shown in Table 6-6, the schedule that provides the somewhat-level worker loading in Figure 6-24 yields the erratic equipment loading shown in Figure 6-27. Any attempt to smooth the equipment loading by adjusting or delaying the schedule will disrupt the worker loading. (As you can verify, the schedule in Figure 6-23 that produced the erratic loading for workers yields a relatively balanced loading for equipment.)

It is impossible to level the loading for all resources at once. The best results arise from applying the scheduling equivalent of the "Pareto optimum"; that is, schedule the activities in the best interests of the project, but try to minimize the number of conflicts and problems in the departments and organizations that supply the resources. When considering multiple resources simultaneously, the schedule is adjusted to level the "priority" resources—resources where irregular loadings are the most costly to the project or demoralizing to workers. The high financial and social costs associated with hiring, overtime, and layoffs often dictate that "human resources"—the workers—be given the highest priority. Some project software packages perform scheduling analysis with simultaneous leveling of multiple resources.

Figure 6-27
Equipment loading for the LOGON project.

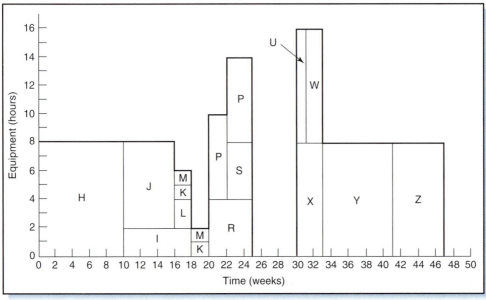

Delaying activities is one method of leveling resource utilization; others are to:

- Eliminate some work segments or activities.
- Substitute resources.
- Substitute less resource-consuming activities.

These methods eliminate or alter work segments and tasks to consume fewer or different resources. For example, when the most qualified workers are not available, either the work that requires their expertise must be eliminated from the plan or else less qualified workers must be called in. These options are compromises that might alter the scope or quality of the work and increase the risk of the project not meeting requirements.

Leveling of a Resource-Constrained Project

What happens when the number of personnel or pieces of equipment, or amount of working capital available restricts a schedule? This is called a *constrained resource* situation, and projects subject to it are called *resource-constrained projects*. Activities in the project must be scheduled so that the loading of a particular resource to the activities does not exceed an available maximum. The focus differs from resource leveling because the issue is not the resource loading's *variability* but its maximum requirement. As each activity is to be scheduled, the sum of its required resources plus the required resource for activities already scheduled at the same time must be checked against the amount available. This problem is more than just leveling of resources; it is rescheduling of jobs, often delaying them until such time when resources become available.

In the LOGON project, for example, suppose only 14 workers are available in any given week. The "leveled" schedule in Figure 6-24 results in a maximum loading of 15 workers. In this example, it is not possible to reduce the maximum loading to any number less than 15 and still complete the project in 47 weeks. To reduce the loading to the 14-worker maximum, some activities will have to be delayed beyond their late start dates, which will delay the project. With a problem like this something has to give: It is infeasible to both satisfy the resource restriction *and* to complete the project by the earliest completion time. Figure 6-28 shows a schedule that satisfies the 14-worker constraint. This schedule was determined by trial and error, making certain not to violate either the precedence requirements or the loading constraint of 14 workers. Notice that the project now requires 50 weeks to complete because Activity X had to be delayed 3 weeks beyond its late start date.

As the example shows, the need for a resource by multiple activities can dictate the project completion time and override the critical path time. Consider another example, again from the LOGON project. Suppose one important project resource is a technical inspector for the contractor, Iron Butterfly. This employee has skills that make her ideal for inspecting and approving a variety of project activities; however her work is quite exacting, which prevents her from working on more than one activity at a time. Suppose the activities in which she will be working are H, J, P, K, L, V, and X. These activities are highlighted in Figure 6-29. Because the same person to work on the activities highlighted can only work on them one at a time, those activities must be done sequentially. Adding the durations of these activities gives the time required for the technical inspector to complete her work, 36 weeks. Add to this the time for the last two Activities, Y and Z, and the total is 50 weeks. Therefore, the project duration will be 50 weeks, not the 47 weeks determined by the critical path. Goldratt distinguishes the path connecting activities that require the same constrained resource (here, H–J–P–K–L–V–X) from the critical path (H–J–M–R–V–X plus Y and Z) and calls it the *critical chain*.[3] In Figure 6-22 the critical path is ACD but the

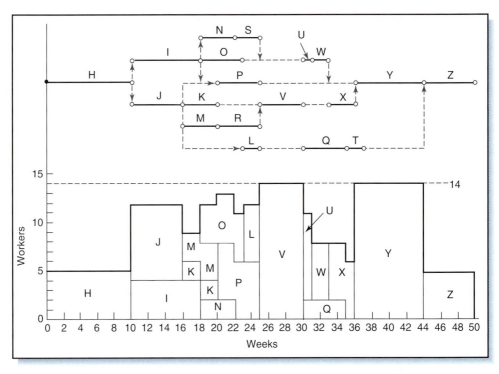

Figure 6-28
Schedule and corresponding worker loading for the LOGON project with 14-worker constraint.

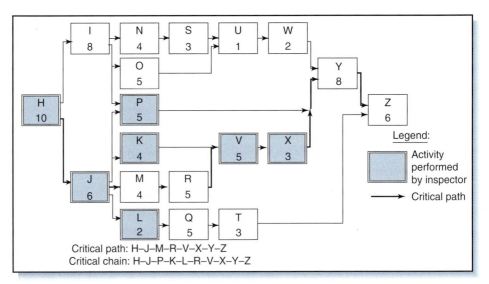

Critical path: H–J–M–R–V–X–Y–Z
Critical chain: H–J–P–K–L–R–V–X–Y–Z

Figure 6-29
Activities in the LOGON project involving the resource of technical inspector.

critical chain is either ACBD or ABCD. The significance of this is that when activities must be delayed and performed sequentially due to a constrained resource, and when the sum of the durations of those activities, the critical chain, exceeds the length of critical path, it is the critical chain—*not* the critical path—that sets the project duration. This is discussed again in the next chapter.

Scheduling with constrained resources involves decisions about which activities should be scheduled immediately and receive resources, and which should be delayed until resources are available. Project management software use procedures based on simple rules (called *heuristics*) for scheduling with constrained resources. Some of these heuristics are discussed in the next chapter.

The constrained-resource problem also occurs in multi-project organizations that draw resources from a common pool. To schedule activities for any one project, managers must take into account the resource requirements of other, concurrent projects. The result is that schedules for projects in these organizations are partly determined by when resources will be freed up from other, higher priority projects.

6.7 CRITICISMS OF NETWORK METHODS

Network methods as described in this chapter have been criticized because they incorporate assumptions and yield results that are sometimes unrealistic. For example, the methods assume that a project can be completely defined upfront in terms of identifiable activities with known precedence relationships. In many projects, however, not all work can be anticipated, and not all activities can be clearly defined at the start. Rather, the project "evolves" as it progresses. But this problem actually relates to scope planning, scope definition, and work definition, not scheduling.

A related problem is that the schedules sometimes require regular modification of activities and timelines; this happens when there are too many activities in the network or the activities are not well defined. The problem can be addressed by initially creating only a rough schedule, then developing more-detailed schedules in a phased approach as discussed in Chapter 4, and by avoiding "proliferation" of activities, i.e., keeping the number of activities in the plan to the essential minimum as prescribed in the work definition guidelines in Chapter 5.

Another criticism relates to the fact that in real projects it is sometimes difficult to demarcate one activity from the next, and the point of separation is more or less arbitrary. This means that successors can sometimes be started before predecessors are finished, and the two "overlap" in the sequence. But again, this is not really a problem. PDM allows for overlap of activities, and hand-over points treat activities as if they did overlap.

A further criticism is that precedence relationships are not always fixed, and that the start of an activity may be contingent upon the outcome of an earlier one that might have to be repeated. The results of a test activity, for example, may require redoing the prior activities of analysis and design, which in the network would be a "loop back" from the test activities to the activities that preceded it. The GERT method discussed in the next chapter deals somewhat with this inadequacy.

In summary, the shortcomings of networks are actually shortcoming in *any* project planning scheme. It can be argued (and innumerable project managers will attest) that the methods, though not perfect, offer a good approach for analyzing and creating project schedules.

6.8 SUMMARY

The advantage of networks is that they clearly display the interdependencies of project activities and show the scheduling impact that activities have on each other. This feature enables planners to determine critical activities and slack times, which is important in project planning and control. Knowledge of critical activities tells managers where to focus; knowledge of slack enables them to address the problems of non-uniform resource requirements and limited resources.

The common methods for network diagramming are AON and AOA (the latter described in the Appendix to this chapter). A variation of the AON method, PDM, allows for a variety of relationships between project activities to better reflect the realities of project work.

The next chapter describes other well-known and more-advanced network scheduling methods: Time–cost tradeoff analysis (CPM), PERT, simulation, critical chain, as well as a project modeling and scheduling method called GERT.

Summary List of Symbols

T_e	*Expected project duration*: the expected length of the project.
T_s	*Target project completion date*: the contracted or committed date for project completion.
ES	*Early start for an activity*: the earliest feasible time an activity can be started.
EF	*Early finish for an activity*: the earliest feasible time an activity can be completed.
LS	*Late start*: the latest allowable time an activity can be started to complete the project on target.
LF	*Late finish*: the latest allowable time an activity can be completed to complete the project on target.
t	*Activity time*: the most likely, or best guess of the time to complete an activity.
FS = n	*Finish-to-start*: an activity can start no sooner than n days after its immediate predecessor has finished.
SS = n	*Start-to-start*: an activity can start no sooner than n days after the start of its immediate predecessor.
SF = n	*Start-to-finish*: an activity can finish no later than n days after its immediate predecessor has started.
FF = n	*Finish-to-finish*: an activity can finish no later than n days after its immediate predecessor has finished.

Summary Illustration Problem

I. AON representation:

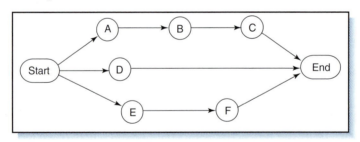

II. AOA representation, same example (refer to following Appendix):

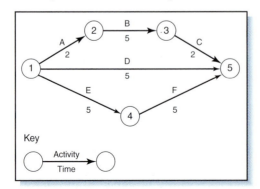

| ACTIVITY | TIME | ES | EF | LS | LF | SLACK | |
						TOTAL	FREE
A	2.0	0	2.0	0	3.0	1.0	0
B	5.0	3.0	7.0	4.0	8.0	1.0	0
C	2.0	8.0	9.0	9.0	10.0	1.0	1.0
D	5.0	0	5.0	5.0	10.0	5.0	5.0
E*	5.0	0	5.0	0	5.0	0	0
F*	5.0	6.0	10.0	6.0	10.0	0	0

* Activities on critical path

APPENDIX: AOA DIAGRAMS AND TIME-SCALED NETWORKS

AOA Diagrams

Besides AON, the most common method for diagramming networks is the *activity-on-arrow (AOA)* or *arrow diagramming* technique. The major feature that distinguishes AOA from AON is the way activities and events are denoted. Figure 6-30 shows the AOA representation for one activity and its events.

Notice that in the AOA method the activity is represented as a directed line segment (called an *arrow* or *arc*) between two nodes (or circles). As shown in Figure 6-30, the nodes represent the start and finish events for an activity, and the arrow between them represents the activity. The number inside each node merely identifies the event. The number need not be in any particular sequence, however it must be unique for the event (each event must have its own number).

The direction of the arrow indicates the flow of time in performing the activity, but like AON the length of the line has no significance (unlike Gantt charts where it is proportional to the activity duration). The number over the line is the activity duration.

As in AON networks, an AOA network should have only *one origin* event and *one terminal* event. All arrows must progress toward the right end of the network and there can be no doubling back or loops.

As with the AON method, the activities follow the order of precedence as defined by their immediate predecessors. When an activity has more than one immediate predecessor, the network must show that it cannot be started until *all* of its immediate predecessors have been completed. This is the purpose of a special kind of activity called a dummy.

Dummy Activities

A *dummy activity* is used to illustrate precedence relationships in AOA networks. It serves only as a "connector," however, it is not a "real" activity and represents neither

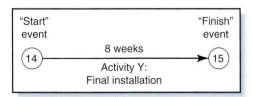

Figure 6-30
AOA representation for an activity and its start and finish events.

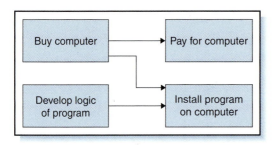

Figure 6-31
AON diagram.

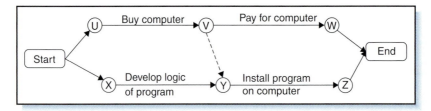

Figure 6-32
Figure 6-31 converted to AOA diagram.

work nor time. The following example demonstrates the need for dummy activities in an AOA network.[4]

A manager decides to have a new computer program written and also to buy a new computer to run the program on. The logic of dependencies between the activities is illustrated in the AON diagram Figure 6-31. There are three dependencies shown:

- The manager will pay for the computer after having bought it.
- The program will be installed on the computer after the logic of the program has been developed *and*
- The program will be installed on the computer after the computer has been bought.

Note that there is no dependency between developing the logic of the program and paying for computer.

The corresponding AOA diagram is shown in Figure 6-32. Note that there are still only three dependencies, although to show the second and third dependencies ("install program" and its immediate predecessors "buy computer" and "develop logic of program") requires a dummy activity between node V and node Y. With this dummy the dependencies are clear, including the fact that there is *no* dependency between "develop logic of program" and "pay for computer." Note that the network has only one "Start" and "End" node each.

Another AOA example is Figure 6-33, which is the network for the LOGON project and includes early and schedule times. Compare this to the AON network in Figure 6-8.

AON versus AOA

Because AON networks are constructed without use of dummies they are simpler and easier to construct; as a consequence, the AON method is somewhat more popular than AOA. Nonetheless the AOA method is often used, perhaps because it was developed first and is better suited for the PERT and CPM time–cost tradeoff procedures

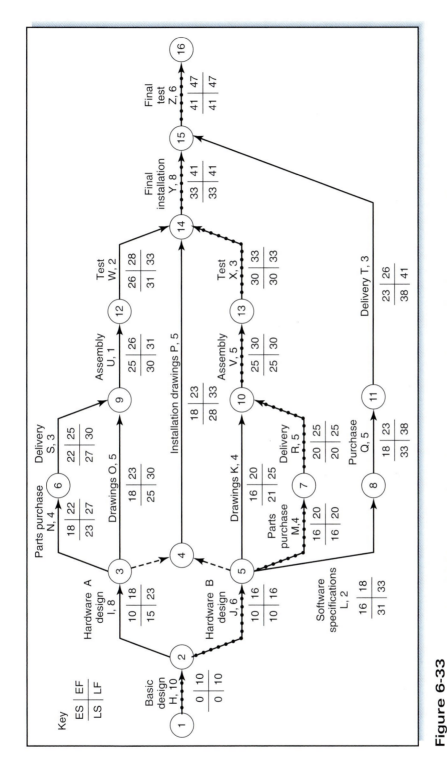

Figure 6-33

AOA network diagram for LOGON project. Note: Numbers in this figure differ from those in Figure 6-8 because in this figure activities are assumed to start *as soon as* their predecessors finish, whereas in Figure 6-8 they are assumed to start in the *next* period. Changing the assumptions would result in identical times in both AOA and AON networks.

229

described in the next chapter. The PERT model emphasizes project *events*, which in the AOA method are specifically designated by the nodes. Also, because AOA diagrams use line segments (the arrows) to represent the flow of work and time, they can easily be converted into time-scaled networks that look like Gantt charts. Most project software packages create time-scaled networks, and some create both AOA and AON networks diagrams. For a particular project, only one method should be used.

Time-Scaled Networks

An AOA network can be converted into a *time-scaled network* such as shown in Figure 6-34, which is for the LOGON project and is analogous to the AOA network

Figure 6-34
LOGON project: (a) Gantt chart, and corresponding time-scaled networks using (b) early start times and (c) late start times.

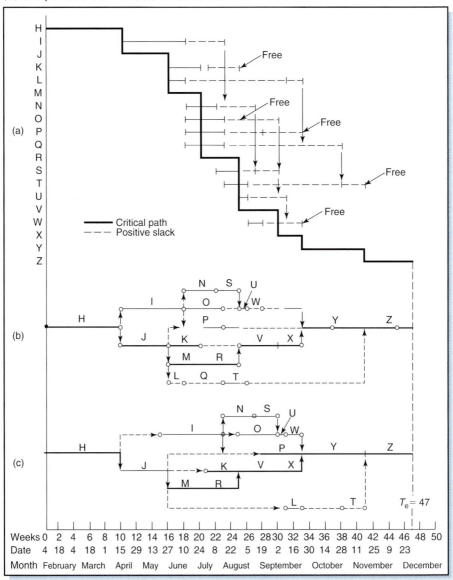

in Figure 6-33. The top of Figure 6-34 is a simple Gantt chart altered to show the critical path. The middle figure is the time-scaled version of the network in Figure 6-33 using the calendar format of the Gantt chart and early times. The bottom figure is the same time-scaled network using late times. The schedule uses weeks and assumes no work on weekends; however, it does not indicate holidays and vacations, which would extend T_e beyond 47 weeks.

Time-scaled networks have the advantages of both Gantt charts and networks because they show the calendar schedule as well as relationships among activities. As with Gantt charts, once the project is underway the network must be monitored and activities kept "current."

REVIEW QUESTIONS AND PROBLEMS

1. What are the advantages of networks over Gantt charts?
2. Draw a logic diagram of your college studies, starting with enrollment and finishing with graduation. Indicate the courses, projects, and exams as well as precedence relationships where applicable.
3. How is a WBS used to create a network and what role does a scope statement play?
4. Can a Gantt chart be created from a network? Can a network be created from a Gantt chart? Which is the preferred way? Explain.
5. Why is it vital to know the critical path? Explain the different ways the critical path is used in network analysis and project planning.
6. Explain the difference between total and free slack.
7. Explain the difference between ES, EF, LS, and LF.
8. Consider each of the following projects:
   (a) Composing and mailing a letter to an old friend.
   (b) Preparing a five-course meal (you specify the course and dishes served).
   (c) Planning a wedding for 500 people.
   (d) Building a sundeck for your home.
   (e) Planning, promoting, and conducting a rock concert.
   (f) Moving to another house or apartment.
   (g) Developing, promoting, manufacturing, and distributing a new packaged food item.
   (h) Developing and installing a computerized information system, both hardware and software.
   (i) Remodel a bathroom.
   (j) Add a bedroom to a house.

   Now, answer the following questions for each project:

   (i) Using your experience or imagination, create a WBS.
   (ii) List the activities or work packages.
   (iii) Show the immediate predecessors for each activity.
   (iv) Draw the network diagram (using the AON scheme).

9. (a) Draw the AON network diagrams for the following four projects:

(i)

Activity	Immediate Predecessor
A	—
B	A
C	A
D	B
E	D
F	D
G	D
H	E, F, G

(ii)

Activity	Immediate Predecessor
A	—
B	A
C	A
D	B
E	B
F	C
G	D
H	D
I	G
J	E, F, H, I

(iii)

Activity	Immediate Predecessor
A	—
B	A
C	—
D	—
E	D
F	B, C, E

(iv)

Activity	Immediate Predecessor
A	—
B	—
C	—
D	C
E	A
F	B
G	E
H	F, G, J
I	A
J	D, I

(b) Convert the networks into event-oriented networks.

10. Refer to Figure 6-1 in the text.

(a) If the person wants to get more sleep by waking up later, which of the following steps would be useful?

(i) Put socks on faster

(ii) Put tie in pocket to put on later

(iii) Put shoes on faster

(iv) Buy a hair dryer that works faster

(b) Calculate the total float and free float of the activity "Put on socks."

11. Eliminate redundant predecessors from the following lists so that only immediate predecessors remain.

(a)

Activity	Immediate Predecessor
A	—
B	—
C	—
D	B
E	C
F	A
G	B, D, C, E
H	A, B, C, D, E, F, G

(b)

Activity	Immediate Predecessor
A	—
B	A
C	A
D	A, B
E	A, B
F	A, C
G	A, B, C, D, E, F
H	A, B, C, D, E, G

(c)

Activity	Immediate Predecessor
A	—
B	—
C	A
D	A
E	B
F	B
G	A, C
H	A, B, D, E
I	B, F
J	C, D, E, F, G, H, I

12. Use Figure 6-5(a) and (b) to draw Gantt charts for the ROSEBUD project.
13. The table below lists activities for constructing a bridge over an operational railway line:[5]

Activity Number	Activity Description	Duration (Months)	Predecessors
A	Detail site investigation and survey	2	—
B	Detail Planning	6	A
C	Detail design	6	B
D	Preparation of site	4	C
E	Relocate services	3	C
F	Re-align overhead track electrification	4	C, E
G	Access road and ramp construction	1	D
H	Piling	2	G
J	Construct foundations and abutments	3	H
K	Construct temporary supports to support bridge deck during construction	2	F, G
L	Fabrication planning of structural steel components	2	C

(*Continued*)

Activity Number	Activity Description	Duration (Months)	Predecessors
M	Manufacture structural steel components (off-site)	2	L
N	Transport structural steel components and erect on-site	1	M
P	Erect pylons and fill with concrete	2	J
Q	Construct main span deck on pre-cast concrete beams	3	H, K, N, P
R	Install cable-stays and lift deck off temporary supports	3	Q
S	Remove temporary supports	1	R
T	Electrical system installation	1	S
U	Roadway surfacing (paving)	2	S
V	Finishing and ancillaries	2	T, U
W	Commissioning—cut-over	1	V
X	Formal hand-over and ceremony	1	W
Y	Project Sign-off	1	X
Z	Administrative closure	1	W
AA	Project End	0 (milestone)	Y, Z

    (a)   Construct a network diagram for the project

    (b)   Do forward and backward pass calculations to indicate early and late start and finish times

    (c)   Indicate the critical path

    (d)   Indicate the total and free slack of each activity

14. Some projects have a fixed due date while others have to be finished as early as possible and the project manager only makes commitments on the completion date once she and her project management team have scheduled the project. Explain how the backward pass differs for these two project types.

15. Explain how it is possible for there to be slack on the critical path. What is the implication of negative slack on the critical path?

16. In the development of a new (first of its kind) complex system, the design of a certain subsystem has large slack. Sufficient resources are available for either an early start or a late start. Discuss the pros and cons of early and late starts. Consider the risk of delaying the project, the risk of changes in the design, management focus, cash flow, and any other factor you can think of.[6]

17. What limitations of AON networks does PDM overcome? What limitations does it not overcome?

18. Give examples of applications of PDM. Take a project you are familiar with (or invent one) and create a PDM network.

19. For the PDM network in Figure 6-20, calculate ES, EF, LS, and LF for all activities.

20. To produce a manual, John has to write the text, after which Ann has to draw sketches and typeset the document. John can start with any section of the book (i.e., he does not have to start with Section 1). The work has to be done within 95 days. The network diagram below shows the precedence relationships and duration of each activity. Draw a Gantt chart to show how the work can be done within 95 days. Take into account that both John and Ann are able to attend to only one task at a time.[7]

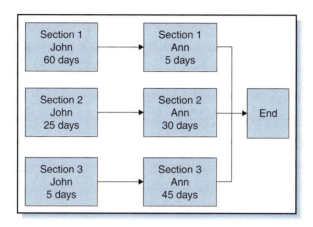

21. Why is leveling of resources preferred to large fluctuation of workload? What negative result could resource leveling cause?

22. Describe how resource leveling of a resource-constrained project differs from resource leveling in a time-constrained project.

23. The network and associated requirements for systems analysts and programmers for the GUMBY project are as follows:

Activity	J	M	V	Y	L	Q	Z
Predecessors	–	J	M	V	J	L	Y,Q
Duration (weeks)	6	4	6	8	2	8	2
Systems Analysts (weekly)	8	5	3	2	5	3	5
Programmers (weekly)	3	4	2	3	3	2	3

(a) Draw the network. Compute ESs, LSs, and total slack times.

(b) Then show the separate resource loadings for systems analysts and programmers, assuming ESs.

(c) Suppose the maximum weekly availability is eight systems analysts and five programmers. Can activities be scheduled to satisfy these constraints without delaying the project?

24. Level the resources for a project with the workload diagram below. In the time-phased diagram at the top of the diagram, dotted lines indicate slack.[8] Discuss pros and cons of the alternatives available.

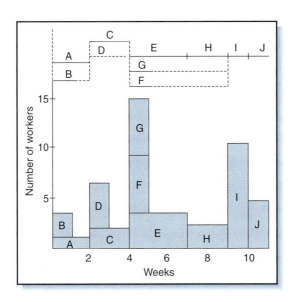

25. The following resources are required to perform the activities listed in Problem 13 above:

Activity Number	Activity Description	Resources
A	Detail site investigation and survey	Surveyors, Engineering, Project Manager
B	Detail planning	Project Manager, Engineering, Construction, Contractors
C	Detail design	Engineering
D	Preparation of site	Construction
E	Relocate services	Engineering
F	Re-align overhead track electrification	Engineering, Contractors
G	Access road and ramp construction	Construction
H	Piling	Construction, Contractors
J	Construct foundations and abutments	Engineering, Construction
K	Construct temporary supports to support bridge deck during construction	Engineering, Construction
L	Fabrication planning of structural steel components	Engineering, Manufacturer
M	Manufacture structural steel components (off-site)	Engineering, Manufacturer
N	Transport structural steel components and erect on-site	Transporter, Engineering
P	Erect pylons and fill with concrete	Construction, Engineering
Q	Construct main span deck on pre-cast concrete beams	Construction, Engineering

Activity Number	Activity Description	Resources
R	Install cable-stays and lift deck off temporary supports	Construction, Engineering
S	Remove temporary supports	Construction, Engineering
T	Electrical system installation	Construction, Engineering
U	Roadway surfacing (paving)	Contractor, Engineering
V	Finishing and ancillaries	Contractors, Engineering
W	Commissioning—cut-over	Project Manager, Engineering, Construction, Contractors
X	Formal hand-over and ceremony	Project Manager, Engineering, Construction, Contractors
Y	Project Sign-off	Project Manager, Engineering
Z	Administrative closure	Engineering
AA	Project End	Project Manager

Allocate the resources to the activities and indicate the workload on the resources. If needed, adjust the schedule.

26. Discuss the implications of resource allocation for organizations involved in multiple projects.

27. Show that the schedule in Figure 6-23 (which produced an erratic loading for workers) yields a more balanced loading for equipment than the one shown in Figure 6-27.

28. Suppose in Figure 6-20 everything is the same except Activity Y can start 4 days after Activity V starts, but cannot be finished until 6 days after Activity V is finished. Show how this changes the values for ES, EF, LS, and LF.

29. Redraw the networks in Problem 9 above, using the AOA method.

30. Redraw Figure 6-6 using the AOA method.

31. For each of the following AOA networks:
    - Draw a corresponding AON network.
    - Compute ES and EF for each activity.
    - Compute LS and LF for each activity. Find the critical path.
    - Determine the total slack and free slack.

(a)

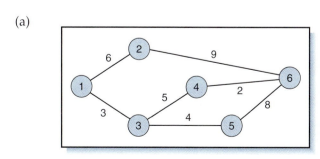

(b)

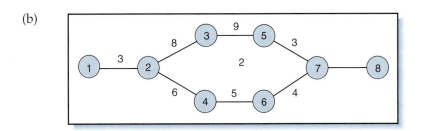

(c)

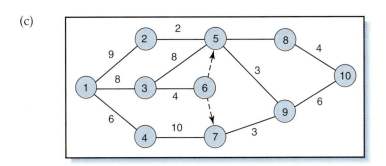

(d)

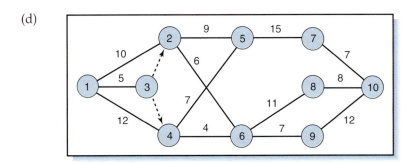

QUESTIONS ABOUT THE STUDY PROJECT

1. Were networks used for scheduling? If so, describe the networks. Show examples. What kind of computer software system was used to create and maintain them? Who was responsible for system inputs and system operations? Describe the capabilities of the software system.

2. At what point in the project were networks created? When were they updated?

3. Was all detailed planning done upfront or was a phased approach followed?

4. How was the schedule reserve (if any) determined and included into the schedule?

5. Were AOA, AON, or PDM networks used? Describe the applications and show examples.

6. Was the workload on resources made visible?

7. If the project was done within a matrix structure, how did communication between the functional and project managers take place?

8. Did the functional manager(s) take responsibility for workload on resources?

9. Was resource leveling done?

10. Were there any complaints about unrealistic workloads?

ENDNOTES

1. W.R. Duncan (ed.), *A Guide to the Project Management Body of Knowledge* (Newton Square, PA: Project Management Institute Standards Committee, 1996). The definition of the critical path in later editions of this document does not state explicitly that the critical path changes from time to time, but that does not change this fact.

2. For more about PDM scheduling, see J.B. Dreger, *Project Management: Effective Scheduling* (New York: Van Nostrand Reinhold, 1992).

3. E.M. Goldratt, *Critical Chain* (Great Barrington, MA: North River Press, 1997).

4. Adapted from J.D. Gordon and R.L. Villoria, *Network-based Management Systems (PERT/CPM)* (New York: John Wiley & Sons, 1967).

5. H. Steyn (ed.), *Project Management a Multi-disciplinary Approach* (Pretoria: FPM Publishing, 2003). Reproduced with permission.

6. Ibid.

7. Ibid.

8. Ibid.

Chapter 7

Advanced Project Network Analyses and Scheduling

Look beneath the surface: never let a thing's intrinsic qualities or worth escape you

—MARCUS AURELIUS
Meditations

*T*he scheduling methods discussed in Chapter 6 assume that activity times are known and fixed, ignoring the fact that in reality they are somewhat unknown and variable. This chapter elaborates on the implications of variable activity times and discusses methods for handling uncertainty about the project completion date. It also addresses that fact that projects often take too long and discusses methods for reducing project duration, starting with CPM.

7.1   CPM AND TIME–COST TRADEOFF

The *critical-path method* (*CPM*) is a systematic approach for allocating resources among activities to achieve the greatest reduction in project duration for the least cost. Developed in 1957 by DuPont Company, Remington Rand, and Mauchy Associates in an industrial setting (a plant construction project for DuPont), it includes a mathematical procedure for estimating the tradeoff between project duration and project cost.[1]

Example 1: The House Built in Less Than 4 Hours[2]

With virtually unlimited resources, suitable project management methods, and meticulous planning, a project can be done *very* fast. On March 13, 1999 the Manukau, New Zealand Chapter of Habitat for Humanity (the international non-profit organization dedicated to eliminating poverty housing) smashed the previous record for building a house (4 hours 39 minutes, set in 1987 in Nashville, USA) by building one in only 3 hours, 45 minutes.

The project specification included construction of a four-bedroom house on an established foundation (Figure 7-1). It incorporated prefabricated wall panels, a wooden floor, roofing iron, ceilings, decks, and steps. Doors, windows, a bath, toilet and plumbing, as well as the electrical system had to be fitted and ready for use; walls, ceilings, and window frames had to be painted; carpets had to be laid and curtains hung. The specifications also included a path to the front door, letter box, installed clothesline, wooden fence around the yard perimeter, three trees planted, and lawn leveled and grassed. The new owners, Mr. and Mrs. Suafoa, watched the construction with their four children while CNN filmed the event. The house passed all local building codes, and the keys were handed over to the family.

What made the speedy completion possible? First was an abundance of resources: 150 people (mostly volunteers). Second, but no less important, was comprehensive and meticulous preparation: 14 months of planning including many iterations of network analysis. The detailed plan was recorded on special task sheets so that team leaders could hand over tasks from one to another without deliberation. With so many people and construction material items at the site, workspace was at a premium and had to be planned carefully. A crane was provided to lift the wooden roof frame onto the wall structure. Third was a systematic computerized method for planning, monitoring, and controlling the project that included the critical chain method (CCM) and time buffers. (The bathroom-fitting task was estimated to take 30 minutes, but took 1 hour; the 30-minute overrun was absorbed in the project buffer.) Finally was the use of suitable technology, including prefabricated wall technology developed by a New Zealand company.

Figure 7-1

The house built in less than 4 hours. (Photo courtesy of Habitat for Humanity.)

Time–Cost Relationship

CPM assumes that the time to perform any project activity is variable depending on the amount of effort or resources applied, and that the completion time for a project can be shortened by applying additional resources (labor, equipment, capital) to particular key activities.

Ordinarily, work on any given activity in a project is performed at a *normal* (usual and customary) work pace. This is the "normal" point shown in Figure 7-2. Associated with this pace is the *normal time*, T_n, i.e., how long the activity will take under normal work conditions, and the *normal cost*, C_n, which is the price of doing the activity in the normal time. (Usually the normal pace is assumed to be the most efficient and thus *least costly* pace. Extending the activity beyond the normal pace will not produce additional savings and might cause a cost increase.)

To reduce the time to complete the activity, more resources are applied in the form of additional personnel or overtime. As more resources are applied, the duration is shortened, but the cost increases. When the maximum effort is applied so that the activity can be completed in the shortest possible time, the activity is said to be *crashed*. The crash condition represents not only the shortest duration, but the *most costly* as well. This is the "crash" point shown in Figure 7-2. Sometimes, however, there is no time–cost tradeoff; the activity is *process limited*, meaning the activity requires a specific time that cannot be changed regardless of resources. An example is the time needed for the fermentation process for wine or beer.

As illustrated in Figure 7-2, the time–cost of completing an activity under normal conditions and under crash conditions define two theoretical extreme points. The line connecting these points, called the *cost slope*, represents the time–cost relationship or marginal tradeoff of cost-to-time for the activity. Every activity has its own unique time–cost relationship. The relationship can be linear, curvilinear (concave or convex), or a step function. Because the shape of the actual time–cost relationship is often not known, a simple linear relationship is assumed.[3] Given this assumption, the formula for the cost slope is:

$$\text{Cost slope} = \frac{C_c - C_n}{T_c - T_n}$$

where C_c and C_n are the crash and normal costs, respectively, and T_c and T_n are the crash and normal times for the same activity. The cost slope is how much the cost of the activity would change if activities were sped up or slowed down.

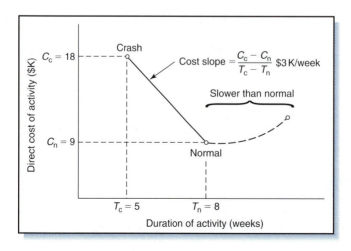

Figure 7-2
Time–cost relationship for an activity.

Using the formula, the cost slope for the activity in Figure 7-2 is $3K per week. Thus, for *each week* the activity duration is reduced (sped up) from the normal time of 8 weeks, the additional cost will be $3K. Completing the activity 1 week earlier (from 8 to 7 weeks) would increase the cost of the activity from the normal cost of $9K to the "sped up" cost of $9K + $3K = $12K; completing it another week earlier (in 6 weeks) would increase the cost to $12K + $3K = $15K; completing it yet another week earlier (in 5 weeks) would increase the cost to $18K. According to Figure 7-2, this last step puts the activity at the crash point, the shortest possible completion time for the activity.

Reducing Project Duration

The cost-slope concept can be used to determine the most efficient way of shortening a project. The AOA network in Figure 7-3 illustrates this with an example. Start with the preliminary project schedule by assuming a normal pace for all activities; therefore, the project in the figure can be completed in 22 weeks at an expense of $55K. Suppose we want to shorten the project duration. Recall from Chapter 6 that the project duration is the length of the critical path. Because the critical Path A–D–G is the longest path (22 weeks), the way to shorten the project is to simply shorten any critical activity—A, D, or G. Reducing an activity increases its cost, but because the reduction can be made *anywhere* on the critical path, the cost increase is minimized by selecting the activity with the smallest cost slope, which is Activity A. Reducing A by 1 week shortens the project duration to 21 weeks and adds $2K (the cost slope of A) to the project cost, bringing it to $55K + $2K = $57K. This step does not change the critical path so, if need be, an additional week can be cut from A to give a project duration of 20 weeks for a cost of $57K + $2K = $59K.

With this second step, the nature of the problem changes. As the top network in Figure 7-4 shows, shortening A uses up all of the slack on Path B–E, so the network now has two critical paths: A–D–G and B–E–G. Any further reduction in project duration must be made by shortening *both* paths because shortening just one would leave the other at 20 weeks. The least costly way to reduce the project to 19 weeks is to reduce both A and E by 1 week, as shown in the bottom network in Figure 7-4. The additional cost is $2K for A and $2K for E, so the resulting project cost would

Figure 7-3
Time–cost tradeoff for example network.

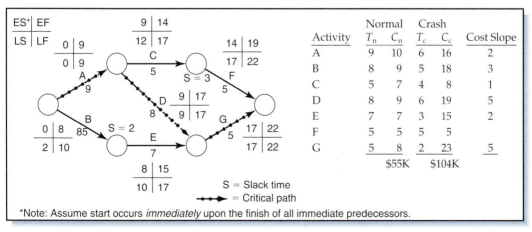

Activity	Normal T_n	Normal C_n	Crash T_c	Crash C_c	Cost Slope
A	9	10	6	16	2
B	8	9	5	18	3
C	5	7	4	8	1
D	8	9	6	19	5
E	7	7	3	15	2
F	5	5	5	5	
G	5	8	2	23	5
		$55K		$104K	

S = Slack time
◄••► = Critical path
*Note: Assume start occurs *immediately* upon the finish of all immediate predecessors.

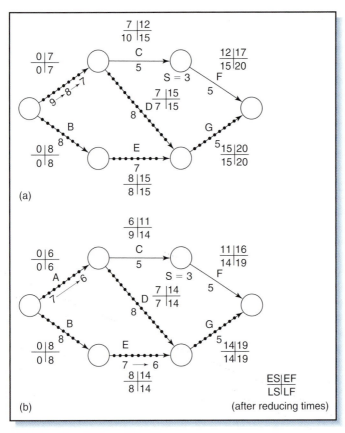

Figure 7-4
Reducing project completion time. (a) Results of steps 2 and 3, and (b) result of step 4.

increase to $59K + $2K + $2K = $63K. This last step reduces A to 6 weeks, its crash time, so no further reductions can be made to A.

If a further reduction in project time is desired, the least costly way to shorten both paths is to reduce G. In fact, because the slack time on the noncritical Path C–F is 3 weeks, and because the crash time for G is 2 weeks (which means, if desired, 3 weeks *can* be taken out of G), the project can be reduced to 16 weeks by shortening G by 3 weeks. This adds $5K per week, or 3 × $5K = $15K to the project cost. With this last step, all slack is used up on Path C–F, and all the paths in the network (A–C–F, A–D–G, and B–E–G) become critical.

Any further reductions desired in the project must shorten *all three critical paths* (A–C–F, A–D–G, and B–E–G). As you may wish to verify, the most economical way to reduce the project to 15 weeks is to cut 1 week each from E, D, and C, bringing the project cost up to $86K. This step reduces the time of C to its crash time, which precludes shortening the project completion time any further. The sequence of steps is summarized in Table 7-1.

Shortest Project Duration

The time–cost procedure described determines which activities to speed up, step-by-step, so as to reduce the project completion time. This stepwise reduction of the project duration eventually leads to the shortest possible project duration and its

Table 7-1 Duration reduction and associated cost increase.

STEP	DURATION (T_E, WEEKS)	ACTIVITIES ON CP WITH LEAST COST SLOPE	COST OF PROJECT (K$)
1*	22		$55
2	21	A ($2)	$55 + $2 = $57
3	20	A ($2)	$57 + $2 = $59
4	19	A ($2), E ($2)	$59 + $2 + $2 = $63
5, 6, 7	18, 17, 16	G ($5)	$63 + $5 + $5 + $5 = $78
8	15	E ($2), D ($5), C ($1)	$78 + $2 + $5 + $1 = $86

*Duration and cost using normal conditions.

associated cost. However, if we want to directly find the *shortest possible project duration* and avoid the intermediate steps, a simpler procedure is to simultaneously crash *all* activities at once. This, as Figure 7-5 shows, also yields the project duration of 15 weeks. However, the expense of crashing all activities, $104K (table in Figure 7-3), is artificially high because, as will be shown, *not* all activities need to be crashed to finish the project in the shortest time.

The project completion time of 15 weeks is the time along the critical path. Because the critical path is the longest path, other (noncritical) paths are of shorter duration and, consequently, have no influence on project duration. Thus, it is possible to "stretch" or increase any noncritical activity by a certain amount without lengthening the project. In fact, the noncritical activities can be stretched until all the slack in the network is used up.

Just as reducing an activity's time from the normal time increases its cost, so stretching its time from the crash time *reduces* its cost. As a result, by stretching noncritical jobs the project crash cost of $104K can be reduced. To do so, start with those noncritical activities that will yield the greatest savings—those with the greatest cost slope. Notice in Figure 7-5 that because Path B–E–G has a slack time of 5 weeks, activities along this path can be stretched by up to 5 weeks without extending the project. Three weeks can be added to Activity B (bringing it to the normal time of 8 weeks) without lengthening the project. Also, 2 weeks can be added to E and 1 week

Figure 7-5
Example network using crash times.

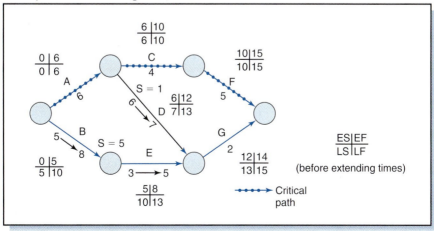

to D, both without changing the project duration. The final project cost is computed by subtracting the savings obtained in stretching B by 3 weeks, E by 2 weeks, and D by 1 week from the initial crash cost:

$$\$104K - 3(\$3K) - 2(\$2K) - 1(\$5K) = \$86K$$

In general, to obtain the shortest project duration, start by crashing all activities, and then stretch the noncritical activities with the greatest cost slopes to use up available slack and obtain the greatest cost savings. An activity can be stretched up to its normal time, which is assumed to be its least costly time (Figure 7-2).

Total Project Cost

The previous analysis dealt only with direct costs—costs immediately associated with individual activities that increase directly as the activities are expedited. But the cost of conducting a project includes more than direct activity costs; it also includes *indirect* costs such as administrative and overhead charges. (The distinction between direct and indirect cost is elaborated upon in the next chapter.) Usually indirect costs are a function of, and increase proportionately to, the duration of the project. In other words, indirect costs, in contrast to direct costs, *decrease as the project duration decreases.*

The mathematical function for indirect cost can be derived by estimation or a formula as established in an incentive type contract. As an illustration, suppose indirect costs in the previous example are approximated by the formula:

$$\text{Indirect cost} = \$10K + \$3K(T_e)$$

where T_e is the expected project duration in weeks. This is represented by the indirect cost line in Figure 7-6. Also shown is the *total project cost*, which is computed by summing indirect and direct costs. Notice from the figure that by combining indirect costs and direct costs it is possible to determine the project duration that gives the lowest total project cost. Figure 7-6 shows that from a cost standpoint, 20 weeks is the "optimum" project duration.

In addition to direct and indirect costs, another cost that influences total project cost (and hence the optimum T_e) is any *contractual incentive* such as a *penalty charge* or a *bonus payment*. A penalty charge is a late fee imposed on the contractor for not completing a facility or product on time. A bonus payment is a reward—a cash inducement—for completing the project early. The specific terms of penalties and bonuses are specified in incentive type contracts such as described in Appendix B at the end of the book.

In the previous example, suppose the contract agreement is to complete the project by week 18. The contract provides for a bonus of $2K per week for finishing before 18 weeks, and a $1K per week penalty for finishing after 18 weeks. Figure 7-7 shows these incentives and their influence on total project cost. Notice that even with incentives, the optimum completion time (for the contractor) is at 19 or 20 weeks, not the contractual 18 weeks. This example reveals that a formal incentive agreement alone is not necessarily enough to influence performance. For the incentive to motivate the contractor it must have "teeth"; in other words, it should be of sufficient magnitude with respect to other project costs to affect contractor performance. Had the penalty been raised to an amount over $2K (instead of $1K) per week for finishing after 18 weeks, the contractor's optimum completion time would have shifted to 18 weeks.

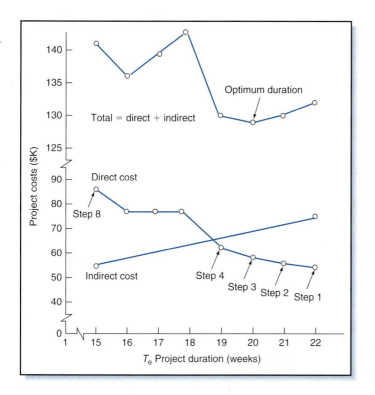

Figure 7-6
Total time–cost tradeoff for the project.

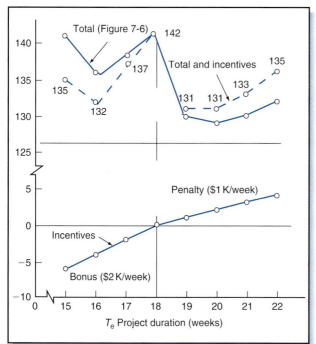

Figure 7-7
Time–cost tradeoff for the project with incentives.

7.2 VARIABILITY OF ACTIVITY DURATION

Suppose you are driving to some destination. Figure 7-8 illustrates the time it will take you to get there and the variability in that time. If everything goes well (little traffic and no mechanical problems) you will get there very quickly; this is the "optimistic duration." Most likely, however, it will take you longer than this. In fact, if you were to repeat the trip several times you would arrive most often in the "most likely duration" time of 30 minutes. Of course, it could take longer than this—say, when traffic is congested or, worse yet, you end up in an accident. Note in the figure that the area below the curve to the left of the most likely duration is much less than the area under the curve to the right of it. This indicates that the chances of you arriving later than the most likely time are greater than the chances of you arriving earlier.

Like your travel time, the activity durations in a project are variable. The question is, given that you cannot say for sure how long each activity will take, how can you possibly say when the project will be completed?

The scheduling approach taken in Chapter 6 ignores variability and assumes that activity durations are constant; this is called the *deterministic* approach. In the following sections we consider that activities durations are variable; this is called the *stochastic* approach.

Variability Effects on a Project Network

Figure 7-8 relates to a single activity. In a project some activities will be completed earlier than expected, others later. When activities are combined in a network, however, the early activities and late activities do not average out: in general, *it is only the late activities that impact the project completion*, which is one reason why projects tend to take longer than estimated.

Consider for example Activity A in Figure 7-9. Should Activity A take longer than planned, it would delay Activity B, which in turn would delay Activities C and D and, thus, the completion of the project. Suppose however that Activity A is finished

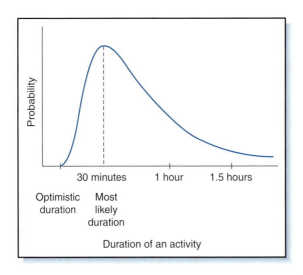

Figure 7-8
Variability of activity duration.

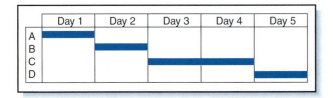

Figure 7-9
Activities delayed if
Activity A is delayed.

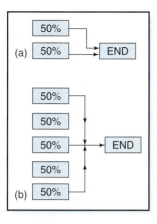

Figure 7-10
Activities delayed where paths merge. (a) Two paths merging, each with 50 percent chance of being on time (b) Five paths merging, each with 50 percent chance of being on time.

earlier than planned. In that case will Activity B start earlier? Not necessarily. Resources needed for Activity B such as people and equipment will likely have other commitments, which would preclude Activity B starting before the scheduled start date.

Consider a second example. Most project networks consist of several paths that merge together or feed into a critical path. Figure 7-10(a) illustrates a project with two critical paths, each with a 50 percent chance of finishing on time. The probability that the project will finish on time is the probability that both paths will finish on time, or $0.5 \times 0.5 = 0.25$ or 25 percent. Figure 7-10(b) shows five paths merging (which is typical of what happens near the end of project networks), each with a 50 percent probability of finishing on time. The probability of finishing the project on time is now $(0.5)^5$ or about 3 percent. This effect is called *merge bias* or *merge-point bias*.

Chapter 6 addressed the fact that the critical path is not necessarily stable but can change if noncritical activities take longer than planned or critical activities take less time than planned. As a result of the variability in activity durations and non-critical paths becoming critical, the project is delayed.

Several methods have been developed to help grapple with the uncertainty about when a project will likely be completed. This chapter addresses some of them, starting with PERT.

7.3 PERT

The PERT method was developed explicitly for application in projects where the activity durations are uncertain. It originated during the US Navy's Polaris Missile System program, the perfect example of a complex research and development program with uncertainty about the kind of research to be done, the stages of development needed, and how fast they can be completed. Projects like this are contracted while new developments are still unfolding and before many of the problems in technology, materials, and processes have been identified. The duration of the project is uncertain and there is great risk the project will overrun the target completion time.

To provide a degree of certainty in the duration of the Polaris program, a special operations research team was formed in 1958 with representatives from the Navy's Special Projects Office, the consulting firm of Booz, Allen, and Hamilton, and the prime contractor Lockheed Missile Systems. The method they devised was called PERT for Program Evaluation and Review Technique.[4]

PERT is a technique to estimate the likelihood (or probability) of a project finishing on time. The purpose of PERT is to analyze the project network (and the Gantt charts resulting from the network), not to create a schedule. The method provides insight on the likelihood of finishing a project by a certain time, though it says nothing about how to increase that likelihood or reduce the duration of a project.

Three Time Estimates

The network methods discussed in Chapter 6 determine the critical path and slack times using *best estimates* for activity duration times. PERT, however, addresses uncertainty in the duration times by using three time estimates—*optimistic, most likely*, and *pessimistic*. Presumably the three estimates are obtained from people who are most knowledgeable about difficulties likely to be encountered and the potential variability in time; usually they are expert estimators or the people who will perform or manage the activity.

The three estimates are used to calculate the "*expected time*" for an activity. The range between the optimistic and pessimistic estimates is a measure of variability that permits making statistical inferences about the likelihood that project events will happen by a particular time.

As seen in Figure 7-11 the *optimistic time, a,* is the minimum time for an activity—the situation where everything goes well and there is little hope of finishing earlier. The *most likely* time, *m*, is the time that would occur most often if the activity were repeated. Finally, the *pessimistic* time, *b*, is the maximum time for an activity—the situation where bad luck is encountered at every step. The pessimistic time

Figure 7-11
Estimating activity duration time.

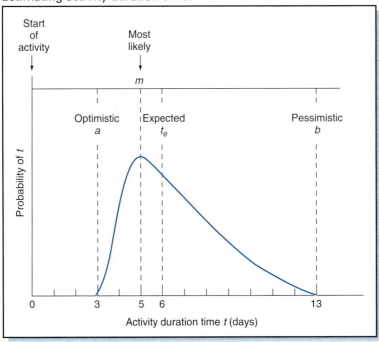

includes likely problems in work, but not highly unlikely events such as natural disasters. In all cases, a normal level of effort is assumed with no extra personnel.

The three estimates in Figure 7-11 are related in the form of a *Beta* probability distribution with parameters a and b as the end points, and m the modal, or most frequent, value. The choice of the Beta distribution was not based on empirical data, but rather because it is unimodal (has a single peak value) and not necessarily symmetrical—properties that seem desirable for a distribution of activity times.[5] Note that whereas the distribution in Figure 7-8 had no end point on the right-hand side, the curve in Figure 7-11 disallows very unlikely events and has cutoff point b.

Based on this distribution and the three time estimates, the *mean* or *expected* time, t_e, and the *variance*, V, of each activity are computed with the following formulas:

$$t_e = \frac{a + 4m + b}{6}$$

$$V = \left(\frac{b - a}{6}\right)^2$$

Since $V = \sigma^2$,

$$\sigma = \frac{b - a}{6}$$

The expected time, t_e, represents the point on the distribution in Figure 7-11 with a 50-50 chance that the activity will be completed earlier or later than it. In the figure:

$$t_e = \frac{3 + 4(5) + 13}{6} = 6 \text{ days}$$

The variance, V, is a measure of variability in the activity completion time:

$$V = \left(\frac{13 - 3}{6}\right)^2 = (1.67 \text{ days})^2 = 2.78 \text{ days}$$

The larger V, the less reliable t_e, and the higher the likelihood the activity will be completed much earlier or much later than t_e. This simply reflects that the farther apart a and b, the more dispersed the distribution and the greater the chance that the actual time will significantly differ from the expected time. In a routine (repetitive) job, estimates of a and b are close to each other, V is small, and t_e is more likely.

Probability of Finishing by a Target Completion Date

The expected time, t_e, is used in the same way as the estimated activity duration time was used in the deterministic networks in Chapter 6. Because statistically the expected time of a sequence of independent activities is the sum of their individual expected times, the expected duration of the *project*, T_e, is the sum of the expected activity times along the critical path:

$$T_e = \sum_{CP} t_e$$

where each t_e is the expected time of an activity on the critical path.

PERT uses a stochastic approach, hence the project duration is not considered a point but rather an estimate subject to uncertainty owing to the uncertainties of the activity times along the critical path. Because the project duration T_e is computed as the sum of average activity times along the critical path, it follows that T_e is also an average time. Thus, the project duration can be thought of as a probability distribution with an *average* of T_e. Thus the probability of completing the project sooner than T_e is 50 percent, and so is the probability of completing it later than T_e.

The variation in the project duration distribution is computed as the sum of the variances of the activity durations along the critical path:

$$V_P = \sum_{CP} V$$

where V is the variance of an activity on the critical path. (For justification, refer to Appendix A).

These concepts are illustrated in the AON network in Figure 7-12.

The distribution of project durations is assumed to be the normal, the familiar bell-shaped curve (see Appendix to this chapter for justification). Given this assumption, it is easy to determine the probability of meeting any specified project target completion date T_s.

As examples, consider two questions about the project shown in Figure 7-12: (1) What is the probability of completing the project in 27 days? (2) What is the *latest* likely date by which the project will be completed? Both questions can be answered by determining the number of standard deviations that separate T_s from T_e. The formula for the calculation is:

$$z = \frac{T_s - T_e}{\sqrt{V_P}}$$

Figure 7-12
PERT network with expected activity times and activity variances.

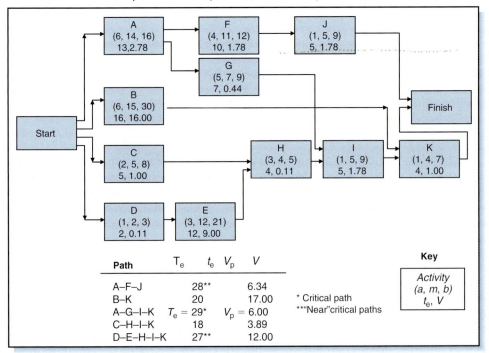

Path	T_e	t_e V_p	V
A–F–J	28**		6.34
B–K	20		17.00
A–G–I–K	$T_e = 29^*$	$V_p = 6.00$	
C–H–I–K	18		3.89
D–E–H–I–K	27**		12.00

* Critical path
***"Near" critical paths

Key

Activity
(a, m, b)
t_e, V

To answer the first question, use $T_s = 27$ days. From the network, the expected project duration, T_e, is computed as 29 days. Therefore:

$$z = \frac{27 - 29}{\sqrt{6}} = -0.82$$

The probability of completing the project within 27 days is equal to the area under the normal curve to the left of $z = -0.82$. Referring to Table 7-2(a), the probability is about 21 percent. (With such a low probability, the project will probably finish later than $T_s = 27$ days.)

To answer the second question, suppose we rephrase it to say: At what date is there a 95 percent probability that the project will have been completed? Using Table 7-1(b), a probability of 0.95 is seen to have a z value of 1.6. As before, we calculate:

$$1.6 = \frac{T_s - 29}{\sqrt{6}}, \text{ so } T_s = 33 \text{ days}$$

In other words, it is "highly likely" (95 percent probable) that the project will be completed within 33 days. (With such a high probability, the project will probably finish earlier than $T_s = 33$ days.)

Note that since we are working with values that are only rough estimates, it makes little sense to compute probabilities of great precision.

Near-Critical Paths

The PERT procedure has been criticized for providing overly optimistic results, a criticism that is well justified since it does not account for the effect of merge-point bias.[6] Notice in the example in Figure 7-12 that two paths are "near critical" in length. The variance of these paths is large enough that either could easily become critical by exceeding the 29 days of the original critical path. In fact, as you may wish to verify using the statistical procedure described previously, the probability of *not* completing Path A and Path E within 29 days is 33 and 28 percent, respectively. So there is more than a slight chance that these paths could become critical. The warning is: Putting too much emphasis on the critical path can lead to ignoring other paths that are near critical in length, paths that could themselves easily become critical and jeopardize the project completion date.

Furthermore, the 50 percent probability of completing the project within 29 days (as presumed with the normal distribution) is overly optimistic. Because *all* activities in the network must be completed before the project is finished, the probability of completing the project within 29 days is the same as the probability of completing *all* five paths within 29 days. Although the probability of completing Paths B and D within 29 days is close to 100 percent, the probabilities of completing Paths A and E within that time is 67 and 72 percent, respectively, and the probability of completing C, the critical path, is only 50 percent. So the chance of completing all paths within 29 days is the product of the probabilities, $(1.0 \times 1.0 \times 0.67 \times 0.72 \times 0.5)$, or less than 25 percent.

Meeting the Target Date

PERT analysis provides the project manager with a level of confidence in estimating the project end date, which is useful when negotiating with customers and other stakeholders. Clearly, one way to increase confidence in the end date is to delay it,

Table 7-2 Normal distribution function for completing a project by time T_s.
(a) Probability that project will be completed sooner than the expected duration (project will probably finish late if committed to the T_s date) duration.
(b) Probability that project will be completed later than the expected duration (project will probably finish early if committed to the T_s date).

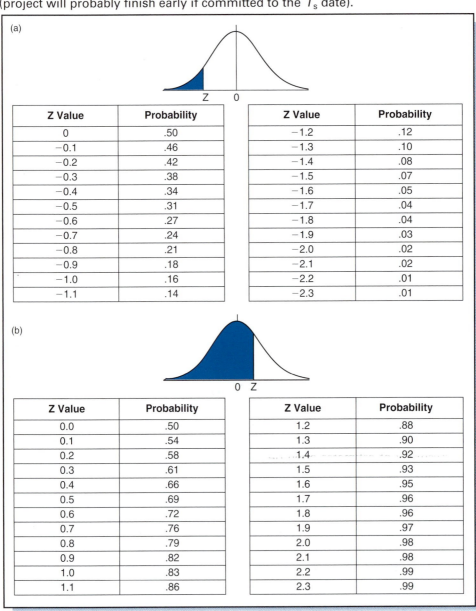

(a)

Z Value	Probability	Z Value	Probability
0	.50	−1.2	.12
−0.1	.46	−1.3	.10
−0.2	.42	−1.4	.08
−0.3	.38	−1.5	.07
−0.4	.34	−1.6	.05
−0.5	.31	−1.7	.04
−0.6	.27	−1.8	.04
−0.7	.24	−1.9	.03
−0.8	.21	−2.0	.02
−0.9	.18	−2.1	.02
−1.0	.16	−2.2	.01
−1.1	.14	−2.3	.01

(b)

Z Value	Probability	Z Value	Probability
0.0	.50	1.2	.88
0.1	.54	1.3	.90
0.2	.58	1.4	.92
0.3	.61	1.5	.93
0.4	.66	1.6	.95
0.5	.69	1.7	.96
0.6	.72	1.8	.96
0.7	.76	1.9	.97
0.8	.79	2.0	.98
0.9	.82	2.1	.98
1.0	.83	2.2	.99
1.1	.86	2.3	.99

although sometimes the end date is considered fixed, in which case the only alternative is to revise the project network to shorten the critical and near-critical paths. Possible ways to do this include:[7]

1. Look for opportunities to fast-track activities on the critical path (i.e., activities that could be removed from and placed in parallel with the critical path). Fast-tracking implies that an activity originally scheduled to succeed a predecessor is rescheduled to start before the predecessor is completed. An

alternative is to split the predecessor into subactivities, and start the successor when only some of the subactivities have been completed.

2. Add more resources to critical activities, or transfer resources from activities that have large slack times to critical and near-critical activities.

3. Substitute activities that are less time-consuming, or delete activities that are not absolutely necessary.

Each of these has drawbacks and must be scrutinized in each project to determine whether it is feasible. Fast-tracking increases the risks of making mistakes and having to repeat activities. Adding resources to speed up activities increases the cost. Transferring resources between activities requires changes to plans and schedules, and increases administrative costs; it also disrupts resources and causes aggravation to the functional managers who supply the resources. The final alternative, substitution or elimination of activities, jeopardizes project performance, especially when it equates to making "cuts" or using poorer quality materials or less-skilled labor.

Criticisms of PERT[8]

The PERT method has been criticized because it is based upon assumptions that sometimes yield results that are problematic. For example, it ignores human behavior and assumes that whenever an activity *is* completed earlier than scheduled that succeeding activities will start straight away—regardless of the fact that resources might not be available or that people procrastinate.

PERT assumes that activity durations are independent. But whenever resources are transferred from one activity to another, the durations of both activities are changed. In other words, activity durations are usually not independent: one's gain is another's loss.

PERT also assumes that three activity estimates are better than one. Estimating three durations instead of one takes more work, although unless based upon good historical data, the three are still *guesses*, which is not much of an improvement over a single "best" guess. The advantage of the pessimistic estimate is that it removes the burden of having to make a single estimate that cannot account for possible setbacks.

Accuracy of estimates often depends on experience. Whenever a database can be formed based upon experience from similar activities from previous projects, a "history" can be developed for each kind of activity that can be used to estimate the times for future similar activities. In fact, reliance on good *historical data* for estimating times makes the PERT method appropriate for projects that are somewhat "repeatable" (and less so for the research and first-of-a-kind projects for which it was originated). Because of this the PERT method tends to be used in construction and standardized engineering projects, but seldom elsewhere.

Despite criticism, PERT remains a useful approach for analyzing the effect of time uncertainty on project schedules. Some of PERT's shortcomings are addressed by simulation.

Monte Carlo Simulation of a PERT Network

Monte Carlo computer simulation is a procedure that takes into account the effects of near-critical paths and merge-point bias. Times for project activities are randomly selected from probability distributions, and the critical path is computed from these times. The procedure is repeated thousands of times to generate a distribution of project durations. It gives an average project duration and standard deviation that is more reliable and accurate than simple PERT probabilistic analysis, and it also gives the probabilities of other paths becoming critical.[9]

Simulation allows the use of a variety of probability distributions besides Beta, including distributions based upon empirical data. As a result, the generated project durations more accurately represent the range of expected durations than the single-network PERT method.

The method can also be used to avoid some limitations of PERT assumptions, such as independence of activity durations and normality of the project duration distribution. The procedure is described in the following example. Another simulation procedure called GERT is described later.

Example 2: Simulation to Determine Project Completion Times

The following example from Evans and Olson illustrates usage of the three time estimates in a simulation to assess the likelihood of project completion time.[10] The project activities and time estimates are in Table 7-3, and the project network is in Figure 7-13.

The critical path is B–F–G–H–I–K–M–O–P–Q; summing t_e and V on this path gives a project duration of 147.5 days with a variance of 56.63 days.

Suppose the customer would prefer that the project be completed within 140 days. Using the PERT method, the probability of completing the project within 140 days is found from:

$$z = \frac{140 - 147.5}{\sqrt{56.65}} = -0.996$$

Table 7-3 Activities and time estimates.

	ACTIVITY	PREDECESSORS	MINIMUM	MOST LIKELY	MAXIMUM	T_E	V
A	Select steering committee	—	15	15	15	15	0
B	Develop requirements list	—	40	45	60	46.67	11.11
C	Develop system size estimates	—	10	14	30	16	11.11
D	Determine prospective vendors	—	2	2	5	2.5	0.25
E	Form evaluation team	A	5	7	9	7	0.44
F	Issue request for proposal	B, C, D, E	4	5	8	5.33	0.44
G	Bidders' conference	F	1	1	1	1	0
H	Review submissions	G	25	30	50	32.5	17.36
I	Select vendor short list	H	3	5	10	5.5	1.36
J	Check vendor references	I	3	3	10	4.17	1.36
K	Vendor demonstrations	I	20	30	45	30.83	17.36
L	User site visit	I	3	3	5	3.33	0.11
M	Select vendor	J, K, L	3	3	3	3	0
N	Volume sensitive test	M	10	13	20	13.67	2.78
O	Negotiate contracts	M	10	14	28	15.67	9
P	Cost–benefit analysis	N, O	2	2	2	2	0
Q	Obtain board of directors' approval	P	5	5	5	5	0

Source: J. Evans and D. Olson, *Introduction to Simulation and Risk Management* (Upper Saddle River, NJ: Prentice Hall, 1998): 116, with permission.

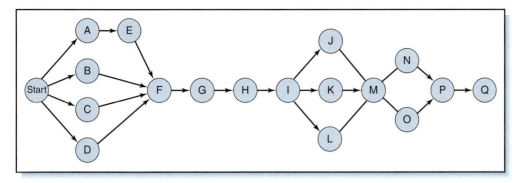

Figure 7-13
Project network.

Referring to Table 7-2, the probability is about 16 percent. This estimate assumes that the activity times have a Beta distribution and the project completion time is a normal distribution.

Using the simulation program Crystal Ball to generate the completion times for 1,000 replications of the project yields the distribution in Figure 7-14. (Various other programs such as Risksim, @Risk, Arena, and Simul-8 can also be used.)[11]

The simulation distribution has a mean of 155 days and gives a probability of completing the project in 140 days of about 6.9 percent (the sum of the probabilities to the left of 140 on Figure 7-14). It is thus unlikely that the project will be finished in less than 140 days, and only 50 percent likely that it will be completed within 155 days. (This compares to the estimated mean completion time of 147.5 days provided by the PERT.)

Simulation provides more accurate, realistic results than PERT because it compensates for noncritical paths that can become critical. But like PERT, it is merely a method for analyzing schedules, not for creating them (such as a Gantt chart or network), and it is based upon guesses or best estimates. It is a "better" analysis tool than PERT but by no means eliminates the uncertainty associated with scheduling.

Figure 7-14
Crystal Ball simulation results for project completion times.

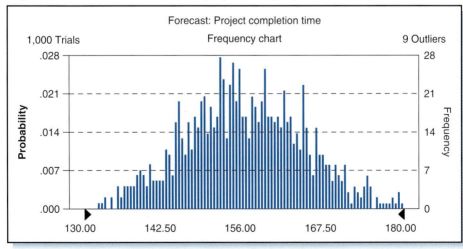

Activities on critical path	Optimistic Duration	Most Likely Duration	Pessimistic Duration
	a	*m*	*b*
A	10	12	15
B	14	15	17.5
C	18	20	22
D	12	13	14.5
E	22	24	27
F	14	15	17
G	13	14	15.5
H	16	17	19
Sum of most likely durations		**130**	

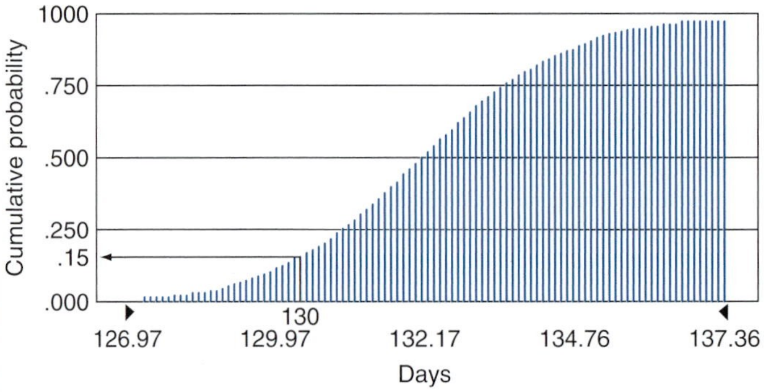

Figure 7-15
Simulation results show low probability of finishing within critical-path time. (Generated by means of Crystal Ball software, assuming triangular distributions.)

Also, neither simulation nor PERT does anything to help planners reduce project risk. Other tools are needed for that, as discussed in Chapter 10.

Why Projects are Often Late

The following example illustrates the risk a project manager takes when committing to a due date based upon the duration of the critical path. A Monte Carlo simulation was used to calculate the probability of finishing a project given the critical-path activity durations shown in Figure 7-15. The critical-path length is 130 days but the simulation reveals only a 15 percent chance of finishing the project within that time. The simulation was applied for the critical path only and did not take into account noncritical paths that could become critical—which would further reduce the probability. This example points out the risk a manager takes in committing to due dates based solely upon the most likely activity durations on the critical path. While individual *m* values might be considered "realistic," the sum of the *m* values is not realistic at all! The manager takes a similar risk by assuming the project cost will be the sum of the most likely activity cost estimates. Yet, many project managers simply add up most likely estimates of activity durations and cost estimates—one reason why projects overrun due dates and budgets.

Another reason has to do with human behavior. During the feasibility or proposal (tendering) stage of a project *optimism* rules as champions and supporters do their best to "sell" the project. Of course, without such optimism many an important project would never come to be. Optimism is necessary to gain buy-in from stakeholders, but it also leads to underestimating the project time and cost. The Chunnel Tunnel is an example. Originally it was believed that 30 million people and 100 million tons of freight would be transported through the Chunnel per year.[12] This claim proved exaggerated when in the first *5 years* only 28 million people and 12 million tons of freight were actually transported! The cost, initially estimated at £7.5 billion, ultimately escalated to £15 billion. And, the project took nearly 18 months longer to complete than originally estimated.

There are other reasons why projects finish late; these—and ways to avoid them—are discussed next.

7.4 THEORY OF CONSTRAINTS AND CRITICAL CHAIN METHOD

The theory of constraints (TOC) is a systems approach to improving the performance of business systems.[13] A premise of TOC is that every system has a goal and that, often, only a few (or one) elements of the system prevents it from achieving that goal. This area or bottleneck is called the *system* constraint; to achieve the goal all management efforts should be directed at eliminating the constraint.

The TOC procedure is:

1. Identify the constraint (s) or bottleneck(s) of the system
2. Decide how to exploit the constraint (s)
3. Subordinate non-constraints to the decision(s) made in Step 2
4. Elevate the constraint (s)
5. Return to Step 1 to determine if a new constraint has appeared (which renders the original one a non-constraint or less critical)

These steps can be illustrated by the analogy of a chain. A chain is as strong as its weakest link; to improve a chain, first you must find out which link is the weakest (Step 1). Step 2 aims at the optimal use of the system without investment in additional capacity; in the chain example, you find ways to use the chain to the maximum load for the weakest link (i.e., to subject all other links in the chain to this maximum load). In Step 3 the system is used to its maximum capacity by ensuring that the load on every link is equal to the maximum capacity of the weakest link. Once the system is used to its maximum, the capacity at the constraint (strength of the weakest link) is upgraded or improved (Step 4). This will enable the capacity everywhere (load on the links) to be increased. Note, however, that the system's capacity is increased only *after* its existing capacity has been fully utilized. Upon strengthening the weakest link, another link will become the weakest link (Step 5), in which case it becomes the new constraint and returns the process to Step 1.

The TOC philosophy applied to project scheduling is called the Critical Chain Method, *CCM*. The constraint of the individual project is its *duration* or due date, and the aim of the method is to reduce the duration or guarantee hitting the due date.[14] CCM acknowledges the stochastic nature of activity durations and also takes into account the impact of human behavior on project scheduling and execution. It can be applied to single projects and to multiple, concurrent projects.[15]

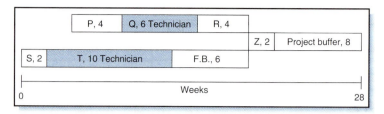

Figure 7-18
Schedule with buffer sizes reduced. F.B.: feeding buffer.

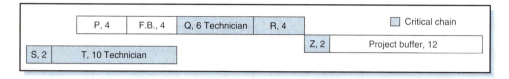

Figure 7-19
Schedule adjusted so that every resource performs only one task at a time. F.B.: feeding buffer.

The second reason why the buffer size can be reduced stems from the obverse of Parkinson's Law, which states "work expands to fill the time available." By removing padding from each activity, people have less time to do the work, hence tend to work faster than when they have more time. For these reasons, the buffer sizes are reduced. In Figure 7-18, they have been reduced by 50 percent.

The project manager commits to completing the project on or before the date at the end of the project buffer, week 28 in the example, although the project team works to complete the project on or before the date at the start of the project buffer, week 20. In theory, there is a high likelihood that this project will be completed *in less than 28 weeks*. With the critical path method, there is a high likelihood the project will be completed *after* the critical-path duration, which is *32 weeks*.

Worth repeating is that in CCM the project manager commits to the completion due date (at the end of the project buffer), while people responsible for the activities in the project *do not commit* to any due dates; they just try to complete their activities within the, hopefully, realistic time estimates they provided.

Critical Chain

But Figure 7-18 reveals a potential problem: Activities Q and T are both performed by the same resource (the "technician"). Assume each requires her full-time attention. To enable her to work on them one at a time, the schedule is adjusted, shown in Figure 7-19. (The technician could have been scheduled to do Activity Q before T, and that would have resulted in slightly shorter project duration.) In the adjusted schedule, Path S–T–Q–R–Z is called the *critical chain*, which is defined as the path connecting activities that require the same constrained resource. Traditional network methods address the resource conflict problem by mean of resource leveling, although the result will not necessarily be the same as with CCM.

Note that the feeding buffer is 4 days, and not 2. The reason is that it follows only one activity, P, hence the principle of aggregation does not apply. Ultimately, the size of the buffer is at the manager's discretion.

If the schedule does not meet a predetermined due date or if upper management wants the project completed sooner, additional resources must be added. But additional resources are costly; hence CCM attempts first to make full use of whatever resources are currently available.

Resource Buffers: Capitalizing on Good Luck

Mentioned earlier was the fact that when activities finish late their successors start late, but when they finish early, their successors *don't necessarily* start early. Resources such as people and equipment that have been scheduled to work on a particular activity are often not available earlier than scheduled because they are working on something else. As a consequence, whenever bad luck occurs, the project suffers; whenever good luck occurs, it's makes no difference!

In CCM the project team is able to capitalize on good luck (predecessors finishing early) through use of *resource buffers*. Unlike project and feeding buffers, resource buffers do not add time to the schedule. A resource buffer is a *countdown* signal or warning to alert resources that an activity on the critical chain will possibly finish earlier than planned and to *be prepared to start early*. This is in accordance with TOC Step 2, exploit the constraint. In a marathon relay race, each runner is prepared to accept the baton from the previous runner, regardless when the latter is expected to arrive; likewise, resources on the critical chain are prepared to take advantage of good luck—i.e., to start earlier than scheduled. In practice a resource buffer can take the form of a series e-mail or other messages to resources counting down the amount of time remaining before they must be ready to start a critical activity. The locations of resource buffers are illustrated in Figure 7-20.

Note that resource buffers are inserted only on the critical chain since feeding buffers are able to adequately deal with the uncertainty on noncritical paths. Note also there is no resource buffer between Activity Q and Activity T since the same resource (technician) does both and, obviously, does not need advance notification about when she will finish Activity Q and must start Activity T.

Milestone Buffers

Sometimes milestone deadlines are set at intermediate times in the project, such as at the scheduled completion dates for project phases. In that case a *milestone buffer* is inserted before the milestone. When milestone buffers are used, the size of the project buffer is reduced; in effect, the project buffer is divided up among the milestone buffers. The different types of buffers are summarized in Table 7-5.

Figure 7-20
Resource buffers providing countdown on when to start critical activities.
F.B.: feeding buffer.

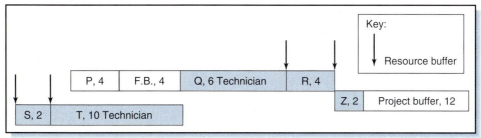

Table 7-5 Summary of buffer types for a single project.

BUFFER TYPE	FUNCTION OF THE BUFFER
Project buffer	Comprised of aggregated contingency reserves taken from activities on the critical chain; provides a contingency reserve between the earliest completion date possible and the committed date.
Milestone buffer	Similar to a project buffer but used when a project phase or milestone has a fixed due date.
Feeding buffer	Comprised of aggregated contingencies taken from noncritical paths; stabilizes the critical chain by preventing noncritical activities from delaying critical activities.
Resource buffer	An early warning or "count down" to the start of a critical activity that ensures that resources are ready to do work on the critical chain as soon as all preceding activities have been completed.

Sizing of Buffers

CCM relies heavily on project and feeding buffers, so making them the right size is important. Goldratt suggests that activity durations be cut by 50 percent and that the project buffer be half the duration of the resulting longest path.[16] The method, which reduces the project duration by 25 percent, was illustrated in the example above and is referred to as the "50 percent of chain" and "cut and paste" method.

As explained in the Appendix to this chapter, the amount by which duration can be reduced is proportional to the square root of the number of activities in the chain. When a path consists of many activities, a buffer of 50 percent of the path length will still be too large.[17] Newbold proposed the *square root of sum of squares (SSQ)* method, where the buffer size is set to the square root of the SSQ of the difference between the low-risk duration and the mean duration for each task along the longest path leading to the buffer.[18] Others have suggested additional methods.[19]

Effects of Human Behavior

Projects take longer than necessary for many reasons, including the following.

First, people build in too much *padding* into time estimates. This effect gets worse as each manager in the WBS adds to the padding. If the person responsible for an activity adds a 10 percent reserve and each person higher in the WBS also adds 10 percent to allow for contingencies, the padding at the project level would be $(1.1)^n$ where n is the number of WBS levels. For a WBS of five levels, this implies a total contingency of 60 percent at the project level. If each adds in 15 percent, the total contingency for the activity would be 101 percent.

Second, they *multitask*. Mentioned in Chapter 6 was the detrimental effect of working on multiple activities and projects at once. For example, a contractor has three independent projects, X, Y, and Z, each of anticipated duration of 10 weeks. The contractor is anxious to finish *all* of them as soon as possible so he divides each into small pieces so that, in a sense, he can work on all of them at the same time. But in doing so, he actually delays the completion of two of the projects. If he had scheduled the projects sequentially X first, Y second, and Z last, without interruption, then, as shown in Figure 7-21(a), he would finish X at week 10, Y at week 20, and at week 30. But when breaks up the projects into small segments of, say, 5-week periods,

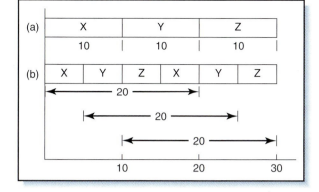

Figure 7-21
Effect of multitasking on elapsed and completion times.

and alternates the work among them, he increases the *elapsed time* for each project from 10 to 20 weeks. As illustrated in Figure 7-21(b), the result is that two of the projects are delayed: X finishes in week 20 and Y finishes in week 25. In general, the more that activities or projects are broken up and intermixed with other projects, the greater the elapsed time to finish any of them.

Compounding the effect is that multitasking precludes people from building the momentum they could have gained by focusing uninterrupted on only one task. This additional effect was illustrated in Figure 6-25.

Multitasking conflicts with TOC Step 2 (exploiting the constraint) and should be avoided, especially on the critical chain. By focusing on one activity at a time, each activity can be completed faster, successor activities started earlier, and project finished sooner.

A third reason projects take longer than necessary is that people procrastinate and waste any scheduled slack time.[20] Given a choice between two scheduled times, one early and one late, people choose to *wait* until the late one, which automatically eliminates slack, puts activities on the critical path, and increases the likelihood of project delay. Whenever there is perceived or real slack time, there is little motivation to complete an activity early. The effect is called the "students' syndrome" because the initial enthusiasm with which students tackle a new course often soon wanes and only resumes just before the final examination. A similar effect in production and project environments is shown in Figure 7-22.

Figure 7-22
Students' syndrome. (a) Students' syndrome in a production operation.
(b) Students' syndrome on a project.

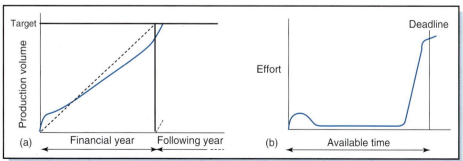

The Challenge of CCM: Changing Behavior

A belief in most project organizations is that because the project manager has to commit to a due date, everybody else throughout the WBS should also commit to due dates. CCM relies on the premise that *only* the project manager needs to make a commitment, and that everyone else works only toward realistic estimates.

While CCM can often be used on small projects without a significant attitude change throughout the company, this is not the case with major projects. To implement CCM on major company-wide projects requires the understanding by everybody that only the project manager commits to the project due date; while nobody else commits to due dates, they all work hard toward meeting realistic due dates. Since most people are accustomed to working toward deadlines, this requires a change in culture and acceptance at all levels of the organization, including top management. Senior managers and customers who do not understand the principles of CCM will try to trim or eliminate the project buffer.

Software Support for CCM[21]

Although many project management software systems do not include provision for CCM, many others do or accept add-ins that make them compatible with CCM. MS Project™ supports CCM only if the Prochain™ add-in is used. The Project Scheduler™ and Concerto™ software fully supports CCM.

7.5 ALLOCATING RESOURCES AND MULTIPLE PROJECT SCHEDULING

Organizations that perform construction, consulting, systems development, or maintenance projects commonly rely on a pool of shared equipment and skilled workers from which all projects draw. In matrix organizations (Chapter 13) all projects share resources from the same functional departments. This section addresses the matter of scheduling multiple projects with constrained resources.

Multiple projects that share resources must be planned and scheduled such that in combination they do not exceed the resources available in the shared pools. Although these projects might in all other ways be considered independent, the fact that they share resources means they are at least somewhat dependent.

As might be expected, the problem of scheduling multiple concurrent projects is analogous to scheduling multiple concurrent activities within a single project, but with modification to account for the economic, technical, and organizational issues that arise when dealing with multiple projects.

First, every project has its own target completion date, and all the projects must be scheduled to finish as close to those dates as possible to avoid deferred payments, penalty costs, or lost sales and revenues. Further, when projects are interdependent, then delays in one project can have a ripple effect on others; the delay of a satellite development and launch project will subsequently cause the delay of a telecommunications project. In any case, scheduling of multiple projects requires first determining the relative priority among the projects to determine which projects should get first dibs on scarce resources.

Because most organizations prefer to maintain a uniform level of personnel and other resources, the combined schedules for multiple projects ideally result in a uniform loading or utilization of these resources. In other words, the resource loading for the combined projects is ideally flat. In theory, projects are scheduled so that as resources are released from one project they are assigned to others. This minimizes costs associated with hiring, layoffs, and idle workers and facilities, and helps maintain efficient use of resources and worker morale.

When limitations on the available resources dictate the project schedule, the schedule is called *resource limited*. When a project must be completed *fast*—either by a due date or as soon as possible, the schedule is called *time limited*. The two situations represent extremes and most schedules are a compromise between them. When time *and* resources contingency reserves are limited, chances are high that the project schedule and budget will run over.

When many activities are ready to start and all require the same resource, to which activities should the resource be allocated? When 10 tasks are ready to start, the number of possible sequences in performing them is 10!, or more than 3.6 million. If n activities are ready to start and all of them require m resources, the number of possible schedules would be $(n!)^m$. Optimization using normal polynomials requires intolerably large amounts of computing time and is usually not feasible (the problem is "NP hard"). Heuristics, on the other hand, provide simple, effective, and acceptable solutions.[22]

Heuristic Methods for Allocating Resources

A heuristic is a procedure based upon a simple rule. Heuristic methods for allocating resources to projects often employ decision rules called *priority rules* or *dispatching rules.* While these methods do not produce optimal schedules (keeping in mind that the duration values are mere estimates), they do produce schedules that are good enough for most situations.

Heuristic methods start with early and late times as determined by traditional network methods, and then analyze the schedule for the required resources (i.e., the resource loading). Whenever a resource requirement exceeds the constraint, the heuristic determines which activities get high priority and receive the resource. The most common heuristic rules for determining scheduling priority are:

(a) *As soon as possible*: Activities that *can* be started sooner should be given priority over (or scheduled ahead of) those that can be started later.

(b) *As late as possible*: Activities that can be finished later are given lower priority than those that must be finished earlier.

(c) *Most resources*: Activities requiring more resources are given priority over those requiring fewer resources.

(d) *Shortest task time*: Activities of shorter duration are given priority over those of longer duration (sometimes referred to as *shortest activity duration, shortest processing time*, or *shortest operating time*).

(e) *Least slack*: Activities with less slack time are given priority over those with more slack time; critical path activities thus have highest priority. (This rule is also referred to as *slack time remaining*).

(f) *First come first served*: Activities that arrive earlier or require the resource earlier are given priority.

(g) *Earliest due date*: This rule is used where a resource is to be allocated to more than one project. Priority is given to the activities in the *project* that has to the earliest target completion date. Alternatively, priority is given to the activity with the *earliest next operation*.

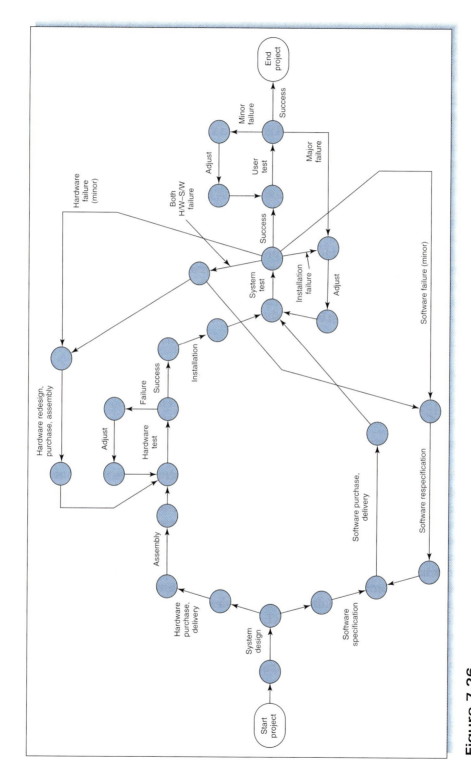

Figure 7-26
Expanded network for the ROSEBUD project.

ROSEBUD network in Chapter 6 except it has been expanded to include the possibility of failure following the tests for hardware, system, and the user. Specifically:

1. A failure in the hardware test would require adjustments to the equipment.
2. A failure in the system test would require either adjustments to the installation, minor redesign of the hardware, or minor respecification of the software, depending on the nature of the failure.
3. A failure in the user test would require either minor or major system adjustments followed by a new system test.

The example is greatly simplified, and you can probably see numerous other places where loops and branches would likely occur in a project such as this. For example, there could be multiple branches at each of the activities for design, delivery, and adjustments.

Figure 7-27 illustrates the corresponding GERT network for the project. Notice that for probabilistic nodes the probabilities are given for the output branches. For example, the node for complete user test (the node following Node 14) ends with success, 0.7; minor adjustments, 0.2; and major adjustments, 0.1. Also, Node 12 represents failure in both hardware and software and the need to redesign both. Each activity would be assigned a probability distribution type (normal, Beta, Erlang, uniform, etc.) as well as distribution parameters (mean, variance, etc.).

Given the network and distributions, Monte Carlo simulation can be used to derive statistics about the project. By simulating the project 1,000s of times, statistics about the mean, variance, and distribution of times to successfully assemble the hardware, administer the system test, and complete the project can be generated. Similar information can be generated about other nodes in the network. Information can also be collected about the distribution of failure times, which is important for estimating the ultimate cost of the project. As the network stands, there is the possibility, though small, that work could loop back infinitely without ever reaching an end.

One criticism of GERT is that in reality seldom is any part of a project ever repeated exactly. For example, in the design and testing of a new system, should the test indicate a problem with the design, the repeated design work will not be the same as the original work.

7.8   DISCUSSION AND SUMMARY

This chapter covered methods for scheduling projects taking into account time constraints, resources constraints, uncertainty in activity and project durations, and multiple projects sharing resources. CPM is a network-based method for analyzing the effect of project duration on cost. It enables managers to determine the least costly way of reducing project duration to complete the project by a due date or in the shortest time. The PERT method enables managers to gauge project risk by estimating the probability of finishing a project by a predetermined due date. The method considers only the current critical path, however, and ignores the fact that noncritical paths could become critical. Monte Carlo simulation takes into account the possibility of any path becoming critical and overcomes this limitation.

The CCM, based on the TOC, is also intended to reduce project duration. Using time buffers it transforms a stochastic problem into a relatively simple deterministic one. Unlike critical-path scheduling, which normally schedules noncritical activities as early as possible, CCM schedules them as late as possible but with buffers. Variability in activity durations can lead to changes in the critical path without warning, but buffers

The standard deviation σ can be used as an indication of risk and, hence, the amount of contingency reserve required. Since $\sigma^2 = V$, it follows that, in the event of aggregation,

$$\sigma_p = (n)^{1/2} \cdot \sigma$$

where σ_p is the standard deviation of the sum.

In the absence of aggregation:

$$\sigma_p < n \cdot \sigma$$

Because $(n)^{1/2}$ is significantly smaller than n, the effect of aggregation of independent risks is significant. The higher the number of risks that are being aggregated, the more marked the effect. CCM applies the principle of aggregation to project schedule risks: contingency reserves for individual activities are reduced so that activity durations are challenging but realistic. Contingencies removed from the individual (lower WBS level) activity durations are replaced by a contingency reserve or "buffer" at the project level. As a result of the effect of aggregation, this buffer can be smaller than the sum of the individual reserves that have been removed from low-level activities. The larger the number of activities on the critical path, the greater the potential reduction in project buffer and, hence, duration.

If the central limit theorem is used to size a project buffer, the probability of the project finishing on time should correspond to the probability indicated by a PERT analysis. The reduction in project duration is dependent on human behavior.

Some authors[36] apply the principle of aggregation to project cost, but before the advent of critical chain there was little evidence of its formal application to project schedules.

REVIEW QUESTIONS AND PROBLEMS

1. Define crash effort and normal effort in terms of the cost and time they represent. When would a project be crashed?
2. How do CPM and PERT differ? How are they the same?
3. What does the cost slope represent?
4. The cost slope always has a negative $(-)$ value. What does this indicate?
5. Time–cost tradeoff analysis deals only with direct costs. What distinguishes these costs from indirect costs? Give examples of both direct and indirect costs.
6. What are the criticisms of CPM? How and where is CPM limited in its application?
7. The following project network and associated costs are given (T in days, C in $1,000s)

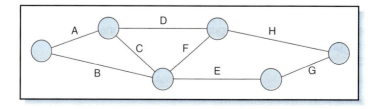

	Normal		Crash		
Activity	T_n	C_n	T_c	C_c	Cost Slope
A	4	210	3	280	70
B	9	400	6	640	80
C	6	500	4	600	50
D	9	540	7	600	30
E	4	500	1	1100	200
F	5	150	4	240	90
G	3	150	3	150	—
H	7	600	6	750	150

(a) Verify that the normal completion time is 22 days and that the direct cost is $3,050.

(b) What is the least costly way to reduce the project completion time to 21 days? What is the project cost?

(c) What is the least costly way to reduce the completion time to 20 days? What is the project cost?

(d) Now, what is the *earliest* the project can be completed and what is the least costly way of doing this? What is the project cost?

8. The following project network and associated costs are given (T in days, C in $1,000s)

	Normal		Crash		
Activity	T_n	C_n	T_c	C_c	Cost Slope
A	6	6	3	9	
B	9	9	5	12	
C	3	4.5	2	7	
D	5	10	2	16	
E	2	2	2	2	
F	4	6	1	10	
G	8	8	5	10	

(a) Compute the cost slopes. What is the earliest the project can be completed under normal conditions? What is the direct cost?

(b) What is the least costly way to reduce the project completion time by 2 days? What is the project cost?

(c) What is the *earliest* the project can be completed and what is the least costly way of doing this? What is the project cost?

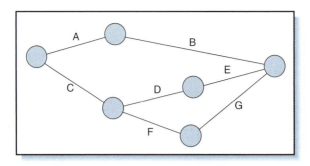

9. The following table gives information on a project (T in days, C in $1,000s$)

Activity	Immediate Predecessors	Normal		Crash	
		T_n	C_n	T_c	C_c
A	—	6	10	2	38
B	—	4	12	4	12
C	—	4	18	2	36
D	A	6	20	2	40
E	B, D	3	30	2	33
F	C	10	10	6	50
G	F, E	6	20	2	100

(a) Draw the network diagram. Compute the cost slopes. Under normal conditions, what is the earliest the project can be completed? What is the direct cost? What is the critical path?

(b) What is the cost of the project if it is completed 1 day earlier? Two days earlier?

(c) What is the earliest the project can be completed? What is the lowest cost for completing it in this time?

(d) If overhead (indirect) costs are $20,000 per day, for what project duration are total project costs (direct + indirect) lowest?

10. Has variability in a time estimate ever caused you to be late for an appointment? Describe.

11. A procurement officer finds that the delivery time for a specific item is never less than 5 days. The worst-case scenario is that it takes 30 days for the item to arrive. A delivery lead time of 10 days is more frequent than any other.

(a) Calculate the expected delivery time.

(b) What estimate would you give for its variance?

(c) What factors would you take into account when deciding the amount of time to be allowed for in the project plan for delivery of the item?

12. Given the immediate predecessors and a, m, b for each activity in the tables below, draw the networks and compute:

(a) t_e and V for each activity.

(b) ES, EF, LS, and LF for each activity.

(c) T_e and V_p for the project.

Activity	Predecessors	a	m	b
A	–	7	9	11
B	A	1	2	3
C	A	7	8	9
D	B	2	5	11
E	C	2	3	4
F	C	1	4	8
G	D, E	6	7	8
H	F, E	2	6	9

Activity	Predecessors	a	m	b
A	–	2	4	6
B	–	2	2	3
C	–	4	8	10
D	A	4	6	7
E	A, B	7	9	12
F	D, E	1	2	3
G	C	2	3	4

13. Refer to the first network in the above problem.
    (a) What is $P(T_e < 23)$?
    (b) What is $P(T_e < 32)$?
    (c) For what value of T_s is the probability 95 percent that the project will be completed?

14. Referring to the network shown in Figure 7-12 of this chapter, what is the probability of completing each of the five paths within 30 days? What is the probability of completing *all* five paths within 30 days?

15. How would you use buffers to ensure that you are on time for appointments? What factors would you take into account when you make a decision on the size of the buffer?

16. Explain in your own words how the principle of aggregation plays a role in reducing project duration.

17. The diagram below shows that Mary must perform both Activity B and Activity F.[37]
    (a) With the realization that Mary has to do the two tasks, indicate two possible critical chains.
    (b) Reschedule the work and indicate the position and the size of the feeding buffer.

18. Refer to the network in number 20 in Review Questions and Problems for Chapter 6.
    (a) Indicate the critical chain on the diagram.
    (b) Which of the two resources is the constraint?
    (c) Construct Gantt charts for this example based on the following heuristics: the shortest task time rule, the least slack rule, and the TOC heuristic.
    (d) Assume that the schedule indicates durations from which contingency reserve has been removed. Insert a project buffer and feeding buffers as required.

19. Refer to Figure 7-20. Scheduling Activity Q before Activity T would also have been a way to resolve the resource contingency. Explain why this alternative was not selected.

20. Consider the data about project activities given in the table below.[38]

Activity	Predecessor(s)	Duration (Days)	Resources
A	—	2	John
B	A	3	Sue
C	—	3	Sue and John
D	C	2	Al
E	D, J	3	Sue and Al
F	E, B	2	John
G	F	2	Ann
H	—	4	Sue
J	H	2	Al

    (a) Schedule the work in such a way that each person always has only one task to perform (do not reduce the durations of activities or insert buffers as yet).
    (b) Indicate the critical chain.
    (c) Indicate where the feeding buffers should be inserted.
    (d) What is the difference in the lengths of the critical path and the critical chain?

21. Discuss the implications of resource allocation for organizations involved in multiple projects.

22. Discuss the differences between fast-tracking, concurrent engineering, and crashing.

23. Write an essay on the reasons why projects are often late.

24. Describe how GERT overcomes the limitations of PERT/CPM.

25. Give some examples of projects where GERT could be used.

26. Take an existing network (such as for LOGON); using your imagination (and the rules of GERT), redraw it as a GERT network.

QUESTIONS ABOUT THE STUDY PROJECT

1. In the project you are studying, discuss which of the following kinds of analysis were performed:
    (a) CPM/time–cost tradeoff analysis
    (b) PERT
    (c) Scheduling with resource constraints
    (d) CCM
    (e) GERT

2. Discuss how they were applied and show examples. Discuss those applications that were not applied but seem especially applicable to the project.
3. How do you rate the risk of not finishing on time, and what are the factors contributing to this risk?
4. Were people (other than the project manager) required to make commitments on the duration of activities? Comment on the possibility of changing this behavior.

Case 7-1: Bridgecon Contractors

Bridgecon is a medium-size construction company that specializes in the detail design and construction of bridges that combine steel and concrete elements.

The Marketing Division is responsible for the first phase in the Bridgecon project management methodology that includes the identification of an opportunity as well as an assessment of the alignment of the opportunity with strategic guidelines. An opportunity has recently been identified by Marketing: A well-known bridge architect has just completed the concept design of a cable-stayed bridge, intended to cross over electrified railway lines. The senior managers are excited about this opportunity, and this marks the end of the first phase. Bridgecon now enters the second phase—the Estimating phase. This phase includes site visits by the estimating team, review of resources and skills available, a more detailed risk review than the one done during the first phase, as well as a preliminary plan for detail design, procurement, logistics, and construction. The deliverable of this phase is an initial presentation to the customer. The third phase (Pre-contract phase) should lead to a contract signed by both Bridgecon and the customer. In Table 7-6, Activities A and B are required for preparing a bid for building the bridge and form part of the second phase.

The project manager who leads the estimating team sets up a number of meetings with stakeholders. First meetings were held with the bridge architect and structural engineers who produced the concept design in order to acquaint the estimating team with the design. The estimating team then meets with subcontractors who might be selected for piling and for fabrication of steel components. The columns "initial duration estimate" and "initial cost estimate" of Table 7-6 are completed subsequent to these meetings. The RFP (request for proposal) for building the bridge indicates acceptance of the plan by the rail authority as one of the criteria for the selection of a contractor. At this stage it is evident that, from the start of Activity D until the completion of Activity S, the operation of one of the railway lines will be impaired, and a preliminary, informal discussion with someone from the rail authority indicates that this might be acceptable. On a subsequent meeting with the rail authorities, concern is expressed about the planned 17 weeks of impaired operation and Bridgecon is requested to reconsider the duration of this period. The estimating team now suggests the following possibilities:

- The duration of Activity N could be reduced from 1 week to half a week by hiring additional trucks. The additional cost would be $33,000.
- An alternative subcontractor for piling has been approached. This subcontractor indicates that it would be able to halve the time of Activity H and provides a first round cost indication of $960,000 for such an expedited piling operation.
- Two steps to shorten the duration of Activity D are possible: First, additional temporary workers could be employed. This would reduce the duration to 3 weeks and increase the cost to $147,000. Second, a team of workers highly skilled in this type of procedure (with their equipment) could be temporarily reallocated from another site to this project, and the estimating team believes that adding this team to the original team and temporary workers would lead to completion of the work within 1 week. The project manager of the other project indicates that such a reallocation would cause him to forfeit an incentive fee of $150,000 for finishing his project early. The two project managers

Table 7.6 Activities for constructing the cable-stayed bridge.

ACTIVITY	ACTIVITY DESCRIPTION	INITIAL DURATION ESTIMATE	PREDECESSORS	INITIAL COST ESTIMATE($1,000)
A	Detail site investigation and survey	2	—	17
B	Detail planning	6	A	16
C	Detail design	6	B	557
D	Preparation of site	4	C	47
E	Relocate services	3	C	28
F	Re-align overhead track electrification	4	C, E	650
G	Access road and ramp construction	1	D	63
H	Piling	2	G	820
J	Construct foundations and abutments	3	H	975
K	Construct temporary supports to support bridge deck during construction	2	F, G	720
L	Fabrication planning of structural steel components	2	C	13
M	Manufacture structural steel components (off-site)	2	L	1320
N	Transport structural steel components and erect on-site	1	M	433
P	Erect pylons and fill with concrete	2	J	840
Q	Construct main span deck on pre-cast concrete beams	3	H, K, N, P	2,800
R	Cable-stay installation and lift the bridge deck off temporary supports	3	Q	875
S	Removal of temporary supports	1	R	54
T	Electrical system installation	1	S	147
U	Roadway surfacing (paving)	2	S	142
V	Finishing and ancillaries	2	T, U	76
W	Commissioning—cut-over	1	V	14
X	Formal hand-over and ceremony	1	W	9
Y	Project sign-off	1	X	1
Z	Administrative closure	1	W	4
AA	Project end (milestone)	0	Y, Z	
				10,621

agree that, should the reallocation be made, the value of incentive fee would be booked as a cost against the cable-stayed bridge project and transferred to the other project.

- The duration of Activity F can also be reduced. A step that would reduce duration to 3 weeks would increase the cost to $730,000 while a further step to reduce duration to 2 weeks would bring the total cost of this activity to $820,000.
- An increase of expenditures on Activity Q to a total of $2,929,000 would reduce the duration of this activity to 2 weeks.

QUESTIONS

1. Compile a list showing the reduced periods for impairment of the rail operation and the associated additional costs.

2. Comment on the impact that crashing might have on the risk of not meeting the committed due date.

ENDNOTES

1. CPM first appeared in the article by its originators: J.E. Kelley and M.R. Walker, "Critical Path Planning and Scheduling," *Eastern Joint Computer Conference* (Boston, MA: 1959): 160–173.

2. Avraham Y. Goldratt Institute, group e-mail messages, March 17–18, 1999; Larry English, Habitat for Humanity, January 2007, Pretoria, South Africa; Habitat for Humanity, *The Fastest House in the World*, accessed January 2007 from http://www.habitat.org/newsroom/1999archive/insitedoc004016.aspx?print=true.

3. A piece-wise approximation can be used for nonlinear relationships. See J.D. Wiest and F.K. Levy, *A Management Guide to PERT/CPM: With GERT/PDM/DCPM and Other Networks* (Englewood Cliffs, NJ: Prentice Hall, 1977), 81–85. As Brooks points out, the relationship between number of workers and activity duration is usually nonlinear; i.e., cutting the number of workers in half will not necessarily double the time but might increase it by, say, only 50 percent, or maybe as much as 150 percent, depending on the task. See F.P. Brooks, *The Mythical Man Month: Essay on Software Engineering* (Reading, MA: Addison-Wesley, 1995): 13–36.

4. The method first appeared in the article by the originators of PERT: D.G. Malcolm, J.H. Roseboom, C.E. Clark, and W. Fazar, "Application of a Technique for Research and Development Program Evaluation," *Operations Research* 7, no. 5 (1959): 646–670.

5. Wiest and Levy, *A Management Guide to PERT/CPM*, p. 43.

6. See A.R. Klingel, "Bias in PERT Project Completion Time Calculation for Real Networks," *Management Science* 13 (1966): 194–201.

7. See R.W. Miller, *Schedule, Cost, and Profit Control with PERT* (New York: McGraw-Hill, 1963): 58; Harold Kerzner, *Project Management: A Systems Approach to Planning, Scheduling, and Controlling*, 5th ed. (New York: Van Nostrand Reinhold, 1995): 653–691.

8. See M. Krakowski, "PERT and Parkinson's Law," *Interfaces* 5, no. 1 (November 1974); A. Vazsonyi, "L'Historie de la grandeur et de la decadence de la methode PERT," *Management Science* 16, no. 8 (April 1970) (written in English). Other problems of PERT/CPM are described by Kerzner, *Project Management*, 679–680; Miller, *Schedule, Cost, and Profit Control with PERT*, 39–45; Wiest and Levy, *A Management Guide to PERT/CPM:* 57–58, 73, 166–173. References to human behavior are in the critical chain literature referenced in this chapter.

9. See R.M. Van Slyke, "Monte Carlo Methods and the PERT Problem," *Operations Research* 11, no. 5 (1963): 839–860.

10. Adapted with permission from J.R. Evans and D.L. Olson, *Introduction to Simulation and Risk Analysis* (Upper Saddle River, NJ: Prentice Hall, 1998): 111–120.

11. Crystal Ball is a registered trademark of Decisioneering, Inc., 1515 Arapahoe, Suite 1311, Denver, CO, 80202, www.decisioneering.com. RiskSim is a registered trademark, Treeplan.com. www.treeplan.com. For information about @Risk, see www.palisade.com; for information about Arena, see www.rockwellautomation.com; for information about Simul8, see www.simul8.com.

12. D.I. Cleland, *Project Management—Strategic Design and Implementation*, 2nd ed. (New York: McGraw-Hill, Inc., 1994): 7.

13. E.M. Goldratt, *What Is This Thing Called Theory of Constraints* and *How Should It Be Implemented?* (New York: North River Press, Inc., 1990).

14. P.H. Pittman, *Project Management: A More Effective Methodology for the Planning and Control of Projects* (Georgia: PhD dissertation, University of Georgia, 1994); E.M. Goldratt, *Critical Chain* (Great Barrington, MA: North River Press, 1997).

15. E.D. Walker, *Planning and Controlling Multiple, Simultaneous, Independent Projects in a Resource Constrained Environment* (Georgia: PhD dissertation, University of Georgia, 1998). A TOC method for allocating resources to multiple projects was developed in this study and, subsequent to the study, the method has been developed further.

16. E.M. Goldratt, *Critical Chain*, 156.

17. W. Herroelen and R. Leus, "On the Merits and Pitfalls of Critical Chain Scheduling", *Journal of Operations Management* 7 (2001): 559–577; L.P. Leach, *Critical Chain Project Management*, 2nd ed. (Norwood, MA: Artech House, Inc, 2003); A. Geekie, Buffer Sizing for the Critical Chain Project Management Method. Unpublished research, University of Pretoria (2006).

18. R.C. Newbold, *Project Management in the Fast Lane—Applying the Theory of Constraints* (New York: St. Lucie Press, 1988).

19. O. Tukel, W.R. Rom, and S. Duni Eksioglu, "An Investigation of Buffer Sizing Techniques in Critical Chain Scheduling", *European Journal of Operational Research* 172 (2006): 401–416; also see D. Trietsch, "The Effect of Systemic Errors on Optimal Project Buffers," *International Journal of Project Management* 23 (2005): 267–274; Y. Shou and K.T. Yeo, "Estimation of Project Buffers in Critical Chain Project Management," *Proceedings of the IEEE International Conference on Management of Innovation and Technology (ICMIT)* (2000): 162–167.

20. E.M. Goldratt, *Critical Chain*.

21. For Prochain software, see www.prochain. com. Project Scheduler software is produced by Sciforma Corporation, see www.sciforma. com while the Concerto program was developed by Realization Corporation, see www. realization.com.

22. D.M. Tsai and H.N. Chiu, "Two Heuristics for Scheduling Multiple Projects with Resource Constraints," *Construction Management and Economics* 14, no. 4 (1996): 325–340; S. Al-jibouri, "Effects of Resource Management Regimes on Project Schedule," *International Journal of Project Management* 20, no. 4 (2002): 271–277 as well as M. Chelaka, L. Abeyasinghe, D.J. Greenwood, and D.E. Johansen, "An Efficient Method for Scheduling Construction Projects with Resource Constraints," *International Journal of Project Management* 19, no. 1 (2001): 29–45.

23. S.S. Panwalkar and W. Iskander, "A Survey of Scheduling Rules," *Operations Research* 25, no. 1 (1977): 45–61.

24. P.J. Viljoen, Goldratt Schools, Personal communication, Pretoria, South Africa, May 2007.

25. J.R. Turner, *The Handbook of Project-Based Management* (UK: McGraw-Hill, 1993).

26. E.M. Goldratt, *The Goal* (Great Barrington, MA: The North River Press, First edition 1984, Second edition 1986, Second revised edition 1992).

27. R.C. Newbold, *Project Management in the Fast Lane—Applying the Theory of Constraints* (Boca Raton, FL: St Lucie Press, 1998) as well as L.P. Leach, *Critical Chain Project Management*. Also see H. Steyn, "Project Management Applications of the Theory of Constraints Beyond Critical Chain Scheduling," *International Journal of Project Management* 20, no. 1 (January 2002): 75–80.

28. In *The Goal* and *The Race* by E.M. Goldratt and R.E. Fox (both Croton-on-Hudson, NY: North River Press, 1986) the notion of using the constraint (drum) to set the pace is described.

29. Adapted from training material of Realization. See www.realization.com.

30. S. Dass and H. Steyn, "An Exploratory Assessment of Project Duration in Multiple-Project Schedules Where Resources Are Allocated by the Theory of Constraints Method," *SA Journal of Industrial Engineering* 17, no. 1 (2006): 39–54.

31. Cohen A. Mandelbaum and A. Shtub, "Multi-project Scheduling and Control: A Process-Based Comparative Study of the Critical Chain Methodology and Some Alternatives," *Project Management Journal* 35, no. 2 (2004): 39–50.

32. E.R. Clayton and L.J. Moore, "PERT versus GERT," *Journal of Systems Management* 23, no. 2 (February 1972): 11–19; L.J. Moore and E.R. Clayton, *GERT Modeling and Simulation: Fundamentals and Application* (New York: Petrocelli/Charter, 1976); Wiest and Levy, *A Management Guide to PERT/CPM*, 150–158.

33. Ibid.

34. J.J. Moder and C.R. Philips, *Project Management with CPM and PERT* (London, Van Nostrand Reinhold Co., 1985).

35. See H. Steyn, "An Investigation into the Fundamentals of Critical Chain Project Scheduling," *International Journal of Project Management* 19 (2000): 363–369.

36. See for example J.R. Turner, "Controlling Progress with Planned Cost or Budgeted Cost," *International Journal of Project Management* 18, no. 3 (2000): 153–154.

37. Adapted from H. Steyn (Ed.), *Project Management—A Multi-disciplinary Approach* (Pretoria: FPM Publishing, 2003).

38. Ibid.

Chapter 8

Cost Estimating and Budgeting

A billion here and a billion there. Pretty soon it starts to add up to real money.

–SENATOR EVERETT DIRKSEN

Cost estimates, budgets, work breakdown structures (WBSs), and schedules are interrelated concepts. Ideally, cost estimates are based upon elements of the WBS and are prepared at the work package level. When the cost of a work task cannot be estimated because it is too complex, the task is broken down further until it can. When the cost cannot be estimated because of uncertainties about the work, the initial estimate is based upon judgment and later revised as information becomes available. Project schedules dictate resource requirements and the rate of expenditures, but as described in the last chapter, the converse is also true: constraints on resources and working capital dictate project schedules. Imposing practical constraints on costs is necessary so that realistic project budgets can be established. Failing to do so results in projects that are prematurely terminated for lack of funds, or are completed but at an exorbitant expense. Both occurrences are relatively commonplace.

Cost estimating, budgeting, and cost control sometimes are thought to be the exclusive concerns of planners and accountants, but in projects they should be of concern to everyone. Project participants who best understand the work—the engineers, scientists, systems specialists, architects, or others who are the closest to the sources of costs—should be involved in the estimating and budgeting process (commonly, however, these same people are disdainful of budgets and ignorant about how they work and why they are necessary). Project managers must also be involved. They do not have to be financial wizards to contribute to the estimating and budgeting process, but they do need skill in organizing and using cost figures.

The project manager oversees the cost estimating and budgeting process, though often with the assistance of a staff cost accountant. Technical projects should also have a *cost engineer*, someone able to track and assess both technical and financial aspects of the project. The cost engineer reviews deliverables, their requirements, specifications and control methods, assesses the project from both cost and technical points of view, and provides cost and technical advice to the project manager.

8.1 COST ESTIMATING

The initial cost estimate can seal a project's financial fate. When project costs are overestimated (too high), the contractor risks losing out to a lower bidding competitor. Worse is when the cost is underestimated. A $50,000 fixed price bid might win the contract, but obviously the contractor will lose money if the cost ends up at $80,000. Underestimates are often accidental—the result of being overly optimistic, although sometimes they are intentional—the result of trying too hard to beat the competition. In a practice called *buy in*, the contractor reduces an initially realistic estimate just enough to win the contract, hoping to cut costs, or renegotiate higher fees after the work is underway. The practice is risky, unethical, and, sadly, relatively commonplace. In large capital projects the tendency is to underestimate costs (and over estimate benefits) to get the needed funding and the project underway, after which the original estimate is soon forgotten.

But a very low bid can signify more than the desire to get a contract. It may imply that the contractor has cut corners, left things out, or was just sloppy in arriving at the estimate. The consequences for both client and contractor can be catastrophic, from operating at a loss to bankruptcy. Cost estimates are used to develop budgets and become the baseline against which project performance is evaluated. After the project begins the rate of actual cost expenditure is compared to the rate of estimated expenditure (indicated in the budget) as an important measure of project work performance. Without good estimates it is impossible to evaluate work efficiency or to determine in advance how much the finished project will cost.

8.2 COST ESCALATION

Accurate cost estimating is sometimes a difficult task—largely because it begins during project conception and well before all necessary, final information about the project is available. The less well defined the project, the less information there is, and the greater the chances that the estimated costs will substantially differ from final, actual figures. As a rule, the difference will be on the side of a cost overrun. The amount by which actual costs increase to overrun the initial estimated costs is referred to as *cost escalation*.[1]

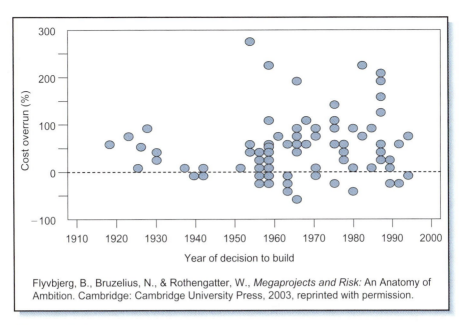

Flyvbjerg, B., Bruzelius, N., & Rothengatter, W., *Megaprojects and Risk:* An Anatomy of Ambition. Cambridge: Cambridge University Press, 2003, reprinted with permission.

Figure 8-1
Projects versus Percent Cost Overrun.

Some escalation can be expected, and up to 20 percent is relatively common. Usually, the larger, more complex the project, the greater the potential for escalation. Cutting edge, high-technology, and R&D projects frequently show cost escalations upwards of several hundred percent. The Concorde supersonic airliner cost more than five times the original estimate, nuclear power plants frequently cost two to three times their estimates, and NASA spacecraft often exceed estimates by a factor of four to five.

Figure 8-1 shows a plot of percent cost overrun versus year of decision to build for 111 transportation-related projects spanning approximately 80 years.[2] The same study that produced this graph also looked at cost overrun versus year of completion for 246 other projects, and got a similar picture. Clearly, overruns have been and remain relatively common. How does that happen? There are many reasons, some avoidable, some not.

Uncertainty and Lack of Accurate Information

Much of the information needed to make accurate estimates is simply not available when early cost figures are first developed. In NASA, for example, lack of well-defined spacecraft design and unclear definition of experiments are the principal reasons for cost overruns. Not until later, when the design is finalized and work activities are well defined (usually during the definition phase or later) can material and labor costs be accurately determined. In most research and development projects the activities are unpredictable, of uncertain duration, or must be repeated.

But sometimes the uncertainty stems from lack of effort. In general, to reduce escalation from uncertainty, management should strive for the most definitive scope of work and clearest, most specific project objectives. The clearer the objectives, scope, and requirements definition, the better the work definition and the more accurate the cost estimates.

Whenever changes in product design or project schedule are needed due to changes in the state of the art or product concept, developmental barriers, strikes, legal entanglements, or skyrocketing wage and material costs, then the original cost estimate should be updated and become the new cost baseline for tracking and controlling project costs.

To make allowances for uncertainty, an amount called a *contingency fund* or *budget reserve* is added to the original estimate.[3] This is the budget equivalent of the *schedule reserve* or *buffer* mentioned in the previous chapter. The contingency amount, which can be added to individual work packages or the project as a whole, is proportionate to the uncertainty of the work; the greater the uncertainty, the higher the contingency amount. The project manager controls the reserve and its allocation to cover overruns.

Contingency funds are intended to offset small variations arising from estimating errors, omissions, minor design changes, small schedule slippages, and so on. Each time the cost estimate is updated, so is the contingency fund. The contingency fund is not a "slush" fund. When no longer needed as intended, it should be cut from the project budget in order not to be used elsewhere; otherwise, the tendency is for costs to rise to expend whatever remains in the fund. Contingencies are discussed later as an aspect of the cost estimating process.

Changes in Requirements or Design

Another source of cost escalation is discretionary, nonessential changes to system requirements and plans. These changes come from a change in mind, not from oversights, mistakes, or environmental changes that would make them imperative. The routine tendency is for users and contractors alike to want to continually modify systems and procedures—to make "improvements" to original plans throughout the project life cycle. These kinds of changes are especially common in the absence of exhaustive planning or strict control procedures.

Contracts occasionally include a *change clause* that allows the customer to make certain changes to contract requirements—sometimes for additional payment, sometimes not. The clause gives the customer flexibility to incorporate requirements not envisioned at the time of the original contract agreement. It can be exercised at any time and the contractor is obligated to comply. Any change, however, no matter how small, causes escalation. To implement a change usually requires a combination of redesign or reorganizing work, acquiring new or different resources, altering previous plans, and undoing or scrapping earlier work. The further along the project, the more difficult and costly it is to make changes.

When accumulated, even small changes have a substantial effect on schedules, costs, and performances. Formal mechanisms such as a *change control system* described in Chapter 11 help reduce the number of changes and contain escalation.

Economic and Social Factors

Even with good initial estimates and few changes, cost escalation occurs because of social and economic forces beyond the contractor's or user's influence. Labor strikes, legal action by interest groups, trade embargoes, and materials shortages all serve to stifle progress and increase costs, but can neither be precisely anticipated nor factored in to plans and budgets. Whenever project work is suspended or interrupted, administrative and overhead costs continue to mount, interest and leasing expenses continue to accrue on borrowed capital and equipment, and the date when payback begins and profit is earned is set back. Rarely can such problems be anticipated and their impacts incorporated into the contingency fund.

One economic factor that has major influence on cost escalation and project profitability is *inflation*.[4] The contractor might try to offset increases from inflation by inflating the price of the project, although the actions of competitors or federal restrictions on price increases often preclude doing that. Some protection from inflation may be gained by including clauses in the contract that allow increases in wage or material costs to be appended to the contract price,[5] but the protection may be limited. Inflation is not one dimensional; it varies depending on the labor, materials, and equipment employed, the geographical region, and the country. Subcontractors, suppliers, and clients use different kinds of contracts that have different inflation protection clauses and that might or might not be advantageous to other parties in the project.

Inflation also causes cash flow difficulties. Even when a contract includes an inflation clause, payment for inflation-related costs is tied to the publication of inflation indices, which always lags behind inflation. Although contractors pay immediately for the effects of inflation, not until later are they reimbursed for these effects.

Trend analysis of inflation in the industry and economy can improve the accuracy of cost estimates. In long-term projects especially, wage rates should be projected to forecast what they will be at the time they must be paid; this is done by starting with best estimates of labor hours and wage costs in current dollars, then applying inflation rates over the project's length.

In international projects, costs escalate also because of changes in *exchange rates*. When the costs are incurred in one currency but paid for in another, a change in the exchange rate will cause the relative values of costs and payments to change, resulting in an escalation of cost or price. This topic is considered further in Chapter 18.

Initial cost estimates are based upon prices at the time of estimating. After that, whenever actual costs are compared with initial estimates, inflation adjustments must be included so there remains a common basis upon which to identify variances and take corrective action.

Inefficiency, Poor Communication, and Lack of Control

Cost escalation also results from work inefficiency, poor management, poor planning, lack of supervision, and weak control. In large projects especially, poor coordination, miscommunication, and sloppy control lead to conflicts, misunderstandings, duplication of effort, and mistakes. This is *one* source of cost escalation where management can have a substantial influence. Meticulous work planning, tracking and monitoring of activities, team building, and tight control all help improve efficiency and contain cost escalation.

Ego Involvement of the Estimator

Cost escalation also comes from the *way* people estimate. Many people are overly optimistic and habitually underestimate the time and cost it will take to do a job, especially in areas where they have little experience. Have you ever estimated how long it would take for *you* to paint a room or tile a floor? How long did it *really* take? Many think of an estimate as an "optimistic prediction." They confuse estimates with goals and see the estimate as a reflection upon themselves, not an honest prediction of what it will take. The more "ego involvement" of the estimator in the job, the more unreliable the estimate. (Of course, sometimes the opposite happens: worried they might not have estimated enough time or cost, people "pad" the estimates to avoid overruns.)

The problem can be reduced by obtaining cost estimates from professional estimators (people other than those who will actually do the work). Remember the earlier contention about the necessity of involving project participants in planning the project? Experienced workers are usually much better at estimating tasks, materials, and time than they are costs. Although the doers (those who do the work) should *define* the work and provide estimates for resources and time, professional estimators should review the estimates for accuracy, check with the doers, and then prepare the cost estimates. A cost estimate should not be a goal; it should be a reasonable prediction of what will happen. Estimators must be, organizationally, in a position where they will not be coerced to provide estimates that conform to anyone's desires.[6]

Project Contract

Chapter 3 describes the relative merits of different forms of contracts, some of which are related to the contract's influence on cost escalation.[7] Consider, for example, the two basic kinds of contracts: fixed price and cost-plus. A fixed price agreement gives the contractor incentive to control costs because, no matter what happens, the amount paid for the project remains the same. In contrast, a strictly cost-plus contract offers little or no incentive to control costs. In fact, when profit is computed as a percentage of costs (rare these days), the contract motivates contractors to "allow" costs to escalate. Other forms of agreements such as incentive contracts permit cost increases, but encourage cost control and provide motivation to minimize escalation.

Bias and Ambition[8]

Finally, it is human for the champions of projects to be optimistically biased toward their projects. In fact, without champions most projects would never start and humankind might be worse off. That bias however might lead to not only overestimating benefits but also underestimating costs. Promoters of big projects have learned that if a project is important enough, sufficient funding to complete it will materialize, no matter the size of the overrun. The result is that the actual project cost, with near certainty, will overrun the estimate.

Example 1: Escalation of the Bandra-Worli Sea Link Project

January 1999—Government Clears Worli-Bandra Cable Bridge
February 2001—Worli-Bandra Sea link Enters Crucial Stage
October 2002—Bandra-Worli Sea Link Toll to Be Costlier
October 2003—Bandra-Worli Sea Link May Hit a Dead End
January 2004—Bandra-Worli Sea Link Project Under Threat
July 2005—Sea link in Trouble Over Extension
May 2006—Bandra-Worli Sea Link to Be Ready by 2008

The headlines from local news media refer to the Bandra-Worli Sea Link (BWSL) roadway and cable-stayed bridge in Mumbai—India's equivalent to San Francisco's Golden Gate Bridge and a good example of megaproject woes. The completed 8-kilometer bridge and its approaches will arc 200 meters into the Arabian Sea to connect downtown Mumbai with its western suburbs. The current route is 12 kilometers and takes an hour travel time; purportedly the link will cut that time in half.

The project was approved in early 1999 following 7 years of study: it was supposed to start in May, cost 650 crores (US $120 million), and finish by mid-2001. But work did not begin until December, and by then the estimated completion date had slipped to mid-2002. Then came the monsoons, which brought the project to a near halt in 2000 and 2001. In late 2001 the project's prime consultant, Sverdrup, was dropped for failure to provide a "competent project engineer." The replacement, Dar Consultants, modified the bridge design by adding 2.8 kilometers to its length and splitting the eight-lane main bridge into two, four-lane roadways. By January 2002 the scheduled completion date had slipped to March 2004. In October it was announced that project costs had increased by 50 crores; due to a "paucity of funds" work had to be slowed and the completion date pushed back to September 2004. A year later, monsoons and rough seas again halted work, delaying the completion date to 2005. Meantime, complaints grew from fishermen concerned about the link's interference with their boats, and from environmentalists about its harm to marine ecology. In 2003, rains again stalled the project for many months. The project's primary contractor, Hindustan Construction Company, requested an additional 300 crores to cover delays and design changes, but the government balked and offered to pay only 120 crores. The controversy stalled the project for almost a year, though eventually funds materialized and the project resumed—as did the delays and cost escalation: by June 2005 the completion date had slipped to September 2006 and the total project cost had risen to 1,306 crores (US $291 M). In May 2006 the completion date was again pushed back, this time to April 2008.

As illustrated, schedule delays and cost escalation are inextricably connected. In the first 7 years of the BWSL project the target date had slipped 7 years and the price doubled. The contributing factors included unknowns (weather), changes in scope and requirements (bridge and roadway design), social factors (livelihood and environmental impact worries), economics (growing land values and interest), and management (dismissal of a major contractor).

8.3 COST ESTIMATING AND THE SYSTEMS DEVELOPMENT CYCLE[9]

Developing the project cost estimate is closely tied to the phases of the project life cycle:

(A) *Conception*: initiation/feasibility
(B) *Definition*: detailed planning/analysis
(C) *Execution*: design/fabrication/implementation

The first cost estimate is made during project conception. At this time very little hard cost information is available so the estimate is the least reliable that it will ever be. Uncertainty about the cost and duration of the project may be large, as illustrated by the largest "region of time–cost uncertainty" in Figure 8-2. How much the project will *really* cost and how long it will *really* take are open questions. The project is compared to other, similar projects, and an estimate is made based upon standards of what it should take—labor time, materials, and equipment—to do the job. This approach is less useful when the project involves research and development because few of the tasks can be classified as "standard" and there are no similar projects. Initial estimates are largely "guesstimates" and might end up being nowhere close to actual costs.

If the project is unique and ill-defined, uncertainty in cost estimates often dictates that contracts awarded be of the cost-plus form. Only after much of the system and project has been defined can the material costs, labor requirements, and

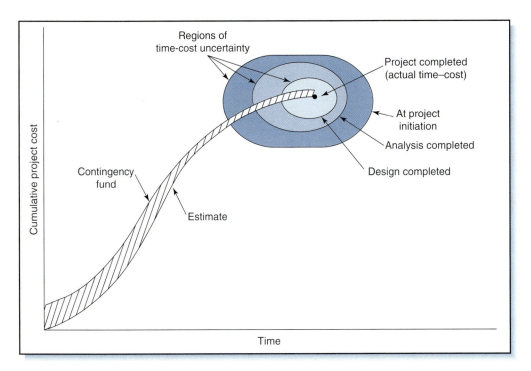

Figure 8-2
Time-cost graph showing cumulative project cost and regions of time-cost uncertainty.

labor rates be nailed down, and reliable cost estimates made. The shrinking time-cost uncertainty regions in Figure 8-2 illustrate this. When the system and project are fairly routine and the estimates somewhat reliable, contractors are willing to accept incentive-type or fixed price contracts. In fact, the awarding of contracts is sometimes put off until designs are somewhat complete so that cost estimates can be more certain. This of course requires contractors to do a lot of front-end work without assurances that they will be awarded the job. When contractors are required to bid before they can attain reliable estimates, they must include substantial contingencies in the estimates to cover the uncertainty.

As the project moves into middle and later phases with work being completed and funds expended, cost estimates become more certain. Often, to control usage of the contingency fund, the amount in the fund is decreased as the project progresses. A project starting out with a contingency of 15 percent of the base estimate might be decreased to a contingency of 8 percent when the project is half completed, then to 3 percent when it is three-fourths completed, and then to just 1 percent to cover small corrections during the final stages of installation and sign-off.

As discussed in Chapter 4, a detailed plan usually is developed only for the next (most immediate) phase of the project, and part of that plan will include a cost estimate and cost commitments for the upcoming phase. At the same time, every attempt is made to look beyond the upcoming phase and to develop realistic, accurate cost estimates for the entire project.

Once developed and approved, the cost estimate is used to establish the budget and becomes the baseline against which progress and performance will be evaluated. It is thus bad practice to frequently change the estimate later in the project life cycle because it destroys the purpose of having a baseline. Sometimes, however, escalation factors render the estimate obsolete and mandate periodic revisions to the budget.

8.4 LIFE CYCLE COSTS

Life cycle costs (LCC) represent all the costs of a system, facility, or product throughout its full cradle-to-grave life cycle. The concept originated in military procurement when it was realized that product development represents but the tip of the cost iceberg—that the cost to operate (e.g., fuel consumption) and maintain (e.g., parts replacement) a system or product is usually far greater. Whereas the emphasis in this chapter is on *project costs*, i.e., costs incurred during the *project* life cycle phases of Definition and Execution, LCC include the reminder of the systems development cycle—the Operations phase and eventual disposal of the end-item—and, sometimes, for the Conception phase too (initiation and feasibility).

Anticipating the LCC is necessary because costs influence many decisions. For example, suppose three contractors submit proposals to build a plant, and each proposal contains not only the plant acquisition (construction) price but also the plant's expected operating costs. If the bids are similar in terms of construction costs and plant features, the bid with the lowest operating costs will likely win.

The LCC similarly affects decisions regarding research and development; indeed, the initial feasibility study of a project should take into account *all the costs* for acquisition, operation, maintenance, and disposal of the system, product, or facility. For example, most US aerospace manufacturers in the 1970s were hesitant to develop a supersonic commercial aircraft because of cost and environmental impact concerns. Costs to develop and produce the aircraft were projected to be high, as were costs for operation and maintenance. At issue were whether enough people would pay the high ticket prices necessary for the airlines to make a profit, and whether enough airlines would purchase the jet for the manufacturers to make money. Ultimately, many felt the answer was no on both counts. Congress canceled subsidies for developing the aircraft, and the program dissolved. Meantime the Europeans decided differently and went on to manufacture the Concorde, only 14 of which went into service. Concordes flew for nearly 27 years and the last one was retired in 2003. The LCC was never recouped, and had not the governments of Great Britain and France provided subsidies, the airlines and manufacturers would have lost money.

Key decisions affecting the operation, maintenance, and disposal of a system are made early in the project life cycle—during Conception and Definition. When a product is conceived and designed so as to have a relatively low operating cost, it becomes more appealing—even if its development cost and purchase price are higher. For example, the high cost of developing more fuel-efficient vehicles might require those vehicles to be priced higher than other less efficient vehicles, but customers will readily pay the price if they know that over the life of the vehicle they will recoup the price excess through fuel savings and lower pollution. Of course, estimating the LCC always involves assumptions about technology, market, and product demand, and relies on historical costs of similar systems and projects; nonetheless, it is a sensible way to approach projects, especially when a choice exists among alternative designs or proposals.

The LCC should also account for the time necessary to develop and build the end-item, i.e., the time before a facility or system becomes operational or a product is "launched" to market. Time is important: it determines how soon the end-item will start generating revenues, gaining market share, and accruing profits or other benefits. The additional benefits gained from an early launch are compared to the higher costs of crashing the project using the time-cost tradeoff approach discussed in Chapter 7. Similarly, the *cost of disposal* at the end of the life cycle must also be estimated; for facilities such as mines and nuclear power plants that require shutdown and rehabilitation after their useful lives, this cost can be substantial.

Analysis of LCC is also necessary for setting targets on development and operating costs, and making design tradeoff decisions to achieve those targets. Following is an example.

Example 2: Life Cycle Costs for an Operational Fleet of Spaceships

(This illustration extends on previous SpaceshipOne examples, but the numbers are purely hypothetical.) Having gained experience from SpaceshipOne, a larger spaceship and mothership are being designed. The new spaceship will carry five people (pilot plus four paying passengers), go as high as 120 kilometers, and be capable of 20 flights per year over an operational life of 5 years. The cost of developing and producing four of these spaceships and two motherships is estimated at $80 million. Meantime, a survey indicates that the number of people worldwide willing to pay the $190,000 ticket price to fly into space is at least 1,000 per year.

A "spaceline" that will use and maintain the fleet of spaceships is being created for a startup cost of $10 million. Operational costs for the spaceline consist of two parts: annual costs for ground operations (reservations, personnel, ground facilities, etc.) and per-flight costs for flight operations (fuel, parts, repairs, etc., for the spaceship and the mothership). Ground operations costs are placed at $2 million per year and per-flight costs at $0.4 million per flight. (The costs are assumed constant for every year and flight, respectively, although realistically they would vary up or down depending on inflation, the learning curve, efficiencies, and economies of scale as more spaceships are added to the fleet. Annual revenues are assumed constant too, though realistically they would start out small and grow over time until the full fleet of spaceships is operational.) Given these costs and ignoring other factors (e.g., time value of money), what is the LCC for the venture?

Assumptions

Four spaceships @ 20 flights/year each = 80 flights/year (320 passengers/year, which lies well within the estimated annual demand). Five years of operation.
Costs:

- *Development and manufacturing*: $80 million
- *Spaceline startup*: $10 million
- *Ground operations*: $2 million per year
- *Flight operations*: $0.4 million per flight

Ticket price: $190,000 (marketing slogan: "Now YOU can go to space for under $200,000!")

LCC Model

LCC ($ million) = Development and production cost
+ Startup cost + Operating cost (5 years)
= $80 + $10 + ([5 year × $2] + [5 year × 80 flights × $0.4])
= $260 million

Total revenues ($ million) = (5 years × 80 flights × 4 passengers × $0.190)
= $304 million.

Bottom line: Assuming the assumptions are correct, revenues will exceed costs by $44 million.

The numbers are of course estimates, but some are more certain than others. For example, based upon experience with SpaceShipOne, the development cost might be fairly certain, but due to lack of long-term operational experience the per-flight cost is fairly uncertain. Startup and ground operations costs, if analogous to airline operations, might be somewhat certain, although passenger demand might be fairly uncertain.

The LCC model plays an important role in system design and development. Using the model a sensitivity analysis can be performed to see what happens when costs are varied up or down and to show best-case, most-likely, and worst-case scenarios. The model can also be used to determine by how much and in what combination the costs must vary before the enterprise becomes lucrative or disastrous.

The LCC model is also used to set cost targets. If the decision is made to proceed with the $80 million development and production cost, then the project must be planned, budgeted, and controlled so as to stay close to that amount. If the per-flight cost is set at $0.4 million, the project must strive to develop a spacecraft and mothership that will cost no more than that to operate. This will affect innumerable design decisions pertaining to many details. Early on, the design analysis must consider major alternatives (e.g., a spaceship to carry five or six passengers instead of four) and the expected costs, revenues, and benefits for each.

The best and only truly comprehensive approach to estimating and analyzing LCC is with a team of people that represents all phases of the system or product life cycle—a cross-functional team of designers, builders, suppliers, and users, i.e., a *concurrent engineering team*. Concurrent engineering for life cycle costing is further discussed in Chapter 13.

8.5 Cost Estimating Process

Estimate versus Target or Goal

Sometimes the word "estimate" is confused with "target" and "goal." It shouldn't be. An estimate is a *realistic assessment* based upon known facts about the work, required resources, constraints, and the environment, derived from estimating methods, whereas a target or goal is a desired outcome, commitment, or promise. Other than by chance, the estimate usually will *not* be the same as the target or goal. That said, once computed the estimate can be compared to a target value or goal, and revised by making hard-headed changes to the cost origins—work tasks, resources, schedules, etc. The point is, an estimate should be determined *independently* of any target or goal; afterward it can be altered by adjusting the work and resources to bring it as close as possible to the target, but never should the estimate be a simple plug-in of the target value.

Accuracy versus Precision

"Accuracy" represents the closeness of the estimated value to the actual value: the accuracy of a project estimated to cost $99,000 but actually costing $100,000 is very good. In contrast, "precision" is the number of decimal places in the estimate. An estimate of $75,321 is more precise than one of $75,000, though *neither* is *accurate* if the actual cost is $100,000. Accuracy is more important than precision: the aim is to derive the most accurate estimate possible.

Classifying Work Tasks and Costs

The cost estimating process begins by breaking the project down into work phases such as design, engineering, development, and fabrication, or into work packages from the WBS. The project team, including members from the involved functional areas and contractors, meets to discuss the work phases or packages, and to receive specific work assignments.

The team tries to identify tasks in the project that are similar to existing designs and standard practices and can readily be adopted. Work is classified either as *developmental* or as an adaptation of existing or off-the-shelf (OTS) designs, techniques, or procedures. Because developmental work requires effort in design, testing, and fabrication, cost estimating is more difficult compared to OTS due to the greater uncertainty about what needs to be done. Overruns for developmental work are common, especially due to inaccurate labor estimates. In contrast, estimating for OTS items or duplicated work is straightforward because it is based upon known prices, or records of material and labor costs for similar systems or tasks. It is thus often beneficial to make use of existing designs and technology as much as possible.

Estimated costs are classified as *recurring* and *nonrecurring*.[10] Recurring costs happen more than once and are associated with tasks periodically repeated, such as costs for quality assurance and testing. Nonrecurring costs happen once and are associated with development, fabrication, and testing of one-of-a-kind items, or procurement of special items.

In the pure project form of organization the project manager delegates the responsibility for the estimating effort, combines the estimated results, and presents the final figures to management. In a matrix organization, estimating is the joint responsibility of the project and functional managers, though the project manager coordinates the effort and accumulates the results. The estimating effort requires close coordination and communication between the estimating groups to avoid redundancies and omissions.

Although this typifies the cost estimating process, the actual method used to estimate cost figures will depend on the required accuracy of and the information available to make the estimate. Cost estimates are determined using variants of four basic techniques: expert opinion, analogy, parametric, and cost engineering.

Expert Opinion

An *expert opinion* is an estimate provided by an expert—someone who from breadth of experience and expertise is able to provide a reasonable, ballpark estimate. It is a "seat of the pants" estimate used when lack of information precludes a more-detailed, in-depth cost analysis. Expert opinion is usually limited to cost estimating during the conception phase and for projects that are poorly defined or unique, for which there are no previous, similar projects to compare.

Analogy Estimate

An *analogy estimate* is developed by reviewing costs from previous, similar projects. The method can be used at any level: overall project cost can be estimated from the cost of an analogous project; work package cost can be estimated from other, analogous workpackages; and task cost can be estimated from analogous tasks. The cost for a similar project or work package is analyzed and adjusted for differences between it and the proposed project or work package, taking into account factors such as dates, project scale, location, complexity, exchange rates, and so on. If, for example, the analogy project was performed 2 years ago and the proposed project is to commence 1 year from now, costs from the analogy project must be adjusted for inflation and price changes during the 3-year interim. If the analogy project was conducted in California and the proposed project will be in New York, costs must be adjusted for site and regional differences. If the "size" (scope, capacity, or performance) of the proposed task is twice that of the analogy task, then the costs of the analogy task must be "scaled" up. However, twice the size does not mean twice the cost, and the size–cost relationship must be determined from analogy or formulas based on physical principles.

Example 3: Estimating Project Costs by Scaling an Analogy Project

So-called process industries such as petrochemicals, breweries, and pharmaceuticals use the following formula to estimate the costs of proposed projects:

$$\text{Cost (proposed)} = \text{Cost (analogy)}[\text{Capacity (proposed)}/\text{Capacity (analogy)}]^{2/3}$$

where "proposed" refers to a new facility and "analogy" to an analogous facility. In practice, the exponent varies from 0.35 to 0.9, depending on the kind of process and equipment used.[11]

Suppose a proposed plant is to have a 3.5 million cum (cubic meter) capacity. Using an analogy project for a plant with 2.5 million cum capacity and a cost of $15 million, the formula gives the estimated cost for the proposed plant as

$$\$15 \text{ million}[3.5/2.5]^{0.75} = \$15 \text{ million}[1.2515] = \$18.7725 \text{ million}$$

Because the analogy method involves comparisons to previous, similar projects, it requires an extant information database about prior projects. Companies that are serious about using the analogy method must rely on good project cost documentation and a database that classifies cost information according to type of project, work package, task, and so on. When a new project is proposed, the database is used to provide cost details about prior similar projects and work packages. Of course, the first assumption in the analogy method is that the analogy to be used is valid; sometimes this is where things go awry.

Example 4: A Case of Costly Mistaken Analogy[12]

In the 1950s and 1960s when nuclear power plants were first being built in the USA, General Electric and Westinghouse, the two main contractors, together lost a *billion* dollars in less than 10 years on fixed price contracts because they had underestimated the costs. Although neither had expected to make money on these early projects, certainly they had not planned to *lose* so much either. The error in their method was assuming that nuclear power plants are analogous to refineries and coal power plants—for which the marginal costs actually get smaller as the plants get larger. But nuclear power plants are not like the other plants. For one thing, they require more safeguards. When a pipe springs a leak in a coal power plant, the water is turned off and the plant shut down until the leak is fixed. In a nuclear plant the water cannot be simply turned off, nor the plant shut down; the reactor continuously generates heat and if not cooled will melt, cause pipes to rupture, and dispersal of radiation. The water-cooling system needs a backup system, and the backup system needs a backup. Typical of many complex systems, costs for nuclear power plants increase somewhat exponentially with plant size—although in the early years of nuclear power nobody knew that.

Parametric Estimate

A *parametric estimate* is an estimate derived from an empirical or mathematical relationship. The parametric method can be used with an analogy project (the case in Example 3) to scale costs up or down, or it can be applied directly—without an analogy project—when costs are a function of system or project "parameters." The parameters can be physical features such as area, volume, weight, or capacity, or performance features such as speed, rate of output, power, or strength. Parametric cost estimating is especially useful when preliminary design characteristics are first being set and a cost estimate is needed quickly.

Example 5: Parametric Estimate of Material Costs

Warren Eisenberg, president of Warren Wonderworks, Inc., a warehousing facilities contractor, wants a quick way to estimate the material cost of a facility. The company's engineers investigate the relationship between several building parameters and the material costs for eight recent projects comparable in terms of general architecture, layout, and construction material. Using the method of least squares (a topic covered in textbooks on mathematical statistics), they develop the following formula—a multiple regression model that relates material cost (y) to floor space (x_1, in terms of 10,000 square feet) and number of shipping/receiving docks (x_2) in a building:

$$y = 201,978 + (41,490)x_1 + (17,230)x_2$$

The least squares method also indicates that the standard error of the estimate is small, which suggests that the model provides fairly accurate cost estimates for each of the eight projects.

Suppose a proposal is being prepared to construct a new 300,000 square feet facility with two docks. The estimated material cost using the model is thus:

$$y = 201,978 + (41,490)(30) + (17,230)(2) = \$1,481,138.$$

Cost Engineering

Cost engineering refers to detailed cost analysis of individual cost categories at the work package or task level. It is a bottom-up approach that not only provides the most accurate estimates of all the methods but also is the most time-consuming; it requires considerable work-definition information—which often is not be available until later in the project. The method starts by breaking down the project into activities or work packages, then further divides these into cost categories. For small projects like Example 6 the approach is simple and straightforward.

Example 6: Cost Engineering Estimate for a Small Project

The project manager for the DMB project at Iron Butterfly Corp. is preparing a project cost estimate. He begins by breaking the project into eight work packages and creating a preliminary schedule. Three labor grades will be working on the project, and for each work package he estimates the number of required labor hours per week for each grade. Hours per week per labor grade are represented in the boxes in Figure 8-3.

For each work package he also estimates the cost of material, equipment, supplies, subcontracting, freight charges, travel, and other nonlabor expenses. Table 8-1 is a summary of the labor hours and nonlabor costs.

Total nonlabor cost (material, equipment, etc.) is thus $26,500. For labor grades 1, 2, and 3, suppose the hourly rates are $10, $12, and $15, respectively, and the overhead rates are 90, 100, and 120 percent, respectively (overhead rate

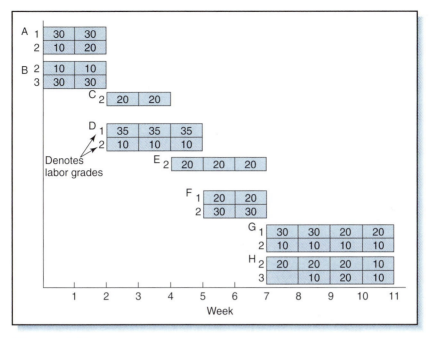

Figure 8-3
Schedule showing hours allocated to work packages by labor grade.

Table 8-1 Labor hours and nonlabor costs.

	Hours by Labor Grade			Nonlabor Costs			
Work Package	1	2	3	Material	Equipment	Subcontracts	Other
A	60	30		$ 500			
B		20	60		$1,000		
C		40			500		$ 500
D	105	30			500		
E		60				$4,500	
F	40	60		8,000	1,000	5,000	500
G	100	40		1,500			500
H		70	40		1,000		1,500
Total	305	350	100	$10,000	$4,000	$9,500	$3,000

is an amount *added* to the labor cost; determining overhead rates is discussed later). Therefore, labor-related costs are:

$$\text{Grade 1: } 305(\$10)(100\% + 90\%) = \$5,795$$
$$\text{Grade 2: } 350(\$12)(100\% + 100\%) = 8,400$$
$$\text{Grade 1: } 100(\$15)(100\% + 120\%) = 3,300$$
$$\$17,495$$

The preliminary estimate for labor and nonlabor cost is $17,495 + $26,500 = $43,995. Suppose Iron Butterfly Corp. routinely adds 10 percent to all projects to cover general and administrative expenses, which puts the cost at $43,995(1.1) = $48,395. To this Ralph adds another 10 percent as a project contingency, giving a final cost estimate for the DMB project of $48,395(1.1) = $53,235.

At the work package or lower level, detailed estimates are sometimes derived with the aid of *standards manuals* and *tables*. Standards manuals contain time and cost information about labor and materials to perform particular tasks. In construction, for example, the numbers of labor hours to install an electrical junction box or a square foot of wall forms are both standard times. To determine the labor cost of installing junction boxes in a building, the estimator determines the required number of junction boxes, multiplies this by the labor standard per box, and then multiplies that by the hourly labor rate. For software development the industry standard is one person-year to create 2,000 lines of bug-free code.

For larger projects the estimating procedure is roughly the same as illustrated in Example 6 although more involved. First, the manager of each work package breaks the work package down into more fundamental or "basic" areas of work. For example, a work package might be divided into two basic areas: "engineering" and "fabrication." The manager of the work package then asks his supervisors to estimate the hours and materials needed to do the work in each basic area. The supervisor overseeing engineering might further divide work into the tasks of structural analysis, computer analysis, layout drawings, installation drawings, manuals, and reproduction, then develop an estimate for each task duration and the labor grade or skill level required. In similar fashion, the fabrication supervisor might break the work down into fabricated materials (steel, piping, wiring), hardware, machinery, equipment, insurance, and so on, then estimate how much (quantity, size, length, weight, etc.) of each will be needed. Estimates of time and materials are determined by reference to previous, similar work, standards manuals, reference documents, and rules of thumb ("one hour for each line of code"). The supervisors submit their estimates to the work package manager who checks, revises, and then passes them on to the project manager. The more developmental and the less standardized the task, the more guesswork involved; even with routine or OTS items, accurate estimating is somewhat of an art.

The project manager and independent estimators or pricing experts on the project staff review the submitted time and material estimates to be sure that no costs were overlooked or duplicated, estimators understood what they were estimating, correct estimating procedures were used, and allowances made for risk and uncertainty.[13] The estimates are then aggregated as shown in Figure 8-4 and converted

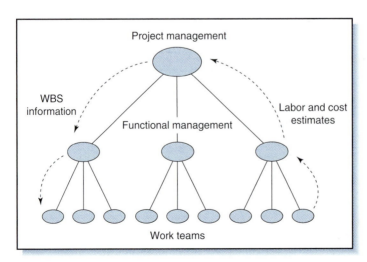

Figure 8-4
The estimating process.

into dollars using standard wage rates and material costs (current or projected). Finally, the project manager tallies in any project-wide overhead rates (to cover project management and administrative costs) and company-wide overhead rates (to cover the burden of general company expenses) to come up with a cost estimate for the total project. The accumulation of work package estimates (upward arrows in Figure 8-4) to derive the project estimate is called the "bottom-up" approach.

Contingency Amount

Contingency amounts are added to estimates to offset uncertainty. In general, the less well defined or more complex the situation, the greater the required amount. Contingency amounts can be developed for individual activities or work packages, or the project as a whole. *Activity contingency* is an amount estimated to account for "known unknowns" in an activity or work package, i.e., sources of cost increases that could or likely will occur; they include scrap and waste, design changes, increases in the scope, size, or function of the end-item, and delays due to weather. Later, when the project budget is established, this amount should be included in a special budget, subdivided into work package accounts and strictly controlled by the project manager. For the project cost estimate, the project manager sums these activity contingencies and adds them to the total project cost, yielding the *base estimate.*

To the base estimate the project manager might add yet another amount, a *project contingency*. This is to account for "unknown unknowns"—external factors that affect project costs but cannot be pinpointed. Examples include unforeseen fluctuation in exchange rates, shortages in resources, and changes in the market or competitive environment. The size of the contingency depends on the perceived risk and likelihood of cost escalation due to unknowns. Computing the contingency based on the perceived project risk is covered in Chapter 10. Any subsequent usage of project contingency funds, like that of the activity contingency, is controlled by the project manager. Adding the project contingency to the base estimate gives the *final cost estimate*, which is the *most likely cost.*

Besides the activity and project contingencies, the corporation might also set aside an additional allowance to cover overruns. This amount, the *overrun allowance*, is added to the most likely cost to yield a cost where the probability of exceeding it is less than 10 percent. The overrun allowance is controlled by a program manager or corporate managers and is ordinarily not available to the project manager without approval.

Top-down versus Bottom-up

In general, the application of the estimating techniques listed previously occur in two ways: top-down and bottom-up. Top-down refers to estimating the cost by looking at the project as a whole. A top-down estimate is typically based upon an expert opinion or analogy to other, similar projects. Bottom-up refers to estimating costs by breaking the project down into elements—individual project work packages and end-item components. Costs for each work package or end-item element are estimated separately and then aggregated to derive the total project cost. Example 6 is a bottom-up approach; Example 3 is a top-down approach. The two approaches can be used in combination: portions of a project that are well defined can be broken down into work packages and estimated bottom-up; other less-defined portions can be estimated top-down. In turn, the cost of each work package can be estimated by breaking the package into smaller elements and estimating the cost of each (bottom-up), or by making a gross estimate from analogy or expert opinion (top-down). The bottom-up method provides more accurate estimates than the top-down method but requires more data and concise definition of tasks.

Reconciling Estimates

The project manager submits the final cost estimate to company management along with forecasts showing the effects of likely, potential escalation factors such as inflation and risks. The estimate is compared against top management's *gross estimate*, the goal or target set by the company or customer. Based on the difference between the gross and bottom-up estimates, management either accepts the estimate or mandates a revision. If the gross estimate is larger, the project manager reviews each work package estimate for possible oversights or over-optimism. If the bottom-up estimate is larger, the project manager reviews the work package estimates for incorrect assumptions, excesses, and other sources of excess cost.

Reducing Costs

What happens if competition or insufficient funding forces management to reduce costs? Managers will want to retain their share of the project and none will want to see budget or staff reduced. Nonmanagement professionals such as engineers, scientists, or systems analysts, unless actively involved in the budgeting process, are often unaware of budget constraints and resist cuts. Here is where communication, negotiation, and diplomacy between project managers and functional managers and staff are necessary to convince the latter to accept a share of budget reductions. When this fails the project manager must look for ways to reduce costs (e.g., reduce work scope or labor requirements or use less costly resources) and convince the team to accept the reductions (dashed arrows in Figure 8-4). If that fails, the final resort is to appeal to top management.[14] To reconcile differences between estimates, top management sometimes exercises an across-the-board cut on all estimates. This is poor practice because it fails to account for judgmental errors or excessive costs on the part of just a few units. It also unfairly penalizes managers who tried to produce fair estimates and were honest enough not to pad them. Such indiscriminate, across-the-board cuts induce everyone to pad estimates for their own protection.

Suppose you are the project manager and it is clear that management insists on a budget that is too low to perform the work. There are only two courses of action: either undertake the project and attempt wholeheartedly to meet the budget, or hand it over to another manager.[15] If you decide on the former, you should document your disagreement and report it to top management; later, the client might agree to changes that would reduce costs and enable it to be completed within budget. If the contract is cost-plus, then the risk is low because additional costs will be reimbursed. If the contract is fixed price and the budget is so underfunded as to likely require cutting corners or stalling the project, then you should suggest to management that they appoint another project manager (who, assuming your argument is valid, might then argue the same case). Not only is this good business practice, it is the only ethical alternative.

8.6 ELEMENTS OF BUDGETS AND ESTIMATES

Budgets and estimates are similar in that both state the cost of doing something. The difference is that the estimate comes first and is the basis for the budget. An estimate may have to be refined many times, but once approved it becomes the budget. Organizations and work units are then committed to performing work according to the budget: It is the agreed-upon contracted amount of what the work should cost and the baseline against which expenditures will be compared for tracking and control purposes. Project budgets and fiscal operating budgets are similar; the difference is that the former covers the life of a project, the latter only a year at a time.

Estimates and budgets share most or all of the following elements:

- Direct labor expense
- Direct nonlabor expense
- Overhead expense
- General and administrative expense
- Profit and total billing

Direct Labor Expense[16]

Direct labor expense is the charge of labor for the project. For each task or work package, an estimate is made as to the number of people needed in each labor grade, and the number of hours or days for each. This gives the distribution of labor hours or days required for each labor grade. The labor hours for the various grades are then multiplied by their respective wage rates. The work package budget in Figure 8-5 is an example, showing the wage rates for three labor grades and the associated labor hours time-phased over a 6-month period.

When the wage rate is expected to change over the course of the work, a weighted average wage rate is used. In Figure 8-5, suppose the initial rate for assistant is expected to increase from $20 to $25 in months 3, 4, and 5. The labor cost for assistant in months 2, 3, 4, and 5 would then increase from $8,000 to 100($20) + 100($25) +

Figure 8-5
Typical 6-month budget for a work package.

Project **CASTLE**   Date **April 1, 1592**

Department **Excavating**   Work package **Moat**

Charge	Rate	Months[+] 1	2	3	4	5	6	Totals Hours	Cost
Direct labor									
Professional	$35/hour	50				50		100	3,500
Associate	$30/hour								
Assistant	$20/hour		100	100	100	100		400	8,000
Direct labor cost		1,750	2,000	2,000	2,000	3,750			11,500
Labor overhead	75%	1,312	1,500	1,500	1,500	2,813			8,625
Other direct cost*			100						100
Total direct cost		3,062	3,600	3,500	3,500	6,563			20,225
General/administrative	10%	306	360	350	350	657			2,023
Total costs		3,368	3,960	3,850	3,850	7,220			22,248
Profit	15%								
Billing total									

[+]Should extend for as many months as required by the project.
*Should be itemized to include costs for materials, freight, subcontracts, travel, and all other nonlabor direct costs.

100($25) + 100($25) = $9,500. (The average wage rate would thus be $9,500/400 hours = $23.75/hour.) Notice that the average wage rate changes whenever the distribution of hours changes. In the example, had the work been evenly distributed 100 hours/month over months 1 through 4 (instead of over months 2 through 5), the average wage for assistant would have been $9,000/400 hours = $22.50/hour.

Direct Nonlabor Expense

Direct nonlabor expense is the total expense of nonlabor charges applied directly to the task. It includes subcontractors, consultants, travel, telephone, computer time, material costs, purchased parts, and freight. This expense is represented in Figure 8-5 by the line "other direct cost." Material costs include allotments for waste and spoilage and should reflect anticipated price increases. Material costs and *freight* charges sometimes appear as separate line items called *direct materials* and *overhead on materials*, respectively; computer time and consultants may appear as *support*.

Direct nonlabor expenses also include items necessary for installation and operation such as maintenance manuals, engineering and programming documentation, instruction manuals, drawings, and spare parts. Note that these are costs incurred only for a specific project or work package. Not included are the general or overhead costs of doing business, unless those costs are tied to the specific project.

On smaller projects all direct nonlabor expenses are individually estimated for each work package. In larger projects, a simple percentage rate is applied to cover travel and freight costs. For example, 5 percent of direct labor cost might be included as travel expense and 5 percent of material costs as freight. These percentages are estimated in the same fashion as the overhead rates discussed next.

Overhead, General, and Administrative Expenses

Although direct expenses for labor and materials are easily charged to a specific work package, many other expenses cannot so easily be allocated to specific work packages, nor even to specific projects. These expenses, termed *overhead* or *nondirect expenses*, are the cost of doing business. They include whatever is necessary to house and support the labor, including building rents, utilities, clerical assistance, insurance, and equipment. Usually, overhead is computed as a percentage of the direct labor cost. Frequently, the rate is around 100 percent but it ranges from as low as 25 percent for companies that do most of their work in the field to over 250 percent for those with laboratories and expensive facilities and equipment.

The overhead rate is computed by estimating the annual business overhead expense, then dividing by the projected total direct labor cost for the year. Suppose projections show that total overhead for next year will be $180,000. If total anticipated direct labor charges will total $150,000, then the overhead rate to apply is 180,000/150,000 = 1.20. Thus, for every $1.00 charged to direct labor, $1.20 is charged to overhead.

Although this is the traditional accounting method for deriving the overhead rate, for project management it results in an arbitrary allocation of costs, which is counterproductive for controlling project costs because most sources of overhead costs are not tied to any particular project. A better way is to divide overhead costs into two categories: *direct overhead*, which are costs that can be allocated in a logical manner; and *indirect overhead*, which cannot. Direct overhead costs can be traced to the support of a particular project or work package; these costs are allocated *only* among the specific projects or activities for which they apply. For example, the overhead cost for a department working on four projects is apportioned among the four projects based on the percentage of labor time it devotes to each. The department's overhead cost is not allocated to projects that it is not involved in.

The other kind of overhead, indirect overhead, includes general expenses for the corporation. Usually referred to as *general and administrative* expense, or *G&A*, it includes taxes, financing, penalty and warranty costs, accounting and legal support, proposal expenses on lost contracts, marketing and promotion, salaries and expenses of top management, and employee benefits. These costs might not be tied to any specific project or work package, so they are allocated across all projects, to certain projects, or parts of projects. For example, corporate-level overhead would be allocated across all projects, project management overhead on a per-project basis, and departmental overhead to specific project segments to which the department contributed. Often, G&A overhead is charged on a time basis, hence the longer the duration of the project, the greater the G&A expense for the project.

The actual manner in which indirect costs are apportioned varies in practice. The example for the SETI Company in Table 8-2 shows three methods for distributing

Table 8-2 Examples of indirect cost apportionment.

SETI Company Company-wide (indirect costs)			
Overhead (rent, utilities, clerical, machinery)		OH	120
General (upper management, staff, benefits, etc.)		G&A	40
		Indirect total	160
PROJECT COSTS	MARS PROJECT	PLUTO PROJECT	TOTAL
Direct labor (DL)	50	100	150
Direct nonlabor (DNL)	40	10	50
	90	110	200 Direct total
		Direct and indirect total	360

Some methods for apportioning indirect costs:

I. Total indirect proportionate to total direct costs

	MARS PROJECT	PLUTO PROJECT	TOTAL
DL and DNL	90	110	200
OH and G&A	72	88	160
	162	198	360

II. OH proportionate to direct labor only; G&A proportionate to all direct costs

	MARS	PLUTO	TOTAL
DL	50	100	150
OH on DL	40	80	120
DNL	40	10	50
G&A on (DL and DNL)	18	22	40
	148	212	360

III. OH proportionate to direct labor only; G&A proportionate to DL and OH and DNL

	MARS	PLUTO	TOTAL
DL and OH and DNL	130	190	320
G&A	16.25	23.75	40
	146.25	213.75	360

indirect costs between two projects, MARS and PLUTO.[17] Notice that although company-wide expenses remain the same, the cost of each project differs depending on the method of allocating indirect costs.

Clients want to know the allocation method used by the contractor, and the contractor should know the allocation method used by subcontractors. For example, Method I is good for the client when the project is labor (DL) intensive, but bad when it is direct nonlabor (DNL) intensive. Method III is the opposite and gives a lower cost when the project is relatively nonlabor intensive (i.e., when labor costs are low but material and parts expenditures are high). This can be seen in Table 8-2 by comparing MARS (somewhat nonlabor intensive) to PLUTO (somewhat labor intensive).

Overhead costs appear in projects in different ways. Any overhead expenses that *can* be traced to specific work packages are allocated directly to them. These appear in the budget, as shown in Figure 8-5. Remaining overhead expenses that cannot be traced to specific work packages are assigned to a special "overhead" work package. This can be a single work package for the entire project, or—if overhead costs can be tied to individual project stages or phases—a series of overhead work packages for each.

Profit and Total Billing

Profit is the amount left over for the contractor after expenses have been subtracted from the contractual price. It is an agreed-to fixed fee or a percentage of total expenses. (Determining profit depends on the kind of contract, discussed in the Appendix to Chapter 3.) Total billing is the sum of total expenses and profit. Profit and total billing are included for estimates of the project as a whole, for large groups of work packages, and for subcontracted work. They usually do not appear on budgets for lower-level work elements.

8.7 PROJECT COST ACCOUNTING SYSTEMS

A project is a system of workers, materials, and facilities, all of which must be estimated, budgeted, and controlled. Hundreds or thousands of items may be involved. To reduce confusion, improve accuracy, and expedite procedures, a system is needed to compute estimates, store and process budgets, and track costs. The term *project cost accounting system (PCAS)* refers to a manual or computerized structure and methodology that enables systematic planning, tracking, and control of project costs. The PCAS is set up by the project manager, project accountant, and involved functional managers. The PCAS focuses on project costs, but by relating project costs to schedules and work performance it also permits tracking and control of schedules and work progress. When combined with other project planning, control, and reporting functions, the PCAS is referred to as the *project management information system (PMIS)*.

During project conception and definition, costs estimates of work packages are accumulated through the PCAS to produce a total project estimate. This estimate later becomes the basis upon which total project and work package budgets are created.

After work on the project begins, the PCAS enables total project and subactivity costs to be accumulated, credited, and reported. Time-phased budgets are created to help managers monitor costs to ensure they are allocated against the appropriate work, and to verify that the work has been completed and charged. The system also provides for revision of budgets.

The functions of the PCAS are summarized in Figure 8-6.

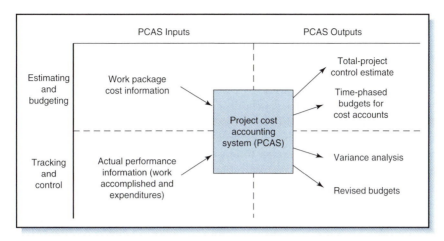

Figure 8-6
Functions of PCAS.

Example 7: Using a PMIS for Estimating Labor Requirements and Costs[18]

Sigma Associates is an architectural/engineering firm with a staff of over 100 architects, engineers, and draftsmen supported by 40 information system and office personnel. The firm has developed its own PMIS that in addition to performing planning and scheduling functions also stores information about all Sigma projects since 1978.

The project manager begins planning a project by creating a WBS to identify the major work activities (e.g., architectural schematics, design administration, construction cost estimating). Using a menu in the PMIS, she then reviews the history of similar work activities in previous projects and the kind and amount of labor they require. By entering factors related to project size, construction costs, and type of clients, she can forecast the labor requirements for every activity in the project.

The PMIS combines these labor requirements with requirements for existing projects to produce a 1-year manpower-loading forecast that enables the project manager to determine whether or not sufficient labor is available. If it is not, the system aids the project manager in reviewing options, including modifying the original schedule, scheduling overtime, and using resource-loading procedures as discussed in Chapter 6.

The labor requirements plan is then given to the comptroller to establish a budget. The comptroller uses the PMIS to apply 1 of 2 possible hourly rates to each activity. The first is the average hourly rate of all employees who might work on the activity, the second the average rate associated with all hours charged to that kind of activity in the last 90 days. The second rate is used more often because it reflects the actual mix of personnel currently employed in similar work. The comptroller then applies factors to incorporate employee benefits and labor overhead. The result is a budget for direct labor cost.

With information from the company general ledger, the comptroller computes the overhead amount per labor dollar. The project is then charged with this rate for its share of company-wide expenses. Project-related, nonlabor expenses that will not be reimbursed by the client (e.g., travel, reproduction, communications) are forecasted and rolled up through the PMIS into the total budget.

When the forecasted total budget is completed, the comptroller analyzes the project plan for profitability. If the plan shows a reasonable profit, the project is accepted. If not, a more profitable plan that maintains the same high-quality standards is sought. When both the comptroller and project manager agree to a plan, the project is accepted.

Time-Phased Budgets

In most projects, simultaneous control of work schedules and cost expenditures can be difficult. The project manager needs a way to keep track of where and when expenses are accruing, how well the project is progressing, and where problems are developing. That way is provided by a *time-phased budget*, which consolidates the project budget and the project schedule, and shows how budgeted costs are distributed over time according to the project schedule. Figure 8-5 is an example showing the distribution of costs over one 6-month period. Throughout the duration of the project the PCAS generates time-phased reports like this for each work package, allowing managers to compare planned expenditures with actual expenditures month-by-month. The reports help ensure that work is completed and accurately charged, and estimates and budgets are revised as needed.

For projects where a substantial amount of the costs originate from purchased items or services, a special separate time-phased budget should be prepared for *procured* materials, equipment, and components, and outsourced work. In large projects this budget will be controlled by a materials or procurement manager.

8.8 BUDGETING USING CONTROL (COST) ACCOUNTS[19]

In small projects, budgeting and cost performance monitoring is done using one simple budget for the project as a whole. This budget, perhaps similar in appearance to the one in Figure 8-5, is used as the basis for comparing actual costs with budgeted costs throughout the project.

On larger projects, however, a single, project-wide budget is too insensitive; once the project is underway, should actual costs begin to exceed budgeted costs it would be difficult to quickly locate the source of the overrun. The better way is to break down the project-wide budget into smaller budgets called *control accounts* (also called cost accounts). Large projects have tens of control accounts; very large projects have hundreds.

The control account is the basic project tracking and control unit of the PCAS. A system of control accounts is set up in a hierarchy, similar or identical to the WBS. Although the lowest level control account usually corresponds to a work package, when the number of work packages is very large, several work packages can be combined into one control account. A multilevel numerical coding scheme is used to organize, communicate, and control the accounts. For example,

LEVEL	NUMERICAL ASSIGNMENT (COST ACCOUNT NUMBER)
1	01–00–0000 . . .
2	01–01–0000 . . .
3	01–01–1000 . . .
3	01–01–2000 . . .
2	01–02–0000 . . .
3	01–02–1000 . . .
4	01–02–1010 . . .

Control accounts and work packages are analogous. Each cost account includes:

- A description of the work
- A time schedule
- Who is responsible

- Material, labor, and equipment required
- A time-phased budget

The time-phased budget is derived from the work schedule and shows the expected distribution of costs throughout the period of the work. In practice, both the schedule and time-phased budget should be developed simultaneously to account for resource and cash flow limitations.

Control accounts also are established for *nondirect* project costs—costs not readily attributable to any work packages or specific tasks. For example, monies allocated to a project for general purpose items, materials, or equipment that can be used by anyone on any task, or for jobs not specific to particular activities such as administration, supervision, or inspection jobs that apply across the project, are budgeted to separate control accounts or, where appropriate, to special work packages for general project items. These accounts are usually set up for the duration of the project and extended, period-by-period, as needed or as funds are appropriated.

With the PCAS and the control-account structure, cost performance can be monitored for a work package, groups of work packages, and the project as a whole. As an example consider again the Robotics Self-Budgeting (ROSEBUD) project. Figure 6-5 in Chapter 6 is the project network for ROSEBUD, and Figure 8-7 is the WBS and organization chart for the ROSEBUD contractor, KANE & Associates. The shaded

Figure 8-7
Integration of WBS and organization structure showing control accounts. (See Figures 8-8 through 8-12 for details.)

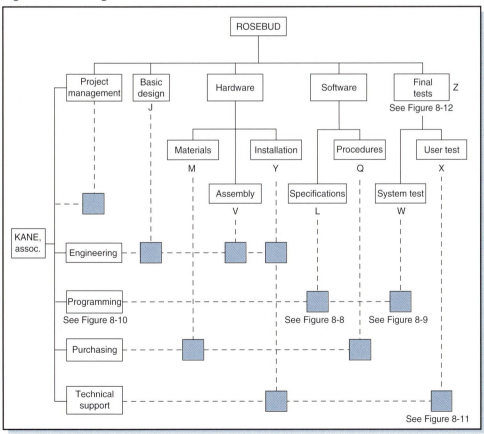

Project ROSEBUD **Date** _____

Department Programming **Work package** L– S/W Specifications

Charge	Rate	Months+						Totals	
		1	2	3	4	5	6	Hours	Cost
Direct labor									
Professional	$35/hour		130					130	4,550
Associate	$30/hour		50	100				150	4,500
Assistant	$20/hour			100				100	2,000
Direct labor cost			6,050	5,000					11,050
Labor overhead	75%		4,538	3,750					8,288
Other direct cost*									0
Total direct cost			10,588	8,750					19,338
General/administrative	10%		1,059	875					1,934
Total costs			11,647	9,625					21,272

+Should extend for as many months as required by the project.
*Should be itemized to include costs for materials, freight, subcontracts, travel, and all other nonlabor direct costs.

Figure 8-8
Budget for programming department for Work Package L.

Project ROSEBUD **Date** _____

Department Programming **Work package** W– System test

Charge	Rate	Months+						Totals	
		1	2	3	4	5	6	Hours	Cost
Direct labor									
Professional	$35/hour						20	20	700
Associate	$30/hour						50	50	1,500
Assistant	$20/hour								0
Direct labor cost							2,200		2,200
Labor overhead	75%						1,650		1,650
Other direct cost*							0		0
Total direct cost							3,850		3,850
General/administrative	10%						385		385
Total costs							4,235		4,235

+Should extend for as many months as required by the project.
*Should be itemized to include costs for materials, freight, subcontracts, travel, and all other nonlabor direct costs.

Figure 8-9
Budget for programming department for Work Package W.

boxes represent locations of control accounts: notice that each represents all or part of a work package for which a single functional area is responsible. For the same project, Figures 8-8 and 8-9 show, respectively, the time-phased budget portions of the cost accounts for the programming department and for work packages L and W.

The WBS for ROSEBUD consists of nine work packages performed by four functional departments plus an additional work package for project management. During the estimating phase each department submits a cost estimate for the work packages in its part of the project. Through the PCAS these estimates are accumulated "bottom-up" to derive the total project estimate. Upon approval, with additions for overhead and G&A, each departmental estimate becomes a budget. Thus, the 10 shaded boxes in Figure 8-7 represent units for which initial cost estimates were made and where budgets and control accounts are set up.

8.9 COST SUMMARIES[20]

As shown in Figure 8-7, the control account structure is a matrix through which higher-level summary accounts can be developed by consolidating control accounts for the WBS and organizational hierarchies. Such consolidation is useful for monitoring the performance of individual departments and segments of the project. For example, consolidating accounts horizontally in Figure 8-7 results in a control account for each functional department. Figure 8-10 shows this in the time-phased budget summary for the programming department, which is the sum of the control accounts for work packages L and W (Figures 8-8 and 8-9). This is the programming department's cost account budget for the ROSEBUD project.

Control accounts also can be consolidated vertically through the WBS. This information is useful for tracking and controlling individual work packages, clusters of work packages, or the project as a whole. Figure 8-12 illustrates this with the budget summary for final tests, which sums the costs from work packages W (Figure 8-9) and X (Figure 8-11).

Figure 8-10
Budget summary for programming department.

Project: ROSEBUD
Department: Programming
Date:
Work package: ALL

Charge	Rate	Months[+] 1	2	3	4	5	6	Totals Hours	Cost
Direct labor									
Professional	$35/hour		130				20	150	5,250
Associate	$30/hour		50	100			50	200	6,000
Assistant	$20/hour			100				100	2,000
Direct labor cost			6,050	5,000			2,200		13,250
Labor overhead	75%		4,538	3,750			1,650		9,938
Other direct cost*									0
Total direct cost			10,588	8,750			3,850		23,188
General/administrative	10%		1,059	875			385		2,319
Total costs			11,647	9,625			4,235		25,507

[+]Should extend for as many months as required by the project.
*Should be itemized to include costs for materials, freight, subcontracts, travel, and all other nonlabor direct costs.

<table><!-- Figure 8-11 -->

Project: ROSEBUD
Date: _____
Department: Technical support
Work package: X - User test

Charge	Rate	Months+ 1	2	3	4	5	6	Totals Hours	Cost
Direct labor									
Professional	$35/hour						10	10	350
Associate	$30/hour						40	40	1,200
Assistant	$20/hour								
Direct labor cost							1,550		1,550
Labor overhead	75%						1,163		1,163
Other direct cost*						1,200	2,107		3,307
Total direct cost						1,200	4,820		6,020
General/administrative	10%					120	482		602
Total costs						1,320	5,302		6,622

+Should extend for as many months as required by the project.
*Should be itemized to include costs for materials, freight, subcontracts, travel, and all other nonlabor direct costs.

Figure 8-11
Budget summary for user test work package.

Project: ROSEBUD
Date: _____
Department: Technical support; Programming
Work package: (W + X) Final Tests

Charge	Rate	Months+ 1	2	3	4	5	6	Totals Hours	Cost
Direct labor									
Professional	$35/hour						30	30	1,050
Associate	$30/hour						90	90	2,700
Assistant	$20/hour								0
Direct labor cost							3,750		3,750
Labor overhead	75%						2,813		2,813
Other direct cost*						1,200	2,107		3,307
Total direct cost						1,200	8,670		9,870
General/administrative	10%					120	867		987
Total costs						1,320	9,537		10,857

+Should extend for as many months as required by the project.
*Should be itemized to include costs for materials, freight, subcontracts, travel, and all other nonlabor direct costs.

Figure 8-12
Budget summary for final tests.

The highest-level control accounts are for the project and the company. Figure 8-13 shows how costs are aggregated vertically and horizontally to derive these costs. Through the PCAS and control-account structure, any deviation from budget at the project level can readily be traced to the work packages and departments responsible. Chapter 11 describes how this is done.

Most PCASs can be used to create a variety of cost summaries, depending on the purpose. Table 8-3, for example, shows the allocation of direct labor, overhead,

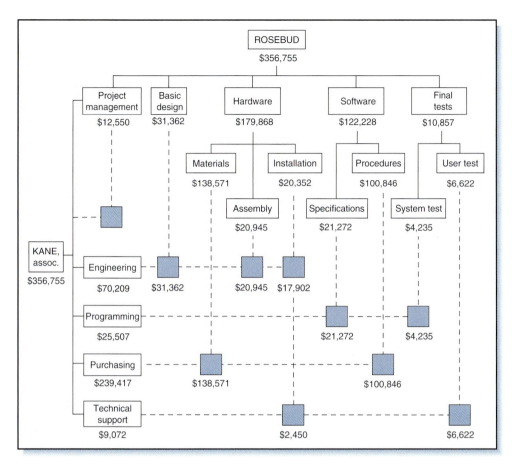

Figure 8-13
Aggregation of control account information by project and organization.

materials, and G&A among the 4 departments and 9 work packages that comprise the ROSEBUD project.

8.10 Cost Schedules and Forecasts[21]

Questions arise during planning and budgeting about what the project expenditures rate will look like, which periods will have the heaviest cash requirements, and how expenditures will compare to income. To answer these and other questions, the project manager analyzes the "pattern of expenditures" using work package cost estimates and cost forecasts derived from the project schedule. Following are some examples.

Cost Analysis with Early and Late Start Times

One simplifying assumption used in cost forecasts is that costs in each work package are incurred uniformly. For example, a 2-week, $22,000 work package is assumed to have a weekly cost of $11,000 per week. With this assumption, a *cost schedule* for the project can be easily created by adding costs period-by-period, for all the work packages scheduled in each period. As an example, look at Figure 8-14, which is the time-based network for the LOGON project using early start times. Also look at

Table 8-3 Cost summary for ROSEBUD project.

	LABOR ($)				OVERHEAD ($)						TOTAL COST
	ENGINEERING	PROGRAMMING	PURCHASING	TECHNICAL SUPPORT	ENGINEERING	PROGRAMMING	PURCHASING	TECHNICAL SUPPORT	MATERIALS	GENERAL AND ADMINISTRATIVE	
Total project	22,800	13,250	2,230	2,850	22,800	9,938	1,673	2,138	235,236	31,290	356,755
Project management											12,550
Activity J	7,200				7,200				14,111	2,851	31,362
Activity L*		11,050				8,288				1,934	21,272
Activity M			1,100				825		124,050	12,596	138,571
Activity Q			1,300				818		89,700	9,168	100,846
Activity V	8,200				8,200				2,641	1,904	20,945
Activity Y	7,400			1,300	7,400			975	1,427	1,850	20,352
Activity W		2,200				1,650				385	4,235
Activity X				1,550				1,163		602	6,622

*Refer to Figure 8-8 to see, for example, how costs in this row were developed.

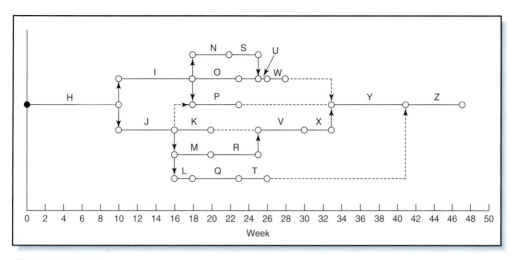

Figure 8-14
Time-based network for the LOGON project using early start times.

Table 8-4 Activities, time, cost, and labor requirements (result of work breakdown analysis).

ACTIVITY	TIME (WEEKS)	TOTAL COST ($K)	WEEKLY DIRECT COST ($K)	WEEKLY LABOR REQUIREMENTS (WORKERS)
H	10	100	10	5
I	8	64	8	4
J	6	96	16	8
K	4	16	4	2
L	2	36	18	6
M	4	84	21	3
N	4	80	20	2
O	5	50	10	5
P	5	60	12	6
Q	5	80	16	2
R	5	0	0	0
S	3	0	0	0
T	3	0	0	0
U	1	14	14	9
V	5	80	16	14
W	2	24	12	6
X	3	36	12	6
Y	8	104	13	14
Z	6	66	11	5
		Total direct cost—$990K		

Table 8-4, which shows LOGON work packages and for each the time, total cost, and resulting average weekly direct cost (derived using the simplifying assumption). For example, the average weekly direct cost for Activity H is computed as $100K/10 weeks = $10K/week.

Using the early start schedule (Figure 8-14), the total weekly project cost can be computed by summing the costs for all activities on a week-by-week basis. The procedure is the same as that described in Chapter 6 for determining the resource loading. In the first 10 weeks, only Activity H is scheduled, so the weekly cost stays at $10K. Over the next 6 weeks, activities I and J are scheduled, so the weekly cost is their sum total, $16K + $8K = $24K. Further along, in weeks 17 and 18, four work packages—I, K, L, and J—are scheduled, so the weekly expense is their sum total, $8K + $4K + $18K + $21K = $51K. These weekly expenses, summarized in the third column in Table 8-5, represent the *cost schedule* for the project. The fourth column in Table 8-5 shows the cumulative project expense, which is interpreted as the forecasted total project cost as of a given week. These costs are graphed in Figure 8-15.

Using the same procedure, project cost schedules and forecasts can be prepared based on late start times. Figure 8-16 is the time-based network for LOGON using late start times; the last two columns of Table 8-5 are the late start weekly and cumulative costs.

Given the early and late cost profiles in Table 8-5 it is possible to analyze what effect delayed activities will have on project costs and budgets. The cost and budget implication of using early start times versus late start times is shown in Figure 8-17; the influence of schedule changes on project costs is clearly apparent. The shaded area in the top figure represents the *feasible budget region*, the range of budgets permitted by changes in the project schedule. The lower part of the figure shows the weekly impact on the cost schedule of delaying activities.

When funding restrictions constrain project expenditures, cost schedules reveal the places of conflict. For example, Figure 8-17 shows a peak weekly expense of $82,000 in Weeks 18 and 19. What if the weekly budget ceiling is only $60,000? In that case the late start times would be preferred because they provide a more "leveled" cost profile and a peak expense of only $54,000. The method for leveling resources discussed in Chapter 6 is also applicable to leveling project costs; costs are treated as just another resource.

The forecasts in the previous example were based upon the total budgeted costs for each work package. Similarly, cost schedules and forecasts can be prepared for other specific kinds of costs or portions of budgets—such as direct labor or materials. Table 8-6 shows the labor cost schedule for the ROSEBUD project using early start times. This kind of cost schedule is useful for identifying periods where scheduling changes may be necessary to meet payroll ceilings (i.e., when the monthly total direct labor cost cannot exceed a payroll ceiling).

Effect of Late Start Time on Project Net Worth

Because of the time value of money, work that is done farther in the future has a lower net present value than the same work if done earlier. Delaying all activities in a lengthy project can thus provide substantial savings because of differences in the present worth of the project. For example, suppose the LOGON project has a long duration, say 47 *months* instead of the 47 weeks used so far. If an annual interest rate of 24 percent were used, compounded monthly at 2 percent per month, the present worth for the project would be $649,276. This is computed by using the monthly expenses in Table 8-5 (again, assuming the weeks shown to be months instead) and discounting the amounts back to time zero. Now, when the late start times are used instead, the present worth is only $605,915—a savings of $43,361.

Does this mean that activities should be delayed until their late start date? Not necessarily. Remember, delaying activities uses up slack time and leaves nothing for unexpected problems. If a problem arises, slack is needed to absorb the

Table 8-5 LOGON project weekly expense using early and late start times ($1000).

	EARLY START			LATE START		
WEEK	ACTIVITIES DURING WEEK	WEEKLY EXPENSE	CUMULATIVE EXPENSE	ACTIVITIES DURING WEEK	WEEKLY EXPENSE	CUMULATIVE EXPENSE
1	H	10	10	H	10	10
2	H	10	20	H	10	20
3	H	10	30	H	10	30
4	H	10	40	H	10	40
5	H	10	50	H	10	50
6	H	10	60	H	10	60
7	H	10	70	H	10	70
8	H	10	80	H	10	80
9	H	10	90	H	10	90
10	H	10	100	H	10	100
11	I, J	24	124	J	16	116
12	I, J	24	148	J	16	132
13	I, J	24	172	J	16	148
14	I, J	24	196	J	16	164
15	I, J	24	220	I, J	24	188
16	I, J	24	244	I, J	24	212
17	I, K, L, M	51	295	I, M	29	241
18	I, K, L, M	51	346	I, M	29	270
19	K, M, N, O, P, Q	83	429	I, M	29	299
20	K, M, N, O, P, Q	83	512	I, M	29	328
21	N, O, P, Q	58	570	I, R	8	336
22	N, O, P, Q	58	628	K, I, R	12	348
23	O, P, Q	38	666	K, R	4	352
24	—	0	666	K, R, N	24	376
25	—	0	666	K, R, N	24	400
26	U, V	30	696	N, O, V	46	446
27	V, W	28	724	N, O, V	46	492
28	V, W	28	752	S, O, V	26	518
29	V	16	768	S, O, P, V	38	556
30	V	16	784	S, O, P, V	38	594
31	X	12	796	U, P, X	38	632
32	X	12	808	W, P, X, L	54	686
33	X	12	820	W, P, X, L	54	740
34	Y	13	833	Y, Q	29	769
35	Y	13	846	Y, Q	29	798
36	Y	13	859	Y, Q	29	827
37	Y	13	872	Y, Q	29	856
38	Y	13	885	Y, Q	29	885
39	Y	13	898	Y, T	13	898
40	Y	13	911	Y, T	13	911
41	Y	13	924	Y, T	13	924
42	Z	11	935	Z	11	935
43	Z	11	946	Z	11	946
44	Z	11	957	Z	11	957
45	Z	11	968	Z	11	968
46	Z	11	979	Z	11	979
47	Z	11	990	Z	11	990

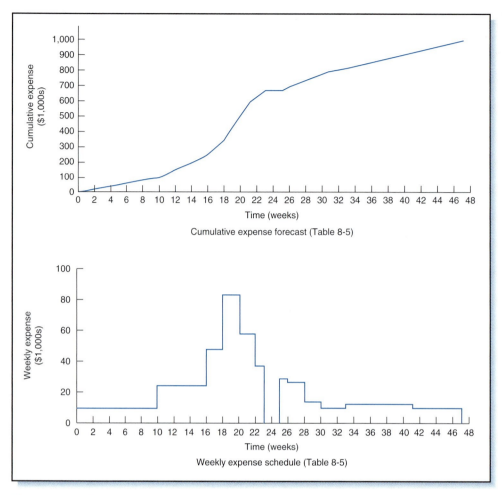

Figure 8-15

Planned weekly and cumulative expenses for the LOGON project.

Figure 8-16

Time-based network for the LOGON project using late start times.

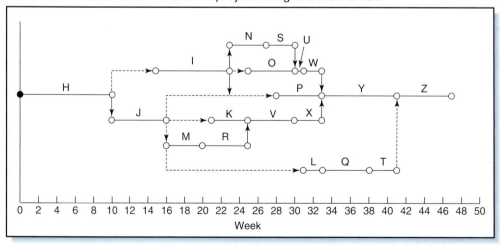

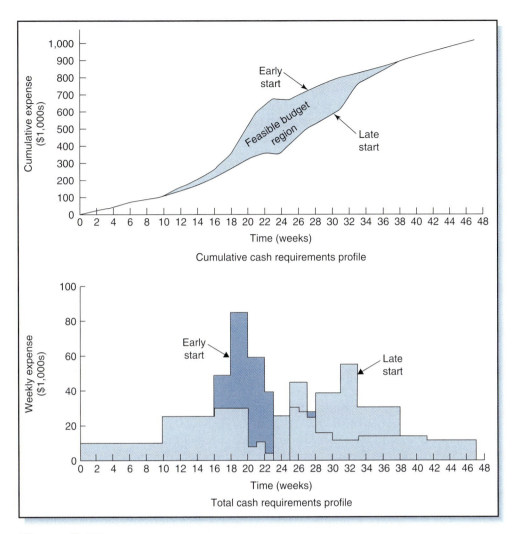

Figure 8-17
Comparison of cash requirements, early versus late start times.

Table 8-6 Labor cost schedule, ROSEBUD project.

| | MONTHLY COST ($) | | | | | | |
DEPARTMENT	1	2	3	4	5	6	TOTAL COST
Engineering (Project)	7,200	4,800	3,300	5,100	2,100	300	22,800
Programming*		6,050	5,000			2,200	13,250
Purchasing		1,100	580	550			2,230
Technical service				800	500	1,550	2,850
Total direct labor cost	7,200	11,950	8,880	6,450	2,600	4,050	41,130

*Refer to Figure 8-11, for example, to see how costs in this row were obtained.

delay and keep the project on schedule. Thus, whether or not an activity should be delayed depends on the *certainty of the work.* Activities that are familiar and unlikely to encounter problems can be started later to take advantage of the time value of money. However, intentionally eliminating slack in schedules of uncertain activities is risky. Activities that are less familiar, such as research and development work, should be started earlier to retain valuable slack that might be needed to absorb unanticipated delays. (This assumes the critical path method; critical chain method (CCM) relies on resource buffers that preclude the need for slack). Also, whether or not to delay activities will depend on the schedule of customer payments. If payments are tied to completion of *stages* of the project, then activities essential to their completion cannot be delayed.

Material Expenditures, Payments, and Cash Flow

Cost schedules and forecasts are also used for estimating cash requirements to meet payments for materials, parts, and equipment.[22] There are several ways to prepare such a cost forecast depending on the purpose. For example, the forecast might represent the cost of materials "when needed"; i.e., the cost of materials corresponding to the date when the materials are needed for use. Alternatively, the forecast might represent the date when payments for materials are due. This forecast will be different from the "when needed" forecast because often a portion of the payment must be made at the time the material is ordered—in other words, the expense *precedes* when the material is needed. Other times, payment can be delayed until after the order is received—in other words, the expense *follows* when the material is needed. The costs shown in the time-phased budget usually reflect costs of materials when needed and not when actual payments are due. Because the times when actual expenditures occur seldom correspond to the times shown on time-phased budgets, forecasts should be made to reveal places of major discrepancy. Figure 8-18 illustrates this point.

A problem often facing the project manager is maintaining a positive cash flow, i.e., that the cumulative cash inflow (payments received) always exceeds the cumulative cash outflow (payments made). Ideally, differences between cash in and cash out throughout the project will be small.[23] The project manager must do a juggling act to hold income from the client in balance with payments for labor, subcontractors, materials, and equipment expenses. To help maintain this balance, management can,

Figure 8-18
Material expenses showing budgeted versus actual expenditures.

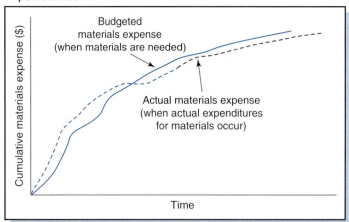

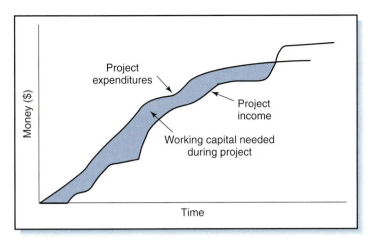

Figure 8-19
Balancing project income and expenditures.

for example, take advantage of the time lag between when materials are needed and the payments for them are required.

Figure 8-19 shows an example of forecast cash flow. All sources of income over the life of the project based on contractual agreements are compared to all foreseeable expenditures—direct and indirect, as well as scheduled payments and any penalty costs, should the project have to be completed late or terminated. The deficit between forecasted income and estimated expenditures represents the amount of invested or working capital needed to meet payment commitments. Based upon this cash flow forecast, a *funding plan* should be created to ensure sufficient working capital will be available throughout the project.[24]

Subcontractors often insist on *milestone payments*, or payments made upon completion of deliverables or phases of the project. Such payments make sense because they help contractors to cover their costs. The drawback is that, should the project encounter serious problems, some unscrupulous subcontractors, having already received several payments, simply walk away from the job and forfeit the final payment, of course leaving the customer in a fix! One way to keep "hold" on the contractor is to withhold a significant portion of the agreed upon payment, called *retention money*, until the work is satisfactorily completed. A second way, called a *performance guarantee*, is to withhold some portion of the final payment for a period following handover of the end-item (called the *guarantee period*, retention period, or defects liability period). During this period any hidden ("latent") defects or visible ("patent") defects discovered by the customer must be rectified. Retention money and performance guarantees need to be agreed upon and included in the contract, and should apply to all project agreements—between customer and prime contractor, as well as prime contractor and its subcontractors. The cost schedule and cash flow plan should include these amounts—payments to be withheld until after handover (to ensure satisfactory delivery) and the guarantee period following the handover (to ensure correction of defects) of any contingency reserves.

8.11   SUMMARY

Cost estimation and budgeting are part of the project planning process. Cost estimation logically follows work breakdown and precedes project budgeting. Accurate cost estimates are necessary to establish realistic budgets and to provide standards against which actual costs will be measured; they are thus a prerequisite for tracking and control, and crucial to the financial success of the project.

Costs in projects have a tendency to escalate beyond original estimates. The accuracy of estimates can be improved and escalation minimized by defining clear requirements and work tasks, employing skilled estimators, being realistic, and anticipating escalation factors such as inflation and project changes. Accuracy is partly a function of the stage in the systems development cycle during which the estimates are prepared; the further along the cycle, the easier it is to produce accurate estimates. However, good estimates are needed early in the project. Besides clearly defining project scope and objectives, accuracy is improved by subdividing the project into activities and work packages, and employing standard technology and procedures. In general, the smaller the work element being estimated and more standardized the work, the greater the accuracy of the estimate. The aggregate of cost estimates for all subelements of the project plus overhead costs becomes the cost estimate for the overall project. Approved estimates become budgets.

The project budget is subdivided into smaller budgets called control or cost accounts. Control accounts are derived from the WBS and project organization hierarchies and are the financial equivalent to work packages. In larger projects a systematic methodology or PCAS is useful for aggregating estimates and maintaining a system of control accounts for budgeting and control.

Cost schedules are derived from time-phased budgets and show the pattern of costs and expenditures throughout the project. They are used to identify cash and working capital requirements for labor, materials, and equipment.

Scheduled and forecasted project expenditures, payments and other cash outflows are compared to scheduled and forecasted payment receipts and income sources to predict cash flow throughout the project. Ideally expenditures and income are balanced so that the contractor can maintain a positive cash flow. The forecasts are used to prepare a funding plan that guarantees adequate financial support for the project.

The last four chapters described aspects of the project planning process, focusing on scope and work definition, scheduling, and budgeting. The next chapter continues in this direction and the topic of project quality management.

REVIEW QUESTIONS AND PROBLEMS

1. Why are accurate cost estimates so important, yet so difficult, in project planning? What are the implications and consequences of overestimating costs? Of underestimating costs?
2. Define cost escalation. What are major sources of cost escalation?
3. What is the purpose of a contingency fund (management reserve)? How is the contingency fund used and controlled?
4. Describe what the term "phased project planning" means.
5. How do changes in requirements cause cost escalation?
6. How does the type of contractual agreement influence the potential for cost escalation?
7. What is the relationship between phases of the project life cycle and cost escalation?
8. Explain: what are LCC's and how are they different from project costs?
9. Explain the difference between a cost estimate and a cost target. What are the problems in confusing the two—in using cost targets as cost estimates?

10. Explain the difference between accuracy and precision. Give two original examples that illustrate the difference.

11. For each of the following estimating methods, briefly describe the method, when it is used, and the estimate accuracy it provides:
    (a) Expert opinion
    (b) Analogy
    (c) Parametric
    (d) Cost engineering

12. Describe the process of using the WBS to develop cost estimates. How are these estimates aggregated into total project cost estimates?

13. What is the role of individual functional and subcontracting units in cost estimating?

14. Describe the different kinds of contingency amounts and the purposes each serves.

15. Describe the PCAS. What is its purpose and how is it used in project planning?

16. What is a time-phased budget? What is the difference between a budget and a cost estimate?

17. Distinguish recurring costs from nonrecurring costs.

18. What are six cost elements shared by most estimates and budgets?

19. How are direct labor expenses determined?

20. What expenses are included under direct nonlabor?

21. How is the overhead rate determined?

22. What is a control account and what kinds of information does it contain? How does a control account fit into the structure of the PCAS?

23. How are control accounts aggregated horizontally and vertically? Why are they aggregated like this?

24. How are time-based forecasts prepared and how are they used?

25. What are the reasons for investigating the influence of schedules on project costs? What is the feasible budget region?

26. What might happen if top management submitted a bid for a project without consulting the business unit or department to be involved in the project?

27. Refer Case 5-1, the Barrage Construction Company, in Chapter 5. In the case, the project manager Sean Shawn employed the analogy method with an adjustment to estimate the cost of constructing a three-car garage. Specifically, he started with the cost of an average two-car garage, $143,000, and increased it by 50 percent to $214,500. Comment on the accuracy of the three-car garage estimate. Suggest a different approach that would probably yield a more accurate cost estimate, then use this approach and made-up time and cost figures to compute the estimate. Argue why your estimate is better than Sean's. Figure 8-20 is Sean's WBS.

Figure 8-20
Sean's garage WBS.

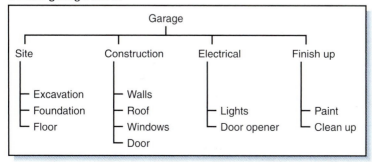

28. The example in Table 8-2 shows three possible ways of apportioning total direct costs. Using the same example, suppose, the direct nonlabor (DNL) cost and G&A are broken down as follows:

	Direct Nonlabor			G&A
	MARS	PLUTO		
Materials	30	5	Freight	8
Other	10	5	Other	32
	40	10		40

Assuming all remaining costs shown in Table 8-2 are unchanged, compute the project costs for MARS and PLUTO using the following apportioning rules:

(a) Overhead (OH) is proportionate to direct labor (DL).

(b) Freight G&A is proportionate to materials.

(c) Other G&A is proportionate to DL, OH, DNL, and freight.

29. Chapter 7 discussed the impact of crashing activities and the relationship of schedules to cost. The method assumes that as activity duration is decreased, the direct cost increases, in some cases owing to increases in direct labor rates from overtime. Overhead rates also may vary, although the overhead rate is often *lower* for overtime work. For example, the overhead rate may be 100 percent for regular time but only 20 percent for overtime. In both cases, the overhead rate is associated with the wage rate being used.

Suppose that in the MARS project in Table 8-2, 1,000 direct hours of labor are required at $50 per hour, and the associated overhead rate is 100 percent for regular time. Now suppose an overhead rate of 10 percent and overtime wage rate of time-and-a-half.

Compare the project cost if it were done entirely on regular time with the cost if it were done entirely on overtime. Which is less expensive?

30. Use the table below and network in Figure 8-21 to answer questions about the ARGOT project:

Activity	Time (Weeks)	Weekly Cost ($K)	Total ($K)
A	4	3	12
B	6	4	24
C	3	5	15
D	4	5	20
E	8	3	24
F	3	4	12
G	2	2	4
			111

(a) Compute the ESs and LSs for the project. Assume Ts is the same as the earliest project completion date.

Figure 8-21
ARGOT project.

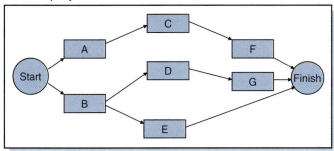

(b) Construct a time-based network for the project such as Figure 8-14 (use early start times).

(c) Construct two diagrams similar to those in Figure 8-15 showing the weekly and cumulative project expenses.

31. Using the data in problem 30, repeat Steps b and c using late start times. Then identify the feasible budget region using the cumulative curves.

32. Explain retention money and performance guarantee.

QUESTIONS ABOUT THE STUDY PROJECT

1. How were project costs estimated? Who was involved? Describe the process.

2. When did estimating take place? How were estimates checked and accumulated? How were they related to the WBS?

3. What, if any, were the principle causes of cost escalation in the project?

4. Was an LCC analysis performed? If so, who did it, when, and using what methods? How did the analysis affect the design, development, and production of the project deliverables or main end item?

5. How often and under what circumstances were cost estimates revised during the project?

6. How were overhead costs determined? What basis was used for establishing overhead cost rates?

7. How were cost estimates tallied to arrive at a total project cost estimate? Who did this?

8. What kind of PCAS was used? Was it manual or computerized? Describe the system and its inputs and outputs. Who maintained the system? How was it used during the project?

9. Describe the process of creating the project budget. Show a sample budget (or portion thereof).

10. How were management and supervisory costs handled in the budget?

11. Was the project budget broken down into cost accounts? If so

    (a) How were they related to the work packages and WBS?

    (b) How were they tied into the PCAS?

12. What kinds of costs summaries were prepared? Who were they sent to? How were they used? Show some examples.

13. Did the PCAS produce time-phased cost schedules and forecasts? Show some examples. How were they used by the project manager?

Case 8-1   Life Cycle Costs for Fleet of Tourist Spaceships

At the time of writing, Burt Rutan and Sir Richard Branson had teamed up to form The Spaceship Company, which will develop and manufacture commercial spacecraft (SpaceShipTwo, or SS2), launch aircraft (WhiteKnightTwo, or WK2), and support equipment. Branson's "spaceline," Virgin Galactic, will handle the operations for space tourist flights. Their hope is to eventually reduce by half the proposed initial ticket price of $190,000.

No information has been released about development and operating costs for the spaceline and equipment, so the figures used in this case are guesses. Refer to Example 2 for *hypothetical* life cycle costs for the spaceline and spaceship fleet, but assume the following changes to the numbers:

- Five spaceships, seven passengers per spaceship
- Development and manufacturing cost, $120 million
- Flight operations cost: $0.5 million per flight
- Ticket price: $190,000 for passengers on the first 100 flights, then $150,000 for passengers on the next 100, and $100,000 for passengers on flights thereafter.

QUESTIONS

1. Assuming all other numbers from Example 2 are the same, what is the "bottom line" profit of the venture for 5 years of operation?
2. If the profit goal is $70 million
   (a) What is the maximum development & production cost for the fleet?
   (b) What is the maximum per-flight operational cost? (Note: assume $120 million development/production cost.)

3. Brainstorm. What are some ways the development cost might be reduced? What are some possible design decisions for the spacecraft and mothership that would reduce the per-flight operational cost? Next, research articles and news releases about SS2 and WK2 to see what the developers, Scaled Composites and The Spaceship Company, have been doing to contain costs.

Case 8-2   Estimated Tunnel Costs for the Chunnel Project[25]

Before construction began on the English Channel Tunnel (Chunnel) Project, the banks underwriting the project hired consulting engineers to review cost estimates prepared by the contractors. The consultants concluded that the tunneling estimates were 20 percent too high. Their analysis was based on comparisons of costs from recent European tunnel projects, including 50 German railroad tunnels ranging in length from 400 meters to 11 kilometers, to the Chunnel, which would be 49 kilometers in length. The costs of the tunnels ranged from £55 to £140 per cum (cubic meter) of open tunnel; the cost of the Chunnel was estimated at £181 per cum on the British side of the channel and £203 on the French side (the difference owing to more difficult geological conditions on the French side). The Chunnel is actually three interconnected tunnels—one for trains going in each direction and a smaller service tunnel between them. Note, however, that the cost estimates are per cubic meter of tunnel, so *presumably*, differences in tunnel lengths and diameters are not major factors. Why might the estimates for the Chunnel be so much higher per cum than the costs for the analogy projects? Discuss possible, logical adjustments to the analogy tunnel project costs to arrive at a cost estimate for the Chunnel tunnel.

1. See F.L. Harrison, *Advanced Project Management* (Hants, England: Gower, 1981): 147–148.

2. B. Flyvbjerg, N. Bruzelius and W. Rothengatter, *Megaprojects and Risk: An Anatomy of Ambition* (Cambridge: Cambridge University Press, 2003): 16.

3. See R.D. Archibald, *Managing High-Technology Programs and Projects* (New York: John Wiley & Sons, 1976): 167–168.

4. See Harrison, *Advanced Project Management*, 148–152.

5. Ibid., 172–173, gives an example of an escalation clause.

6. Politically, how independent should the estimators be? So independent, says DeMarco, that the project manager has "no communication with the estimator about how happy or unhappy anyone is about the estimate." See Tom DeMarco, *Controlling Software Projects* (New York: Yourdon Press, 1982): 19.

7. A more complete discussion is found in Harrison, *Advanced Project Management*, 162–171.

8. B. Flyvbjerg, N. Bruzelius and W. Rothengatter, *Megaprojects and Risk: An Anatomy of Ambition.*

9. Harrison, *Advanced Project Management*, 154–161.

10. Archibald, *Managing High-Technology Programs and Projects*, 171.

11. J. Dingle, *Project Management: Orientation for Decision Makers* (London: Arnold/John Wiley & Sons, 1997): 105.

12. R. Pool, *Beyond Engineering: How Society Shapes Technology* (New York: Oxford University Press, 1997); T.A. Heppenheimer, "Nuclear Power," Invention and Technology, *Fall* 18, no. 2 (2002): 46–56.

13. A complete discussion of the pricing review procedure is given by Harold Kerzner, *Project Management: A Systems Approach to Planning, Scheduling, and Controlling*, 5th ed.

14. Discussed in M. Rosenau, *Successful Project Management* (Belmont, CA: Lifetime Learning, 1981): 91.

15. *Ibid.*, 91–92.

16. A thorough discussion of labor pricing is given by Kerzner, *Project Management*, 728–732. This example is derived from Kerzner.

17. This example is derived from a similar one in Rosenau, *Successful Project Management*, 89–91.

18. This example is derived from Thomas Wilson and David Stone, "Project Management for an Architectural Firm," *Management Accounting* (October 1980): 25–46.

19. See Harrison, *Advanced Project Management*, 199–202 for further discussion of cost accounts.

20. The kinds of cost summaries used often depend on what is available in the software, though many software packages permit customizing of reports.

21. J.D. Wiest and F.K. Levy, *A Management Guide to PERT/CPM*, 2nd ed. (Upper Saddler River, NJ: Prentice Hall, 1977): 90–94.

22. See Kerzner, *Project Management*, 396–398, for an example of a material expenditure forecast.

23. Harrison notes that keeping cash in balance in foreign contracts is especially difficult because foreign currency use must be managed: "In many cases, the profits from [currency dealings] can exceed the profits from the project; in others, if this is not managed effectively, the losses from foreign currency commitments can bring about large losses on a project and lead to bankruptcy." See Harrison, *Advanced Project Management*, 185.

24. See Archibald, *Managing High-Technology Programs and Projects*, 168.

25. Drew Fetherston, *The Chunnel* (New York: Times Books, 1997): 141–142.

Chapter 9

Project Quality Management

> *I have offended God and mankind because my work didn't reach the quality it should have.*
>
> —Leonardo da Vinci

Project success is measured in terms of how well a project meets predetermined budgetary, schedule, and performance requirements. Performance requirements are the project's *quality criteria*, which more generally relate to the needs and expectations of the customer, the contractor, and other stakeholders about the functioning and performance of the project end-item system or other deliverables. A high-quality project benefits the stakeholders and society at large and does not harm the environment.

9.1 THE CONCEPT OF QUALITY

Back in the 1950s *quality* was seen merely as the screening or sorting of products that had already been manufactured to the separate good ones from the bad. But in the current competitive business environment, so the thinking goes, you have to *prevent* defects and failures rather than perform inspections. "You cannot inspect to make it right." The modern emphasis is on *processes* to ensure getting it right the first time, every time, and a culture of involving all project team members and other stakeholders in quality-focused processes.

Figure 9-1
London Tower Bridge. (Photo courtesy of Herman Steyn.)

But the quest to be competitive often strains project teams to accelerate project schedules and cut costs. This can lead to increased rework, required changes, and greater workload on the project team. This in turn can result in a "quality melt-down." Once the project manager has committed to the budget, schedule, and deliverables, the project cost, schedule, and performance requirements are somewhat fixed and, often, cannot be changed without serious consequences and extensive negotiation. However, "… the bitterness of poor quality lives long after the sweetness of cheap price or timely delivery has been forgotten."[1]

To illustrate the consequences of project quality—and the staying power of those consequences long after project schedules or budgets have been forgotten—Michael Carruthers uses the case of the London Tower Bridge (Figure 9-1).[2] The bridge was opened in 1894—4 years late and at a cost nearly twice the estimated £585,000. In terms of time and cost the project was a failure, but in many other ways it was a success. It has withstood the test of time: more than a century later the bridge's design and construction quality are still apparent. The original requirement was that it enable pedestrians and horse-drawn vehicles to cross the river; today it carries 10,000 vehicles per day and is a major tourist attraction. The bridge has survived floods, pollution, and bombs (World War II)—problems never considered at its inception. It is a true testament to project quality.

In contrast is the space shuttle Challenger. While engineers claimed to have warned managers about a potentially serious quality problem, commitments on a launch due date promised to politicians took precedence: in other words, quality was compromised in order to meet a schedule. On January 28, 1986, defective seals on the rocket boosters allowed hot gases to escape and ignite the main fuel tank shortly after launch, causing a massive explosion and killing the seven astronauts onboard.

What Quality Is

Quality implies meeting specifications, but it is much more than that. While meeting specifications will usually prevent a customer from taking the project contractor to court, it alone does not ensure the customer is satisfied or that the contractor has gained a good reputation or will win repeat business.

Ideally, a project should aim *beyond* specifications and try to meet customer expectations—including those not articulated. It should aim at delighting the client. A common shortfall of project managers is they assume that the needs, expectations, and requirements of the customer are evident or will require little effort to research and define.

Quality implies that the product or end-item is *fit* for the intended purpose. Fitness normally involves a wide range of criteria such as performance, safety, reliability, ease of handling, maintainability, logistical support, as well as environmental safety. While a luxury item such as a piece of clothing might have superior style, material, finish, or workmanship, the customer will also consider its *value for the money* and whether it is priced right for the intended purpose. Optimizing only one aspect of a product—fitness for purpose, client satisfaction, value for the money, or strategic benefit to the organization—will not optimize the whole product, and the project manager must seek a balanced compromise among the multiple aspects and define specifications to reflect that compromise.

Quality also implies the absence of defects, which is why people often associate the terms *quality* and *defect*. A defect is a *nonconformity*—something other than what the customer had expected. Quality management attempts to identify and correct as many nonconformities—problems, mistakes, and defects—as possible. It also seeks to identify nonconformities as soon as possible. In general, the longer a nonconformity is allowed to persist before it is discovered, the more costly it is to remedy. It may be easy and inexpensive to fix a defect in an unattached component, but it is usually more expensive to fix after the component has been assembled with others, and even more so after it has been imbedded inside a system. The most expensive defects are the ones that cause a malfunction or failure while the customer is using the end-item system.

But "absence of defects" requires qualification, and the presumption that zero defects equate to high quality is not always true. A quality project is one that satisfies multiple requirements, and devoting too much attention to any particular one, such as eliminating *all* defects, may detract from fulfilling other, more important requirements.[3] For example, project requirements relate to time and cost, as well as end-item performance. When the schedule must be maintained, removing *all* defects can prove exceptionally costly. The customer might prefer keeping costs down and holding to the schedule rather than eliminating all defects. Of course, in some cases it is necessary to make every effort to remove defects.[4] In an air traffic control system and pacemakers for human hearts, all critical or major defects and even most minor defects have to be removed. The point is, it depends on the customer. In many cases the customer would prefer that an end-item be delivered on time at lower cost with a *few* defects than delivered late at a higher cost with no defects.

In removing defects, the focus is on those that would prevent the system from meeting its most important requirements. This is the concept of "good enough quality"—where preset priorities on performance requirements, time, and cost preclude satisfying all of the requirements and force the project team to meet only those that are the most important. Says Bach, creating systems "of the best possible quality is a very, very expensive proposition, [although] clients may not even notice the difference between the best possible quality and pretty good quality."[5] The customer, of course, is the judge of what is "good enough," and to be able to make that judgment must be kept constantly updated as to project problems, costs, and schedules.

Ideally, everyone on the project team contributes to quality; this implies that each person:

1. Knows what is expected of her
2. Is able and willing to meet those expectations
3. Knows the extent to which she meets the expectations
4. Has the ability and authority to take necessary corrective actions

For that to happen might require extensive training and motivation efforts, although once everyone is contributing, attention to quality becomes automatic and requires little influence from the project manager.

What Quality Is *Not*

Quality of a product implies that the product is fit for its purpose. But fit for purpose does not necessarily relate to the expense, reliability, or number or sophistication of features, all of which refer to the *grade* of the product. In other words, the *quality* and *grade* of a product are not the same. Good quality implies value for the money and, therefore, not necessarily *high* quality. For example, coal mines produce coal of different grades. The highest grade is used in steelmaking while lower grades are used in chemical products and coal-fired power stations. Even though the coal for a power plant is lower grade than for steelmaking, it is the appropriate—hence good—quality coal for the purpose. In fact, it would be inappropriate and uneconomical for power plants to use higher-grade coal to generate steam. Of course, coal mines should strive toward *high-quality processes* to deliver all grades of coal to meet the specifications and requirements of all of their clients, including specifications for price and reliable delivery.

Quality Movements

What could be described as the "quality revolution" started in the 1950s in Japan under the influence of an American, Dr. W. Edwards Deming. He proposed a new philosophy of quality that included continuous improvement, skills training, leadership at all levels, elimination of dependency on inspections, retaining single-source suppliers rather than many sources, and use of sampling and statistical techniques. Since then a number of quality movements have come and gone—some that could be described as fads. The most lasting and popular movement since the 1980s is total quality management (TQM). TQM is a set of techniques and more—it is a mindset, an ambitious approach to improving the total effectiveness and competitiveness of the organization. The key elements of TQM are identifying the mission of the organization, acting in ways consistent with the goals and objectives of the organization, and focusing on customer satisfaction. TQM involves the total organization, including teams of frontline workers and the visible support of top management. Quality problems are systematically identified and resolved to continuously improve processes. In projects, this purpose is served by closeout sessions or post-mortems, discussed later.

Another management philosophy called just in time (JIT), or lean production, complements TQM. In a production environment, JIT recognizes that quality problems are often hidden by excessive work-in-progress inventory. By continuously reducing inventory and other sources of non-value added waste in processes, problems are exposed and solved as part of a continuous improvement drive. The JIT approach includes relatively easy-to-implement measures that improve quality and reduce costs and lead times.[6]

Another influential quality movement is Six Sigma, started in the 1980s at Motorola and later popularized by General Electric. Advocates claim that Six Sigma provides a more structured approach to quality than TQM. The term "six sigma" refers to the fact that in a normal distribution, 99.99966 percent of the population falls within -6σ to $+6\sigma$ of the mean, where "σ" (sigma) is the standard deviation. If the quality of a process is controlled to the Six Sigma standard, there would be less than 3.4 *parts per million* scrap or defects in the process—near perfection!

But the Six Sigma approach goes beyond statistics and includes a philosophy for reducing process variability. It also includes a five-step improvement system for existing processes and another five-step process for designing new processes or products, both aimed at Six Sigma quality levels. The process for incremental improvement is called *DMAIC* (Define, Measure, Analyze, Improve, Control), which involves defining the best measures to improve a process, implementing those measures, tracking the measures, and reducing defects so that fewer outcomes fail to meet specifications. (*Designing* for Six Sigma employs a similar process called DMADV for Define, Measure, Analyze, Design, and Verify.) In projects, the Six Sigma approach translates into defining clear deliverables that are approved by management and relate to the mission of the organization. The DMAIC process is sometimes used as the project methodology, where the steps of the process define the stages of the project.

Quality Product: Meeting Mutually Agreed Specifications

Quality starts with a process where the product or end-item requirements and specification have been clearly laid out and agreed upon by the project team and the customer. In contrast, when the requirements have not been defined in sufficient detail or agreed upon, the result is neglected important features, unnecessary "gold-plating" or added "bells and whistles," and an unsatisfied customer. Whenever the customer provides a requirement or specification that seems unrealistic, the contractor should review it with the customer and alter it so the desired end-result can be attained. The approved modified specification should reflect the client's expectations, the product's fitness for its intended purpose, and any negotiated compromises.

The comprehensive specification of the product or end-item should be included as part of the project scope definition. Identifying important product specifications, the associated components, their configuration in the product, and subsequently controlling these components and their configuration is called *configuration management*, which was discussed in Chapter 2. We will revisit the topic later in this chapter and again in Chapter 11.

Project Quality Management

Project quality management includes quality management processes as well as certain techniques to reduce the risk of products or end-items not meeting requirements. Section 9.2 discusses the processes in project quality management, and Section 9.3 the techniques for quality assurance. Section 9.4 covers techniques for quality control.

9.2 THE PROCESSES OF PROJECT QUALITY MANAGEMENT

Project quality management consists of quality planning, quality assurance, and quality control, illustrated in Figure 9-2. *Quality planning* is a process to guide future quality activities; it sets the requirements and standards to be met, as well as the actions necessary to meet those requirements and standards. *Quality assurance* is the process to perform the planned quality activities and to ensure that the project utilizes processes necessary to meet the quality standards and project requirements. *Quality control* is the process to ensure that quality assurance activities are being performed (or have been performed) according to approved quality plans, and that project requirements and standards are being met. In the event that unsatisfactory

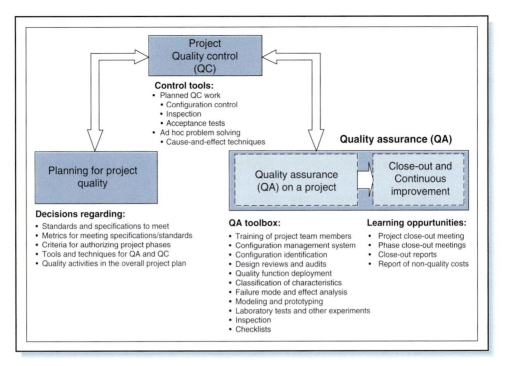

Figure 9-2
The project quality management process.

performance or nonconformities (defects) are discovered, the causes must be determined and eliminated. Quality control can be thought of as "the medicine" to eliminate nonconformities, while quality assurance the "healthy lifestyle" to prevent nonconformities.

As shown in Figure 9-2, project quality control overarches quality planning and quality assurance. This is to emphasize quality control's role in ensuring that quality assurance is performed according to the quality plan. In turn, project quality assurance helps guarantee compliance with project requirements, while systematic project closeout and continuous improvement help future projects by providing lessons learned from completed projects.

Quality Planning

Quality planning should provide the confidence that all steps necessary to ensure quality have been thought through. Quality planning has two aspects: (1) establishing organization-wide project quality management procedures and policies and (2) establishing a quality plan and including it in the project plan for each project.

Responsibility for establishing organization-wide policies and procedures to improve project quality management typically falls on functional managers and especially the quality manager. The ISO 9001 standard specifies the requirements for such a quality management system.[7] For design and development projects, the ISO 9001 standard prescribes that an organization shall determine (a) the design and development stages; (b) the necessary review, verification, and validation appropriate to each design and development stage; and, (c) the responsibilities and authorities for design and development.

Planning for quality for each project should be an integrated part of the project planning process and make use of the principles discussed in Chapters 4 through 8 for identifying, scheduling, budgeting, and assigning responsibility for quality assurance and control tasks. The project quality plan (or quality management plan) should be integrated with the procurement plan, risk plan, human resource plan, and communications plan. It should indicate how the project team will implement organizational quality policies to maintain quality assurance and quality control in the project.

The quality plan should specify the requirements to be met in each phase for the project to be approved and to continue to the next phase. It should also indicate the quality techniques that will be used (described in Sections 9.3 and 9.4) and when. It should specify at what stages formal design reviews will be held, how product or end-item characteristics will be classified, what models or prototypes will be produced and how they will be tested, how quality assurance will be managed for work done by subcontractors, as well as when and how deliverables will be inspected.

The Cost of Quality

Since quality is always related to *value for the money spent*, the quality planning process should consider the cost and benefits of quality activities. A cost–benefit analysis is performed to evaluate and justify proposed quality activities, and to compare the savings or benefits from fewer or eliminated nonconformities to the costs of quality assurance and control activities. Money spent on quality assurance and control should be justified in terms of the reduced risk of not meeting requirements.

Costs of quality are commonly classified as *prevention*, *appraisal and control*, and *internal failure* and *external failure*.

1. Prevention costs include costs of quality training, design reviews, and other activities aimed at preventing errors. The cost of quality planning is a prevention cost.
2. Appraisal and control costs relate to the evaluation of products and processes, including product reviews, audits, tests, and inspections.
3. Internal failure costs are costs associated with nonconformities discovered by the producer, such as the cost of scrap, rework, and retest.
4. External failure costs are costs incurred after delivery to a client and include costs for replacements, warranty repairs, liability, and lost sales as a result of a damaged reputation. All of these costs are associated with failures discovered by the customer.

While the cost of quality in a company with a sound quality management system could be as little as 2 percent of the proceeds of a company, the cost of quality in a company with a poor quality management system could be 20 percent or more.[8] It therefore makes sense to invest in a quality management system, i.e., spend more on appraisal and prevention activities and, hence, reduce the costs of internal and external failures. This would involve devoting more attention to design reviews, audits, and classification and control of product characteristics, and more extensive modeling and testing.

The costs of external failures normally occur only after project completion, but the costs of prevention, appraisal, and control are incurred during the project lifespan. Therefore, prevention and appraisal costs must be estimated in the project plan and covered in the project budget. They are among the many costs in the budget that the project manager must justify to executive management.

Quality Assurance

Project quality assurance reduces the risks related to features or performance of deliverables, and provides confidence that end-item requirements will be met. Since quality assurance relies heavily on human resources, it usually involves considerable training of project team members.

As indicated in Figure 9-2, quality assurance comprises the following:

1. Activities done in a specific project to ensure that requirements are being met. This includes demonstrating that the project is being executed according to the quality plan.
2. Activities that contribute to the continuous improvement of current and future projects, and to the project management maturity of the organization.

Quality assurance should provide confidence that everything necessary is being done to ensure the appropriate quality of project deliverables.

Project Closeout and Continuous Improvement

You might say that continuous improvement is the keystone to progress: without it, humankind would not have moved beyond the Stone Age. Project organizations should strive to continually improve their technical operations and managerial processes; one way is to conduct a formal closeout or *post-completion review* for every project. The review takes place upon completion of the project, although, ideally, also upon completion of each phase of the project. The purpose of these reviews is to understand what happened, to learn lessons that can be applied to other projects and avoid repeating mistakes. The reviews enable the organization to improve its technical and managerial processes, including its project management processes. (The organization's level of competency in project management—its *project management maturity*—is discussed in Chapter 16.)

The responsibility of the project manager during closeout reviews is to facilitate candid and constructive discussion about what happened—what worked and what did not, and to make sure that everyone participating is heard. The discussion is formally documented and includes a list of lessons learned from the project. The process is essential for continuous improvement, although unfortunately it is often neglected because people lose interest as the project winds down, do not think it will benefit their careers, and become busy with new or upcoming projects. The result is that organizations repeat mistakes, "reinvent the wheel," and do not benefit as much as they could from their experiences.[9] Post-completion reviews are covered again in Chapter 12.

Quality Control

Quality control is the ongoing process of monitoring and appraising work, and taking corrective action so that planned-for quality outcomes are achieved. The process verifies that quality assurance activities are being performed in accordance with approved quality plans, and that project requirements and standards are being met. Whenever nonconformities are uncovered, the causes are determined and eliminated. In the same way that quality planning should be integrated with other aspects of project planning, quality control should be integrated with the other aspects of project control. Quality control cannot be performed in isolation; it must be integrated with project scope control, cost control, and progress and risk control. It is a responsibility of the project manager.

Quality control is a subset of *scope verification*, but whereas scope verification refers to the acceptability of project deliverables or end-items *by the customer*, quality control refers to conformance to specifications set by *the contractor*. It is therefore a narrower concept related to verifying adherence to specifications and standards previously set, whereas scope verification also includes verifying the general acceptability of those specifications and standards.

The quality control process includes inspections to verify that deliverables are meeting specifications, as well as acceptance tests just before handover of deliverables to the customer. In the event that a minor characteristic is found to be out of specification, the contractor might request a waiver, deviation, or modification, which would release the nonconforming item from the specified requirement. A *waiver* applies to an unplanned condition that is discovered only after the item has been produced. It authorizes a temporary nonconformity, such as a scratch discovered on the paint of a hardware item. A *deviation* is also a temporary departure from specification, but might affect more items and extend for a longer period of time. For example, if a specified material is temporarily unavailable, the contractor can apply for a deviation to allow usage of an alternative material. In contrast, a *modification* is any change to a design or manufacturing process specification that is considered permanent.

Control activities as illustrated in Figure 9-2 include both planned quality control activities and ad hoc problem solving. Planned activities include, for example, site inspections on a construction project, tests on a pressure vessel, or an audit of a supplier to ensure that correct materials are being used. Ad hoc problem solving relates to handling unforeseen problems, risks, and opportunities. Common techniques for analysis and problem solving are discussed later.

Quality of Procured Items

Often the quality requirements for items that are procured from suppliers are set by industry standards, in which case the main criterion for choosing a supplier is price. When a procurement officer receives instructions to buy a batch of standard items such as bolts, she would obtain quotes from a number of suppliers and pick the least expensive; when the batch arrives, an inspector checks the bolts to determine whether they are acceptable. But in the case of a subsystem or item to be newly developed, there likely is no industry standard. In that case, to assure the item meets specifications, the contractor ordering the item to be developed should be involved in planning the quality assurance and quality control of the work of the supplier.

Even for procured items that are standard, better than just selecting the cheapest supplier is for the contractor to develop a mutually beneficial long-term relationship with a supplier that has the proven capability and is willing to meet the contractor's requirements. The contractor and the supplier work together as partners and share responsibility for each other's success. Establishing this kind of relationship is not always easy, especially when the supplier is much larger than the contactor or does not value the relationship or consider the contracted work high priority.

Contractors often invest heavily to make sure they get the appropriate-quality subsystems and components from their suppliers. It is common for a contractor to have a special vendor quality section within its procurement division to oversee quality assurance of all procured items—including their development and manufacture or construction. The role of the vendor quality section is to assist in selection of suppliers, monitor suppliers' processes to ensure quality, and perform acceptance tests and inspection of purchased items. Additional responsibilities are described in the example.

Example 1: Companies Working Together for Quality Assurance and Control

Company A develops mining equipment. As part of a new mining system, it contracts with Company B in a "sole source" relationship to develop, manufacture, and provide support for a new mining vehicle. Company B realizes that the vehicle needs a new transmission and selects another company to develop, manufacture, and support the transmission. Since standardization and compatibility with existing equipment are important, Company A's vendor quality section works with Company B in the selection of the company to supply the transmission, which is Company C. (More than that, Company A actually nominated Company C as a potential supplier to Company B.) Company B's engineering division develops a functional specification for the transmission that includes functional characteristics, maintenance requirements, interfaces with the rest of the vehicle, and test requirements. Its vendor quality section then verifies that Company C's engineers will be using appropriate processes to ensure cost-effective compliance with the specification, and that the transmissions will be tested according to Company B's functional specification to insure compliance to Company B's performance criteria before any transmissions are shipped.

9.3 Techniques for Quality Assurance during System Development

System developers employ a wide range of techniques to ensure the quality of the project end-item or products. This section discusses a "toolbox" of these techniques.

Configuration Management[10]

During the design of a system, vast amounts of data and information are generated for use in the design process and later for manufacturing (or construction), maintenance, and support. The design can involve many hundreds or even thousands of documents (specifications, schematics, drawings, etc.), each likely to be modified in some way during the project. Keeping track of all the changes and knowing the most current version of every item can be difficult. Thus, any project aimed at delivering a technical product should include provision to keep up with and control all this information; such is the purpose of *configuration management*. Configuration management represents policies and procedures for monitoring and tracking design information and changes, and ensuring that everyone involved with the project and, later on, the operation of the end-item has the most current information possible. Policies and procedures that form the configuration management system for a project should be included as a section in the quality plan. As with all procedures, the best configuration management system is whatever enables the desired level of control and is the simplest to implement. Two aspects of configuration management are configuration identification and configuration control.

Configuration Identification

Configuration identification is an inherent part of systems design that involves defining the structure of the system, its subsystems, and components. Mentioned in Chapter 2, any subsystem, component, or part that is to be tracked and controlled as an individual entity throughout the life cycle of the system is identified as a *configuration item (CI)*. A CI can be a piece of hardware, a manual, a parts list, a software package, or even a service. A subsystem that is procured is also treated as a CI. All physical and functional characteristics that define or characterize and are important for controlling the CI are identified and documented. Ultimately, every functional and physical element of the end-item system should be associated in some way with a CI, either as a CI on its own or as a component within a subsystem that has been identified as a CI. Ideally, each CI is small enough to be designed, built, and tested individually by a small team.

Master copies (electronic or paper) of the configuration documents for every CI are retained in a secure location (the "configuration center") and managed by someone not involved in the functions of design, construction, manufacture, or maintenance.

(Additional documentation such as the design premises, assumptions, and calculations are not considered configuration documentation and are normally retained by the design authority.)

Any modifications, waivers, or deviations to a CI are recorded so that all CI documentation reflects the "as-built" status of the system. In the case of an end-item such as a building, ship, or other one-of-a-kind system that becomes operational, the "as-built" specification will later be used for its operation and maintenance. Where multiple units are produced (such as cars, airplanes, appliances) and modifications and improvements are introduced over time, the specific configuration for each individually produced unit must be known, which requires that each specific CI in the product must be traceable to its specific "as-built" specifications. This is necessary, so that, for example, the correct spare parts, training, and operating manuals can be supplied, and problems can be traced and analyzed in the event of accidents, customer complaints, or claims regarding product liability. This concept of "traceability" was introduced in Chapter 4 and is illustrated in the following example.

Example 2: Traceability and the Apollo Spacecraft[11]

The way to establish the reliability of an item is to test many of them until one fails, or to design-in the reliability through methods of engineering analysis. Either way, everything about the item must be known—its manufacturing processes, the composition of it parts and materials, even the sources of those materials. For the Apollo space mission the goal of achieving mission success was set at 99 percent, and of crew survivability at 99.9 percent. To meet such high-level goals, every CI (subsystem, component, part, etc.) as it moved through the design and manufacturing process was accompanied with a package of documents that established its genealogy and pedigree. The saying went, "If you ordered a piece of plywood, you wanted to know from which tree it came." Half-inch bolts for the Apollo spacecraft involved an 11-step manufacturing process with certification tests at each step. Every bolt was subjected to rigorous testing, as were the steel rods from which they were made, the billets from which the rods were extruded, and the ingots from which the billets were forged. Everything about the process and tests for the bolts was documented, including the original source of the iron for the bolts—Minnesota—and even the *mine* and the *mine shaft*. This extreme tracking and control is necessary to insure high reliability, and to enable problem diagnosis in case things go wrong. It comes with a price though, which is why bolts available for 59 cents at the hardware store cost $8 or $9 apiece on rockets and spacecraft.

Configuration Control

Configuration control is the second aspect of configuration management; it is a technique more for quality control than quality assurance but is covered here for the sake of continuity. The design of a system is normally specified by means of a large number of documents such as performance specifications, testing procedures, drawings, manuals, lists, and others that are generated during the design process. As the design evolves, these documents are subject to change, and an orderly scheme is needed to manage and keep track of all these changes. Such is the purpose of configuration control.

Configuration control is based on the following principles:

1. Any organization or individual may request a change—a modification, waiver, or deviation.
2. The proposed change and its motivation should be documented. Standard documents exist for this purpose; for modifications, the document is called a *change proposal* or *request*, *change order*, or *variation order*.

3. The impact of the proposed change on system performance, safety, and the environment is evaluated, as is its impact on all other physical items, manuals, software, manufacturing or construction, and maintenance.
4. The change is assessed for feasibility, which includes estimating the resources needed to implement the change and the change's impact on schedules.
5. The change proposal is either rejected or accepted and implemented. The group responsible for making the decision, called a *configuration board* (CB) or a *configuration control board* (CCB), should include the chief designer as well as representatives from manufacturing or construction, maintenance, and other relevant stakeholders. Often the project manager or program manager chairs the group.
6. When a proposed change is approved, the work required to implement the change is planned. This includes actions regarding the disposition of items that might be affected by the change such as items in the inventory, equipment and processes used in manufacturing or construction, and manuals and other documentation.
7. The implemented change is verified to ensure it complies with the proposed, approved change proposal.

Change requests are sometimes classified as Class I or Class II. Class I requests are for changes that can be approved by the contractor or the developer; Class II changes must gain the approval of the client. Configuration control is an aspect of project control and, in particular, change control, both discussed in Chapter 11.

Design Reviews

Since the fate of an end-item is often sealed by its design, the project manager must insure that the proposed design is acceptable in all respects. This is the purpose of *design reviews*—to ensure that the users' requirements and inherent assumptions have been correctly identified, and that the proposed design is able to meet those requirements in an appropriate way. Design reviews (not to be confused with *general project reviews*, described in Chapter 12) provide confirmation of the data used during the design process, design assumptions (e.g., load conditions), and design calculations. They should ensure that important life-cycle aspects of the product or end-item have been addressed and pose no unacceptable risks; examples of these aspects include:

1. Omissions or errors in the design
2. Compliance to regulations, codes, specifications, and standards
3. Cost of ownership
4. Safety and product liability
5. Reliability
6. Availability
7. Ability to be constructed or manufactured (manufacturability)
8. Shelf life
9. Operability
10. Maintainability
11. Patentability
12. Ergonomics

The reviews should involve representatives from all disciplines, functions, and users who are or will be connected to the end-item throughout its life cycle and include outside designers and subject matter experts. (This relates to the concurrent engineering process, discussed in Chapters 4 and 13.) For example, a design review of a production facility (e.g., a chemical plant, mine, or factory) would include:

- Representatives from the technical support area that will eventually be responsible for maintenance of the facility.
- People from the construction area or company that will build the facility.
- Representatives from the marketing, procurement, legal services, and quality areas that in some way will occupy, make use of, or have to deal with the consequences of the facility.

Early in the conceptual phase the reviews might involve representatives from only a few functions, but as the project moves to later phases many more representatives will be involved. For the design of a simple part or component, a single review upon completion of the design but preceding manufacture might be sufficient. In the case of a complex system, however, it will be necessary to convene several reviews at successive stages of the project. The quality plan should indicate when these reviews will be held, the stakeholders to be involved in each, who will chair them, and to what extent the designer is bound to comply with the reviewers' directions or recommendations. The review dates, subjects, and attendees should be noted in the project communication plan.

Formal Reviews

Formal design reviews are planned events, preferably chaired by the project manager or someone else who is *not* directly involved in designing the product. For projects aimed at developing and delivering a product, the kinds of reviews commonly include:

1. *Preliminary design review*: The functional design is reviewed to determine whether the concept and planned implementation fit the basic operational requirements.
2. *Critical design review*: Details of the hardware and software design are reviewed to ensure they conform to the preliminary design specifications.
3. *Functional readiness review*: For high-volume or mass-produced products, tests are performed on early-produced items to evaluate the efficacy of the manufacturing process.
4. *Product readiness review*: Manufactured products are compared to specifications to ensure that the controlling design documentation results in items that meet requirements.

Formal reviews serve several purposes: minimize risk, identify uncertainties, assure technical integrity, and assess alternative design and engineering approaches. Unlike peer reviews, the actual oversight and conduct of formal reviews are handled by a group of outsiders, although the project team accumulates information for the reviewers. These outsiders are technical experts or experienced managers who are intimately familiar with the end-item and workings of the project and the project organization, but are not formally associated with the project organization or its contractors. Since a formal review may last for several days and involve considerable preparation and scrutiny of results, the tasks and time necessary to prepare and conduct the review and to obtain approvals should be incorporated in the project schedule.

A prerequisite for the design review is thorough design documentation, so a common practice is to convene a "pre-review meeting" at which the design team gives the review team a brief overview of the design, documentation describing the design premises, philosophy, assumptions, and calculations, and specifications and drawings for the proposed design. The review team is then allowed sufficient time (typically 14 days) to evaluate the design and prepare for the formal review meeting. Sometimes the review team uses a checklist to ensure that everything important is covered. In recent years the Internet has become an effective medium for conducting design reviews and has reduced the cost of the reviews.[12]

Informal Design Reviews

In addition to the formal reviews, the project manager should encourage many informal design reviews. These include informal discussions among designers, and between designers and other stakeholders. Good suggestions can come from different places, but it is up to the designer to decide whether or not to use them. Draft designs, reports, and other deliverables should be presented regularly and (ideally) voluntarily to peer designers and other stakeholders for informal review. In a healthy quality culture, brainstorming is commonly used to evaluate and edit not only designs, but also reports and other deliverables of all kinds. The principle behind brainstorming is to freely generate as many ideas as possible, withholding any form of evaluation or criticism until after numerous ideas have generated. Only later are the ideas assessed and the good ones separated from poor ones.

Example 3: Formal and Internal Reviews in the Mars Pathfinder Project[13]

Outside review boards conduct formal reviews for all of major NASA projects. These reviews are important since termination or continuation of a project depends on the board's findings. Preparation for a formal NASA review can take an enormous amount of time. Senior project management for the Mars Pathfinder project (see also Example 5, Chapter 11) estimated that preparation for one such review, the *critical design review*, would require about *6 weeks* of their devoted attention. This would divert time from the actual management of the project, which, paradoxically, could increase the likelihood of the project falling behind schedule and failing the review. To prepare for the review, project manager Brian Muirhead first ordered an internal review.

Internal (or peer) reviews at NASA address a narrow range of topics and require only a few days preparation. The main value of these reviews lies in making sure that everyone understands the decisions being made, that nothing is overlooked, and that the project is kept on track. Over 100 peer reviews were conducted during the 3 years of Pathfinder development.

The Pathfinder internal review revealed a slew of problem areas, including lack of progress in defining system interfaces, rapid growth in the mass of the Mars lander (the prototype weighed too much), and a shortage of good engineers. These findings did little to inspire confidence about the project's ability to pass scrutiny of the design review board.

The verdict from the critical design review is an all-or-nothing decision. The project earns either a passing or failing grade. A failing grade initiates a cancellation review, a process that can result in project termination. A project such as Pathfinder could be canceled if budget overruns ran as little as 15 percent. The Pathfinder design review board comprised 25 consultants and seasoned managers from NASA and JPL (Jet Propulsion Laboratory, the site responsible for most of the Pathfinder design work), none of whom was associated with the project.

Besides determining the future of a project, design reviews serve another purpose: to give it a kick in the pants. Preparation for the review sessions is a laborious endeavor and forces the project team to make decisions about unresolved issues. Formal reviews may be held 3 or 4 times during the project.

The review board for the Pathfinder critical design review was not happy with many aspects of the project; nonetheless, they did not initiate a cancellation review. Instead, they approved the project, but instructed Pathfinder managers to be more critical of designs, focus less on performance and more on cost, and stop obsessing over business innovations. These recommendations later proved useful and helped to make the Pathfinder project one of the most successful in the history of space exploration.

The design review process is significant to quality, no matter how highly competent the design staff. There is always more than one means to an end, and a designer can be expected to think of only some of them. Even the most competent people overlook things. Mature designers appreciate the design review process in terms of the networking experience, innovative ideas provided by others, knowledge gained, and reduction of risks, but less mature designers tend to feel insulted or intimidated by it. It is human nature for people to be less than enthusiastic about others' ideas and to resist suggested changes to their own. The design review process seeks to achieve "appropriate quality" (a balanced compromise agreed upon by the stakeholders) and refrains from perfecting minor features and faultfinding. Review meetings are also discussed in Chapter 12.

Audits

Unlike design reviews, which relate only to the design of a product, audits have broader scope and include a variety of investigations and inquiries. The purpose of audits is to verify that *management processes* comply with prescribed processes, procedures, and specifications regarding, for example, system engineering procedures, configuration management systems, contractor warehousing and inventory control systems, and facility safety procedures. They are also performed to verify that *technical processes* such as welding adhere to prescribed procedures, and to determine the *status of a project* whenever a thorough examination of certain critical aspects of the work is required. Any senior stakeholder such as a customer, program manager, or executive can call for an audit. Like formal design reviews, audits are relatively formal and normally involve multifunctional teams. Unlike design reviews where sometimes innovative ideas originate, audits focus strictly on verifying that the work is being performed as required. They are performed by internal staff or by independent, external parties who are deemed credible and, ideally, unbiased, fair, and honest.

Preparation for an audit includes agreement between the auditor and stakeholder requesting the audit as to the audit's scope and schedule, and the responsibilities of the audit team. The audit team prepares for the audit by compiling checklists and sometimes attending training sessions to learn about the project. Each auditor is required to prepare a report within a few days following the investigation detailing any nonconformities found, rating the importance of the nonconformities, describing the circumstances under which they were found and the causes (if known or determinable), and providing suggestions for corrective action. While the focus is on uncovering nonconformities, commendable activities are sometimes also noted in the audit report. A typical thorough audit will take 1 to 2 weeks.

Classification of Characteristics

A system (deliverable or end-item) is "specified" or described in terms of a number of attributes or characteristics, including functional, geometrical, chemical, or physical properties and processes. Characteristics can be specified or described in terms of numerical specifications, which often include tolerances of acceptability. In a complex system there are typically a large number of characteristics defined on drawings and other documents. As a result of the Pareto principle (which states that, in general, the large majority of problems in any situation are caused by a relatively small number of sources), the most cost-effective approach to quality assurance is to attend to the system or component characteristics that have the most serious impact on quality problems or failures. This does not mean to imply that other characteristics should be ignored, but rather that limited resources and activities for inspection and acceptance testing should be directed first at those items classified as most crucial or problematic.

Characteristics are typically classified into four categories: *critical, major, minor,* and *incidental* (or, alternatively, *critical, major A, major B,* and *minor*). The *critical* classification is reserved for characteristics where a nonconformance would pose safety risks or lead to system failure. Quality plans often specify that items with critical characteristics be subjected to 100 percent inspection. The *major* classification is for characteristics where nonconformance would cause the loss of a major function of the deliverable. The *minor* classification is for characteristics where nonconformance would lead to small impairment of function or to problems with manufacturability or serviceability. Characteristics classified as *incidental* would have minimal effect or relate to relatively unimportant requirements. The classification assigned to a characteristic is determined by the designer of the system in collaboration with others such as the designer of the next higher-level system, designers of interfacing systems, or staff from manufacturing or construction. Together they analyze the design characteristics regarding safety and other requirements, and classify them using a set of ground rules.

Classification also applies to kinds of nonconformities or defects, but this should not be confused with the classification of characteristics. In welded structures, for example, the specified characteristics often include the "absence of any cracks or of certain amounts and kinds of impurities" in the weld metal. A crack (a nonconformity that could lead to a catastrophic failure) would be classified as "very serious," whereas a small amount of an impurity in the weld (a nonconformity that would have no effect on the integrity of the structure) would be classified as "minor."

Classification of characteristics serves as a basis for decisions regarding modifications, waivers, and deviations at all levels of a system. For example, classification of characteristics in a higher-level system provides guidance to designers of the lower-level subsystems and components that comprise the system. Classifying the braking performance of an automobile as critical (e.g., that the automobile when traveling at 25 miles per hour should be able to stop within 40 feet on dry pavement) tells the braking system designers that components of the brakes should be classified critical as well. Failure mode and effect analysis (FMEA), discussed below, sometimes plays an important role in this classification process.

Sometimes the characteristic classifications are listed in a separate document, although it is more practical to indicate the classifications directly on drawings and other specifications by means of symbols such as "C" for critical, "Ma" for major, "Mi" for minor, and so on. Absence of a symbol normally indicates the lowest priority, although some organizations denote even the lowest classification with a symbol as well. Only a small percentage of characteristics should be classified as critical. Too large a number of characteristics classified as critical could be the sign of poor design: if everything is critical, nothing in particular is critical!

Failure Mode and Effect Analysis

Any system can potentially fail as the result of a variety of conditions such as the short-circuiting, cracking, collapsing, or melting of its components, or inadequate, missing, or incorrect steps and procedures in its design production, or operation. FMEA (also called *failure mode, effect, and criticality analysis,* FMECA) is a technique to determine in what ways a technical system might fail, and what effects the identified failures would have on the system's performance and safety, and on the environment.

FMEA is a procedure normally used during the early stages of system development; it involves the following steps:

1. List the *relevant components* of the system.
2. Identify all the *possible ways* in which the component or system might *fail* (the *failure modes*). This is best done by a team that brainstorms all the conceivable failure modes. The causes of each failure mode and conditions under which they are likely to occur are also listed.
3. Assess the *probability* of each failure mode occurring.
4. Describe and assess the probable *effects* (or impacts) of each failure mode; these are impacts on the performance and safety of the system, and on the environment.
5. Assess the *severity* or seriousness of the effects.
6. Rate the *criticality* of each identified failure mode. Criticality is a function of both the probability of the failure and the seriousness of the effects.
7. Prepare a plan to circumvent the failure mode and/or mitigate the effects of the failure. Where applicable, describe an appropriate response in case the failure occurs. In cases where conformance to a specific characteristic is necessary to prevent a particular failure, the characteristic is classified as critical.

Table 9-1 illustrates: The columns "Sev" (severity), "Prob" (probability), and "Det" (detectability—potential failure will be easy or difficult to detect) are each rated 1 to 10 for each of the potential failure modes. RPN (risk priority number), which is the criticality of the failure mode, is:

$$RPN = Sev \times Prob \times Det$$

Items are categorized by RPN and the highest-priority ones are addressed first.

Although a failure by itself might not be critical, combined with other failures it could have a very serious effect. The Chernobyl disaster is an example where a chain of errors (each alone not very serious) led to a catastrophic failure—the meltdown of a nuclear reactor. Thus, FMEA must consider combinations of possible failures modes as well individual failure modes. Although used primarily in design and engineering analysis, FMEA can also be used to identify issues affecting project costs and schedules—a tool in project risk management, described in Chapter 10.

Modeling and Prototyping

Designers use a variety of models to ensure the quality of their products, including computer simulation models, mathematical models, three-dimensional scale models, and full-scale prototypes, each to gain a better impression of how the final product, system, or subsystem will look and perform. Models and prototypes also serve a marketing role by helping others to understand and see a "vision" of the product or system. A full-scale wooden or plastic mock-up of the driver's cab of a new truck or the cockpit of a new airplane, for example, helps the producer to sell its products and to obtain suggestions or criticisms about features and configurations.

In product development projects, constructing models helps minimize the risk of failure to meet technical requirements. As shown in Table 9-2, it is customary in development projects to build and test different types of models coinciding with project phases to eliminate different risks. (Table 9-2 applies to development projects where the deliverable is the detailed definition and specification for the product and its production process, but not the manufactured product itself; hence the absence of a "production" or a "building" phase.)

Table 9-1 FMEA Table.

<table>
<tr>
<td colspan="13" align="center">**Potential**
Failure Mode and Effect Analysis
(Design FMEA)</td>
</tr>
<tr>
<td colspan="7">System _____
Subsystem _____
Component _____
Design Lead _____
Core Team _____</td>
<td colspan="6">FMEA Number _____
Prepared By _____
FMEA Date _____
Revision Date _____
Page _____ of _____</td>
</tr>
<tr>
<td colspan="7">Key Date _____</td>
<td colspan="6"></td>
</tr>
<tr>
<td rowspan="2">Item/Function</td>
<td rowspan="2">Potention
Failure Mode(s)</td>
<td rowspan="2">Potention
Effect(s)
of Failure</td>
<td rowspan="2">S
e
v</td>
<td rowspan="2">Potential
Cause(s)/
Mechanism(s)
of Failure</td>
<td rowspan="2">P
r
o
b</td>
<td rowspan="2">Current Design
Controls</td>
<td rowspan="2">D
e
t</td>
<td rowspan="2">R
P
N</td>
<td rowspan="2">Recommended
Action(s)</td>
<td rowspan="2">Responsibility &
Target
Completion
Date</td>
<td rowspan="2">Action Taken</td>
<td>Action Results</td>
</tr>
<tr>
<td>New Sev | New Occ | New Det | New RPN</td>
</tr>
<tr>
<td></td><td></td><td></td><td></td><td></td><td></td><td></td><td></td><td></td><td></td><td></td><td></td><td></td>
</tr>
<tr>
<td></td><td></td><td></td><td></td><td></td><td></td><td></td><td></td><td></td><td></td><td></td><td></td><td></td>
</tr>
<tr>
<td></td><td></td><td></td><td></td><td></td><td></td><td></td><td></td><td></td><td></td><td></td><td></td><td></td>
</tr>
<tr>
<td></td><td></td><td></td><td></td><td></td><td></td><td></td><td></td><td></td><td></td><td></td><td></td><td></td>
</tr>
</table>

Table 9-2 Phases of equipment development.

Project Phase	Model Built and Tested	Objectives Relating to the Elimination of Risks	Risks Eliminated
Concept	Exploratory development model (XDM) (Breadboard models) Such models could be built for the entire system or for specific high-risk subsystems	Proof that the concept would be feasible	The risk that the concept would not be feasible
Validation	Advanced development model (ADM)	Proof that the product would perform according to specifications and interface well with other systems (form, fit and function)	The risk that the performance of the system and its interfaces with other systems would not be acceptable
Development	Engineering development model (EDM) manufactured from the intended final materials	Proof of reliability, availability, and maintainability	The risk of poor operational availability or reliability
Ramp-up	Pre-production models (PPM)	Proof that the product could be manufactured reliably in the production facility and could be deployed effectively	The risk of unforeseen problems in manufacturing

Projects for the development of new chemical or metallurgical processes often include similar project phases and models (Table 9-3). The models for such processes usually start out as laboratory equipment but ultimately grow in sophistication and capacity to enable a pilot operation, then ultimately a demonstration plant that closely replicates the proposed facility.

The kind of models used in a project, whether full-scale physical mock-ups, scale models, mathematical models, computer simulation models, breadboards, or prototypes, depends on the information needed versus the expense of creating and using them. For a small product comprising only a few components, building and testing

Table 9-3 Phases for development of chemical or metallurgical development.

Project Phase	Objective
Laboratory experiments	To prove the basic concept.
Pilot plant	To learn how the process works when scaled up. This provides inputs for the design of the final plant.
Demonstration plant	To provide a full-scale plant that demonstrates to potential customers the economic feasibility as well as operational aspects.

a full-scale model that closely resembles the final product is probably cost-effective; for a complex system with innumerable components, it usually is not and computer simulation and mathematical models are normally more effective.

Example 4: Modeling the Form and Fit of Boeing 777 Components[14]

One of the most pervasive problems in the development of large aircraft is aligning vast numbers of parts and components so that during assembly there is no interference or gaps between them. In the mid-1980s Boeing invested in three-dimensional CAD/CAM (computer-aided design/computer-aided manufacture) technology that would enable designers to see components as solid images and simulate their assembly into subsystems and systems on a computer screen. By 1989 Boeing had concluded that "digital preassembling" of an airplane could significantly reduce the time and cost of rework that usually accompanies introducing a new airplane into the marketplace. In 1990 it launched the Boeing 777 twinjet program and began involving stakeholders such as customers, design engineers, tool makers, manufacturing representatives, and suppliers in the concurrent engineering design process (see Example 7, Chapter 4). The physical geometry of the airplane's components was determined with CAD/CAM technology instead of with physical mock-ups that are time-consuming and expensive to build. As a result, the 777 program exceeded its goal of reducing changes and rework by 50 percent.

Testing of Prototypes and Models

As shown in Table 9-2, a goal of building and testing models is to systematically reduce the risk that the final product will not be satisfactory. Models enable data to be gathered about systems and subsystems that will assist in later stages of development. Experiments with models reveal design shortcomings. Data about stresses and strains in components, for example, provide information about potential failure modes in the final product. (Occasionally, the engineers and technologists who design and build models become attached to them and do not want to see them get broken or damaged, and they actually resist doing tests on them. Of course, the objective of modeling is not to create perfect models but to generate data that will result in a high-quality final product.) While early tests on components to acquire technical data should be supervised by designers and test personnel, functional tests on full-scale models should involve people who most resemble typical users.

For products that are to be manufactured in quantities, the design should be verified by means of a *qualification test* before manufacturing ramp-up. The qualification testing process happens in the opposite way of the system design process. While typically the design process happens top-down, starting with the overall system design and cascading down to the design of individual subsystems and components, qualification testing happens bottom-up, starting with the testing and qualification of individual components, then of subsystems, and finally of the full, completed system.

9.4   PROCESSES AND TECHNIQUES FOR QUALITY CONTROL

When a development project terminates with handover to an operational process (e.g., repetitive manufacture of a product), the deliverables of the project include the product design, the production process design, and a plan or specification to insure the production process will provide *repeated* delivery of a quality product. The last of these is the subject of quality control, which concerns anything that must be done to insure that the output of a repetitive process remains at the required, specified quality level and does not deteriorate.

Inspection and Acceptance Testing of the Final Product

Quality control of items produced repetitively includes inspections on the product and its components throughout the production process. Characteristics classified as critical are always inspected, whereas minor or incidental characteristics are not. In automobile production, for example, the braking and steering performance on every vehicle is tested. When items are produced in large quantities, some of them might be subjected to destructive tests; when only one or a small batch of an item is produced, the inspection and testing procedures must involve non-destructive methods such as radiographic, infrared, and ultrasonic imaging of critical components.

For certain critical components produced in high volume, sampling is commonly used to reduce the cost of inspection. Based on the results of tests from a few samples, a statistical inference is made about the quality of the entire batch or process. Obviously, this method is mandatory when the testing destroys the product. To check the heat treatment of engine blocks, for example, a piece must be cut from a heat-treated engine block and tested in a laboratory. Testing of samples is common whenever a process produces a large number of identical products.

Although testing of the end product from a production process does not lie within the realm of *project* quality management, per se, the testing procedures and other quality assurance processes to be used during production should be specified during any development project where the result is a mass-produced item, and included as project deliverables. Product designers—who have intimate knowledge of the key characteristics of the product and its components—are well suited to specify the ways those components should be quality checked once production begins.

Basic Tools of Quality Control

In 1982 professor Kaoru Ishikawa of the Tokyo University defined what have come to be known as the "seven basic tools' or "magnificent seven" of quality control:"[15]

1. Check sheet
2. Flowchart
3. Run chart and control chart
4. Scatter diagram
5. Pareto diagram
6. Histogram
7. Cause-and-effect diagram

Although Ishikawa worked in a production environment (Kawasaki Steel Works) and not a project environment, most of the seven basic tools are applicable in everyday situations and some in particular to projects.[16] Ishikawa's tools are aimed at identifying the sources of defects and nonconformities in products and processes, but are equally applicable for identifying sources of and resolving all kinds of potential problems, including those associated with project risks. The application of some of the tools to project risk analysis and management is discussed in the next chapter.

Check Sheet

A check sheet is a sheet created especially for collecting data about a problem from observations. The content and format of the sheet are uniquely designed by the team investigating the problem. Data recorded on the sheet is subjected to analysis using the other six tools. A check sheet should not be confused with a *checklist*, the latter being a list of steps, issues, or pointers based upon prior experience to be considered (e.g., in planning a project).

Flow Chart

Flowcharts show the steps in a procedure and their relationships. Process flowcharts show the steps or tasks in a process. Project networks are a form of flowcharts that show the sequence of activities in a project. For problem analysis, usually more detailed flowcharts are needed to reveal the steps and tasks within the activities. An example is the diagram showing material flow in Figure 3-5. Close scrutiny of a flowchart often can reveal the steps or relationships that cause quality problems.

Run Chart

A run chart is a graph of observed results plotted versus time to reveal potential trends or anomalies. The plot of schedule performance index versus cost performance index as illustrated in Figure 11-16 is a form of run chart that tracks project performance and indicates whether a project is improving or worsening in terms of schedule and cost.

Control Chart and Scatter Diagram

Control charts and scatter diagrams are widely used for tracking and control of repetitive events (e.g., mass production). For projects that include the development of production processes, however, one of the deliverables would be specification of the relevant charts for controlling the quality of the process. Readers involved in projects aimed at the delivery of continuous operations systems should refer to books on statistical control techniques, such as *Juran's Quality Control Handbook*.[17]

Pareto Diagram and Histogram

Vilfredo Pareto, a nineteenth century Italian economist born in Paris, formulated "Pareto's Law" of income distribution. This law states that the distribution of income and wealth in a country follows a regular logarithmic pattern: 20 percent of the people own 80 percent of the wealth. This principle, also dubbed the "80/20 rule," has since been found to apply in principle to a wide variety of situations, including those relating to quality. Quality consultant Dr. Joseph Juran in the late 1940s posited that the large majority of defects are due to a small minority of the causes and, thus, for economic reasons it makes sense to separate the vital few causes of defects from the trivial many, and to direct improvement efforts to those few.

Figure 9-3 is a Pareto diagram. The histogram in the bottom part of the diagram shows the number of defects versus kinds (sources) of quality problems; the line in the top of the figure represents the cumulative effect of the problems corresponding to scale on the right. As shown, the first sources account for roughly 43 percent of the problems; the first and second combined account for roughly 70 percent. Thus, resolving just the first two problems would eliminate 70 percent of the problems.

In project environments, Pareto analysis would be used to track the sources of recurrent problems, and to identify those causing the most problems and most in need of attention.

Cause-and-Effect Diagram

Quality problems and risks are often best addressed through the collective experience of project team members. Team members meet in brainstorming sessions to generate ideas about problems or risks. These ideas can be recorded on a *cause-and-effect (CE) diagram* (also called a *fishbone* or Ishikawa diagram), which is a scheme for arranging the causes for a specified effect in a logical way. Figure 9-4 shows a CE diagram

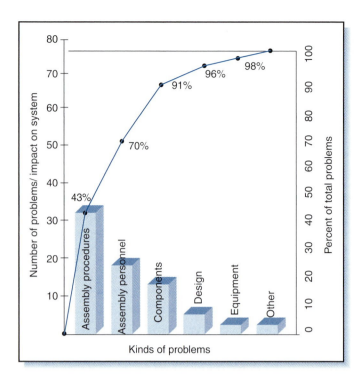

Figure 9-3
Pareto diagram.

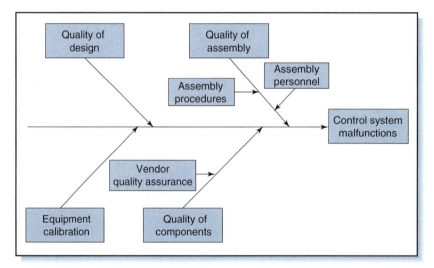

Figure 9-4
CE (fishbone or Ishikawa) diagram.

to determine why a control system does not function correctly. As the team generates ideas about causes, each cause is assigned to a specific branch (e.g., "assembly procedures" on the Quality of Assembly branch). CE diagrams and brainstorming can be used in two ways: (1) given a specified or potential outcome (*effect*), to identify the potential *causes* and (2) given a cause (or a risk), to identify the outcomes that might ensue (*effects*). CE diagrams do not solve problems but are nonetheless useful for identifying problem sources and planning actions to resolve them.

The seven basic tools are relatively simple. Following are two techniques that are more sophisticated.

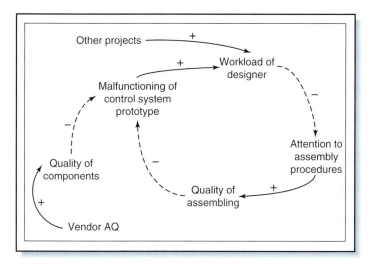

Figure 9-5
Casual loop diagram for control system problem.

Causal Loop Diagram

As the name suggests, a *causal loop diagram* shows the causes of a certain problem or situation. It can be used to illustrate the structure of a complex system and the influence that variables in the system have on one another.[18]

As shown in Figure 9-5, variables in a causal loop diagram are connected by arrows to indicate cause–effect relationships. The positive and negative signs indicate the direction in which the variable at the arrow's head changes when the variable at the arrow's tail changes. That is, a positive sign indicates a reinforcing effect—the variable at the arrow's head increases as the variable at the arrow's tail increases. A negative sign indicates that the variable at the arrow's head decreases when the variable at the arrow's tail increases. For example, in Figure 9-5 when the number of projects increases, the designer's workload also increases, and when that happens the designer's attention to assembly procedures decreases. Causal loop analysis is a way of modeling the dynamics of a complex system, but it involves considerations beyond the scope of this book. In many cases the more superficial analysis afforded by CE diagrams is sufficient.

Current Reality Tree

A *current reality tree* (CRT) is a technique for analyzing an existing situation or system. It starts with an identified (observed) undesirable *effect* (UDE) or symptom, and then is used to identify relationships between the UDE and other undesirable effects. Unlike CE and causal loop diagrams, a CRT also considers whether the causes identified are *sufficient* to have resulted in the specified UDE. This "hard logic" requires that assumptions about the situation be identified, and that as many facets of the problem as possible be uncovered, which leads to the identification of underlying causes (root causes or core problems)—much in the same way that symptoms in a patient lead to diagnosis of health problems.[19]

For example, suppose a control system is malfunctioning, and one possible source is the procedure used to assemble the system (UDE 900). Figure 9-6 shows the CRT for the situation; it is read from the bottom to the top as follows: Entities 100, 200, 300, and 400 are causes for the UDE numbered 500. The oval around the

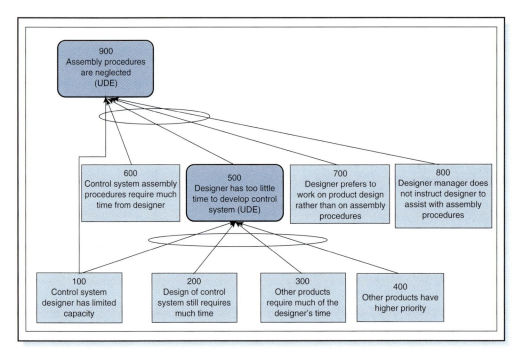

Figure 9-6
Example of a CRT.

arrows indicates that these four entities are sufficient to have caused UDE 500. In the same way, entities 500, 600, 700, and 800 are sufficient to have caused UDE 900. The CRT approach requires more effort than simple CE analysis and, hence, would be applied only to problems that are considered more severe (the first 20 percent of the causes that lead to 80 percent of the problems). The CRT is one of several techniques and tools described in the literature on theory of constraints, which include the *future reality tree* (describes the desired future situation after a problem has been resolved), the *prerequisite tree* (a process for overcoming barriers), and the *transition tree* (a process for problem solving).[20]

Other Tools for Quality Assurance and Control

Mentioned elsewhere in this book are planning and control methods that also apply to quality assurance and control. For example, much of the quality assurance effort in a product design project is directed at keeping the project team focused on customer requirements, and making sure that those requirements do not become distorted or misinterpreted as the project moves from stage to stage and the work changes hands. Quality function deployment (QFD) discussed in Chapter 4 is a method for defining customer requirements and ensuring that those requirements remain in the focus throughout the design and production process.

Likewise, checklists as described in this book for preparing plans, assessing risks, and monitoring work progress help maintain quality by assuring that important issues or items are not overlooked. These checklists can be used for inspections, testing, design reviews, and FMEA. A potential disadvantage of checklists is that people rely on them too much and ignore issues or items not on the list. The last item on every checklist should be "Now, list and scrutinize all perceived important items not on this checklist!"

9.5   SUMMARY

Quality management is necessary to ensure compliance with the quality criteria of a project. Along with scheduling and budgeting, quality management addresses one of the dimensions of the project target—satisfying requirements and specifications.

Quality takes into account project end-item compliance to specifications, fitness for the purpose, and customer expectations. It does not necessarily imply the highest grade or most product features, nor does it imply the highest cost or even zero defects. It implies simply the "best" based upon customer expectations and the intended usage of the end-item.

Quality management can be divided into three processes: *quality planning*, *quality assurance*, and *quality control*. Quality planning is an integral part of project planning and involves setting the standards and specifications to be met, identifying all the quality-related activities, and scheduling and budgeting of these activities. Quality assurance is performing the planned quality activities and ensuring that the project utilizes all processes considered necessary to meet the requirements. Quality control is the ongoing process of monitoring and appraising work, and taking corrective action. It is an integral part of project control and includes inspection, testing, and solving ad hoc problems.

Project management has benefited primarily from two quality philosophies—TQM and Six Sigma, both of which emphasize continuous improvement. In a project environment, continuous improvement is facilitated by a quality assurance process and a systematic project closeout process with documented lessons learned.

Project management has also benefited from many of the techniques popularized by the so-called quality movements, including statistical methods and basic problem-solving tools used for manufacturing and production. Beyond these, however, project quality management utilizes techniques and processes applicable to all engineering and technical endeavors; these include design reviews, configuration identification and configuration control, classification of characteristics, FMEA, as well as experimenting, modeling, and prototyping. Many of the techniques used for project quality assurance and quality control are also applicable to project risk management, the subject of the next chapter.

REVIEW QUESTIONS

1. Describe your understanding of "quality."
2. A Rolls Royce is a high-quality vehicle. Is this always true? Consider different users and uses.
3. How does compliance to specification differ from satisfying requirements?
4. Is there a difference between *satisfying requirements* and *fitness for purpose*? Explain.
5. Explain the difference between *quality* and *grade*.
6. How does the role of the quality manager (a functional manager) regarding quality planning differ from that of the project manager?
7. For each of the following, indicate whether you would apply for a modification, a deviation, or a waiver:
   (a) The supplier of oil filters to a motor car manufacturer indicates that it plans to terminate the production of an oil filter that is specified on a car that is being developed.

(b) An inspector discovered a kink in reinforcing steel and the structural engineer is of the opinion that, while the steel does not meet her drawings, the defect would have no negative effect.

(c) A damaged ship has to be repaired at a foreign port. The corrosion protective coating specified is not available. However, a more expensive (but probably acceptable) type of coating is available.

8. Describe the differences between design reviews and audits.

9. Discuss how design reviews contribute to the approach of concurrent engineering.

10. Explain how a narrow tolerance on a manufacturing drawing differs from the characteristic being classified as critical or major.

11. Explain how classification of *defects* differs from classification of *characteristics*.

12. Discuss the relationship between project risk management and project quality management.

13. Describe how FMEA resembles the risk management approach described in Chapter 10.

14. Do an FMEA on an electric kettle with cord and plug.

15. How do tests for acceptance by the client differ from tests to obtain design information?

16. How would you expect the bars of a Pareto diagram to change as the result of an improvement program?

17. How does the information on the x-axis of a Pareto diagram in project control differ from the information on the x-axis of a Pareto diagram constructed to analyze defects in a mass production environment?

18. Describe the pros and cons of CE diagrams, causal loop diagrams, and CRT.

19. Why does it make sense to construct a Pareto diagram before constructing a CRT?

QUESTIONS AND ASSIGNMENTS REGARDING THE STUDY PROJECT

1. In which ways would you be able to uncover client expectations that have not been articulated explicitly?

2. Develop a quality plan for your project to form part of an integrated project management plan. Include quality management policies, standards, and specifications to meet metrics for meeting specifications/standards, training, criteria for authorizing project phases, and discuss the use of specific tools and techniques for quality assurance and quality control.

3. Discuss how the quality plan is integrated with the schedule, budget, risk management plan, and, if applicable, with the procurement plan.

4. Identify project budget items that aim at reducing the cost of probable external failures.

5. Draw a CE diagram, a causal loop diagram, a CRT, and a Pareto diagram to illustrate a project management problem that you experience in your study project.

6. Compile a list of "lessons learned," and indicate how these lessons could contribute to more successful future projects.

Case 9-1   Ceiling Panel Collapse in the Big Dig Project

(For more about the Big Dig Project—Boston's Central Artery/Tunnel Project, see Chapter 14, Example 4 and Case 14-3.)

Boston, July 11, 2006—Four concrete panels, each weighing about three tons, fell from the ceiling of a Big Dig tunnel, crushing a woman to death in a car. The accident occurred in a 200-foot section that connects the Massachusetts Turnpike to the Ted Williams Tunnel. Said the Modern Continental Company, the contractor for that section of the project, "We are confident that our work fully complied with the plans and specifications provided by the Central Artery Tunnel Project. In addition, the work was inspected and approved by the project manager."[21]

The panels, which were installed in 1999, are held from metal trays secured to the tunnel ceiling with epoxy and bolts. The epoxy–bolt system is a tried-and-true method: holes are drilled into the concrete ceiling, cleaned, and filled with high-strength epoxy; a bolt is screwed into the hole, and as the epoxy cures it develops a secure bond. "That technique is used extensively," said an engineering professor at the Massachusetts Institute of Technology (MIT).[22] For a design like the Big Dig's ceiling, he said, engineers often add safety "redundancies," in other words, enough epoxy-and-bolt anchors to hold the ceiling panels even if a few of them failed. But for the connector tunnel, he contends, too few anchors were used. "They didn't have enough to carry the load. There was no room for error." He added, however, that the evidence was preliminary and to draw conclusions would be premature.

Some bolts from the ceiling wreckage showed indications of having very little epoxy, and three of them had none. State Attorney General Thomas Reilly's investigation is focusing on whether the epoxy used in the tunnel failed or if construction workers who installed the bolts misused or omitted the epoxy. An accident caused by improper installation or errors in mixing the epoxy, he said, would implicate the tunnel's design and designers. (Epoxy often requires on-site mixing before use.) However, he added that some documents reflected a "substantial dispute" among engineers over the anchor system's adequacy to hold the weight of the ceiling panels.

Seven years before the accident, safety officer John Keaveney wrote a memo to one of his superiors at contractor Modern Continental Construction Co. saying he could not "comprehend how this structure can withhold the test of time."[23] He said his superiors at Modern Continental and representatives from Big Dig project manager Bechtel/Parsons Brinckerhoff (B/PB) assured him that the system had been tested and proven to work. Keaveney told the *Boston Globe* that he began to worry about the ceiling panels after a third-grade class visited the Big Dig for a tour in 1999. He showed the class some concrete ceiling panels and pointed to the bolts in the ceiling. A girl raised her hand and asked, "Will those things hold up the concrete?""I said, 'Yes, it would hold,' but then I thought about it."

Some have argued that the investigation should look at the tunnel's design: Why were the concrete panels so heavy, weighing 2½ to 3 tons apiece? Why were they there at all? And why did the failure of a single steel hanger send 6 to 10 of the panels crashing down? Reports from eyewitnesses indicate the accident began with a loud snap as a steel hanger gave way, which set off a chain reaction that caused other hangers holding up a 40-foot steel bar to fail and send 12 tons of concrete smashing below. Were the 40-foot bars under-designed to handle the weight?

Investigators are also looking at whether the use of the wrong epoxy may have played a role.[24] Invoices from 1999 show that at least one case of a quick-drying epoxy was used to secure ceiling bolts rather than the standard epoxy specified by the designers. The epoxy holds 25 percent less weight than standard epoxy and is not recommended for suspending heavy objects.

Additional issues raised during the early stages of the investigation include the following:[25]

- Design changes that resulted in the use of heavier concrete ceiling panels in the connector tunnel instead of lighter-weight panels as used in the Ted Williams Tunnel.

- The lack of steel supports in sections of the connector tunnel ceiling to which bolts holding the concrete panels could have been connected.
- Possible tunnel damage caused by blast vibrations from nearby construction of an office tower.
- Use of diamond-tipped drill bits, instead of carbide bits, in drilling holes for the bolts (epoxy may not hold as well in smoother holes drilled with diamond bits).
- The impact of cold weather during installation of the epoxy–bolt system in some tunnel sections.

B/PB, the project management contractor for the Big Dig, said in a statement "Determining the causes of this specific failure will require a thorough forensic analysis of design, methods, materials, procedures, and documentation." As investigators scrutinize the construction history of the $14.6 billion project, criticism is reviving that Massachusetts lacked adequate supervision of private contractors. B/PB was involved in both the design and construction efforts—an arrangement that some say may have compromised oversight. "There was no one checking the checkers," said one US Representative. Wrote one blogger, "I wouldn't want to be the registered engineer whose signature is on the design. It will be his fault if the materials and workmanship are found not to be up to specifications. But who knows if it is his fault. This is a huge mess and the whole bunch of them, engineers, managers, inspectors, and testers, should be investigated."[26]

QUESTIONS

1. With 20-20 hindsight, draw a CE (fishbone, Ishikawa) diagram to illustrate possible causes and effects. Include the possible causes mentioned in the case. The diagram should have been developed before construction, therefore also indicate other possible failure modes and other causes you can think of. How would the diagram (developed after the accident) be of value during litigation?
2. List the characteristics that should have been classified as critical.
3. Propose guidelines for a process to ensure that the epoxy would provide sufficient bonding to the concrete ceiling.
4. Explain the role that configuration management should have played in preventing the accident.

5. What role could modeling/prototyping, laboratory tests, checklists, and training have played?
6. Explain how someone within B/PB would be accountable regardless of the findings of a forensic investigation. Would B/PB be off the hook if a subcontractor would be found guilty?
7. What would the implications have been if the engineer who signed off a specific design or construction aspect was an engineer-in-training instead of a registered engineer?
8. Comment on the relationship between project quality management and project risk management. How could risk management have prevented the accident? How does project quality management relate to project cost management?
9. Comment on the contribution that inspection and audits could have played.

ENDNOTES

1. M.C. Carruthers, *Principles of Management for Quality Projects* (London: International Thompson Press, 1999).
2. Ibid.
3. See E. Yourdan, *Rise and Resurrection of the American Programmer* (Upper Saddle River, NY: Yourdan Press/Prentice Hall, 1998): 157–181.
4. P.B. Crosby, *Quality Is Free* (McGraw-Hill, 1979).
5. James Bach, "The Challenge of 'Good Enough' Software," *American Programmer* (October 1995).
6. John Nicholas and Avi Soni, *The Portal to Lean Production: Principles and Practices for Doing More with Less* (Boca Raton, FL: Auerbach, 2006).
7. International Systems Organization, *ISO 9001, Quality Management Systems—Requirements*, 3rd ed. (Geneva, Switzerland, 2000).

8. P.B. Crosby, ibid.

9. A. Kransdorff, "The Role of the Post-project Analysis,"*The Learning Organization* 3, no. 1 (1996): 11–15.

10. The ISO/CD 10007 standard offers guidelines on configuration management systems: International Standards Organization, *ISO/CD 1007 Quality Management Systems—Guidelines for Configuration Management* (Geneva, Switzerland, November 2001).

11. Mike Gray, *Angle of Attack: Harrison Storms and the Race to the Moon* (New York: W.W. Norton, 1992): 170–171.

12. E.W. East, J.G. Kirby , and G. Perez, "Improved Design Review through Web Collaboration,"*Journal of Management in Engineering* (April 2004).

13. Adapted from Brian Muirhead and William Simon, *High Velocity Leadership: The Mars Pathfinder Approach to Faster, Better, Cheaper* (New York: Harper Business, 1999): 86–89, 178–179.

14. http://www.boeing.com/commercial/777family/pf/pf_computing.html accessed in August 2006.

15. K. Ishikawa, *What Is Quality Control?* (Englewood Cliffs, NY: Prentice Hall, 1982).

16. D.R. Bamford and R.W. Greatbanks, "The Use of Quality Management Tools and Techniques: A Study of Application in Everyday Situations,"*International Journal of Quality and Reliability Management*, 22, no. 4 (2005).

17. J.M. Juran and F.M. Gryna, *Juran's Quality Control Handbook*, 4th ed. (McGraw-Hill, 1988).

18. D. Sherwood, *Seeing the Forest for the Trees—A Manager's Guide to Applying Systems Thinking* (London: Nicholas Brealey Publishing, 2002); J.D. Sterman, *Business Dynamics: Systems Thinking and Modeling for a Complex World* (McGraw-Hill, 2000).

19. L.J. Steinkopf, *Thinking for a Change—Putting the TOC Thinking Processes to Use* (New York: St Lucie Press, 1999).

20. E.M. Goldratt, *What Is This Thing Called Theory of Constraints* and *How Should It Be Implemented?* (New York: North River Press, Inc, 1990).

21. Pam Belluck and Katie Zezima, "Accident in Boston's Big Dig Kills Woman in Car,"*New York Times* (July 12, 2006).

22. Matt Bradley, "Bolt Failure at Big Dig: An anomaly?"*The Christian Science Monitor* (July 21, 2006).

23. Sean Murphy, "Memo Warned of Ceiling Collapse: Safety Officer Feared Deaths in '99, Now Agonizes Over Tragedy,"*Boston Globe* (July 26, 2006).

24. Scott Allen and Sean Murphy, "Big Dig Job May Have Used Wrong Epoxy,"*Boston Globe* (May 3, 2007).

25. Bob Drake, "Investigators Probe Boston Tunnel Design," CENews.com (September 1, 2006), www.cenews.com/article.asp?id=1108; accessed May 15, 2007.

26. Russ Waters, Physics forums, www.physicsforums.com/showthread.php?t=126374, russ_waters, July 17, 2006, 9.30 P.M.; accessed May 20, 2007.

Managing Risks in Projects

Life "looks just a little more mathematical and regular than it is;
its exactitude is obvious, but its inexactitude is hidden;
its wildness lies in wait."

—G. K. Chesterton[1]

When our world was created, nobody remembered
to include certainty.

—Peter Bernstein[2]

*E*very project is risky, meaning there is a chance things won't turn out exactly as planned. Project outcomes happen as a result of many things, including some that are unpredictable and over which project managers have little control. Risk level is associated with the certainty level about technical, schedule, and cost outcomes. High-certainty outcomes have low risk; low-certainty outcomes have high risk. Certainty derives from knowledge and experience gained in prior projects as well as from management's ability to control project outcomes and respond to emerging problems.[3] This chapter discusses how sources of risk in projects are identified, how risks are assessed in terms of likelihood, impact, and consequences, and appropriate ways of dealing with risks.

10.1   RISK CONCEPTS

Risk is a function of the uniqueness of a project and the experience of the project team. When activities are routine or have been performed many times before, managers can anticipate the range of potential outcomes and manipulate aspects of the system design and project plan to achieve the desired outcomes. But when the project is unique or the team is inexperienced, the potential outcomes are more uncertain, making it difficult to anticipate problems or know how to avoid them. Even routine projects have risks because outcomes may be influenced by factors that are new and emerging or beyond anyone's control.

The notion of project risk involves two concepts:

1. The *likelihood* that some problematical event will occur.
2. The *impact* of the event if it does occur.

Risk is a joint function of the two; that is,

$$Risk = f(\text{likelihood, impact})$$

Given that risk involves both likelihood and impact, a project will ordinarily be considered risky whenever the combination of the likelihood and the impact is large. For example, a project will be considered risky when the potential impact is human fatality or massive financial loss even when the likelihood is small.

Managers are accustomed to dealing with facts and figures; especially in technical projects, they work with hard numbers derived from rigorous procedures. Many of them find the concept of risk hard to deal with; faced with uncertainty, they prefer to ignore the fact that something might go wrong. Of course, ignoring a potential problem will not make it go away.

Risk cannot be eliminated from projects, but it can be reduced and plans readied in case things go wrong; this is the purpose of risk management. The main process and aspects of risk management are shown in Figure 10-1: identify the risks, assess

Figure 10-1
Risk management elements and process.

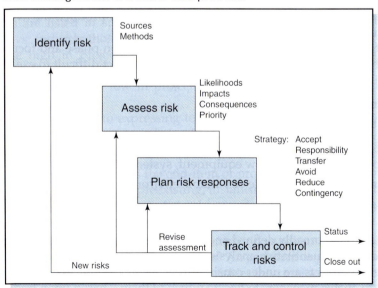

and a failure with terrible impact should never be ignored, regardless of how small the expected value. For example, the chemical plant accident at Bhopal, India has been attributed to over 30 separate causes, their joint probability being so small as to be beyond consideration. Yet they *all* did happen, causing an accident that resulted in between 1,800 to 10,000 deaths and 100,000 to 200,000 more injuries.[18] Similarly, the nuclear meltdown at Chernobyl was the result of *six errors* in human action, any one of which, if absent, would have precluded the accident. Despite the minuscule likelihood, all six did happen resulting in an accident that immediately caused several dozen deaths, several hundred hospitalizations, and 135,000 evacuations. More disturbing is the long-term impact: an estimated 5,000 to 24,000 additional cancer deaths in the former Soviet Union, and many more throughout Europe and Asia.[19] The lesson: Any risk with a severe impact should never be ignored, no matter how small the likelihood.

10.4 RISK RESPONSE PLANNING

Risk response planning addresses the matter of how to *deal* with risk. In general, the ways of dealing with an identified risk are to transfer the risk, alter plans or procedures to avoid or reduce the risk, prepare contingency plans, or accept the risk.

Transfer the Risk

Risk can be transferred partly between the customer, the contractor, or other parties using contractual incentives, warranties, penalties, or insurance policies.

Insurance

The customer or contractor might purchase insurance as protection against a wide range of risks, including risks associated with

- Property damage or personal injury suffered as a consequence of the project.
- Damage to materials while in transit or in storage.
- Breakdown or damage of equipment.
- Theft of equipment and materials.
- Sickness or injury of workers, managers, and staff.
- Forward cover: insure against exchange rate fluctuations.

Contract Type

A popular way to transfer or allocate risk is through the use of an appropriate contract type, as discussed in the Appendix to Chapter 3. When the statement of work is clear and little uncertainty foreseen, the contractor should be willing to quote a *fixed price*. An example would be the building of a wall according to a well-defined drawing and specifications, in which case the contractor perceives little risk and is willing to accept it. However when the scope of the work is unclear and changes foreseen, it is less likely a contractor will commit to a fixed price and accept the risk of an overrun. In such cases a *cost-plus* contract would be more appropriate since the contractor is covered for all expenses incurred in the performance of the work.

Whereas in fixed-price contracts the contractor assumes most of the risk for cost overruns, in fixed-price with incentive fee contracts the contractor accepts roughly 60 percent of the risk, and the customer 40 percent; in cost-plus incentive fee contracts the contractor assumes roughly 40 percent, the customer 60 percent. With a cost-plus fixed fee (CPFF) contract the customer assumes all or most of the risk of an overrun because the contractor has no incentive to contain the costs.

In large projects, a variety of contracts are used depending on the risk associated with individual work packages or deliverables. In the Chunnel, the most uncertain part of the project was tunneling under the English Channel, so the tunneling work was contracted on a CPFF basis. The electrical and mechanical works for the tunnels and terminals, perceived as low risk, were done on a lump-sum basis. Procurement of the rolling stock, perceived as slightly riskier, used a cost-plus-percentage-fee contract.[20]

Not all risks can be transferred from one party or another. Even with a fixed-price contract where ostensibly the contractor takes on the risk of overruns, the customer will nonetheless incur damages and hardship should the project overrun the target schedule or the contractor declare bankruptcy. The project still must be completed and someone has to pay for it. To avoid losses, a contractor might feel pressured to cut corners, which of course increases the risk of the customer of receiving an end-item of sub-par quality. To lessen such risks, the customer will stipulate in the contract rigid quality inspections and penalties.

Subcontract Work

Risk often arises from uncertainty about how to approach a problem or situation. One way to avoid such risk is to contract with a party who is experienced and knows how to do it. For example, to minimize the financial risk associated with the capital cost of tooling and equipment for production of a large, complex system, a manufacturer might subcontract the production of the system's major components to suppliers familiar with those components. This relieves the manufacturer of the financial risk associated with the tooling and equipment to produce these components. But, as mentioned, transfer of one kind of risk often means inheriting another kind. For example, subcontracting work for the components puts the manufacturer in the position of relying on outsiders, which increases the risks associated with quality control, scheduling, and the performance of the end-item system. But these risks often can be reduced through careful management of the suppliers. If the manufacturer feels capable of handling those management risks, it will happily accept them to forego the financial risks.

Risk Responsibility

The individuals or groups responsible for all risks in a project should be specified. Risks may be transferred, but they can never be simply "offloaded." For instance, when an item is procured and shipped from abroad, the risk of damage usually remains with the seller as long as the item is onboard the ship; as soon as the item is hoisted over the rail of the ship the risk is transferred to the buyer.

A party willing to accept responsibility for high risk in a project will usually counter by demanding a high level of *authority* over the situation. For example, a customer agreeing to accept the risk of poor quality or cost overrun will almost certainly require a large measure of management control over aspects of the project that influence quality and cost. Furthermore, a party willing to bear high risk will usually insist on *compensation* to cover the risks. The CPFF contract illustrates: the contractor's risk is covered by compensation for all expenses, but the customer's risk is covered by his management oversight of the contractor to prevent abuses.

Avoid Risk

Risk can be avoided by altering the original project concept (e.g., eliminating risky activities, minimizing system complexity, reducing end-item quality requirements), changing contractors, incorporating redundancies and safety procedures, and so on. Sometimes it can be avoided by removing from the project the work causing the risk, thus reducing the scope of the project. Even though many risk factors can be avoided, not all can be eliminated, especially in large, complex, or leading-edge projects. Attempts to eliminate risk often entail adding innumerable management controls and monitoring systems that tend to increase system complexity and, perversely, introduce new sources of risk. Attempts to avoid risk can result in diminished payoff opportunities. Projects for research and innovative, new product development are inherently risky, but can offer potential for huge benefits later on. Because the potential benefits in such projects are proportionate to the size of the risk, the preferred approach is to reduce risk to an acceptable level rather than completely avoid it.

Reduce Risk

Among the ways to reduce the technical risk (its likelihood, impact, or both) are to:[21]

- Employ the best technical team.
- Base decisions on models and simulations of key technical parameters.
- Use mature, computer-aided system engineering tools.
- Use parallel development on high-risk tasks.
- Provide the technical team with adequate incentives for success.
- Hire outside specialists for critical review and assessment of work.
- Perform extensive tests and evaluations.
- Perform a risky task earlier in the project to allow time to reduce the impact of the risk.
- Minimize system complexity.
- Use design margins.

The last two points deserve further explanation. In general, system risk and unpredictability increase with system complexity: the more elements in a system and the greater their interconnectedness, the more likely that something—an element or interconnection—will go wrong. Thus, minimizing complexity through reorganizing and modifying elements in end-item design and the project tasks can reduce the project risk. For example, by *decoupling activities* and subsystems, i.e., making them independent of one another, the failure of any one activity or subsystem will be contained and not spread to others.

Incorporating *design margins* into design goals is another way to reduce risk associated with meeting technical requirements.[22] A design margin is a quantified value that serves as a safety buffer to be held in reserve and allocated by management. In general, a design margin is incorporated into a requirement by setting the target design value *stiffer* or more rigorous than the design requirement. In particular,

$$\text{Target value} = \text{Requirement} + \text{Design margin}$$

By aiming for the target value, a designer can miss the target by as much as the margin amount and still satisfy the requirement. Striving to meet target values that are stiffer than the requirements reduces the risk of not meeting the requirement.

Example 5: Design Margin Application for the Spaceship

Suppose the weight requirement for the spaceship navigation system is 90 pounds. To allow for the difficulty of reaching the requirement (and the risk of not meeting it), the design margin is set at 10 percent, or 9 pounds. Thus, the *target weight* for the navigation system becomes 81 pounds.

A design margin is also applied to each subsystem or component within the system. If the navigation system is entirely composed of three major Subsystems, A, B, and C, then the three together must weigh 81 pounds. Suppose C is an OTS item with a weight of 1 pound that is fixed and cannot be reduced. But A and B are being newly developed, and the design goals for them have been set at 50 pounds for A and 30 pounds for B. Suppose a 12 percent design margin is imposed on both subsystems; in that case, the *target weights* for A and B are 50 (1.0 − 0.12) = 44 pounds, and 30 (1.0 − 0.12) = 26.4 pounds, respectively.

Design margins provide managers and engineers a way to flexibly meet problems in an evolving design. Should the target value for one subsystem prove impossible to meet, then portions of the margin values from other sub-systems or the overall system can be reallocated to the subsystem. Suppose Subsystem B cannot possibly be designed to meet the 26.4-pound target, but Subsystem A *can* be designed to meet *its* target value, then the target value for B can initially be increased by as much as 3.6 pounds (its margin value) to 30 pounds; if that value also proves impossible to meet, the target can be increased by another 6 pounds (the margin value originally allocated to Subsystem A) to 36 pounds; if even that value cannot be met, the target can be increased again by as much as another 9 pounds (the margin value for the entire system) up to 45 pounds. Even with these incremental additions to B's initial target value, the overall system would still be able to meet the 90-pound weight requirement.

Design margins not only help reduce the risk in meeting requirements, they encourage designers to exceed requirements—in the example to design a system that weighs less than required. Of course, the design margins must be set carefully so as to reduce the design risk yet not increase design cost.

Design margins focus on technical requirements. Among ways to reduce risks associated with *meeting schedules* are:[23]

- Create a master project schedule and strive to adhere to it.
- Schedule the riskiest tasks as early as possible to allow time for failure recovery.
- Maintain close focus on critical and near-critical activities.
- Put the best workers on time-critical tasks.
- Provide incentives for overtime work.
- Shift high-risk activities in the project network from series to parallel.
- Organize the project early and be careful to adequately staff it.
- Provide project and feeding buffers (contingency reserves), as discussed in Chapter 7.

To reduce the risk associated with meeting project cost targets:[24]

- Identify and monitor the key cost drivers.
- Use low-cost design alternative reviews and assessments.
- Verify system design and performance through modeling and assessment.
- Maximize usage of proven technology and commercial off-the-shelf equipment.
- Provide contingency reserves in project budgets.
- Perform early breadboarding, prototyping, and testing on risky components and modules.

The last way is especially powerful for reducing risk.[25]*Breadboards* and *prototypes*, i.e., test mock-ups and models that enable ideas to be tested through experiment and trial and error so designs can be corrected early in the project, greatly reduce the need for changing designs and suffering schedule and cost overruns.[26] Breadboards, prototypes, and modeling are discussed in Chapters 2 and 9. The following explains other ways to reduce schedule and cost risk.

Example 6: Managing Schedule and Cost Risk at the Vancouver Airport Expansion Project[27]

The expansion project at Vancouver International Airport involved constructing a new international terminal building (ITB) and a parallel runway. The schedule for the $355 million project called for full operation of the ITB less than 3.5 years after the project was approved, and opening of the new runway only 5 months after that. The project team identified the following as major risk areas in meeting the tight budget and schedule constraints:

1. *Risk in Structural Steel Delivery and Erection.* Steel is the most critical aspect of big construction projects in Canada. Long procurement lead times from steel mills and difficulties in scheduling design, fabrication, and erection make big-steel projects problematic. Recognizing this, the project team awarded the structural steel contract very early in the project so there would be ample time to design, procure, fabricate, and erect the 10,000 tons of steel required for the ITB. As a result, the ITB was completed on time.

2. *Material Handling Risk.* Excavation, moving earth, and material handling comprised the second critical area. Millions of cubic meters (cum) of earth had to be moved, and over 4 million cum of sand were required for concrete runways and taxiways. The project team developed an advance plan to enable coordinated movement of earth from one locale to another, and used local sand as a component in the concrete. This saved substantial time and money, and resulted in the runway being completed a year ahead of schedule.

3. *Environmental Risk.* Excavations and transport of earth and sand by barges threatened the ecology of the Fraser River estuary. These risks were mitigated by advance planning and constantly identifying and handling problems as they arose through cooperative efforts of all stakeholders.

4. *Functionality Risk.* Because new technology poses risk, the project team adopted a policy of using only proven components and technology. Whenever a new technology was in doubt, its usage and success at other existing sites was evaluated. Consequently, all ITB systems were installed and operational according to schedule with few problems.

One additional way to reduce the risk of not meeting budgets, schedules, and technical performance is to do whatever is necessary to achieve the requirements, and *nothing* more (excepting design margin).[28] The project team might be aware of many things that could be done beyond the stated requirements, but in most cases these will consume additional resources and add time and cost. Unless the customer approves the added time and cost, these things should be avoided. Avoiding "non-essential" needs reduces the risk of failing to meet the essential needs.

Contingency Planning

Contingency planning implies identifying the risks, anticipating whatever might happen, and then preparing a plan of action to cope with them. The initial project plan is followed, yet throughout execution the risks are closely monitored. Should a risk materialize as indicated by an undesired outcome or trigger symptom, the contingency course of action is adopted. The contingency can be a post-hoc remedial action to compensate for a risk impact, an action undertaken in parallel with the original plan, or a preventive action initiated by a trigger symptom to mitigate the risk impact. Multiple contingency plans can be developed based upon "what-if" analyses of possible outcome scenarios for multiple risks.

Accept Risk (Do Nothing)

Not all impacts are severe or fatal, and if the cost of avoiding, reducing, or transferring the risk is estimated to exceed the benefit, then "do nothing" might be the best alternative. Of course, this response would never be chosen for risks where the impacts or consequences are potentially severe. In Figure 10-4, the accept-risk strategy would be chosen for risks falling in the "low consequence" region (except when the impact is potentially catastrophic, which is off the chart). Sometimes nothing can be done to avoid, reduce, or transfer a risk, in which case the risk must be accepted, regardless of the consequence. Fortunately such situations are rare.

Responding to a risk sometimes creates a new, *secondary risk.* Having planned a risk response, the project management team should check for possible secondary risks before implementing the plan.

10.5   RISK TRACKING AND RESPONSE

The identified risks are documented and added to a list called a *risk log* or *risk register* and rank ordered, greatest risk consequence first. For risks with the most serious consequences, mitigation plans are prepared and strategies adopted (transfer, reduce, avoid, or contingency); for the least important ones, nothing is done (accept).

The project should be *continuously monitored* for trigger symptoms of previously identified risks, and for symptoms of risks newly emerging and not previously identified. Known risks may take a long time before they begin to produce problems. Should a symptom reach the trigger point, a decision is made as to the course of action. The action might be to institute an already prepared plan or to organize a meeting to determine a solution. Sometimes the response is to do nothing; however, nothing should be a conscious choice (not an oversight) closely tracked to ensure it was the right choice and no further problems ensue.

All risks deemed critical or important are tracked throughout the project or the phases to which they apply; to ensure this, someone is assigned responsibility to track and monitor the symptoms of each important risk.

Altogether, the risk log, mitigation strategies, monitoring methods, people responsible, contingency plans, and schedule and budget reserves constitute the project risk management plan. The plan is continuously updated to account for changes in risk status (old risks avoided, downgraded, or upgraded; existing risks reassessed; new risks added). The project manager (and sometimes other stakeholders such as management and the customer) is alerted about emerging problems; ideally, the project culture embodies candor and honesty, and people readily notify the project manager whenever they detect a known risk materializing or a new one emerging.

10.6   PROJECT MANAGEMENT *IS* RISK MANAGEMENT

Risk management supplements and is a part of other project management practices such as requirements and task definition, scheduling, budgeting, configuration management, change control, and performance tracking and control. With all of these, managers learn and assess the risks so they can proactively reduce them or plan for the consequences. If, for example, a project must be completed in 9 months but knowledgeable people estimate that it will take closer to 12, management can take a multitude of actions to increase the likelihood of it finishing in 9.

Ideally, risk identification, assessment, and response planning are treated as formal aspects of project planning, and the resulting risk management plan is a part of the integrated or master project plan—along with the quality management plan, change and configuration management plan, human resource plan, communications plan, procurement plan, schedule, budget, and so on. Also ideally, the identification, assessment, and response planning for risks, and subsequent tracking and reduction of risks involve many project team members and other stakeholders. And like cost variances and earned value, it should be included as a measure in project tracking and control.

Of course, not all projects *need* comprehensive risk analysis and risk management. On small projects, a small, highly paid and motivated staff can usually overcome difficulties associated with the risks, and, if not, the consequences are usually small anyway. In larger projects, however, where the stakes and/or the risks of failure are high, risk management is especially important. These projects require awareness and respect for all the significant risks—safety, legal, social, and political, as well as technical and financial. Application of risk management principles can make the difference between project success and project failure.

Risk Management Principles

Following are general principles for managing risks:[29]

- Create a *risk management plan* that specifies ways to identify all major project risks. The plan should specify the person(s) responsible for managing risks as well as methods for allocating time and funds from the risk reserve.

- Create a *risk profile* for each risk that includes the risk likelihood, cost and schedule impact, and contingencies to be invoked. It should also specify the earliest visible symptoms (trigger events) that would indicate when the risk is materializing. In general, high-risk areas should be visible and have lots of eyes watching closely. Contingency plans should be kept up-to-date and reflect project progress and emerging risks.

- Appoint a *risk officer* to the project, a person whose principle responsibility is the project's risk management. The risk officer should not be the same person as the project manager because the role involves matters of psychology and politics. He should *not* be a can-do person, but instead, to some extent, a devil's advocate identifying, assessing, and tracking all the reasons why something might not work—even when everyone else believes it will.

- Include in the budget and schedule a calculated *risk reserve*, which is a buffer of money, time, and other resources for dealing with risks as they materialize. The risk reserve is used at the project manager's discretion to cover risks not specifically detailed in the risk profile. The reserve may include the RT or RC values (described later) or other amounts. It is usually not associated with a contingency plan, and its use might be constrained to particular applications or areas of risk. The size of the risk reserve should be held confidential by the project manager (otherwise, projects have a tendency to consume whatever time–cost resources are available, even if in reserve form).

- Establish *communication channels* (perhaps anonymous) within the project team to ensure that bad news gets to the project manager quickly. Ensure that risks are continually monitored, current status of risks is assessed and communicated, and the risk management plan updated.

- Specify procedures to ensure that the project is accurately and comprehensively *documented*. Documentation includes proposals, detailed project plans, change requests, summary reports, and a postcompletion summary. In general, the better the documentation of past projects, the more information available for planning future, similar projects, estimating necessary time and resources, and identifying possible risks.

In every project the identified risks are documented. Figure 10-5 illustrates a template for the profile and management plan for an identified risk; it summarizes everything known about the risk. Such a document would be retained in a binder or library, to be updated as necessary until the risk is "closed out" (believed to no longer exist).

Expect the Unexpected

Having identified and analyzed myriad risk hazards and possible consequences, and prepared all kinds of controls and safeguards, people might be led to believe that everything that could possibly go wrong has been anticipated and covered; then when something *still* goes wrong, it catches them *completely off guard*. Although it is true that risk planning can cover many or most risks, it is rare that it can cover all of them. Thus, risk planning should be tempered with the concept of "nonplanning" or Napoleon's approach, which is *to expect that something surely will go wrong*, and that ways will have to be found to deal with it *as it emerges*. Expecting the unexpected is as important for coping with risk than preparing extensive plans and believing that the unexpected has been eliminated.[30]

Example 7: Successful Management of Risks as They Arise—
Development of the F117 Stealth Fighter[31]

An example of how to manage risk in R&D projects is the F117 Stealth Fighter program, aimed at developing a revolutionary new "low observable" (difficult to detect with radar) combat aircraft capable of high-precision attacks on enemy targets. The success of this program gave the USA a minimum 15- to 20-year lead over other nations in this technology. The F117 involved high risk because of the many lessons to be learned during the program and the significant challenges that had to be overcome. In the F117 program, however, challenges were *expected* in all phases of the program, from early design and test, through evaluation and final deployment. To handle the risks, numerous decisions were made on the spot between program managers for Lockheed (contractor) and the Air Force (customer). The program was set up for rapid deployment of resources to solve problems *as they arose*. Managers from the customer and the contractor worked closely to minimize bureaucratic delay. Schedules were optimistic and based on assumptions that everything would work; however, everyone throughout the management chain *knew the risks* and the significant challenges to overcome, so problems and delays never came as a surprise or threatened program support. This is a good example of *managing* risk as opposed to *avoiding* risk, and it illustrates how to pursue aggressive, revolutionary advances when a technological opportunity exists.

Risk Management Caveats

For all the good it can provide, risk management itself can *create* risks. Almost every philosophy, procedure, or prescription has exceptions and caveats, and that is true

Risk Profile and Management Plan				
Risk Number	Last Update	Originator		Risk Category
Project	Phase	Department		WBS Number
Likelihood	Impact	Consequence		Priority
Risk Assessment				

Risk description
_____
_____
_____
_____
_____

Risk sources
_____
_____
_____
_____
_____

Risk assessment
_____
_____
_____
_____
_____

Strategy:	Risk Plan
☐ Accept	1. _____
☐ Avoid	2. _____
☐ Contingency	3. _____
☐ Reduce	4. _____
☐ Reserves	5. _____
☐ Transfer	6. _____
	7. _____

Risk Tracking	
Member Responsible	Risk Officer
Measures/Symptoms	Comments
Trigger Event	Comments

Signoffs			
Cost Engineer	System Engineer	Quality Manager	Project Manager
Date:	Date:	Date:	Date:

Figure 10-5
Document for the profile and management plan of an identified risk.

of risk management as well. Misunderstanding or misapplication of concepts associated with risk management can stymie a project by fooling people into thinking they have nothing to worry about, and actually leave project personnel worse prepared for dealing with *emerging* problems.

Having created a risk management plan, project managers and supporters might be emboldened to charge ahead and take risks they might not take otherwise. Much of the input to risk analysis is subjective; after all, a likelihood is just that—it does not indicate what *will* happen, only what *might* happen. Data analysis and planning gives people a sense of having power over events, even when the events are chancy. Underestimating the risk likelihood or impact can make consequences seem insignificant, leading some people to venture into dangerous territory that common sense would disallow. For example, the security of seat belts and air bags encourages some drivers to take risks such as driving too close behind the next car or accelerating through yellow lights. The result is an actual *increase* in the overall number of accidents (even though the seriousness of injury is reduced).

Repeated experience and good documentation are important ways to identify risks, but they cannot guarantee that some important risks will not remain unknown. Same and similar outcomes that have occurred repeatedly in past projects eventually deplete peoples' capacity to imagine anything else happening. As a result, some risks become unthinkable and are never considered. Even sophisticated computer models are worthless when it comes to dealing with unthinkable risks because a computer cannot be instructed to analyze events that have never occurred and are beyond human imagination. Risk analysis models are based on the occurrence frequency of past events in a finite number of cases. History provides a sample, not the population of all possibilities.

Managing risk does not mean eliminating it, although the management of some projects makes it seem as though that is the goal. The prime symptom of "trying to eliminate risk" is management overkill or micromanagement: excessive controls, unrealistic documentation requirements, and trivial demands for the authorization of everything. By definition, projects inherently entail uncertainty and risk. Micromanagement is seldom appropriate and may prove disastrous for some projects, particularly those for product development and R&D. When management tries to eliminate risk, it stifles innovation and, say Aronstein and Piccirillo, "forces a company into a plodding, brute force approach to technology, which can be far more costly in the long run than a more adventurous approach where some programs fail but others make significant leaps forward."[32] The appropriate risk management approach, particularly for development projects, is not to try to avoid or eliminate risk altogether, but to accommodate and mitigate risk by reducing the cost of failure.

10.7 SUMMARY

Project risk management involves identifying the risks, assessing them, planning the appropriate responses, and taking action.

Identifying project risks starts early in the project conception phase. Areas of high risk that can significantly influence project outcomes are hazards to be dealt with. Risks in projects stem from many sources such as failure to define and satisfy customer needs or market requirements, technical problems arising in the work, extreme weather, labor and supplier problems, competitors' actions, and changes imposed by outside parties. Risk hazards are identified from experience with past projects and careful scrutiny of current projects.

Projects have innumerable risks, but only the important ones need to be addressed. Importance depends on the likelihood, impact, and overall consequence of the risk. Likelihood is the probability a risk will occur as determined by knowledgeable, experienced people. Risk impact is the effect of the risk, its seriousness or potential influence on project schedule, cost, or performance outcomes. Risk consequence is a combination of both likelihood and impact, a way of expressing the two concepts as one. Risk consequence measures are used to decide which risks should receive attention and which can be ignored. As a precaution, every risk with severe impact should be carefully considered, even when the likelihood of occurrence is very small.

Risk response planning addresses the way identified risks will be dealt with. Some risks can be transferred to other parties or spread among many stakeholders or subcontractors. Some risks can be avoided, and should be. On the other hand, high risk might be associated with high benefits, so trying to eliminate the risk could also reduce the payoff. Thus, better than trying to avoid risk is to try to reduce it to a manageable level. For areas of high risk, contingency plans with alternatives for dealing with new problems should be developed.

Good risk management accommodates or mitigates risk and reduces the cost of failure. Principles for risk management include having a risk management plan that specifies the risks, their symptoms and backup plans, a risk officer responsible for identifying and tracking the risks, and a budget and schedule reserve. The plan must specify the ways that risks will be monitored and emerging problems will be communicated to the project manager. Good project documentation furnishes insurance against perilous situations in the future because lessons learned about risks can be referenced. No amount of preparation can anticipate all risks; therefore, project managers should expect the unexpected and be prepared to find ways to deal with risks as they arise.

This and the last several chapters focused on aspects of project planning—work definition, scheduling, quality, budgeting, and risk management. The next several chapters move into the project execution phase and, in particular, methods for tracking and controlling project performance, creating and sharing information, and bringing the project to successful completion.

The Appendix to the chapter that follows discusses common analytical methods for assessing risk consequences and deciding between alternative risk responses. Some of these methods are also employed in project selection—the topic of Chapter 17.

APPENDIX: RISK ANALYSIS METHODS

Four common methods for risk analysis are expected value, decision trees, payoff tables, and simulation.

Expected Value

Selection of the appropriate risk response is sometimes based on analysis of risk consequences in terms of the expected value of project costs and schedules.

In general, expected value is the average or mean outcome of numerous repeated circumstances. For risk assessment, expected value represents the average outcome of a project, if it were repeated many times, accounting for the possible occurrence of risk. Mathematically, it is the weighted average of all the possible outcomes, where the respective likelihoods of the possible outcomes are the weights, that is

$$\text{Expected value} = \Sigma[(\text{Outcomes}) \times (\text{Likelihoods})]$$

To account for risk, the risk project time and cost consequences are determined using expected value.

The risk consequence on project duration is called the *risk time, RT*. It is the expected values of the estimated time required for risk correction, computed as

$$RT = (\text{Corrective time}) \times (\text{Likelihood}) \tag{5}$$

The risk consequence on project cost is called the *risk cost, RC*. It is the expected value of the estimated cost of correcting for the risk, computed as

$$RC = (\text{Corrective cost}) \times (\text{Likelihood}) \tag{6}$$

For example, suppose the baseline time estimate (BTE) for project completion is 26 weeks and the baseline cost estimate (BCE) is $71,000. Assume that the risk likelihood for the project as a whole is 0.3, and, should the risk materialize, it would delay the project by 5 weeks and increase the cost by $10,000. Also, because the probability of the risk materializing is 0.3, the probability of it *not* materializing is 0.7. If the risk does not materialize, no corrective measures will be necessary, so the corrective time and cost will be nil. Hence

$$RT = (5)(0.3) + (0)(0.7) = 1.5 \text{ weeks}$$
$$RC = (\$10,000)(0.3) + (0)(0.7) = \$3,000$$

These figures, RT and RC, would be included as reserve or buffer amounts in the project schedule and budget to account for risk. RC and RT are the *schedule reserve* and *project contingency* (budget reserve), respectively, as mentioned in Chapters 6 and 8.

Accounting for the risk time, the *expected project completion time, ET*, is

$$ET = BTE + RT = 26 + 1.5 = 27.5 \text{ weeks}$$

and accounting for the risk cost, the *expected project completion cost, EC*, is

$$EC = BCE + RC = 71,000 + 3,000 = \$74,000$$

When the corrective time and cost cannot be estimated, then ET and EC are computed as

$$ET = BTE(1 + \text{likelihood}) = 26(1.3) = 33.8 \text{ weeks} \tag{7}$$
$$EC = BCE(1 + \text{likelihood}) = \$71,000(1.3) = \$92,300 \tag{8}$$

These examples account for risk factors that affect the project as a *whole*. Another way to determine risk consequence is to first disaggregate the project into work packages or phases and then, *for each* element, estimate the risk likelihood and corrective time and cost. These individual corrective estimates are then aggregated to determine ET and EC for the entire project. This approach tends to give more credible RT and RC estimates than do equations (5) through (8) because risks so pinpointed to individual tasks or phases can be more accurately assessed. Also, it is easier to identify the necessary corrective actions and estimate the time and costs associated with particular tasks.

For example, a project has eight work packages, and for each the BCE, risk likelihood, and corrective cost have been estimated. The following table lists the information for each work package and gives EC, where EC is computed as

$$EC = BCE + [(\text{corrective cost}) \times (\text{likelihood})]$$

WBS Element	BCE	Corrective Cost	Likelihood	EC
J	$10,000	$2,000	0.2	$10,400
M	8,000	1,000	0.3	8,300
V	16,000	4,000	0.1	16,400
Y	10,000	6,000	0.2	1,200
L	8,000	2,000	0.3	8,600
Q	9,000	2,000	0.1	9,200
W	5,000	1,000	0.3	5,300
X	5,000	1,500	0.3	5,750
Total		$71,000		$75,150

Therefore, the project EC is $75,150. Because this is only 5.8 percent above the project BCE of $71,000, the overall cost consequence of project risks is small.

Now, for the same eight work package project, assume the BTE, risk likelihood, and corrective time have been estimated for each work package. These figures are listed below along with ET, computed as

$$ET = BTE + [(\text{Corrective time}) \times (\text{Likelihood})]$$

WBS Element	BTE	Corrective Time	Likelihood	ET
J	6	1	0.2	6.2
M	4	1	0.3	4.3
V	6	2	0.1	6.2
Y	8	3	0.2	8.6
L	2	1	0.3	2.3
Q	8	1	0.1	8.1
W	1	1	0.3	1.3
X	1	1	0.3	1.3

The project network is used to determine ET for the overall project. Suppose the network is as shown in Figure 10-6. Without considering the risk time, the critical path would be J-M-V-Y-W-X, which gives a project BTE of 24 weeks. Accounting for risk consequences, the critical path does not change but the duration is increased to 27.9 weeks. This is the project ET.[33]

Figure 10-6
Project network, accounting for risk time.

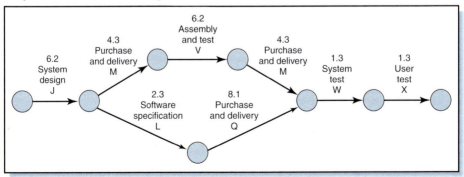

Although activities on critical and near-critical paths should be carefully monitored, in general, *all* activities that poses a high-risk consequence (high likelihood and/or high impact) should also be carefully monitored, even those not on the critical path.

Increasing the project schedule and budget to account for the expected risk time and expected risk cost cannot guarantee adequate protection against risk. Expected value is equivalent to the long-run average, which results from repeating something many times. Project activities are never identical or repeated over and over, but even if they were, that would not preclude a bad outcome in a particular instance. The point: No attempt to prepare for risk using expected value criteria offers any guarantee. Such is the nature of risk.

Decision Trees[34]

A decision tree is a diagram wherein the "branches" represent different chance events or decision strategies. Decision trees can be used to assess which risk responses among alternatives yield the best-to-be-expected consequence.

One application of decision trees is in weighing the cost of potential project failure against the benefit of project success. Assume a project has a BCE of $200,000 and a failure likelihood of 0.25. If the project is successful, it will yield a net profit of $1,000,000.

The expected value concept can be used to compute the average value of the project assuming it could be repeated a large number of times. If it were repeated many times, then the project would lose $200,000 (BCE) 25 percent of the time, and generate $1,000,000 profit the other 75 percent of the time. The average outcome or expected value would be

$$\text{Expected outcome} = (-\$200,000)(0.25) + (\$1,000,000)(0.75) = \$700,000.$$

This suggests that although there is potential to net $1,000,000 maximum, it is more reasonable to use $700,000 for the BCE. It also implies that all project costs plus any action taken to reduce or eliminate the failure risk should not exceed $700,000.

Another application of decision trees is in deciding between alternative risk responses. Suppose a project has a BCE of $10 million, risk failure likelihood of 0.6, and a risk impact of $5 million. Two strategies are being considered to reduce the risk likelihood (but not the risk impact):

Strategy 1 will cost $2 million and will reduce the failure likelihood to 0.1.
Strategy 2 will cost $1 million and will reduce the failure likelihood to 0.4.

The decision tree and resultant expected project costs are shown in Figure 10-7. The analysis suggests Strategy 1 should be adopted because it has the lowest expected cost.

An application of decision tree analysis is the expected commercial value method used in project selection, discussed in Chapter 17.

Uncertainty and Payoff Tables

When no prior experience or historical data exists upon which to estimate likelihood, then the expected value risk consequence cannot be computed; hence, other criteria must be used to assess courses of action in the face of risk. This situation is referred to as *uncertainty*, which implies no information is available about what may occur. To determine the best strategy under uncertainty, begin by identifying possible alternative routes the project could take in response to factors over which

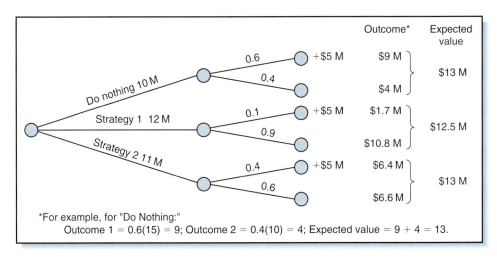

Figure 10-7
Decision tree.

management has no control. These different routes are called *states of nature*. Consider different possible strategies or actions, and then indicate the likely outcome for each state of nature. The outcomes for different combinations of strategies and states of nature are represented in a matrix called a *payoff table*.

For example, suppose the success of a project to develop "Product X" depends on market demand that is a known function of particular performance features of the product. The development effort can be directed in any of three possible directions, referred to as strategies A, B, and C, each of which will result in a product with different performance features. Also, assume that another firm is developing a competing product that will have performance features similar to those under Strategy A. One of three future states of nature will exist when the product development effort ends: N1 represents no competing products on the market for at least 6 months, N2 represents the product competing with Product X introduced between 0 and 6 months later; N3 represents the product competing with Product X introduced first. The *payoff table* shown in Table 10-6 gives the likely profits in millions of dollars for different combinations of strategies and states of nature.

The question is: Which strategy should be adopted? The answer: It depends! If project sponsors are optimistic, they will choose the strategy that maximizes the potential payoff. The maximum potential payoff indicated in the table is $90 million, which happens for Strategy C and state of nature N1. Thus, optimistic project sponsors will adopt Strategy C. In general, the strategy choice that has the potential of yielding the largest payoff is called the *maximax* decision criterion.

Table 10-6 Payoff table.

	STATES OF NATURE		
STRATEGY	N_1	N_2	N_3
A	60	30	−20
B	60	50	60
C	90	70	40

Now, if project sponsors are pessimistic, they instead will be interested in minimizing their potential losses, in which case they will use the *maximin* decision criterion and adopt the strategy that gives the best outcome under the worst possible conditions. For the three strategies A, B, and C, the worst-case payoff scenarios are –$20 million, $50 million, and $40 million, respectively. The best (least bad) of the three is $50 million, or Strategy B. Thus, pessimistic sponsors would adopt Strategy B.

Any choice of strategy other than the best one will cause the decision maker to experience an opportunity loss called *regret*. If, for example, Strategy A is adopted, and the state of nature turns out to be N2, the sponsor will regret not having chosen Strategy C, which is the best for that state of nature. A measure of this regret will be the difference between the unrealized payoff for Strategy C and the realized payoff for Strategy A, or $70 – $30 = $40 million. This way of thinking suggests another criterion for choosing between strategies, the *minimax regret* decision criteria, which is the strategy that minimizes the *regret* of not having made the best choice.

Regret for a given state of nature is the difference in the outcomes between the best strategy and any other strategy. This is illustrated in a *regret table*, shown in Table 10-7. For example, given the payoffs in Table 10-6, for state of nature (N1) the highest payoff is $90 million. Had Strategy C, the optimal strategy, been selected, the regret would have been zero, but had strategies A or B been selected instead, the regrets would have been $30 million each (the difference between their outcomes, $60 million, and the optimum, $90 million). The regret amounts for states of nature N2 and N3 are determined in a similar fashion.

To understand how to minimize regret, first look in the regret table at the largest regret for each strategy. The largest regrets are $80 million, $30 million, and $20 million for strategies A, B, and C, respectively. Next, pick the smallest of these, $20 million, which occurs for Strategy C. Thus, Strategy C is the choice to minimize regret.

Another approach for selecting a strategy is to assume that every state of nature has the same likelihood of occurring by using the *maximum expected payoff* criterion. Referring back to the payoff table, Table 10-6, where the likelihood of each state of nature is assumed to be one-third, the expected payoff for Strategy A given outcomes from the payoff table is

$$1/3(60) + 1/3(30) + 1/3(-20) = 23.33, \text{ or } \$23.33 \text{ million}$$

The expected payoffs, computed similarly for strategies B and C, are $56.66 million and $66.66 million, respectively. Thus, Strategy C would be chosen as giving the maximum expected payoff. Notice in the previous examples that three of the four selection criteria point to Strategy C. This in itself might further convince decision makers about the appropriateness of selecting Strategy C.

Table 10-7 Regret table.

	STATES OF NATURE		
STRATEGY	N_1	N_2	N_3
A	30	40	80
B	30	20	0
C	0	0	20

Simulation

Application of simulation to project management was illustrated in Chapter 7. In general, simulation gives the probability distribution of outcomes, which can be used to determine the probability (or likelihood) of a particular outcome such as completion cost or time, which in turn can be used to establish an appropriate target budget or completion date, or to prepare contingency plans. For instance, although the critical path example in Chapter 7 indicated that the project would be completed in 147 days, the simulated completion time distribution (Figure 7-14) indicated that it would be 155 days, *on average*. Thus, at the *earliest*, the target completion should be set at 155 days, although the likelihood of not meeting that date would be 50 percent. Using the simulated probability distribution, a target completion date can be set such that the likelihood of not meeting it is more acceptable. Alternatively, given a prespecified date by which the project must be completed, management can use simulation to estimate the likelihood of failure and, hence, decide whether to prepare contingency plans or change the project requirements, activities, or the network.

REVIEW QUESTIONS AND PROBLEMS

1. Should risks that have low likelihood be ignored? Explain.
2. How does a person's risk tolerance affect whether a risk is rated as high, medium, or low?
3. What is meant by risk of failure?
4. What factors make a project high-risk?
5. Discuss the difference between internal risk and external risk. List sources of risk in each of these categories.
6. Describe each of the following sources of technical risk: maturity, complexity, quality, and concurrency or dependency.
7. Briefly describe the following risk identification techniques: analogy, checklists, WBS analysis, process flowcharts, and brainstorming.
8. Describe a CE diagram. Pick a problem (effect) of your own choice and use a CE diagram for illustration.
9. A project involves development of a system with state-of-the-art hardware and software, both of which are very complex, and where system performance depends on another, external system that is being developed concurrently. Based on Table 10-3, and assuming all risk factors are independent and equally weighted, what is the CLF for the project?
10. What is an influence diagram? How is it used to identify and analyze risk sources and to assign priorities to those sources?
11. Tables 10-3 and 10-4 are for illustration purposes. Discuss the general applicability of these tables to rating risks in projects. Would *you* use these tables to assess the risk likelihood and impact in a project of your choice? Why or why not?
12. Do equations (1), (2), and (3) present good ways for rating the overall likelihood, impact, and consequences of risk? Discuss pros and cons of using these equations.
13. Discuss briefly each of the following ways to handle risk: transfer risk, avoid risk, reduce risk, do contingency planning, and accept risk.
14. Think of a project you are familiar with and problems the project encountered. List some ways that risk could have been reduced in the project and explain each.
15. What is a design margin? How does its application reduce risk?
16. One requirement of a power-generating system states that it must provide 500 kilowatt hour minimum output. The system has three power-generating

Subsystems, X, Y, and Z. Constraints on physical size indicate that the output capacity of the overall system will be split among the three subsystems in the approximate ratio of 5:3:2. Suppose a design margin of 3 percent is applied to the system and the subsystems. Note that because the power requirement is stated as *minimum* output, the design margin would set the target output at 3 percent *higher than* the requirement.

(a) What is the target requirement output for the overall system?
(b) What are the target requirement outputs for each of the subsystems? (Remember, subsystem margins are *in addition* to the system margin.)
(c) Suppose that, at best, Subsystem X can be designed to meet only 47 percent of the power output requirement for the overall system. Assuming the Subsystems Y and Z can be designed to meet their respective design targets, will the output requirement for the overall system be met?

17. List and review the principles of risk management.

18. How does risk planning serve to increase risk-taking behavior?

19. Risk management includes being prepared for the unexpected. Explain.

20. Can risk be eliminated from projects? *Should* management try to eliminate it?

21. How and where are risk time and risk cost considerations used in project planning?

22. Where would criteria such as minimax, maximin, and minimax regret be used during the project life cycle to manage project risk?

23. Below is the network for the Largesse Hydro Project:

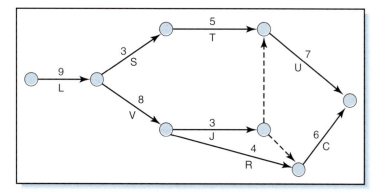

The following table gives the baseline cost and time estimates (BCE and BTE), the cost and time estimates to correct for failure, and the likelihood of failure for each work package in Largesse.

WBS Element	BCE	BTE (weeks)	Corrective Cost	Time	Likelihood
L	$20,000	9	$4,000	2	0.2
V	16,000	8	4,000	2	0.3
T	32,000	5	8,000	2	0.1
U	20,000	7	12,000	3	0.2
S	16,000	3	4,000	1	0.3
J	18,000	3	4,000	1	0.1
R	10,000	4	4,000	3	0.3
C	15,000	6	5,000	2	0.3

(a) Determine the risk time and risk cost for all the WBS elements of the project.

(b) Consider the risk times on noncritical paths. Which activities and paths should be watched carefully as posing the highest risks?

(c) What is the project expected cost (EC) and expected time (ET)?

24. Because of its geographical location, the Largesse Hydro project is threatened with delays and costs associated with bad weather. The likelihood of bad weather is estimated at 0.30 with a potential impact of delaying work by 10 weeks and increasing the cost by $20,000.

(a) Ignoring the time and cost risks in Problem 23, what are the expected project completion time and completion cost considering the weather risk?

(b) What is the estimated expected project completion time and cost considering the weather risk *and* the risks listed in Problem 23?

25. Softside Systems has a $100,000 fixed-price contract for installation of a new application system. The project is expected to take 5 weeks and cost $50,000. Experience with similar projects suggests a 0.30 likelihood that the project will encounter problems that could delay it as much as 3 weeks and increase the cost by $30,000. By increasing the project staff 20 percent for an additional cost of $10,000, the likelihood of problems would be reduced to 0.10, and the delay and cost would be 1 week and $8,000, respectively. Set up a decision tree to determine whether Softside should increase the size of the project staff.

26. Corecast Contractors has been requested by a municipality to submit a proposal bid for a parking garage contract. In the past, the cost of preparing bids has been about 2 percent of the cost of the job. Corecast project manager Bradford Pitts is considering three possible bids: cost plus 10 percent, cost plus 20 percent, and cost plus 30 percent. Of course, increasing the "plus percent" increases the project price, decreasing the likelihood of winning the job. Bradford estimates the likelihood of winning the job as follows:

	Bid price	P(win)	P(lose)
P1	C + 0.1C = 1.1C	0.6	0.4
P2	C + 0.2C = 1.2C	0.4	0.6
P3	C + 0.3C = 1.3C	0.2	0.8

In all cases, the profit (if the bid is won) will be the bid price minus the pro-posal-preparation cost, or 0.02C; the loss (if the bid is not won) will be the pro-posal-preparation cost.

Prepare a decision tree for the three options. If Bradford uses the maximum expected profit as the criterion, which bid proposal would he select?

27. Iron Butterfly, Inc. submits proposals in response to RFPs and faces three possible outcomes: N1, Iron Butterfly gets a full contract; N2, Iron Butterfly gets a partial contract (job is shared with other contractors); N3, Iron Butterfly gets no contract. The company is currently assessing three RFPs code named P1, P2, and P3. The customer for P3 will pay a fixed amount for proposal preparation; for P1 and P2 Iron Butterfly must absorb all of the proposal-preparation costs, which

are expected to be high. Based upon project revenues and proposal-preparation costs, the expected profits ($1,000s) are as shown:

	N1	N2	N3
P1	500	200	–300
P2	300	100	–100
P3	100	50	25

To which RFPs would Iron Butterfly respond using the various uncertainty criteria?

28. Iron Butterfly, Inc. project manager for the LOGON project, Frank Wesley, is concerned about the development time for the robotic transporter. Although the subcontractor, Creative Robotics has promised a delivery time of 6 weeks, Frank knows that the actual delivery time will be a function of the number of other projects Creative Robotics is working on at the time. As incentive to speed up Creative Robotic's delivery of the transporter, Frank has three options:

S1: Do nothing.

S2: Promise Creative Robotics a future contract with Iron Butterfly.

S3: Threaten to never contract with Creative Robotics again.

He estimates the impact of these actions on delivery time would be as follows:

Payoffs: Strategy	Creative robotics workload		
	Slow	Average	Busy
S1	4	6	8
S2	3	4	7
S3	3	6	6

What strategy should Frank adopt based upon uncertainty criteria? Use criteria similar to the maximax, maximin, minimax regret, and maximum expected payoff, except note that the criteria need to be adapted because here the goal is to *minimize* the payoff (time), which contrasts to the usual case of maximizing the payoff (profit).

QUESTIONS ABOUT THE STUDY PROJECT

1. What did the project manager and stakeholders believe were the major risks in the project?
2. In your own judgment, was this a risky project? Why or why not?
3. Was formal risk analysis performed? When was it done (during initiation, feasibility, planning, etc.)?
4. Was a formal risk management plan created? Discuss the plan.
5. Was there a risk officer? Discuss her duties and role in the project.
6. How were risks identified?

7. How were risks dealt with (through risk transfer, acceptance, avoidance, reduction, etc.)?

8. Discuss the use of contingency plans and budget and schedule reserves to cover risks.

9. What risks materialized during the project and how were they handled?

Case 10-1   The Sydney Opera House[35]

The Sydney Opera House (SOH) is a top tourist attraction and landmark for Sydney and all of Australia. It has become a major arts center (although, owing to the design, it is not necessarily the best place to hear opera). The SOH is visually spectacular and a magnificent structure (Figure 10-8), but designing and building it was somewhat nightmarish.

The original concept for the SOH was a sketch submitted by Danish architect, Jorn Utzon. Judges selected it from an open competition that ended with 233 entries from 11 countries. Though happy to win the competition, Utzon was mildly shocked. Although his concept had caught the attention of the judges, it consisted only of simple sketches with no plans or even perspective drawings. Utzon faced the task of converting the concept into a design from which a structure could be built, but he had no prior experience in the design and construction of such a large building. Because plans, detailed design drawings, and estimates of needed materials were lacking, little existed from which the cost could be determined. No one knew how it would be built, and some experts questioned that it could be built at all. (Interestingly, though, because the design was *so* unique, some people presumed it would also be inexpensive to build.) Despite all the uncertainty, the initial project cost estimate was put at $7 million, which the government would pay

Figure 10-8
Sydney Opera House. (Photo courtesy of Australian Information Service.)

through profits raised from a series of state-run lotteries.

Engineers who reviewed the concept noted that the roof shells were much larger and wider than any shells seen so far. Further, because they stuck up so high, they would act like sails in the strong winds blowing up the harbor. Thus, the roof would have to be carefully designed and constructed to prevent the building from blowing away.

The government was worried that people scrutinizing the design might raise questions about potential problems that would stall the project. They thus quickly moved ahead and divided the work into three main contracts: the foundation and building except the roof, the roof, and the interior and equipment.

As many experts had feared, the SOH project became an engineering and financial debacle, lasting 15 years and costing $107 million ($100 million over the initial estimate). Hindsight is 20/20, yet from the beginning this should have been viewed as a risky project. Nonetheless, risks were either downplayed or ignored, and not much was done to mitigate or keep them under control.

QUESTIONS

1. Identify the obvious risks.
2. What early actions should have been taken to reduce the risks?
3. Discuss some principles of risk management that were ignored.

Case 10-2 Infinity & Beyond, Inc.

Infinity & Beyond, Inc. is a producer of high-tech fashion merchandise. The company's marketing department has identified a new product concept through discussions with potential customers conducted in three focus groups. The marketing department is excited about the new "concept" and presents it to top management who gives the approval for further study. Lisa Denney, senior director of the new product and website development, is asked to create a plan and cost breakdown for the development, manufacture, and distribution of the product. Despite the enthusiasm of top management and the marketing department, Lisa is unsure about the product's market potential and the company's ability to develop it at a reasonable cost. To Lisa's way of thinking, the market seems ill-defined, the product goals unclear, and the product and its production technology uncertain. Lisa asks her chief designer to create some product requirements and a rough design that would meet the requirements and marketing concept, and to propose how the product might be manufactured and marketed.

After a few weeks the designer reports back with requirements that seem to satisfy the marketing concept. She tells Lisa that because of the newness of the technology and the complexity of the product design, the company does not have the experience to develop the product on its own, let alone manufacture it. Lisa checks out several design/development firms, asking one, Margo-Spinner Works Company, MSW, to review the product concept. MSW assures Lisa that although the technology is new to them, it is well within their capability. Lisa reports everything to top management who tells her to ignore any misgivings and go ahead with the development.

Lisa sets a fixed-price contract with MSW and gives them primary responsibility for the entire development offer. MSW management had argued for a cost-plus contract, but when Lisa stipulated that the agreement had to be fixed-price, MSW said okay, only under the condition that it be given complete control of the development work. Lisa, who has never worked with MSW, feels uncomfortable with the proposition, but knows of no other design company qualified to do the work, so she agrees. Several people from Infinity & Beyond, Inc. will be assigned to work at MSW during the development effort, and during that time will determine whether Infinity & Beyond, Inc. has the capability to make the product or must outsource its production.

QUESTIONS

1. Discuss the major sources of risk in this project.
2. What do you think about Lisa's handling of the project so far? If you were her, what would you have done differently?
3. Discuss the handling of stages of the project—product concept, definition, development, and production—and what Lisa and other parties did that served to increase or decrease the risks.

Case 10-3   The Nelson Mandela Bridge[36]

Newtown, South Africa is a suburb of Johannesburg that boasts a rich cultural heritage. As part of an attempt to help rejuvenate Newtown, the Nelson Mandela Bridge was constructed to link it to important roads and centers of commerce in Johannesburg. The bridge (Figure 10-9), which opened in 2003 and spans 42 electrified railway lines, has been acclaimed for its functionality and beauty.

Lack of space for the support pylons between the railway lines in the marshaling yard dictated that the bridge design have a long span. This resulted in a structure with the bridge deck supported by stay cables from pylons of unequal height. The northern side pylons are 48 meters (157 feet) high and the southern side ones (toward Newtown) are 35 meters (115 feet) high.

The pylons are composite columns consisting of steel tubes that had to be filled with concrete after being hoisted into the vertical position. The decision was made to pump the concrete into the tubes through a port at the bottom of each tube. This had to be done in a single operation. Although the technology for casting concrete this way was not new, the steel columns were the highest known in South Africa; in fact, filling them with concrete would set a world record for bottom-up pumping of self-curing concrete.

The pump for the concrete was placed at ground level between the electrified railway lines. In addition to risks of working in the presence of continuous rail operations, several risks relating to the casting of the concrete were identified. One risk was that the aggregate (stone) and cement in the concrete mixture might segregate in the pylon tubes before the concrete solidified, which would compromise the strength of the concrete. This risk was assessed through tests performed in an experimental column. Another risk was that the pump might fail during construction, resulting in the solidification of concrete in an uncompleted pylon, thus rendering further pumping of concrete from the bottom impossible.

Figure 10-9
Nelson Mandela Bridge, Johannesburg. (Photo courtesy of Jorge Jung, BKS (Pty) Ltd., Pretoria.)

Two mitigation strategies were considered: an additional pump on standby and, alternatively, completing the process by pouring concrete from the top of the pylon. The concrete mixture had to be transported by trucks to the site, which posed yet another risk: interruption of the concrete supply owing to traffic congestion in the city.

Despite the risks of working over a busy area with trains running back and forth, no serious accident occurred during the 420,000 man-hours spent on the project. The pump never failed, and construction finished on time. The stay cables—a total length of 81,000 meter, (50 miles)—were installed and the bridge deck lifted off temporary supports, all while the electrified railway lines underneath remained live. Upon completion of the bridge, some wondered whether the costs incurred to manage the risks were not excessive, while others held that the engineers had been too frugal and taken unacceptably high risks.

QUESTIONS

1. How would you have identified the risks? (Refer also to methods in Chapter 9.)
2. Using the table below, discuss how the risks were addressed (as described in the text) and/or how risks could have been addressed. Also indicate any additional risks you can think of.
3. Indicate whether the risks listed in the table above are internal or external.
4. Describe how you would determine the expected values of the risks listed in the table.
5. Compile a complete list of information that you would require in order to make an assessment of the risk of a pump failure.

Possible risk event	Plans to address risk				
	Accept	Avoid	Reduce	Transfer	Contingency plans and/or contingency reserves
Failure to make an acceptable profit					
Not finishing the construction by July 20, 2003 (Nelson Mandela's 85th birthday)					
Interference with rail activities					
Geological structures necessitating expensive foundations					
The concrete mixture segregating when pumped into the columns					
A pump failure while concrete is being pumped					
Interrupted supply of concrete due to city traffic delaying trucks transporting concrete to the site					

6. How available do you think this information would have been early in the project and where would you obtain it?
7. Draw a CE diagram to indicate how different factors could have contributed to delaying project completion.

8. Describe how risks are reduced over the lifespan of a project such as this.
9. With reference to the concerns expressed upon completion of the construction, discuss the statement: "Risks always relate to the future. There is no such thing as a *past risk.*"
10. Discuss the difference between good decisions and good luck.
11. How could a manager protect himself against the risk of making a decision that might later have negative implications?

ENDNOTES

1. Quoted in Peter Bernstein, *Against the Gods: The Remarkable Story of Risk* (New York: John Wiley & Sons, 1996): 331.
2. Ibid., 207–208.
3. Asked once to define certainty, John Von Neumann, the principle theorist of game theory and mathematical models of uncertainty, answered with an example: To design a house so it is *certain* the living room floor never gives way, "calculate the weight of a grand piano with six men huddling over it to sing, then triple the weight" and design a floor to hold that weight. That will guarantee certainty! *Source:* Bernstein, *Against the Gods,* 233.
4. See Robert Argus and Norman Gunderson, *Planning, Performing, and Controlling Projects* (Upper Saddle River, NJ: Prentice Hall, 1997): 22–23.
5. Adapted from Jack Michaels, *Technical Risk Management* (Upper Saddle River, NJ: Prentice Hall, 1996): 208–250.
6. Murray Turoff and Harold Linstone (eds), *The Delphi Method: Techniques and Applications,* 2002; http://is.njit.edu/pubs/delphibook/ http://is.njit.edu/pubs/delphibook/
7. The term "likelihood" is sometimes distinguished from "probability." The latter refers to values based on frequency measures from historical data; the former to subjective estimates or gut feel. If two of three previous attempts met with success the first time, then Ceteris paribus, the probability of success on the next try is 2/3 or 0.67 (and the probability of failure is 1/3). However, even without numerical data, a person with experience can, upon reflection, come up with a similar estimate that "odds are two to one that it will succeed the first time." Although one estimate is objective and the other subjective, that does not imply one is better than the other. Frequency data will not necessarily give a more reliable estimate because of the multitude of factors that influence outcomes;

a subjective estimate, in contrast, might be very reliable because humans often can do a pretty good job of assimilating lots of factors.
8. W. Roetzheim, *Structured Computer Project Management* (Upper Saddle River, NJ: Prentice Hall, 1988): 23–26; further examples of risk factors and methods of likelihood quantification are given in Michaels, *Technical Risk Management.*
9. See J. Dingle, *Project Management: Orientation for Decision Makers* (London: Arnold, 1997).
10. See Robert Gilbreath, *Winning at Project Management: What Works, What Fails, and Why* (New York: John Wiley & Sons, 1986).
11. Roetzheim, *Structured Computer Project Management,* 23–26.
12. Robert Pool , *Beyond Engineering: How Society Shapes Technology* (New York: Oxford University Press, 1997), 197–202.
13. Ronald Kotulak, "Key Differences Seen in Columbia, Challenger Disasters,"*Chicago Tribune* (February 2, 2003): 5, Section 1.
14. Robert Pool, *Beyond Engineering,* 207–214.
15. Michaels, *Technical Risk Management,* 40.
16. Edmund Conrow, *Effective Risk Management* (Reston, VA: American Institute of Aeronautics and Astronautics, 2000), 135–140.
17. Statistics make it easy to ignore risks by depersonalizing the consequences. For example, it is less distressing to state that there is a 0.005 likelihood of someone being killed than to say that 5 people out of 1000 will be killed.
18. I. Mitroff and H. Linstone, *The Unbounded Mind* (New York: Oxford, 1993): 111–135.
19. Ibid.
20. F. T. Anbari (ed.), *The Chunnel Project,* Case studies in Project Management, Project Management Institute, 2005.
21. Howard Eisner, *Computer-Aided Systems Engineering* (Upper Saddle River, NJ: Prentice Hall, 1988): 335.

22. See Jeffrey Grady, *System Requirements Analysis* (New York: McGraw-Hill, 1993): 106–111.

23. Eisner, *Computer-Aided Systems Engineering*, 336.

24. Ibid.

25. A breadboard is a working assembly of components. A prototype is an early working model of a complete system. The purpose of both is to demonstrate, validate, experiment, or prove feasibility in a concept or design.

26. Roetzheim, *Structured Computer Project Management*, 96.

27. Henry Wakabayashi and Bob Cowan, "Vancouver International Airport Expansion,"*PM Network* (September 1998): 39–44.

28. Neal Whitten, "Meet Minimum Requirements: Anything More is Too Much,"*PM Network* (September 1998): 19.

29. Tom DeMarco, *The Deadline* (New York: Dorset House, 1997): 83; Edward Yourdan, *Rise and Resurrection of the American Programmer* (Upper Saddle River, NJ: Prentice Hall, 1998): 133–136.

30. Dietrich Dorner, *The Logic of Failure* (Reading, MA: Addison-Wesley, 1997): 163.

31. D. Aronstein and A. Piccirillo, *Have Blue and the F117A: Evolution of the Stealth Fighter* (Reston, VA: American Institute of Aeronautics and Astronautics, 1997): 79–80.

32. Ibid., 186–190.

33. For other approaches to risk time analysis, see Michaels, *Technical Risk Management*.

34. This section and the next address the more general topic of decision analysis, a broad topic that receives only cursory coverage here. Most textbooks on production/operations management and quantitative analysis for management cover the topic in depth. A classic book on the subject is R. D. Luce and H. Raiffa, *Games and Decisions* (New York: John Wiley & Sons, 1957).

35. Adapted from O. Kharbanda and J. Pinto, *What Made Gertie Gallop: Learning from Project Failures* (New York: Van Nostrand Reinhold, 1996): 177–191.

36. *Source*: Frans Kromhout, Divisional Director, Bridges, BKS (Pty) Ltd, Pretoria.

Chapter 11

Project Execution and Control

> *The rider must ride the horse, not be run away with.*
>
> —DONALD WINNICOTT,
> *Playing and Reality*

> *Prediction is very difficult, especially about the future.*
>
> —NIELS BOHR

*U*pon completing the Definition phase the project manager and team will have prepared a complete set of requirements and specifications, and a comprehensive project plan. The plan will include details about the immediate, upcoming stages of the project, as well as a comprehensive outline for all remaining stages. These stages constitute the remainder of the project, the *Execution* phase of the project life cycle, one of the topics of the chapter.

Entering the Execution phase it would be comforting to know that the prepared specifications and plans have accounted for all remaining aspects of the project and covered every potential problem. But of course, no project plan is ever complete or perfect. Things rarely go entirely as anticipated, although every effort is made to keep the project moving toward preestablished specifications and objectives. Keeping the project moving forward and on target, tracking progress, and overcoming obstacles is the purpose of *project control*, which is the other main topic of the chapter.

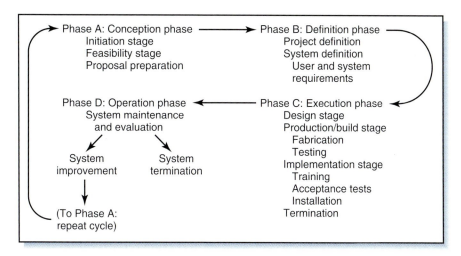

Figure 11-1
Phase and stages systems development life cycle (Phases A–C = project life cycle).

11.1 PHASE C: EXECUTION

The Execution phase typically includes the stages of *design, production/build*, and *implementation* (Figure 11-1), although in each project the actual stages will depend on the purpose of the project. For example, in hardware development projects the stages are design, development, and production; in construction projects they are design and construction; and in consulting projects they are background research and report outline, compilation, and presentation. Some companies have methodologies with custom-made project phases and stages; these are discussed in Chapter 16. Most projects that produce a physical end-item—a product, building, system, or report—also have an implementation stage, which is when the end-item is handed over to the user. This chapter looks at the stages of design and production/build. The implementation stage, project closeout, and Phase D are covered in the next chapter.

11.2 DESIGN STAGE

During the design stage system specifications are converted into plans, schematics, and drawings. The output of design varies depending on the industry and the type of system, but usually is in the form of pictorial representations—blueprints, flow charts, and schematic diagrams—or models showing system components, dimensions, relationships, and overall configuration.[1]

During the design process the system is conceptually broken down into tiers of subsystems, components, and parts. Various design possibilities for elements in each tier are reviewed for compatibility with each other and with elements at higher-level tiers, and for ability to meet specifications and system cost, schedule, and performance requirements. The breakdown into tiers and components uses the block-diagramming (Chapter 2), requirements breakdown structure (RBS) (Chapter 3), and work breakdown structure (WBS) (Chapter 5) approaches.

The design process is composed of two interrelated activities. First is preparation of a *functional* design that shows the system components and their relationships. The purpose of this design activity is to determine the *logical*, functional elements of the system and how they should be interconnected to achieve the system's objectives. This is the thrust of the systems engineering process described in Chapter 2.

The second kind of design is preparation of a *physical* design, which is what the actual system and its components will look like, their sizes, shapes, and relative location. This design activity results in engineering, manufacturing, architectural, and other types of drawings and models that show details necessary for later fabrication, assembly, production, and maintenance of the system. Sometimes they reveal places where the functional design is impractical or infeasible because of assembly, maintenance, or appearance considerations, in which case it is necessary to redo the functional design.

Design often follows an evolutionary, trial-and-error process as illustrated in Figure 2-8 in Chapter 2 and Figure 4-7 in Chapter 4. A trial design is prepared, modeled, and then tested against system performance specifications. If it fails, the design is modified and retested. This design-build-test process of iteration is followed to varying degrees in virtually all development projects for new or innovative systems.

When a complex system is being designed, the iteration occurs in many places throughout the system, and changes in one subsystem have a ripple effect on others. One subsystem may require, for instance, a bigger motor, which robs space from another subsystem that must then be moved to another part of the system, which displaces something else, and so on. Uncontrolled, the result is a never-ending system redesign. Thus, one responsibility of the project manager and systems engineer is to try to minimize the number of changes and design iterations for each subsystem, and to keep redesigns local and minimize interference on other subsystems.

Example 1: Design Complexity in the Chunnel[2]

One of the mandated changes in requirements for the English Channel Tunnel (Chunnel) project was that trains running through it must be resistant to fire damage for at least 30 minutes. That would enable every train car to be capable of continuing along with a fire raging inside until out of the tunnel. But because the frame of a normal train car would deform from the heat and soon immobilize the train, the car frames would have be made of special metal alloys that are unlike the metals used in trains everywhere else in the world. This would make the trains heavier, 2,400 tons instead of 1,600 tons, and would require heavier locomotives needing six axles instead of four. The locomotives would have to be specially designed, and because they needed more power, the tunnel's electrical power system would have to be specially designed too.

In many projects, the stages of design and production/build do not occur as discrete, sequential stages, but rather overlap. The building or construction of a part of the system commences as soon as the detail design for that part has been completed, then building begins on another part when more of the detail design has been completed, and so on. In other words, the system is being built *while* it is still being designed—a practice referred to as *fast-tracking* or *design-build*. Fast-tracking is common in the construction industry: the foundation is being dug and steel being raised even though the roof and interior designs have not yet been completed. The practice speeds up the work and can save up to 1 year on a major construction project, but it is also risky. Problems with a design often do not appear until the details have been worked out, but by then portions of the system or building will have been fabricated and might have to be torn down and rebuilt—increasing costs and schedules, of course. The usual sequential or "slow-tracking" method takes longer but allows more time for design problems to surface and be resolved before construction begins.

The Project Manager in the Design Stage

The project team size and level of project activity continually grow as the project moves through execution. As the system and project plan are defined in greater detail, the project manager assigns project tasks to group leaders and subcontractors. As the size of the project organization increases, so does the project manager's workload. Design activities require participation from groups throughout the contractor organization and its subcontractors. The project manager coordinates their efforts, facilitates communication and effective interfacing, and tries to keep the effort on schedule, within budget, and directed toward system and project objectives.

Interaction Design[3]

Why is it that so many software-based products are difficult to use, do things that people don't need, and contain obscure features that many people don't want? Examples are DVD players, software products, digital watches, and entertainment systems all that contain numerous features and functions that most people do not need and never learn to use. Yet in an effort to continuously "improve" the product, developers keep adding ever more features, a process that leads to "bloatware." Compare, for instance, all the things you presumably *could do* with word-processing and spreadsheet software with the few features that you actually use. The problem is not only that these products have too many features, but that they inter-mix never-used features with often-used ones, making the product more difficult to use and understand, and leaving the user feeling frustrated and stupid. In the eyes of customers, the products are too complex.

Complex systems have always been around, but in the past they were operated only by *trained* personnel. Farm and construction equipment, aircraft, trains, and electrical generators are complex but are designed for use by someone specially trained, not the average person. Commercial products (digital watch, camera, ATM, car console, cell phone, etc.) are complex too, however, but are used by amateurs, not skilled operators.

Complexity and bloatware occur when the product design is *controlled* by engineers and programmers, people who are technically astute but often ignore "interaction design"—those aspects of design that include product functions and how they are presented to the user. This happens when product goals and user requirements are poorly defined, no one guides the design process to meet user requirements, and the user–system interaction is not a central design issue. Whenever a programmer adds a pet function to a product or a marketing manager insists on another feature, they are adding to bloatware and ignoring the average end-user.

The project manager and systems engineer must retain focus on interaction design throughout the design process. This starts with identifying and describing the end-users in detail, their wants, aptitudes, skill levels, and behaviors with the product, incorporating these into user requirements, and thereafter considering the end-user in every design decision that will influence the function and operation of the product.

Controlling Design

Project reviews are conducted during the design stage at key milestones to ensure that objectives, requirements, and specifications are being met. Although scheduled by the project manager, reviews are ideally conducted and chaired by objective "outsiders" to ensure that functions and interfaces satisfy requirements, and that the final design suits the user's personal tastes, needs, and budget.

During the design stage, changes to initial designs may be necessary as a result of new technology, technical problems, or new requirements of the user. These inevitably require changes in work activities and affect project plans, schedules, costs, and budgets. Project management is responsible for monitoring these changes, determining their impact on the project, communicating the impact to stakeholders affected, obtaining approvals, and updating schedules, budgets, and plans. Changes should be reviewed and approved by project management; those that drastically alter the project plan may require user approval and changes to the contract.

Design changes tend to increase project costs, but as shown in Figure 11-2, typical design costs are a small fraction of production costs. Consequently, prolonging this stage to get the design right is usually less costly than fixing design-related problems later during the stages of production and operation. But design changes cannot be allowed to continue indefinitely and sometimes management imposes a freeze date after which no discretionary changes are allowed.

Project management is also responsible for ensuring that results of the design effort are well documented. Good documentation is necessary, so everyone knows the design requirements, its features, configuration, strengths, and limitations; it is the precursor for preparing plans and procedures for subsequent system production, operation, and maintenance.

Planning for Production/Build and Later Stages

The project manager is always looking beyond the current stage, and during the design stage is preparing the plan for the production stage. This plan will address tool and machine design, equipment and materials procurement, assembly, functional tests, component tests, integration tests, packaging, and so on, and include a detailed production/build schedule. Because all of the design materials (specs, drawings, etc.) might not be completed in time, production tasks might have to be scheduled in phases, which will require coordination of design and production tasks.

The overall plan for the production/build stage must also account for the systems, tasks, and resources that will be needed to produce, operate, and maintain the end-item system; these are *side-items*, so-called to distinguish them from the main contract

Figure 11-2
Relative costs for design and production.

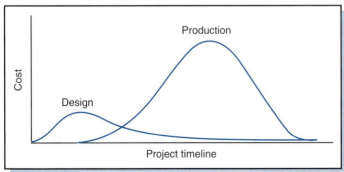

end-item of the project. Side-items are no less important than the main end-item, for without them the production, operation, or maintenance of the end-item would be impossible. Although side-items are usually developed and produced by subcontractors, the manager of the overall project is responsible for ensuring that they have all been identified and contractors are developing and producing them.

11.3   PRODUCTION/BUILD STAGE

Detailed designs in hand, the contractor is ready to move into the next stage, which is to produce or build the end-item. The main activities in this stage are fabrication, testing, and planning for subsequent stages of the project.

System Fabrication

System fabrication begins when sufficient design work is completed for the project manager to authorize fabrication. Components prepared by the contractor and its suppliers are gathered together and assembled into the final end-item. As in earlier stages, the project manager monitors the work, coordinates efforts among departments, and tracks expenditures and completed work against the budget and master schedule. The principal management tasks during this stage are releasing work orders; monitoring, inspecting, and documenting progress; comparing planned versus actual results; and taking corrective action. The project manager and the manufacturing or construction manager share responsibility for these tasks.

During system fabrication, work quality is constantly being assessed. As with most tasks in the production/build stage, quality control of components and fabrication is not, per se, the responsibility of the project manager; nonetheless, because the quality of the final system *is* the responsibility of the project manager, she must make sure that other managers involved in the production/build stage have implemented a quality plan to achieve the quality objectives of the project. Quality planning and control are discussed in Chapter 9.

System Testing

Throughout the Execution phase a variety of tests are performed on the end-item system. Tests fall into three groups: tests conducted by the contractor to make sure that the system design (1) meets requirements and (2) is being followed by the producer or builder, and (3) tests conducted by the user to make sure the system meets user requirements and other contractual agreements. Tests for quality to be performed, test criteria, and test conditions are defined in the quality plan.[4]

The first group is aimed at verifying the design. If these tests should reveal inadequate performance because of faulty or poor design, then the design stage must be repeated. Since repeating steps is costly and time-consuming, the tests should be devised to catch problems as early as possible. Of course, even if the design is perfect, unless the builders conform to it and do not cut corners on materials and procedures, the system will be inadequate; hence, the second group of tests is necessary to verify that the builders have correctly followed the design and that the components and workmanship meet specifications. The final group of tests includes verification tests, reviews, and audits conducted by the customer to ensure that user requirements have been met and that test documentation is complete and accurate. These tests often reveal design deficiencies not identified during the first group of tests;

unlike the design engineers who perform the first group of tests, user personnel may experience difficulties in operating the system or induce system failures.

To minimize the chances of having to redesign the entire system because of faulty components, testing should follow the sequence of components first, subsystems next, then the whole system last. Each part is tested to ensure it functions individually; parts are integrated into components and tested to ensure that they work together; components are integrated into subsystems and tested to ensure that each subsystem performs; and finally subsystems are integrated and tested to ensure that the entire system meets performance requirements.

Tests are performed against earlier developed systems specifications and user requirements. Sometimes, in addition, they are often performed *in excess* of specifications for normal operating conditions to determine the actual capacity or point of failure of the system. In *stress tests* an increasingly severe test load is applied to the system to determine its ability to handle heavier than probable conditions. In *failure tests* the system is loaded or submitted to repeated load cycles until it fails in order to determine its ultimate capacity. Contracts for development projects sometimes set the design requirements and performance criteria, and specify the test criteria and types of tests to verify them.

The project manager oversees preparation of the test plan and schedule to be included in the production/build plan. She ensures that the necessary resources are available to perform the tests, and that test results are well documented and filed for later reference.

Planning for Implementation

With phased project planning, details in the project plan are filled in as information becomes available. Hence, during production/build the detailed plan for implementation is prepared.

Implementation is the process of turning the system over to the user. The two prime activities in implementation are installing the system in the user's environment and training the user to operate the system. The project manager must develop plans in advance so that the implementation stage can begin at or before completion of system fabrication. The plans must ensure that needed side-items will be available in time for user training, system installation, and operation. Planning for implementation should start early in the project—in the definition phase, but be substantially completed by the end of the production/build stage. The implementation strategy to replace an existing system with a new one should address:[5]

1. Approach for converting from the old system to the new system.
2. Sequencing and scheduling of implementation activities.
3. Acceptance criteria and a test plan that will enable the customer to sign off on the system.
4. Approach to phasing out the old system and phasing in the new.
5. User training.
6. Installation details (for installation, check out, and acceptance of the end-item and side-items).
7. Site preparation details (addressing security, access, power, space, equipment, etc.).

An initial implementation plan might have been developed earlier as part of the project master plan; now a more detailed plan is prepared with the participation of the customer to address all the above points. As this plan is being prepared, the contractor accumulates materials to train the user in system operation and maintenance. Simple systems require only a brief instruction pamphlet and a warranty. Complex systems require much more—lengthy manuals for procedures, system operation, repair, and servicing; testing manuals; manuals for training the trainers; training materials and simulators; and schematics, drawings, special tools, and servicing and support equipment. Much of the information for manuals is derived from documentation created during the design stage.

Agreement must be reached with the customer about how and when the project can be closed out—that is, how and when the customer will consider the system acceptable and the project completed. Misunderstandings about this, such as "acceptance only after modification," can cause a project to drag indefinitely. To prevent that, the user requirements as defined early in the project ideally should include conditions and criteria for customer acceptance of the system. Other aspects of the implementation stage, which can consume a big part of the project life cycle, are discussed in the next chapter.

11.4 THE CONTROL PROCESS

A major function of project management during the Execution phase is to control the project. Author Daniel Roman defines the project control process as:

> Assessing actual against planned technical accomplishment, reviewing and verifying the validity of technical objectives, confirming the continued need for the project, overseeing resource expenditures, and comparing the anticipated value with the costs incurred.[6]

The process can be compared to an air-conditioning system:

1. The desired temperature is set on the thermostat.
2. The actual temperature is measured, and the temperature variance determined (actual temperature minus desired temperature).
3. If the variance is positive, the air conditioner turns on until the actual temperature coincides with the desired temperature (i.e., variance drops to zero).

Every control process has the same three steps: (1) set the performance standards, (2) compare these standards with actual performance, and (3) take necessary corrective action.

The first step, set *performance standards*, happens in a project during the Definition phase. The standards are derived from the user requirements, technical specifications, budgeted costs, schedules, and resource requirements in the project plan.

The next step, compare the standards with *actual project performance*, happens during execution. Planned schedules, budgets, and performance specifications are compared to actual expenditures and work completed. The time and cost of work still to be done are estimated, and a forecast of the anticipated date and cost of the completed project prepared.

Corrective action follows whenever the actual performance significantly differs from the performance standards. The work is altered or expedited to achieve the standards, or the standards are revised. If work performance is deficient, resources are added or shifted. If the original expectations and plans prove unrealistic, then project objectives are changed and the standards and plans revised accordingly.

To keep the project aimed at requirements, schedules, and budgets, obviously there must initially be a plan! In fact, you could say that the first step to project control is project definition: *without clear and complete requirements and a good plan, there can be no project control.*

11.5   PROJECT MONITORING

The purpose of *project monitoring* is to observe and track how well the project is doing, and to forecast how well it will do in the future. Project monitoring involves collecting and interpreting data, and reporting information.

The data collected must relate directly to the project performance standards, i.e., to project plans, schedules, budgets, and requirements. Typical sources of data include materials purchasing invoices, worker time cards, change notices, test results, purchase and work orders, and expert opinion. A balance must be struck in the amount and variety of data collected: too much data will be costly to collect and process, and will be ignored; too little will not adequately capture project status and allow problems to go unchecked. The collected data must be analyzed, and the results reported in sufficient detail and frequency to enable managers to quickly spot deviations and take corrective action.[7]

How frequently should data be collected, assessed, and reported? In general, the frequency of assessment should be less than the average length of work packages. A good rule of thumb is to assess work progress every week. For small projects this ensures that small work packages lasting only 2 to 3 weeks will be checked at least twice. For projects with work packages of several months' length, an assessment every 2 to 3 weeks might be adequate. The goal is to check the work often enough to be able to measure progress accurately and spot problems early, yet not so often that it becomes burdensome. Sometimes the frequency depends on the people doing the work: highly competent and motivated people do not need to be monitored as closely or often as those less competent or less motivated.

11.6   INTERNAL AND EXTERNAL PROJECT CONTROL

Monitoring and regulating project activities happens both internally and externally. *Internal control* refers to the contractor's systems and procedures for monitoring work, reporting status, and taking action. *External control* refers to additional procedures and requirements imposed by the customer, including oversight of project coordination and administration functions. Government contracts sometimes impose external control by stipulating:[8]

- Frequent reports by the contractor on schedules, cost, and technical performance.
- Inspections of work by government program managers.
- Inspection of the contractor's books and records by government auditors.
- Strict terms imposed on the contractor on allowable project costs, pricing policies, etc.

External control can be a source of annoyance and aggravation to the contractor, and with managers overlooking managers it adds to bureaucratic turmoil and increases administrative costs. Nonetheless, it is sometimes necessary to protect the customer's interests, especially in cost plus fixed free (CPFF) projects. To minimize conflicts and costs, the contractor and customer must work together to establish agreed-upon plans, compatible specifications, and methods for monitoring the work.

11.7 TRADITIONAL COST CONTROL

In traditional cost control, work performance is measured with *variance analysis,* which compares actual costs with planned costs to determine the difference between the amount spent and the amount budgeted. For project control, cost variance analysis is inadequate.

Example 2: Cost Variance Analysis

Consider the following weekly status report for a software development work package:

Budgeted cost for period = $12,000	Actual cost for period = $14,000	Period variance = $2,000
Cumulative budget to date = $25,000	Cumulative actual costs to date = $29,000	Cumulative variance = $4,000

The report indicates apparent overruns for both period and cumulative costs, with cumulative costs running $4,000 over budget. But because we do not know how much work has been completed for the $29,000, it is impossible from the data to determine if the project is really over budget.

Suppose that $25,000 was the amount budgeted for completing 50 percent of software development work; i.e., as of the week of this report, 50 percent of the work package should have been completed. If 50 percent of the work had actually been completed (as intended), then the project would, in fact, be over budget and something would have to be done to reduce future expenditures and eliminate the $4,000 overrun. Now, suppose only 30 percent of the work had been completed; in that case the project would not only be over budget, but also behind schedule, and further cost overruns could be expected just to get caught up. As a third possibility, suppose that 70 percent of the work had been completed, which is more than was scheduled, so the project would be ahead of schedule. In this case, the project might not be over budget because substantially more work has been completed than was planned for this date.

As the example shows, to be able to assess project status, besides cost variance you also need information about *work progress*—information such as percentage of work completed, milestones achieved, and so on, as discussed later.

11.8 COST-ACCOUNTING SYSTEMS FOR PROJECT CONTROL

In the early 1960s the US government developed a combined PERT-based scheduling and cost-accounting system called *PERT/Cost.*[9] The system became mandatory for military and R&D contracts with the US Department of Defense and NASA (DOD/NASA). Any contractor wanting to work for DOD/NASA had to demonstrate the ability to use the system and to produce the necessary reports. The mandate increased usage of PERT/Cost but also created resentment because many firms found PERT/Cost an expensive duplication of, or incompatible with, their existing accounting systems. Interestingly, many firms not working for DOD/NASA voluntarily adopted PERT/Cost with few complaints. PERT/Cost was an improvement over traditional cost-accounting techniques and spurred the development of other more-sophisticated systems to track work and report progress and costs. It was the original network-based project cost-accounting system (PCAS) mentioned in Chapter 8.

Most PCASs integrate information about work packages, cost accounts, and project schedules into a unified project control package. They permit cost and scheduling overruns to be identified and the causes pinpointed among numerous work packages or control accounts. Two features common to most of these systems are use of *work packages* or *control accounts* as the basic data collection units, and the concept of *earned value* to measure project performance.

11.9 WORK-PACKAGE AND CONTROL (COST) ACCOUNTS

Earlier chapters described the central role of work packages and cost accounts in project planning; by no coincidence, they are also major elements of project control. Each cost account consists of one or more work packages; each work package is considered a contract for a specific job, with a manager or supervisor, description, time-phased budget, work plan and schedule, resource requirements, and so on. Work packages and cost accounts are also the focal points for data collection, work progress evaluation, problem assessment, and corrective action.

Large projects may be composed of hundreds of work packages, making it potentially difficult to identify the ones causing a cost or schedule overrun. An advantage of a PCAS is that it can readily sort through all of the work packages to locate the problem-causing ones. Although the individual work package remains the central element for control, a PCAS can consolidate and report information for *any* level of the project, from the individual control-account or work-package level up to the project level. Additionally, most permit consolidation and reporting of project information using a functional breakdown as well. This means that when control accounts are established for work packages, the PCAS can aggregate them either vertically through the WBS or horizontally through the project-functional organization. An example is Figure 8-13 in Chapter 8, which shows levels of control-account aggregation for the Robotics Self-budgeting (ROSEBUD) project. Because higher-level accounts in the cost-account structure are built up through the WBS and organizational hierarchies, variances in costs and schedules at any project level can be traced down through the structure to identify work packages causing the variances.

Work Authorization

Part of the control process is *work authorization*, also known as start–stop control, which means that work is started only after formal authorization and ended only upon review and acceptance. This control applies to all levels of work, from the project level to the work-package level. At the project level, authorization formally begins upon the customer's and top management's acceptance of the project plan, which authorizes the project manager to execute the project. The project manager then authorizes the managers of subprojects to begin, who authorize managers and supervisors at the next level lower, as shown in Figure 11-3. The process is a continuation of the initiation and authorization process described in Chapter 3 and shown in Figure 3.8.

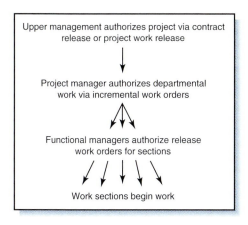

Figure 11-3
Project work authorization process.

The same process can also be used to authorize the *phases* of a project: the customer or other stakeholders evaluate the detailed plan for a project phase and, if they find it and the risks acceptable, they authorize the project to proceed to the next phase (the "gating process" described in Chapter 16). Alternatively, authorization can also be based upon *results* of the last phase. In contracted projects, if the work during a phase is not up to expectations, the contractor is paid the amount owed and the project terminated at the end of the phase.

On large projects, authorization is subdivided into the stages of *contract release, project release,* and *work order release* or *work requisition*. After the customer gives the okay and the contract is awarded, the contract administrator prepares a contract release document that specifies contractual requirements and gives project management the go-ahead. The comptroller or project accountant then prepares a project release document, which authorizes project funding.

Work begins only upon receipt of a *work order* by the department or contractor responsible. The work order (or "engineering order," "shop order," "test order," or similar document depending on the kind of work) specifies that the work package or task is authorized to start. As the scheduled start date for the task draws near, the project manager or project office releases a work order and other authorization documents such as purchase orders, test requests, and tool orders, as needed. For simple activities, verbal authorization might suffice.

Collecting Cost, Schedule, and Work Progress Data

For each work-package, data about *actual* costs and work progress is periodically collected and entered into the PCAS or project management information systems (PMIS) (discussed in Chapters 8 and 12). The PCAS tallies and summarizes information up through the WBS and project organization structure in a process similar to creating the budget summaries described in Chapter 8. The PCAS generates performance reports periodically or as needed for every work package, department or section, and the entire project.

Assessing work progress is the responsibility of the functional manager or team supervisor in charge of the work package. Each week the supervisor tallies the labor hours spent on each task as indicated on time cards. She notes tasks completed, tasks still "open," and the estimated time needed to complete open tasks. Progress is recorded on a Gantt chart showing completed and open tasks. Figure 11-4 is an example showing the status of the LOGON project as of week 20. Notice that work packages K, L, M, and Q are all open and behind schedule.

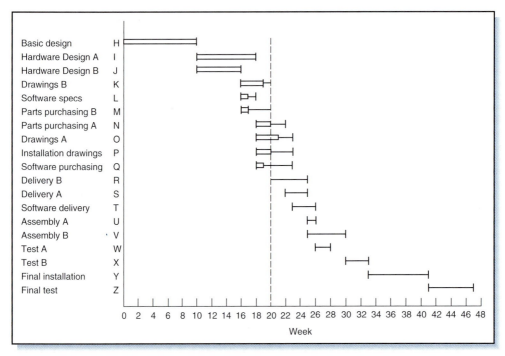

Figure 11-4
Gantt chart showing work status as of week 20.

How is work progress measured? Costs and time elapsed are measured easily, but neither say much about actual progress made toward completing the project. Unfortunately, sometimes it is difficult or impossible to assess work progress precisely or reliably using quantitative measures. As a consequence, managers often must rely on the subjective estimates. In a survey of conventional ways to measure project progress, Thompson identified the following:[10]

1. *Supervision*: Managers and supervisors assess progress by direct observation, asking questions, and reviewing written reports and project documentation.
2. *Milestones*: These are easily measured end-points of tasks, or transition points between tasks. Milestones are usually considered critical to the project and represent achievement of a desired level of performance, including, for example, completion of drawings, reports, design documents, or solutions to specific technical problems.
3. *Tests and demonstrations*: Described earlier, these can range from simple tests of system components to full-system and user acceptance tests. They are a good way of obtaining periodic, objective measures of technical progress at intermediate stages of the project.
4. *Design reviews*: These are meetings with managers and technical personnel (engineers, systems analysts, designers, etc.) to review the design progress against the plan.
5. *Outside experts*: The project manager or other stakeholder invites a person or "expert panel." Such experts assess project status by observation, talking to project personnel, and reviewing documentation.
6. *Status of design documentation:* Experienced project managers can determine when a design is nearly finished by the "completeness" of documentation such as drawings, schematics, functional diagrams, manuals, and test procedures.

7. *Resource utilization:* A request for or change in resources may reflect progress; for example, tasks nearing completion often require special testing or implementation facilities, personnel, and equipment.
8. *Telltale tasks:* Certain tasks such as concept design, requirements and specification definition, feasibility analysis, and repeated testing usually happen early or midway in a project; happening later in the project can signify *lack* of progress.
9. *Benchmarking or analogy:* Certain tasks, or the entire project, may be compared to similar tasks or projects as a crude way to weigh relative progress.
10. *Changes, bugs, and, rework:* The rate of changes to elements of the plan (design, schedule, budget), the number of system bugs, and amount of rework are also measures of progress. Because, ordinarily, the number of changes and bugs decreases as the project nears completion, a sustained high number may *indicate* lack of progress.

While collecting data about completed or in-progress work reveals existing or emerging problems, measures to *anticipate* problems are also necessary, including those identified in the risk management plan (Chapter 10), personal observations of the project manager (walk-throughs of offices and worksites), and informal discussions with team members.

Any changes to estimates or schedules for remaining work are documented by the work-package supervisor and submitted to the project manager for approval. Each week the work-package supervisor also tallies current expenses. Labor hours reported on timecards are converted into direct labor cost. The supervisor adds direct labor, material, and level-of-effort costs for completed and open tasks to the cost of work in prior periods, and then applies the overhead percentage rate to applicable direct charges. Late charges and outstanding costs (a frequent source of cost overruns) are also included.[11]

Each week a revised report is prepared to show costs of all work completed in prior periods plus work accomplished in the current period. This is reviewed, verified, and signed by the supervisor before forwarding it to the project manager. Once work-package information has been validated by the project manager it is entered into the PCAS wherein costs to-date are accumulated for all work packages and summary reports prepared. Periodically the project manager reviews the summary reports to reassess the project and prepare estimates of the work and cost still needed to complete the project. These estimates plus the record of project costs and work progress to date provide a forecast of the completion date and project cost at completion; the forecast procedure is described later. Once a task or work package is completed, the project manager closes its cost account and any associated budget reserve (contingency) to prevent additional, unauthorized billing.

11.10 PROJECT CONTROL EMPHASIS

The emphasis in project control is on project scope, quality, schedule, procurement, and cost.

Scope Change Control

Projects have a natural tendency to grow over time because of changes and additions in the scope, a phenomenon called "scope creep." Changes or additions to the scope reflect changes in requirements and work definition that, usually, result in time and cost increases. The aim of scope change control is to identify where changes have occurred, ensure the changes are necessary or beneficial, contain or delimit the changes wherever possible, and manage the implementation of changes. Because changes in scope directly impact schedules and costs, controlling scope changes is an important aspect of schedule and cost control. Scope control is implemented through the *change control system* and *configuration management*, both described later.

Quality Control

Quality control is managing the work to achieve the contracted or desired requirements and specifications, taking preventive measures to keep errors and mistakes out of the work process, and identifying and eliminating the sources of errors and mistakes.

Project quality control starts with the *quality management plan* described in Chapter 9. The quality plan specifies necessary "quality conditions" for every work package—the prerequisites or stipulations about what must exist before, during, and after the work package to ensure quality. It also specifies the measures and procedures (tests, inspections, reviews, etc., as discussed earlier) to assess conditions and progress toward meeting requirements. In technical projects, progress toward meeting technical performance targets is tracked using a methodology called *technical performance measurement (TPM)*, discussed later.

Projects employ a variety of methods for testing and inspection to eliminate defects and ensure that end-items meet requirements. The following illustrates an inspection approach used in design engineering and software development projects.

Example 3: Team Inspection Process[12]

The purpose of the team inspection process is to improve quality, shorten development time, and reduce costs by avoiding defects. The process occurs in a team meeting of four or five people who inspect requirements and design documentation and software code. The roles of the team members are:

- *Moderator:* The person who oversees the inspection and records defects spotted in the document or code.
- *Reader:* The individual who reads the document or code, line by line, during the inspection meeting.
- *Inspector(s):* The person who is the most knowledgeable, has the most information, and is best able to detect errors in the documentation or code.
- *Author:* The engineer or programmer who created the document or code.

The process works like this:

Upon completing the requirements document, design document, or code the author schedules an inspection meeting. At least 2 days prior to the meeting every member of the inspection team receives a copy of the material being inspected and all supporting documentation.

The inspection meeting lasts for about 2 hours during which an average team can inspect 10–15 pages of text or 400 lines of code. Defects are documented, and the team decides whether it should meet again after the defects have been corrected. When the inspector signs off on the document or code, the process is considered completed and the materials approved.

As part of a continuous improvement effort, the identified defects or mistakes can be entered into a database that when referenced during other projects can reduce the chances of similar mistakes recurring.

To deal with quality problems that are both unique and repetitive, the project manager can appoint a *quality-improvement team*, which is a small group of individuals responsible for identifying and eliminating the sources of quality problems. On a small project, one cross-functional team might serve the function; on a large project, several specialized teams might be needed to address particular problems in certain phases or technical areas of the project. To help eliminate problem sources and improve processes in future projects, the contractor or customer can incorporate the findings of these teams into larger, ongoing continuous improvement efforts.

Schedule Control

The intent of schedule control is to keep the project on schedule and minimize schedule overruns. Even when projects are carefully planned and estimated, they can fall behind for reasons beyond anyone's control, including, for example, necessary changes in project scope, weather problems, and materials shortages. Causes of schedule overruns discussed in Chapter 7 include multitasking, procrastination, and task time variability (the uncertainty in knowing how long tasks will task).[13] The following are guidelines for controlling schedule variability and keeping projects on target.

Use Time Buffers

Described in Chapter 7, a time buffer is a schedule reserve, an amount of time included in the schedule to account for uncertainty in completion time. To implement a time buffer, the computed, expected finish date is increased by the buffer amount. If the estimated finish date is July 31 and the desired time buffer is 4 weeks, the target finish date is set for August 31.

Time buffers are an important aspect of the critical chain methodology (CCM), which prescribes locating them at the end of the critical chain for the entire project and the ends of every subpath feeding into the critical chain.[14] Once a project is underway, the amount of buffer "consumed" is tracked. Each time a task in the critical chain or a feeding chain is delayed, it "eats" into the time buffer. The more of the buffer consumed, the greater the likelihood the buffer will be exhausted and the target finish date overrun. Hence, the project should be managed so as to minimize consumption of the buffer.[15] Example 4 illustrates the process.

Example 4: Abbott Laboratories' Fever-Chart Tracking and Control[16]

Abbott Laboratories' Diagnostic Division (ADD) started using CCM for some projects in 1999. Prior to that, most projects were scheduled and tracked using the traditional critical-path approach. Doug Brandt, a biochemist with over 20 years of project management experience and founding director of ADD's PMO at the Lake County site, estimates that prior to use of CCM only about 20 percent of projects were completed on time; since, for those using CCM it has been over 80 percent.

Brandt attributes part of the success to CCM's tracking and control capability. The main tool for this purpose is the "fever chart," a graph that shows for each project the percentage of project buffer consumed versus the calendar time (Figure 11-5). (Actually, ADD tracks percentage of CCM used, not calendar time, but the latter is simpler for illustration purposes.) Early on, a "healthy project" will have consumed little or none of its buffer. As the project progresses, the percentage of buffer consumed can be expected to increase, and the plot of percentage of buffer consumed versus time to rise diagonally. Monitoring the graph, the project manager can determine whether a project will be completed early, on time, or late; a sharp upward trend, for example, indicates that the project is stalled—little progress is being made on critical chain tasks. In a *well-managed healthy* project the slope of the line is shallow and a large part of the project buffer remains unconsumed by the end of the project. Completing

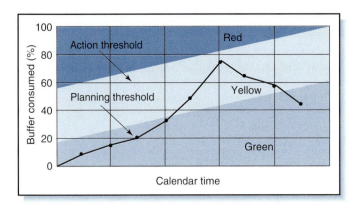

Figure 11-5
Chart of buffer consumed versus time.

a project with buffer remaining is equivalent to completing the project *ahead of target*. Thus, to complete the project early, the project must be managed so as to avoid consuming project buffer; the more buffer remaining, the more the project is completed ahead of schedule.

The fever chart is divided into three regions, green, yellow, and red, to denote a project's status or health (its "fever"). Yellow indicates a potential for the project to overrun its target date, and red means a strong potential. Whenever a project falls into yellow or red, a flag is raised telling the project manager to seek out the task in the project causing the problem (i.e., the task consuming the buffer). A sharp upward line anywhere on the chart also indicates a problem—that little progress is being made on the critical chain. Once the problematic task is identified, managers feed more resources to the task, decouple the task from the critical chain, or employ other strategies to remedy the problem. Every week the fever chart is updated and reviewed, and quick remedial action taken whenever the project veers out of the green zone.

The buffer status of a project indicates the *risk* of not meeting the due date. In companies where multiple projects are executed concurrently, the relative buffer status of projects can be used to reallocate resources to the projects with the highest risk of not meeting due dates.

The fever chart is but one way to manage time buffers.[17] The following explains another.

Example 5: Doling Out the Reserves: The Mars Pathfinder Project[18]

The goal of the Pathfinder project was to land on Mars a skateboard-sized, self-propelled, six-wheel rover that would move over the terrain and send back photos and scientific data (Figure 11-6). The project had a budget reserve of $40 million, which represented 30 percent of the total project budget (a large percentage, common in risky technological projects) and schedule reserve of 20 weeks out of the project's 37-month design, build, and test schedule.

Once the project was underway the question arose: How should the reserves be used? Use them too freely and too early and you have nothing left for later when they might be needed. Use them too stingily and you stifle progress, increase risk, and end up with leftover reserves that might have been put to good use. The guideline adopted for use of the reserves was to set hard limits on the amount to be released in each period of the project. For example, *none* of the schedule reserve was to be used (no slippage allowed) until the start of system assembly and test—near the halfway point in the project. But when problems arose, something had to give way so the project wouldn't fall behind; hence the guideline was to commit whatever budget reserves necessary to keep the project on schedule. (Time was a strategic issue and had priority because the launch date had to coincide with the exact relative positioning of Earth and Mars.)

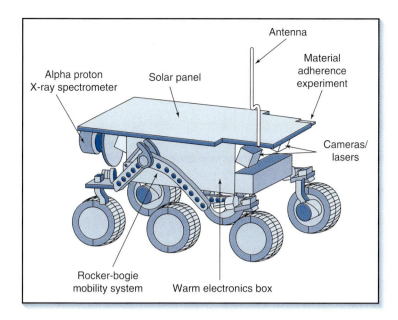

Figure 11-6
The Mars
Pathfinder rover.

The project was a success. Pathfinder landed safely and the little rover sent back thousands of pictures. The project established a new standard in its use of imaginative new approaches to design, build, and land a spacecraft in half the time and at 1/20th the cost of previous Mars missions.

Fight Tendency to Multitask
Do not interrupt work on a particular task or project by interspersing it with work from other tasks or projects. Determine the priority of the tasks or projects and then work continuously on the high priority ones until they are completed. As discussed in Chapter 7, this reduces the total elapsed time to complete the work and eliminates worker confusion about what they should be concentrating on.

Frequently Report Activity Status
Tasks or work packages on the critical path should be prepared to start at the earliest possible time, but for that to happen they need to know the status of their predecessors. Especially in time-sensitive projects like Pathfinder, the status of every activity should be reported to successor activities on a daily basis stating the expected days remaining to complete and the earliest date when successors should expect to begin. In priority projects, the mandate is that *as soon as* immediate predecessors of a critical activity are completed, the group assigned the next activity will begin work immediately, even if it has to stop doing something else. In CCM, this capability is called a *resource buffer*.

Publicize Consequences of Schedule Delays and Benefits of Early Finish
Everyone—team members, subcontractors, and suppliers—should be informed about the negative consequences of a schedule overrun and the possible reward of finishing early. The project contract might include incentive payments for early project completion, or the budget extra money for bonus payments to workers and subcontractors who finish on time or early.

Other measures are also used to keep projects on schedule, as illustrated next.

Microsoft meets product launch dates by utilizing visual freeze, internal target ship dates, and time buffers in schedules. A "visual freeze" is a halt imposed on aspects of the product design that affects visual appearance to customers. The freeze date usually occurs at approximately the 40 percent mark of the schedule. Upon reaching that date, developers lock into the product its major features. Thereafter, few if any changes are allowed in major interface features (menus, dialog boxes, and document windows). Any change requests must be negotiated with the program manager, lead developer, and product manager. The freeze enables the user education group to prepare training and system documentation (side-items) in parallel with product final debugging and testing so the documentation will be ready in time for product release. Despite the apparent benefits of this tactic, managers say that sticking to the visual freeze date is difficult, late changes still happen, and many hours are spent redoing the documentation so it conforms to late changes in the product.

Microsoft also sets somewhat fixed "internal target dates" that pressure developers into deciding which product features must absolutely be included and which may be forgone. Without fixed dates, developers tend to keep adding product features and ignore the schedules. Given fixed ship dates, they must determine in advance which features to include so the product can be released to market on time.

To account for overlooked or poorly understood tasks, difficult bugs, and unforeseen changes in features, Microsoft also includes time buffers in project schedules. The buffers are used exclusively for uncertainties, not for routine or planned tasks. A time buffer can range from 20 percent of the total schedule time for application projects to 50 percent for totally new projects. Schedules for project teams do not show time buffers but only the internal ship dates, which are the launch dates announced to the public minus the time buffer.

Procurement Control[20]

The main contractor is responsible for the quality, schedule, and cost of all procured items in the project. Often, the project manager will visit and inspect the facilities of suppliers responsible for designing and producing these items to make sure they meet requirements. After the project is underway, each supplier's progress is monitored by visits to the supplier's site and frequent status reports from the supplier. The project manager reviews the subcontractors' and suppliers' progress and expenses, and does whatever necessary to prompt or assist them when problems arise. For all major outsourced material, equipment, and components, a contingency plan should be prepared, including possibly a contractual provision to transfer work to another supplier in case the original supplier encounters serious or unrecoverable problems. Such contingencies should be addressed in the procurement plan and the project risk plan.

Cost Control

Cost control tracks expenditures versus budgets to detect variances, and seeks to eliminate unauthorized or inappropriate expenditures and minimize or contain cost changes. It identifies why variances occur, when changes to cost baselines are necessary, and what cost changes are reflected in budgets and cost baselines.

Cost control happens at both the work-package level and the project level using the control accounts and the PCAS, described earlier. Through the PCAS, actual expenditures are tallied, validated, accumulated, and compared to budgeted costs. Periodically the project manager reviews actual and budgeted costs, compares the costs to assessments of the work completed, and estimates the project's completion cost and completion date using the methods described next.

11.11 PERFORMANCE ANALYSIS

Cost and Schedule Analysis with Earned Value

The status of the project or any portion of it can be assessed with three variables: BCWS, ACWP, and BCWP. These are industry-standard acronyms, but to save ink and conform with the project management institute (PMI) we will use the abbreviated terms PV, AC, and EV.

1. *PV* is the *planned value*—the sum cost of all work and apportioned effort scheduled to be completed in a given time period as specified in the *original budget*. It is the same as the amount in the time-phased budget mentioned before. For example, Table 8-5 and Figure 8-15 in Chapter 8 shows the cumulative and weekly PV for the LOGON project. In week 20, for example, to date PV is $512,000 and weekly PV is $83,000. PV is also referred to as *BCWS*—the *budgeted cost of the work scheduled*.

2. *AC (ACWP)* is the *actual cost of the work performed*—the actual expenditure incurred in a given time period. It is the sum of the actual costs for all completed and started (but not completed) work packages plus the associated overhead.

3. *EV* is the *earned value* (also termed the *budgeted cost of the work performed—BCWP*), which is determined by looking at the amount of work performed thus far (fully and partially completed work packages) as well as the amount that work was supposed to have cost according to the *budget*.[21] Thus,

   • The EV for a completed work task is the same as the PV for that task.

   • The EV for a partially completed work task is computed based upon the estimated *percent complete* or the task. (It is alternatively computed by taking 50 percent of PV when the task is started, then the other 50 percent when the task is completed.)

Following is an example that illustrates how to compute EV.

Example 7: EV Versus PV in the Parmete Company

The Parmete Company has a $200,000 fixed-cost contract to install 1,000 new parking meters. The contract calls for removing old parking meters from their stands and replacing them with new ones. The cost for this is $200 per meter.

Parmete estimates that 25 meters can be installed each day. At that rate and a cost of $200 per meter the project should take 40 working days to finish and have a final PV of $200,000. Also on that basis, the planned value of the work scheduled (PV) as of any given day can be determined by multiplying the number of working days completed as of that day by the cost of installing 25 meters ($200 times 25). For example, as of day 18,

$$PV = 18 \text{ days} \times (25 \text{ meters}) \times (\$200) = \$90,000$$

That is to say, as of the 18th day work on the project, according to the project schedule and budget $90,000 worth of work should have been done. Notice that PV is always associated with a specific date on the project schedule.
In contrast, the *earned value* (EV) for any given day represents the value of the work *actually* done in terms of the budget. In this project, EV is the number of meters *actually* installed to date times the $200 budgeted for each. Suppose, for example, that as of the 18th 400 meters had been installed; thus,

$$EV = (400 \text{ meters}) \times (\$200) = \$80,000$$

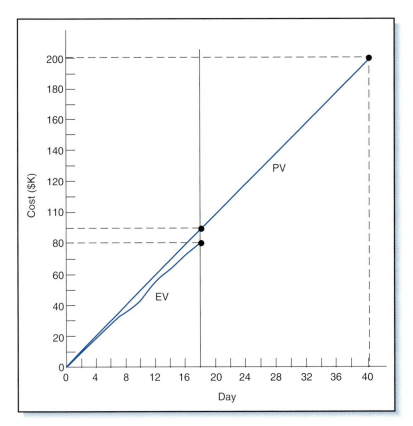

Figure 11-7
Graph of PV and EV.

In other words, as of the 18th day, $80,000 worth of work has been performed. Now, given that $90,000 was the amount of work that was *supposed* to have been performed, the project is $10,000 worth of work *behind schedule*. Notice, the $10,000 does not represent a cost savings, but rather the value of work that should have been but was not done. It represents 50 parking meters, or 2 days worth of work, meaning that as of the 18th day the project is 2 days behind schedule. (The 2 days is referred to as the *time variance*, or TV.) Thus, EV represents a translation of project cost into work progress. As of day 18, this project has made only 16 days' worth of work progress. This is represented on the graph for PV and EV in Figure 11-7.

As stated, besides completed tasks, the EV must also reflect tasks started but not yet completed (open tasks). For example, suppose that before quitting at the end of the 18th day the meter installer had just enough time to remove an old meter but not to put in a new one. Therefore, the work on that meter was 50 percent completed. If this was the 401st, then the EV would be the full cost for the first 400 meters plus 50 percent of the cost for the 401st.

$$EV = \$80,000 + (0.50)(\$200) = \$80,100$$

Thus, as of day 18 the EV would be $80,100, which is slightly more than 16 days of work completed. (Actually, it represents $80,100/(25 × $200) = 16.02 days of work, which puts the project 1.98 days behind schedule, but such precision is usually unwarranted.)

When taken together, the variables PV, AC, and EV can be used to compute variances that reveal different aspects about the status of a project. For example, assume for the LOGON project as of week 20, shown in the graph in Figure 11-8.

$$PV = \$512,000$$
$$AC = \$530,000$$
$$EV = \$429,000$$

Using these figures, four kinds of variances can be determined:

1. *Schedule variance*: SV = EV − PV = −$83,000.
2. *Time variance*: TV = SD − BCSP (where SD is the "status date" (here week 20) and BCSP is the date where PV = EV (about week 19 from Figure 11-8)).
   = (20 − 19) = 1 week.
3. *Cost variance*: CV = EV − AC = −$101,000.

The SV shows that the total work completed as of week 20 is $83,000 less than planned, suggesting that the project is behind schedule (the negative value indicates that the project is behind schedule; a positive value would suggest the project is ahead of schedule).

Figure 11-8
LOGON project status as of week 20.

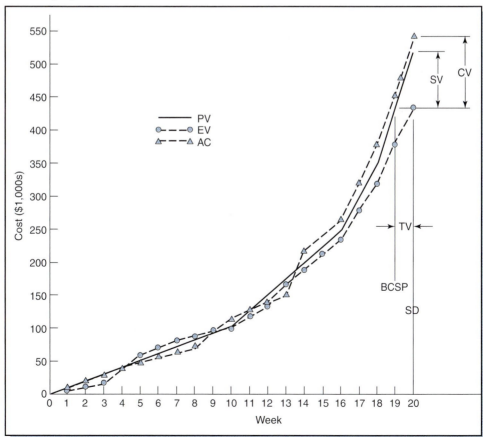

The TV represents how much the project is behind schedule, in this case about 1 week because only $429,000 worth of work has been completed (EV), which is roughly the value of work scheduled (PV) to have been completed a week earlier.

The CV of –$101,000 indicates the financial status of work, indicating that LOGON is overspending. Given that it compares the earned value of work completed with actual costs, a negative CV indicates that the project is overspending while a positive figure indicates underspending for the work performed.

Work-Package Analysis and Performance Indices

Determining the status of the project requires information about the performances of all work packages. With information from the PCAS, charts similar to Figure 11-4 and Figure 11-8 can be prepared for every work package and cost account.

Consider the status of the LOGON project as of week 20. Referring to Figure 11-4, activities H, I, and, J have been completed and are closed, and activities K–Q are "open" and in progress. This Gantt chart gives a general *overview* of work package and project status, but to determine the origins and sizes of project problems it is necessary to assess each activity in more detail. This is done by computing two *performance indices* for each work package:

1. *Schedule performance index*: SPI = EV/PV
2. *Cost performance index*: CPI = EV/AC

Values of SPI and CPI greater than 1.0 indicate that work is ahead of schedule (SV positive) and underbudget (positive CV), respectively; values less than 1.0 indicate the opposite.

Table 11-1 shows cost and variance information for all LOGON activities as of week 20. The performance indices CPI and SPI show trouble spots and their relative magnitude: L, M, and Q have fallen the most behind schedule (they have the smallest SPIs), and L and M have had the greatest cost overruns relative to their sizes (they have the smallest CPIs). The overall project is "somewhat" behind schedule and over cost (SPI = 0.84; CPI = 0.81).

Focusing on *only* the project level or *only* the work-package level to determine project status can be misleading, and the project manager should scan both, back

Table 11-1 LOGON performance report week 20 cumulative to date.

ACTIVITY	PV	AC	EV	SV	CV	SPI	CPI
H*	100	100	100	0	0	1.00	1.00
I*	64	70	64	0	–6	1.00	0.91
J*	96	97	96	0	–1	1.00	0.99
K	16	12	14	–2	2	0.88	1.17
L	36	30	18	–18	–12	0.50	0.60
M	84	110	33	–51	–77	0.39	0.30
N	40	45	40	0	–5	1.00	0.89
O	20	28	24	4	–4	1.20	0.86
P	24	22	24	0	2	1.00	1.09
Q	32	16	16	–16	0	0.50	1.00
Project	512	530	429	–83	–101	0.84	0.81

*Completed

and forth. If she looks only at the project level, good performance of some activities will overshadow and hide poor performance in others. If she focuses only on individual work packages, the cumulative effect from slightly poor performance in many activities can easily be overlooked. Even small cost overruns in many individual work packages can add up to a large overrun for the project.

The importance of examining variances at both project and work-package levels is illustrated in the following example. The SV in Figure 11-8 (which is $-\$83,000$) suggests that the LOGON project is behind schedule, and TV = 1. However, scrutinizing Figure 11-4 reveals that one of the work packages behind schedule is Activity M, which happens to be on the critical path (see Chapter 6, Figure 6-8). Thus, because activity M appears to be about 3 weeks behind schedule (Figure 11-4), the project must also be 3 weeks behind schedule—*not* 1 week as estimated by the project level analysis.

The importance of monitoring performance at the work-package level is further illustrated by an example in the ROSEBUD project. Figure 11-9 is the cost report for Work Package L for month 2. This report would likely be available to managers about 2 or 3 weeks into month 3. The numbers in the PV columns are derived from the month 2 column in the budget plan in Figure 8-7, Chapter 8. Current and cumulative numbers are the same because Work Package L begins in month 2.

The performance indices for ROSEBUD Work Package L are

$$SPI = EV/PV = 0.80$$
$$CPI = EV/AC = 0.74$$

indicating both schedule and cost overruns as of month 2. Suppose the project manager investigates the costs for Work Package L and finds the following:

First, although AC and PV for direct labor are equal, PV reflects the estimate that only 80 percent of work scheduled for the period was actually performed (EV = PV × SPI = 6050 × 0.80 = 4850). Second, although AC and PV for direct labor are equal, the AC and PV for labor overhead are different. Suppose the difference was due to an increase in the labor overhead rate from 75 percent to 90 percent during month 2. Whereas PV would reflect the old rate (0.75 × 6050 = 4538), AC would

Figure 11-9
Cost chart for ROSEBUD project as of month 2.

Project ROSEBUD						Date Month 2				
Department Programming						Work Package L Software specifications				

Charge	Current Period					Cumulative to date				
	PV	EV	AC	SV	CV	PV	EV	AC	SV	CV
Direct labor Professional Associate Assistant										
Direct labor cost Labor overhead Other direct cost	6,050 4,538	4,840 3,630	6,050 5,445	−1,210 −908	−1,210 −1,815	6,050 4,538	4,840 3,630	6,050 5,445	−1,210 −908	−1,210 −1,815
Total direct cost General/administrative	10,588 1,059	8,470 847	11,495 1,150	−2,118 −212	−3,025 −303	10,588 1,059	8,470 847	11,495 1,150	−2,118 −212	−3,025 −303
Total costs	11,647	9,317	12,645	−2,330	−3,328	11,647	9,317	12,645	−2,330	−3,328

Note: EV is for 80 percent of work scheduled and labor overhead is increased to 90 percent of labor cost.

SPI: EV/PV = 0.80   CPI EV/AC = 0.74

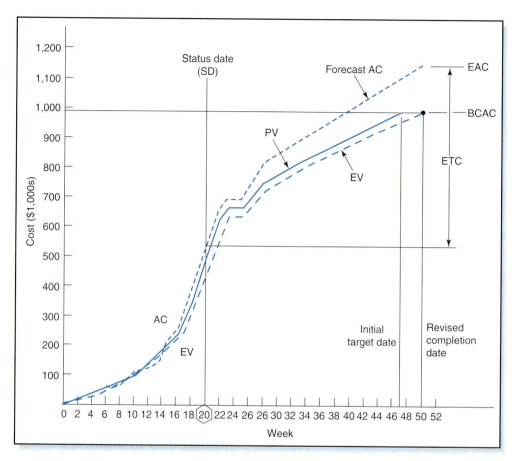

Figure 11-13
LOGON Project status chart and forecast as of week 20.

is probably more realistic than week 50 because it accounts for current ability to meet the schedule.

Effect of Uncertainty

The EAC is based upon a single-value assessment of progress—the EV as of the SD. Often this assessment is based upon opinions about the percent complete, which means it is subject to uncertainty. If the EV is subject to uncertainty, then so is the EAC. A way to account for this uncertainty is to consider a *range* of EACs.[23] The range would consider optimistic, pessimistic, and most likely values of EAC and be interpreted probabilistically, as illustrated next.

Example 12: Uncertainty in Forecasted EAC and Completion Date

For the LOGON project the EV as of week 20 is $429,000. With the project budgeted at $990,000, this means the project is 43.3 percent completed. Suppose that an expert looks at the project and concludes that in actuality it is somewhere between 35 percent and 48 percent completed. These represent the pessimistic and optimistic scenarios, respectively. The corresponding EVs are:

Pessimistic	0.35($990,000)	= $346,500
Most likely	(given)	= $429,000
Optimistic	0.48($990,000)	= $475,200

Given that as of week 20 the AC = \$530,000 and PV = \$512,000, the range of possible CPIs, SPIs, EACs, and forecast completion dates are:

	CPI	EAC (\$)	SPI	Week, PV scheduled[a]	Revised week of completion[b]
Pessimistic	0.65	1,322,308	0.68	18	62.6
Most likely	0.81	1,222,593	0.84	19	53.3
Optimistic	0.90	1,102,222	0.93	19.5	49.6

[a]Approximate week where EV = current PV (see PV curve, Figure 11-13). For example, pessimistic EV = 346,500 since from Figure 11-13, PV = 346,500 at about Week 18.
[b]20 weeks + (47 weeks − (PV, scheduled))/SPI.

Figure 11-14 shows three points representing the forecasted costs (EAC) and revised completion times, and the associated EAC and completion-time probability distributions.

The estimated completion times do not reflect which, if any, of the current behind-schedule activities are on the critical path; they reflect only the current rate at which the work is being done and assume that the pace of work is uniform everywhere in the project, on critical and noncritical tasks alike.

Figure 11-14
Estimated cost at completion (EAC) and completion times.

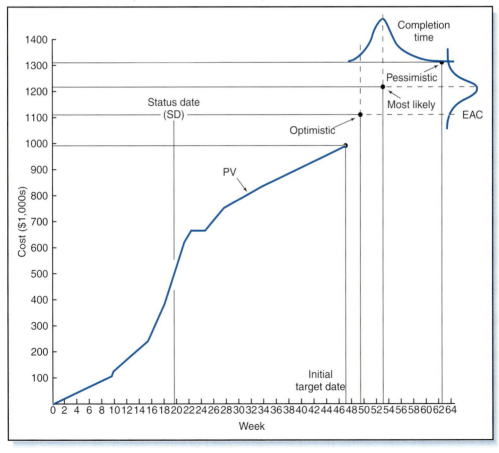

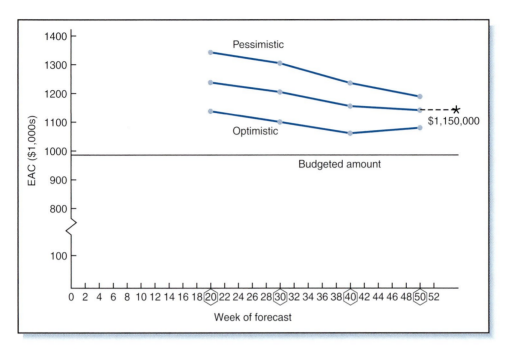

Figure 11-15
Plots of pessimistic, most likely, and optimistic EACs at four review periods.

The three measures for cost and time (optimistic, most likely, pessimistic) can be forecasted at periodic intervals throughout the project. The procedure for forecasting at week 20 (Example 11) may be repeated, for instance, at weeks 30, 40, and 50. Figure 11-15 shows plots of pessimistic, most likely, and optimistic EAC forecasts made at 10-week intervals starting at week 20. (Similarly, plots of periodic forecasts for optimistic, most likely, and pessimistic *completion times* can also be constructed.) The convergence of the pessimistic and optimistic forecasts in the figure as the project moves toward completion illustrates increasing certainty about the EAC and suggests that the project is heading toward a most likely EAC of $1,150,000.

11.13 MONITORING PERFORMANCE INDEXES AND VARIANCES

Projects are largely monitored and controlled at the work-package level, though project managers also do periodic quick checks at the project level. They often have so many work packages that it is impossible to check every one on a frequent basis; with a project level check, the project manager can get a quick "ballpark" estimate of the project's performance. Although the estimate is somewhat inaccurate, in general, frequent, slightly inaccurate information on time is better than very accurate information that is too late.

One way to track project performance trends is to follow a plot of SPI against CPI, as shown in Figure 11-16 for the LOGON project. According to the plot, which shows performance for 20 weeks, LOGON started out in the marginal and poor regions, briefly recovered, and then drifted disturbingly back to and *remained* in the poor region. In such a case, the project manager would talk to team leaders and functional

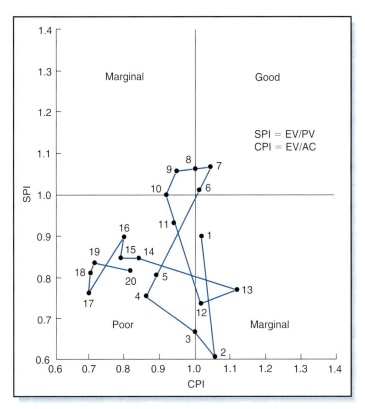

Figure 11-16
LOGON project cost/schedule performance plotted for months 1–20.

Table 11-2 Example of variance boundaries.

Work Package A	Variances greater than $2,000
Work Package B	Variances greater than $18,000
Department C	Variances greater than $6,000
Department D	Variances greater than $38,000
Project	Variances greater than $55,000

managers to identify detailed causes of the problems. Plots like Figure 11-16 can be maintained for individual work packages to quickly spot troublesome trends.

Seldom do actual and planned performance measures coincide; as a result, nonzero variances are more often the rule than the exception. This leads to the question: what amount of variance is acceptable before action must be taken?

At each level of the project organization—work package, departmental, and project—critical values or *variance limits* are established as being "acceptable." Limits can be set on variances for any level or element of the project, shown in Table 11-2. Only when a variance falls beyond the limit are corrective measures considered. Some variance limits are set to remain constant throughout the entire project, others to vary. In research projects, for example, variance limits are set somewhat large early in the project, and are reduced as stages of the project are completed. This coincides with project uncertainty, which starts out large but diminishes as the project progresses.

and operation of the end-item system, its subsystems, and components, which is the *configuration management* process covered in Chapter 9. Whenever an aspect of the design (e.g., a performance criterion) or element of a project plan (e.g., scope statement, schedule, or budget) is first approved, it is referred to as the *baseline*; subsequently, anytime the baseline is altered to incorporate approved changes, it is referred to as second baseline, third baseline, and so on.

The change control system includes strict procedures to control and minimize design and work changes; these include:[26]

- Requiring that original work scope and work orders (with specific schedules, budgets, and statements of work) are clearly stated and *agreed to* by persons responsible.
- Close monitoring of work to ensure it is *meeting* (not exceeding) specifications.
- Careful screening of tasks for cost or schedule overruns (potentially signifying a change in work scope) and quick action to correct problems.
- Requiring a prespecified request and approval process of all discretionary changes.
- Requiring similar control procedures of all subcontractors and suppliers for all purchase orders, test requests, and so on.
- Assessing the impact of all necessary or de facto changes on the end-item and project, and revising designs and plans to reflect the impact.
- Freezing the project against all nonessential changes at a predefined phase. The freeze prohibits additional changes to the design so that the next stage (procurement, fabrication, construction, or coding and testing) can begin. The freeze point must be agreed to by management early in the project and project personnel reminded of it.

The process, summarized in Figure 11-17, ensures that all design and work changes are (1) documented as to their effect on work orders, budgets, schedules, and contractual prices; (2) formally reviewed; and (3) assessed and accepted or rejected. The process

Figure 11-17
Change control process.

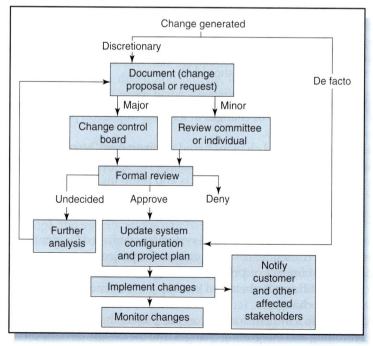

IRON *Butterfly Corp*			
Change request			Page ... of ...
Title:			
Project no.	Task no.	Revision no.	Date issued
Description of change			
Reason for change			
Documentation attached			
Originated by:	Date:		
Request logged by:	Date:		
Cost implications			
Schedule implications			
Implications on performance of deliverable(s)			
Other implications (risks & issues)			
Proposed plan for implementation			
Implications evaluated by:		Date:	
Recommendation			
Recommended by:		Date:	
Documentation attached			
Approved by:	Date:	Approved by:	Date:

Figure 11-18
Example of change request document.

accounts for both discretionary changes as well as de facto changes. The former are those subject to a formal review and approval or denial decision; the latter are those that *must* be approved either because they are mandated or, in fact, have already occurred.

An essential part of the process is the change proposal or change request document (Figure 11-18), which provides the information and rationale for the proposed change. Any project team member or other stakeholder can request a change by filing a change proposal. The same change control process is applied to everyone, regardless of role, title, or position.

Often, a committee called a *change control board* handles the process. In large projects, the change board consists of the project manager and managers from engineering, manufacturing, purchasing, contract administration, the customer, and other areas, and meets weekly to review change requests. The effects of proposed changes are estimated prior to the meeting, at which time the board decides which changes to reject and which to accept.

Any proposed or enacted change that impacts the time, cost, or nature of work of a single task or other related tasks must be documented. Because everyone involved in the project has the potential to recognize or originate changes, everyone must be on the watch for changes and held accountable for bringing them to the attention of the project manager.

11.15 CONTRACT ADMINISTRATION

Project control includes the ongoing comparison of project activities, changes, and accomplishments to requirements as stipulated in the contract, as well as invoicing the customer and the payment of bills. Ensuring that commitments of the developer/contractor and the customer as specified in the contract are met is the function of *contract administration*.[27]

As an aspect of project control but pertaining exclusively to contracted work, contract administration includes authorizing work to begin; monitoring work with respect to budgets, schedules, and technical performance; ensuring quality; controlling changes; and sending or receiving payments for work completed. Contract administration ensures that change requests for contracted work are assessed against the conditions stated in the contract, and that any necessary changes are made to the contract before proceeding with work. It also assures that all necessary approvals are secured before the contract is modified and the changes implemented. The project manager administers all of this through procedures similar to those already described for task authorization, performance tracking and reporting, and change control. When the contract incorporates customer-specified measures or requirements for project monitoring and reporting, the project control system must incorporate the specified measures into the usual performance tracking and progress reporting system.

The process must also ensure that customers are invoiced for services and materials as specified in the contract, and that subcontractors and suppliers are paid. For simple projects, billing and payment tracking is done through the contractor's accounts receivable system; for large, complex projects, it is handled through a dedicated billing and payments tracking system.

11.16 CONTROL PROBLEMS

Regardless of the thoroughness and conscientiousness of the project manager, or of the sophistication of the project control system, problems still occur. Roman notes the following:[28]

1. The control process focuses on one factor such as cost, and ignores others such as schedule and technical performance. This happens when control procedures are issued by one functional area such as accounting or finance, and other areas are not involved. Forcing compliance to one factor distorts the control process and usually results in excesses or slips in other areas. For example, overemphasis on costs can lead to schedule delays or shoddy workmanship.
2. Project team members resist or do not comply with control procedures. They do not understand the benefits or necessity of using formal controls, and resent attempts to evaluate and control their work. Managers encourage this noncompliance when they fail to exercise sanctions against people who defy the procedures.
3. Project team members aware of problems do not accurately or fully report them. They may not understand the situation or, if they do, may be hesitant to reveal it. The information they report may be fragmented and difficult to piece together.
4. Control systems that rely entirely on self-appraisal of work progress and quality may force people to act defensively and provide prejudiced information. Bias is one of the biggest obstacles to achieving accurate reporting and control.
5. Managers act indifferently about controversial issues, believing that with time they will resolve themselves. This leads some workers to believe that management doesn't care about the control process, an attitude likely to spread to others throughout the project.

6. Managers overseeing several projects sometimes misrepresent charges so as to offset poor performance in one project by good performance in others. The practice is somewhat common in organizations having multiple contracts with the same customer as a means of avoiding the bureaucracy and overall satisfying requirements on all the contracts, but it distorts the historical data that might be used for planning and estimating future projects, and is unethical because it can result in mischarging the customer.

7. The information reporting and accounting mechanisms are inaccurate or misleading. Full reliance on subjective measures such as the earned value of open work packages can suggest that more work was completed than actually was; similarly, a bad situation can be made to look favorable simply by altering accounting procedures.

To minimize these problems, upper, functional, and project managers must actively support the control process, and everyone in the project must understand the relevancy of the control process and how it benefits the project. The control process and performance measures must be impersonal, objective, and uniformly applied to all people, tasks, areas, and suppliers.

11.17 SUMMARY

The Execution phase typically includes the stages of *design, production/build*, and *implementation*. During the design stage the system concept is broken into tiers of subsystems, components and parts, and for each of these designs, drawings, schematics, and models are created. The process has two interrelated activities: one is preparation of a *functional* design that shows the system components and their relationships; the other is preparation of a *physical* design, which shows what the actual system and its components will look like. Project management is responsible for coordinating the design activities, and for controlling changes to the design throughout the process

The main activities in the production/build stage are fabrication and testing. In this stage, components are assembled and the end-item system is produced. Work quality is constantly assessed through a variety of tests to ensure that requirements for the system and its components are met. A detailed plan for system implementation and project closeout is prepared.

Throughout the Execution phase, the project control process guides work, ensures effective utilization of resources, and corrects problems. It monitors cost, time, and work progress and keeps the project moving toward scope, budget, schedule, and quality objectives. The focal point of the control process is individual work packages and cost accounts. Virtually all control activities—authorization, data collection, progress evaluation, problem assessment, and corrective action—occur at the work-package/cost-account level. Because higher-level cost accounts are built up through the WBS and organizational hierarchies, project cost and schedule variances can be traced through the cost-account structure to locate the sources of problems.

The control process begins with authorization; once authorized, work is continually tracked with reference to the project plan for conformance to scope, quality, schedules, and budgets. Key technical measures are monitored to gauge progress toward meeting technical objectives. Performance to date is reviewed using the concept of earned value, and estimates of project cost and completion date are revised.

Variances in costs and schedules are compared to preestablished limits. Whenever variances move beyond acceptable limits, or when new opportunities or intractable problems arise, the work must be replanned and rescheduled. Such changes are inevitable, though every effort is made to minimize their impact on cost and schedule overruns. A formal change control and configuration management process ensures that all changes are authorized, documented, and communicated.

The next chapter concludes the discussion of project control and covers the topics of project evaluation, reporting, and communication. It also covers the remainder of the project life cycle—system implementation and project closeout—and the last phase of the systems development cycle, operation.

Summary of Variables

PV = BCWS = budgeted cost of work scheduled (planned value)
AC = ACWP = actual cost of work performed
EV = BCWP = budgeted cost of work performed (earned value)
SV $\qquad$ = schedule variance = EV − PV
CV $\qquad$ = cost variance = EV − AC
BAC $\qquad$ = budgeted cost of project at completion
SPI $\qquad$ = schedule performance index = EV/PV
CPI $\qquad$ = cost performance index = EV/AC
ETC $\qquad$ = forecast cost to complete project = (BAC − EV)/CPI
EAC $\qquad$ = estimated cost of project at completion = AC + ETC

REVIEW QUESTIONS AND PROBLEMS

1. What is the practice of "fast-tracking?" What are the associated potential benefits and dangers?
2. What happens during the design stage? Who is involved? What do they do? What is the role of the project manager? How are design changes monitored and controlled?
3. What is the role of interaction design in design and development?
4. What does the plan for production/build include?
5. What happens during the production or building stage? How is work planned and coordinated? Who oversees the work?
6. What is the distinction between the project end-item and project side-items? What role does the project manager have regarding each?
7. What is contract administration?
8. What are the three phases of the project control process?
9. Explain the differences between internal and external project controls.
10. How are overhead expenses allocated in work packages?
11. If a cost or schedule variance is noticed at the project level, how is it traced to the source of the variance?
12. Describe the typical pattern of work authorization. What is usually included on a work order?
13. Describe the process of collecting data about the cost, schedule, and work accomplished.
14. Discuss different ways of measuring ongoing work progress.

15. Why is scope change control an important part of the project control process?

16. Discuss quality control as applied to projects.

17. What are the principal causes of project schedule overruns? Discuss at least four practices that may be used to reduce schedule variability and keep projects on schedule.

18. Explain PV, AC, and EV, and how they are used to determine the variances AV, SV, CV, and TV. Explain the meaning of these variances.

19. What does it signify if cost or schedule index figures are less than 1.00?

20. Explain TPM, its purpose, and how it is conducted.

21. Explain what is meant by a forecast "to complete" (ETC) and how this forecast is related to the "at completion" forecast (EAC).

22. Discuss reasons why the project manager frequently resists project changes.

23. What should a change control system guarantee? Describe procedures that minimize unnecessary changes.

24. What aspects of project control fall under contract administration?

25. What are some difficulties encountered when attempting project control?

26. Use the networks in Figure 11-19 to determine ES, LS, EF, and LF for all the activities (activity numbers indicate duration in days). Apply the buffer concept to the critical path. For network (a) use a 3-week time buffer for the critical path, a 1-week time buffer for every path that connects to the critical path. For network (b) use a 4-week time buffer on the critical path, and a 2-week time buffer for every path that connects to the critical path.

27. In the LOGON project suppose the status of the project as of week 22 is as follows (note usage of the longer acronyms; some project management software use these and not the shorter acronyms PV, AC, and EV).

$$BCWS = \$628{,}000$$
$$ACWP = \$640{,}000$$
$$BCWP = \$590{,}000$$

Figure 11-19
Two project networks.

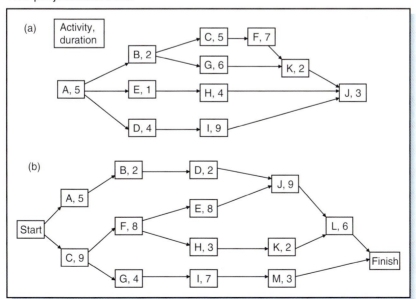

Answer the following questions:

(a) What is the earned value of the project as of week 22?

(b) Compute SV and CV.

(c) Draw a status graph similar to Figure 11-13 and plot BCWS, ACWP, and BCWP. Show SV and CV. Determine TV from the graph.

(d) Compute SPI and CPI. Has the project performance improved or worsened since week 20?

(e) Using BAC = $990,000, compute ETC and EAC. How does EAC compare to the week 20 estimate of $1,222,593? From your status chart determine the revised completion date. How does it compare to the revised date (week 48–49) as of week 20?

(f) Are the results from (e) consistent with the results from (d) regarding improvement or deterioration of project performance since week 20?

28. For a particular work package, as of April 30 the budgeted cost is $18,000. The supervisor determines that only 80 percent of the scheduled work has been completed and the actual expense is $19,000. What is the BCWP? Compute SV, CV, SPI, and CPI for the work package.

29. Using the status chart in Figure 11-20:

(a) Estimate SV, CV, and TV, and compute SPI and CPI for week 30. Interpret the results.

(b) Compute ETC and EAC. Estimate the revised completion date and sketch the lines for forecast AC and forecast EV.

30. Assume for the following problems that work continues during weekends.

(a) A task is planned to start on April 30 and takes 20 days to complete. The actual start date is May 3. After 4 days of work the supervisor estimates that the task is 25 percent completed. If the work rate stays the same, what is the forecast date of completion?

(b) Task C has two immediate predecessors, tasks A and B. Task A is planned to take 5 days to complete; Task B is planned to take 10 days. The early

Figure 11-20
Project status as of week 30.

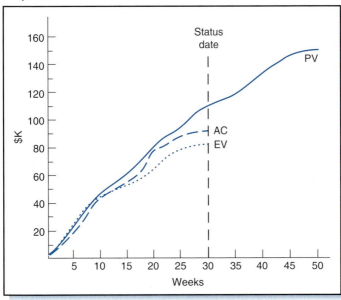

start time for both tasks is August 1. The actual start dates for tasks A and B are August 2 and August 1, respectively. At the end of August 4, Task A is assessed to be 20 percent completed and Task B, 30 percent completed. What is the expected early start time for Task C?

31. Refer back to Problem 27. Assume the $590,000 indicated for week 22 is the most likely EV. Given a BAC of $990,000, this represents 59.6 percent of the project completed. Suppose an expert assesses the LOGON project at that time using various measures and concludes that LOGON is between 50 percent and 65 percent completed. Let these represent pessimistic and optimistic scenarios. Compute the corresponding pessimistic, most likely and optimistic scenarios. Compute the corresponding pessimistic, most likely, and optimistic CPIs, SPIs, EACs, and forecast the corresponding completion dates for the project.

32. Refer back to Problem 26, Figure 11-19.

   (a) For network (a), suppose after 7 weeks, activities A, B, and E have been completed, D is 50 percent completed, and C is 80 percent completed. What is the revised early completion date for the project?

   (b) For network (b), suppose after 25 weeks, activities A, B, C, F, E, G, and I have been completed, and D and H are ready to begin in week 26. What is the revised early completion date for the project?

33. For the following questions refer to Figure 11-21.

   As of week 5, for the project:

   (a) What is the planned value (PV)?

   (b) What is the earned value of the work completed (EV)?

   (c) What is actual cost of the project (AC)?

   (d) What is the value of work remaining?

   (e) What is the CPI?

Figure 11-21
Project status as of week 5.

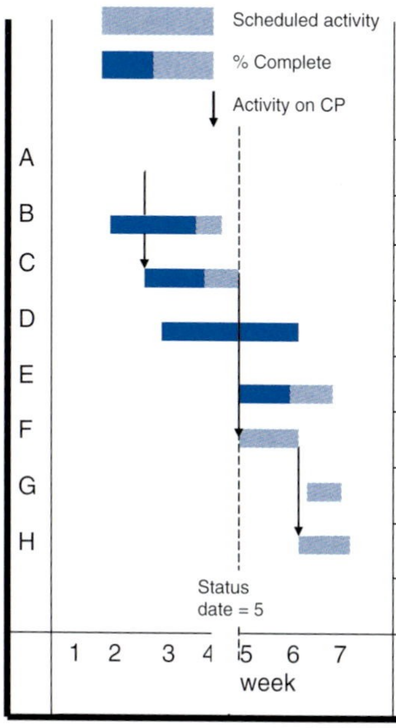

Project status as of Week 5

	Budget at completion	% Sched uled	PV = BCWS	% Comp lete	EV = BCWP	AC = ACWP
A	A 200	100	0	100	200	240
B	B 1,000	100		70		900
C	C 400	100		60		300
D	D 1,200	50		100		500
E	E 800	0		50		440
F	F 900	0		0		0
G	G 300	0		0		0
H	H 500	0		0		0
	4300					

Status date = 5

1 2 3 4 5 6 7 week

(f) What is estimated cost to complete the project (ETC)?

(g) What is the forecasted cost at completion (EAC)?

(h) What is the estimated cost variance at completion, and the percent overrun or underrun?

(i) According to EV, is the project ahead or behind schedule?

(j) According to the critical path, is the project ahead or behind schedule?

QUESTIONS ABOUT THE STUDY PROJECT

1. What kinds of external controls, if any, were imposed by the client on the project?
2. What kinds of internal control measures were used? (For instance, work package control, cost-account control, etc.) Describe.
3. Describe the project control process:

   - How was work authorized to begin? Describe examples of work authorization orders.
   - How was data collected to monitor work? Explain the methods and procedures (time cards, invoices, etc.).
   - How was the data tallied and summarized?
   - How was the data validated?

4. Was the concept of earned value used?
5. How was project performance monitored? What performance and variance measures were used? Who did it? How often?
6. How were problems pinpointed and tracked?
7. Were forecasting "to complete" and "at completion" used? If so, how and by whom?
8. Were variance limits established for project cost and performance? What were they? How were they applied?
9. When cost, schedule, or performance problems occurred, what action did the project manager take? Give examples of problems and what the project manager did.
10. What changes to the product or project goal occurred during the project? Describe the change control process used in the project. How were changes to the project plan and systems specifications reviewed, authorized, and communicated? Show examples of change request and authorization documents.

Case 11-1 *The Cybersonic Project*

The Cybersonic project is off to a good start. Careful attention was given to preparing detailed objectives and requirements, well-defined work packages, assignments and responsibilities, a schedule, and a budget.

The project manager, Miles Wilder, considers himself a "project manager's project manager." He claims to know and use the principles of good project management, starting with having a good plan and then carefully tracking the project. He announces to his team leaders that status meetings will be held on alternating Mondays throughout the duration of the year-long project. All 18 project team leaders are instructed to attend these and give a brief rundown on the tasks on which they are currently working.

At the first status meeting, all of the team leaders show up. Seven of them are currently managing work for the project and are scheduled to give reports; the other 11 are not yet working on the project (as specified by the project schedule), but attend because Miles wants to keep them informed about the project progress. The meeting is scheduled for 3 hours, during which the team leaders are to give oral reports about whatever they think is important. After almost 5 hours of reports by five of the leaders, Miles ends the meeting. Several major problems are reported that Miles tries to resolve at the meeting. Specific actions to resolve some of the problems are decided, and Miles schedules another meeting for the afternoon 2 days later to address remaining problems and hear the remaining two reports. Some of the team leaders are miffed because they will have to change their schedules to attend this new meeting.

Miles arrives an hour late at the next meeting, which, after 3 hours, gives the team only enough time to resolve problems raised at the first meeting. There is not enough time for two team leaders to give their first reports. Miles asks these leaders whether any major issues or problems with their tasks have occurred. When they respond, "no," he lets them skip their reports, promising to start with them at the next meeting in 2 weeks. A few of the team leaders are assigned actions to address current problems. Some of the attendees feel the meeting was a waste of time.

Before the next status meeting, a few of the team leaders inform Miles they cannot attend and will send representatives. This meeting becomes problematic for three reasons. First, several new problems about the project are raised and, again, the ensuing discussion drags out so that there is not enough time for everyone to give a status report. Second, during the 5-hour long meeting, only six team leaders of a scheduled eight give their reports. Also, some of the team leaders disagree with Miles about actions assigned at the previous meeting. Because no minutes had been taken at that meeting, each leader had followed his/her own notes about actions to take, many of which now conflict with Miles' expectations. Further, people at the meeting who are "representatives" are not fully aware of what was discussed at the previous meetings, do not have sufficient information to give complete reports or answer questions, and are hesitant to commit to action without their team leaders' approval.

The next several meetings follow the same pattern. They run longer than scheduled. Fewer team leaders and more representatives attend. Some status reports are not given because of inadequate time. Attendees disagree over problems identified and actions to be taken. Some meetings are rescheduled or canceled because Miles cannot attend. The project falls behind schedule because problems are not addressed adequately or quickly enough.

Miles feels that too much time at the meetings has been spent resolving problems and that many of them should instead have been resolved by the team leaders. He instructs the leaders to work out solutions and changes on their own, and to report at status meetings only the results. This reduces the length of the meetings but creates other complications: some of the team leaders take actions and make changes that ignore project dependencies and conflict with the schedules and work tasks of other team leaders. Even though everyone is working overtime, the Cybersonic project falls further behind schedule.

QUESTIONS

1. Why is Miles' approach to tracking and controlling the Cybersonic project ineffective?

2. If you were in charge, what would you do?

Case 11-2   SA Gold Mine: Earned Value After a Scope Change[29]

The team at SA gold mine was tasked to sink a 2,000 meter deep ventilation shaft, and then to excavate room for a station at the bottom of the shaft. The approved plan was to sink the shaft within 20 months at a cost of R65,000 (approximately US $10,000) per meter of shaft depth. For the station at the bottom, 30,000 cubic meter of rock would have to be excavated within 3 months

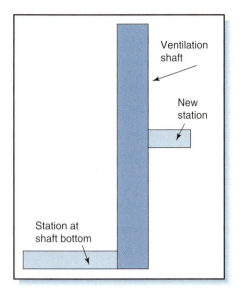

Figure 11-22

at a cost of R700 per cubic meter. The plan assumed a straight line earned value over time.

After the work had begun, the scope of the project was changed to include excavation for a new station halfway down the shaft (Figure 11-22) with a volume of 20,000 cubic meters. It was agreed that the additional work had to be done at the same excavation rate as the bottom station, but since removal of the rock required hoisting of only 1,000 meters instead of 2,000 meters for the bottom station, the team agreed on the cost of R500 per cubic meter (compared to the R700 budgeted for the bottom station). Since working space

and other resources available would limit the amount of work that could be done simultaneously, everyone agreed that the new station would delay the sinking of the shaft. After 13 months, the shaft had reached a depth of 1,400 meters below surface and excavation for the halfway station was completed. The actual cost at this time was R90 million, which was more than was budgeted for the period. This aggravated a cash-flow problem at that stage. The executive management requested an earned value report. Information on the relative amounts of time spent on excavating the new station and sinking the shaft was not available.

QUESTION AND PROBLEMS

1. Calculate the CV, SV, TV, CPI, and SPI.
2. Prepare a graph to illustrate the initial plan for the work, including the excavation for the station at the shaft bottom, as well as the changed plan to the executive management. Indicate the earned value and the actual cost after 13 months.

3. Regarding the cash-flow problem that has been aggregated by the high rate of spending, discuss the desirability of performing projects faster than planned.

ENDNOTES

1. The design output is normally in the form of a master record index or data pack that lists all drawings, material specifications, process specifications (e.g., for heat treatment of materials, welding, etc.). One guide for specification practices is MIL-STD 490A.
2. Drew Fetherston, *The Chunnel* (New York: Times Books, 1997): 198–199.

3. Alan Cooper, *The Inmates are Running the Asylum: Why High-Tech Products Drive Us Crazy and How to Restore the Sanity* (Indianapolis: Sams, 1999).

4. Where a number of units of the system are produced, the first and second groups of tests are performed on a prototype. When the system is a single-copy, the second group of tests takes place during construction, and the design is verified afterward.

5. C.L. Biggs, E.G. Birks, and W. Atkins, *Managing the Systems Development Process* (Englewood Cliffs, NJ: Prentice-Hall, 1980): 187–193.

6. Daniel Roman, *Science, Technology, and Innovation: A Systems Approach* (Columbus, OH: Grid Publishing, 1980): 369.

7. The terms "variance" and "deviation" are used here interchangeably, although in some contracts variance refers to small changes in the project plan for which compensation or correction is expected, whereas deviation refers to large changes that require a formal contractual response.

8. Roman, *Science, Technology, and Innovation*, 383.

9. DOD & NASA *Guide, PERT Cost Accounting System Design* (Washington, D.C.: U.S. Government Printing Office, June 1962).

10. Adapted from Charles Thompson, "Intermediate Performance Measures in Engineering Projects."*Proceedings of the Portland International Conference on Management of Engineering and Technology*, Portland, OR, July 27–31, 1997: 392.

11. Archibald, *Managing High-Technology Programs and Projects*, (New York: John Wiley, 1976): 195.

12. Information for this application provided by Elisa Denney and Jennifer Brown.

13. Eliyahu Goldratt describes the impact of multitasking, procrastination, and task variability in *The Critical Chain* (Great Barrington, MA: North River Press, 1997).

14. Ibid.

15. An approach to sizing time buffers is discussed in K. Hoel and S.G. Taylor, "Quantifying Buffers for Project Schedules, "*Production and Inventory Management Journal* 40, no. 2 (Second quarter, 1999): 43–47; Project Control Using Percentage of Buffer Consumed is described in Lawrence Leach, *Critical Chain Project Management, 2nd ed.* (Norwood, MA: Artech House, Inc., 2005), 117–120.

16. Interview with Doug Brandt, PMO Director, Abbott Diagnostics Division, May 2006.

17. Commercial software such as Project Scheduler by Sciforma Corporation support fever chart and related ways to track buffer status.

18. From Brian Muirhead and William Simon, *High Velocity Leadership: the Mars Pathfinder Approach to Better, Faster, Cheaper* (New York: Harper-Business, 1999): 40–42.

19. Michael Cusumano and Richard Selby, *Microsoft Secrets* (New York: Free Press, 1995): 204, 221, 256–257, 417.

20. P.K. Joy, *Total Project Management: The Indian Context*, Updated ed. (Delhi: Macmillan India, 1993): Chapter 11.

21. Ways to determine EV (BCWP) are explained in T. G. Pham, "The Elusive Budgeted Cost of Work Performed for Research and Development Projects,"*Project Management Quarterly* (March 1985): 76–79; for earned value approach, see Q. W. Fleming and J. M. Koppleman, *Earned Value Project Management* (Upper Darby, PA: Project Management Institute, 1996).

22. For examples of analytical models used for TPM, see Howard Eisner, *Computer-Aided Systems Engineering* (Upper Saddle River, NJ: Prentice Hall, 1988): 297–326.

23. Arild Sigurdsen, "Method for Verifying Project Cost Performance,"*Project Management Journal 25* no. 4 (December 1994): 26–31.

24. F.L. Harrison, *Advanced Project Management* (Hants, England: Gower, 1981): 242–244.

25. Ibid., 245–246.

26. Ibid., 244; Archibald, Managing High-Technology Programs and Projects, 187–190.

27. W. Hirsch, *The Contracts Management Deskbook*, rev. ed. (New York: American Management Association, 1986), Chapter 6.

28. Adapted from Roman, *Science, Technology, and Innovation*, 327–328, 391–395.

29. Source: Mr. P. Joubert, Anglo Platinum.

Project Evaluation, Communication, Implementation, and Closeout

We look at it and we do not see it.

—Lao-Tzu,
Sixth century B.C.

*An individual without information cannot take responsibility;
an individual who is given information cannot help but
take responsibility.*

—Jan Carlzon,
Riv Pyramidera!

*T*he last chapter described how a project is tracked, assessed, and guided so that schedules, expenditures, and technical performance targets can be met. The project manager oversees the work, assesses progress, and issues instructions for corrective action; as information is received, she judges the status of the project and communicates directives or progress reports to workers, upper management, and the client. The first half of this chapter discusses how project information is received, reviewed, and reported for evaluation and decision making. It also discusses the broader topic of project communication and information systems for project management.

As the project nears completion the end-item system is turned over to the customer. This is the last stage of the project life cycle—system implementation. The last duty of the project manager is to close out the project, whereupon the end-item system is handed over to the customer and becomes operational. The second half of this chapter describes system implementation and operation, and the project manager's role in each.

12.1   PROJECT EVALUATION

A project is an open system—it is goal-oriented and utilizes feedback information to determine how well it is doing and what it needs to reach its goals. The purpose of evaluation in project management is to assess performance, reveal areas where the project deviates from goals, and uncover extant or potential problems so they can be corrected. Although it is certain that problems and deviations will occur, it is not known a priori where or when. Evaluation throughout the life cycle for the purpose of guiding the project is called *formative evaluation*; it addresses the questions "What is happening?" and "How is the project proceeding?" Evaluation after the project is completed for the purposes of appraising the project and assessing the end product or end-results is called *summary evaluation*; it addresses the questions "What happened?" and "What were the results?"

Project Formative Evaluation

Methods and Measures

As described in Chapter 11 a wide variety of methods, measures, and sources (instead of a few) are used to obtain evaluation information about schedule, cost, and technical performance. These methods and measures should be specified in the project plan before the project begins. Using a variety of measures and sources increases the validity of the evaluation, particularly when multiple sources all lead to the same conclusion. The primary ways for obtaining and/or conveying project evaluative information are written reports with charts and tables, oral reports, first-hand observation, and review meetings.

Written reports with charts and tables are the most expeditious way to review cost, schedule, and work performance information since they reduce large amounts of information into simple, comprehensible formats. The danger is that they can hide or obscure information, leading to facile and erroneous conclusions. For example, as noted earlier, because project-level measures tend to hide lower-level problems, conclusions need to be substantiated by a more detailed investigation at the work package level. Charts and tables alone neither reveal the underlying causes of problems nor suggest opportunities. Thus, better sources of evaluative information are oral *and* written reports, and first-hand observation. Oral reports about project status are an easy, quick way to obtain information, although their accuracy and reliability depend on the interpretative and verbal skills of the presenter, and the number of channels through which the information had to pass to get to the presenter. In general, the greater the number of channels, the more distorted the message becomes. Because of this, project managers are seldom in their offices; they walk around the project, making observations and gathering first-hand information from supervisors and workers.

Site Visits

Most project managers would never rely solely on second- or third-hand reports or remote sources (e.g., e-mail) for tracking progress. If they cannot always be at the project site, they make a point to visit it often—unannounced and uninvited. While at the site the project manager tries to catch members of the team at lunch or on break and speak to them informally. In this way she demonstrates that she is involved in the project, and cares about the team and values their work. It is the best way to build relations and learn what is happening.

Just because no one reports problems or complains does not mean everything is okay. Instead of inquiring about project "status," sometimes it is better to ask people about how work is going, how life is going, what is going well or not so well, and what additional resources or support they need. Subtle signs that problems might be brewing include team members being quiet or not participating in meetings, avoiding discussion about the project during breaks, or giving conflicting reports about what is happening. The project manager watches peoples' reactions—their facial expressions and body language. Rather than trying to talk to everyone, she concentrates on people working on those tasks that traditionally are the most problematic. She tries to validate any reported problems and issues by getting at least two points of view.

Technology

In geographically dispersed projects, the project manager cannot visit every site and meet face-to-face with the workers and staff. This is not a good situation, but it happens. In such cases the project manager is forced to rely on technology—to use video- and audio-conferencing, websites, e-mail, and the telephone. Video-conferencing can be effective but is expensive and requires appropriate technical facilities; audio-conferencing can be good too, but involves careful scheduling so as not to waste peoples' time. The Internet is effective for broadcasting plans, reports, documents, and memos; however, it is passive and does not *require* that people see or respond to documents.

The overall best form of long-distance communication is frequent one-on-one conversations on the *telephone, not e-mail.* Over the telephone, the project manager can listen to tone of voice, probe for details, and obtain real-time feedback. But site managers, workers, and contractors are not always completely truthful, so the project manager should also have a trusted source onsite to oversee work and report back progress. But the best communication remains face-to-face, and for sensitive issues it is worth traveling the distance to visit the site and meet with team members in person. A good rule of thumb is: the more sensitive the issue, the lower the technology to communicate it! For highly sensitive issues, use face-to-face; for relatively sensitive issues, the telephone is okay; for less or non-sensitive issues, use e-mail and fax. Important discussions and commitments should always be followed up in writing.

12.2 COMMUNICATION PLAN

As part of the project master plan the project manager should prepare a communication plan. The communication plan addresses all forms of project communication—formal and informal, verbal and written. It includes a tentative schedule for all formal design and management reviews and milestone meetings and describes the meeting formats, expected itineraries, advance preparations, time limits on presentations, attendance policy, and who will lead. It also specifies important points of contact in the project (a Who's Who among the customer, contractor, subcontractors and vendors, supporters, other interest groups).

Role/type / Meeting/report	Status meeting (frequency)	Status meeting minutes (frequency)	Business feasibility	Information request	Technical feasibility	Business brief	Project plan (frequency)	Problems and issues (frequency)	Business study	Use case analysis	System architecture	Detailed technical design	Other
Client	X	X	X			X	X	X	X	X			
Relationship manager		X	X	X	X	X	X	X	X	X	X		
Business analyst	X	X	X			X	X	X	X	X	X		
Project manager	X	X	X	X	X	X	X	X	X	X	X		X
Client project team	X	X	X			X	X	X	X	X			
IT project team	X	X					X	X	X	X	X		X
Client director		X	X			X		X	X				X
IT director		X	X	X	X	X	X	X	X	X	X		
Project sponsor		X	X			X			X				
IT VP		X	X						X				
Architect	X	X	X	X	X	X	X	X	X	X	X		X
Security/audit	X	X	X		X			X	X	X	X		
Internet operations	X	X	X		X		X	X	X	X	X		X
Intranet operations	X	X	X		X		X	X	X				
Legal/corporations communication		X	X		X			X	X				
Other													

Figure 12-1
Sample communication plan.

The matrix in Figure 12-1 shows part of a communication plan that specifies the expected meetings and reports, and the key stakeholders who will participate in each. This would be supplemented by other documents giving details about the what, where, when, and how for each kind of meeting and report.

The communication plan should be distributed to the project team and discussed before the project begins. To make sure that everyone understands the forms of required written communication and the content and format of each, the plan should include examples of good and bad documentation from previous projects. Many of these documents can be posted online.

12.3 Project Review Meetings

Purpose of Review Meetings

Review meetings are one of the most common and important ways to communicate and assess project evaluative information. The main function of these meetings is to identify deviations from the project plan and quickly correct them. During the meetings, participants focus on project progress and current problems, opportunities, and anticipated problems.

Review meetings can be informal and scheduled weekly or daily, or formal and scheduled whenever needed or according to project phases. Most large projects require both.

Informal Reviews

Informal reviews are held frequently and regularly, and involve members of the project team. The reviews (called "peer reviews" because they are attended by a group of peers) focus on project status, special problems, emerging issues, and performance of the project. Meeting participation depends on the phase of the project and issues at hand; only the team members, customer representatives, functional or line managers, and project managers who need be involved are invited. Before the meetings, status reports and forecast time and cost-to-complete are updated. Attendees with assignments are expected to give presentations.

To encourage honesty and candor, the project manager takes on the role of group facilitator. Because reviews are intended to uncover problems and issues, bad news and problems should be *expected* and openly confronted. Finger-pointing, passing blame, or smoothing over of conflict should be avoided; such behavior wastes time, discourages attendance, and negates the purpose of the meetings—to identify issues or problems and agree on the course of action.

Standup Meetings

A variation of the informal review is the "daily standup meeting." Intended more as an update on status than a progress review, the meeting is short (15 minutes) and to-the-point. Usually held at the start of every day, a small group of team members give a quick run-through of yesterday's progress and today's next steps. (The occasional surprise attendance of a prominent person—senior manager from the contractor or customer—adds spice and helps keep everyone on their toes.) Problems that require more than a minute's reflection are deferred for a later meeting.

Formal Reviews

Formal reviews are scheduled at milestones or critical project stages. In projects that involve significant design and development effort, two common formal reviews are the *preliminary review* and the *critical review*. The purpose of the preliminary design review is to assess how well the functional design specifications fit the basic operational requirements. At the critical design review, details of the hardware and software design are checked for conformance to the preliminary design specifications.

Formal reviews can be a precondition for continuing the project. In the phased project planning approach, the decision to continue or terminate the project is based upon the results of a formal review of project performance so far. Formal design reviews were discussed in Chapter 9.

Another kind of formal review is the *project audit*, also discussed in Chapter 9. In all projects, regardless of contractual obligations, the customer or sponsor should assume some responsibility for being the project watchdog. The project audit is a special review initiated by the customer to provide an independent assessment of project progress. It can be conducted early in the project, during design or construction, or upon any significant change in the budget, schedule, or project goals. The purpose of the audit is similar to a formal critical review: to verify project progress, identify constraints to progress, and assess the effectiveness of the organization in doing its job. Audits scrutinize the plans, schedules, budgets, constraints, communications, and overall management of the project.

Action Plan

Whenever a problem surfaces at a review, an action plan is formulated to resolve it; should the problem require further investigation, a person is named responsible to convene another meeting soon and prepare the action plan.

Problem area	Objective	Actions	Who	When completed
1. Planning and scheduling	1. Establish backup support for each system.	1. (A) Discuss systems with analysts who support them; formulate plan for each system.	Project leaders and analysts	January 1
	2. Review all systems. Eliminate those not used; clean up others.	2. (A) Prepare questionnaire on system status.	Ron Gilmore	November 15
		2. (B) Complete questionnaires.	Analysts and programmers	December 1
		2. (C) Determine status and specific actions.	PL, analysts and programmers	January 31
	3. Provide information on purposes and uses of new project management system.	3. Prepare seminar on PMS and present to staff.	Joan Gibb	Before March 1

Figure 12-2
Sample action plan.

Each action plan might include a statement of the problem, objectives for resolving it, the required course of action, a target date, and person responsible (Figure 12-2). To make sure the plan fits with other plans, the project manager or person responsible should seek approval from everyone who will contribute to or be affected by the plan.

Another example of an action plan is a *problem failure report*. NASA, for instance, uses such a report for tracking all problems and keeping focus on the most important ones. A problem failure report is prepared for every problem identified. The problem is assigned two ratings: one to indicate its impact on mission success (1 = negligible impact; 4 = mission catastrophic); the other to indicate both certainty about an identified cause and confidence in the proposed solution (1 = known cause and known solution; 4 = unknown cause, unverified solution). Problems with a 3 or 4 rating on either are potentially mission-threatening and require the project manager's personal sign-off. The reports are retained electronically; on the Mars Pathfinder project mentioned in Chapters 9 and 11, over 800 of them were generated and subsequently evaluated.[1]

At each meeting, one of the first topics covered is the status of items on the action plan. The person taking notes on the meeting—and afterward writing them up and distributing them—should be the person leading the meeting—usually the project manager—not a secretary. This reinforces the perception (and reality) that the leader is committed, involved, and in charge.

Project Meeting Room

Project-related meetings and conferences are typically convened in a central meeting place or project office. The chosen location should serve as a physical reminder of the project and provide adequate space for preparing, storing, and displaying project information. Gantt charts, networks, and cost charts comparing planned and actual performance are prominently displayed for easy reference. The room has a conference table, chairs, cabinets with project files, computers, a projector, and, sometimes, teleconference equipment.

12.4　REPORTING

Company management must be kept apprised of the status, progress, and performance of ongoing and upcoming projects. Problems affecting profits, schedules, or budgets, as well as their expected impacts and recommended actions should be reported promptly. Stakeholders such as the customer, professional, citizen, and activist groups, public agencies, stockholders, and others who have a genuine interest in the project should also be kept up-to-date about project status.

Reports to Top Management and the Project Management Office

Top management and the project management office (PMO) should be sent monthly progress reports that provide[2]

1. A brief statement summarizing the project status.
2. Red flag items where corrective action has or should be taken.
3. Accomplishments to date, changes to schedule, and projections for schedule and cost at completion.
4. Current and potential problem areas and actions required.
5. Current cost situation and cost performance.
6. Manpower plan and limitations.

When several projects are simultaneously underway, the PMO compiles and provides management monthly summaries showing the relative status of the projects. Each summary includes names of the customer and the project manager; monetary and labor investment; scheduled start and finish dates; possible risks, losses, and gains; and other information for top management review. These summaries enable management to assess the relative performance of the projects and their combined influence on the company. They also enable the PMO to coordinate plans, authorizations, and resource allocations for the projects. When the projects are managed as a portfolio (Chapter 17) the summaries allow top management to decide which projects to continue, which to devote more or less resources to, and which to terminate. Reports to top management and the PMO are prepared by the project manager and project staff from information generated by the project cost accounting system (PCAS) or project management information system (PMIS).

Reports to Project, Program, and Functional Managers

On large projects, project or program managers receive reports from work package leaders about the value of work completed, current and forecasted costs, and updated schedules for completion (similar to Table 11-1 and Figure 11-13, aggregated up to second or third level). They also receive monthly financial status reports showing costs incurred and cumulative planned costs versus actual costs. These reports are also sent to the company financial manager or controller. Functional managers also receive monthly status reports showing labor-hours and costs expended for work packages in their respective areas. The reports shown in Figures 8-8 through 8-12, modified to include actual expenditures, are representative.

Reports to Customers/Users

The customer should be sent monthly reports about work progress and the impact of any requested or unavoidable changes on work scope, schedule, or cost. These reports should be presented in a clear, understandable format. Although the contractor's marketing or customer relations director might be assigned the job of communicating contract-related information to the customer, the project manager is ultimately responsible for ensuring the customer is kept well informed. She must always be available to the customer to answer questions and satisfy requests for project information. Keeping the customer well informed avoids later "surprises."

12.5 PROJECT MANAGEMENT INFORMATION SYSTEMS

The formal methods for planning and control described in this book do not require any more input data or information than is, or should be, available in any project. What they *do* require, however, is a framework or tool—a *system*—for collecting, organizing, storing, processing, and disseminating that information. Such a framework or tool is the *PMIS* mentioned earlier in the book.

PMISs assist project managers in planning, budgeting, and resource allocation. Additionally, many perform assorted analyses such as variance, performance, and forecasting at any level of the work breakdown structure (WBS) and project organization. A good PMIS enables quick review and easy updating of plans, schedules, and budgets, and facile control of changes to system configuration and project plans. It filters and reduces data to provide information on a summary, exception, or "what if" basis.

PMIS Software

If you think about it, methods such as earned value analysis, forecasting, change control, and configuration management for large projects involve processing and integrating a hefty amount of information. As computers are good at this, PMIS software has become an essential tool for project planning and control. In fact, without software it would be difficult to do much of the analysis necessary to plan and control large projects.

Benefits

The major benefit of project management software is speed. Once data have been collected and entered, revisions in plans, schedules, and budgets can be done rapidly. Most PMIS software is also good at handling and integrating complex data relationships; for large projects with hundreds of work tasks, tens of organizations, and thousands of workers, software is essential.

There are dozens of kinds of PMIS project software packages to choose from, but they vary greatly in capability, flexibility, and price.[3] Simpler PMIS software are limited in what they can do but are usually good at whatever that is; once this software has been mastered, it is easy to upgrade to more sophisticated software.

Features of PMISs

Following is a rundown of the kinds of analytical capabilities, outputs, functions, and features offered by various PMIS software. Important to note is that among the many available software packages, most do not have all of these capabilities; in fact, some do little more than perform the most basic functions.

Scheduling and Network Planning. Virtually all project software performs project scheduling using network-based algorithms. These systems compute early and late schedule times, slack times, and the critical path. Among the capabilities to look for are the type of procedure (CPM, PERT, PDM, CCM), whether outputs are event- or activity-oriented, maximum number of allowable activities, the coding format for activities and events (some use a WBS scheme), the quality and clarity of outputs (e.g., network, Gantt chart, tabular reports, or multiple types), and whether multiple projects can be simultaneously planned and tracked. All software allow calendar input of non-work periods such as weekends, holidays, and vacations for producing schedules.

Resource Management. Most software systems also perform resource loading, leveling, allocation, or multiple functions, but the analytical sophistication and quality of reports varies. Major considerations are the maximum number of resources permitted per activity or project; the kind of resource loading/scheduling techniques used (resource-limited, time-limited, or both); split scheduling (stopping and restarting activities); interchangeable usage of different resources; and rate of resource usage.[4]

Budgeting. Software systems vary greatly in the way they handle fixed, variable, and overhead costs, and in their ability to generate budget and cost summary reports. In some, cost and expense information are not treated explicitly; in others, cost accounting is a major feature. The PMIS software for large projects should have a cost and budgeting module—the PCAS described in Chapter 8—that is integrated with the software's planning, scheduling, procurement, tracking, and other modules.

Cost Control and Performance Analysis. Here is where project software capabilities differ the most. To perform the control function, a system must be able to compare actual performance (actual costs and work completed) to planned and budgeted performance. Among the features to consider are the software's capability to compute and report cost and schedule variances, earned values, and performance indices, and to forecast by extrapolating past performance. The most sophisticated PMIS software "roll up" results and allow aggregation, analysis, and reporting at all levels of the WBS. They also permit modification and updating of existing plans through input of actual start and finish dates and costs. Plus, they *integrate* network, budget, and resource information and allow the project manager to ask "what if" questions under various scenarios while the project is underway. They allow the user to access, cross-reference, and report information from multiple sites or databases linked via web-based technology.

Reporting, Graphics, and Communication. Project software also vary in the number, kind, and quality of reports they produce—an important consideration since all of this can affect the speed and accuracy of the information communicated. Many systems provide only tabular reports or crude schedules; others generate networks and resource histograms; still others offer a variety of graphics including pie charts and line graphs.

Some PMIS software makes use of the Internet, which allows geographically dispersed team members everywhere easy access to project information and a common place to send and store information. Some systems automatically flag problems, such as excessive buffer consumption as illustrated by the fever chart in the previous chapter.

Interface, Flexibility, and Ease of Use.   Some software systems are compatible with and can tie in to existing databases such as payroll, purchasing, inventory, enterprise resource planning (ERP), cost-accounting, or other PMISs; some can be used with popular DBMS and spreadsheet systems and some with systems for modeling and risk analysis.

Many larger software systems allow data to be pooled from different projects for *multi-project* analysis, planning, and control. With this feature, information from several simultaneous projects can be combined to form a picture of the overall state of the organization. Some software provides a "dashboard" or overview of each project. By "clicking" on a particular project, a manager can zoom-in to view more detailed information about the project. Managers can readily distinguish which projects are performing as expected from those experiencing problems or overruns—an essential capability for project portfolio management (Chapter 17).

Systems vary widely in their flexibility. Many perform a narrow set of functions that cannot be modified. Others allow the user to develop new applications or alter existing ones, depending on needs. Among the applications sometimes available are change control, configuration management, responsibility matrixes, expenditure reports, cost and technical performance reports, and technical performance summaries. Many software systems utilize Internet technology and protocols that enable easy access through a browser to a variety of management applications and databases.

Finally, there is the consideration of user friendliness: How easy is it to learn and operate the system? Systems vary greatly in the style of system documentation, thoroughness and clarity of tutorials, ease of information input, clarity of on-screen presentation and report format, helpfulness of error messages, and the training and operating support offered by the developer.

12.6 WEB-ENABLED PROJECT MANAGEMENT[5]

Many project management software products take advantage of web-enabled technology that offer "paperless" plans and reports on interactive websites. This technology is especially well suited for situations where project team members and stakeholders are situated at different sites. Putting information on a project website or other network utilizing Internet standards affords the benefits of immediate availability of information, efficiency and accessibility for communication between workers, ease of usage, and reliability and currency of information because it is communicated in real time.

With web-browser integrated project management software, team members can report progress and retrieve assignments through their own individual web pages. The manager can aggregate information from scattered worksites to get an overview of the entire project.

In most cases, the necessary tools are already at hand. Web-enabled project software requires only one thing: access to a web browser such as Internet Explorer or Netscape. Since Internet and intranet networks are easy to learn and use, team members readily adapt to a web-based PMIS for sending and accessing project information. Special website administration is usually not necessary since team members maintain their own sites, and the costs associated with overhead, update, and maintenance of web-based communication are very low.

Intranets, Virtual Private Networks, and Security

The security of project information on a network is an important matter. Project websites may contain information that an organization does not want to share with outsiders, in which case the company should use an intranet, virtual private network, or password-controlled website.

An *intranet* is a private computer network that uses Internet standards and protocols to allow communication among people within an organization. It provides access to a common pool of information from computers within organizational walls. The intranet is owned by the organization it serves and is accessible only by organizational members and other authorized parties. Access can be extended to trusted external organizations, partners, or clients through an extended network called an *extranet*.

Organizations take steps to keep unauthorized people out of their intranet systems by using firewalls and other mechanisms that either block unauthorized access or make internal information unreadable to unauthorized computers that gain access. When employees are allowed to access the Internet from inside the company's property, the company can keep its stored information secure with the use of firewalls and *virtual private networks*, the latter which offer access by authorized users to an organization's intranet from the Internet.

Group Productivity[6]

Intranets employ browser-based software to enable users to move easily among different kinds of software tools that perform a wide variety of functions. With an intranet it is easy to access *group productivity software* and to store reports, profiles, calendars, and schedules. It is also easy for users to locate information in these documents using special *document sharing tools* such as newsgroups, chat rooms, and electronic whiteboards. These tools are especially useful for sharing pictorial information about product design requirements and descriptions.

One of the most common ways that project managers use intranets is for collecting information about time spent on projects. The information is retained in a project database, then processed by project management software to report and tally time spent and time still needed to complete the project.

E-mail is another important communication tool, although experienced project managers readily admit it is no substitute for face-to-face meetings or the telephone. Other means for collectively sharing information include *discussion forums* and *chat rooms*. Members of a discussion forum can view others' contributions and add comments. Chat rooms are similar to e-mail and discussion forums but permit immediate response by participants to incoming messages.

It used to be that video- or audio-conferencing were the only ways for geographically dispersed teams to hold meetings. Today, video, voice, and data can be shared over the intranet or Internet at desktop locations. The information shared can be in the form of a spreadsheet, text document, slide presentation, chart, graphic, photo, engineering schematic, or video file. At Boeing, all designs are stored electronically; they are available immediately to anyone who needs them and are kept current to reflect the most recent changes. Specific notification of any change is sent via e-mail to everyone who needs to know, as specified on a responsibility matrix (persons with "N" responsibility). As long as team members have access to a computer and browser, they can participate in meetings. Engineers in Seattle having trouble assembling a mock-up can send video images to designers in New York who can *see* what the mock-up looks like, assess the problem, and offer suggestions; without that technology, the New York team would have to *go* to Seattle.

12.7 PMIS IN THE PROJECT LIFE CYCLE

A computer-based PMIS can assist the project manager throughout all phases of the project life cycle. Figure 12-3 shows the range of managerial tasks and functions where a PMIS can help. The following example illustrates this use.

Example 1: Sigma Associates' PMIS for Project Planning and Control

Sigma Associates, the architectural/engineering firm mentioned in Chapter 8, Example 4, uses a computer-based PMIS for most planning and control functions.

Figure 12-3
PMIS function in the project life cycle (*Source*: Project/2).

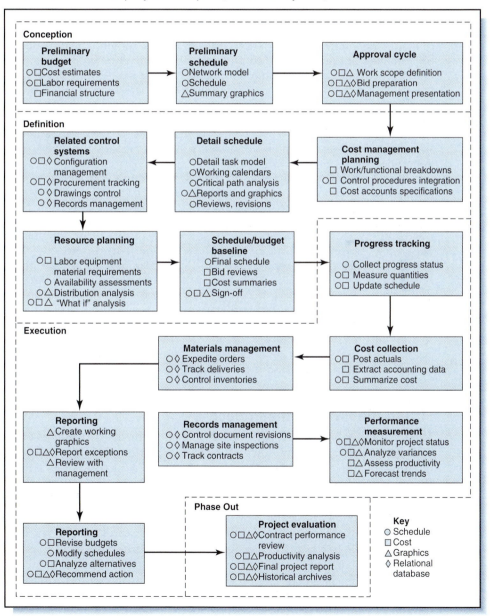

So ubiquitous is Sigma's PMIS in its operations that employees think of it as a member of the team; they call it "Sally."

Once a project is approved, Sally's main function changes from planning assistance to monitoring and control. Sally's major purpose is to routinely compare the original or current baseline project plan with actual performance, to raise warnings about discrepancies, and to forecast project outcomes (schedule and cost at completion).

Each week, Sally receives information about current costs. Estimates of weekly time spent on each activity are accumulated from all project participants. Non-labor expenses and client reimbursements are input through the company's general ledger system.

Project managers make biweekly estimates of hours anticipated to complete each activity. Sally converts the anticipated hours-to-complete into a percentage completed for each activity. The system multiplies budgeted labor hours by the percentage completed to determine the estimated labor hours intended to bring the activity to its current level of completion (a form of earned value). By comparing this estimate with actual labor expenditures from time cards, the project manager can determine whether the activity is moving at its budgeted pace. Sally makes actual-to-plan comparisons and reports discrepancies, which managers rely on to spot problems and locate the causes. Whenever project managers fail to make the biweekly estimates of anticipated hours, Sally prompts them about the missing estimate entries.

Sally uses the anticipated hours-to-complete to prepare estimates of labor requirement loads for the remainder of the project. These estimates are used to adjust the remaining labor loadings and to make necessary revisions to schedules.

The comptroller uses Sally to forecast the timing and amounts of client billing, and the timing of expected payments according to each client's payment history. Based on the percentage of work completed, the system computes an estimate of earned client fees. These fees are compared to actual labor costs, overhead costs, and non-labor expenses in a monthly profit/loss analysis. Sally generates monthly reports of net profit for project-to-date and year-to-date, summarized by office, department, and project manager. It also combines net profit for all projects to give a picture of the company's financial health.

Sally also checks for the correctness of the hours charged on time cards. Hours charged are compared with dates on the schedule, and a card with discrepancies is withheld and a memo describing the error is sent to the employee. A summary report of rejected or uncorrected cards is sent each week to the comptroller. Sally is an example of a sophisticated, comprehensive PMIS: it serves all the functions (and more) of a high-end PMIS.

Fitting the PMIS to the Project

Most computer-based PMI software is no match for the capabilities of Sally, however that is not a problem since all such capabilities are seldom required. Just as the project team should carefully plan and define the project before it begins, so too should it plan and define the information requirements of the PMIS; it should then choose the PMIS that satisfies these requirements most economically and effectively. The purpose of a PMIS is, in the words of Palla, to "get the right information to the right person at the right time so the right decision can be made for the project."[7] Any PMIS able to do this is the right one. Many firms use more than one kind of PMI software package—say, Microsoft Project™ for smaller projects and Primavera™ or Artemis™ for large ones. For a comprehensive review of PMIS software, see the *Project Management Software Survey* and the Project Management Knowledge Base at http:pmkb.com.http://www.pmkb.com.[8]

While PMISs are essential for effective and efficient handling of computational aspects of project management, the role of PMISs should be seen in context: computer systems do little to help the project manager identify key stakeholders, negotiate the project scope with them, decide on key subcontractors, or motivate the team. Too many novices start off by going on a 2-day computer software course where they get the impression that project management is all about using the century old Gantt chart tool on a modern computer.

12.8 INFORMAL COMMUNICATION

Much of the communication in organizations happens informally (the most familiar form being the *grapevine*) and projects are no exception. Certainly informal communication has its drawbacks; neither thorough nor dependable, it tends to garble messages from one person to the next (even jokes lose their punch lines after going through just a few people), and does not guarantee that people who need information will ever get it. Nonetheless, it is largely beneficial and essential. It fulfills social and work needs, and conveys information more quickly and directly than most formal systems. Some management theorists posit that vast networks of informal communication are essential for any organization to perform well.

Managers cannot control informal communication, but there are several ways they can influence it.[9] One is to *insist* on informality, remove status barriers, and inspire casual conversation, particularly between managers and workers. As examples, at Walt Disney, everyone—from the president to down—wears a name tag; at Hewlett Packard, people are urged to use first names; and at Delta Airlines and Levi Strauss, the management philosophy is "open door." MBWA (management by walking around), or getting managers out of the office and talking to people (instead of relying solely on presentations or e-mail reports), stimulates informal information exchange. The physical layout of the office is also instrumental. Intermingling of the desks of workers from interrelated functional areas, removing walls and partitions, "family groupings" of chairs and desks, and spot placement of lounges are ways of increasing face-to-face contact.

Project management attempts to do what the informal organization sometimes does: allow the people involved in a problem or decision to directly communicate and make decisions. One way or another, people affected by a decision or problem talk about it, form ideas, and make decisions, though often the formal organization overlooks or stifles these ideas. After management has adopted the appropriate formal structure it should then encourage supportive informal processes.

12.9 IMPLEMENTATION STAGE

The final stage of the systems development life cycle is implementation—the stage where the end-item system or other deliverable is completed and the user takes on responsibility for its operation. Implementation sometimes happens in an instant, sometimes takes months. Take a clock. If the clock is simple, you just plug it in and set it. If it is a digital alarm clock with a radio, you might need to read the instructions first to learn how to set it. If it is a nuclear clock such as the one used by the US Bureau of Standards, you may need several manuals and a training program to install and learn how to operate it. If the clock is a replacement for an existing clock connected to a timing device that controls lighting and heating in a large skyscraper, you will have to develop a *strategy* for substituting one clock with the other so as to minimize disruption and inconvenience to the people in the building. This section discusses these and other issues associated with implementation, starting with user training and acceptance testing.

User Training

The purpose of user training is to teach the user how to operate, maintain, and service the system. At one extreme, training is a simple instruction booklet; at the other, it is an extensive, ongoing program with an annual budget of many thousands of dollars. The first step is to determine the training requirements—the type and extent of training required. This will dictate the kind of materials needed (manuals, videos, simulators); personnel to be trained (existing or newly hired personnel); techniques to be used (classroom, independent study, role plays); training schedule (everyone at once, in phases, or ongoing); and staffing (contractor, user, or subcontracted training personnel). Users should review and approve all training procedures and documents before training begins, and provide input afterward to improve the training. Often the user takes over training after the contractor's trainers have trained the user's trainers.

User training should address the issue of how the newly installed system will fit into the user's environment. It should provide an overview of the system's objectives, scope, and operation, and how the system interfaces with the user organization. This will enable the user to understand the system as part of his larger environment and integrate it with existing systems. All new systems create fear, stress, and frustration; one aim of training should also be to relieve or eliminate these.

User Acceptance Testing

The final tests of the end-item that happen before or during installation are the user acceptance tests. Based on the results of these tests the user determines if the system warrants (1) adoption or installation as is, (2) installation pending modifications or adjustments, or (3) complete rejection.

User tests will differ from tests conducted by the contractor during design and production, though the latter should have anticipated and rigorously exceeded the user's tests. Nonetheless, the contractor should be prepared for the possibility that aspects the system might fail some of the user tests.

Ideally, users perform the tests of acceptance with minimal assistance from the project team. In cases where the user is unable to perform the tests, the project team must act as surrogate user and make every effort to test the system as the user would. This means putting aside biases or vested interests and assuming a role somewhat devoid of system-related technical expertise. Lack of user participation in acceptance testing can lead to later long-term problems; therefore, even in the role of surrogate user–tester, the contractor must insist that the user is on hand to witness the tests.

System Installation and Conversion

The system installation and conversion stage is conducted according to the implementation plan. During conversion, equipment must be installed, tested, fine-tuned, and deemed operable to the fulfillment of requirements.

Virtually all new systems are, in a sense, designed to substitute other, existing systems, so a major implementation issue is the strategy to be used for replacing the

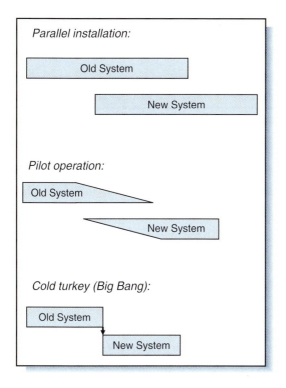

Figure 12-4
Three strategies for system conversion.

old system with the new one—the process of *conversion*. Three possible strategies, illustrated in Figure 12-4, are:

Parallel installation: Both new and old systems are operated in parallel until the new system is sufficiently proven.
Pilot operation: The new system is operated in a limited capacity until proven, then the old system is phased out as the new one is phased in.
Cold turkey (Big Bang): In one fell swoop, the new system is moved in and the old one is moved out.

Selecting the best conversion strategy is no simple matter; it involves complicated considerations of costs, risks, and logistics. For example, the first strategy seems the safest: If the new system fails there is still the old one. But it is also the most expensive because two complete systems must be operated simultaneously, plus adequate staff must be on hand to operate both systems at once. With the second strategy, costs and risks are low, and staff can be trained in stages; the problem is, a pilot operation is not necessarily representative of full system operation. Often, only after the full new system has been phased in (and the old one phased out) do certain critical problems become apparent. The last strategy is the fastest and potentially least costly, but it is also the riskiest and raises questions about: "When will there be time to train the staff to operate the new system and what happens if the new system fails?."

Prior to actual installation, the project manager updates all plans and schedules, gains approvals for revisions, and renews the commitment from teams in the contractor and customer organizations. Implementation is a high-stress stage, and the project manager and team must be patient with users and sensitive to their questions, concerns, and fears.

After the new system has been installed, the contractor will continue monitoring it and performing tests to ensure that the system design is adequate, the system was installed properly, and that it smoothly interfaces with other systems in the user environment.

12.10 PROJECT TERMINATING AND CLOSEOUT

Projects are by definition endeavors of limited duration; they all come to an end. When this happens, it is the project manager who ensures that all project-related work has been completed and formally closed out by a specified date. It is the project manager's responsibility to put an end to the project, which can be a tough assignment, especially when there is no follow-up project.

At closeout the project product or deliverable is handed over to the customer. Contracts sometimes provide for a first handover at completion as well as a second handover after a *defects liability period* (a.k.a. retention period, guarantee period, and maintenance period). At the first handover the customer should ensure that all *patent defects* (defects that can readily be detected by a person qualified in the field) are identified and reported. After the first handover the contractor is only liable for rectifying *latent defects* (those that could not be detected through a reasonable inspection at first handover). If, for instance, it is not raining at the time of the first handover, a roof that later leaks would be considered a latent defect. The purpose of the second handover is to afford the customer more time to identify deviations from specifications or substandard workmanship. After the second handover the contractor is no longer liable for defects, and any *retention fees* withheld by the customer to ensure compliance are paid to the contractor.

The Last Step

By the time the end-item has been delivered and installed, many members of the project team will have lost enthusiasm and be anxious to move on to something new. Managers eagerly shift emphasis to upcoming projects and, as a result, give the termination little attention. Yet, as common sense indicates, terminating a project is no less important than any other project activity. In fact, the method of termination can ultimately determine the project's success or failure.

Termination can occur in a variety of ways. The best way is according to a planned, systematic procedure. The worst ways are abrupt cancellation, slow attrition of effort, or siphoning off of resources by higher-priority projects. A project can go sour simply by being allowed to "limp along" until it fizzles out. Unless *formally* terminated, some projects will drag on indefinitely, sometimes from neglect or insufficient resources, sometimes intentionally for lack of follow-up work. In the latter case, workers remain on the project payroll long after their obligations have been met. Unless the project has been officially terminated, work orders remain open and labor charges continue to accrue.

Reasons for Termination

Project terminations essentially fall into three categories: achievement of project objectives, changing environment or intractable problems, or poor customer/contractor relations.[10]

Even in the first case—when the project is terminated because all work has been completed and contractual objectives successfully met—it takes a skilled project manager to orchestrate termination and ensure that no activities or obligations are left uncompleted or unfulfilled. The seeds of successful termination are sown early in the project. Because termination requires customer acceptance of the project results, the criteria for acceptance should have been clearly defined, agreed upon, and documented at the beginning of the project, and any changes made during the project approved by the contractor and customer.

Some projects never reach successful completion because of factors such as changing market conditions, skyrocketing costs, depleted critical resources, changing priorities, or other factors. The decision to abort before completion occurs when the financial or other losses from termination are considered less than those expected from completing the project. The customer may simply change his mind and no longer want the project end-item.

Projects sometimes are also halted because of changing market conditions or technology, unsatisfactory technical performance, poor quality of materials or workmanship, violation of contract, poor planning and control, bad management, or customer dissatisfaction with the contractor. Many of these reasons are the fault of the contractor and project management, and could have been avoided had management exercised better planning and control, showed more respect for the user, or acted in a more ethical manner. These terminations leave the user with unmet requirements and cast doubt over the contractor's technical competency, managerial ability, or moral standing.

Termination and Closeout Responsibilities

As with earlier stages of the project work, the project manager is responsible for planning, scheduling, monitoring and controlling termination, and closeout activities. The responsibilities listed by Archibald include:[11]

A. Planning, scheduling, and monitoring closeout activities:
- Obtain and approve termination plans from involved functional managers.
- Prepare and coordinate termination plans and schedules.
- Plan for transfer of project team members and resources to other projects.
- Monitor completion of all contractual agreements.
- Monitor the disposition of any surplus materials and project equipment.

B. Final closeout activities:
- Close out all work orders and approve the completion of all subcontracted work.
- Notify all departments of project completion.
- Close the project office and all facilities occupied by the project organization.
- Close project books.
- Ensure delivery of project files and records to the responsible managers.

C. Customer acceptance, obligation, and payment activities:
- Ensure delivery of end-items, side items, and customer acceptance of items.
- Notify the customer when all contractual obligations have been fulfilled.
- Ensure that all documentation related to customer acceptance as required by contract has been completed.
- Expedite any customer activities needed to complete the project.
- Transmit formal payment and collection of payments.
- Obtain from customer formal acknowledgment of completion of contractual obligations that release the contractor from further obligation (except warranties and guarantees).

Responsibility for the last group of activities, particularly those relating to payment and contractual obligations, is shared with the contract administrator or other person responsible for company-client negotiations and legal contracts. The final activity, obtaining the formal customer acknowledgment, may involve contractor claims if the customer has failed to provide agreed-to data or support, or requested items beyond contract specifications. In such cases the contractor is entitled to compensation.

Before the project is considered closed, the customer reviews the results or end-item with the contractor to make sure everything is satisfactory. Items still open and in need of attention, and to which the contractor agrees, are recorded on a list, sometimes called a "punch list". The items on the list then are checked off by the contractor as they are rectified.

Example 2: Punch List for the Chunnel[12]

Five months before the scheduled completion date of the Chunnel, the punch list still contained a lot of items—over 22,000. Incredibly, with only a day remaining before handover of the Chunnel to its owner/operator, that number had been whittled down to only 100. Problem was, the contract allowed for *no* (zero) items on the punch list; any open items at the handover would void the agreement and stop payments. A simple solution would be to delay the handover until the remaining items were fixed, which was estimated to take only a week. But few things associated with the Chunnel were simple. Invitations for the handover ceremony had already gone out, and preparations for the big gala celebration had all been completed. Besides, the project was financed by a syndicate of some 200 banks located around the world, and any proposed delay in the handover would require their approval.

What followed was a series of frenzied, harried negotiations via telephone and fax that lasted throughout the night. By dawn, the bank syndicate had agreed to amend the contract. The gala signoff ceremony went off as planned, complete with fireworks, champagne, a choral group, and a Dixieland jazz band. The ceremony, attended by corporate executives and project managers from the Chunnel's 10 prime contracting companies plus a thousand other guests, was in itself a minor project.

The importance of doing a good job at termination cannot be understated; neither can the difficulty. In the rush to finish the project and the accompanying confusion, it is easy to overlook, mishandle, or botch the termination. To make sure that does not happen, termination responsibilities should be systematically delegated and checked off as completed. Project termination requires the same degree of attention and service as do other project management responsibilities.

12.11 CLOSING THE CONTRACT

Delivery, installation, and user acceptance of the main contract end-item (hardware, software, or service specified by the project contract) does not necessarily mean that the project is closed. Project completion can be delayed pending delivery of necessary, ancillary articles—*side items*—or payment of compensation for failure to meet contractual agreements.

Side Items

The installation, operation, maintenance, and monitoring of the contract end-item is often contingent upon availability of numerous contract side items such as special tools, instruments, spare parts, reports, drawings, courses of instruction, and user operating and maintenance manuals. Side items are usually provided by subcontractors and can range from the simple and mundane to the complex and innovative. An operating manual for a network server is an example of the former; a high-fidelity computer simulator for training operators of a large chemical processing facility is an example of the latter. Simple or complex, side items are important to successful system implementation and project closeout.

Side items are deliverable contract items, and their cost may contribute to a significant percentage of total project cost. Yet, however, perhaps because they are deemed "side" items, the time and effort they require to develop and produce are often underestimated. The result is a delay in implementing the end-item and closing out the project.

Side items should be included in all aspects of project planning and control. The project manager must make certain that the scope of work for side items is well understood and that qualified personnel are assigned with adequate time to fulfill their requirements.[13] Side items must be looked upon as part of the contracted work, not as afterthoughts or project extensions. To ensure that the project can be closed out on schedule, side items must be given full consideration in the WBS, project schedule, and budget.

Negotiated Adjustments to Final Contract

In many high-cost projects, the contractor receives payment for only a portion of the total project cost, say 80 to 90 percent, and the remainder is conditional upon the performance of the end-item, the contractor's compliance with contractual agreements, or the quality of the working relationship with the contractor.[14]

These final payment contingencies are considered post-acceptance issues because they occur after the user has accepted the major end-item. If the delivered end-item is satisfactory yet does not perform to the contracted specifications, if it is found defective after a trial period due to design or production inadequacies, or if it is delivered late, the contractor may be responsible for paying negotiated compensation to the user.

Contract sign-off might also be contingent upon how well the product functions after installation or delivery. In that case, the project manager oversees installation, setup, and initial operation at the customer's site, and might also provide on-site user support, at no additional fee, until any operating deficiencies have been removed.

Sometimes the customer or contractor seeks to negotiate aspects of the contract price or completion date *after* the project is completed. The US government and other customers retain the right to negotiate overhead rates *after* they receive the final price on cost-plus contracts. Likewise, a contractor sometimes seeks to negotiate a revised completion date on the contract *after* the project is completed—usually because it has overrun the originally scheduled date and wants to salvage its reputation.

12.12   PROJECT SUMMARY EVALUATION

One of the final activities of the project team after the project has been closed out and the system made operational is to perform a formal evaluation. This final *summary evaluation* gives project and company management the opportunity to learn from its mistakes and successes in the project. Without a summary review, there is a tendency to mentally suppress problems encountered and to understate the impact of errors or misjudgments. ("Things weren't really so bad, were they?") Project summary evaluation reviews and assesses the performance of the project team and the end-item system. The purpose of the review is to determine and assess what was done and what remains to be done—not to find fault or pass blame. As mentioned earlier, finger-pointing and reprimanding are counterproductive because they lead people to cover up the very problems and mistakes that evaluation seeks to reveal. Two forms of summary evaluation are the post-completion project review and the post-installation system review.

Post-completion Project Review

The *post-completion project review* (also perversely called a *postmortem*) is a summary review and assessment of the *project*. It is conducted by the contractor immediately after the end-item system has been implemented and the project closed out—early enough so project team members are still around and available to participate and their memories fresh. It is an important task for which funds and time should be included in the project's budget and schedule.[15] Post-completion reviews are part of the process to continuously improve future projects through experience gained from completed projects—an opportunity that many companies forgo.

The post-completion project review should review:

1. Initial project objectives in terms of technical performance, schedule, and cost; and the soundness of the objectives in view of the needs and problems the system was supposed to resolve.
2. Changes in objectives, and reasons for changes, noting which changes were avoidable and which were not.
3. The activities and relationships of the project team throughout the project life cycle, including the interfaces, performance, and effectiveness of project management; relationships among top management, the project team, the functional organization, and the customer; cause and process of termination; customer reactions and satisfaction.
4. The involvement and performance of all stakeholders, including subcontractors and vendors, the client, and outside support groups.
5. Expenditures, sources of costs, and profitability; identify organizational benefits, project extensions, and marketable innovations.
6. Areas of the project where performance was particularly good, noting reasons for success and identifying processes that worked well.
7. Problems, mistakes, oversights, and areas of poor performance, and the causes.
8. A list of lessons learned from the project and recommendations for incorporating them into future projects.

The review includes a half- or day-long meeting with representatives from all functional organizations that substantially contributed to the project—marketing, design, engineering, production, quality assurance, testing, contract administration, and so on. To encourage maximal openness and candor, the managers of these areas should *not* be at the meeting. An outside facilitator might be selected to guide the process to ensure the review is comprehensive, unbiased, and accurate. During the meeting the participants independently list the things that went right and wrong with the project; they then share their notes and create lists of rights, wrongs, lessons learned, and future recommendations. The completed lists are then formally presented to stakeholders, project, functional, and senior managers, and others on the project team.

The review seeks not to criticize or place blame for mistakes or problems, but to determine lessons that may be applied to future projects. The review results are documented in a *project summary report*, which becomes the authoritative document on the project. The project summary report describes the project, its evolution, and its eventual outcome. It describes the project plan, how the plan worked, and where it failed. Because projects affect different parties in different ways, the individual opinions and assessments of the customer, the project team, and upper management should be considered separately. A project that was profitable for the contractor might not have effectively resolved the client's problem; a project that resolved a client problem might have put the contractor into financial jeopardy.

The project summary becomes the reference for project-related questions that might arise later. Thoroughness and clarity are essential since people who worked on the project usually will not be available to answer questions later. The summary report is retained in a project library, and lessons learned and recommendations promoted in other projects, sometimes by the PMO. Post-completion reviews and summary reports are ways to capture and reapply knowledge to future projects—tools for project *knowledge management,* discussed in Chapter 16.

Example 3: Microsoft Postmortems[16]

Product development projects at Microsoft often conclude with a written postmortem report that is circulated to the highest levels of management, which for major projects includes the company president. A report can require as much as 6 months to prepare and range from under 10 pages to over 100 pages in length. Its purpose is to describe what worked well in the project, what did not, and what should be improved for the next project. Descriptive information is also included such as *the size of the project team, duration of the project, aspects of the product* (size in thousand-lines-of-code (KLOC), languages and platform used), *quality issues* (number of bugs per KLOC, type and severity of bugs), *schedule performance* (actual versus planned dates), and the *development process* (tools used, interdependencies with other groups). Functional managers prepare the initial draft and then circulate it via e-mail to other team members for comment. The final draft is sent to team members, senior executives, and the directors of product development, coding, and testing.

Post-installation System Review

Several months after its delivery, the fully operational end-item system should be evaluated to assess its performance in the user environment and under ongoing operational conditions. This *post-installation system review* focuses on the end-item system and serves a variety of purposes for the contractor and user, such as providing operation and maintenance information for the system's designers, and revealing possible needed enhancements for the system's users. Based upon the original user requirements, the post-installation system review attempts to answer the questions: Now that the system is fully operational, is it doing what it was intended to do? Is the user getting the expected benefits from the system? What changes to the system, if any, are necessary to better fulfill the user's needs?

It is important that the evaluated system is *unaltered* from the one delivered. Frequently the user makes system modification and improvements after installation; although there is nothing wrong with this per se, the system is physically or functionally changed from the one delivered or installed, a fact that must be considered when evaluating its performance.

During the course of the review the evaluation team might discover elements of the system in need of repair or modification. Design flaws, operating problems, or necessary enhancements that could not have been foreseen earlier sometimes become obvious after the system has been in routine operation.

Results of the review are summarized in *a post-installation report* that describes the system's performance compared to its objectives, any maintenance problems, and any suggested possible enhancements. The post-installation system report and the project summary report are filed together and retained as references for planning future projects.

12.13   AFTER THE PROJECT—PHASE D: OPERATION

What happens next after the conclusion of Phase C depends on whether the end-item or deliverable is a physical system or procedure that must be maintained and operated, or a service for which no physical product remains.

Examples of the latter are rock concerts, company relocations, and corporate mergers and audits. Each of these projects provides a service rather than develops, produces, or installs a product or system.

But when the project does develop and/or build a system or product, the result is a physical end-item system that then moves into the next and final stage of the systems development cycle: operation. The contractor sometimes remains involved with the customer and operational system during this phase in two ways: (1) an agreement to maintain/repair the system or (2) a new project to enhance or replace that same system.

System Evaluation and Maintenance

The contractor may perform evaluation of the system either as part of the original contract agreement or by an additional agreement. The evaluation may occur as the last scheduled activity of the contractor in the form of a post-installation review, described earlier, or as an *extended agreement* to provide periodic review and/or service of the system on a continuing basis. Sometimes the agreement is a warranty-type arrangement whereby the contractor provides review and maintenance for a prespecified time period as part of the original contract. Other times, it is an "extended" type of arrangement that continues the contractor's involvement for a longer time period. As part of the agreement the contractor may assign *system representatives* and technicians to the user site to perform preventive maintenance (parts replacement at regular intervals) and system upgrades on a scheduled basis or when requested by the user.

Enhancing or Replacing the System

When the customer needs or desires to enhance or replace the originally contracted system, a new project emerges. From the original contractor's perspective, this is an *extension* to the original project.

There are two kinds of extensions: discretionary and essential. *Discretionary extensions* are requested by the user or proposed by the contractor for the purpose of improving the operation, performance, or convenience of the original project end-item. The environment remains the same, but new and better ways now exist that can improve the system. The other kind, *essential extensions*, are compulsory; without them the system will cease to operate or become obsolete. Whenever the end-item as originally implemented is no longer adequate because of changes in the environment or design or other deficiencies, it *must* be enhanced or replaced.

A decision to expand, enhance, or replace a system marks the beginning of a new systems development cycle. The cycle is initiated either by a request from the user (e.g., a request for proposal (RFP)) or with a proposal from the contractor. Any extension itself becomes a project. Humankind engages in few dead-end projects; each spurs others, and the systems development cycle keeps rolling along—hence the term "cycle." (See Figure 11-1, the arrow "To Phase A; repeat cycle.")

12.14   SUMMARY

Project evaluation uses a variety of sources and measures for collecting and communicating formative evaluation information, including written and oral reports, observations, and review meetings. Site visits and one-on-one conversations are the best sources, as are informal reviews and formal review meetings. Informal reviews are internal reviews held regularly and conducted by peer members of the project team. Formal reviews are special reviews or audits held at key stages or milestones in the project, and conducted by experienced outsiders and consultants. They provide independent assessments of overall project performance, suggestions or instructions for improving the project, and sometimes recommendations about whether or not to continue the project. The kinds of reports and reviews, details about contents, formats, schedules, participants, and points of contact are specified in the project communication plan.

For many projects, the management functions associated with planning and control are enhanced by using PMIS software. Most PMIS software perform the functions of network scheduling, resource management, budgeting, tracking, cost control, and performance analysis. Many also take advantage of web-based technology, which provides the benefits of ready accessibility at remote sites, ease of usage, and reliability and currency of information.

Implementation is the final stage of the systems development life cycle; this is when the end-item system or other deliverable is completed and turned over to the user. Among the important tasks during implementation are user training, user tests of acceptance, and system installation and conversion. The contractor trains the user how to operate, maintain, and service the system, and develops a strategy for installing the system in the user's environment; three possible strategies are parallel, pilot, and cold turkey. The user performs his own set of tests to determine whether or not the installed end-item system is acceptable.

The project is terminated through a series of formal procedures. The project manager oversees all termination activities and conducts the project closeout. Following project completion, a post-completion review or postmortem is conducted to assess the effectiveness of the project organization. The results of this review are compiled in a project summary report for future reference. Additionally, after the main end-item system has been in operation for a while, a post-installation system review is conducted to assess its performance and determine possible maintenance or enhancements needs. The documented results are combined with the project summary report to provide a reference document for future project teams.

The preceding two sections of the book described how project managers, organizations, and teams plan, organize, and guide projects from start to finish, but did not say much about the managers, organizations, or teams *themselves*. The following section of the book focuses on managers and teams. It addresses project *organizational behavior* and the topics of organization structure, leadership, teamwork, and conflict and stress, all of which are crucial to effective management of projects.

REVIEW QUESTIONS

1. Describe the difference between formative evaluation and summary evaluation in project management.

2. Why is it better to rely on a variety of information sources for evaluation than just a few? Give some examples of how several sources are used in project evaluation.

3. What are the advantages and disadvantages of the following sources of information: (a) charts and tables, (b) oral and written reports, (c) first-hand evaluation?

4. What is the purpose of internal peer reviews? When are they held? Who participates?

5. What is an action plan? What must it include?

6. What is a formal critical review? When is a formal review held and what does it look at? Why do outsiders conduct it? Why would a customer or project supporter want a formal review?

7. What should be included in summary status reports to top management? What should be included in comparative summary reports?

8. What reports should the project manager receive? How does the project manager use these reports?

9. What reports are sent to functional managers?

10. When and what kind of reports are sent to the customer? Why is reporting to customers so important?

11. What is the role of the PMIS in project management?

12. Discuss the applications and benefits of web-based project management.

13. Discuss the uses of the PMIS throughout the phases of the project life cycle.

14. How is a system implemented? Describe the important considerations for turning the system over to the user.

15. Discuss user training and why it is sometimes included in the implementation stage.

16. How is the project end-item tested and checked out for approval?

17. Describe the different strategies for installing or converting to the new system.

18. What are the reasons for project termination? How can termination for reasons other than achievement of project goals be avoided?

19. What is involved in planning and scheduling the project termination?

20. What is the role of the project manager and contract administrator in receiving customer acceptance of the work and final payment?

21. What are side items? Give examples not used in this book. How can they delay project completion?

22. What kinds of negotiated adjustments are made to the contract, post-acceptance? Why would a user or contractor want to specify the terms of a contract *after* the project is completed?

23. What is a punch list?

24. What is a project extension and how do project extensions originate? How is a project extension managed?

25. What are the differences between the two kinds of reviews in project summary evaluation: the post-completion project or postmortem review and the post-installation system review? Describe each of these reviews.

26. Describe what happens during the operation phase? What is the role of the systems development organization (contractor) in this phase?

QUESTIONS ABOUT THE STUDY PROJECT

1. How often and what kinds of review meetings were held in the project? Why were they held? Who attended them?
2. When and for what reason were special reviews held?
3. How was follow-up ensured on decisions made during review meetings?
4. Was there a project meeting room? How often and in what ways was it used?
5. Describe the kinds of project reports sent to top management and the customer. Who issued these reports? What kinds of reports were sent to project and functional managers? Who issued them?
6. Describe the PMIS used in the project you are studying. Was it the same one used for cost-accounting (PCAS) and project scheduling? Does it combine scheduling, budgeting, authorization, and control, or were several different systems used? If several systems were used, how were they integrated?
7. What are the strong and weak points of the PMIS? Does the system adequately satisfy the information requirements needed to plan and control the project? Is a web-based system used? Are inadequacies in the system the fault of the software, or of the manual support system that provides inputs and utilizes the outputs? What improvements would you suggest to the system?
8. Did the project manager encourage open, informal communication? If so, in what way? If not, why not?
9. How was the project terminated? Describe the activities of the project manager during the final stage of the project and the steps taken to close it out.
10. If the end-item is a building or other "constructed" item, how was it turned over to the user? Describe the testing, acceptance, training, and authorization process.
11. How was the contract closed out? Were there any side items or negotiated adjustments to the contract?
12. Did any follow-up projects grow out of the project being investigated?
13. Describe the project summary review (prepared at the *end* of the project). Who prepared it? Who was it sent to and how was it used? Where is it now? Show an example (or portion of one).
14. Was there a review of the product or project output after it was installed? When? By whom? What did they find? Did the client request the review or was it standard procedure?
15. What happened to the project team when the project was completed?
16. Does the contractor remain involved with the customer and end-item through an extended agreement?

ENDNOTES

1. Brian Muirhead and William Simon, *High Velocity Leadership: The Mars Pathfinder Approach to Faster, Better, Cheaper* (New York: Harper Business, 1999): 179.
2. R.D. Archibald, *Managing High-Technology Programs and Projects* (New York: John Wiley & Sons): 191.
3. First to run on a PC was Harvard Project Manager in 1983, followed soon by an explosion of products—well over 100. All but the strongest products have since disappeared.
4. D. Roman, *Managing Projects: A Systems Approach* (New York: Elsevier, 1986): 181, 184; L. F. Suarez, "Resource Allocation: A Comparative Study,"*Project Management Journal* 18, no. 1 (March 1987): 68–71, 76, 231.
5. Portions of this section were prepared with the assistance of Elisa Denney.

6. Tyson Greer, Understanding Intranets (Redmond, WA: Microsoft Press, 1998); see also Stephen Mead, "Project-Specific Intranets for Construction Team,"*Project Management Journal* (September 1997), 44–51.

7. R. W. Palla, "Introduction to Micro-computer Software Tools for Project Management,"*Project Management Journal* (August 1987), 61–68.

8. *Project Management Software Survey* (Newtown Square, PA: Project Management Institute, 1999), http://www.pmkb.com/forum/showthread.php?t=45.

9. Thomas Peters and Robert Waterman, *In Search of Excellence* (New York: Warner Communications, 1984): 121–125.

10. D. Roman, *Managing Projects: A Systems Approach*, 392–394.

11. See Archibald, *Managing High-Technology Programs and Projects*, 235–36 and 264–70, for a complete checklist of close-out activities.

12. Drew Fetherston, *Chunnel* (New York: Time Books, 1997): 372–375.

13. V.G. Hajek, *Managing Engineering Projects*, 3rd ed. (New York: McGraw-Hill, 1984). See pp. 233–240 for a good description of monitoring and support side items for both engineering hardware and computer software projects.

14. Ibid., 241–242.

15. A procedure for conducting post-project reviews is discussed in Neal Whitten, *Managing Software Development Projects*, 2nd ed. (New York: John Wiley & Sons, 1995), 343–357.

16. Michael Cusumano and Richard Selby, *Microsoft Secrets* (New York: Free Press, 1995): 331–334.

Part IV

Organization Behavior

CHAPTER 13

   Project Organization Structure and Integration

CHAPTER 14

   Project Roles, Responsibility, and Authority

CHAPTER 15

   Managing Participation, Teamwork, and Conflict

*P*roject outcomes depend on the way individuals and groups are organized and interact. As human endeavors, projects are both influenced by and have influence on the behavior and well-being of the groups and individuals that belong to them.

   The three chapters in this section focus on the organizational and behavioral issues surrounding projects, and the teams and individuals that comprise them. They describe the ways that groups are organized into projects, styles of leadership used by project managers, roles and responsibilities of project team members, and ways groups and individuals are managed to maximize effectiveness and minimize the negative consequences of working in projects.

   Chapters 13 and 14 in this section cover topics discussed in the PMBOK guide under project management "process." Chapter 15 addresses the PMBOK knowledge area of human resource management.

Chapter 13

Project Organization Structure and Integration

> *How can you expect to govern a country that has 246 kinds of cheese?*

—Charles de Gaulle

*O*rganizations are systems of human and physical elements interacting to achieve goals. As with all systems, organizations are partly described by their *structure*—the form of relationships that bond their elements. In all organizations two kinds of structures coexist. One is the *formal* structure, the *published* one that describes normative superior–subordinate relationships, chains of command, and subdivisions and grouping of elements. The other is the *informal structure*, the unpublished one that describes relationships that *evolve* through the interactions of people. Whereas the formal organization prescribes how people are supposed to relate, the informal organization is how they actually do relate. It is the groupings, authority relationships, and lines of communication that exist in the organization but nowhere appear on the organization chart.

This chapter deals primarily with formal organization structure, particularly the kinds of structures applicable to projects. There is no one best way to structure project organizations, but there are structural patterns and specific roles that enhance project performance. Though project managers are seldom involved in organizational design decisions, they should understand the kinds of organizational designs used in project management and their relative advantages and disadvantages. Sometimes project managers can affect the project structure, even if only through suggestions to top management.

The chapter also deals with project integration, which is the way that individual functional groups, subunits, project phases, and work tasks are interlinked and coordinated to achieve project goals. The discussion covers various kinds of integration roles used in projects, and the special case of integration in large-scale projects (LSPs) and development projects.

13.1 FORMAL ORGANIZATION STRUCTURE

Concepts of organizational structure apply to all kinds of organizations—companies, institutions, agencies—as well as to their subunits—divisions, departments, projects, and teams. Formal organization structure is publicized in a chart such as the one for NASA in Figure 13-1; a quick glance reveals both the organizational hierarchy and groupings for specialized tasks. By looking at the chart in Figure 13-1, for example, one can see:

1. The range of activities in which the organization is involved and the major subdivisions of the organization (exploration, space operations, science, aeronautics research).
2. The management hierarchy and reporting relationships (under "Mission," e.g., directors at Ames, Goddard and Jet Propulsion Laboratory all report to the associate administrator for Science).
3. The type of work and responsibility of each subdivision (e.g., projects at research centers focus on specific disciplines or goals such as space exploration, space operations, etc.).

Figure 13-1
NASA organization chart, 2006.

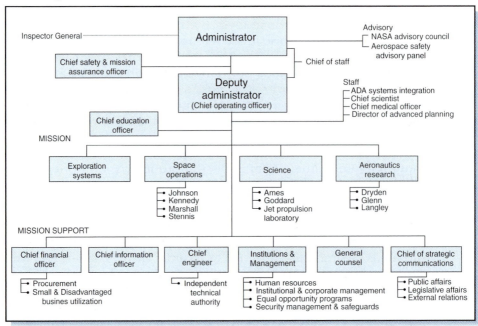

4. The official lines of authority and communication (the administrator is the highest authority, the deputy administrator the next highest, and so on; communication moves formally along the lines from one box to the next, up or down).

There are many things the chart does not show. For example, it does not show informal lines of communication and personal contacts whereby, for example: workers at Jet Propulsion Laboratory talk directly to workers at Dryden via e-mail and telephone, not (as the chart implies) via the directors of these centers, nor does it indicate places of status and power that develop at lower levels. Nonetheless, the chart does give a fundamental overview of elements and relationships of the formal organization, and in this way it is useful.

13.2 ORGANIZATIONAL DESIGN BY DIFFERENTIATION AND INTEGRATION

There is no "best" kind of organization structure. The most appropriate structure depends on the organization's goals, type of work, and environment. Organization structures typically develop through a combination of planned and evolutionary responses to ongoing problems. Organizations create specialized roles and units, each with suitable expertise and resources needed to deal with certain classes of situations and problems efficiently. As organizations grow or the environment changes, additional subdivisions and new groupings are implemented to better handle new situations and emerging problems. For example, as a company increases its product lines, it may subdivide its manufacturing area into product-oriented divisions to better address problems specific to each of the lines. As a company expands its sales territory, it may subdivide its marketing force geographically to better handle problems of regional origin. This subdivision into specialized areas is called *differentiation*.

Obviously, subunits of an organization do not act as independent entities but must interact and support each other. The degree to which they interact, coordinate, and mutually adjust their actions to fulfill organizational goals is called *integration*.

Traditional Forms of Organization

How an organization is subdivided is referred to as the *basis* for differentiation. The six bases for differentiation are functional, geographic, product, customer, process, and project. The project form will be discussed in detail; first, we will look at the other five "traditional" forms of differentiation and the ways subunits in each are integrated.

Functional Differentiation

The functional form of organization is so-called because it is divided into functional subunits such as marketing, finance, production, personnel, and research and development; the structure of the Iron Butterfly Company in Figure 13-2 is an example. Most of the integration between subunits is handled by rules, procedures, coordinated plans, and budgets. When discrepancies occur that cannot be resolved by these measures, the managerial chain of command takes over. When a problem involves several subunits, it is collectively resolved by managers of all subunits affected.

This form of organization works well in repetitive, stable environments because there is little change, and the rather low level of integration afforded by rules,

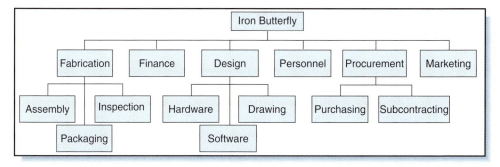

Figure 13-2
Formal organization structure for Iron Butterfly Company showing functional differentiation.

procedures, and chain of command gets the job done. The functional form has a long history. The Roman army was an early organization that used functional differentiation, rules and procedures, and chain of command. The functional form remains today as the most prevalent basis for organization differentiation.

Geographic Differentiation

Most organizations have more than one basis for differentiation. The Roman army was also geographically differentiated; that is, structured according to region or location. Organizations subdivide according to region (e.g., Atlantic, Mid-Western, and Pacific states; European branch; Far East command; etc.) to tailor themselves to the unique requirements of local customers, markets, suppliers, enemies, and so on. Within each geographic subunit, functional differentiation is often retained. Regional subunits may operate relatively autonomously, and any necessary integration between them is usually achieved through standardized accounting and reporting procedures.

Product Differentiation

Firms that produce a variety of products use product-based differentiation. Corporations such as General Motors, General Foods, and General Electric are split into major subdivisions wherein each designs, manufactures, and markets its own product line. Within each subdivision is a functional, geographic, or other form of breakdown. As with geographically differentiated organizations, integration between product subdivisions tends to be limited to standardized financial and reporting rules and procedures.

Customer Differentiation

Organizations may also differentiate by customer type. For example, companies with large military sales often establish a separate division because federal requirements for proposals, contracting, and product specifications differ substantially from those for commercial customers. The level of integration between customer divisions depends on the degree of interdependency between their product lines; typically, however, integration is low.

Process Differentiation

In the process differentiated form, some logical process or sequence of steps (e.g., design, then development, then assembly, then inspection, etc.) is the basis for differentiation. This basis is used for the subunits in the fabrication department of Iron Butterfly (assembly, testing, then packaging), shown in Figure 13-2. A higher level of integration is required among process differentiated subunits because they are sequentially related and problems in one area directly impact the other areas. These subunits tend to rely on coordinated plans and schedules as the primary means of integration. Other means such as task forces and teams are necessary when unanticipated problems arise or as task uncertainty increases. These will be discussed later.

Drawbacks of Traditional Forms of Organization

By their very design, traditional forms of organization can address only certain anticipated, classifiable kinds of problems. As the environment changes and new kinds of problems arise, they react by further differentiating subunits and adding more rules, procedures, and levels of management. The price they pay for this is—in a word—bureaucracy, which translates into less flexibility and greater difficulty integrating the subunits.

Most traditional organizational forms work on the assumption that problems or tasks can be neatly classified and resolved within specialized areas. Thus, subunits in traditional forms tend to work independently and toward their own goals. When a problem arises that requires participation from multiple subdivisions, there may be no person or group to see that it gets resolved. Such problems fall through the cracks.

One way to handle unanticipated, unclassifiable problems is to adapt (redesign) the organization whenever they arise. However, the process of adapting organizational structure to suit unique problems is slow and expensive, reflecting both the inertia of organizations as well as peoples' resistance to change. The alternative to redesign is to bump problems up the chain of command. This works as long as it is not done too often because the chain of command gets quickly overloaded as the number of unanticipated problems increases. Management's response to overload is to add more managers and staff groups, which adds to the size of the management structure, eventually making the organization even less flexible. In short, traditional organizations are not well suited for environments where there is high uncertainty and frequent change. Nonetheless, as described later, most projects are conducted within or using resources provided by organizations with a traditional functional structure.

13.3 REQUIREMENTS OF PROJECT ORGANIZATIONS

Project environments are characterized by complexity, change, uncertainty, and unpredictability. Projects typically require the resources and coordinated work effort of multiple people, subunits, and organizations. Each project is a new undertaking to satisfy a new goal. Subunits must combine their resources according to a coordinated project plan, and be able to allocate and utilize their resources according to that plan. Changes or mistakes in one area have consequences in all others. Because each project is unique and may have no precedent, uncertainty is inherent. As the size of the project increases so do the number of subunits involved and the potential for errors or mistakes.

Organizations working in technologies such as software development, pharmaceuticals, biomedicine, space exploration, advanced product development, and weapon systems development routinely encounter the unexpected. As a result, they need to be adaptable to changing goals and environmental forces, and be able to deal with the uncertainty that accompanies these changes. They must be, in a word, *organic*, which means highly differentiated to accommodate a large variety of potential problems, highly integrated to respond rapidly to situations and problems that require involvement of multiple subunits, and highly flexible to alter structure as goals change.

To achieve this, all project organizations have two properties:

- They integrate subunits using horizontal relations.
- They differentiate their structure to suit the unique requirements of the project and the environment.

These properties are discussed next.

13.4 INTEGRATION OF SUBUNITS IN PROJECTS[1]

Traditional organizations are characterized by their verticalness, or reliance upon up-and-down patterns of authority and communication. As mentioned, this makes them clumsy, slow, and ineffective in dealing with rapidly changing or highly uncertain situations. In contrast, project organizations are characterized by their *horizontalness* or use of direct communication between the parties involved in a problem. Horizontal relations cut across lines of authority and move decisions to the level of the parties affected.

All organizations have horizontal relations, most in the form of personal contacts, informal relationships, and friendships. These contacts are particularly helpful for expediting communication and getting problems resolved between subunits. For example, whenever the assembly department in Figure 13-2 experiences a minor parts shortage, George, the assembly foreman, phones Helen in purchasing for a "rush order" favor. The call bypasses the formal structure (George and Helen's respective managers) and speeds up the ordering procedure.

The drawback with informal processes is that they do not ensure everyone who needs to know is involved or gets the necessary information. For example, Helen must charge all purchases to an account, but if George is not privy to the dollar amount in the account it is possible that his informal requests will deplete the account before additional funds can be credited, which involves someone in the finance/accounting area who is not aware of George's request. Also, if George does not tell anyone else about the parts shortages, the reason for the problem—pilferage, defective parts, or underordering—will never get resolved. In short, informal processes in many respects are inadequate.

Project organizations improve upon informal contacts by incorporating horizontal relations into the formal structure. They do this through the use of functions referred to as *integrators*. Integrators reduce the number of decisions referred up the chain of command and facilitate communication between units working together on a common task. Like informal processes, integrators bypass traditional lines of authority and speed communication. They are better, however, because they ensure that everyone affected by a problem is involved and gets the necessary information.

Several kinds of integrators are used in projects. They are listed below in order of increasing authority, need, and cost; in the list, the latter kinds take on all the authority and responsibility of the former kinds.[2]

Liaison role
Task forces and teams
Project expeditors and coordinators

Project managers
Matrix managers
Integrating contractors

13.5 LIAISON ROLES, TASK FORCES, AND TEAMS

The *liaison role* is a specialized person or group that links two departments at lower levels. In Figure 13-3, the dotted line represents the liaison role of "inventory controller." In addition to performing duties in the assembly department, this person links the assembly and purchasing departments by notifying purchasing of impending shortages and keeping track of orders placed. The role relieves the assembly foreman of this responsibility and, by legitimizing the process, ensures that orders get placed and are documented.

However, the liaison role is not always effective. Though the inventory controller in the example expedites parts ordering, the reason for part shortages goes unresolved. To unravel the problem it is necessary to involve people from other areas of the company. This is where the next kind of integrative function, an *interdisciplinary task force* or *team*, comes into play.

A *task force* is a temporary group of representatives from several areas that meets to solve a problem. (Toffler termed this phenomenon "adhocracy."[3]) When such a group is formed and actively begins addressing the problem, they are, in fact, conducting a project. For example, when a shortage problem occurs, the assembly foreman might call together liaison people from the areas of inspection, accounting, purchasing, and others who should be involved. The task force meets once, several times, or as needed until the problem is solved, after which it disbands. The most effective task forces have a team leader or coordinator, 10 members or less, and are short-lived.[4]

Both the leader and members are selected by (and the leader reports directly to) the person responsible for the project—a functional manager, vice president, or CEO. Leaders are responsible for expediting and coordinating efforts and may have authority to direct tasks to certain individuals or units, or to contract work out. Usually though, they have little formal authority over team members who, often,

Figure 13-3
Liaison role linking assembly and purchasing departments.

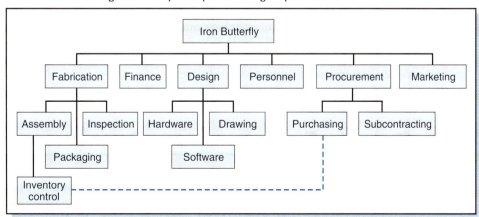

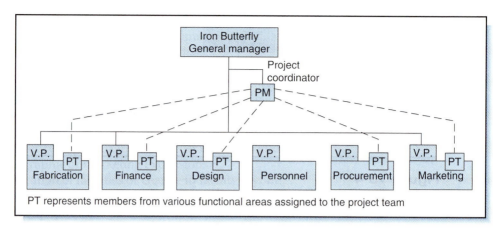

Figure 13-5
Multifunctional project team.

development budget.[6] Concurrent engineering is discussed in Chapter 4 and later in this Chapter.

The multifunctional project team may be located either in the functional area most responsible for the project or at a higher-level position, such as reporting to the general manager as shown in Figure 13-5. The latter arrangement imputes greater importance to the project and improves coordination between the areas involved. The person managing such a project is designated the project *coordinator*. Though this person has no line authority over team members, he does have authority to make and execute decisions about project budgets, schedules, and work perform-ance. Besides the high-level position of reporting to the general manager, the coordi-nator's influence, like that of the expediter, originates in his project knowledge and being placed at the center of everyone involved.

13.7   PURE PROJECT ORGANIZATIONS

Projects that entail high-level complexity, major resource commitments, and heavy stakes in the outcome require a *pure project* or *projectized* form of organization. A pure project is a separate organization, similar to its own company, created espe-cially for and singularly devoted to achievement of the project goal. Whatever the project must have to afford it the highest priority—all necessary human and physi-cal resources—are incorporated into the pure project organization. These organiza-tions are able to react quickly to changing demands of the environment, the user, and the parent organization. Often, found within the pure project are liaisons, task forces, and teams.

Heading the pure object organization is the *project manager*. Unlike the coordi-nator, the project manager has full authority over all people and physical resources assigned to the project and, thus, maximum control. The project manager has authority to contract out for resources, both from internal functional areas as well as from exter-nal subcontractors and suppliers. The pure project manager is involved in the project from start to finish: During proposal preparation, she requests plans from functional areas, reconciles discrepancies among plans, and prepares preliminary budget and schedule estimates; after acceptance, she allocates budgeted money to procure resources and hire personnel; during the project, she allocates resources and approves

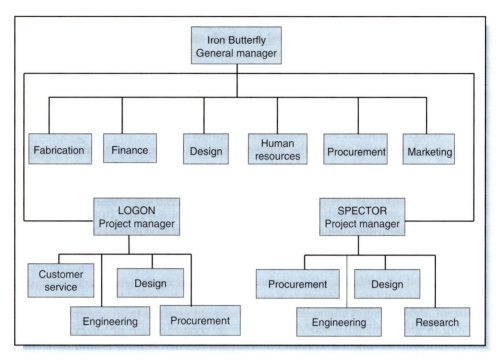

Figure 13-6
Pure projects as "arms" to the functional organization.

all changes to requirements and the project plan. When personnel must be "borrowed" from functional areas, she is the one who negotiates to get the best people.

When resources are not internally available, the project manager heads selection of and negotiations with subcontractors. She oversees their work and coordinates it with other projects. The project managers at LogiCircuit, disaster recovery, and NASA project described in Chapter 1 are examples of pure project managers.

Pure Project Variations

Three common variations of the pure project structure are the *project center*, the *stand-alone project*, and the *partial project*.

In the *project center*, the structure of the parent organization remains the same except for the addition of a separate "project arm" and project manager. This form is shown in Figure 13-6 for the Iron Butterfly Company and two of its pure project arms, LOGON and SPECTOR. (Of course, pure project organizations are not like people; they can have any number of arms, one for each project.) Resources and personnel are borrowed from functional and staff areas for as long as needed. General Motors used a project center when it chose 1,200 key people from various divisions for the task of determining how to downsize all of its automotive lines. The project center developed suggestions, turned them over to the automotive divisions for implementation, and then disbanded. In another corporation, a project center was used to oversee the relocation of its offices. By creating a project center to work full-time on the tricky problems of relocation, the rest of the organization was able to continue its work as usual.

The *stand-alone project* is an organization created especially for the purpose of accomplishing the project. It does not represent only one organization but consists of members from several participating organizations. It is typically used for large-scale

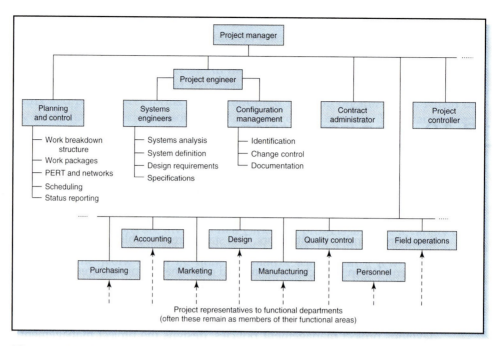

Figure 13-10
Project office for a large development project.

for example, putting everyone in the project staff work in the same physical office, keeping the office open and accessible to all functional areas, and encouraging frequent meetings and consensual decision making among representatives. Additional techniques for facilitating interaction are discussed in Chapter 15.

In staffing the project office, the project manager must avoid duplicating the efforts of the functional areas. The purpose of the project office is to *coordinate* work and advise the functional areas on *what* they should do, not *how* they should do it. Nor should the office try to *do* the work. To minimize the size of the full-time project office staff in smaller projects, all functional representatives and most specialists physically remain located at their functional areas.

Office of Projects, PMO, and the Program Office

Multi-project organizations also have an *office of projects* (not to be confused with the project office), program office, or *PMO*. This was shown in Figure 13-8 as the "vice president of projects." In pure project organizations, the office is located at a level between senior management and project managers (in Figure 13-6, it would be located below the general manager and on the line connected to the LOGON and SPECTOR projects). When projects are small, the office of projects substitutes for individual project offices and handles proposals, contracting, scheduling, cost control, and report preparation for every project. When projects are large or overlap, the office of projects or PMO is used *in addition* to project offices and coordinates the combined requirements of all the projects.[13]

When projects are part of a program, *a program office* is set up to ensure that the projects supplement one another and "add up" to overall program goals. The program office handles interfaces external to each project, maintains user enthusiasm and support, keeps project managers informed of potential problems, and handles interfaces and integration between projects. The NASA program office described in

Chapter 1 is an example. When programs are very large, the integration work of the program office is supplemented by outside "integration contractors," discussed next.

13.11 INTEGRATION IN LSPs

Any party that works toward the project goal is a part of the project organization. In large-scale projects (LSPs) or megaprojects, numerous parties—sponsors, prime contractors, subcontractors, consultants, and suppliers—contribute to one effort. Figure 13-11 shows the principal contributors and relationships in an LSP. Relationships are complex and lines of authority connecting the parties are often weak (sometimes based entirely on contracts and purchase orders). If Figure 13-11 appears somewhat confusing, well, that simply reflects the fact that relationships in LSPs *are* sometimes confusing. Examples of LSPs include space systems (e.g., the international space station), construction projects (Canada's LaGrande hydroelectric venture, Holland's Delta flood control project, English Channel Tunnel, China's Three Gorges Dam), as well as company relocations (involving the client, movers, construction companies, recruiters, consultants, and suppliers) and corporate mergers (dual sets of clients, consultants, and attorneys).

Integration between contractors in LSPs is achieved through use of project managers, coordinators, liaisons, and task forces. Notice in Figure 13-11 the relationships, both horizontal and hierarchical, among contributors' management as well as

Figure 13-11
Integration relationships in an LSP.

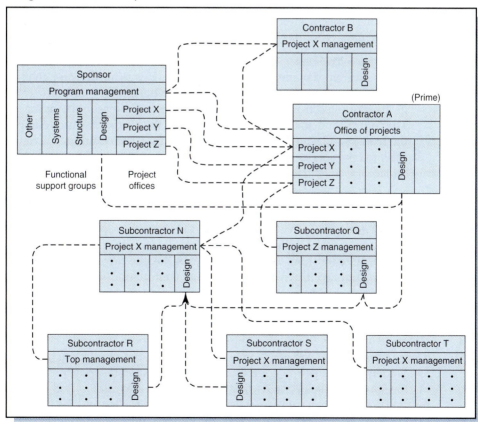

between their functional areas. Direct relationships and communication between, for instance, the design groups of the sponsor, its contractors, and subcontractors accelerate decision making and tighten integration.

Most LSPs are devoted to development and/or construction of complex systems. The total effort is subdivided among a number of contributors, each responsible for a specific subsystem or component to be integrated with others to form the overall system. Figure 13-12, for example, shows the major components in the international space station. The figure is simplified and excludes the launch vehicles to get the components into Earth's orbit, the support systems, and the numerous organizations working to develop, produce, launch, and integrate the components (prime contractors, subcontractors, and suppliers).

Oversight and Integration Contractors

In public works and government projects, integration is usually the responsibility of the sponsoring agency. Sometimes, however, the engineering and management tasks are quite difficult or extensive, and outside help is required.

Among the first LSPs to experience the integration problems inherent to large systems were weapons system development projects during World War II.[14] For instance, the components that made up a system such as a bomber were purchased by separate offices within the Army Air Corps. These components—airframe, engines, and electronics—were then furnished to the airframe manufacturer to assemble. As systems grew more complex, procurement by several separate organizations no longer worked. Sometimes the subsystem interfaces were different so plugs and fasteners would not fit, or the size of the components was greater than planned and the entire system had to be redesigned. To overcome these difficulties, the military established detailed specifications and committees to coordinate subsystem interfaces. This resulted in massive red tape and long delays, as exemplified by Livingston:[15]

> A contractor wished to change the clock in an airplane cockpit from a one-day to an eight-day mechanism. A justification was written and given to the military representative, who forwarded it to the military technical group. The group requested from the contractor more detailed reasoning for the change. The contractor acknowledged and sent it to the group. The group approved the request and sent it to the change committee. The committee reviewed it, accepted the change, then sent an authorization back to the coordinator to replace the clock. This simple request took *three months* to process.

Today, the integration process is expedited by giving responsibility to a single "oversight" body, similar to the role of a wedding consultant or general contractor, but on a larger scale. The job of integrating an LSP requires considerable manpower and a wide range of technical skills. Usually, the *lead* or *prime* contractor is assigned the responsibility for systems integration. Meantime, the project sponsor retains responsibilities such as contracting with *associate* contractors (subsystem manufacturers), and making major decisions, as well as resolving conflicts between the prime and associates. The associates become subcontractors to the prime contractor, taking their orders from the prime, and subjecting themselves to its surveillance and approval. Figure 13-13 shows the relationships among the sponsor, prime, and contractors for a large urban transit project. Notice the different types of relationships.[16]

Sometimes the prime contractor is given greater responsibility, such as assisting the sponsor in selecting associates, pricing of subsystems, and allocating project funds. This presents a problem when the prime contractor and the subcontractors are competitors, because subcontractors are understandably hesitant to divulge design

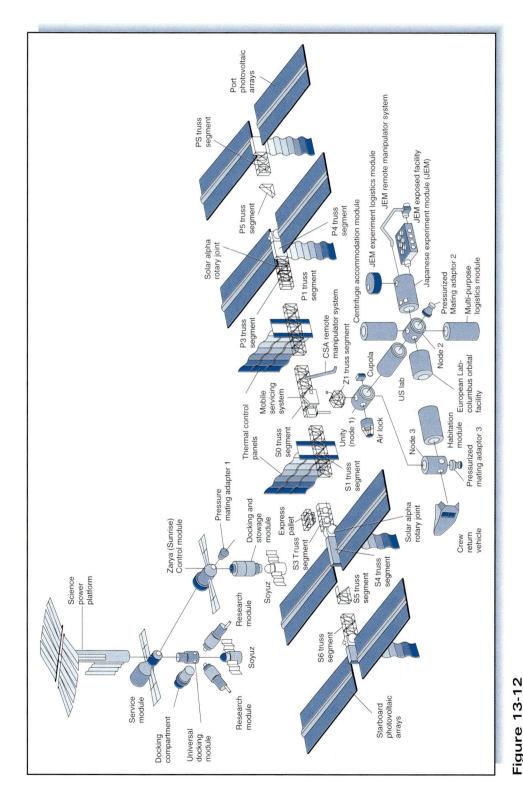

Figure 13-12

Major components in the hardware and assembly of the international space station (Diagram, courtesy of NASA).

503

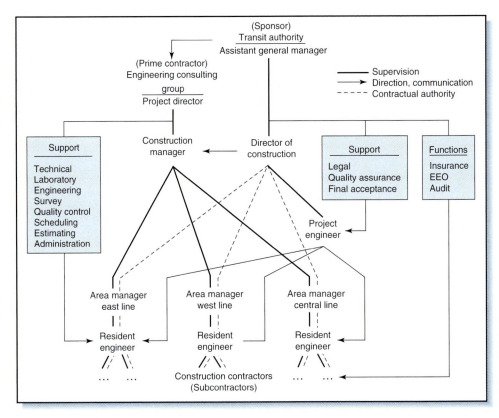

Figure 13-13
Management and authority relationships in a large construction project.

concepts or subsystem details, even though the prime needs them to integrate the overall system.

Sometimes even the largest prime contractors need assistance. At such times they submit a joint proposal as a *team* where one company serves as leader, assuming responsibility for systems engineering and management of the others. This appeals to small- and medium-sized firms that ordinarily would not have the resources to contract independently. The problem with this approach is that unless the lead company is strong, serious interface problems may arise. It also reduces competition, and because no team is likely to have all the best subsystems, the sponsor may require the team leader to open up the subsystem development to competition and, if necessary, change the members of the team.

When the prime contractor lacks the capability to perform the integrating work, a separate consulting firm, or *integration contractor*, is engaged entirely for providing integration and engineering advice.[17] These contractors, which sometimes employ thousands of workers, are able to quickly pull together all the necessary resources. The problem is that they often operate in the same business as the contractors they integrate, which puts them in the awkward position of managing their competitors and being able to learn their secrets.

Example 3: Corporate Merger—Large-Scale Non-technical Project[18]

Special integration management is necessary not only in technical projects, but in any *large*, *complex* project. In 2000, one of the US's largest pharmaceutical companies acquired one of Europe's largest for $6.9 billion. The acquisition involved 10,000 people, 18 manufacturing locations, and 30 international affiliates. The US company engaged a well-known global consulting firm to oversee the integration, which initially assigned as many as a dozen representatives to work on the effort. The consultant first established a program management office, then a global acquisition integration management (AIM) team with 18 full-time director-level individuals from the US corporation. The purpose of the AIM team was to plan, manage, and execute the integration across all divisions and functional areas of the corporation. This team went on to create other teams, eventually numbering 24 and including more than 500 people from both corporations. The consulting group determined the composition of the teams, structured the work of these and other teams, participated in the teams' major decisions, kept watch over critical path activities, and consulted extensively with managers and functional teams in the European company. By hiring the consulting firm as integration contractor, the project benefited from best practices and lesson learned through the consultant's many years of merger and acquisition experience—experience lacking in the two pharmaceutical corporations. The project structure, consisting of the integration consultant, AIM team, and other teams was a pure project organization devoted entirely to the corporate merger.

13.12 INTEGRATION IN SYSTEMS DEVELOPMENT PROJECTS

Integration in projects can be conceptualized in two ways: integration of the *functional areas* of the project organization to achieve project goals, and integration of the *phases* of the project so that issues concerning later phases influence decisions made in the early phases. The former, which has been the subject of the chapter thus far, is called *horizontal integration*; the latter is called *vertical integration* (Figure 13-14). The two aspects are not independent because integration of the project phases also usually requires integration of the functional areas.

Achieving high-level integration in large-scale systems development projects such as new product development and software development can be difficult. These projects require the integrated efforts of many functional units throughout the stages of conception, definition, design and development, testing, production, and installation.

Figure 13-14
Horizontal and vertical integration in systems development projects.

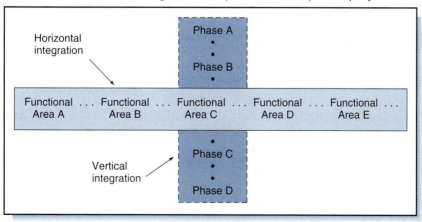

Nonintegrated Systems Development

In a traditional development project, a different functional group is responsible for each phase. For example, first the marketing group specifies the initial concept and customer requirements, then the design group produces the technical specifications and the system design, then the manufacturing and purchasing groups determine ways to make the product and obtain the parts and materials.

Even when a project manager oversees the process, the level of horizontal and vertical integration is rather low. Work at each stage remains largely centered in one functional area and receives minimal involvement from others. With each new stage of the project, a new functional area takes over, "inheriting" and being forced to accommodate the output of the previous stage. As a result, the design group is forced to create a product design that conforms to the requirements it inherited ("thrown over the wall") from marketing, and, in turn, the manufacturing group is forced to develop a production process that conforms to the design it inherited from the design group. The process, illustrated in Figure 13-15, involves little interaction between marketing, design, and manufacturing groups.

Decisions regarding definition, design, and production are made sequentially and independently; they are often incomplete or incorrect because not all of the right people and functional areas are involved at the time. The consequence is, for example, that marketing fails to specify an important requirement, or else specifies one that is not necessary; later, the engineering design group creates a product design that meets all the requirements but the manufacturing group finds difficult or costly to produce. Each new functional group stepping into the process must struggle to accommodate commitments made by earlier groups. When a group encounters commitments it cannot implement, it must send the design (or decision/commitment) back to the other groups for modification. This back-and-forth exchange between areas results in numerous *change requests*, with detrimental consequences to project schedules, budgets, and end-item quality. The problem is lack of integration, failure of early decisions to account for the complete systems life cycle, and the requirements and knowledge of the functional areas and stakeholders that will eventually inherent the project or the end-item.

Figure 13-15
Traditional interaction between functional areas during the phases of systems development.[19]

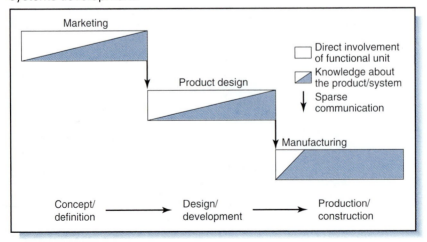

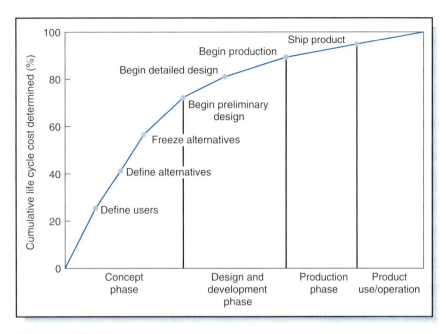

Figure 13-16
Percent of life cycle cost set during stages of the systems development life cycle.

Impact on Life Cycle Costs

The nonintegrated approach to system development has a big impact on life cycle costs too. As described in Chapter 8, *life cycle costs* include all costs of materials, production, distribution, and operation of the end-item for as long as it continues to be produced and used. Fact is, most of this cost is predetermined by decisions made very early in the systems development life cycle. As Figure 13-16 shows, about 80% of a product's life cycle cost is determined in the project's conceptual and design stages, well before the product is manufactured. This means that whatever the total product cost, 80% is based upon choices made during the early stages of the life cycle.[20] Unless important decisions affecting the later stages of production, system installation, and operation are made correctly at the start, the consequences are not only a protracted systems development cycle and delayed launch of the product or system, but high production and operating costs too.

The integrated approach to systems development is *concurrent engineering*.

13.13   CONCURRENT ENGINEERING

Concurrent engineering is implemented with a cross-functional team that can be structured as a matrix team or pure project team. Every group, department, or organization responsible for some piece of the project or influenced by the project is given the opportunity to contribute to the team and provide early input to key decisions. The team invites functional areas to participate in decisions long before those areas actually begin design, production, testing, or operational work on the system (Figure 13-17). Horizontal integration and vertical integration are achieved in one fell swoop.

other managers. Most project managers have a good deal of responsibility not much authority, so they need different skills and leadership
approaches than traditional managers.

14.1   THE PROJECT MANAGER

Project Manager's Role

Without the role of project manager there would be no such thing as project management. The project manager is the glue holding the project together and the mover
and shaker spurring it on. To be a project manager, a person wears many different
hats, many at the same time; they include the hats of an integrator, communicator,
decision maker, motivator, evangelist, entrepreneur, and change agent.

The importance of integration in project work was emphasized earlier. Project
management integrates diverse activities and scattered elements to achieve time,
cost, and performance goals. As the central figure in the project, the project manager's prime role is to *integrate everything and everybody* to accomplish these goals. The
project manager has been called the organizational "metronome," the person who
keeps the project's diverse elements responsive to a single, central beat.[3]

The project manager is the *project communication hub*, the end of the funnel for all
reports, requests, memoranda, and complaints. She takes inputs from more sources
and directs information to more receivers than anyone else in the project. Between
sources and receivers, she refines, summarizes, and translates information to make
sure that project stakeholders are well informed about policies, objectives, budgets,
schedules, requirements, progress, and changes.

Being at the hub puts the project manager in the central position of making *decisions* about allocating resources, setting project scope and direction, and balancing
schedule, cost, and performance criteria. Even when lacking the authority to make
high-level decisions, she is often well situated to influence the decisions and actions
of those who do.

The prime motivational factor in any diverse group is strong commitment to a
central goal. In a project organization, it is the project manager who instills a *sense
of direction* and commitment to action. There are many motivating factors in project
work such as spontaneity, achievement, and excitement, but these are sometimes difficult to uphold, especially in a project that is long and stressful. Lack of precedent,
part-time personnel, diverse specialties, infrequent contact, and spatial distance
between workers are among the factors that can drain motivation from projects.
Despite these, the successful project manager is able to foster enthusiasm, team
spirit, confidence, and a drive toward excellence.

The project manager is a sort of *evangelist* who conveys faith in the project, its
value, and workability. During the conceptual phase, the would-be project manager is often the only person who sees the big picture. Whether or not it gets funded
depends on her ability to gain the endorsement of influential stakeholders.

The project manager is an *entrepreneur*, driven to procure funds, facilities, and
people to get the project off the ground and keep it flying. She must win over reluc-
tant functional managers who will question assigning their better people to the
project. Even after work is underway, she must continue to champion the cause, and
at any stage of the project she might find herself fighting for the project's very exist-
ence. In the end, whether the project succeeds or fails, the project manager is ultimately held accountable.

Finally, the project manager is the *change agent* who initiates passage into new and promising, though sometimes murky, areas. She is always alert to developments that could impinge on the project, ready to adopt new and innovative ideas, and strives to overcome resistance to change. As the composition and size of the project change (and so the communication and reporting channels), the project manager is the person who orchestrates and facilitates the change. At the same time, while facilitating big changes, she resists those little ones that would unnecessarily increase the scope, cost, or duration of the project.

Example 1: Gutzon Borglum: Project Manager and Sculptor[A]

If you are familiar with the carvings in Figure 14-1, then you know the handiwork of Gutzon Borglum. More than 2 million people a year visit Mount Rushmore National Memorial. Most of them who hear the name Gutzon Borglum think that it was he who *sculpted* the faces. And, of course, he *was* the sculptor, though not of the *actual faces* on the mountain. The contract for the project specified that the memorial was "to be carved . . . by . . . and/or under the direction of Gutzon Borglum" and that Borglum was to enjoy "full, final, and complete freedom of authority in the execution of the monument's design." He did carve the faces, but on a miniature model exactly 1/12 the size of the ones on the mountain. The model served as a guide for workers who did the actual sculpting of the monument. Much of this "sculpting" consisted of removing huge quantities of granite using dynamite and heavy drills and pneumatic jackhammers; the usual sculptor's tools of chisels and hammers were used only for detail work.

Projects of such grandiose size are never the work of just one person; however, in the case of Rushmore if anyone should get credit, it would have to be Gutzon Borglum. Although many others contributed to the project in important

Figure 14-1
Gutzon Borglum's most famous work attracts millions of visitors a year. (Photo courtesy of John Nicholas.)

ways, it was Borglum's tireless efforts that yielded much of the project funding, and his genius and stubborn dedication that made it happen. He picked the site; he wrote letters and articles, and he spoke personally to businessmen, wealthy industrialists, senators, congressman, and US presidents; he determined that the faces would be of Washington, Jefferson, Roosevelt, and Lincoln; he hired and organized the work crew; he created the innovative means for transferring the design from the model to the mountain; and, *in addition to that*, he attended to myriad details, from designing the scaffolding, work platforms, tramway, hoists, and grounds buildings to orchestrating events in the pageants for the initial dedication and final unveiling ceremonies. Meantime, he also kept trying to revive his Stone Mountain project in Georgia, which he had started years earlier but not finished. People wondered when he ever rested or if he ever slept. Of course, he was by no means perfect; he did not always have project problems under control, and his efforts were criticized for being uncoordinated and unorganized, especially in the early years. When the project began in 1927, Borglum wasn't completely sure what the monument was going to look like. At the time, however, all that mattered to South Dakotans was that it would bring recognition to their obscure state, and to Borglum that it was an opportunity to do something never before accomplished and a chance at artistic immortality.

People familiar with Borglum were impressed with his artistic talent, but they were even more impressed with his "capacity for affection, wrath, generosity, stinginess, nobility, pettiness, charm, and sheer obnoxiousness."[5] He was short on modesty and humility, and long on "mulish stubbornness." He thought big, dreamed big, talked big, and was not afraid to tackle any undertaking. His enthusiasm was contagious.

The project work crew consisted of 22 men. Most of the carving they had to do was with 80-pound drills and jackhammers while dangling on the side of a cliff. They sat in harnesses designed by Borglum that were lowered down the mountain face with hand winches. Imagine their feelings, as described by biographer Rex Smith: "You do your drilling while hanging on the side of a stone wall so lofty that you feel at first like you are hanging on the back fence of creation. From where you sit you can look down upon mountains and plains that stretch farther than the eye can see. Surrounded by these vast spaces, suspended against a stone cliff, you feel dwarfed and insignificant . . . and uneasy."[6] Borglum was a stickler for safety, so despite the dangers there were few accidents and no fatalities throughout 14 years of work. Borglum was never chummy with his crew, but he cared and looked out for them, and, in return, they were extremely loyal to him, the project, and each other.

Seeing the monument today, we realize that its construction must have posed great challenges, but that, obviously, those challenges were overcome. Borglum, however, was never sure they would be overcome because a sculpture of such scale had never before been attempted. Although he had selected the mountain, he knew there was the risk that it might contain some disastrous hidden flaws—a crack or bad rock—that could not be worked around. In fact, besides funding, it was the shape of the mountain and its deep fissures that determined that the number of presidential busts had to be four and no more. Time and again obstacles arose, funds ran out, and the project had to be stopped. But Borglum and other believers persevered so that the project would again be revived. In the end, however, the carving was abandoned and the monument left uncompleted according to its original design because the nation was about to become embroiled in World War II and would no longer support the effort. Just months before the project was canceled, Borglum died. Up until then he had been the prominent driving force, and you have to ask, had he lived beyond the war years, how much more of the monument would have been completed? Borglum was a sculptor, but when it came to turning a mountain into a monument, he was the ultimate project manager.

Job Responsibilities

The project manager's principal responsibility is to deliver the project end-item within budget and time limitations, in accordance with technical specifications, and, when specified, in fulfillment of profit objectives. Other specific responsibilities vary depending on the project manager's capabilities, the stage of the project, the size and nature of the project, and the responsibilities delegated by upper management. Delegated responsibility ranges at the low end from the rather limited influence of a project expeditor (where, in essence, the real project manager is the manager to whom the expeditor reports) up to the highly centralized, almost autocratic control of a pure project manager.

Though responsibilities vary, they usually include:[7]

- Planning project activities, tasks, and end-results, which includes creating the work breakdown, schedule, and budget, and coordinating tasks and allocating resources.
- Selecting and organizing the project team.
- Interfacing with and influencing stakeholders.
- Negotiating with and integrating functional managers, contractors, users, and top management.
- Providing contact with the customer.
- Monitoring project status.
- Identifying technical and functional problems.
- Solving problems directly or knowing where to find help.
- Dealing with crises and resolving conflicts.
- Recommending termination or redirection of efforts when objectives cannot be achieved.

Spanning all of these is the umbrella responsibility for integration, coordination, and direction of all project elements and life cycle stages. This responsibility involves (1) identifying interfaces between the activities of functional departments, subcontractors, and other project contributors; (2) planning and scheduling so the efforts are integrated; (3) monitoring progress and identifying problems; and (4) communicating the status of interfaces to stakeholders, and initiating and coordinating corrective action.

Risk is unavoidable in project environments, and the likelihood of a minor or major crisis is always greater than in non-project situations. The project manager is responsible for the advance planning necessary to anticipate and avoid crisis situations.

Most managers of medium- and large-sized projects report in a line capacity to a senior-level executive. They are expected to monitor and narrate the technical and financial status of the project and to report current and anticipated errors, problems, or overruns.

Domain Competency and Orientation

Because project managers work at the *interface* between top management and technologists, they must have managerial ability, technical competency, and other broad qualifications. They must feel as much at home in the office talking with administrators and customers about policies, schedules, budgets, and user needs as in the plant, shop, or on-site talking to specialists and supervisors about technical issues.

Broad background is also essential. The more highly differentiated the functional areas, the more prone they are to conflict and resistant to integration. To effectively integrate multiple, diverse functional areas, the project manager needs to understand each of the areas, its techniques, procedures, and contribution to the project. Referred to as *domain competency*, the project manager must have a good understanding of all areas of the project. Another way of saying this is that the project manager's competency must cover the full scope of the project; she should be familiar with all the areas described in the project scope statement and first-level breakdown of the work breakdown structure (WBS). Most project managers cannot possibly be expert in all areas of the project, but they must be familiar enough with the areas to intelligently ponder ideas offered by specialists and to evaluate and make appropriate, balanced decisions. Along the same lines, to deal effectively with top management and the user, they must know about the workings and business of the parent and customer organizations. In complex, technical projects, the project manager often receives technical assistance from a project engineer, discussed later.

Studies indicate that the most effective project managers have goals, time, and interpersonal orientations intermediate to the functional units they integrate. In other words, they take a balanced outlook.[8] For instance, to integrate the efforts of a production department and a research department, the project manager's time perspective should be intermediate between production's short-term, weekly outlook and research's long-term, futuristic outlook.

As far as the relative importance of technical ability versus managerial competency, that depends on the project. In R&D projects, project management requires greater technical competency because of the greater complexity of technical problems and the technical orientation of the project team. In product development and non-technical projects, however, project management requires greater managerial ability because of the greater involvement of multiple, diverse functional areas. In general, project managers must have sufficient technical ability to understand the problem, although too much technical emphasis can lead project managers to neglect their managerial role. There is no substitute for strong managerial competency in the role of the project manager.

14.2 PROJECT MANAGEMENT AUTHORITY

Authority is an important subject in project management. In general, it refers to a manager's power to command others to act or not to act. There are different kinds of authority, the most familiar is that conferred by the organization and written in the manager's job description, called *legal authority*. Given legal authority, people in higher organizational positions are viewed as having the "right" to control the actions of people below them. Often associated with legal authority is *reward power*, the power to evaluate and reward subordinates.

Another kind of authority, *charismatic authority*, stems from the power one gains by personal characteristics such as charm, personality, and appearance. People both in and outside the formal authority system can increase their ability to control others by being charismatic.

Traditional Authority

Traditional management theory says that authority is always greater at higher levels in the organization and is delegated downward from one level to the next. These are presumed best because managers at higher levels are assumed to know more and, therefore, able to make decisions, delegate responsibility, and "command" workers at lower levels. This point has been challenged on the grounds that modern managers, particularly in technology-based organizations, cannot possibly know everything needed to make complex decisions. They often lack the necessary technical expertise and so, increasingly, must rely upon subordinate specialists for advice. Even managers who are technically skilled cannot always manage alone; they rely upon staff groups for personnel and budgetary assistance. Especially in projects, this aspect of "participatory management" (described in the next chapter) has become commonplace.

Influence

In project management it is important to distinguish between legal authority and the *ability* to influence others. Managers with legal authority have the power to influence subordinates by giving orders and controlling salaries and promotions. Generally, however, the most effective managers are able to influence others *without* "ordering" them or making issue of their superior–subordinate relationship (this is especially true when subordinates are well educated or highly experienced). In fact, managers who rely solely on legal authority are often relatively ineffective; effective managers rely more on two other sources of influence: *knowledge* and *personality*.[9] The first source, called *expert power*, refers to a special level of knowledge or competency attributed to the power holder. Others believe that the power holder possesses knowledge and information that is important and that they themselves do not have. Simply, the expert power holder is viewed as being right because he knows more, and others readily defer to his opinions or requests.

The other, called *referent power*, is derived from rapport, personal attraction, friendship, alliances, and reciprocal favors. The recipient in some way identifies with the power holder and defers to his requests.

Given expert power and referent power, influence in organizations can be achieved irrespective of the formal hierarchy and legal authority. Clearly these two kinds of power enable people to gain influence over others *despite* the formal authority system. In the informal organization, for example, they allow one member in a team to influence all the rest (sometimes more than the team's leader). Even within the formal organization, referent and expert power can subtly reverse the authority relationship. A subordinate may exert considerable influence over her superior if the superior comes to rely upon the subordinate for information or advice, or if a bond of trust, respect, or affection develops between them. Everyone has seen this, and history is replete with examples of people of "lower" social or organizational stature controlling actions of people of higher stature: Alexandria was Queen of Russia; Rasputin was a lowly priest.

Authority in Projects

Most managers rely upon multiple forms of influence—knowledge, expertise, persuasion, and personal relationships, although when these fail, however, they are able to fall back on their legal authority. But project managers seldom have legal authority. Except in the case of the manager of a pure project, the typical project manager *lacks any form of traditional legal authority*.

Unlike traditional organizations where influence and authority flow vertically, influence and authority in project management flow horizontally and diagonally. The project manager exists *outside* the traditional hierarchy. The role is temporary, superimposed on the existing structure, and so is not afforded the leverage inherent to a hierarchical position. Project managers work across functional and organizational lines and, except for members of the project office, have no subordinates reporting to them in a direct line capacity. The issue is further complicated in matrix organizations wherein project managers have a permanent role, yet must share formal authority with functional managers.

Thus, despite the considerable degree of responsibility they carry, most project managers lack a comparable level of formal authority. Instead they have *project authority*, meaning they can make decisions about project objectives, policies, schedules, and budgets, but cannot give orders to back up those decisions.

The disparity between high formal responsibility and low formal authority has been referred to as the *authority gap*.[10] This gap means that project managers must rely on other forms of influence. "How to make friends and influence people" is not an academic issue for project managers.

Project Manager's Authority

Most project managers handle the authority gap similarly. In cases where they are given no legal authority, they have no choice but to rely entirely upon influence derived from expert power and referent power. They must do this because in virtually all projects—task force, matrix, or pure project—they *depend* on others to get the job done. They have few resources under their direct control and must rely upon functional managers, support units, and contractors for personnel and facilities. Many decisions must be made for which the project manager has neither the time nor expertise, so they depend on others to investigate and suggest courses of action.

Another source of the project manager's influence is her network of alliances, the quality of which depends heavily upon her reputation and personal achievements. Such reputations are gained through recognition of accomplishments. Even when project managers have legal authority, they seldom resort to using it because unilateral decisions and commands are inconsistent with the need for reciprocity and tradeoffs in projects. Recognizing that not all information and decisions need to be channeled through them, effective project managers encourage direct contact between individuals involved, regardless of organizational level.

In summary, successful project managers tend to rely upon knowledge, experience, and personal relationships as sources of influence (Figure 14-2). To build expert-based power, they must be perceived as technically and administratively competent as demonstrated by their experience and reputation. To build referent-based power, they must develop effective interpersonal, persuasion, and negotiation skills.

Figure 14-2
Project manager's sources of influence.

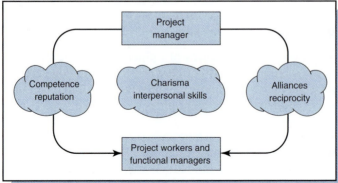

Sometimes the project manager possesses legal authority or the power of command, in which case there are doubtless many instances where she will need to use it. These are situational, depending on the task at hand and the willingness of subordinates to take responsibility. This subject is discussed more in the next chapter.

Example 2: Effective Project Managers, Contrast in Styles[11]

Two examples of how different project managers uniquely influence people are Kelly Johnson and Ben Rich, both former management heads of the advanced projects division of Lockheed-Martin Company, the "Skunk Works" mentioned in Chapter 13.

Kelly Johnson was a living legend, not only at the company but in the whole aerospace industry. With the help of a highly cohesive team of 150 engineers and shop workers, he created over 40 airplanes, including the fastest, highest-flying ones in the world. Yet, he was strictly business, without humor, hot tempered, and reputed to eat "young engineers for between-meal snacks." He made people with whom he had dealings sweat—whether bureaucrats or engineers—particularly excuse makers and faultfinders, so he had as many detractors as friends. Nonetheless, when it needed someone to head up the most difficult and challenging projects, company management and the military repeatedly selected Kelly. Why? Beneath the bad temper and paunchy, somewhat unkempt appearance was an unquestioned, sure-fire genius. He knew everything, it seemed, and his ability to make accurate, on-the-spot deductions was amazing. For a new engine inlet, Kelly simply glanced at the initial design and pronounced it wrong, being about 20 percent too big. His engineers worked nearly 1 full day to recompute the design only to discover that, sure enough, the engine inlet was 18 percent too big. In another instance, he looked at a design and said "the load here is 6.3 pounds per square inch." After an hour of complicated calculations, his people measured it as 6.2 pounds per square inch. When he retired, Kelly Johnson was recognized as the preeminent aerodynamicist of his time.

Kelly chose as his successor Ben Rich. Ben was the first to acknowledge that he didn't possess Kelly's genius and, therefore, would rely on his teams for most decisions. His first move was to loosen the reins and allow the teams latitude to make most calls on their own. Ben was decisive in telling a team what he wanted, but he then let the members decide which methods and procedures to apply. He stuck to schmoozing and cheerleading through an endless supply of one-liners. As one employee puts it, "Whereas Kelly ruled by his bad temper, Ben ruled by his bad jokes." Ben believed in using a non-threatening approach. Whereas he didn't shirk from scolding deserving individuals, he preferred complimenting people and boosting morale. According to one colleague, Ben was the perfect manager: he was there to make the tough calls, defend and protect his project teams, obtain more money and new projects, and convince the government and senior management of the value of his teams' work.

Johnson and Rich led using different styles and different strengths, yet both have been acknowledged by the industry as exemplary project managers. Kelly Johnson accomplished great things, despite his temperament, and most engineers considered it an honor to have worked with him. Competency and reputation were his strengths; people tolerated his personality. Ben Rich, no technical slouch, acknowledged that he had a few smarter people working for him. Unlike Kelly, however, he had charisma and many personal friends, and with that he too was able to accomplish great things at the Skunk Works.

The Balance of Power

Because most project managers must share authority with functional managers, what relative balance of power between them is optimal? Some theorists say that project and functional managers should share power equally. However, the concept of power has several dimensions, and according to some research not all of these dimensions should be balanced equally.[12] In the best performing projects, authority is clearly differentiated: project managers are given the power from top management to procure critical resources, coordinate work efforts, and mediate conflicts; in contrast, functional managers are given the power to make decisions over technical problems and the technology used.

Even in the usual circumstance where project managers do not have reward power, it is usually beneficial for them to be *perceived* by workers as having the same reward power as functional managers. Whether or not the perception is accurate, project personnel tend to follow the manager who they perceive as having the greatest influence over their salaries and promotions.

14.3 SELECTING THE PROJECT MANAGER

Qualifications of successful project managers fall into four categories: personal characteristics, behavioral skills, general business skills, and technical skills.

Personal Characteristics

Archibald lists the following as essential personal characteristics:[13]

- Flexible and adaptable
- Preference for initiative and leadership
- Confidence, persuasiveness, verbal fluency
- Effective communicator and integrator
- Able to balance technical solutions with time, cost, and human factors
- Well organized and disciplined
- A generalist rather than a specialist
- Able to devote most of his time to planning and controlling
- Able to identify problems and to make decisions
- Able to devote the time and effort and to maintain a proper balance in use of time

These characteristics make sense given the environment in which the project manager works and the responsibilities and restrictions placed on the role. Obviously, project managers must be able to work in situations where there are constant deadlines, great uncertainty, startups and closeouts, and constant change in goals, tasks, people, and relationships. At the same time, they must be able to gain the respect, trust, and confidence of others.

Behavioral Skills

A project manager needs strong behavioral and interpersonal skills.[14] In particular she must be an active listener and active communicator. Active listener means that the project manager has mastered the art of questioning for clarification and paraphrasing to make sure she understands verbal messages. This requires the ability to:

- Ask leading questions
- Keep quiet to give the other person sufficient time to talk

- Reflect on the person's answer and check for correctness
- Reflect on the person's emotions

The acronym for active listening is LEAR: Listen, Explore, Acknowledge, Respond.

The project manager must be sensitive to the attitudes of project stakeholders regarding policies, time limits, and costs. Many specialists in the project will disdain anything non-technical and resent schedule and budgetary constraints. The project managers must be able to convince them about why project budgets, schedules, and policies matter.

The project manager must also know how to build trust, promote team spirit, and reward cooperation through praise and credit—often the only forms of reward she can give, and she must be able to work *with* people and delegate responsibility. She must understand personalities, attitudes, and characteristics of people both as team members and as individuals, and know how to best utilize talent even when it does not measure up to her standards. The project manager must be sensitive to human frailties, needs and greed, and be skilled at resolving conflict, managing stress, and coaching and counseling. It seems like a tall order, but good project managers can do all of that.

General Business Skills

The project manager is, after all, a *manager* and so must also have general business skills that include:

- Understanding of the organization and the business.
- Understanding of general management—marketing, accounting, contracting, purchasing, law, personal administration, and (in profit environments) the concept of profitability.
- Ability to translate business requirements into project and system requirements.
- Strong, active, continuous interest in teaching, training, and developing subordinates.

Since project managers have cost responsibility, they must understand the concepts of cost estimating, budgeting, cash flow, overheads, incentives, penalties, and cost sharing. They are involved in contract agreements, so they must be informed about contract terms and implications. They are responsible for the phasing and scheduling of work to meet delivery dates, so they must be familiar with the tasks, processes, and resources necessary to execute the project. And they are responsible for enforcing project schedules, and hence must be knowledgeable about tools and techniques for tracking and control—as covered elsewhere in this book.

Technical Skills

To make informed decisions, project managers must be able to grasp the technical aspects of the project. As mentioned, their "domain competency" must span the full scope of the project. In non- or low-technology environments, grasp can be developed through experience and informal training. In high-technology projects, qualifications are more rigorous and usually require a career molded in the technology environment and knowledge of science or engineering.[15]

Although project managers seldom do technical analysis, they must be qualified to make technical judgments and capable of technical analysis and integration. Many technically qualified people are not very good at integration because most education and training in engineering and technology emphasizes analysis and ignores integration.[16] To be able to communicate with everyone and integrate their work, the project manager must understand and speak the language of the technical specialists on the project.

To meet the management requirements for both technical competency and general business competency, projects sometimes utilize two managers—one technical and one administrative. This often happens in construction projects where the architect is responsible for technical matters while the so-called project manager handles administrative "paperwork." Having two managers tends to complicate problems of coordination, communication, and authority because both must share responsibility. Further, when the project manager becomes subservient to the architect, his ability to manage the project is compromised. This split is also common in the motion picture industry. The movie *producer* manages the resources, schedules, and budgets (in essence, the project manager), while the *director* oversees technical–artistic matters. Only occasionally are they the same person. Because the shooting of a motion picture is an artistic pursuit, directors need flexibility in budgets and shooting schedules, but costs matter too, and the producer faces the question "at what price creativity?" It comes as no surprise that the two do not always have an amicable relationship.[17] Still, the movie industry highly regards the role of the project manager. When an Academy Award is given for "Best Picture," it is awarded to the picture's producer—the person who manages resources, budgets, and schedules.

Ideally, there is but one project manager, and all others also serving in some managerial or administrative capacity in the project (engineers, architects, directors, etc.) report to her.

Selection and Recruiting

The project manager for a given project is selected from among the ranks of product and functional managers, functional specialists, and experienced project managers. The last source is the best though often the least feasible. It might be difficult to find an experienced project manager who has the right mix of qualifications and whose current project ends just before the new one begins. As a result, when an experienced project manager is needed, often he must be recruited from the outside—as is readily observable in the Sunday job listings of major metropolitan newspapers (Figure 14-3 shows a sampling). One problem with bringing in outsiders is that it takes time for them to make friends, build alliances, and learn organizational procedures and policies. On the plus side, an outsider is likely better suited to objectively take on the task (without political influence), and not have any enemies—at least initially.

The role of project manager is also filled by transferring or promoting functional managers. One problem with this is the difficulty some managers experience in shifting from a functional to a project perspective. A functional manager must adjust from exclusively working in one area to overseeing and integrating the work of many areas, a transition that requires considerable effort and inclination. Unless the manager has abundant, well-rounded experience he will likely be perceived by other managers as just another functional manager.

The project manager role is also filled by promoting non-managerial specialists (engineers, scientists, system analysts, product specialists, etc.). The problem with this is the same as with putting any non-manager into a management role: he must first learn how to manage. Administrative and technical abilities are not the same, and just because a person is a good engineer or auditor does not mean he will be a good project manager. Besides learning how to manage, a specialist must learn how to remove himself from his area of specialty and become a generalist. Ideally, the

Figure 14-3
Advertisements for project management positions.

project management assignment will not conflict with existing lines of authority or reporting relationships. It is a bad idea, for example, to put a functional specialist in a project management role that would give him authority over his former boss.

Training

Because project management skills cannot be learned quickly, organizations devote substantial time and expense to prepare individuals for careers in project management. Some sponsor internal training programs that focus on the special requirements of their organizations; others use external seminars and university programs. Recent years have seen a rapid proliferation in both kinds of training programs, as well as the rise of training oriented toward professional certification, such as the

PMI's Project Management Professional, or PMP. Often, a project support office or PMO assists with this training and professional development.

Still, there is no substitute for experience. Many organizations allow promising people who aspire to become project managers the benefit of on-the-job training.[18] As part of their career paths, technical specialists work full or part time as administrative assistants to experienced project managers—similar to serving an apprenticeship. While this gives them exposure to management, it also tests their aptitude and talent for being managers. Valued specialists with little managerial aptitude or ability should be given other career opportunities commensurate with their skills and interests.

Example 3: On-the-Job Training of Project Managers[19]

Microsoft Corporation's approach to preparing project managers (which they term "program managers") is typical. There is neither an official training program for program managers nor guidelines that spell out requirements for writing specifications, scheduling projects, or making prototypes. Program managers can attend an optional, 3-week training session. Microsoft occasionally holds videotaped luncheons where managers present their experiences. The videotapes then may be circulated.

Program managers at Microsoft learn the job primarily by "doing" it. Microsoft carefully selects and mentors the right people, then expects them to learn on the job. For about 90 percent of program managers, training happens by pairing a new program manager with an experienced, successful program manager; the other 10 percent receive formal training.

Moving into the Role

Project management responsibilities range from few and mundane on simple projects to extensive and challenging on complex projects. Presumably, the person in the project manager role is qualified and wants the responsibility; still, the burden of moving into the role can be eased if the project manager:[20]

- Understands what has to be done.
- Understands his authority and its limits.
- Understands his relationship with others in the project.
- Knows the specific results that constitute a job well done.
- Knows when and what he is able to do exceptionally well, and when and where he falls short.
- Is aware of what can and should be done to correct unsatisfactory results.
- Believes that his superiors have an interest and believe in him.
- Believes that his superiors are eager for him to succeed.

Not feeling or knowing these can diminish the project manager's effectiveness. Senior management should give project managers the necessary assurances and information; ultimately, however, the project manager might have to seek these out from management.

14.4 WAYS OF FILLING THE PROJECT MANAGEMENT ROLE

Organizations use various titles for the role of project manager including "program manager," "project director," "task force chairman," and others. The titles "task force coordinator" and "project engineer" are also used, though these usually imply more focused roles with less managerial responsibility than other forms. The most effective project management role occurs when one person becomes involved during proposal preparation and stays on until the project is completed. When it is difficult to find someone available and competent enough to see the project through, the role is filled in other ways. For example, the role may be assigned to the general manager or plant manager, though these managers usually have neither the necessary time to devote to a project nor the flexibility to shift roles. Alternatively, the role may be assigned temporarily to a functional manager. Here, the consequence is that she must divide her time between the project and her department, whereby both may suffer. Also, these combination functional–project managers may have trouble gaining cooperation from other functional managers when they are seen as competitors for resources. In long-term projects, responsibility may pass from one functional manager to the next as the project progresses. The problem here is that the process lacks an oversight person who can ensure continuity from one phase to the next. The managers at later stages inherit problems created by manager in earlier stages. This "two-hat" role includes additional problems, described in Chapter 13.

Sometimes project responsibilities for scheduling, budgeting, marketing, technical performance are divided among several people. This is common practice in technological projects where, as mentioned earlier, responsibility is split between a technical project manager and an administrative project manager. The problem with this arrangement is in having two or more project management roles with no one to oversee and integrate *them*.

Some projects, especially large ones in the public sector, require exceptional presentation, negotiation, and political skills to deal with broad constituencies and powerful public and private interest groups. In such cases it is also common to see two people heading up a project—one to deal with the technical side, the other with stakeholders.

Although ideally the person filling the project management role devotes full time to managing the project, it is very common for managers to oversee multiple projects, and is acceptable as long as the manager can adequately fulfill her responsibilities in all of them. In fact, the practice can be advantageous because it puts the project manager in a position to resolve resource and priority conflicts between projects and to simultaneously negotiate resources for all the projects he oversees.

14.5 ROLES IN THE PROJECT TEAM

In the early stages of a project, the project and functional managers divide the overall project objective into work tasks. This division determines skill requirements and serves as the basis for personnel selection and subcontracting. Those who contribute to the project at any given time, such as people from functional support areas, contractors, and the project office, become part of the *project team*. This section describes roles and responsibilities of members of the project team.

Members Serving the Project Office

Chapter 13 described the purpose of the project office and its placement within the organization. This section focuses on specific roles of members of the project office. The example shown in Figure 14-4 is for an engineering-development project such as the one discussed in Chapter 13. In addition to the project manager and representatives since these packages produced contiguous road and tunnel sections that had to dovetail. A Joint Venture team coordinated everything from the CAT "control center," where contractors poured over data about progress, graphics of the interface connections, critical paths, and schedules.

The CAT project also involved architectural design, landscape design, and urban design for which Joint Venture subcontracted the small local firm of Wallace, Floyd Associates. The architects like to point out that, while Joint Venture engineers designed what the public does not see, they, the architects, designed what the public does see. Joint Venture—a large engineering team of international reputation—felt that partnering with a small architectural firm intimately familiar with the locale would better enable them to meet the project's complex set of needs.

Getting a project off the ground involves negotiating hoops and hurdles held by many stakeholders. After the project gets underway, the project manager remains mindful of all of those stakeholders, and works to retain their support in ways big and small.

Example 5: McCormick Place West[29]

Some project managers and contractors go to great lengths to build and sustain relations with stakeholders in the nearby community. McCormick Place West is a major multi-year project, part of a multi-phase expansion to Chicago's existing McCormick Place convention complex. The group of companies that teamed up to design and build the structure (another "joint venture") has engaged a number of programs to build relations with nearby residents and businesses. For example, project managers and staff visit local high schools to educate students about practices and careers in construction, engineering, and architecture, and they offer a similar program geared to sixth graders. Another program hires and teaches trade skills to local workers through hands-on experience, and offers an opportunity to become union certified; about 20 people a year have become certified in this way. The contractor donates old computers to the local schools and cars to their shop classes. Copying a popular reality-TV series, the company remodeled the home of a local needy family. Through these and other charitable programs the contractor has provided benefits to the local community and substantially gained its support.

14.7   SUMMARY

The most defining aspect of project management is the role of project manager. Project managers work at the project–functional–user interface, integrating project elements to achieve time, cost, and performance objectives. They have ultimate responsibility for the success of the projects, yet in most cases work outside the traditional hierarchy and have little formal authority. To influence decisions and behavior, they tend to rely on negotiations, alliances, favors, and reciprocal agreements. Their strongest source of influence is the respect they gain through skillful and competent administration, technical competency, or charisma.

Successful project managers are perceived as both technically and administratively competent. They have a good understanding of the business as well as strong domain competency—broad knowledge encompassing the full scope of the project. They also have strong behavioral and communication skills and are able to function effectively in uncertain, changing conditions.

The role of project manager is best filled by one person who is involved in the project from start to finish. Sharing or rotating the role among several people is usually less effective, although sometimes necessary to meet technical, administration, and political challenges.

Project managers get work done through a team composed of people from various functional and support groups scattered throughout the parent company and from outside subcontractors. The project office provides administrative assistance and services. Functional managers contribute primarily to the technical content of the project and share responsibility for developing tasks, plans, schedules, and budgets for work required of their areas. They maintain the technical base from which projects draw.

Top management, the manager of projects or PMO director, and the project champion and project sponsors all play key roles in the project. Top management establishes the policies, responsibilities, and authority relationships through which project management is conducted. The manager of projects or PMO director ensures that projects are consistent with organization goals and receive the necessary resources. The champion rallies support for the project and convinces others of its virtues, benefits, or value. The sponsor is a person with organizational clout who supports the project and works to get it the necessary priority and resources. Numerous other stakeholders support or resist the project and often have a big impact on its success or failure.

People find project work challenging, rewarding, and exhilarating, but without question they often also find it taxing and stressful. Maximizing the chances of project success—and minimizing human casualties along the way—requires special behavioral skills for dealing with groups and individuals, including skills for assembling disparate individuals and groups into a single, cohesive team, and for handling work conflicts, personal problems, and emotional stress. These are covered in the next chapter.

REVIEW QUESTIONS

1. What is the project manager's primary role?
2. What is meant by "the project manager is an evangelist, entrepreneur, and change agent?"
3. Does the project manager's resistance to change contradict her roles as a change agent?
4. Describe the typical responsibilities of a project manager. In what ways are responsibilities such as budgeting, scheduling, and controlling considered as integration and coordination responsibilities?
5. Discuss the relative need for both technical and managerial competence in project management.
6. Why is a broad background essential for the project manager? What *is* a broad background?
7. Describe what is meant by legal authority. How does it differ from charismatic authority?
8. Describe how and in what ways people in organizations, regardless of hierarchical position, influence others.
9. How does the authority of the typical project manager differ from authority of other managers?
10. What is meant by the "authority gap?"
11. What is the most frequently used source of influence among project managers? How does the project manager use this and other sources of influence to induce functional managers to release their personnel to the project?

from Nuwave's current processes. Some portions of the process will be highly automated, others will not. Software for the new process will integrate information from the sales and finance departments with information from the manufacturing department and suppliers to create production schedules and purchase orders.

Ordinarily the manufacturing department assigns a project manager to projects that involve new processes. However, no one in the department has had experience with a project of this scope, with the software and hardware equipment to be implemented, or with lean production concepts. The president of Nuwave thinks that in addition to designing the software, Noware should oversee the entire project, including equipment procurement and installation and worker training. In contrast, the manufacturing department manager thinks that one of his senior engineers, Roberta Withers, could handle the project. She has a thorough knowledge of Nuwave's current manufacturing processes and experience in manufacturing machine design. Also, she is considered the department's expert in mechanical systems. Ms. Withers has a degree in mechanical engineering and has been with Nuwave for 6 years in the manufacturing department. Her boss thinks that the project would be a good opportunity for Roberta to learn about concepts such as lean production and computer integrated manufacturing systems.

QUESTIONS

1. Assume that you must act on the information available in the case. If it was your choice, who would you select to manage the project: Noware, Roberta, or someone else? Explain.

2. If you could get more information before making a choice, what would you want to know?

Case 14-3   The Big Dig: Boston's Central Artery/Tunnel Project[30]

(Refer to Example 4.) Before the Massachusetts congressional delegation could seek federal funding for the CAT project, it first had to poll constituents about sensitive transportation issues. Then-speaker of the House Philip "Tip" O'Neal wanted to know where his supporters—voters of East Boston—stood. When first told about the project, he said, "What tunnel? We're not building any tunnel." He changed his mind when supporters predicted that "the trade unions are going to be marching on you (if you veto the tunnel)" and assured him that in East Boston "no homes would be lost." The delegation then faced formidable opposition from the Reagan administration and Federal Highway Administration, both which initially argued that CAT was ineligible for federal funding.

An early responsibility of Joint Venture/DPW was to prepare an environmental impact statement, the draft of which consisted of several thick volumes. Part I described impacts in 17 categories, including "transportation," "air quality," "noise and vibration," "energy," "economic characteristics," "visual characteristics," "historic resources," "water quality," "wetlands and waterways," and "vegetation and wildlife." Under "economic characteristics" it described commercial and industrial activity, tourism, and employment patterns in the affected areas. According to the report, the project would not displace any residences, but would relocate 134 businesses with 4,100 employees.

At the first public hearing 175 persons spoke, including some from the EPA and the Sierra Club, and 99 provided written commentary. The magnitude and complexity of the project is reflected in a sampling of the public interest groups represented: The 1000 Friends of Massachusetts, American Automobile Association, Archdiocese of Boston/Can-Do Alliance, Beacon Hill Civic Association, Bikes Not Bombs, Boston Building

Trades Association, Boston Society of Architects, Charles River Watershed Association, Conservation Law Foundation of New England, and Haymarket Pushcart Association. Project officials quickly dispelled public concern about large-scale building demolitions and displacement of businesses and neighborhoods.

In January 1991 the Massachusetts secretary of the environment issued a certificate of approval; construction could proceed assuming certain mitigation measures were implemented to ease environmental impacts. The certificate recommended a planning process for utilization of the 27 new acres of downtown Boston that would be created by the removal of the elevated Central Artery, and urged project managers to formulate "creative strategies" for integrating the new highway system with mass transit facilities, limiting downtown parking spaces, and reserving highway lanes for high-occupancy vehicles.

Beyond environmental matters, the project had to respond to issues and conditions raised by hundreds of groups, businesses, and agencies. CAT officials put the number of early mitigation commitments at 1,100 and the added cost to the project at $2.8 billion. The commitments address state and federal requirements, as well as reduction of construction impacts, including $450 million for temporary lanes, curbs, and sidewalks that would enable businesses to continue during construction, and $230 million for the City of Cambridge and the Metropolitan District to build a park along the Charles River.

QUESTIONS

1. From the information provided here and in Example 4, create a list of stakeholders for the project and revise Figure 14-6 to include them, showing possible or likely links between them. For each stakeholder, state its likely interests in the project and in what ways it could shape or influence the conduct of the project and its tunnels, roadways, bridges, etc.
2. Considering the technical aspects of the project (building tunnels, roadways, and bridges; demolishing the old roadway structure and replacing it with parks) and its political, economic, environmental, and social impacts (and the stakeholders with interests in each), what characteristics (skills, background, competencies) would you expect of the "ideal" manager or managers overseeing a project of this scope and magnitude?

ENDNOTES

1. L.R. Sayles and M.K. Chandler, *Managing Large Systems: Organizations for the Future* (New York: Harper & Row, 1971): 204.
2. Ibid., 212.
3. Ibid., 204.
4. Portions adapted from Rex Alan Smith, *The Carving of Mount Rushmore* (New York: Abbeville Press, 1985).
5. Ibid., 17–18.
6. Ibid., 164.
7. Russell Archibald, *Managing High-Technology Programs and Projects* (New York: Wiley-Interscience, 1976): 35; William Atkins, "Selecting a Project Manager," *Journal of Systems Management* (October 1980): 34; Daniel Roman, *Managing Projects: A Systems Approach* (New York: Elsevier, 1986): 419.
8. Paul Lawrence and Jay Lorsch, *Organization and Environment: Managing Differentiation and Integration* (Boston, MA: Graduate School of Business, Harvard University, 1967): Chapter III.
9. These bases of interpersonal power were first described by J.P.R. French and B. Raven, "The Bases of Social Power," reprinted in *Group Dynamics*, 3d ed., D. Cartwright and A. Zander, eds. (New York: Harper & Row, 1968): 259–269.
10. Richard Hodgetts, "Leadership Techniques in the Project Organization," *Academy of Management Journal*, 11 (June 1968): 211–219.
11. Ben Rich and Leo Janos, *Skunk Works* (Boston, MA: Little, Brown & Co, 1994).
12. R. Katz and T.J. Allen, "Project Performance and the Locus of Influence in the R&D Matrix," *Academy of Management Journal* 28, no. 1 (March 1985): 67–87.

13. Archibald, Managing High-Technology Programs, 55.

14. J.R. Adams, S.E. Barndt, and M.D. Martin, *Managing by Project Management* (Dayton, OH: Universal Technology, 1979): 137.

15. P.O. Gaddis, "The Project Manager," *Harvard Business Review* (May–June 1959): 89–97.

16. Ibid., 95.

17. An example is the 1984 movie *Heaven's Gate* where the director was allowed to virtually dominate the movie's producers. Originally scheduled for completion in 6 months at a cost of $7.5 million, the production ended up being released a year late and $28 million *over* budget. The movie was a box office flop and helped clinch the demise of United Artists Corp. which had to underwrite the expense. From Steven Bach, *Final Cut* (New York: William Morrow, 1985).

18. D. Roman, *Managing Projects: A Systems Approach* (New York: Elsevier, 1986): 439–440.

19. Michael Cusumano and Richard Selby, *Microsoft Secrets* (New York: Free Press, 1995): 105–106.

20. Harold Kerzner, *Project Management: A Systems Approach to Planning, Scheduling, and Controlling* (New York: Van Nostrand Reinhold, 1979): 99.

21. These responsibilities are for project engineers in engineering-development projects, as described in W.P. Chase, *Management of Systems Engineering* (New York: Wiley-Interscience, 1974): 25–29.

22. According to Archibald, *Managing High-Technology Programs*, 124–128, 199.

23. Ibid., 128–131.

24. Katz and Allen, "Project Performance and the Locus of Influence," 83–84.

25. David Cleland and William King, *Systems Analysis and Project Management*, 3d ed. (New York: McGraw-Hill, 1983): 358.

26. Ibid., 362–363.

27. Thomas P. Hughes, *Rescuing Prometheus* (New York: Vintage Books, 1998): Chapter V (this book provides interesting and relevant historical perspective on the Big Dig and several other large, complex projects); David Luberoff, Alan Altshuler, and Chritine Baxter, *Mega-Project: A Political History of Boston's Multibillion Dollar Artery/Tunnel Project* (Cambridge, MA: Taubman Center, John F. Kennedy School, Harvard University, 1993); http://www.lfmsdm.mit.edu/news_articles/sdm_business_trip_fall03/sdm_business_trip_fall03.html.

28. Figure 14-6 represents stakeholders prior to 1992. After that B/PB-Joint Venture accountability shifted from the Massachusetts DPW to the Massachusetts Highway Department (MHD), and after 1997 to the Massachusetts Turnpike Authority (MTA). In 1998, key B/PB personnel combined with personnel in MTA to form an "integrated project office" with the purpose of combining "the expertise of the management consultant (B/PB) with the longer-term dedication and specialized experience of the owner (MTA)." *Source: Completing the "Big Dig": Managing the Final Stages of Boston's Central Artery/Tunnel Project (2003)* (National Academies Press): Chapter 5; http://www.books.nap.edu/openbook.php?record_id=10629&page=31; accessed May 8, 2007.

29. Amanda Klinger, Debra Belmonte, Emily Chou, Chris Phares, Nate Volman, and Ricardo Pina, *The McCormick Place West Expansion Project* (Loyola University Chicago Report, February 2005).

30. *Source*: Thomas P. Hughes, *Rescuing Prometheus*.

Chapter 15

Managing Participation, Teamwork, and Conflict

Eh! je suis leur chef, il fallait bien les suivre.
Ah well! I am their leader, I really ought to follow them!

—ALEXANDRE AUGUSTE LEDRU-ROLLIN,
1857

A leader is best when people barely know that he exists.
Of a good leader, who talks little, when his work is done,
his aims fulfilled, they will say, "We did this ourselves."

—LAO-TZU,
The Way of Life

Kenka ryosei bai.
In a quarrel, both sides are at fault.

—*Japanese proverb*

*D*uring the manned landings on the moon, a study was conducted of NASA project management by researcher Richard Chapman.[1] This was during NASA's heyday—a period marked by extraordinary achievements and a time when NASA was upheld as exemplar of a large agency that worked well. It is interesting and instructive to begin this chapter with a few of Chapman's comments about the project managers of that era:

> [In addition to technical competency and management capacity] all agree that the project manager must have the ability . . . to build a cohesive project team. (p. 93)

> Those project managers who [developed the most closely-knit project teams emphasized] decentralized decision making [and] technical problem-solving at the level where both the problem and most experience reside. [They encouraged project members] to feel a sense of responsibility for problem-solving at their respective levels, within the assigned guidelines . . . (p. 83)

> Most project staffs believe that they receive generous support and attention from the project manager. Most also acknowledge that the project manager is vigorous and fair in bestowing recognition on team members and in rewarding them to the best of his capability. (p. 82)

In another study of NASA, Kloman compared the performance of two large projects, Lunar Orbiter and Surveyor. Lunar Orbiter was a success and fulfilled objectives within time and resource limits; Surveyor was not as successful and experienced cost escalation and schedule delays. The study characterized Lunar Orbiter's customer/contractor organizations as being tightly knit *cohesive* units, with good *teamwork* and mutual *respect* and *trust* for their project counterparts. In contrast, teamwork in Surveyor was characterized as "slow and fitful" to grow and "spurred by a sense of anxiety and concern."[2] Kloman concluded:

> What emerges perhaps most forcefully from a broad retro-spect-ive view is the importance of the human aspects of organization and management. Both projects demonstrated the critical nature of human skills, interpersonal relations, compatibility between individual managers, and teamwork. (p. 39)

These remarks are the crux of this chapter: Behavioral issues such as decentralized decision making, interpersonal skills, supervisory support, and teamwork are important factors in effective project management. It is unfortunate that such issues are often overlooked in project practice, or given short shrift in project management education, largely because inexperienced managers and specialists in the "hard" disciplines (technicians, engineers, and businesspeople) see them as "soft" issues of little consequence and with no precise answers. But in reality these issues are not soft. They are as hard as nails. As experienced managers know, they have a profound effect on project performance and success.

This chapter discusses issues broached by the two studies cited: participative decision making, teamwork, conflict resolution, and the related matter of emotional stress in work. Behavioral scientists have been investigating practical methods for building cohesive teams, resolving interpersonal and intergroup conflict, and managing stress for many years. We will review the methods most relevant to the project environment.

15.1 LEADERSHIP IN PROJECT MANAGEMENT

Leadership Style

Chapter 13 described a variety of organizational forms apropos for different purposes and types of work. Likewise, there is a variety of suitable leadership styles depending on the situation. Leadership is the ability to influence the behavior of others to accomplish what is desired; *leadership style* is the way in which a leader achieves that influence.

Leadership style can generally be divided between the two extreme approaches of *task-oriented* and *relations-oriented*. Task-oriented leaders show higher concern for the goal and the work and tend to behave in a more autocratic fashion. Relations-oriented managers show greater concern for people and tend to exercise a more democratic leadership style.

Numerous studies have attempted to discern the most appropriate or effective leadership style. Most management theorists agree that no one leadership style is best for all situations. Effective style depends upon characteristics of the leader, the followers, the leader's interpersonal relationship with followers, and the nature and environment of the task. This perspective is called the *contingency approach* or *situational approach* to leadership. There are many different contingency models; all suggest that the leader should use the style that best fits the work situation and try not to apply the same style to all employees and situations. Brief mention will be made of two of these models—those of Fred Fiedler and Hersey and Blanchard.

Contingency and Situational Approaches

According to Fiedler,[3] the three variables that most affect a leader's influence are whether (1) the work group accepts or rejects the leader, (2) the task is relatively routine or complex, and (3) the leader has high or low formal authority. Although the project manager might encounter any of these situations, the most common (as described in the previous chapters) is likely to be:

- He has relatively low formal authority.
- He gets along with team members and is respected for his ability and expertise.
- The task is relatively complex and requires a good deal of judgment or creativity.

Fiedler's research indicates that under these three conditions a *relations-oriented* style is the most effective. The most prominent behavior in this style is the leader's positive emotional ties with and concern for his subordinates.

Hersey and Blanchard[4] use a model called *situational leadership* that weighs the interplay of three variables: (1) the amount of direction and guidance a leader gives (task behavior), (2) the amount of socio-emotional support he gives (relations behavior), and (3) the readiness of followers to perform the task (maturity). The last variable, "maturity," has two aspects: the person's *skill* or *ability* to do something and the person's *motivation* or *willingness* to do it. According to the model the most effective leader behavior depends upon the maturity level of the followers. Project managers seldom manage laborers or even shop-floor people. Usually they deal with technical specialists, managers, professionals, tradespeople, and other highly trained people. Thus, they tend to work with people who are either (1) able but perhaps unwilling to do what the manager wants or (2) both able and willing to do what he wants. For Group (1) the model suggests a *participative* style as more effective. The thrust of a participative leadership style is toward facilitating, supporting, and communicating with followers. Both managers and followers share decision making. For Group (2), the model suggests a delegating style as more effective. The manager identifies the problem or goal and gives the followers responsibility to carry out the task. Followers are permitted to solve the problem and determine how, where, and what to do.

In their research on managing scientific and technical personnel, Hersey and Blanchard found that people with high-level education and experience responded

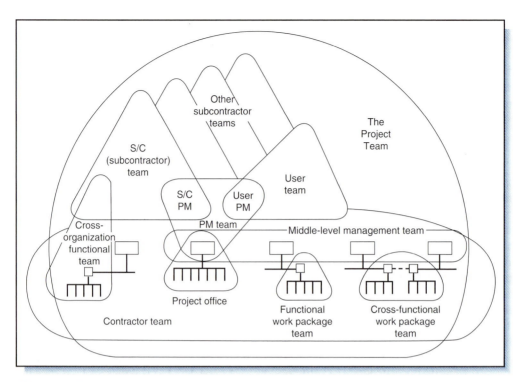

Figure 15-1
Groups comprising the project team.

team is that the former is simply a collection of people, whereas the latter is a collection working toward a common goal. Thus, virtually all work accomplished in a project, whether mental or physical labor, is the product of teams. To be successful, a project needs *teamwork*.

The Trouble with Teams

Failures in projects often can be traced to the inability of a team to make the right decisions or perform the right tasks. These failures often stem from the maladies that teams suffer: internal conflict, member anxiety, and frustration; time wasted on irrelevant issues; and decisions made haphazardly by senior people, coalitions, or default. Team members often are more concerned with getting the task *done* than with doing it *right*. Many teams never know what their *purpose* is, so they never know when, or if, they have achieved it.

In projects with multiple teams, each might have different attitudes, orientation, and goals. Some teams might be physically isolated and maintain separate offices, creating and reinforcing separating boundaries. Or teams might develop an "us versus them" attitude leading to intergroup competition, resentment, and conflict. These occurrences make for a portentous project environment and bode ill for project success.

High-Performing Teams

In contrast, successful projects are the result of the efforts of *effective* teams, those that succeed in achieving whatever they have set out to do. In an effective team, individuals and groups work together as a single cohesive unit.

What makes a team effective? Peter Vaill has studied a large number of highly effective teams that "perform at levels of excellence far beyond those of comparable systems."[10] The prominent feature he found for all of them is that they know and are committed to team goals. Members are never confused about why the team exists or what their individual roles are. Leaders inculcate belief in the team's purpose, eliminate doubts, and embody a team spirit. He also found the following:

- Commitment to the purpose of the system is never perfunctory and motivation is always high.
- Teamwork is focused on the task. Distinctions between task and process functions dissolve. Members develop behaviors that enable them to do what they must.
- Leadership is strong, clear, and never ambivalent. Leaders are reliable and predictable, regardless of style.
- The team is clearly separated from others; members uniformly feel that "we are different."

Vaill found three characteristics *always* present in the behavior and attitudes of leaders and members of high-performing systems. He calls them *time, feeling,* and *focus*.

First, leaders and members devote extraordinary amounts of time to the task. They work at home, in the office, in taxicabs—anywhere. They fully commit themselves for the duration of the project. Second, they have very strong feelings about the attainment of the goal. They care deeply about the team's purpose, structure, history, future, and the people in it. And third, they focus on key issues; they have a clear list of priorities in mind. In high-performing teams, time, feeling, and focus are always found together.

Vaill encourages would-be leaders to "Seek constantly to do what is right and what is needed in the system (focus). Do it in terms of your energy (time). Put your whole psyche into it (feeling)."[11]

High-performing teams function as a whole. Everyone devotes lots of time, intensely values the team and its purpose, and is clear about priorities. Successful project organizations are high-performing teams. For project managers, Vaill's findings underscore the importance of clear definition of project objectives, clarification of the roles and tasks of team members, strong commitment to achieving objectives, and a "project spirit" that bonds everyone together.

Example 1: Time, Feeling, and Focus in Project Management: Renovating the Statue of Liberty

The renovation of the Statue of Liberty is a good example of the kind of commitment and effort required for successfully managing a large-scale project.[12] Over 25 firms submitted proposals for the task of leading the team of 500 engineers, architects, artisans, and craftsmen who would do the renovation. Selected for the job was the small construction management firm of Lehrer/McGovern, Inc.

As Hofer describes the firm's partners: Lehrer is soft-spoken and generally conservative in appearance; McGovern clean-shaves his head, has a handlebar mustache, and wears cowboy boots. Despite differences in appearance, the two share similar goals and broad experience as civil engineers and construction managers.[13]

Did they devote a lot of time to the project? To coordinate the more than 50 businesses doing the job, Lehrer and McGovern worked as many as 16 hours each day. As managers they handled everything from helping architects and craftsmen implement plans, to making arrangements with subcontractors and ensuring that materials were ordered and delivered on time.

Did they instill feeling for the project? Said Lehrer, "this project is a labor of love. The spirit and pride of hundreds of men and women involved bring out the best of us as Americans."[14] They expected and they inspired feelings like that of managers representing the client, contractor, and several subcontractors. Typical problems include inability to reach agreement, lack of innovative ideas, too much conflict, or complacency of team members.

Initially a human relations consultant or other person with facilitation skills is called in by the project manager or manager of projects to facilitate the effort. Her function is to help the group solve its own problems by drawing attention to the *way* the group's behavior is affecting its decision quality and work performance.

The consultant collects data from members using personal interviews or questionnaires. She then summarizes the data, but keeps individual sources anonymous. This summary will later be presented to the team so that members may discuss problems and analyze behavior.

The consultant first shares the results with the team leader (project manager, functional leader, or work package supervisor) and coaches him on how to prepare for the upcoming team building workshop. The consultant remains impartial to the team leader and team members. The *entire team* is her client.

A workshop is convened so that members can review and analyze the group's problems. This workshop differs from ordinary staff meetings in many ways. It convenes at an off-site location away from interruptions, can last up to several days, and includes all team members. The atmosphere is open and candid, without the usual superior–subordinate restrictions. Usually the workshop is facilitated by the consultant who may alternate this role with the group leader, depending on the agenda.

The workshop specifics vary.[19] One common format is this:[20]

1. The workshop begins with an open discussion of the agenda. Team members describe what they would and would not like to happen.
2. The consultant presents the summary results from the interviews or questionnaires. These are posted on the wall for easy reference. Discussion may be necessary to make sure everyone understands the issues. The consultant may post quotes (anonymous) from interviews. A variety of problems can be expected, for example:

    "Our meetings are always dominated by the same two or three people."
    "Our way of getting things done is slow and unorganized."
    "I have no voice in decisions that affect my functional group."
    "Even though the team leader asks for our opinions, I know she ignores them."
    "This group works a lot of overtime because there is no scheme for how we should fit new tasks into our existing workload."
    "There is no clear-cut definition distinguishing between the roles of engineers and researchers in this project."
3. Given the summary results and the time constraint of the workshop, the team sets priorities for problems it wants to resolve including additional ones generated during the workshop.
4. The group works to resolve the priority issues. In the meantime
    (a) The consultant monitors the session and reports her observations about the group, pointing out dysfunctional group behavior, encouraging members to express their feelings, confronting behaviors of individuals that lead to defensiveness or distrust, and reinforcing effective behavior.
    (b) The group periodically critiques itself. After working through a problem, the group pauses to evaluate what they did that helped or hindered the process.
    (c) The group prepares a formal action plan with solutions, target dates, and people responsible. The plan may include "operating guidelines" specifying *how* the group will function. (Typical guidelines are described in Section 15.6, Step 4.)

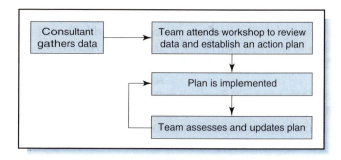

Figure 15-2
The team building cycle.

The author has worked with project groups where problems ranging from technical issues to interpersonal conflict were resolved with team building workshops.[21]

The purpose of the workshop is twofold: It provides a structure for the team to resolve interpersonal or group process issues as well as a forum where the group examines itself as a team. Participants often find these sessions refreshing. They gain stimulating insight into group dynamics and develop a model of behavior to follow in the future.

To ensure that action steps are implemented and process issues continue to be addressed, the workshop always includes follow-up sessions. These take place formally at 2–3-month intervals or less formally during regular meetings. The team takes stock of its functioning, what improvements it has made, and what still is needed. As the group becomes more effective, the group itself takes over the consultant's role. Whenever follow-up sessions reveal new problems, the process is repeated. The full cycle is summarized in Figure 15-2.

Two conditions are necessary for team building to succeed. First, management's *support* is needed. The team leader and upper managers must face the issues uncovered and assist in (or provide resources for) working toward solutions. Second, team members must *want* to resolve the group's problems. They must be open and honest in providing information, willing to share in the responsibility for having caused problems, and eager to work toward solutions.

15.6 BUILDING NEW TEAMS

With small variation, team building can be applied to *new* project teams. The new team might be a concurrent engineering team, a work package team, or a management or design team with representatives from the client and contractor. The purpose of team building for a new team is similar to those of an experienced one—to develop a plan for working together and build good working relationships and a good working environment. New teams have the advantage of not having established bad habits and poor working relationships.

The first task of a newly formed team is to reach agreement on its purpose, how it will achieve its purpose, and the roles of its members. It then asks itself: How can we effectively work together in a manner that will allow us to accomplish our purpose and leave us feeling good about one another?

A team building workshop led by a facilitator is convened to help members become acquainted, reach agreement on objectives, and decide how they will function as a team. In *Team Building: Issues and Alternatives*, William Dyer describes several building teamwork in new groups. IGPS is useful for building teamwork between two or more groups. With slight variation these methods may be adapted to bring customers, subcontractors, and suppliers together at the start of a project. They may also be used to unify work groups following changes in project organization or plans, and to prepare team members for new job assignments just before a project is completed.

Conflict is inevitable in organizations and, if properly managed, is beneficial. The primary sources of conflict in projects are schedules, priorities, manpower levels, technical opinions, administrative issues, interpersonal conflicts, and cost issues. The relative importance of these varies with the stage of the project life cycle. Conflict is generally best dealt with through confrontation, i.e., examining the issues and attempting to resolve the conflict at its source. Confrontation presumes, however, that people will be open, honest, and willing to work together to resolve the conflict. Lacking these conditions or poorly handled, confrontation can lead to hostility and personality conflicts.

Conflict often occurs because of a violation of expectations between parties. Sharing, clarifying, and mutual agreement of expectations is one way to eliminate such conflict. This is the basis for conflict resolution using the role clarification and intergroup conflict resolution techniques.

Stress in projects is inevitable, though distress is not. Stress induces energy, increases vitality, and helps people deal with the demands of work. However, stress from too few or too many work demands can be debilitating. In projects, the main sources of stress are demanding goals and schedules, work tasks, roles, and social relations. Good project planning can help reduce many of the technical sources of stress. Participative management and social support can reduce stress originating from work tasks, roles, and social relations.

REVIEW QUESTIONS

1. Explain the difference between task-oriented and relations-oriented leadership styles.
2. Describe the contingency approach to leadership. According to this approach, what is the best way to lead?
3. What are the differences between the leadership models of Fiedler and Hersey–Blanchard? What do they say about leadership in the situations faced by project managers?
4. In what ways is participative management useful for motivating and gaining commitment?
5. Why is teamwork important in projects? Isn't it enough that individual workers are highly skilled and motivated?
6. What characteristics are common to Vaill's high-performing systems?
7. What is meant by group process issues? What kinds of issues do they include?
8. What is the purpose of team building? Where is team building needed?
9. Outline the steps in a team building session for a group that has been working together. Outline the steps for building a new project team.
10. Outline the steps in the IGPS process.
11. What conditions of management and the team members are necessary for team building interventions to succeed?
12. Describe some situations that you know of where team building could be used.
13. What do you think are the reasons why team building is not used more often? What barriers are there to applying team building?

14. What are the sources of conflict between the user and the contractor? How do contracts lead to conflict?
15. What are the sources of conflict between parties in the project organization?
16. Describe how the sources of conflict vary with the phases of the project life cycle.
17. What are the negative consequences of conflict in projects?
18. Explain why some conflict is natural and beneficial.
19. Describe some ways of dealing with conflict.
20. Explain how the project manager uses confrontation to resolve conflict.
21. What are the assumptions in using confrontation (i.e., what conditions must exist for it to be successful)?
22. Describe the "expectation theory" of conflict. How does the expectation theory compare with your experiences of conflict in work situations?
23. Describe the RCT. What sources of conflict does it resolve?
24. Describe what happens in IGPS. What sources of conflict does it resolve?
25. Describe each of these major sources of stress in a project environment: project goals and schedules, work overload, role conflict and ambiguity, and social/interpersonal relations. Describe your work experiences with these sources of stress.
26. Describe the means by which (a) participative management and (b) role clarification help to reduce work stress.
27. What is "social support?" What are the sources of social support? How does social support reduce job stress?
28. What are some ways of improving social support among project team members?

QUESTIONS ABOUT THE STUDY PROJECT

1. How would you characterize the leadership style of the project manager in your project? Is it authoritarian, laissez faire (do-nothing), or participative? Is the project manager more task-oriented or more relations-oriented, or both?
2. What kind of people must the project manager influence? Given the theories of this chapter, is the style of leadership used appropriate? Despite the theories, does the style used by the project manager seem to be effective?
3. What do you think are the primary work motivators for people in this project? Discuss the relative importance of salary, career potential, formal controls, and participation in decision making.
4. Describe the different groups (management teams, project office, functional groups) that comprise the project team in this project.
5. What mechanisms are used to link these teams—for example, coordinators, frequent meetings, or close proximity?
6. What kinds of formal and informal activities are used to increase the cohesiveness of the project team? Can any of these be termed as team building?
7. What kinds of activities are used or steps taken to resolve problems involving multiple groups?
8. How would you characterize the level of teamwork in this project?
9. Ask the project manager if he or she knows about formal team building and IGPS procedures like those described in this book.
10. At the end of this (or other projects), what does the organization do to disband a team? Are there any procedures for giving recognition or dealing with members' feelings about disbanding?
11. How prevalent is conflict and what effect does conflict have on individual and project performance?

12. What responsibility does the project manager take in resolving these conflicts?

13. How does the project manager resolve conflict? Is confrontation used?

14. Are any formal procedures used, such as RCT or IGPS, to resolve conflicts?

   Emotional stress is a personal issue and most people are hesitant to speak about it other than on a general level. Still, you might ask the project manager or other team members about stresses they personally feel or perceive in the project.

15. Is this a high stress or low stress project? Explain. If it is a high stress environment, is it taken for granted that that is the way it must be, or do people feel that steps could be taken to reduce the stress?

16. Does the project manager try to help team members deal with job stress? Explain.

17. Does the organization make available to its employees programs on stress management?

Case 15-1 *Mars Climate Orbiter Spacecraft*[46]

NASA designed the Mars Climate Orbiter spacecraft to collect data about Mars' atmospheric conditions and serve as a data relay station. Instruments aboard the Orbiter would provide detailed information about the temperature, dust, water vapor, and carbon dioxide in Mars' atmosphere for approximately 2 Earth years. The Orbiter would also provide a relay point for data transmissions to and from spacecraft on the surface of Mars for up to 5 years.

   The Orbiter was launched in December of 1998 and arrived in the vicinity of Mars 9 months later, firing its main engine to go into orbit around the planet. Everything looked normal as it passed behind Mars as seen from the Earth; after that the Orbiter was never heard from again. Presumably it had crashed into the planet. Paraphrasing project manager Richard Cook, "We had planned to approach the planet at an altitude of about 150 kilometers, but upon review of data leading up to the arrival, we saw indications that the approach altitude was much lower, about 60 kilometers. We believe the minimum survivable altitude for the spacecraft would have been 85 kilometers."

   Later, an internal peer review attributed the $280 million mission loss to an error in the information passed between the two teams responsible for the spacecraft's operations, the Climate Orbiter spacecraft team in Colorado and the mission navigation team in California. In communicating back and forth, one team had used English units (inches, feet, pounds), while the other used metric units (meters, grams). Without knowing it, the two teams were using different measurement systems for information critical for maneuvering the spacecraft into proper Mars orbit.

QUESTIONS

1. How could such a mistake have occurred between the two teams?

2. What does the mistake suggest about the degree of interaction and coordination between the teams?

3. How might this problem have been prevented?

ENDNOTES

1. Richard L. Chapman, *Project Management in NASA: The System and the Men* (Washington, DC: NASA SP-324, NTIS No. N75-15692, 1973). The project team Chapman refers to is the project office staff, which numbered from one or two members on small matrix projects to as many as 70 in large pure project organizations.

2. E.H. Kloman, *Unmanned Space Project Management* (Washington, DC: NASA SP-4102, 1972): 23.

3. Fred Fiedler, *A Theory of Leadership Effectiveness* (New York: McGraw-Hill, 1967).

4. P. Hersey and K. Blanchard, *Management of Organization Behavior: Utilizing Human Resources*, 4th ed. (Upper Saddle River, NJ: Prentice Hall, 1982): 150–173.

5. Paul Hersey and Kenneth Blanchard, Managing Research and Development Personnel: An Application of Leadership Theory, *Research Management* (September 1969).

6. Bryman, M. Bresnan, A. Beardsworth, J. Ford, and El. Keil, The Concept of the Temporary System: The Case of the Construction Project, *Research in the Sociology and Psychology of Organizations* 5 (1987): 253–283.

7. L.R. Sayles and M.K. Chandler, *Managing Large Systems: Organizations for the Future* (New York: Harper & Row, 1971): 219.

8. For a discussion of the interpersonal and leadership requirements for the matrix, see S.M. Davis and P.R. Lawrence, *Matrix* (Reading, MA: Addison-Wesley, 1977): 108–109.

9. Warren Bennis and Burt Nanus, *Leadership: Strategies for Taking Charge* (New York: Harper & Row, 1985): 224–225.

10. Peter Vaill, The Purposing of High-Performing Systems, *Organizational Dynamics* (Autumn 1982): 23–39.

11. Ibid., 38.

12. This discussion is largely based on W. Hofer, Lady Liberty's Business Army, *Nation's Business* (July 1983): 18–28; see also Alice Hall, Liberty Lifts Her Lamp Once More, *National Geographic* (July 1986): 2–19.

13. Hofer, ibid.

14. Ibid., 28.

15. Ibid., 21.

16. John Nicholas, Developing Effective Teams for System Design and Implementation, *Production and Inventory Management* (Third Quarter 1980): 37–47; and John Nicholas, Organization Development in Systems Management, *Journal of Systems Management* 30, no. 11 (November 1979): 24–30. Much of the following discussion is derived from these sources.

17. See Chapman, *Project Management in NASA*, 59–62. The other functions of project management were defined to be project planning, information and control, and consultation.

18. R.T. Keller, Predictors of the Performance of Project Groups in R&D Organizations, *Academy of Management Journal* 29 no. 4 (December 1986): 715–726.

19. See, for example, William Dyer, *Team Building: Issues and Alternatives*, 2d ed. (Reading MA: Addison-Wesley, 1987) and Nicholas, Organization Development in Systems Management, 24–30.

20. J. Reilly and J.E. Jones, Team Building, in *Annual Handbook of Group Facilitators*, J.W. Pfeiffer and J.E. Jones, eds. (LaJolla, CA: University Associates, 1974).

21. Nicholas, Organization Development in Systems Management.

22. This discussion is largely based on Dyer, *Team Building*, 100–106.

23. Davis and Lawrence, *Matrix*, 134.

24. R.R. Blake, H.A. Shepard, and J.S. Mouton, *Managing Intergroup Conflicts in Industry* (Houston: Gulf Publishing, 1965).

25. Sayles and Chandler, *Managing Large Systems*, 277–278.

26. Ibid., 278.

27. H.J. Thamhain and D.L. Wilemon, Conflict Management in Project Life Cycles, *Sloan Management Review* (Spring 1975): 31–50; and H.J. Thamhain and D.L. Wilemon, Diagnosing Conflict Determinants in Project Management, *IEEE Transactions of Engineering Management* 22 (February 1975).

28. W.H. Schmidt, Conflict: A Powerful Process for (Good or Bad) Change, *Management Review* 63 (December 1974): 5.

29. Fred Moody, *I Sing the Body Electronic* (New York: Viking, 1995): 110–115.

30. This section focuses on managing conflict from a group level perspective. For an individual level perspective, see Marc Robert, *Managing Conflict from the Inside Out* (Austin: Learning Concepts, 1982).

31. It is not only the best approach, it is also the one most favored by project managers (followed by compromise, then smoothing, then forcing and withdrawal). See Thamhain and Wilemon, Conflict Management in Project Life Cycles, 42–44.

32. Ibid., 46–47.

33. Sayles and Chandler, *Managing Large Systems*, 216.

34. This discussion is based upon Dyer, *Team Building*, 116–118. See Herb Bisno, *Managing Conflict* (Newbury Park, CA: Sage, 1988) for another perspective.

35. This discussion is based upon Dyer, *Team Building*, 109–116.

36. Ibid., 111.

37. Ibid., 112.

38. Ibid., 113–114.

39. Ibid., 116–117, 135.

40. Portions of this section are adapted from E.F. Huse and T.G. Cummings, *Organization Development and Change*, 3d ed. (St. Paul: West,

1985): Chapter 12; J.C. Quick and
J.D. Quick, *Organizational Stress and
Preventive Management* (New York: McGraw-
Hill, 1984): and J.C. Williams, *Human Behavior
in Organizations*, 2d ed. (Cincinnati: South-
Western, 1982): Chapter 9.

41. Bryman et al., The Concept of the Temporary
System: The Case of the Construction Project,
253–283.

42. Portions of this section are adapted from Huse
and Cummings, *Organization Development
and Change*; Quick and Quick, *Organizational
Stress and Preventive Management*; Williams,
Human Behavior in Organizations; J.S. House,
Work Stress and Social Support (Reading, MA:
Addison-Wesley, 1981); and L.J. Warshaw,
Managing Stress (Reading, MA: Addison-
Wesley, 1982).

43. See research cited in Quick and Quick,
*Organizational Stress and Preventive
Management*, 170.

44. House, *Work Stress and Social Support*, 22–26,
30–38.

45. Ibid., 98, 99.

46. NASA website, December 1999.

Part V

Project Management in the Corporate Context

CHAPTER 16

The Management of Project Management

CHAPTER 17

Project Selection and Portfolio Management

CHAPTER 18

International Project Management

*T*he first two chapters in this part address the question: "Beyond having skilled project managers and good project management tools and methods, what else can an organization do to improve its project success?" Part of the answer is that the organization must ensure that its managers are competent in project management best practices and are able and provided support to apply those practices; this is the topic of Chapter 16. The other is that the projects must have been selected according to sound criteria based upon organizational objectives and available resources—the topic of Chapter 17. Chapter 18 covers a topic of increasing importance given the growing globalization of industries, businesses, and technology: international project management. The chapter is a virtual review of most everything else covered in this book, so it is fitting that it be the book's last chapter.

Chapter 16's material is addressed by PMBOK as project management "process"; ensuring that projects pursued support the corporate strategy is the topic of Chapter 17. Chapter 18 covers nearly all the PMBOK knowledge areas, but in the international context.

Chapter 16

The Management of Project Management

> If you can't describe what you are doing as a process,
> you don't know what you're doing.
>
> —W. EDWARDS DEMING

> I know what I know
> I'll sing what I said
> We come and we go
> That's a thing that I keep
> In the back of my head
>
> —PAUL SIMON

> He attacked everything in life with a mix of extraordinary
> genius and naïve incompetence, and it was often difficult
> to tell which was which.
>
> —DOUGLAS ADAMS

The material in this chapter concerns policies and practices that span the conduct of *all* projects in a particular organization. In most cases, such policies and practices stem from senior management decisions about what is necessary or desirable in the management of projects, and what the organization, as a whole, must do to improve project execution and outcomes. In other words, the topics in this chapter describe measures that project organizations (not individual project managers) take, once a project has been approved, to increase the likelihood the project will succeed; these measures relate to project management methodology, project management maturity, knowledge management, and the project management office (PMO).

16.1   PROJECT MANAGEMENT METHODOLOGY[1]

Project management methodology is a framework and process that an organization mandates or recommends for the management of its projects. It often includes many of the topics of this book, though organized in a way that suits the organization and its projects, and incorporates lessons learned by the organization. It provides a structure so that all projects are managed and performed in a standardized, disciplined, and systematic manner, using practices that increase the likelihood of projects meeting requirements and being completed on time and within budget. The methodology is created or adopted by the organization so as to uniquely fit its business requirements, procedures, and culture, and the size, scope, technology, and complexity of its projects.

Although some methodologies prescribe the technical tasks of the project, our focus is on those that emphasize the *management* of projects.

Why Methodology?

By developing and requiring conformance to a prescribed project management methodology, an organization is assured that all of its projects will be conducted and managed in a consistent manner. Lacking a methodology, most everything associated with the management of a project falls to the discretion of individual project managers who tend to use their own management practices and styles—some good, some not so good. Without a prescribed methodology every project is managed differently, even those managed by the same person.

The aim of the methodology is to ensure that recognized "good" and "best" project management practices are identified and applied across all projects, and to elevate the management practices of all project managers to those of the best in the organization. The methodology provides a common way to do things and a common terminology. When everyone does things in similar ways, communication, accountability, learning, and continuous improvement about those ways are enhanced.

Of course, for the organization and managers to benefit from the methodology, they must accept and practice it. Managers accustomed to a structured, documented approach to project management will gladly adopt the methodology, but many of those not accustomed will find it burdensome.

Creating the Methodology

The two ways an organization can develop a methodology are to create it from scratch or adopt it from elsewhere. In the first way a small group of the organization's best project managers meet with the purpose of creating a methodology that incorporates methods they all use or recognize as good and believe should be adopted for use in every project. In the second way, managers look at methodologies created by other organizations that represent industry standards, and adopt the ones they find most suitable. An example of a "standard" project management methodology is Prince2 (meaning Project In Controlled Environments), widely used in the UK. Another is the Project Management Body of Knowledge (PMBOK, published by Project Management Institute, PMI), which includes many processes, tools, and techniques that can be incorporated into a methodology. Many companies have developed their own methodologies, some of which can be viewed publicly online or in training brochures. Many of these have much in common in terms of scope and details, and are a good source for ideas.

When an organization adopts an industry standard or extant methodology from another organization, it uses that standard or methodology as a starting point or baseline from which to expand and create a tailored methodology that precisely fits its own projects and business practices. The tailoring is ideally done by a group of the organization's best project managers (not by senior managers or outside consultants); this helps ensure that the methodology will be appropriate for the organization's projects and resources, and accepted by its project managers.

What Does the Methodology Mandate?

The methodology specifies the stages of the project life cycle and the roles and particular management tasks of the project manager and project stakeholders during each stage. For instance, it specifies who is responsible for initiating projects, proposing projects, and reviewing and selecting projects. It specifies the roles and responsibilities of the project review board (discussed in the next chapter) and the project management office (discussed later in this chapter). The methodology also spells out the individuals who must sign off on budgets and schedules, and approve performance results at each project stage.

Phases and Gates

All projects are conducted in stepwise fashion. The project management methodology defines the phases or stages of the project and what management tasks must happen during each. For example, the methodology might specify that projects occur in five stages—initiation, feasibility, definition, development, and launch—and then state what should happen in each. Often, at the end of each stage is a "gate," so-called because at that point the project is assessed and a decision made to approve, hold, or cancel it. The number of stages and gates varies; the minimum is usually four or five; Motorola has 12 for its Cellular Systems Group. The gates represent decision points including, for example, approve project initiation; approve project definition and systems requirements; approve system validation and certification; and approve launch of system into the market. Each gate has specified forms, documents, or scorecards to review the project for a decision.

This gating process is common in organizations that conduct numerous, concurrent internal projects. Examples are projects in product development (PD), IT, or infrastructure and process improvement that in a sense must "compete" for product or market goals and resources. The gating process is one way of culling out weaker, less-promising projects so that scarce resources are available for the stronger, more-promising projects. Additionally, for large, individual projects, the process helps reduce risk. Application of the gating process in project selection and portfolio management is described in the next chapter.

Relationship with Project Life Cycle

Figure 16-1 illustrates a project management methodology with seven stages within a five-phase project life cycle (Conception through Post-project). In general, a methodology should conform to the technical and business practices of the organization, so in Figure 16-1, for example, whatever development methodology the organization employs in stages 4 and 5 (waterfall, spiral, iterative, Scrum, etc.), the project management methodology must be able to accommodate and manage it. Different organizations use different development methodologies, which is one reason why the project management methodology must be uniquely tailored to the organization.

Elements of the Methodology

The content of the project management methodology has been the subject of most of this book. In fact, one way to create and implement a methodology is to look at the topics and methods described in this and other project management books, and for each determine a procedure for addressing or performing it, and then specify who in the organization will do it and when in the project life cycle it should be done.

But the actual content and details of the methodology—its tasks and requirements—depend on the scope and scale of the organization's projects. For large, complex, risky projects, the methodology would specify detailed tasks and methods for analysis, definition, planning, monitoring, control, and closeout. For small, straightforward no-risk projects, a somewhat simplistic methodology would be more appropriate.

The goal in creating the project management methodology is simple: to provide a framework and set of structured tasks, tools, and techniques to better conceive, define, plan, schedule, budget, track, control, and close out projects. Anything beyond the minimum necessary to enable this should be excluded. Choices about

Figure 16-1
Project life cycle phases versus project management methodology.

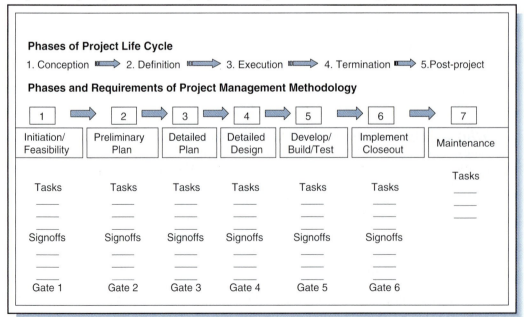

which aspects of the methodology can be bypassed and which must be followed for a particular project should be stated in the methodology and not left to the discretion of the project manager.

Key elements of the methodology are:

- Phases and stages of the project life cycle
- Required tasks and deliverables
- Who is responsible

Phases and Stages of the Project Life Cycle

The methodology should start by defining the nominal phases or stages through which a project progresses. Though this book has used the three phases of Conception, Definition, and Execution, each with a series of stages, a particular project can be defined using any number of phases or stages, whatever best represent the "natural" progression of the organization's projects, and the initiation, approval, definition, execution, and close out of the projects. The methodology can even identify pre- and post-project phases—what happens before and after the project (the methodology in Figure 16-1 includes the post-project stage of maintenance). The methodology would specify at each phase the details and requirements of the gating process, if one exists.

Required Tasks and Deliverables

For each phase or stage the methodology specifies project management tasks and deliverables such as documents, plans, reports, and performance metrics. As an example, *Stage 1: Initiation/Feasibility* of the methodology in Figure 16-1 might specify the following tasks and deliverables:

- Assemble team and identify stakeholders
- Prepare project initiation form
- Complete preliminary task list
- Perform risk analysis and prepare key-risk list
- Develop requirements list
- Prepare funding request
- Prepare resource plan, timeline, spending plan
- Prepare project proposal

Typically the methodology will include tasks and deliverables that cover virtually all of the topics covered in this book, including those in Table 16-1.

Who Is Responsible—Signoffs and Approvals

As exemplified in Figure 16-1, the methodology might also include gates at which a project must be approved before it can move on. The methodology would specify persons at each stage who have signoff authority, and the roles for stakeholders such as the client, sponsor, champion, steering committee, and project manager.

An example of the methodology for a large corporation is in Figure 16-2. Interesting in its details, it is an excellent example of the scope and depth of tasks and deliverables that comprise a comprehensive project management methodology.

One Size Fits All?

Most methodologies are somewhat flexible. They specify project management requirements at a high level for a generic kind of project but allow for inclusion

Table 16-1 Project management tasks and deliverables.

Project initiation/proposal	Procurement/contract management
Stakeholder identification	HR recruiting, training, layoffs
Project selection	Project tracking/review
Proposal development	Data entry
Project planning	Reporting to management
Requirements/specifications	Project auditing
Work definition	Quality control/assurance
Resource needs	Process control
Time and cost estimating	Change control
Scheduling	Project closeout
Budgeting/accounting	Post-project review
Risk analysis	Post-implementation review
	Knowledge management

of other requirements, depending on the unique features of each project. When all projects in an organization tend to be the same in terms of scope, size, and complexity, then a single methodology might be suitable for all of them.

In general, the scope and number of requirements, tasks, and deliverables specified by the methodology tends to increase with the scope, size, risk, and complexity of the projects to which it is applied. To accommodate projects of different size and complexity the methodology can be made "scalable." It might come in, say, three or four versions, and the particular one to be applied will depend on the capital resources, labor hours, duration, number of high-level work packages and contractors, number of different technologies involved, and the risk of the project. One problem with multiple methodologies, however, is deciding which one is appropriate for a given project.

Many organizations have one basic—perhaps scalable—methodology because all of their projects tend to be similar. In contrast, organizations such as oil and gas companies that are involved in a variety of different categories of projects (PD, exploration, construction of refineries and pipelines, applied research, marketing) have multiple, different methodologies, one for each category. One methodology would be applied to, say, projects in search of new oil sources, another for projects to construct new refineries or ocean-drilling platforms. The technical stages, tasks, and even life cycles of these projects differ and call for somewhat different project management methodologies.

Evolving, Continually Improving Methodology

A project management methodology is not a static thing. Like all frameworks or systems, it is subject to change and improvement based upon experience and the changing environment. New tasks and deliverables judged to improve project performance are added; others thought unnecessary or without sufficient benefit are dropped. The methodology must be periodically reviewed to incorporate changes in projects, technology, and business practices; as new steps and requirements are added, others are pruned to prevent the methodology from becoming cumbersome and burdensome. Of course, the ability to improve the methodology depends on how much the organization is able to learn from its past projects, a subject covered later.

Project Approval	Customer Requirements	Solution Analysis/ Recommendation	Detailed Design	Attain the Solution	Solution Implementation
Preliminary Plan	**Preliminary Plan**	**Detailed Plan**	**Working Plan**	**Working Plan**	**Working Plan**
Project initiation form	Updated project initiation form	Updated project initiation form	Updated project initiation form	Updated project initiation form	Updated project initiation form
Preliminary task list	Preliminary task list	Preliminary task list	Detailed task list	Detailed task list	Detailed task list
Risk analysis	Risk analysis	Risk analysis	Risk analysis	Risk analysis	Risk analysis
Issue log	Issue log	Issue log	Issue log	Issue log	Issue log
Prelim customer business unit analysis	Scope management	Scope management	Scope management	Scope management	Scope management
	Prelim customer business unit analysis	Prelim customer business unit analysis	Final customer business unit analysis	Final customer business unit analysis	Final customer business unit analysis
			Benefits realization plan	Benefits realization plan	Testing plan/QA
			Implementation plan	Implementation plan	Implementation plan
			Conversion plan	Conversion plan	Conversion plan
			Training plan	Training plan	Training plan
			Resource plan	Resource plan	Resource plan
			Procurement plan	Procurement plan	Procurement plan
			Documentation plan	Documentation plan	Documentation plan
			Operations/support plan	Operations/support plan	Operations/support plan
					Benefits realization plan
Deliverables	**Deliverables**	**Deliverables**	**Deliverables**	**Deliverables**	**Deliverables**
Project initiation form	Process definition	Conceptual design	Business impact plan	QA/user test documentation	Closure document
• general business case	Business function requirements	Solution evaluation	• detailed work flow	Implementation checklist	Final communication
• project description	• business model	Feasibility/proof of concept	• organization impact	Change management	Shut-down old systems
• project timeline	• work process flows	Customer sign-off document	• business process		Hand-off to operations
• project spending plan	Define target population	Contingency plan	• reengineering		Project post-completion review
• assumptions	Current and proposed states	Fit analysis	• operations impact		Schedule benefits review
• dependencies	Outputs/inputs	• architecture	• resource plan		
• potential risks	Budget cap	• functionality	QA/user test plan		
• project team	Business rules	• skills	Back-out plan		
• governance team	Policy changes	• training	Security		
• requirements for next phase	Metrics				
• ROI	Security				
• sign-offs	Regulatory				
Resource plan	Environmental				
High-level requirements	Interfacing				
Change control process	Recovery requirements				
Communication strategy					
Phase Review: Governance Team	**Phase Review: Governance Team**	**Phase Review: Governance Team**	**Phase Review: Governance Team**	**Phase Review: Governance Team**	**Phase Review: Governance Team**
Go / No-Go	Go / No-Go	Go / No-Go	Go / No-Go	Go / No-Go	Go / No-Go
Sign-offs	**Sign-offs**	**Sign-offs**	**Sign-offs**	**Sign-offs**	**Sign-offs**
Project sponsor	Project sponsor	Project sponsor	Project sponsor	Project sponsor	Project sponsor
Project champion	Project champion	Project champion	Project champion	Project champion	Project champion
Project manager	Project manager	Project manager	Project manager	Project manager	Project manager
Governance team	Governance team	Governance team	Governance team	Governance team	Governance team
Customer business unit manager		Customer business unit manager	Customer business unit manager		

Figure 16-2

Comprehensive six-stage project management methodology.

583

Perhaps the most important consideration about the methodology is that the payoff from using it must exceed the effort in creating and maintaining it. The methodology must not become yet more red tape, forcing managers to attend more to paperwork than manage projects. It should be the means to an end—successful projects—not an end in itself, which is something its creators and enforcers must continually be mindful of.

16.2 PROJECT MANAGEMENT MATURITY AND MATURITY MODELS

How good are we really? How well do we measure up to our competitors? What strengths do we have that could be exploited? In which areas should we improve? These are questions that competitive companies continually ask themselves about their capabilities and competencies. The degree or extent of capability or competency regarding project management is referred to as "maturity."

Maturity Continuum

In the same way that humans grow and develop physically and intellectually, so do organizations grow and develop competency in project management, referred to as levels of maturity. Typical levels of maturity are shown in Figure 16-3.

The process begins when one person or a few people who understand the principles of good project management initially introduce them to the organization. At first these individuals tend to practice the principles on their own, in isolation of other project managers. Of course, for the organization to further develop its project management capability *many* people must practice the principles. For that to happen requires awareness at the executive level as to the importance of project management and willingness to support project management initiatives.

Spreading the principles of good project management practice throughout the company involves a number of steps, including documenting lessons learned from each project for the benefit of other projects, and developing a common language and glossary of project management terms to be used everywhere in the company. A company that operates across the globe might actually create a glossary of terms

Figure 16-3
Levels of project management maturity/competency.

0	1	2	3	4
No project management ability	Basic awareness of project management principles	Lessons learned are applied across projects	Company-wide use of a standardized methodology	Project management competency used as a strategic weapon
	Isolated use of project management techniques by individual project managers	Use of a common vocabulary	Established project management office	

in multiple languages. Naturally, moving to higher-level maturity also requires that the organization develop a project management methodology. Ultimately the organization benchmarks its project management capabilities against leader project organizations in industry, and then presumably uses its superior capabilities (speedy delivery of projects, cost effectiveness, and superior quality) to attain an edge on its competitors.[2]

Maturity Models

Ways to gauge or measure an organization's project management maturity have been expressed in so-called "maturity models"; currently there are more than 30 of these models[3] although none has achieved acceptance worldwide.[4]

Maturity models fall into three general categories[5]

- Technical Delivery Process Models
- Project Management Process Models
- Total Organization Models

Technical Delivery Process Models originated in the Total Quality Management movement of the 1980s when companies first started measuring their quality management capabilities. An example of these models is the Capability Maturity Model (CMM) developed by the Software Engineering Institute of Carnegie-Mellon University during the 1980s and 1990s in response to a US Department of Defense request for ways to identify competent software contractors. The model, which emphasizes documentation of processes similar to those emphasized in ISO quality standards, assesses project management practices against standard criteria and identifies five levels of maturity.

The next category of models, Project Management Process Models, generally focuses on knowledge areas.[6] Many of these models are based on the nine knowledge areas in the Guide to the Project Management Body of Knowledge (PMBOK)[7] of the PMI. The level of maturity achieved in each knowledge area is determined by an assessment of standardized criteria during an audit. Figure 16-4 illustrates an example showing the results of such an audit and the relative maturity levels among the relevant knowledge areas.

Figure 16-4
Result of a maturity assessment regarding project management knowledge areas.

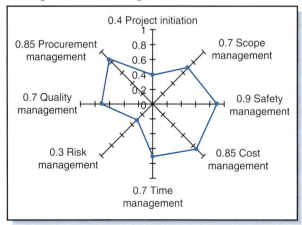

Several of these process models specify five possible levels of maturity:[8]

- Ad hoc: no formal procedures or plans
- Individual Project Planning
- Systematic Project Planning and Control
- Integrated Multi-project and Formal Planning and Control
- Continuous project management Improvement

Following the development of CMM, the PMI sponsored research at the University of California Berkeley and George Washington University,[9] and produced the Organizational Project Management Maturity Model (OPM3).[10] This is an example of a Total Organizational Model, so-called because it takes into account the entire organization, not only projects, and applies to all organizations, not just project-oriented ones.

How Good Should We Be?

It would be incorrect to presume that an organization should strive for the highest-level maturity in all aspects of project management as prescribed by these models. Different companies have different needs that each requires different levels of maturity. For example, whereas a company doing research using limited internal funding needs strong capability in project selection, a construction contractor with ample capacity to take whatever work comes along does not. Likewise, whereas a company that develops nuclear reactors should have a high maturity in environmental protection and safety practices, a company that develops computer games can get by with low maturity in those areas. In their study of project management maturity in hardware and software PD, Milosevic and Patanakul found that standardization of project management processes and use of standard tools increase project success up to a point, beyond which it can reduce success; in other words, conformity to industry standards can only take you so far.[11]

As an organization's business environment changes, so do its requirements for managing projects. No one maturity model provides an adequate metric for project success across all industries and types of projects. Each organization must identify which areas of competency are important, and avoid spending time and resources achieving high maturity in those areas less important.

Benefits and Shortcomings of Maturity Models[12]

Having achieved a high rating according to a standard maturity model, a company can potentially use that rating to its advantage. In responding to a request for quotes, for example, it can point out the high-level maturity it has achieved for a recognized model.

By their very nature, however, maturity models emphasize formal processes and procedures, and focus only on explicit knowledge, which is knowledge that can be readily documented and transferred. The weakness they all share is ignoring tacit knowledge, which is knowledge that cannot be easily written or described. Leadership, communication, teamwork, and the knowledge and skills held by project managers and team members also play a big role in project success; being tacit, however, this knowledge cannot be accounted for by the maturity models.[13]

Project Maturity and Project Success

Studies indicate that about two thirds of all organizations rate at level 2 or lower on the 5-level maturity scale. Engineering industries such as petrochemical and defense show relatively high maturity, while insurance, financial and health services, pharmaceutical R&D, and telecommunications show lower maturity.[14]

Does achieving higher maturity according to the models automatically confer greater project success? The empirical evidence is paltry, but the answer seems: not necessarily. Project success depends on many things, including aspects of the project environment, the team, and the project manager, none of which the maturity models can account for. According to one study, senior managers see little association between maturity level and project performance;[15] the few studies that claim to show a correlation between maturity and project success lack a theoretical basis[16] and, not surprisingly, are those conducted by consultants, not researchers. As to the question, Does maturity offer a competitive advantage? The answer is also be mixed. The models measure only explicit knowledge—that which can be standardized and documented and, hence, copied or adopted by other companies. An organization that mimics standard practices and ignores its own unique strengths can never become better than its competitors.[17]

16.3   KNOWLEDGE MANAGEMENT IN PROJECT MANAGEMENT

One potential pitfall in project planning and execution is to treat each project as if it were completely unique and ignore the lessons of other projects. Solutions to problems are invented . . . and reinvented. Mistakes in projects are repeated ... and repeated again. Why does that happen? As the saying goes, "Fool me once, shame on you. Fool me twice, shame on me!"

As an example, consider a project that is truly unique—a first time, one-of-kind project for which apparently the organization has no prior experience. The project manager must ponder what to expect and how to proceed, and plan the project starting with a clean slate. There is no one in the organization to help because—after all—the project is unique. But is there really no one? In most organizations rarely can it be said that there is no one who can help. Almost always there is someone, *somewhere*, with experience and knowledge that is relevant to the project. If only the project manager knew whom that someone is!

Authors O'Dell and Grayson describe the problem in the title of their book *If Only We Knew What We Know*.[18] In many organizations critical knowledge is wasted; the knowledge exists but people don't know it exists or how to gain access to it. Often the waste occurs because the organization has no formal process for capturing and disseminating knowledge, a process called *knowledge management*. In a project organization, a knowledge management process would help ensure that in every project people learn something and that whatever they learned will be available to be shared with others who could use it. Knowledge management can provide project managers with the knowledge they need, even in cases where they themselves don't know they need it!

Organizational Forgetting

According to the classic learning curve, knowledge accumulates with experience: the more of something you do, the more you learn about it and the better you get,

definition, project managers at CorCom are not involved until after a project has been approved and defined. The stance of CorCom managers is, "Tell us exactly what you want, and we'll give it to you." This contrasts to the old way of "Let us help you define your needs and requirements, and suggest the best alternatives." In other words, CorCom project managers have no say in project definition or the solutions they are responsible for implementing. The concern of some at MCA is that this lack of early user–developer interaction precludes thorough and accurate identification of customer needs. But it is too early to tell if this concern is more than just a perception.

FUTURE OF THE PMO

The Director is convinced about the continued importance of the IT PMO but is concerned about what senior management thinks. He has scheduled a meeting with the Global CIO to discuss the future of the PMO.

QUESTIONS

1. Does the IT PMO at MCA have a future? What, if any, role can it retain?

2. How does the IT PMO Director's role compare to the Vice President of Projects discussed in Chapter 14?

ENDNOTES

1. Information in this section obtained from interviews with project managers and PMO directors at 11 organizations: Doug Brandt (Abbott Laboratories); Jacki Koehler (ABN-Amro); Ruta Kulbis (Accenture); Holly Wells (Aon); Carson Neally, Jim Yeck, Robert Wunderlick, and Jeff Roberts (Argonne National Laboratory); Douglas Gilman, Joe Wolke, and Eileen Will (Chicago Board of Trade); Martin Wills (Information Resources, Inc.); Cynthia Reyes (Nicor); Thomas Foley (Sears Roebuck); Gurran Gopal (Tellabs); and Carol Bobbe (TransUnion).

2. Common language, processes, methodology, benchmarking, and continuous improvement are the five levels of maturity defined by H. Kerzner in *Strategic Planning for Project Management using a Project Management Maturity Model* (New York: Wiley, 2001).

3. T.J. Cooke-Davies, "Project Management Maturity Models: Does it Make Sense to Adopt One?"*Project Manager Today* (May 2002).

4. K. Jugdev and J. Thomas, "Project Management Maturity Models: The Silver Bullets of Competitive Advantage?"*Project Management Journal* 33, no. 4 (December 2002): 4–14.

5. T.J. Cooke-Davies, J. Schlichter, and C. Bredillet. "Beyond the PMBOK Guide," *Proceedings of the 32nd Annual Project Management Institute*, 2001 Seminars and Symposium.

6. K. Jugdev and J. Thomas, *Project Management Maturity Models: The Silver Bullets of Competitive Advantage*?

7. *A Guide to the Project Management Body Of Knowledge (PMBOK Guides)*, 3rd ed., PMI; November 2004.

8. Project Management Process Maturity (PM)2 Model (the Berkeley PM Model) by Y. Kwak and C. W. Ibbs, www.ce.berkeley.edu/~ibbs/yhkwak/pmmatrutiy.html; see also J.K. Crawford, *Project Management Maturity Model—Providing a Proven Path to Project Management Excellence* (New York: Marcel Dekker, Inc, 2002).

9. C.W. Ibbs and Y.H. Kwak, "Assessing Project Management Maturity," *Project Management Journal* 31, no. 1 (March 2000): 32–43.

10. PMI, *Organizational Project Management Model* (PA, USA: PMI Inc, 2003).

11. D. Milosevic and P. Patanakul, "Standardized Project Management May Increase Development Project Success," *International Journal of Project Management* 23 (2005): 181–192.

12. J.S. Pennypacker and K.P. Grant, "Project Management Maturity: An Industry Benchmark", *Project Management Journal* 34, no. 1 (March 2003): 4–11; K. Jugdev and J. Thomas, *Project Management Maturity Models: The Silver Bullets of Competitive Advantage*?

13. G. Skulmoski, "Project Maturity and Cost Interface," *Cost Engineering* 43, no. 6

(2001): 11–18; E.S. Andersen and S.A. Jessen, "Project Maturity in Organizations," *International Journal of Project Management* 21 (2003): 457–461.

14. T.J. Cooke-Davies and A. Arzymanow, "The maturity of project management in different industries: An investigation into variations between project management models," *International Journal of Project Management* 21, (2003): 471–478; Pennypacker and Grant, "Project Management Maturity: An Industry Benchmark"; Crawford, "Senior Management Perceptions of Project Management Competence," *International Journal of Project Management* 23 (2005): 7–16.

15. Crawford, "*Senior Management Perceptions of Project Management Competence.*

16. Jugdev and Thomas, *Project Management Maturity Models: The Silver Bullets of Competitive Advantage?*; example of an industry study: A. Nietro Rodriguez and D. Evrard, *A First Global Survey on the Current State of Project Management Maturity in Organizations Across the World* (Price Waterhouse Cooper, 2004).

17. Jugdev and Thomas, *Project Management Maturity Models: The Silver Bullets of Competitive Advantage?*

18. Carla O'Dell and C. Jackson Grayson, *If Only We Knew What We Know* (New York: Free Press, 1998).

19. For examples of organizational forgetting see Linda Argote, *Organizational Learning:*

Creating, Retaining, and Transferring Knowledge (Boston: Kluwer Academic Publishers, 1999).

20. Nancy Dixon, *Common Knowledge: How Companies Thrive by Sharing What They Know* (Boston: Harvard Business School Press, 2000).

21. Ernst and Young, Knowledge Management, downloaded April 13, 2007, http://www. ey.com/global/content.nsf/Middle_East/ Knowledge_Management_-_Tools.

22. *A Leader's Guide to After Action Review (TC 25-20)*, 1993, US Department of the Army.

23. Dixon, *Common Knowledge*, 77–79, 81–82.

24. Ernst and Young, Knowledge Management; National Library for Health, Knowledge Management Specialists Library, Peer assist; downloaded April 143, 2007, http://www. library.nhs.uk/knowledgemanagement/ ViewResource.aspx?resID=125167.

25. Dixon, *Common Knowledge*, 82–85.

26. Other examples provided by Ibid, 103–104, and Nathaniel Welch, *Peer Assist Overview*, accessed April 12, 2007, http://003cce4. netsolhost.com/PeerAssit.htm.

27. O'Dell and Grayson, *If Only We Knew What We Know*, 51–52.

28. Cumsumano and Selby, *Microsoft Secrets* (New York: Free Press, 1995): 243.

29. *Sources*: see note 1.

Chapter 17

Project Selection and Portfolio Management

> Lilies that fester smell far worse then weeds.
>
> —SHAKESPEARE,
> *Sonnets*

> Errors, like straws, upon the surface flow; he who would search for pearls must dive below.
>
> —JOHN DRYDEN

*P*ursuing the right projects is crucial for business success and a determinant of whether a company is an industry leader or follower. From the top-management viewpoint, projects are the means by which the organization pursues and achieves its strategic goals and objectives. If the organization proclaims it wants to "be the low-cost leader,""expand market share in Europe,""develop state-of-the-art technologies," or "preserve the natural environment" then you would expect that many or most of its projects would be directed at or incorporate those objectives.

But often that is not the case. In many companies projects have little or nothing to do with strategic goals or objectives. Instead they represent narrow, short-term interests, focused merely on easily seized opportunities or the pet agendas of a few people. Projects that are the hobbyhorses of senior executives get "sacred cow" status despite questionable benefits and excessive risk or cost. Even worse, they hog resources and squeeze out projects that have obvious business value.

A study of 35 predominantly North American firms revealed relatively little overall spending on projects that contributed directly to company goals and strategies.[1] In general, project resources were spread too thinly because the companies had too many projects and no systematic way to prioritize them. Most projects were "low-hanging fruit"—relatively easy to do but offering little in the form of business potential. Pursuing the "wrong" projects, companies inadvertently waste resources and deprive potentially superior projects of opportunities.

17.1 PROJECT PORTFOLIO MANAGEMENT

A project portfolio is a group of projects or programs in an organization or business unit that aim at strategic objectives, share resources, and must compete for funding. Any organization that funds, manages, and allocates resources to more than one project has a project portfolio—even though managers may not know what it looks like, how it contributes to strategic objectives, or how to actively manage it.[2] The term *project portfolio management* refers to a formal process wherein:

- Project proposals are assessed for costs, risks, benefits, and contributions to objectives.

- Decisions are made conscientiously to authorize certain projects, retain some on the "back burner," and dispose of those with limited potential.

- Scarce resources are allocated effectively so as to insure that approved, priority projects get adequate funding and support.

- Projects as a whole are "balanced" in terms of high versus low risk, large versus small size, long-term versus short-term focus, etc.—whatever balance the company deems best.

- Projects are *continually* tracked, compared, and managed collectively; decisions about each project are based upon benefits and required resources compared to other projects.

There is no best process for managing a project portfolio. Academics and consultants have proposed many approaches, and software firms offer numerous products. The breadth of the subject fills books; hence, treatment in this chapter is limited to an overview of the process and a survey of common methods.

Process for Successful Projects[3]

Successful projects depend upon two things: doing the *right projects* and doing those *projects right*. Managers make both happen in the following ways, as shown in Figure 17-1:[4]

- **Strategic management: focus the organization.** Top management articulates the vision and mission of the organization, defines organization objectives and strategic initiatives, decides on the total budget, and allocates resources to business units. Common themes for strategic initiatives are to be the low-cost leader or technology

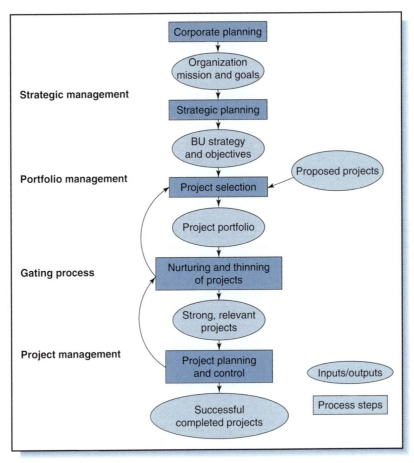

Figure 17-1
The management of projects.

leader, to be innovative or imitative, or to pursue mass markets or niche markets. The objectives should be clearly articulated and not changed too frequently.

- **Portfolio management: select the right projects.** Business unit managers develop goals, strategies, and initiatives that are consistent with corporate objectives and initiatives. These become specific criteria for selecting projects from proposals that are generated internally, requested by customers, or resulting from ad hoc problems or obligations.

- **Gating methodology: nurture or get rid of projects.** Managers assess each project as it moves through gates. They compare project performance to gating criteria and make decisions: important but struggling projects are allocated more resources; poorly performing or mediocre projects are put on hold or canceled.

- **Project management: manage the projects right.** Projects are managed using sound principles and practices of project management.

Project Review Board

Responsibility for project selection and portfolio management rests with a team called the *Project Review Board* or *PRB* (aka, Portfolio Management Team, Project Governance Board, Project Steering Committee, or Project Council). Membership in the PRB typically includes a project portfolio manager, chief financial officer (CFO), chief risk manager (CRO), chief human resource officer (CHRO), the project management office (PMO) director, and the chief technical officer (CTO) (from IT, engineering, or product development, depending on the organization). The CFO weighs each project's costs and financial benefits; the CRO assesses each project's risk; the CHRO assesses the human resource requirements; and the CTO assesses each project's technical benefits and difficulties.[5] The PMO director assures that documentation necessary to make selection and gating decisions is complete for every project under consideration. The project portfolio manager, who typically acts as PRB chairperson, investigates any strategic benefits not addressed by the members, integrates their views, and finally approves project additions or deletions in the portfolio.

For research and engineering projects the PRB will include a group of technically competent "peer reviewers," each of whom independently appraises and rates each proposal according to its scientific and/or technical merit, the competency or capability of the proposal originator, likelihood of success, and so on. If all the reviewers assign low scores to a proposal then the project is rejected. If all assign high scores then the project is approved, given that others on the PRB also approve it and funds are available. If funding is tight, few projects are approved, regardless of high scores. If funding is abundant, even mediocre-rated projects might be approved.[6]

17.2 FRAMEWORK FOR PROJECT SELECTION AND PORTFOLIO MANAGEMENT

When an organization has excess capacity it readily takes on all the projects it can get. But when it does not—when it has insufficient resources (talented people, finances, technological capacity) to support every proposed project that comes along—then logically it pursues only those that contribute the most to its objectives and initiatives. Organizations in which most projects are generated internally rely on the portfolio management process to evaluate proposals and approve projects; those where projects are generated externally rely on the process to determine to which RFPs they should respond.

Since projects differ with regard to resource requirements, risk, cost, and strategic value, choosing the right projects for the portfolio can be a complex problem. Projects are in fact investments, and many of the methods used in project portfolio management derive from general principles of investment management. Just as an investment portfolio might reduce risk by, say, investing in multiple currencies (pound, euro, yen, or dollar), a project portfolio might reduce risk by spreading projects across more than one business sector. Managers use the logic and techniques of project selection and portfolio management to decide in which among alternative areas of business, business partners, and technologies to invest.

Selection Process

Since organizations habitually face project selection decisions, they should have a prescribed means for assessing and comparing projects. A company should also have a set of *measurable* criteria that reflects its strategic goals and initiatives, as well as a process for evaluating projects in terms of those criteria. The selection process and its relation to other aspects of portfolio management are shown in the two phases in Figure 17-2. In Phase I each project is independently evaluated and screened; in Phase II, all projects are considered together and only a subset is approved.[7]

Screening and selection of project proposals rely on results from project selection analysis. All analysis is based upon assumptions about business conditions and technology, some that later might prove to be wrong. For this reason the assumptions in analysis should always be explicit and the analysis work always documented. Among the many popular methods for analysis, the most common are financial models and scoring models.

Financial Models

Financial models measure project proposals in terms of economic or financial criteria such as net present value (NPV), internal rate of return (IRR), return on original investment (ROI), payback period, and so on. Another common method is the expected commercial value (ECV) model diagrammed in Figure 17-4; this model is an application of decision-tree analysis, described in the Appendix to Chapter 10. The model illustrated in Figure 17-4 takes into account the development and launch phases of product development, associated costs, and likelihood of success.[11] Suppose the development cost of a proposed product is $10 M, launch cost is $1.5 M, and the NPV for the future stream of earnings is $50 M. If the probabilities for success are 80 percent in development and 60 percent in the market, then

$$\text{ECV} = [(\$50)0.6 - \$1.5\text{ M}]\,0.80 - \$10\text{ M} = \$12.8\text{ M}.$$

In general, projects with higher ECV values are preferred over those with lower values.

Another financial model is the benefit/cost ratio, or B/C, which weighs the benefits of a project against the costs. A simple example is

$$\text{B/C} = \frac{\text{Estimated revenues} \times \text{probability of success}}{\text{Estimated cost}}$$

Figure 17-4
Model for computing ECV.

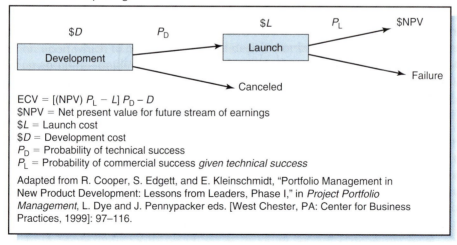

ECV = [(NPV) P_L − L] P_D − D
$NPV = Net present value for future stream of earnings
$L = Launch cost
$D = Development cost
P_D = Probability of technical success
P_L = Probability of commercial success *given technical success*

Adapted from R. Cooper, S. Edgett, and E. Kleinschmidt, "Portfolio Management in New Product Development: Lessons from Leaders, Phase I," in *Project Portfolio Management*, L. Dye and J. Pennypacker eds. [West Chester, PA: Center for Business Practices, 1999]: 97–116.

Values in the numerator and denominator are all expressed in the same form, either as annualized or present worth amounts. For example, if estimated annual revenue is $100,000, probability of success is 50 percent, and estimated annualized cost of the project is $25,000, the resulting ratio is 2.0. This says that for each dollar spent on the project, two dollars in benefit can be expected back. B/C can be computed regardless whether benefits are expressed in terms of revenues or cost reductions.[12] For instance, in the ratio

$$B/C = \frac{\text{Worth of benefits}}{\text{Capital recovery cost} + (\text{Operating cost} + \text{Maintenance cost})}$$

the "worth" can be cost savings. Suppose, for example, renovation of a plant and installation of new equipment is expected to provide a present worth savings of $6 M for a present worth cost (for facility renovation, equipment installation, and annual operating and maintenance expenses) of $3 M. The B/C ratio for the project is 2.0.

Of course the accuracy of the ratio depends on having assigned accurate numbers to *all* significant, relevant costs and benefits, including "hidden" or external ones such as impact on society, the economy, and the environment.[13] Although hidden benefits and costs can be difficult to identify and measure, often they exceed by far the obvious benefits and costs that are included in the analysis. In the renovation example, suppose after the project is begun the factory electrical system is found to be out-of-code and must be entirely replaced, and portions of the flooring are determined to be unsound and must be reinforced; or, suppose the environmental regulations are changed and require installation of equipment to clean up smoke and liquids discharged from the factory. Not anticipating these costs, the B/C ratio would be erroneous and misleading.

The main weakness of B/C, ECV, and all financial models of project value is total reliance on *estimates* for development costs, commercialization and capital expenditures, future streams of earnings, probabilities, etc., and lack of data for estimation during project conception (plus project supporters' tendency to understate costs and overstate benefits). Another weakness is sole emphasis on financial and economic criteria, and neglect of other criteria of equal or potentially greater importance.

Scoring Models

Scoring models rate projects in terms of *multiple* criteria that include quantifiable measures as well as non-quantifiable ones such as market risk, fit with company mission and goals, customer excitement, and so on.

The simplest scoring models incorporate whatever criteria are considered important and thought to discriminate between projects. A project is rated for each criterion according to a scale (say, 5 = excellent, 4 = good, 3 = adequate, 2 = poor, 1 = bad), and the scores for all criteria are summed to yield a total project score. A weighted rating method (described in Chapter 3) is used when some criteria are considered more important than others.

Table 17-1 shows another rating method that includes both probabilities and weights. The first column lists the scoring criteria, and the next five ("very good" through "very poor") *the expected probability* that the project will fit the criteria. For example, the probability that the long-range outlook for the product will be "very good" is 80 percent, and will be "good" is 20 percent. How these probabilities are obtained depends on the information available to the scoring team and can range from complete gut-feel to sophisticated quantitative analysis. The score in the table for risk level acceptability, e.g., can be based on an opinion about the project as a whole, or derived from influence diagrams or analysis of the risk impacts and probabilities, as

Table 17-1 Project Weighted Scoring Model.

Criteria		Very Good 4	Good 3	Fair 2	Poor 1	Very Poor 0	Expected Rating	Weighted	Weight Expected Score
Long-range	1. Product	0.8	0.2				3.8	10	38
outlook	2. Market	1.0					4.0	10	40
Meets	1. ECV	0.8	0.2				3.8	5	19
objectives	2. ROI		1.0				3.0	6	18.0
	3. Image		0.6	0.4			2.6	4	10.4
Fits strategy	Phase 1	0.8	0.2				3.8	10	38
	Phase 2	1.0					1.0	5	5
	Phase 3	0.6	0.2	0.2			3.4	5	17
Goal	Goal A	0.2	0.8				3.2	10	32
contribution	Goal B	1.0					4.0	5	20
	Goal C		0.2	0.2	0.6		1.6	4	6.4
Risk level acceptability		0.7	0.3				3.7	10	37
Competitive advantage		0.9	0.1				3.9	8	31.2
Compatibility with other systems		0.2	0.7	0.1			3.1	8	24.8
	Total							100	336.8/400

Adapted from David Cleland in *Project Management: Strategic Design and Implementation*, 3rd ed., (McGraw-Hill, 1999); reprinted in *Project Portfolio Management*, L. Dye and J. Pennypacker, eds. (West Chester, PA: Center for Business Practices, 1999): 3–22.

explained in Chapter 10. As with all project analysis, the more data available and the greater the experience of the scoring team, the more accurate are the estimates.

Numbers in the expected rating column in Table 17-1 are calculated as the sum of the probabilities times the score weights. The expected rating for long-range outlook for the product, for instance, is 0.8(4) + 0.2(3) = 3.8.

The next column, weight, reflects the relative importance of the criteria (e.g., a criterion weighted 10 is considered twice as important as one weighted 5); sometimes the weights are set to total to 100. The next column, weighted expected score, is the weight multiplied by the expected rating. For the long-range outlook of the product, the weighted expected score is 3.8 × 10 = 38.

The bottom of Table 17-1 shows the total weighted expected score—the sum over all criteria—of 336.8 out of a possible 400 maximum. This score will be used to screen the proposal or rank-order it with other current and proposed projects in the selection phase, discussed in the next section.

One drawback of scoring methods is that they ignore the resources needed to implement projects. Big projects tend to be more attention-getting and score higher than smaller projects, but they also consume more resources and shut out other projects, regardless of how important those others might be to survival or growth. This drawback can be offset by simultaneously considering a project's required funds, cost, or resources with its score or rating, as in the cost–benefit grid and cost-effectiveness methods, described later.

17.4 Methods for Comparing and Selecting Projects

After proposed projects have been analyzed, scored, and screened, the next step is to compare the surviving ones with current and proposed projects and determine which of them combined constitute the best portfolio. Projects that are technically or commercially interdependent need to be considered in combination. The result is some proposed projects will be added to the portfolio; some current projects dropped.

In their review of project portfolios in product development, Cooper et al. found that companies tend to use project selection approaches aimed at some combination of the following goals:[14]

- Maximizing the value or utility of the portfolio
- Achieving balance in the portfolio
- Fitting the portfolio with organization objectives and strategic initiatives

Value or Utility
Single-Criterion Methods
Value or utility methods select projects with the highest "value" or usefulness as determined from financial models or scoring methods. Projects are rank-ordered according to some value or utility measure (e.g., B/C ratio, ECV from model in Figure 17-4, score from Table 17-1, etc.), and the highest-ranked ones are selected subject to resource availability. A minimum value threshold can be applied for screening projects; for example, any proposal having a B/C ratio of less than 1.5 or a score of less than 50 percent maximum (200/400 in Table 17-1) is rejected immediately.

Beyond our scope are other value methods, including optimization techniques based on mathematical programming that select the combination of projects that maximizes portfolio value subject to project dependencies, limited resources, and other constraints. An advantage of some of these methods is that they allow *sensitivity analysis* for a *range* of input conditions (e.g., what happens if expected revenues drop 20 percent, costs rise 30 percent, and the exchange rate increases by 10 percent ?).[15]

The main drawback of single-criterion methods is their reliance on a single criterion to rank-order projects; this can be risky because underlying estimates of costs, benefits, probabilities, etc. are usually fraught with inaccuracies. Also, the methods tend to be laden with assumptions that if incorrect or overlooked can lead to erroneous conclusions. Rank-ordering of projects according to B/C, for instance, assumes that all the projects are of comparable size (order of magnitude) in terms of expected costs and benefits. Project A with a B/C of 3.0 would be ranked ahead of Project B with a B/C of 2.0 even if Project B had a benefit of $2 million and Project A a benefit of only $200,000.

Multiple-Criteria Methods
There are many ways to value a project, and projects valued high in one way might be considered very poor in another. The way to account for this is with a scoring method that uses several criteria.[16] For example, in Table 17-2 each project is rated for three criteria: Fit with Corporate Strategy (subjective rating 0–4, where 0 is poor

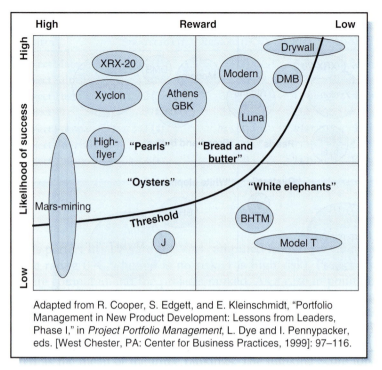

Adapted from R. Cooper, S. Edgett, and E. Kleinschmidt, "Portfolio Management in New Product Development: Lessons from Leaders, Phase I," in *Project Portfolio Management*, L. Dye and I. Pennypacker, eds. [West Chester, PA: Center for Business Practices, 1999]: 97–116.

Figure 17-6
Bubble chart for likelihood of success, reward, and range of uncertainty.

the charts to decide which projects to analyze more carefully and which to cancel. Conceptually, at least, every organization has a "threshold" line, shown in Figure 17-6, above which projects are accepted and below which they are rejected. White elephants and some oysters and bread and butters would be cut from further consideration, but all others would be retained for further analysis, scoring, and rank-ordering.

Strategic Fit

A third way to select projects is by how well they fit organizational goals and strategies. Starting with the organization's mission, strategic initiatives, and objectives, top management decides on the "kinds" or categories of projects needed to achieve them.

Some typical ways to categorize or group projects are according to:[19]

- Strategic goals (defending the product base, growing the base, diversifying products, etc.)
- Product lines (product A, B, C. etc.)
- Project type (R&D, capital improvement, process improvement, product development, etc.)
- Geography (Toronto, California, Indonesia, Central America, etc.)
- Business unit (marketing, manufacturing, product development, etc.)

Examples of categories are the five headings in Table 17-3. Associated with each category is an allocated funding amount that is the total budget or resources available to projects in the category. In Table 17-3 the allocated amounts are $12.5 M, $8.5 M, $10 M, $8 M, and $7.2, respectively.

In small companies these categories would be consolidated into a single portfolio and managed by one portfolio group. In large companies, each category would be a *separate portfolio* managed by its own PRB. In the latter case, top management first reviews all projects and proposals, and divides them among the categories. The PRB for each category then reviews the projects to determine which it will approve and which it will deny.

Companies routinely undertake more projects than they can handle, and even a short list of the most "desirable" projects might exceed available funding. For example, in Table 17-3 the totals at the bottom of the columns indicate that projects in four of the five categories require funding in excess of the allocated funding. To decide which projects to select, the PRB creates a rank-ordered list of projects (using methods described earlier), and starting at the top approves projects until funds runs out. Supposing the projects in Table 17-3 have been rank-ordered, the underlined projects are the cutoff projects. In the last category, for instance, Project S is the cutoff, and Projects A1 and E1 will not be supported.

An approved project is admitted to the portfolio and enters a queue. But the ultimate execution of the project depends on availability of key resources. Someone, somewhere (perhaps the PMO) is keeping track of deployment of key limited resources. Only when the needed resources become available can the project be scheduled to begin.

Deciding on the categories and appropriate funding for each is the responsibility of top management. These decisions presumably are based upon consideration of organization mission, strategies, and objectives, although sometimes the allocation is debatable. The mission of NASA, for instance, is to support research and development in aeronautics, manned spaceflight, and unmanned space exploration, although currently the overwhelming share of NASA funding goes to manned spaceflight programs, which leaves little remaining for unmanned space exploration, and even less for aeronautics research. This has lead critics to charge that NASA's skewed funding allocation and project portfolio does not support the agency's full range of purported objectives.

Table 17-3   Projects Rank-Ordered by Category.

PROJECTS RANK-ORDERED WITHIN CATEGORIES									
ASIAN OPERATIONS $12.5 M		EUROPEAN OPERATIONS $8.5 M		OEM PRODUCT LINE DEVELOPMENT $10 M		DOMESTIC PRODUCT LINE DEVELOPMENT $8 M		PROCESS IMPROVEMENT $7.2 M	
Project E	3.2	Project B	0.2	Project A	3.4	Project D	2.2	Project C	2.2
Project G	1.4	Project F	2.2	Project H	0.8	Project J	1.2	Project 1	0.8
Project O	0.6	Project N	0.4	Project L	1.7	Project M	0.1	Project K	1.2
Project Q	3.7	Project P	1.5	Project R	31[a]	Project T	1.3	Project S	2.7[a]
Project W	2.3[a]	Project U	1.3	Project C1	1.6	Project V	0.2	Project A1	0.7
Project B1	1.8	Project X	0.6	Project G1	1.1	Project Y	0.8	Project E1	1.2
Total	13.0[b]	Project F1	1.9[a]	Total	11.7[b]	Project Z	1.2[a]	Total	8.8[b]
		Total	8.1			Project D1	2.2		
						Project H1	0.2		
						Total	9.4[b]		

[a] Cutoff project.
[b] Required funding exceeds allocation.

Cost–Benefit Grids

A method well suited for prioritizing and selecting projects according to several criteria is Buss's cost–benefit grid.[20] Suppose two important criteria are financial benefits and project cost. The PRB reviews each project proposal and rates the project's financial benefits as high, medium, or low, and its cost as high, medium, or low. The outcome is a rating for each proposal in terms of both financial benefits and cost, which can be displayed on a 3 × 3 grid. When several projects are rated in this way, the result looks like Grid A in Figure 17-7, which shows the ratings for 12 projects. Comparing the positions of the projects on the grid, the team should be able to justify why it rated one project high and another medium or low.

After reaching agreement on the ratings for the first grid, the team repeats the procedure for other criteria such as technical benefits, intangible benefits, fit with company business strategy, and so on, and plots the results on other grids (Figure 17-7).

How are intangible benefits assessed? First, the team must agree on the intangible benefits it wants to consider for every project, e.g., company image, customer satisfaction, employee turnover, and so on. Teams with members who represent different perspectives—i.e., where some members see projects in terms of financial return and others see them in terms of technical capabilities or difficulties or strategic benefits—are usually better able to identify intangibles than those where everyone thinks alike. Once the team has agreed on the list of intangibles, it chooses a scoring method. If, for example, each benefit is scored on a scale of 1–5 and there are six intangible benefits, each project's total score for intangibles will range from 30 (score of 5 on all six benefits) to 0. To locate a project in the grid, scores are converted into simple categories, e.g., 21 or more is high, 10 or less is low, and in between is medium.[21]

Figure 17-7
Buss's cost–benefit grids, ratings for 12 projects.

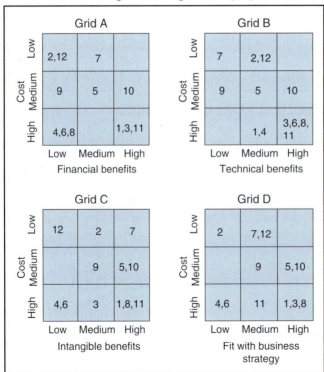

Using the completed grids, the team creates a rank-ordered list. Projects in the lower right cell would be listed at the top; those in the upper left, at the bottom. But besides location in the grids, rank-ordering also depends on organizational priorities. In Figure 17-7 projects 1, 3, 8, and 11 appear in the lower right cell in three of the grids, yet if the organization's top priority is financial return, then project 8 will be ranked lower and might even be rejected; if strategic fit is top priority, then project 11 might be rejected. Final selection will also depend on the size of the project and available funding and resources, as described earlier.

The main advantage of this method is clear exposition of the comparative benefits of projects and reliance on the collective judgment of a team to assess those benefits. For this method (and all team assessment and selection methods), the team ideally includes members representing a broad range of perspectives (technical, product/market, financial, environmental, social, etc.).[22]

Although this approach might seem to rely too much on subjective judgment and too little on formal analysis, there is nothing to prevent the team from using formal analysis methods and sophisticated quantitative models to arrive at their ratings. (As mentioned, though, even quantitative analysis sometimes relies on inputs that are little more than mere guesses, which makes them little more accurate or valid than subjective methods—despite creating false perceptions to the contrary.)

Cost-Effectiveness Analysis[23]

Cost-effectiveness analysis is similar to the cost–benefit grid method but uses numerical values for cost and benefits. The term "effectiveness," which refers to the degree to which a project is expected to fulfill project requirements, is interchangeable with the terms "benefits", "value", "utility", "efficiency", and "performance". As with those terms, assessing effectiveness typically involves consideration of multiple factors. In assessing commercial aircraft alternatives, for instance, effectiveness would account for some combination of passenger capacity, passenger comfort, aircraft weight, range, speed, fuel efficiency, and maintainability, which are interrelated in complex ways. One method for deriving a single measure incorporating multiple factors is to rate the factors subjectively (but with the results from quantitative analysis and advice of technical experts), weigh the ratings, and add them up—similar to the weighted scoring model discussed earlier in Table 17-1. The factors chosen for the analysis are assumed to represent significant ways to distinguish the projects; in all other important respects the projects are assumed identical.

The example in Table 17-4 shows three proposed projects and seven factors.[24] Each project is scored for each factor 0–100 for effectiveness (E) and for weighted effectiveness (WE = weight $\times E$). Total WE, the sum of the weighted effectiveness across all seven factors, represents the project effectiveness.

The method does not rank the projects but does suggest which ones should be dropped from consideration and allows tradeoff analysis of those projects remaining. For example, Figure 17-8 shows the three projects from Table 17-4 and five other projects. Projects j, h, and m (in the shaded area) fall below the minimal effectiveness threshold of 75 percent and should be dropped from consideration. The line connecting the uppermost points (j, A, n, C)—sometimes called the "efficient frontier"—represents the *maximum effectiveness* attainable for a given cost, or minimum cost for a given level of effectiveness. Projects that fall below this line (Projects B and k) are inferior to at least one other project in terms of both cost and effectiveness and can also be dropped. Hence only Projects A, n, and C are worthy of further consideration.

of the developer or contractor, although US contractors working overseas must confusingly also comply with US law, and the trick is to not violate laws in either country.

In countries like China some rules are not always enforced, leading local contractors and customers to argue that they can be ignored (this, of course, ignores the fact that at anytime the rules *could* be enforced).[7] Contractors working overseas must be careful to verify anything the locals say about the law and not do anything that would violate the law.

Because of differences in language, formalities, terminology, regulations, and laws, international contracts take longer to finalize than domestic contracts. Getting the wording and terminology right on contracts is extremely important, and the littlest details (like initialing changes and pages) matter.[8] The project manager must be involved in contract negotiations from the beginning and—this is essential—have access to his own legal counsel or sound legal advice.

To minimize confusion about contract terminology, the International Chamber of Commerce has created a list of International Commercial Terms, or "Incoterms," which its website describes as "standard trade definitions most commonly used in international sales contracts . . . (and) at the heart of world trade"; usage of Incoterms in contracts helps clarify expectations and "goes a long way to providing the legal certainty upon which mutual confidence between business partners must be based."[9]

The contractor must be sure to include stipulations and actions in the contract to protect its intellectual rights and be prepared to take action should it discover that its ideas, products, or technology are being pirated.

Litigation, Payment, Meeting Contract Terms

Contracts should be designed to avoid legal disputes, which in the international arena can be a nightmare—messy, slow, expensive, and sometimes corrupt. They should specify that any legal struggles would be conducted in a neutral country, i.e., neither the country of the contractor nor the customer. US contractors often specify England.

The contract should provide stipulations to assure that the customer will receive its deliverables and the contractor its payment. This would seem customary even in single-country, domestic projects, yet because of the extreme difficulties of litigation in international projects the stipulations must be such as to remove even the slightest chance of problems. To protect the customer, the contract might include severe penalties for schedule slippage or failure to meet requirements, and strong incentives to exceed them (such incentives assume that the contractor is in the position to perform work to meet requirements—which is not always the case in developing countries).

To protect the contractor, the contract might specify a substantial first payment followed by frequent payments upon meeting time-phased targets. Payments are often delayed, not because of the customer but because international funds transfer typically require approval by an agency of the host government, which can take 60 days. In some cases payments to foreigners must be made via tax agents, which further impact the payment process.

As common practice, contractors should never perform work or sell anything for unsecured payment after completion or delivery. In many countries, including China, the system for managing credit and receivables is not very good and customer creditworthiness is difficult to ascertain.

Politics

National and local political stability and the government's position regarding the project are potential risk factors. Radical political reform, overthrow of the government, local political strife, military intervention, and labor strikes are clearly situations that could threaten a project. While phenomena such as labor strikes are seldom experienced in countries such as the USA, they are common in some other countries. But such events rarely materialize on short notice and without early warning signs. A contractor considering or involved in international projects must have reliable people at the site or region to monitor these signs and keep project management informed.

It should be obvious from this section that international projects are fraught with problems absent in single-nation projects. The following example illustrates a few more problems—plus what happens when cross-cultural teams don't try to integrate.

Example 1: The Chunnel Project[10]

The initial construction phase of the 32-mile (51 kilometer) Channel Tunnel between Britain and France was managed almost as two separate projects—one starting from Britain, the other from France, both in a race to see which would reach the halfway mark first. Competition, it was felt, would speed things up. But the teams represented two cultures and two countries, and the competition only aggravated differences between them and exacerbated problems typical to international projects.

For starters, contracts should ideally be written in one language and governed by one legal system. In the Chunnel project there were *two* contracts, one each in English and French, neither having precedence over the other. Although the contracts were purportedly based on principles common to the two legal systems, legal approaches to health, safety, trade unions, and taxation differed significantly, and a panel appointed to resolve disputes was put in the situation of having to make very tough decisions.

The two countries also differ with regard to specifications and standards, e.g., for rolling stock (train engines and cars), railway width, voltages, and signaling systems, although, clearly, in every case the Chunnel would have to have only one. It was decided that where a difference existed between the standards of the two countries, the more rigorous or higher should prevail. It was not always obvious however which standard was the higher (e.g., the way concrete should be poured).

Decisions by any democratic government require substantial deliberation, but when *two* democratic governments are involved the process can be even more time-consuming. Simply deciding whether to increase door width from 600 to 700 millimeters took 9 months.

18.4   LOCAL STAKEHOLDERS

Contractors[11]

Project teams operating in foreign countries are often required to hire nominated local contractors. Subcontracting to local contractors can reduce costs for labor and relocation but it also increases costs for training and supervision. Sometimes lower labor cost equates to lower productivity, which translates into more workers needed and erases any potential savings; but many countries like India, however, have low labor costs yet productivity as high as in Western nations. A local contractor who has connections to local officials and is familiar with customs and bureaucracy can sometimes cut through red tape and avoid hassles that would stymie a contractor from the outside.

Selecting a local contractor requires considerations beyond the usual criteria of skill, experience, resources, and financial stability. One is the likely quality of communications as determined by the local contractor's language and culture. Another

Offset requirements are specified in the RFP, and sometimes a contractor wins the job based primarily on the offset plan described in the proposal. In essence, the offset is the deal-clincher, exceeding in importance the principle work of the project.

Export/Import Restrictions

The export/import of certain US technology, software and hardware are regulated by government agencies such as the US Departments of Commerce, State, and Agriculture. Systems designers and project planners should try to identify the restricted items early in the project since those that are essential for the project but restricted or prohibited from import/export will have to be substituted with non-restricted alternatives.

Time Zones[16]

Project stakeholders living in different regions of the globe might have no overlap in their business hours, so a message sent by one might take days for others to learn about and react to it. Avoiding communication delays is mostly a matter of planning, such as scheduling business hours in different time zones so there is a minimal 2 to 3 hours overlap across all of them. During critical stages of the project, the project manager and other key participants should be 24-hour accessible from anywhere via cell phone messaging and e-mail.

18.6 PROJECT MANAGER

Typical problems in an international project:[17]

- Someone on the team does not have a valid passport
- Team members need travel visas
- A coworker needs health tests and inoculations before heading to the project site
- Someone on the team gets sick or injured at the project site
- Someone gets arrested for a local traffic violation

At times like these the first place people go is to the project manager. They expect she will personally be able to handle the predicament or know where to get help. Of course, while dealing with issues like these the manager must also continue to deal with project related problems at the site and back home as well.

Self-Sufficiency

In unfamiliar surroundings, faced with unique challenges and without support from nearby business associates and family, the project manager must be adaptable to the local environment and able to resolve problematic situations that would perplex or immobilize a lesser person. A sense of humor helps, as does prior experience working in international projects.

Sensitivity and Acceptance

The project manager must understand local norms and customs and be able to develop trusting relationships with business associates, supporters, and customers in the host country. Project staff, contractors, and laborers might come from many nations and have no prior experience or know what to expect from or how to deal with foreign managers. No matter what their country of origin, the project manager must be able to demonstrate respect for and acceptance of their cultures; sometimes she does this is subtle ways, like emulating aspects of their social customs, eating local popular foods, or wearing forms of local dress. This will help in earning their trust and confidence.

Every Culture a New Experience

Each project in a new country or region requires new learning and familiarization, and experiences from one culture or country cannot be generalized to another. For example, although local laborers might *appear* unmotivated or lacking in creativity, the fact is, sometimes they simply do not know what they are supposed to do; not lacking in motivation, they might just need careful instructions and explanations. It rests on the project manager to seek out whatever sources of motivation are effective. Sometimes it is a simple matter of modifying the workday hours to conform to local biological clocks!

Nor can it be assumed that just because a process or method succeeded in one country that it will be workable in another, or that local laborers and suppliers will automatically accept the process or method. Making assumptions without considering the local environment, sentiments, and attitudes can lead to resentment and resistance among the local staff.

Fully Engaged, Fully in Charge

The project manager must be in the middle of everything in the project. Ideally, she manages the project not from a remote office but at the site. She is always or frequently there to see what is happening and to discuss problems with local managers, staff, and workers. She is fully committed to the project and willing to remain in the host country until the project is completed and the customer is satisfied and has signed off.

People on the project team witness the project manager making decisions that affect the project and them personally. The project manager stays in touch with her team and is available to assist them when they need help with documents, currency, local housing, or medical assistance; in this way she earns their gratitude, respect, and commitment to the project.

Local Project Manager

In cases where the project manager is seldom able to be on site, then day-to-day responsibility for the project should be delegated to the local project manager, someone who is visibly engaged and fully in charge. Thus each subproject has two project managers, the global project manager who plans and coordinates from the home office and travels among sites, and the local project manager responsible for on-site, detailed planning and day-to-day management. The local manager reports to the global manager, and the responsibilities and authority of the two are clearly delineated and understood by everyone on the project.

At time of hiring, the local project manager should be informed about expectations, responsibilities, and performance targets, and then again reminded periodically. Hiring and training a local project manager is not easy, so should a problem arise she should be given every opportunity to work it out. If the problem is thought to be serious and getting worse, the contractor should "parachute in" a trusted person to assess

The project manager kicks off the international project with a team-building session for key members from the project team, including local managers and staff. The goal is to develop a common purpose and shared expectations, identify possible or likely problems, and develop guidelines to reduce those problems. The project guidelines address familiar matters such as collaboration, conflict management, and role assignments, but also problems unique to international projects such as coordination across multiple countries and time zones, and cross-cultural, language, and social factors likely to impact communication and decision making.[21] A useful exercise is for each participant to express how much he assumes people from other cultures will conform to his culture and way of doing things, and how much he is willing to adapt to others' cultures and ways—a variation of the role clarification technique described earlier.

The contractor should also hold a team-building session with each local subcontractor, at which time they discuss issues that might arise, and prepare a plan for ways to prevent or resolve them. They also agree on which tasks each will do exclusively and which they will do jointly. To encourage teamwork and joint accountability, the contractor should arrange that a large proportion of the work packages (20 to 30 percent) are performed jointly by team members from both the host and the home countries. This will assist local people in taking ownership of the project while enabling the project manager to maintain control over the work.

Beyond building relationships among project team members, it is essential that the project manager develop relationships with other key stakeholders in the host country. Should the project become embroiled in problems, having strong personal ties with local and national vendors and officials—government, trade, labor—will come in handy, especially if the problems become serious. To this end, the project manager should allow ample time to attend social events with project staff and local stakeholders, welcoming parties for newly arriving staff, and celebrations for kickoffs, milestones, and local holidays and cultural events.

18.10   PROJECT DEFINITION

An international project cannot be approached in exactly the same way as a domestic project. The issues and unknowns in each project associated with culture, country, laws, people, and politics are numerous and must be identified.

Where to Start

How do project managers learn about the important issues they need to be aware of in each international project? Common ways are:[22]

- *Look at examples of similar, successful projects* done in the country by your company or others and try to learn what they did. Seek out project managers who have experience in similar projects in that country or region and ask for advice.

- *Hire a credible consultant or freelance expatriate* to provide advice and guidance and serve as a cultural intermediary with local stakeholders. Seek those who have project experience in the host region and have developed a social network of important local acquaintances.

- *Seek trusted guides, professionals, or international advisory groups* for advice about local politics, norms, customs, business practices, and economic environment. Although they might not know about the business or technology of a particular project, they will know about local labor, resources, and laws.

- *Send project managers and team members to formal training programs* to learn about foreign stakeholders, institutions, and environment, and strategies for coping with them.

- *Start with a small pilot project* in the country to allow time to become familiar with the culture and laws before committing to larger, riskier projects or partnerships.

- *Create a culture risk management team* to identify multi-cultural, multi-national issues and steps to reduce or avoid them. The membership of this team should mirror the national and ethnic groups of the project stakeholders.

Scope and Customer Requirements

In most projects the customer provides a list of needs and wants expressed in non-technical terms, and the contractor then expands upon the list and converts it into technical requirements. In a multi-language project, the process is more complicated because the customer's list of needs has to be translated into the contractor's language, and the contractor's list of technical requirements has to summarized and translated back into the customer's language for approval. Because the process can be lengthy and risky, typical Western managers are eager to get through with it as soon as possible and start the project. But managers from other cultures often take a different stance, preferring to hold off on defining details, and build relationships and establish areas of agreement first. The attitude is, not to worry, disagreements about details are bound to happen, but they will be worked out. This process of building trust and establishing areas of common ground is so critical that it must be handled by the project manager and not left to others in business development, sales, or marketing, as is common in domestic projects.

Scope and SOW in Global Projects[23]

When the project has global reach, i.e., consists of subprojects at multiple international locations, the global steering committee prepares a scope statement, SOW, and a preliminary plan that specifies the countries or regions of all the subprojects. The preliminary plan identifies goals, strategies, targets, costs, etc., for each country and subproject, although only in the form of estimates, proposals, or suggestions.

The preliminary plan for each subproject is given to the local project manager, local sponsor, and local steering committee, who then review it and expand it into a more detailed plan, taking into account what they know about the region and site. The local group also makes suggestions to the global committee as to the subproject's purpose, goals, estimated benefits, and costs. The process is repeated for every subproject, resulting in information as illustrated in Table 18-2.

Because of differences in culture, norms, and languages, subprojects that start out with almost identical purpose, scope, and SOW often end up varying substantially. To accommodate differences in purposes, goals, strategies, etc. (Table 18-2, rows 1 through 8), the global steering committee must adjust the scope and SOW for each subproject (rows 9 and 10). After a few back-and-forth iterations between the global and local committees, the scopes and SOWs of the subprojects and the global project (row 11) are mutually adjusted and made compatible.

Table 18-2 Impacts of country differences on scope and SOW.[24]

	SUBPROJECT IN COUNTRY A	SUBPROJECT IN COUNTRY B	SUBPROJECT IN COUNTRY C
1. Purposes			
2. Goals			
3. Strategies			
4. Cost			
5. Schedule			
6. Benefits			
7. Issues			
8. Risks			
9. Scope			
10. SOW			
11. Goals, scope, and SOW of global project			

The intended outcomes of the process are:[25]

1. Each local project manager and team has been brought into and become fully committed to the subproject.
2. Each local sponsor agrees to the goals and scope of the subproject and promises support.
3. The scope, goals, and SOW of the subprojects conform with local customs, regulations, and laws.
4. Stakeholders at the global level and local level are in agreement.
5. Goals, scope, and SOW of the subprojects align with those of the global project.

Work Definition[26]

Work definition must account for the many factors that distinguish an international project from a domestic project. One approach is to start with a generic work breakdown structure (WBS) template for the technical part of the project and then expand it to include international factors. The starting template lays out the first-level breakdown of activities or end-items, general areas of work to be completed, general resources needed, and predecessors or preconditions for each, and at first might look no different from a one-country, domestic project.

Each first-level activity is assigned to the project team member who will be responsible for managing it (someone who, presumably, knows the most about it). This person, who might be the local project manager, subdivides the activity into detailed task definitions, and estimates for resources, time, and cost.

Thus far the work definition process is not much different than for a domestic project. In an international project, however, as activities are broken down into greater detail, relevant local and international matters begin to surface. It is at the lower levels of the WBS where an international project becomes truly unique. Although a generic kind of project repeated in each of several countries might look the same in terms of high-level technical activities, subprojects in different countries look quite different at the work package level owing to differences in local and international matters—culture, institutions, geography, infrastructure, and so on. The local or cross-national issues (e.g., Table 18-3) identified in each work package must be addressed by detailed tasks in the work package, or by additional work packages.

Table 18-3 Issues in international projects.

- Team members speak different languages
- Expatriate team members need vaccinations, passports, visas, etc.
- Expatriate team members need local room, board, transportation
- Local team members lack knowledge and skills about project work
- Local communication infrastructure is poor
- Project leader lacks prior international experience
- Team members lack experience and knowledge about the local culture and host country
- Local team members are unfamiliar with business practices of the contractor
- Work status might be difficult to determine
- Project will at times require people from the home office with critical skills
- Local transportation infrastructure is poor
- The business needs of the local office differ from home-office needs
- Project will depend on vendors who do no have strong presence in the country
- Business processes in the host country differ from those in the home country
- Technology or material require export licenses and import approvals
- Project is a joint venture and may be difficult to control
- Project (or task) startup is dependent on success of another project or task
- Team members might be pulled off the project due to other higher-priority needs

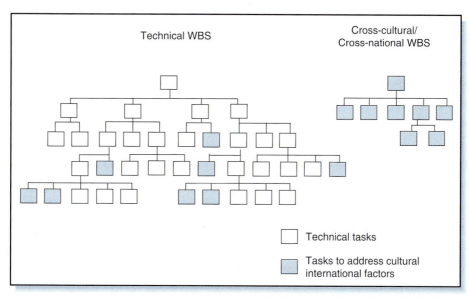

Figure 18-1
WBSs for an international project.

How does the project team know what unique issues and factors need to be addressed in an international project? Besides discovering issues through the traditional WBS process, the team can create a separate cross-cultural/cross-national WBS devoted entirely to international issues (Figure 18-1). This special WBS can be created by a special "culture risk team" whose sole purpose is to identify and deal

Table 18-4 Summary matrix of task versus subproject.[28]

Task	Subproject in Country A	Subproject in Country B	Subproject in Country C
Technical Tasks			
Survey		X	X
Site development		X	X
Site construction		X	X
System implementation	X	X	X
System test	X	X	X
Training	X	X	
Tasks addressing local issues			
Labor		X	X
Subcontractors		X	X
Permits	X		X
Customs	X		X
Time zone	X	X	
Language	X		X

with cultural/international issues. The work packages in the first-level breakdown of this special WBS would specify the tasks of the team, e.g.:[27]

1. Identify important international and local issues and factors in the project.
2. Assess risks associated with these issues and prepare plans to address them.
3. Provide support for overseas personnel on the project.
4. Provide team building and relationship building support.
5. Manage knowledge obtained for this and other international projects.

As Figure 18-1 illustrates, the two WBSs can be used to identify work packages wherein international issues reside, and to address and resolve the issues. This dual-pronged approach helps assure that no important issues are overlooked; any redundancies that appear in both WBSs are simply consolidated.

One way to keep track of the detailed tasks and work packages in a global project is with a summary matrix, shown in Table 18-4. The matrix reveals which tasks are unique to certain subprojects and countries and which are common among many or all. It also suggests places where knowledge gained from one subproject might be used in another, and helps insure that important tasks or issues are not overlooked.

Work Package Size

Tracking technical tasks in an international project can be difficult. Since in general, smaller work packages are easier to track and control than larger ones, the technical WBS should ultimately be subdivided into packages of short-duration and measurable outcomes. Early in the definition process, however, a detailed breakdown for all activities will neither be possible nor—because of the many unknowns—desirable. Nonetheless, after the project gets underway and the picture of pending activities becomes clearer and the unknowns fade, the work is defined in greater detail. As with phased project planning for other aspects of the project, the WBS and plan are continually reviewed, and the immediate, upcoming work packages are subdivided into detailed, short-duration tasks (ideally, no more than 2 weeks each).

While the WBS is being created, so is the responsibility matrix. The matrix should show the responsibilities of all individuals and groups working on or supporting the project—customer, subcontractors, and other supporting stakeholders, both at home and at the project site/host country.

Resources, Schedule, and Budget[29]

Estimates for resources, time, and cost based upon experience in the home country must all be revised when applied to overseas projects. Planned resources must account for differences in equipment and labor productivity levels, and the schedule and budget must be adjusted for additional time and costs for communication (fax, phone, courier, translators), travel (air fares, car rentals, taxi and limo fares), and arrangements for conferences and local services. The budget must include fees and costs for insurance, licenses, governmental reviews, local housing, overseas work salary incentives, automobile, daycare, schooling, security, and medical care. Expenses and lead times for obtaining passports and visas, and for transporting managers, workers, and replacements in accordance with project schedule requirements must also be accounted for.

In addition to those already mentioned, other factors adding to time and cost in international projects must be included. Time for shipping includes shipping preparation, transport between countries, clearing port-of-entry customs, and transportation in the host country to the site. Time for customs inspection and clearance depends on the item shipped and local politics. Transport time in the host country depends on the quality of roads and on available airport, harbor, trucking, and other local services. The available transportation to or from the project site might depart only once a week, and missing it by an hour will result in a week's delay. Material or equipment to be exported from the USA but considered by the government as "transfer of technology" must first be approved and licensed by the Department of State, which can take months. Fluctuations in exchange rates should also be anticipated, for example by preparing forecasts showing the impact on Estimated cost At Completion (EAC) of, say, a change of ± 10 percent in the Euro. All of these extra activities make international projects, ceteris paribus, more costly, lengthy, and risky than domestic projects.

Example 4: Added Time and Cost of an International Project

A contractor working on an overseas project encountered bad weather that fouled the equipment and brought the project to a standstill. Back home, the contractor would have resolved the problem simply by bringing in other equipment appropriate for the weather. That equipment however was not available in the host country and had to be imported. Because of problems associated with international transport (export licensing, shipping schedules), local transport (local roads and hauling services), and local bureaucracy (customs inspection, and import regulations on equipment), this substantially added to project time, cost, and risk. What would have been a relatively straightforward solution of little consequence in a domestic project had grown to a lengthy, costly, and risky proposition in the overseas project.

The skills and work ethic of local professionals and laborers must also be factored into time estimates and schedules. Owing to language differences the productivity of a local engineer might be considered equivalent to only half that of, say, an American engineer, which would be compensated for in the project by extending the engineering work schedule. On the other hand, if lower labor costs of local engineers would allow the hiring of several of them to replace one American, then changes to the project schedule might not be necessary. But never are the tradeoffs easy to determine in advance.

Example 5: Productivity in International Projects

One of the authors has worked with American, Canadian, and German engineers in several projects in South Africa. Despite their professional competency, in all cases these engineers needed a significant amount of time before they became as productive as the local engineers due to many factors including time to "settle in," lack of personal networks, lack of knowledge about local companies and their processes, poor understanding of the cultural environment, and communication problems. Such factors put expatriate project staff at a handicap and reduced their productivity, at least initially, and as a result, restricted them to working on tasks somewhat below their full potential. In the South African projects the expatriate engineers were given only technical assignments, whereas local engineers with similar qualifications and experience were given additional responsibility for management and coordination.

Training

Often, much advance preparation goes into training and coaching expatriate managers and staff in the culture, traditions, and regulations of the host country. Typically overlooked but sometimes as important is to train local managers and staff in the culture, expectations, common business practices, and technical procedures of the contractor and the home country. Cultural adjustment is a two-way street. For training of locals, the strategy and setting must be carefully designed; in some cultures the Western mode of classroom lecture discussion is not very effective.

18.11 PROJECT MONITORING

Tracking and Updating the Plan[30]

The project manager should require that every local subcontractor understands his expectations and procedures for communication and reporting progress. She should also require that the local project manager and team leaders review the project plan and submit task updates on a weekly basis; in an international project this is simplified by posting the plan and updates on the Internet. Assuming that technical work packages have been subdivided into tasks of short duration—the recommended 2 or 3 weeks, the project manager will then be able to easily discern whether a task has been completed, is on schedule, or is falling behind.

Should a subcontractor start to fall behind or fail to meet requirements, the project manager should take a more direct role in managing the subcontractor's work; if that is not possible, he should assign a local person to assist the subcontractor. Because of the hassles of international litigation, it is always better to first coach a subcontractor into getting back on track before resorting to legal action.

Site Visits

The project manager of an international project must make his presence known; if he cannot always be onsite, then he should make frequent visits—unannounced. In general, nowhere is the value of site visits more important than in international projects.

18.12 COMMUNICATION

Communication Plan[31]

As in any project, the project manager should prepare a communication plan. Besides the usual contents as described in Chapter 12, the plan for an international project must address communication difficulties stemming from differences in languages and time zones. It should specify important points of contact (Who's Who) in the host country, home country, and elsewhere. The project staff at home and abroad, and domestic and foreign contractors should understand the required reports and written communication, and the content and format of each. Foreign contractors and local project staff might not be familiar with "common" project documents and have to be taught why they are important and how they will be used.

A common "working language" should be adopted for all or specific portions of the project. Those not familiar with the working language should be given accelerated language lessons; everyone using the common language should be reminded to speak slowly and use simple terms and no slang. The project newsletter should be published in multiple versions for the different languages of the key stakeholders on the project.

Meetings

The communication plan should include a tentative schedule for all formal design and management reviews and milestone meetings, and describe the format of meetings, expected content, advance preparations, time limits on presentations, attendance policy, and who will lead. Since formal meetings in international projects tend to be difficult to schedule, require time-consuming preparation, and expose people to cultural gaffes or imbroglios, it is best to restrict them to a relative few key milestones and reviews. No one should be shocked by anything revealed in a formal meeting. Especially with attendees from different cultures and countries, the project manager should try to meet in advance to report any major problems.

The primary method for status tracking and identifying problems should be one-on-one communication and frequent informal meetings, convened as needed, the time and place determined by urgency and purpose, e.g., meet on alternate weeks if everything is okay, more often if not, and at the location experiencing the problems or issues. Attendance should be restricted to those who can contribute to the meeting or benefit from being there. As with domestic projects, the person who takes notes, writes them up, and distributes them should be the project manager.

18.13   RISKS AND CONTINGENCIES

By definition, an international project is a project that is fraught with risks; many of these risks are subtle or hidden and can be exposed only by looking at the project from the multiple perspectives of the different cultures of the project stakeholders. Any standing risk policies of the contractor or customer (described in Chapter 10) should be applied in a consistent manner across all projects in all countries. In other words, the risk tolerance upon which the policy is based should remain constant, no matter the project or country.

Risk analysis begins during project conception and definition by imagining different scenarios about what could go wrong, and developing a contingency strategy for each scenario. The project master plan and budget should incorporate these contingency plans, including an exit strategy in case problems get out of hand.

As discussed in Chapter 10, project risk is associated with level of uncertainty: the less you can say for certain about something, the greater the risk. In an international project much of the uncertainty relates to ignorance about local and international customs, conditions, and stakeholders. The more you know about culture, customs, language, institutions, and infrastructure, the better you can identify and mitigate the risks. In other words, learning is a strategy for reducing risks in international projects.

Another strategy is to decrease the amount that has to be learned. In international projects, companies avoid having to learn about or deal with local regulations, laws, and resources by doing the following:[32]

- *Outsource activities that are heavily restricted by local regulations*: Activities such as purchasing land, obtaining permits, hiring of locals, and moving materials through customs are risky because they require knowledge about local laws and customs. By outsourcing these activities to knowledgeable subcontractors and consultants, the burden of responsibility (and much of the risk) for those activities is shifted to the subcontractors.

- *Perform technology-intensive work* before *systems or subsystems are shipped*: Rather than dealing with the uncertainties of local labor, materials, and infrastructure, perform most work for major components of the project at home and then transport them overseas for simple assembly or installation.

- *Sign contracts under international law or third-country law*: Rather than learn the intricacies of local laws and depend on local lawyers, finalize all contract agreements according to international law or in a neutral country where the laws are more familiar. This practice is almost mandatory in countries where local laws are unclear or enforcement unpredictable.

Most companies employ a mix of the above—they learn about and deal with some aspects of the host country and culture, but avoid having to learn and deal with others. The mix depends on the kind of project. In general, the more that the project success depends on the contractor being "imbedded" in a foreign country, the more the contractor must learn about the country, its laws, and culture. For example, contractors such as Fluor and Bechtel performing large construction projects are heavily imbedded in the local environment because the projects take years, are of large scope, and rely somewhat on local resources. Hence, the firms must learn about the country or region of the project, which they do by hiring local contractors and laborers and selecting expatriates who have experience and language ability in the country. They also methodically accumulate knowledge about the host country. At the same time, they reduce their need to learn about *everything* by outsourcing to local suppliers and contractors, utilizing prefabricated components made at home wherever possible, and hiring host-country natives to manage relations with local stakeholders, and freelance expatriates to manage technology and contracts.

But, of course, the onsite project manager of an international project is always imbedded in the host country—even when the contractor (his employer) is not. Although much about the local environment might not matter to his firm, knowing the local ways and protocols does matter to the manager who has to live and work in the host country for as long as the project takes. Of all the ways to reduce the risks in an international project, perhaps the overall best is to learn and adapt to the local customs, laws, infrastructure, and social norms, and to build trusting relationships with laborers, leaders, subcontractors, and officials in the host country.

18.14   SUMMARY

A project that is international automatically inherits more issues and greater risk than a project that is not. These issues touch most everything about project management—leadership, interpersonal relations, stakeholder involvement, communication, planning, estimating, risk management, and tracking and control.

The project manager must be able to work with local subcontractors and suppliers, customers, business associates, and officials. Often these stakeholders withhold effort, collaboration, or support until they feel that they know the project manager personally. Thus, gaining personal familiarity and building trusting relationships is a fundamental aspect of managing international projects. Besides "domain competency" over the technical aspects of the project, the project manager must possess the qualities of self-sufficiency, ability to adapt to unfamiliar environments, and willingness and ability to understand and respect and accept local culture and customs.

When the project manager cannot always be on site, a local project manager should be appointed to handle detailed planning and day-to-day management. In addition, the project should have a permanent "local representative" to update the project manager on local matters, mediate with local stakeholders, and help resolve other local issues.

Each global project should have an executive steering committee to oversee governance and funding, and to set goals and coordinate work and resources among subprojects at different sites. It should also have a local steering committee to plan and execute the details, and handle problems at the site or host country.

Definition and planning for an international project requires identifying many issues and unknowns associated with culture, country, laws, people, etc., and accounting for them in project plans, schedules, and budgets. Managers, representatives, consultants, and others familiar with the local environment must be consulted and involved in preparing detailed plans. The project might have two WBSs, one to address technical aspects of the project, the other cultural or international aspects. Most everything takes more effort, time, and cost, which must be factored into tasks, schedules, and budgets.

The project manager should convey a strong presence—explaining to local managers and subcontractors the project goals, her expectations, and procedures for communication and reporting progress. Ideally she is onsite; if not, she makes frequent visits. She should prepare a communication plan that addresses the forms of communication, identifies points of contact, and includes a schedule for formal reviews and meetings.

Many of the risks in international projects stem from ignorance about local and international customs and conditions; thus, one of the best ways to reduce risk is to learn about and adapt to local customs, laws, infrastructure, and social norms, and build trusting relationships with local stakeholders.

REVIEW QUESTIONS

1. The analogy was made between an international project and a play. In international projects, who are the actors, what are the scripts, what are the sets, and what are the props?
2. What are the four main categories of "unknowns" in an international project?
3. In the above list, which unknowns are implicit and which are explicit? Why are implicit unknowns potentially more problematic for the project manager?
4. Consider two countries you are familiar with (say, your native country and one other). Compare and contrast them in terms of the following: language, formality, gift giving, attitudes about age and about time, social behavior, food and drink, holidays and time off, and customary labor time.
5. Why might worker layoffs following the project cause legal problems for the contractor or employer?

for automatic placement and retrieval of parcels and record keeping. The new system will be derived from a combination of advances in robotic technology, as well as application of existing technology. Our company has 35 years' experience in design and installation of parcel handling and associated information processing systems, and in recent years has installed eight robotic transporter systems for companies in North America and Europe. (This experience is explained in Section 6, Qualifications and Key Personnel.) Despite the use of advanced technology, the proposed system will incorporate design information about existing MPD systems to avoid duplication of effort and result in a fully operational system less than 12 months from start.

The proposed systems work like this:

Upon a parcel's arrival at the distribution center receiving dock, it is placed into one of three standard-sized parcel "buckets." The buckets are electronically coded as to parcel item and shipping destination. This code is relayed to a master database from any of four terminal workstations located at the dock. The workstations are connected via a DEM-LAN network to a CRC Model 4000 server. The Model 4000 has 64-gigabyte storage with backup for retaining information about parcel description, status, storage location, and destination. The system keeps track of available, remaining storage space, and, if need be, reallocates buckets for optimal space utilization. Allocation for space utilization relies on neural network technology, which enables the system to "learn" and improve its reallocations over time. The CRC4000 will also provide reports about system status and performance on request by management.

The parcel buckets are manually attached to a robot transporter mounted on an overhead track-conveyor system (Item 1). The robot transporter carries the bucket to a "suitable" vacant storage slot within a shipping container located on a rack in the facility. The computer determines which shipping container has a vacant slot of sufficient size and containing parcels going to the same or nearby destination as parcels in the transporter's parcel bucket. The robot transporter then conveys the bucket to the appropriate shipping container and unloads it into the vacant slot. Shipping containers are stacked three high in seven rows of racks (Items 2 and 3). The storage facility has capacity for 400 shipping containers, each with 150 cubic feet of storage capacity.

When a truck or rail car going to a specific destination is to be loaded, the destination is keyed in at the dock terminal workstation so the database system can identify all shipping containers having buckets with parcels going to the same or nearby destinations. The system then routes the robot transporters to the appropriate shipping containers for retrieval of parcel buckets. The system has four robot transporters that operate independently and simultaneously. The robot transporters retrieve the buckets and transport them back to the loading dock for placement of parcels into departing truck or rail cars. The longest specified retrieval time in the system is 8 minutes.

Based upon structural tests performed at our request by M&M Engineering Corp., the ceiling structure of the MPD Chicago facility was found to be capable of supporting additional loads of up to 600 pounds per square inch. The system we are proposing would add at most 325 pounds per square inch, including parcel weight, and, hence, can be installed directly to the existing ceiling frame without additional reinforcement. Structural tests performed by M&M Engineering on walls and floors also indicate sufficient strength to support the system with a safety factor of 2.1. The system can be directly connected to the existing main electrical harness hookup.

(Discussion continues about features of the robotic system and neural network software, including the benefits and advantages over alternative designs.)

C. Project Plan and Schedule (Forms II to V from RFP)

Form II: Work Packages
1. Perform functional design of overall system.
2. Prepare detailed design specifications for subcontractors of robotic transporter, conveyor track, storage rack systems, and shipping and parcel containers.
3. Prepare specifications for the software system and for DEM-LAN and CRC4000 system interface.
4. Prepare detailed assembly drawings for robotic transporter units, conveyor track system, and storage rack system.
5. Prepare plan for system installation and test at the site.
6. Fabricate robotic transporter units, conveyor track, and rack support subassemblies at IBC facility.
7. Perform preliminary functionality tests on robotic transporter units.
8. Perform structural and functional tests of conveyor track and storage rack systems.
9. Perform installation of all subsystems at MPD Chicago facility site.
10. Perform checkout of subsystems and final checkout of overall system at MPD facility site.
11. Codes and Standards (*List of requirements and standards for local, state, and federal agencies, and measures for compliance*)

Form III: Deliverables
Hardware Group A
7 storage racks, 10′ × 15′ × 6′, installed at site
Final structural, functional checkout of racks
400 shipping containers installed at site
1,000 size D43A parcel buckets
600 size D25B parcel buckets
600 size D12C parcel buckets
Overhead track-conveyor system (1567′ non-contiguous linear section, 18 crossover points, distribution uniform balance, weld supported at 6″ intervals), installed at site
Final structural, functional checkout

Hardware Group B
4 robot transporter units (each 300 pounds maximum load capacity compatible with three-size parcel buckets, 380 Mh, retrieval at farthest point 8 minutes), installed at site
Four unit functional checkout
Integration checkout, Groups A and B
Software Group
DEM-LAN network, four CRC2950 workstation terminals and CRC4000 server, operating system software (CRC)
Vista-Robotic software (Creative Robotics)
Triad warehousing system; Mobius transaction processing (CRC)
Support
Two copies, system operation/maintenance manuals
Robot transporter/CRC4000 integration
User training to competency
Final system checkout, user

Form IV: Work Schedule	
1. Commence basic design	May 2010
2. Basic design review	July 2010
3. Process/Track Design approval	September 2010
4. Computer system specs review	October 2010
5. Hardware Groups A and B received	December 2010
6. Begin installation at site	January 2011
7. Finish installation of complete system+/−	March 2011
8. Final user approval	May 2011

Form V: Subcontractors
1. Creative Robotics, Inc., Newton, MA, will supply the robot transporters and necessary software.
2. Steel Enterprises, Inc., West Arroyo, OH, will supply the parts for the overhead track-conveyor system and storage racks.
3. United Plastics Co., Provo, UT, will supply the shipping containers and parcel buckets.
4. CompuResearch Corp., Toronto, Ont., will supply terminal workstations, DEM-LAN network, and CRC4000 computer; will provide neural network software, support and installation of software and related hardware.

4 BUDGET AND PRICE (PROJECT PRICE: $14,413,905)

A. Budget and Price (Form VI from RFP)

TASK	LABORCOST	O/H @0.25	MATERIAL COST	S/C	G/A @0.10	TOTAL
Project coordination	800,000	20,000	20,000		12,000	852,000
Project design and development	260,000	65,000	51,000		143,000	519,000
Basic hardware	684,000	171,000	54,100		90,910	1,000,010
Hardware design and drawings	1,165,200	291,300	143,400		160,000	1,759,900
Software specs	150,400	37,600	23,300	116,000	32,730	360,030
Parts purchase	10,320	2,490	600	1,477,500	149,100	1,640,010
Drawings	703,000	175,750	121,200	0	100,000	1,099,950
Software purchase	6,080	1,520	2,000	2,550,000	72,720	2,632,320
Assembly	562,800	140,700	151,000	0	85,450	939,950
Test	343,000	85,750	117,000	0	54,580	600,330
Final installation and test	997,600	249,400	133,500	165,000	154,550	1,700,050
Totals	5,682,400	1,240,510	817,100	4,308,500	1,055,040	13,103,550
Price		Profit	10%	1,310,355		14,413,905

B. Variations, Changes, Contingencies

(List conditions under which costs will change: change in the scope of work, cost of steel-fabricated materials, work stoppages for labor disputes, etc.)

C. Billing and Payments

(Proposes the method for billing and payment.)

5 PROJECT ORGANIZATION AND MANAGEMENT PLAN

Our company knows project management and has the experience, skills, procedures, and software to successfully perform this project. The project manager, Mr. Wesley, will be responsible for managing project work, which includes all client contact work, reporting of progress, adherence to contractual commitments regarding

Project Master Plan for Logistical Online System

CONTENTS

Attachments

Item 1.   Robot transporter
Item 2.   MPD site layout
Item 3.   Storage rack assembly
Item 4.   LOGON organization chart
Item 5.   Responsibilities
Item 6.   Principal subtasks
Item 7.   Project schedule
Item 8.   LOGON project cost estimate

Iron *Butterfly, Corp.*

Elegant design. Built to last.

Memorandum

To: SEE DISTRIBUTION

Ref. Job No.: 904-01

From: Frank Wesley, Project Manager

Date: 1-3-10

Subject: Logistical Online System Project

<u>Project Summary Plan</u>

The Project Summary Plan for the Logistical Online System Project for the Midwest Parcel Distribution Company's Chicago distribution center has been modified to include your suggestions and approved by everyone in distribution. Copies of this document are herewith sent for use in the performance of contract requirements.

FW:es
Enclosure

<u>Distribution:</u>

Julia Melissa, Project Engineer
Sam Block, Fabrication Manager
Noah Errs, Quality Control Supervisor
Larry Fine, Software Manager
Sharry Hyman, Design Manager
Brian Jennings, Assembly Supervisor
Frank Nichol, Site Operations Manager
Emily Nichol, Assembly Supervisor
Robert Powers, Drawing Supervisor
Burton Vance, Purchasing Manager

LOGISTICAL ONLINE SYSTEM PROJECT SUMMARY PLAN

I MANAGEMENT SUMMARY

On September 5, 2009, the Midwest Parcel Distribution (MPD) Company of New York awarded the Iron Butterfly Company (IBC) the contract for the Logistical Online (LOGON) System Project. The system is to be installed at MPD Co.'s main Chicago distribution facility.

The project consists of designing, fabricating, and installing a parcel transport, storage, and database system, for automatic placement, storage, and retrieval of standardized shipping containers. The system uses an overhead conveyor track system, conveyor-robot transporter units, racks with standard size shipping containers and storage buckets, and a computerized database for automatic placement and retrieval of parcels and record keeping.

Iron Butterfly is the prime contractor and is responsible for the design of hardware and software, fabrication of component parts, system installation, and checkout. The major subcontractors are Creative Robotics, Inc. (CRI), Steel Enterprises, Inc. (SEI), United Plastics Co. (UPC), and CompuResearch Corp. (CRC). Iron Butterfly will provide overall project management between CRI, SEI, and UPC Corp. and related contract administration; legal, accounting, insurance, auditing, and counseling services as may be required. The project manager is Mr. Frank Wesley, and the project engineer is Ms. Julia Melissa.

The project will commence with basic design on or before May 17, 2010; installation at the site will begin on or before January 10, 2011; and final system approval by MPD Co. will be made on or before May 2, 2011. The principle subtasks are shown in the schedule, Item 7.

The price of the contract is $14,520,000, fixed fee with limited escalation, based on a target final approval date of May 2, 2011. Total expenses, tabulated in Item 8, for labor, overhead, materials, subcontracting, and general/administrative are $13,140,270. The agreement provides for an escalation clause tied to inflation indices for material expenses for the steel conveyor track and rack support systems. Because the facility will be unusable for MPD Co. during most of the later part of the project, an agreed-to penalty of $10,000 a day will be imposed on IBC for target completion overruns. Contingency arrangements in the agreement allow for reconsideration of the penalty in event of disruption of work for labor dispute with management.

II PROJECT DESCRIPTION

On September 5, 2009, IBC was awarded the contract for the LOGON System Project. The award followed a 4-month competitive bidding review by the MPD Company of New York. The system is to be installed at MPD Co.'s main Chicago distribution facility.

The project consists of designing, fabricating, and installing a parcel transport, storage, and database system, hereafter called LOGON, for automatic placement, storage, and retrieval of standardized shipping containers. The system will substantially improve the speed of parcel handling, increase the utilization of storage facility space, enhance record keeping, and reduce labor costs at the facility. Anticipated ancillary benefits include reduced insurance premium and shrinkage costs.

The system uses an overhead conveyor track system, conveyor-robot transporter units, racks with standard size shipping containers and storage buckets, and a computerized database for automatic placement and retrieval of parcels and recordkeeping.

The LOGON system works as follows:

Upon a parcel's arrival at the distribution center receiving dock, it is placed into one of three standard-sized parcel "buckets." The buckets are electronically coded as to parcel item and shipping destination. This code is relayed to a master database from any of four terminal work stations located at the dock. The work stations are connected via a DEM-LAN network to a CRC Model 4000 server. The Model 4000 has 64 gigabytes storage with backup for retaining information about parcel description, status, storage location, and destination. The system keeps track of available, remaining storage space, and, if needed, reallocates buckets for optimal space utilization. The CRC4000 will also provide reports about system status and performance on request by management.

The parcel buckets are manually attached to a robot transporter mounted on an overhead track-conveyor system (Item 1). The robot transporter carries the bucket to a "suitable" vacant storage slot within a shipping container located on a rack in the facility. The computer determines which shipping container has a vacant slot of sufficient size and containing parcels going to the same or nearby destination as parcels in the transporter's parcel bucket. The robot transporter then conveys the bucket to

Item 1
Robot transporter.

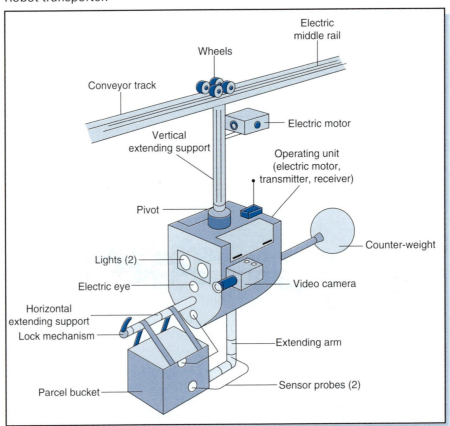

the appropriate shipping container and unloads it into the vacant slot. Shipping containers are stacked three high in seven rows of racks (Items 2 and 3). The storage facility has capacity for 400 shipping containers, each with 150 cubic feet of storage capacity.

When a truck or rail car going to a specific destination is to be loaded, the destination is keyed in at the dock terminal workstation so the database system can identify all shipping containers having buckets with parcels going to the same or nearby destinations. The system then routes the robot transporters to the appropriate shipping containers for retrieval of parcel buckets. The system has four robot transporters that operate independently and simultaneously. The robot transporters retrieve

Item 2
MPD site layout.

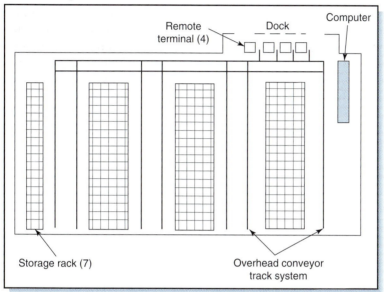

Item 3
Storage rack assembly.

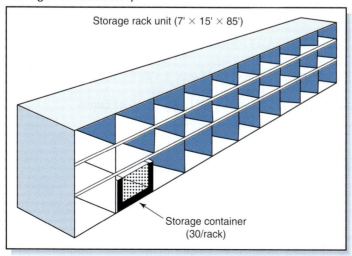

the buckets and transport them back to the loading dock for placement of parcels into departing truck or rail cars. The longest specified retrieval time in the system is 8 minutes. As in our previous applications, this system will employ neural network technology that will enable it to improve on its ability to place and retrieve containers.

Iron Butterfly is the prime contractor and is responsible for the design of hardware and software, fabrication of components parts, system installation, and checkout. The major subcontractors are CRI, which will supply the major components for the robot transporters; SEI, which will supply the parts for the overhead track-conveyor system and storage racks; UPC, which will supply the shipping containers and parcel buckets; and CRC, which will supply the terminal workstations, DEM-LAN network, neural network software, and CRC4000 computer. CRC will also provide support for software development and installation of all computer hardware items.

Structural tests performed by M&M Engineering Corp. indicate that the present ceiling structure of the facility can support additional loads of up to 600 pounds per square inch. The LOGON system would add a maximum of 325 pounds per square inch, including parcel weight, and thus can be installed directly to the existing ceiling frame without additional reinforcement. Structural tests performed on walls and floors also indicate sufficient strength to support the system with a safety factor of 2.1. The system can be directly connected to the existing main electrical harness hookup.

During system installation, MPD has arranged for alternate, temporary storage at another facility and rerouting of most parcel traffic to its other sites.

As much as possible, design information about existing systems, such as MPD's Tulsa facility, will be utilized to try to initially move the project to an advanced stage. Remaining design work will use as much as possible of work that has been done already, without compromising confidentiality of clients, on previous, similar projects.

III ORGANIZATION SECTION

III.1 Project Administration

All correspondence on project matters will be between the project manager for IBC and the project director for MPD. When specifically authorized, project personnel may correspond directly with the client or subcontractors for information, keeping the project manager and project director informed with copies of all correspondence and memos of telephone conversations.

The account number assigned to the LOGON project is 901-0000. Work packages and tasks will be assigned subaccount numbers at the time when work package instructions and schedules are authorized. A single invoice for the project accounts as a whole is acceptable for billing at monthly intervals.

III.2 Project Organization and Responsibility

The organization of IBC for the performance of the LOGON project is shown in Item 4. Specific administrative and managerial responsibilities are summarized in the responsibility chart, Item 5.

The project manager, Mr. Wesley, is responsible for managing project work, which includes all client contact, reporting of progress, adherence to contractual

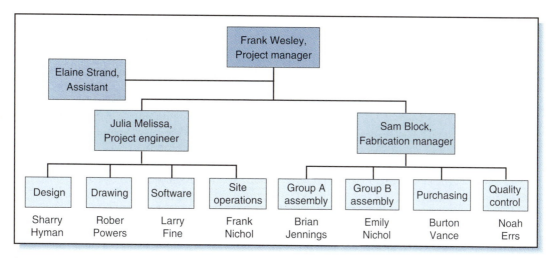

Item 4
LOGON organization chart.

commitments regarding schedule and technical performance, and monitoring of budgetary expenditures. Changes in scope of contractual services will be recorded in communications with the client. He and his staff will report directly to Mr. Ed Demerest, vice president and project director for MPD Co.

The project engineer, Ms. Melissa, is responsible for establishing specifications and ensuring system delivery to meet technical requirements. She will supervise the preparation of design requirements and drawings depicting system elements, estimate quantities, check drawings and requirements calculations, and ensure that system technical requirements are fulfilled at the site.

The fabrication manager, Mr. Block, is responsible for managing procurement, assembly, and related work at the IBC plant. He will direct procurement and assembly operations, ensure that the quality of delivered parts from subcontractors meets requirements, coordinate assembly operations of robotic transporters, track conveyor, and storage rack subsystems, and sign off final approval for assemblies prior to shipment to the MPD site.

III.3 Subcontractor Administration

The four primary subcontractors of the project are CRI, SEI, UPC, and CRC. Key personnel associated with each are:

Bill Plante	Project coordinator, CRI
Terry Hemmart	Manager, manufacturing, SEI
Delbert Dillert	Customer representation, UPC
Lynn Duthbart	Systems engineering representative, CRC
Elmer Hyman	Customer representative, CRC

Changes or modifications to the respective agreements requested by a subcontractor or by IBC will be acted upon by the IBC project manager, Mr. Wesley, upon receipt of a written proposal from the subcontractor.

Responsibility code

P Primary responsibility
S Secondary responsibility
N Must be notified
A Must give approval

Persons responsible

Manager group	Sub-group	Individuals
Project manager	—	F.W., J.M.
Project engineer	Design	S.E.H., R.L.Q., P.J., D.V.R., R.I.P.
Project engineer	Drawing	O.E.M., P.V.P.R., D.M.N., R.L.
Project engineer	Software	L.S.F., L.L.L., J.R.S., D.V.Q., F.W.N.
Project manager	Site operations	J.M.M.N., L.O.T., A.U.A., D.A.R., S.O.B.
Fabrication manager	Assembly A	E.N., G.G.F., R.T.T., B.V.L., B.J.
Fabrication manager	Assembly B	T.T.Y., H.R.D.
Fabrication manager	Purchasing	B.V.

Project task or Activity	F.W.	J.M.	S.E.H.	R.L.Q.	P.J.	D.V.R.	R.I.P.	O.E.M.	P.V.P.R.	D.M.N.	R.L.	L.S.F.	L.L.L.	J.R.S.	D.V.Q.	F.W.N.	J.M.M.N.	L.O.T.	A.U.A.	D.A.R.	S.O.B.	E.N.	G.G.F.	R.T.T.	B.V.L.	B.J.	T.T.Y.	H.R.D.	B.V. Purchasing
Project coordination	P	S																			S								
Project development	A	P	A	P	S	S										A													
Project design	A		A	P	S											N					N								
H Basic design	N		A				N					N																	N
I Hardware design A	A		A									N																	
J Hardware design B	A											N																	
K Drawings B							A	S	P																				
L Software specs													A	P	S	S													
M Parts purchase B		N																											P
N Parts purchase A		N					A	P												A	N								P
O Drawings A							A	A		S	P																		
P Installation drawings									S																				
Q Software purchase	N															N	N			A	N								P
U Assembly A	N															N	N			A	N	A	P	S	S				
V Assembly B	N															N	N				N						P	S	
W Test A	N															N	N			A	N								
X Test B	N															N	N			A	N								
Y Final installation	N															A	A	P	S	A	P	P					A	P	
Z Final test	N															A	A	P	S	A	A	A	P	S			A	S	

Item 5
Project responsibilities.

Correspondence to subcontractors concerning technical matters will be directed to the previously named first four parties or their substitutes. Software specifications related work with CRC will be coordinated by, and communications should be directed to, the CRC customer representative. Project telephone conversations between IBC and subcontractors shall be noted in handwritten memos and copies sent to the IBC project engineer.

Progress reports shall be prepared by Mr. Plante, CRI project coordinator, Ms. Hemmart, SEI manufacturing manager, Mr. Dillert, UPC customer representative, and Mrs. Duthbart, CRC systems engineering representative for presentation at weekly meetings to be held at IBC's Chicago office for the duration of scheduled involvement as noted in the respective agreements. Other meetings may require attendance by other individuals as required by the subcontractors or requested by the project manager. The following number of meetings has been included in the respective subcontractor agreement budgets.

CRI	5 meetings
SEI	3 meetings
UPC	2 meetings
CRC	5 meetings (software development)
CRC	8 meetings (site system integration)

The subcontractors will provide information and perform services on the project as follows:

1. CRI will perform all elements of work associated with procurement, manufacturing, and component functional tests of parts and subassemblies according to specifications, plans, and drawings provided by IBC. Parts and components for four robotic transporters will be delivered to IBC according to the criteria and dates specified in the agreement.
2. SEI will perform all work associated with procurement, manufacturing, and component functional tests of parts and subassemblies according to the specifications, plans, and drawings provided by IBC. Parts and components for the complete overhead conveyor track system and seven storage racks will be delivered to IBC according to the criteria and dates specified in the agreement.
3. UPC will perform all work associated with procurement, manufacturing, and component functional tests of parts and subassemblies according to the specifications, plans, and drawings provided by IBC. Plastic containers and parcel buckets will be delivered to the MPD Chicago distribution facility in quantities and according to dates specified in the agreement. One plastic container and one each of three-size parcel buckets will be delivered to the IBC facility for tests according to the date specified in the agreement.
4. CRC will perform all work associated with development, programming, and tests of LOGON system robotic transporter control and neural networking software, system database, and reporting functions according to the specifications provided by IBC. Software will be delivered to the IBC facility according to dates specified in the agreement.
5. CRC will transport, install, and perform component and integration tests for checkout of four terminal work stations, DEM-LAN network, CRC4000 server, NN software, backup system, and peripheral hardware according to criteria and dates specified in the agreement.

Iron Butterfly will provide overall project management between CRI, SEI, and UPC Corp. and related contract administration, legal, accounting, insurance, auditing, and counseling services as may be required by the project.

III.4   Client Interface

Key personnel associated with the project for MPD Company are:

Ed Demerest	Project director, Chicago
Lynn Joffrey	Administrative assistant, Chicago
Cecil Party	Financial manager, Chicago
Mary Marquart	Operations manager, New York

Changes or modifications to the agreement requested either by MPD or by IBC will be acted upon by the operations manager, Mrs. Marquart, upon receipt of a written proposal from IBC.

All correspondence with MPD regarding the project will be directed to the project director, Mr. Demerest. If he requests our contacting another person or contractor, he will receive a copy of each item of correspondence between parties. Project telephone conversations between IBC and outside parties shall be noted in handwritten memos and copies sent to Ms. Joffrey.

Progress reports shall be prepared by Mr. Wesley, IBC project manager, for presentation at monthly meetings to be held at MPD Co.'s Chicago office. Other meetings may require attendance by other individuals as required by MPD or requested by Mr. Wesley. Mr. Wesley shall also convene two other meetings, a mid-project review and a project summary, at the New York office of MPD. A total of 15 meetings are included in the agreement budget. MPD Co. will provide information and perform services on the project as follows:

1. MPD will perform all elements of work associated with vacating the site prior to the date in the agreement for commencing of system installation.
2. MPD will provide surveys, design criteria, drawings, and preliminary plans prepared under previous agreements or received through requests for proposals for the LOGON system.
3. MPD will provide design criteria, drawings, and plans prepared for the automated parcel storage and retrieval system at MPD Co.'s Tulsa facility.
4. MPD will obtain all internal, municipal, state, and federal approvals as may be necessary to complete the project.
5. MPD will provide overall project management between MPD, IBC, and CRC Corp.; contract administration; legal, accounting, insurance, auditing, and consulting services as may be required by the project.

The contract administrator is the operations manager. Changes or modifications to the agreement with MPD, requested either by MPD or IBC, shall be subject to a written proposal by IBC to MPD's contract administrator through Mr. Demerest.

The financial manager, Mr. Party, is responsible for approvals of monthly expense summaries provided by STING and monthly payment to IBC. MPD is responsible for securing necessary support from electrical and telephone utilities for system hookup, and for making available to IBC all criteria, drawings and studies prepared for the Chicago site facility and the Tulsa facility automated system.

III.5   Manpower and Training

No additional manpower requirements beyond current staffing levels are envisioned to perform services for this project. Five personnel from the design group for this project have been enrolled in and will have completed a robotics seminar at a local university before the project begins.

III.6   User Training

Two systems operations manuals and 16 hours of technical assistance will be provided. Thereafter, ongoing operator training will be the responsibility of MPD Co.

IV   TECHNICAL SECTION

IV.1   Statement of Work and Scope

The major tasks to be performed are the design, fabrication, installation, and checkout of the LOGON system for the Chicago distribution center of MPD Co. The work will be executed in accordance with the terms, conditions, and scope as set forth in the applicable drawings and specifications prepared by IBC in the written proposal and confirmed in the agreement.

Subtasks required to perform the major tasks noted above are shown on the network in Item 6. The major subtasks are (letters refer to task designations on Item 6):

1. Perform basic design of overall system (H).
2. Prepare detailed design specifications for robotic transporter, conveyor track, storage rack systems, and shipping and parcel containers to be sent to Creative Robotics, Steel Enterprises, and United Plastics, subcontractors (J, I, M, N).
3. Prepare specifications for the software system and for DEM-LAN and CRC 4000 system interface (L).
4. Prepare detailed assembly drawings for robotic transporter units, conveyor track system, and storage rack system (O, K).
5. Prepare drawings and a master plan for system installation and test at the site (P).
6. Fabricate robotic transporter units, conveyor track, and rack support subassemblies at IBC facility (U, V).
7. Perform preliminary functionality tests on robotic transporter units at IBC facility (X).
8. Perform structural and functional tests of conveyor track and storage rack systems at IBC facility (W).
9. Perform installation of all subsystems at MPD Chicago facility site (Y).
10. Perform checkout of subsystems and final checkout of overall system at MPD facility site (Z).

IV.2   Schedule and Calendar

The project will commence with basic design on or before May 11, 2010; installation at the site will begin on or before January 10, 2011; and final system approval by MPD Co.

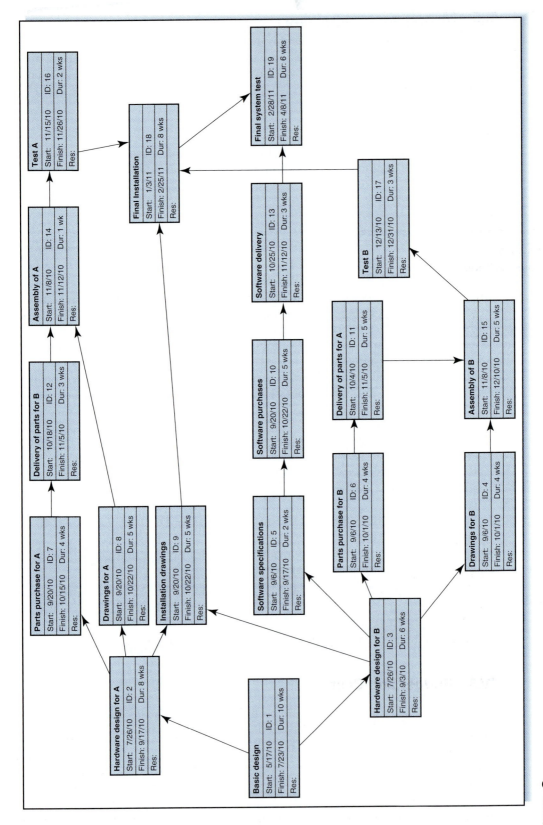

Item 6
Principal subtasks.

684

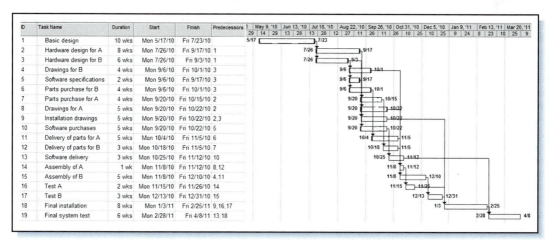

Item 7
Project schedule.

will be made on or before May 2, 2011. The project master schedule for the most significant portions of the project is given in Item 7. The significant project milestones indicated are:

1. Commence basic design   May 11, 2010
2. Basic design review   July 26, 2010
3. Transporter and conveyor   September 6, 2010
   design review
4. Computer system specs review   September 20, 2010
5. Hardware group A and B review November 29, 2010
6. Begin installation at site   January 10, 2011
7. Final user approval   May 2, 2011

Starting dates for activities that are dependent on results of reviews will be adjusted to allow for significant changes in the length of predecessor activities, although no adjustments are anticipated.

Work package instructions and a detailed schedule for basic design has been distributed. Subsequent schedule and work package information will be distributed and discussed at review meetings.

The schedule of contract deliverables is given in Section IV.9.

IV.3   Budget and Cost

The price of the contract is $14,520,000, fixed fee with limited escalation, based on a target final approval date of May 2, 2011. Expenses and fees will be billed and are payable monthly as incurred. The agreement provides for an escalation clause tied to inflation indices for material expenses for the steel conveyor track and rack support systems. Because the facility will be otherwise unusable for MPD Co. during the last 5 months of the project, completion by the contracted date is imperative. An agreed-to penalty of $10,000 a day will be imposed on IBC for target completion overruns. Contingency arrangements in the agreement allow for reconsideration of the penalty in event of disruption of work for labor dispute with management.

Principal tasks, subtasks, man-hours, and dollars to perform them have been estimated. Total expenses, as tabulated in Item 8, for labor, overhead, materials, subcontracting, and general/administrative are $13,140,270.

Expenditures of direct labor, the largest single cost factor, are under immediate control of department heads in design, fabrication, procurement, and customer service departments because they assign personnel to the project.

Item 8
LOGON project cost estimate.

TASK	LABOR TIME	LABOR RATE	LABOR COST	O/H @ 0.25	MATERIALS	S/C	G/A @ 0.1	TOTAL
Project	5,000	112	560,000	140,000				
coordination	5,000	48	240,000	60,000				
		Total	800,000	200,000	20,000		102,000	1,122,000
Project	1,000	112	112,000	28,000				
development	1,000	80	80,000	20,000				
		Total	192,000	48,000	45,000		28,500	313,500
System design	125	112	14,000	3,500				
	375	96	36,000	9,000				
	375	48	18,000	4,500				
		Total	68,000	17,000	6,000	1,550,000	164,100	1,805,100
H Basic hardware	750	120	90,000	22,500				
	4,000	96	384,000	96,000				
	3,500	60	210,000	52,500				
		Total	684,000	171,000	54,100		90,910	1,000,010
I Hardware	450	104	46,800	11,700				
design A	2,750	96	264,000	66,000				
	2,250	60	135,000	33,750				
		Total	445,800	111,450	24,500		58,175	639,925
J Hardware	625	104	65,000	16,250				
design B	3,375	96	324,000	81,000				
	3,250	80	260,000	65,000				
		Total	649,000	162,250	61,500		87,275	960,025
K Drawings B	400	104	41,600	10,400				
	400	72	28,800	7,200				
		Total	70,400	17,600	57,400		14,540	159,940
L Software specs	400	112	44,800	11,200				
	600	96	57,600	14,400				
	600	80	48,000	12,000				
		Total	150,400	37,600	23,300	116,000	32,730	360,030
M Parts	5	112	560	140				
purchase B	40	96	3,840	960				
		Total	4,400	1,100	250	758,000	76,375	840,125
N Parts	10	112	1,120	280				
purchase A	50	96	4,800	1,200				
		Total	5,920	1,480	350	719,500	72,725	799,975
O Drawings A	1,625	104	169,000	42,250				
	1,750	72	126,000	31,500				
		Total	295,000	73,750	85,800		45,455	500,005
P Installation	1,125	112	126,000	31,500				
drawings	1,500	104	156,000	39,000				
	1,750	72	126,000	31,500				
		Total	408,000	102,000	35,400		54,540	599,940

LOGON Project Cost Estimate (in dollars)

Task	Labor time	Labor rate	Labor cost	O/H @ 0.25	Materials	S/C	G/A @ 0.1	Total
Q Software	20	112	2,240	560				
purchase	40	96	3,840	960				
			6,080	1,520	1,600	717,500	72,670	799,370
U Assembly A	25	112	2,800	700				
	250	96	24,000	6,000				
	300	80	24,000	6,000				
		Total	50,800	12,700	64,000		12,750	140,250
V Assembly B	250	112	28,000	7,000				
	2,750	96	264,000	66,000				
	2,750	80	220,000	55,000				
		Total	512,000	128,000	87,000		72,700	799,700
W Test A	50	104	5,200	1,300				
	750	96	72,000	18,000				
	750	80	60,000	15,000				
		Total	137,200	34,300	47,000		21,850	240,350
X Test B	75	104	7,800	1,950				
	1,125	96	108,000	27,000				
	1,125	80	90,000	22,500				
		Total	205,800	51,450	70,000		32,725	359,975
Y Final installation	800	112	89,600	22,400				
	3,000	96	288,000	72,000				
	2,250	88	198,000	49,500				
		Total	575,600	143,900	121,000	105,000	94,550	1,040,050
Z Final test	500	112	56,000	14,000				
	2,500	96	240,000	60,000				
	1,500	84	126,000	31,500				
		Total	422,000	105,500	12,500	60,000	60,000	660,000
Totals			5,682,400	1,420,600	816,700	4,026,000	1,194,570	13,140,270

Item 8
(continued)

Responsibility for expenditures of man-hours and direct expenses belongs to the project manager, who receives biweekly accounting of all expenditures of time and money.

IV.4 Information Requirements

Most of the information required by IBC to perform under the terms of the agreement has been supplied by MPD Co. A limited amount of site information will be obtained from additional required surveys performed by an IBC survey party. MPD has expressed a willingness to dispatch some of its own personnel for minor survey work to expedite the project.

IV.5 Documentation and Maintenance

Minutes and action plans of review meetings will be formally documented and sent to the project manager. Biweekly expense and progress reports will be sent from functional managers to the project manager. Monthly project summary reports will be sent from the project manager to functional managers and to other managers and supervisors listed in distribution.

Cost, performance, and progress documentation will be maintained and reported through the company project cost accounting system.

A final summary report will be prepared by the office of the project manager for the company archives.

The project manager is responsible for maintenance of all project files. All copies of project documents sent outside IBC will leave only under his direction.

IV.6 Work Review

Internal review of work produced in each of the design, fabrication, procurement, and customer service divisions is a responsibility of the division head for each of the functional disciplines.

IV.7 Applicable Codes and Standards

Track conveyors, storage racks and supporting structures, electrical harnesses, and radio transmitters are to be designed to the applicable standards of AATOP, ASMER, OSHA, the Illinois Building Requirements Board, and the City of Chicago.

IV.8 Variations, Changes, Contingencies

The agreement with MPD defines the conditions for considering a change in compensation or penalties due to a change in the scope of work or cost of steel-fabricated materials, or unanticipated stoppage of work for labor dispute. It describes the procedure whereby authorization for such a change may be obtained from MPD.

The agreement, Paragraph 9.2, under prime compensation, states:

> "Whenever there is a major change in the scope, character, or complexity of the work, or if extra work is required, or if there is an increase in the expense to the CONTRACTOR for steel-fabricated materials as negotiated in the agreement with the responsible SUBCONTRACTORS, or if there is a stoppage of work resulting from a labor dispute with management, the CONTRACTOR shall, upon request of the CLIENT, submit a cost estimate of CONSULTANT services and expenses for the change, whether it shall involve an increase or a decrease in the Lump Sum. The CLIENT shall request such an estimate using the form provided herein (Attachment F). Changes for reasons of labor dispute with management will be reviewed and determined according to the conditions specified (Attachment G)."

During system installation and tests, MPD has made arrangements to reroute about 70% of its Chicago parcel business to other distribution centers. The remainder will be stored at an alternate facility near Chicago. In the event of an unforeseen schedule overrun, the reroute plan will remain in effect. MPD requires 30 days notice of anticipated schedule overrun to extend the agreement with the alternate Chicago storage facility.

IV.9 Contract Deliverables

All items are to be assembled, installed, and in operation at the site in accordance with technical specifications in the agreement.

Transport of components and parts from subcontractors to the IBC plant will be scheduled by subcontractors. The respective agreements specify the following items as deliverable to IBC:

Item	Date
Parts and components for robot transporters from CRI	November 1, 2010
Parts and components for overhead conveyor track and storage rack systems from SEI	November 4, 2010.
One shipping container and one each of three-size parcel buckets from UPC	November 10, 2010
Robotic transporter system control software from CRC	October 25, 2010

Transport of Group A and Group B subassemblies from the IBC plant to the MPD site will be accomplished in one-half day. Agreement for delivery is with Acme Systems Contractor, Co.

Following are the items identified in the agreement as deliverable to MPD:

Item	Date
Hardware (Group A):	
7 storage racks, 10′ × 15′ × 6′	
Installed at site	November 15, 2010
Final structural, functional checkout	November 29, 2010
Delivered 400 shipping containers installed at site	December 6, 2010
Delivered 1,000 size D43A parcel buckets	December 13, 2010
Delivered 600 size D25B parcel buckets	December 13, 2010
Delivered 600 size D12C parcel buckets	December 13, 2010
Overhead track-conveyor system (1567′ noncontiguous linear section, 18 crossover points, distribution uniform balance, weld supported at 6″ intervals)	
Installed at site	November 1, 2010
Final structural, functional checkout	November 8, 2010
Hardware (Group B):	
4 robot transporter units (each 300 pounds. maximum load capacity compatible with three-size parcel buckets, 380 Mh, retrieval at farthest point 8 minutes)	
Installed at site	November 8, 2010
Four unit functional checkout	November 10, 2010
Integration checkout, groups A and B	January 3, 2011
Software Group:	
Submission of software specifications to CRC	September 19, 2010
(Installation of DEM-LAN network, four CRC2950 workstation terminals, and CRC4000 server, all performed by CRC)	February 7, 2011
(Software-integration checkout, performed by CRC)	March 7, 2011
Final checkout:	
Two copies, system operation/maintenance manuals	March 7, 2011
Robot transporter/CRC4000 integration	April 4, 2011
Benchmark systems test, with parcels	April 8, 2011
User training	April 11–12, 2006
Final system checkout, user	On or before May 2, 2006

Author Index

SUBJECT INDEX

Executive steering committee (*See also* Project review board), 641

Exit conditions, 169

Expectation theory of conflict, 564

Expectations, team, 556

Expected commercial value, 610

Expected completion date, uncertainty of (*See also* Target completion date), 389–390

Expected completion time/cost, 209, 277

Expected duration, activity, 250

Expected payoff, 393

Expected value, 375, 388–391, 393

Expeditors, project, 488–490
  (*illus.*), 489

Expense
  direct labor, 307
  direct nonlabor, 308
  material, 308
  overhead, general, and administrative, 308–310
  weekly and cumulative, 180–182

Expense charts, 180
  (*illus.*), 182

Expenses, elements (line items), 306–310
  materials, 324–325
  payments for, 324–325

Expert opinion, 300, 416

Expert power, 523

Export/import restriction, 638

External control of project, 412

External risks, 366

Extranet, 462

F

F-111, 42

F-117, 120, 385, 510

Fabrication, system, 409

Failure
  during project termination, 468–469
  risk of, 34, 377–378
  tests, 410

Failure mode and effects analysis (*See* FMEA)

Failure report, 457

Fast-tracking, 81, 406

Feasibility stage, 83–85
  (*illus.*), 84

Feasibility study, 56, 86–93

Feasible budget region, 320
  (*illus.*), 323

Federal Aviation Administration, US, 49

Fee, in contract, 107

Fee swing, 112

Feedback, in systems and organizations, 38–39

Feeding buffer, 261–262
  (*illus.*), 262

Fever chart, 419–420
  (*illus.*), 420

Feynmen, Richard, 628

FIDIC, 195

Field manager, 533

Financial models, 610–611

Finish-to-finish node, PDM, 213
  (*illus.*), 213

Finish-to-start node, PDM, 213–214
  (*illus.*), 214

Firewall, 462

Fitness for purpose, 334

Fixed-price contract, 102, 108
  and risk, 378–379

Fixed-price incentive fee contract, 111

Fixed-price with redetermination contract, 108–109

Float time (Slack time), 208–209

Flowchart, process, 353
  risk identification tool, 368

Fluor Corp., 650

FMEA, 347–348, 375
  (*illus.*), 349

Food and drink customs, 632

Ford Motor Co., 489–490

Forecasting
  at-completion and to-complete, 431–436
  costs, 317–325

Foreign currency, 331

Foreign projects (*See* International projects)

Formal reviews, 344–345, 456

Formality customs, 631

Forward cover, 637

Free slack, 209

Freeze, design, 440

Functional areas (departments)
  in concurrent engineering, 508–509
  (*illus.*), 508
  integrating, 505–507
  (*illus.*), 505
  project office representatives, 533

Functional design of system, 59–60, 406

Functional differentiation, 483–484

Functional flow block diagrams (FFBD), 56–57, 59–60, 63, 128
  (*illus.*), 57, 58, 60

Functional leader in project, 534

Functional managers
  reports to, 458–459
  role, 533–534

Functional readiness review, 344

Functional representative, 499–500

Functional requirements, 56–57, 128–129

Functions, subsystems, definition and grouping of, 59–60

Funding plan, 325

Funnel, selection process, 609
  (*illus.*), 609

G

Gantt, Henry L., 177

Gantt chart, 8, 177–179
  (*illus.*), 178, 179

disadvantages of, 182–183
  multi-level
  (*illus.*), 184
  from network, converting, 210–211
  showing work status, 415
  (*illus.*), 416

Gates and gating process, 606, 609
  in methodology, 578–579
  and portfolio management, 611

Gencor Co., 653, 654

General and administrative expense, 308–310

General Electric Corp., 301, 628

General Motors Corp., 491

Geographic differentiation, 484

George Washington University, 586

GERT, 272–276
  network, (*illus.*), 275
  nodes, 272–273
  (*illus.*), 273
  vs. PERT/CPM, PDM, 228–229

GERT, 8, 272–275

Gestalt, 33

Gift-giving customs, 631–632

Global projects (*See also* International projects)
  scope and SOW definition, 643–644
  (*illus.*), 644
  steering committee, 641, 643

Global system, 41–42

Goal
  vs. estimate, 299
  project, three dimensional, xxxii–xxxiii
  (*illus.*), xxxi
  system, 34–35

Goman Publishing Company, 13–14

Government/nonprofit project management, 17–18

Grade vs. quality, 335

Graphical evaluation and review technique (GERT), 8, 272–275

Great pyramids of Egypt, xxiii–xxiv
  (*illus.*), xxiv

Group process
  guidelines, 556–557
  issues, 552, 554

Group productivity software, 462

Groupthink, 562

Guarantee period, 325

Guidelines, team operating, 555–557

H

Habitat for Humanity, 241

Hammock activity, 204

Hand-over points, 221–222
  (*illus.*), 221

Have Blue project, 120

Hazard, risk, 365, 372

Hedging, 637

Heuristic methods, resource allocation, 267–269

Hewlett Packard Corp., 465

criticisms of, 225
effect of due date, 209–210
free slack, 209
last start time and last finish time, 206–208
multiple critical paths, 205
network diagrams
    AON diagrams, 197–201
    event–oriented networks, 201
    formation of network, 201–202
precedence diagramming method
    finish-to-finish, 213
    finish-to-start, 213–214
    multiple PDM relationships, 214–216
    start-to-finish, 213
    start-to-start, 212
scheduling, with resource constraints
    leveling multiple resources, 222–223
    leveling of resource-constrained project, 223–225
    leveling of time-constrained project, 218–220
    resource allocation, workload and loading, 218
    resource availability and project duration, 217
    splitting activities, multi-tasking and hand-over projects, 221–222
total slack, 208–209
Network scheduling (*See also* Scheduling)
criticisms of, 225
Networks and network diagrams (*See also* Activity-on-arrow diagram; Activity-on-node diagram; CPM; PERT), 197–202
GERT, 272–275
    (*illus.*), 275
PDM, 215–216
    for risk identification, 368
    time-scaled, 230–231
    (*illus.*), 230
New engineering contract (NEC), 195
New venture management, 16–17
Nodes (*See*: Activity-on-arrow diagram; Activity-on-node diagram; GERT; PDM)
Nonconformities (defects), 334, 336
Noncritical activities, 204–205
Nondirect costs, 313
Non-integrated system development, 506
    (*illus.*), 506
Nonprofit fund-raising campaign project, 23
Normal distribution
    project duration, 278
    table of *z*-values, 254
Normal time-cost, 242
Normandy invasion, xxvi–xxvii
North American Aviation Space Division, 104–106

Nuclear power plants
    costs, 301
    meltdown likelihood, 373

O

Objectives
    as requirements, 54
    system, 44
    team, 556
Off-the-shelf, 58–59, 300
Office of projects (*See* PMO)
Offsets, 637–638
O'Neal, Philip "Tip", 542
Open systems, 38–40
Operation phase
    in systems development cycle, 80–81
    in systems engineering, 67
Operation phase, 80–81, 474–475
Operational modes, requirements for, 55, 90
OPM3, 586
Optimistic activity times (*a*), 250
Oracle, 369
Oral reports, 369
Organization
    chart (*illus.*), 482
    differentiation forms, 483–485
    goals, 616–617
    integration, traditional, 483–485
    project
        conflict in, 560–561
        forms of, 485–499
    projectized, 490
    strategic management of, 605
Organization structure
    formal, 483–485
    integrated with WBS, 312–314
        (*illus.*), 313
    project, 485–499
Organizational common knowledge, 588
Organizational forgetting, 587–588
Organizations
    matrix, 593–596
    pure project, 490–493
    as systems, 35–36
    traditional, 483–485
Outputs, system, 37
Overhead expense, 308–310
Overrun allowance, 305
Overseas projects (*See* International projects)

P

Parametric estimate, 302
Pareto diagram, 353
    (*illus.*), 354
Partial project, 492
Participative management, 548–549, 568–569
Pathfinder project, xxviii–xxix, 345–346, 420–421, 457
    Mars rover vehicle (*illus.*), 421
Paup, John, 106

Payments, project, 469, 470, 634
Payoff table, 391–392
    (*illus.*), 392
PDM, 197, 212–216
    vs. AOA and AON, 197, 227–228
    relationships, 214, 312
        (*illus.*), 212, 214
Peer consulting, 590–592
Peer review, 607
Penalty, in contract, 102–103, 246
Percent complete, 413, 423
Performance analysis,
    dashboards, 596–597
    project, 423–431
    software, 460
    technical (TPM), 418, 429–431
Performance guarantee, 325
Performance index, 426–428
Performance measures, 430
Performance requirements, 57–58, 129
Performance standards, 411
Performance target, contract, 107
PERT, 8, 249–259, 275, 279, 376
PERT/Cost, 413–414
PERT/CPM, 228
Pessimistic activity time (*b*), 250
Phased project planning, 81, 122–125
    (*illus.*), 123, 124
Physical design, 59–60, 406
Physical model, 45
Plan (*See also* Project master plan)
    action, 456–457
    communication, 454–455
        (*illus.*), 455
    risk management, 384, 386
        (*illus.*), 386
Planned value (PV), 423
Planning (*See also* Project planning)
    contingency, 382
    implementation, 410–411
    management function, 4
    risk response, 378–383
    role in stress reduction, 568
Planning and control process, 157
    project failure, cause of, 539–541
    role of WBS, 164, 165, 172, 173
    role of work package, 169, 170, 171
PLUTO, xxvi
PMBOK, xxxv–xxxvi, xxxviii, 575, 585
    book chapters vs. (*illus.*), xxxvii
PMI, xxxvi, 579, 585, 586
PMIS, 310
    benefits of, 459
    features of, 460–461
    project, fit to, 464–465
    project life cycle, role in, 463–464
        (*illus.*), 463
    reports by, 458
    software, 459
    web-based, 461–462
PMO, 70, 589, 593–598
    conflict resolution, role in, 496
    evolution of, 597
    functions, 594–597
        (*illus.*), 594

T

Tacit Knowledge, 589–590
Target completion date (*See also* Project duration), 206, 209–210
  commitment to, 260, 262
  meeting, ways of, 253–255
  probability of finishing by, 251–253
Target cost, 299
  vs. actual cost in contracts, 107, 110–111
Target date
  meeting, 253–254
  probability of meeting, 251–252
Target value in design margin, 380–381
Task force, 487
Task-oriented leadership, 547, 549
Tasks in project methodology, 581
  (*illus.*), 580
Team, project, the
  groups comprising, 549–550
  (*illus.*), 550
Team building, 552–559
  international projects, 642
  new team, 555–557
Teams
  building, 552–559
  clarifying members' roles, 565
  cohesiveness, 552
  concurrent engineering, 507–509
  conflict within, 550, 556, 559–566
  disbanding, 557
  effective, 552
  heavyweight, 510–511
  high-performing, 550–552
  improving ongoing, 553–555
  inspection process, 418
  interdisciplinary, 487
  multifunctional, 489–490
  (*illus.*), 490
  permanent, 488
  project
    roles outside of, 534–538
    roles with, 531–534
  resolving problems between, 557–559
  trouble with, 550
Teamwork, 549–551
Technical delivery process models, 585
Technical performance measurement (TPM), 418, 429–431
Termination, project, 339
  reasons for, 468–469
  responsibilities, 469–470
Testing
  acceptance, 352
  models and prototypes, 351
  system, 409–410
  user acceptance, 466
Tests, 416
  failure, 410
  qualification, 351

stress, 410
system, 409–410
Theory of Constraints (TOC), 259
  resource allocation, multiple projects, 269–270
Three Gorges Dam project, China, 501
Three time estimates, PERT, 250
Time, attitudes about, 632–633
Time and materials contract, 110
Time buffer (*See* Buffer, time)
Time-constrained project, 218–222
Time-constrained schedule, 267
Time–cost relationship, 242–243
  (*illus.*), 242
Time–cost tradeoff analysis (*See* CPM)
Time–cost uncertainty
  in system development cycle, 295–297
  (*illus.*), 296
Time estimates, updating, 429
Time-phased budgets, 312
Time-scaled networks, 230–231
  (*illus.*), 230
Time variance, 425
Time zones, international, 638
To-complete estimate, 432–436
Top-down estimate, 305–306
Top management
  in international projects, 640–641
  organization goals, 616–617
  reports to, 458
  role in project management, 535–536
Total organization models, 585–586
Toyota Co., 143
TQM, 335
Traceability, 57, 132–133, 342
Traceability matrix, 61–62
  (*illus.*), 62
Tracking and control (*See* Control; Project Control)
Tracking risks, 383
Training
  for overseas projects, 648
  project manager, 529–530
  user, 466
Transfer of risk, 378–379
Trigger, risk, 369, 383
Tsunami, Indian Ocean, 24
Two-hat problem, manager's, 496

U

Uncertainty
  effect on estimated completion, 434–436
  in project cost estimate, 295–297
  (*illus.*), 296
  as source of cost escalation, 291
Uncertainty condition, risk, 391–392
Unexpected, expect the, 385
University of California, Berkeley, 586
Unsolicited proposal, 86

User
  acceptance testing, 466
  conflict with contractor, 560
  needs, 87–89
  training, 466
User requirements, 89–90, 125–128
  example, 92
  vs. system requirements and specifications (*illus.*), 131, 132
Utzon, Jorn, 398

V

V-model, (*illus.*), 50
Value for the money, 334, 338
Vancouver Airport expansion project, 382
Variance, 451
  activity time, 250
  limits, 437
  project, 252
  schedule, time, cost, 425
  (*illus.*), 425
Verification requirements, 57–58
Vice president of projects, 494
  position in organization (*illus.*), 495
Vickers Corp., 41
Virtual private network, 462
Vision statement, 82
Von Neumann, John, 402

W

Waiver, specification, 340, 342
Wallace, Floyd, Associates, 538
Walt Disney Co., 465
  Epcot, 11
WBS (*See* Work breakdown structure)
Web-enabled tools, 461–462
Well-defined work unit, 169
Westinghouse Co., 301
Work
  authorization, 414–415
  (*illus.*), 415
  definition, 163–173
  international projects, 644–646
Work breakdown structure (WBS), 164–169
  (*illus.*), 165, 166, 167, 168
  creating Gantt chart from, 178
  for integrated planning and control, 172–173
  integrated with organization structure, 312–314
  (*illus.*), 313
  in international projects, 644–646
  (*illus.*), 645
  for proposal, 94
  for risk identification, 367–368
Work definition, 163–173
Work order/requisition, 103, 415
Work overload/underload, 567–568